Patria

LAURENCE BLAIR

Patria

Lost Countries of South America

THE BODLEY HEAD
LONDON

1 3 5 7 9 10 8 6 4 2

The Bodley Head, an imprint of Vintage, is part of the Penguin Random House group
of companies whose addresses can be found at global.penguinrandomhouse.com

First published by The Bodley Head in 2024

Copyright © Laurence Blair 2024

Laurence Blair has asserted his right to be identified as the author of this
Work in accordance with the Copyright, Designs and Patents Act 1988

Maps by Bill Donohoe

penguin.co.uk/vintage

Typeset in 10.2/13.87pt Sabon LT Std by Jouve (UK), Milton Keynes
Printed and bound in Great Britain by Clays Ltd, Elcograf S.p.A.

The authorised representative in the EEA is Penguin Random House Ireland,
Morrison Chambers, 32 Nassau Street, Dublin DO2 YH68

A CIP catalogue record for this book is available from the British Library

HB ISBN 9781847924681
TPB ISBN 9781847924698

Penguin Random House is committed to a sustainable future
for our business, our readers and our planet. This book is made
from Forest Stewardship Council® certified paper.

To my parents and grandparents

... almost everything I've written has been for someone who can no longer read me, and this book itself is nothing more than a letter to a ghost.

Héctor Abad Faciolince,
El olvido que seremos, 2006

Con la espada y con la pluma

By sword and pen
Coat of arms drawn by Garcilaso de la Vega 'El Inca', 1609

Contents

Cast of Characters

ANDEANS AND AMAZONIANS

The Inca emperors

Manco Capac, the legendary progenitor of the Inca dynasty
Viracocha, the eighth Inca, fled the Chanca invasion
Pachacuti, the ninth Inca, founder of Tawantinsuyu, the Inca Empire
Túpac Inca Yupanqui, the tenth Inca, defeated by the Mapuche
Huayna Capac, the eleventh Inca, conqueror of Ecuador, father to
   around 250 children

	Huáscar, Huayna Capac's heir, who ruled in Cuzco
	Atahualpa, a rebel who governed Ecuador
His sons	**Túpac Hualpa,** a short-lived Spanish puppet
	Paullu, baptised as Cristóbal, who also sided with Spain
	Manco, an adept rider and swordsman, founder of the Vilcabamba dynasty

Sayri Túpac, Manco's son, later baptised as Diego
Titu Cusi, Manco's eldest son, not of full royal blood
Túpac Amaru I, Manco's son and posthumous high priest, later
   baptised as Felipe

Inca queens, consorts and children

Cura Occlo, Manco's beloved wife, sister, queen and co-commander
María Cusi Huarcay, Sayri Túpac's wife and sister
Beatriz, their daughter and heir to their estates, raised in Cuzco
Angelina Quilaco, a wife of Titu Cusi
Quispe Titu, their son, died young
Juana Quispe, wife of Túpac Amaru

Captains, courtiers and relatives

Guavia Rucana, ruler of the Chincha Kingdom
A Chincha Lord, Atahualpa's steward
Don Pedro Guanuque, post-conquest guardian of the Chincha Islands

Villac Umu, high priest of the Sun and commander of Manco's armies
Atoc-Sopa, regent for Sayri Túpac
Martín Pando, scribe and interpreter to Titu Cusi
Don Melchor Carlos Inca, son of Paullu, a libertine
Puma Inca
Curi Paucar   nobles and captains at Túpac Amaru's court
Colla Topa
Paucar Inca
Chimpu Ocllo, a granddaughter of Huayna Capac
Inca Garcilaso de la Vega, her illegitimate son, a half-Spanish soldier,
    writer and historian

Andean rebels, 1780–82

José Gabriel Condorcanqui, a revolutionary leader known as **Túpac
    Amaru II**
Micaela Bastidas, his wife and trusted general
Juan Bautista Túpac Amaru, his half-brother, later a pretender to the
    Inca throne
Túpac Katari, leader of a great Andean insurrection in Upper Peru,
    later quartered
Bartolina Sisa, his wife and fellow commander, also executed

The Diaguita

Juan Calchaquí, leader of a 1560 revolt against the Spanish
Pedro Bohórquez, a false Inca, chosen to lead the Diaguita in rebellion
    in 1658
A Mapuche woman, his consort and captain
Francisco, his son
Luis Enríquez, the false Inca's lieutenant, who fought on until 1664
Milanka, a Diaguita woman

Amazonian rulers

Aparian
Machiparo
Nurandaluguaburabara
The Coniu Puyara, fearsome queens and captains of war, also known
    as the Amazons

SPANIARDS, SAILORS AND SOLDIERS

In the Caribbean

Cristoforo Colombo, also known as Columbus, a Genoese navigator in Spanish service

Amerigo Vespucci, a Florentine merchant, also sailing for Spain

Hernán Cortés, a lesser Spanish noble who conquered the Mexica

Juan Ponce de León, first Spanish governor of Puerto Rico, failed colonist of Florida

Sebastián de Belalcázar, a bloodthirsty pacifier of modern-day Colombia

In Peru

Francisco Pizarro, pirate of the Caribbean, conqueror of Tawantinsuyu

His brothers   **Juan**
               Gonzalo
               Hernando

Pedro, his cousin, page and chronicler

Diego de Almagro, conquistador and invader of Chile, Pizarro's bitter rival

Francisco de Toledo, a ruthless colonial administrator, viceroy of Peru

Diego Rodríguez de Figueroa, Spain's ambassador to Vilcabamba

Atilano de Anaya, another emissary to the Vilcabamba Incas

Martín García Óñez de Loyola, captor of Túpac Amaru, later governor of Chile

Pedro Sarmiento de Gamboa, standard-bearer, secretary, sailor and occultist

Marcos García and **Diego Ortiz**, Augustinian friars in Vilcabamba

Martín de Murúa, a Spanish historian of Vilcabamba

In the Amazon –

Francisco de Orellana, the first European to sail down the Amazon, later slain by locals

Gaspar de Carvajal, chaplain and chronicler of their expedition

In the Río de la Plata

Pedro de Mendoza, failed founder of Buenos Aires, wracked by syphilis

Ulrich Schmidel, one of his 1,500 men, a Bavarian mercenary who traversed the Chaco

Isabel de Guevara, one of twenty European women to accompany their expedition

Alonso Mercado y Villacorta, Catalonian soldier and governor of Tucumán

Hernando de Torreblanca, Jesuit missionary and chronicler of the Third Calchaquí War

In Chile

Francisco de Aguirre, a soldier who laid waste to northern Chile

Pedro de Valdivia, governor of Chile, captured and slain by the Mapuche

Alonso de Ercilla, veteran of Wallmapu, poet and author of *La Araucana*

Francisco Núñez de Pineda y Bascuñán, a captain of pikemen, author of *Cautiverio feliz*

Antonio de Erauso, formerly **Catalina,** a nun turned soldier and brigand

Francisco López de Zúñiga, a veteran of the Netherlands, governor of Chile

Ambrosio O'Higgins, an Irish farmer turned Marquess of Osorno and viceroy of Peru

Casimiro Marcó del Pont, a Galician aristocrat and governor of Chile

Vicente San Bruno, royalist commissar and captain of the Talavera Regiment

In Spain

	Charles V, also Holy Roman Emperor
	Philip II
Kings of Spain	**Philip III**
	Eight others
	Carlos IV
	Fernando VII

Juan Ginés de Sepúlveda, a churchman and defender of Spanish colonialism

Bartolomé de las Casas, priest and ex-slaver turned critic of the conquistadors

PALMARIANS, BRAZILIANS AND PORTUGUESE

In Palmares

Ganga Zumba, king and high priest of Palmares
          Aca Inene, his mother
          Gana Zona, his brother
          Anajubá, his son
          Tuculo, another son, a fearsome general
          Andalaquituxe, their cousin, all rulers of Palmarian towns
          Pedro and **Brás**, his youngest sons, raised in Portuguese
             Pernambuco
Zumbi, Ganga Zumba's nephew and commander of his armies, later
  ruler of Palmares
Dandara, Zumbi's legendary warrior-queen
João Tapuya
Ambrosio
Pedro Capacaça   captains and commanders
Quiloange
Quissama
Camuanga

In Pernambuco

Johan Maurits of Nassau, governor of Dutch Pernambuco
Bartolomeu Lintz, his spy
Henrique Dias, a Black soldier and war hero against the Dutch
Filipe Camarão, a native Potiguara knight, also a decorated veteran
Fernão Carrilho, a soldier, victorious against rebels in Bahia
António Vieira, a Jesuit priest and diplomat
Domingos Jorge Velho, a feared enslaver and soldier of fortune
Borba Gato, a frontiersman and miner in Minas Gerais

Monarchs and emperors

Pedro II, King of Portugal, a correspondent of Zumbi
Four others

João VI, King of Portugal, who fled to Brazil in 1808
Pedro I, his son and independent Emperor of Brazil
Pedro II, his son and heir, who reigned for over fifty-eight years

Isabel, his daughter and regent

Rebels and abolitionists

Maria Felipa de Oliveira, a fisherwoman who burned a Portuguese fleet

José de Santa Eufrásia, a Black militia officer and revolutionary

Luísa Mahin, a Guinean shopkeeper and fighter in the Malê and Sabinada revolts

Luís Gama, her son and biographer, a lawyer, poet and crusading emancipator

André Rebouças, an engineer and transatlantic opponent of slavery

Maria Firmina dos Reis, schoolteacher and author of *Úrsula*

Machado de Assis, Afro-Brazilian author of *The Posthumous Memoirs of Bras Cubas*

Chico da Matilde, a sailor and strike leader, also known as the Sea Dragon

PATRIOTS

Revolutionary leaders

Juan José Castelli, radical abolitionist, commander of the first Army of the North

Bernardo de Monteagudo, a Black public defender and agitator for Spanish American unity

Andrés Jiménez de León Mancocapac, a seditious cleric, descended from the Incas

Juan Manuel Belgrano, a lawyer from Buenos Aires, proponent of the Inca plan

José de San Martín, soldier and liberator of Argentina, Chile and Peru

Bernardo O'Higgins, bastard son of Ambrosio and Supreme Director of Chile

Simón Bolívar, Venezuelan liberator, visionary of a united continent

Francisco de Miranda, Venezuelan exile, ideologue of Latin American independence

Dionisio Inca Yupanqui, a dragoon lieutenant-colonel, defender of Indigenous rights

Heroes of Buenos Aires, 1806–12

María Remedios del Valle, enslaved maidservant and combat nurse, praised for her valour

Pablo Jiménez, an enslaved man, handy with a pickaxe, later immortalised in poetry

Manuel Macedonio Barbarín, a militia sergeant from Angola, later a lieutenant colonel

Valerio, an enslaved man who helped foil a royalist conspiracy

Gauchos and guerrillas

Juana Azurduy, forgotten heroine of South American independence

Manuel Padilla, her husband, fellow commander of the Lagunas Republiqueta

Martín Miguel de Güemes, a well-off gaucho commander with the popular touch

Antonio Visaura, a Black cobbler, militiaman and gaucho colonel

Vicente 'Panana' Martínez, a mixed-race sergeant and revolutionary plotter

Juan José Feliciano Fernández Campero, Marquis of Yavi, aristocrat and Incaphile

Diego Cala, his second-in-command and spy chief

Joaquín Fretes, a Guinean music teacher, ringleader of a conspiracy in Mendoza

The Army of the Andes

Andrés Ibañez, a West African prince, aide to San Martín, later innkeeper

María Demetria, the general's cook

Juan Isidro Zapata, his doctor and chief medical officer

Falucho, hero of the Battle of Maipú

Francisco Fierro, also from Guinea, wounded, deserted and sent to sea

Dámaso Moyano, a formerly enslaved drummer sergeant, later Spanish brigadier

William Miller
Samuel Haigh   officers and aides
Enrique Martínez
Juan Gregorio las Heras

MAPUCHE AND WINKA

Lonkos, toquis and weichafes

Lautaro, a shrewd war chief, formerly a conquistador's page

Caupolicán, his right hand, a warrior of prodigious strength

Pelantaro, a cunning rebel commander

Nabalburi, his spy among the Spanish

Antonio de Meneses, captured as a child, twelve years enslaved, now escaped

Antuwenu and **Lienkura,** battle-scarred diplomats

Francisco Mariluán, statesman and survivor who recognised Chilean independence

Cheuquante, Pinoleo, Colissi, chiefs who rescued the crew of HMS *Challenger*

Cadin, a warlord who tried to plunder the wreck

Mañilwenu, an old ally of the Spanish crown

Kilapán, his son, later minister of war to Aurelio I and elected war chief

Calfucurá, suzerain of Puelmapu, also known as the Emperor of the Pampas

Ambrosio Paillaléf, a lord made rich by raiding

Orélie-Antoine de Tounens, provincial French lawyer proclaimed King of the Araucanía and Patagonia, also known as Aurelio I

Lemunao, his loyal retainer

Frédéric I, modern-day pretender to the steel crown

Pichi Juan, a Huilliche, ordered to burn down the forest of Chan Chan

Melín, a chief near the border

Alejo, his son, a primary school teacher

Epulef, owner of the ruins of Spanish Villarrica

Manuel Aburto Panguilef, a twentieth-century Mapuche intellectual and organiser

Chileans, Argentines and other foreigners

Ignacio Domeyko, a Polish mineralogist and traveller in Wallmapu

Edmond Reuel Smith, a travel writer and oil painter from New York

Francisco Antonio Pinto, a diplomat and second president of Chile

Diego Portales, a powerful Chilean minister of the 1830s

Vicente Pérez Rosales, Chile's agent of colonisation in Wallmapu

Cornelio Saavedra, a soldier, landowner and sworn enemy of the Mapuche

Justo José de Urquiza, president of Argentina

Julio Roca, Argentine general and genocidaire of Puelmapu

Gregorio Urrutia, Chilean colonel, occupier of Gulumapu

Ambrosio Letelier, lieutenant of a battalion of engineers

Jack, a sheep, mascot of the *Challenger*'s crew

Dagoberto Godoy, aviator from Temuco, the first man to fly over the Andes

Marmaduke Grove, eccentric flying ace, socialist and inventor of sabre-rattling

Salvador Allende, a doctor, senator and moderate Marxist elected Chile's president

Augusto Pinochet, Chile's military dictator between 1973 and 1990

Sebastián Piñera, conservative Chilean president and businessman

Gabriel Boric, former student leader, Chile's youngest-ever president

THE PATRIA OF LÓPEZ AND THE TRIPLE ALLIANCE

The Great War

Dr Francia, dictator and defender of Paraguayan independence, also known as *El Supremo*

Carlos Antonio López, his nephew, president of Paraguay

Francisco Solano López, his son, successor and grand marshal of Paraguay's armies

Madame Eliza Lynch, an Irishwoman, consort to López junior

Juan Francisco 'Panchito' López, a colonel, their fifteen-year-old son

José Eduvigis Díaz, a low-born career soldier and victor of Curupayty

Bernardino Caballero, López's lieutenant and founder of the Colorado Party

George Frederick Masterman, chief military apothecarist to Paraguay's armies

Juan Crisóstomo Centurión, a Paraguayan colonel, joint editor of *Cabichuí*

Ramona Martínez, an enslaved combat nurse, later called the American Joan of Arc

Nimia Candía, a twice-wounded riflewoman

Major James Manlove, Confederate exile and failed privateer

Richard Francis Burton, British celebrity explorer

Bartolomé Mitre, Argentine president and historian

Domingo Faustino Sarmiento, his successor, author of *Facundo: Civilization and Barbarism*

Domingo Fidel Sarmiento, his adoptive son, a twenty-one-year-old infantry captain

Cándido López, a cobbler, veteran and one-armed painter of the Triple Alliance War

Post-war Paraguay

Rafael Barrett, Spanish essayist, whistleblower on the yerba mate industry

Emilio Aceval, president and former child soldier, overthrown by Caballero

Justo Pastor Benítez, a *Lopizta* writer and intellectual

Juan O'Leary, a schoolteacher, journalist, Colorado and chief acolyte of *Lopizmo*

Rafael Franco, leftist-nationalist revolutionary leader who disinterred López

Arturo Bray, an Anglo-Paraguayan veteran of the Somme and the Chaco War

The Stronato

Alfredo Stroessner, dictator between 1954 and 1989

Freddy, his son, a cocaine addict

Augusto Roa Bastos, author of *I the Supreme* and *Son of Man*, exiled by the regime

Josef Rudolf Mengele, mass murderer of Auschwitz, given asylum by Stroessner

Auguste Ricord, Nazi collaborator, cosy with the regime, supplied the US half its heroin

POPULISTS AND PRESIDENTS

Fidel Castro, revolutionary leader of Cuba for fifty years until 2008

Ernesto 'Che' Guevara, Argentine medical student turned Cuban guerrilla leader

Juan Domingo Perón, twice Argentine president, founder of nationalist, pro-worker movement *peronismo*

Eva 'Evita' Perón, an actress and his first lady, died young and beautiful

Carlos Saúl Menem, a peronist

Néstor Kirchner, a peronist

Cristina Fernández de Kirchner, his wife and successor, sentenced in a $1bn fraud case

Mauricio Macri, a conservative

Alberto Fernández, a peronist

Javier Milei, a libertarian, communes with his dead dog for political advice

Hugo Chávez, former colonel, Venezuelan president, founder of the Bolivarian Revolution

Nicolás Maduro, his authoritarian successor, a former foreign minister

Horacio Cartes, cigarette baron and Paraguayan president, accused of mass bribery

Mario Abdo Benítez, his successor, pallbearer to Stroessner and son of his secretary

Santiago Peña, president of Paraguay, protégé of Cartes

Hilarión Daza, Bolivian presidential guard turned president, stabbed to death by his guards in 1894

Narciso Campero, his successor, an old soldier and oligarch, nephew of the Marquis of Yavi

Evo Morales, former coca-grower, three times elected president of (the Plurinational State of) Bolivia

David Choquehanca, his foreign minister

Luis Arce, finance minister to Morales turned his enemy, Bolivian president

Jeanine Áñez, interim president in 2019–20, now in jail

Juan Velasco Alvarado, army officer and left-leaning caudillo of Peru, 1968–75

Alberto Fujimori, president in the 1990s, convicted for corruption and ordering massacres by death squads

Luiz Inácio Lula da Silva, thrice elected Brazil's president with the Worker's Party (PT)

Michel Temer, a conservative interim president and writer of romantic poetry

Jair Bolsonaro, a far-right, disgraced former paratrooper and dictatorship nostalgic

Gustavo Petro, former guerrilla, Colombia's left-wing president

Nayib Bukele, president of El Salvador, 'philosopher king' and 'world's coolest dictator'

ROYALTY, RAPPERS, REBELS AND RUBBER BARONS

Toussaint Louverture, formerly enslaved general and leader of the
  Haitian Revolution
Jean-Jacques Dessalines, his successor, Emperor of Revolutionary Haiti
Francis Burdett O'Connor, an officer in Bolívar's Irish Legion
William Gibbs, British guano baron, builder of Tyntesfield, Somerset
André Bresson, French mining engineer
Miguel Grau, the Knight of the Seas, Peruvian admiral killed in the
  War of the Pacific
Arturo Prat, his Chilean former comrade, shot down boarding his ship
Maximilian I, a Habsburg archduke installed by France as emperor of
  Mexico
Euclides da Cunha, a Brazilian engineer and author of *Os Sertões*
Carlos Fermín Fitzcarrald, genocidal Peruvian rubber extractivist
Nicolás Suárez Callaú, Bolivian rubber magnate and Europhile
Henry Wickham, British explorer of the Amazon and rubber thief
Karl Marx, philosopher, guano enthusiast, author of *Das Kapital*
Alexander von Humboldt, polymath, naturalist and early backpacker
  in Latin America
Mariano de Rivero, Peru's leading scientist of the nineteenth century
Chapman Todd, captain of the U.S.S. *Wilmington*, hero of the
  Spanish-American War
Roger Casement, diplomat, humanitarian investigator and Irish
  nationalist
Rosa Luxemburg, Polish-German revolutionary socialist, executed in
  1919
Hiram Bingham III, US senator and tomb raider who popularised
  Machu Picchu
William M. Branham, a faith healer and self-declared prophet from
  Kentucky
Afeni Shakur, political activist and Black Panther
Tupac Amaru Shakur, her son, a West Coast rapper, named after
  Túpac Amaru II

Author's Note

Patria is based on many years of research. To keep the text uncluttered for the general reader, notes are compiled by page number at the end of the book, and key works cited are included in the acknowledgements. Some names in the present-day narrative have been changed or omitted.

Latin Americans often use the word *América* not to mean the United States, but all of the Americas, North and South. This book does the same. Based on a geographical misconception that stuck, European empires referred to the original inhabitants of the American landmass as Indians. Except when quoting others, I employ the terms Indigenous, native peoples and first nations, as used by their modern-day descendants.

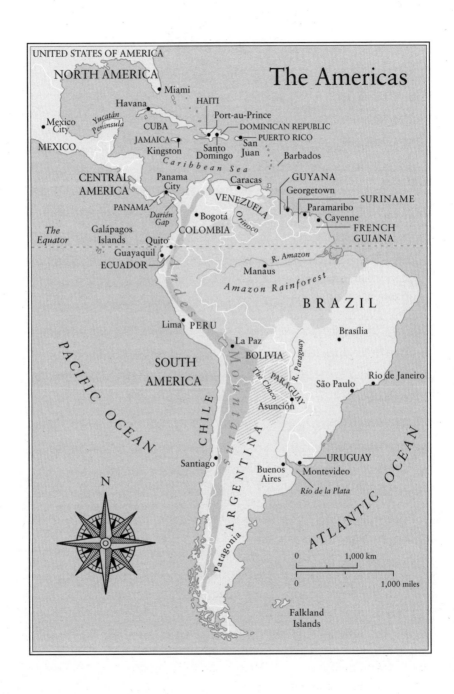

The Americas

UNITED STATES OF AMERICA

NORTH AMERICA

Miami

Havana
HAITI
Port-au-Prince
Mexico City
Yucatán Peninsula
CUBA
DOMINICAN REPUBLIC
PUERTO RICO
MEXICO
JAMAICA
San Juan
Kingston
Santo Domingo

Caribbean Sea
Barbados

CENTRAL AMERICA
Panama City
Caracas
GUYANA
Georgetown
SURINAME
PANAMA
VENEZUELA
Paramaribo
Cayenne
Darién Gap
Bogotá
Orinoco
FRENCH GUIANA
The Equator
Galápagos Islands
COLOMBIA
Quito
Guayaquil
R. Amazon
ECUADOR
Manaus
Amazon Rainforest
BRAZIL

Lima PERU
La Paz
Brasília
BOLIVIA
R. Paraguay
SOUTH AMERICA
PARAGUAY
São Paulo
Rio de Janeiro
The Chaco
CHILE
Asunción

Mountains
URUGUAY
Santiago
Buenos Aires
Montevideo
ARGENTINA
Río de la Plata

PACIFIC OCEAN

N

ATLANTIC OCEAN

Patagonia

0   1,000 km

0   1,000 miles

Falkland Islands

Introduction
One Hell of a Drug
Cerro Corá, Paraguay

We fly around fists of orange rock that punch out of the jungle. The horizon, a cloudless blue, pitches and rolls. Fuzzy chatter over the headsets, a gloved finger pointing out red triangles on a screen. From the air, you see them as rectangles of a spiky, lurid green amid the darker forest: marijuana plantations, spotted earlier on by reconnaissance flights. The men check their assault weapons, flick safety catches off.

Then we are down on the ground, ducking below the spinning rotors and running through flattened bushes of weed. It's not long past 9 a.m., and already swelteringly hot. I follow Major Aldo Pintos and his unit through the thicket to a clearing. Black tarpaulins stretched over wooden poles cover a sleeping area: wooden bunks, duvets, a jar of toothbrushes tied to a tree – and bulging sacks of the harvest. The air is heavy with the dank, cloying aroma. A pot bubbles atop glowing embers. 'They hide when they hear the helicopter,' says Pintos. 'They're probably still nearby.'

The growers are impoverished farmers on the bottom rung of the international drug trade. They rarely pack more heat than a shotgun, used to hunt wild pigs. At most, they blast off a cartridge to cover their escape. Still, the major is taking no chances. Cradling his assault rifle under one arm, he grabs a bottle of cooking oil from a table, pours it over one side of the rudimentary tent, and touches a match to the plastic. It goes up in seconds, the flames shooting in all directions. The space beneath the forest canopy turns opaque with the fumes of a tonne of burning weed. The men and women of the SENAD – Paraguay's anti-drug force – probably hotbox more pot than the most dedicated stoner.

Nearby, another SENAD unit hacks three-metre-high plants to the ground with their machetes. 'Here, in a single day, I can take thousands of kilos of marijuana out of circulation,' says Captain Óscar Chamorro, a stentorian soldier with cropped silver hair and wraparound shades.

We watch as his men torch a giant wooden press, used to make com-pacted bricks of weed known as *prensado*. A couple of scrawny, mewling kittens inspect the flaming wreckage. Major Pintos picks up a child's T-shirt – the word *amor* picked out in sequins – and tosses it into the inferno. Another blow struck in the War on Drugs, now well into its sixth decade.

On this front – like most others – the drugs are winning. Squeezed between Brazil, Bolivia and Argentina in the entrails of South America, Paraguay is relatively small: about the size of California or Sweden, home to little more than six million people. But its red, fertile earth yields two or three harvests a year, making it a marijuana powerhouse: the continent's biggest producer of weed, second only to Mexico in the hemisphere.

The country is too flat to grow coca, the Andean bush whose leaves are steeped in gasoline and other chemicals to make cocaine. But it sits right on a key pipeline for the white bricks that head south-east from Bolivia bound for Brazil, Africa and Europe. In recent years, police in Europe have made record busts of the powder, stashed amid Paraguayan soybean, lea-ther and paint in hauls of up to sixteen tonnes. That's only a fraction of what the PCC – a ruthless Brazilian narco multinational – and the 'Ndrangheta mafia ship across the Atlantic via Paraguay every year.

Paraguay is the perfect transit country. Not only because of its geog-raphy: long, unguarded borders, rivers flowing down to ports in Uruguay and Argentina. The state is weak and permeable; in South American rankings, only Venezuela is more corrupt. SENAD agents are routinely accused of collusion with narcos. They rely on hand-me-down helicopters that saw service against the Vietcong. The country has no radar coverage of its north to detect planes landing at clandestine cocaine labs; its customs officials have few scanners to check containers. One in four people lives in poverty. They have little to lose by working as drug mules or growers.

Meanwhile, Paraguay's crammed jails are ideal recruiting grounds for the cartels. Their commanders live it up in 'VIP cells' with sex work-ers on call, and regularly tunnel to freedom – or simply walk out the front door. A full legalisation of marijuana, at least, could undercut the gangs and provide poor *campesinos* with an honest living. But Paraguay is probably too conservative. Ninety per cent of the population is Cath-olic: a statistic only rivalled by San Marino, East Timor and the Vatican.

The grisly consequences are mostly concentrated in the nearby city of Pedro Juan Caballero in Paraguay's remote north-east. A grid-plan of bars, garages and gun shops running along the unmarked border with Brazil, it has a murder rate to rival Baltimore or Tijuana. A few days earlier, I called in on Cándido Figueredo, a journalist who has spent decades covering the narco takeover of his hometown. He takes out a stack of crime-scene photos of those who crossed the gangs: mass graves, charred corpses, SUVs turned into colanders, torsos torn limb from limb.

'In this country,' he says, 'you can buy anyone: from a journalist to a minister.' Reporters who blow the whistle on this cosy arrangement, known as *narcopolítica*, are gunned down in the street. Hitmen have shot up Cándido's bungalow twice. He is now guarded 24/7 by a trio of police with sub-machine guns. A 9mm handgun also sits below his paunch. 'Here, a life is worth absolutely nothing,' he grimaces. 'The police sometimes find a body near the border in the morning, and they dump it on the other side. It's less paperwork.'

I meet up with Néstor, a stocky forty-something in a pink-chequered cardigan. He was fourteen, he says, when he was first hired to help bring in the marijuana harvest. His father, a cattle wrangler, was away for months at a time; his mother washed clothes. The offer of 80,000 guaraníes a day – around £8 – was irresistible. 'You know how much your family is in need, so you're forced to take it. That's why everyone gets corrupted and goes to work there.'

Néstor has since risen to middle management in the criminal underworld. He's done time in Brazil and Uruguay for smuggling cocaine. Now he's back home, running a marijuana operation in the nearby hills. In his back garden in Pedro Juan Caballero, a pair of parrots watch as he digs up six blocks of prensado. The bricks of weed are usually flecked with mud and insects – and sometimes doused with cheap cola to make them stick together. It's hardly the finest kush, but it delivers a potent chemical high. Inside, a baby *jaguarundi* wildcat – another souvenir from Néstor's plantation in the forest – scurries from under a wardrobe to snatch raw meat from his fingers.

The SENAD roll into town and Néstor stops answering his phone. Maybe it's his workers' meagre belongings that Major Pintos burns to a cinder. Another plantation set aflame, we jog back to the landing site, the smell of prensado clinging to our clothes. As we take off, the updraft blasts a giant tarpaulin covered with the drying harvest, scattering the emerald flowers to the breeze.

On 1 March 1870, a wheezing, corpulent figure crashed through the undergrowth below us on an emaciated white horse that foamed with sweat. His navy-blue uniform and gold epaulettes are filthy and torn to shreds. Blood pours from a slash to his forehead and drips from his beard; it pools in his crotch from a wound in his gut. Francisco Solano López – grand marshal and president of Paraguay – and his three followers are all that's left of an army of tens of thousands.

He topples off his mount into the mud. His soldiers lever him down into a stream called the Aquidabán-Nigüí and try to haul him onto the far side. One of them runs off. Enemy riflemen appear along the banks, demanding his surrender. López, pallid and waist-deep in the water, curses and swings his sabre. 'Muero con mi patria!' he is said to have bellowed: I die with my country. A shot rings out. The man who styled himself the Napoleon of the New World collapses forward, blood from a fresh bullet wound in his back swirling into the muddy current.

It's the final act of the deadliest international war ever fought in the western hemisphere: a conflict that redrew South America's borders, appalled and fascinated observers, and almost wiped Paraguay off the map. Fought over six long years from 1864 against Brazil, Argentina and Uruguay, the War of the Triple Alliance left half of Paraguay's population dead – hundreds of thousands of men, women and children. The country was bankrupted, in ruins, and under enemy occupation for eight years. López was declared a tyrant and a monster. The state was shackled with an unpayable war debt, chunks of its territory were annexed forever and its natural resources were auctioned off. 'The Paraguayans exist no longer,' wrote one eyewitness to the cataclysm. 'There is a gap in the family of nations.'

But as well as this devastating material legacy, the conflict would leave a permanent psychological scar. The nation's heroic resistance would linger in popular memory. Before long, a beguiling half-truth would supersede it: that Paraguay was an emerging superpower, destined for greatness under López. That is, before foreign rivals – and internal traitors – stabbed the South American Sparta in the back, forbidding any mention of its martyred marshal so it could never rise from the ashes. One party, founded by López's trusted lieutenant, would later cement its control by vowing to make Paraguay great again. Seventy years later, it is still in power, and Paraguay is still poor.

In August 1954, two generals are driven in an open-top car through the crowded streets of Asunción, the capital, flanked by bodyguards in suits and helmeted cavalrymen. One is the Argentine president Juan Domingo Perón, on a diplomatic visit to return cannons, uniforms, drums and sabres seized during the Triple Alliance war. The other is

Alfredo Stroessner. He has just been sworn in as Paraguay's president after being elected with one hundred per cent of votes. He was the only person allowed to run.

Armoured cars bring the war trophies forward in giant cases. A bald, bespectacled history teacher takes to the podium in the square outside the cathedral. For Juan O'Leary, today is a vindication of his life's work. For fifty years, he has tracked down and interviewed toothless veterans, navigated swampy battlefields on horseback and canoe, and scribbled flowery verses for obscure literary journals. His guiding mission: 'to return to our nationality its lost faith, to unify its conscience, to cure it of its defeat and its defeatism.'

Above all, he has sought to be an 'agitator', an 'apostle', to resurrect 'the gigantesque figure of Marshal López ... the binding knot of our history, the beginning and end of our epic, the key to our past'. López, he has long argued, 'was and is Paraguay'. And now, when he looks up from his notes in the presence of the nation's new commander-in-chief, he sees the marshal's ghost 'illuminate before my eyes'. For history, O'Leary proclaims, 'is not a cemetery where the dead dwell, but the mother of the future; a fecund womb where fertile ground must grow, not sterile desert earth; the laboratory from whence come all the good and evil from which our lives are moulded.'

Stroessner will go on to rule Paraguay for almost thirty-five years, armed and bankrolled for most of them by the United States. The longest dictatorship in South American history, his regime will murder and torture thousands in the name of an anti-communist crusade, force tens of thousands more into exile, traffic drugs, smuggle contraband, and plunder its own people on an unfathomable scale: claiming all the while to be resurrecting the lost fatherland of López.

The history of South America is littered with such nations: dreamed-up, dismembered, or disappeared altogether. You won't find most of them on a map. But these places, and their long afterlives, still shape the continent to this day. This book is about what connects then and now: the lost country and the actual one, the marshal and the marijuana, cut down and growing forth again endlessly from the same remote patch of jungle.

Two years out of a history degree and a few months on from a breakup, I fly out to Colombia and backpack down through the Andes to Chile for an internship at a newspaper. On my first morning at their office in Santiago, the editors admit they're broke and shutting down in a few weeks. 'We didn't want you not to come,' one shrugs.

I've got few bylines to my name and zero contacts in the media. My pitches moulder in unattended inboxes. Chile is a news desert, the same two centrist sexagenarians swapping the presidential sash for sixteen years. In the evenings, I pace along the churning dishwater of the Río Mapocho, looking up at the snowcapped peaks shining pink above the smog.

Searching for stories, I start to read about a catastrophic war, and its long shadow over a landlocked, poor and oppressively hot land that foreign desks covered – if they bothered to at all – from Buenos Aires or London. Six months and a thirty-six-hour bus ride later, I'm in a motel in Pedro Juan Caballero, waking at 5 a.m. to revving trucks, waiting for drug lords to pick up my calls. To pass the time, I catch the bus out to the forested sierra where Paraguay's destiny was decided.

I take the trail through the trees to a watchman's hut. He waves me through with a warning to look out for jaguars. I come to a scar in the jungle – an airstrip bulldozed for Stroessner's visits. A monument of white concrete is freckled with plaques from trips by schools, regiments, diplomats and presidents. Nearby, a cross rises above the tomb of Colonel Panchito López: the marshal's fifteen-year-old son, also shot dead after refusing to come quietly. Down at the fateful creek, a silvery, insubstantial bust indicates the spot where López left behind his hefty physical form and passed into immortality. A broken bough lies across the water, recalling the unlucky palm frond that the marshal leaned on as he expired.

A few days later, I pass the same national park again, as Captain Chamorro of the SENAD drives me out to the helicopter landing spot in the hills. Conversation inevitably turns to López. 'Paraguay in 1870 was the most advanced country in Latin America,' Chamorro claims. 'It had railways two years before Brazil, today's economic power.' His ringtone sounds: 'Danger Zone' from the *Top Gun* soundtrack. He lets it play for a while before fielding the call.

'And whatever you think of López,' the captain continues, 'he died sword in hand, on the battlefield. How many modern leaders can you say that about?'

In October 2019, in Temuco, southern Chile, a statue of a sixteenth-century conquistador was lassoed around the neck and yanked to the ground. Cheering protesters – many wearing the ponchos of the Indigenous Mapuche people – stamped on the broken effigy of Pedro de Valdivia and hammered it with wooden staffs. In nearby Concepción, a crowd felled a bust of the Spanish coloniser, impaled it on a spike, and barbecued it at the feet of another statue: Valdivia's nemesis, the Mapuche chieftain Lautaro. A few months later, locals jostled to film with their smartphones as a bronze of General Cornelio Saavedra – who directed Chile's conquest of the Mapuche in the late nineteenth century – was manhandled over a bridge and into the frigid Lumaco River.

The historical reckoning spread across Latin America. In Popayán, Colombia, the native Misak, Pijao and Nasa peoples put Sebastián de Belalcázar – a man who had been dead for five centuries – on trial. They found the Spaniard guilty of the mass murder, enslavement, torture and rape of their ancestors. Then they tore down his equestrian monument, erected in 1937 atop a sacred pre-Columbian pyramid. In São Paulo, Brazil, masked men heaped tyres beneath a statue of Manuel de Borba Gato – an eighteenth-century frontiersman – and set them ablaze. The leader of Entregadores Antifascistas, a union of delivery workers, handed himself in. Borba Gato, he said, was guilty of genocide. Days before the king of Spain visited San Juan, Puerto Rico – today a US territory – to mark the capital's 500th anniversary, locals awoke to find a steel effigy of the explorer Juan Ponce de León knocked off his plinth and shattered from impact. 'No kings, no gringo invaders', read a statement by the Fuerzas Libertarias de Borikén, named after the Indigenous term for the island. Monuments to Christopher Columbus in Mexico City, Barcelona, Madrid and London were meanwhile taken down, torched, or spattered with blood-red paint.

Some were inspired by protests against police brutality in the United States, where more than 200 memorials to enslavers and Confederate generals were meanwhile being dismantled. But the challenge to traditional heroes across South America began much earlier. Back in 1986, a Benin-style bronze appeared in downtown Rio de Janeiro. It depicted Zumbi, ruler of Palmares, a powerful realm of runaways who resisted colonial slavery for a century. At the turn of the millennium, authorities in Lima shunted Francisco Pizarro, the conqueror of the Inca Empire, from the capital's main square to a tiny square of grass beside a highway. In 2015, Buenos Aires replaced a statue of Columbus with Juana Azurduy – a forgotten heroine of independence who battled with Indigenous guerrillas against Spanish rule in the Andes.

It wasn't just a question of rearranging the furniture: entire countries went by new names. Bolivia became the Plurinational State of Bolivia in 2009. A decade earlier, Hugo Chávez – a radical army colonel turned president – rebaptised Venezuela. It was henceforth to be prefixed as the

Bolivarian Republic, after Simón Bolívar, who liberated swathes of the continent in the 1810s. Not content with the rebrand, Chávez later unveiled a new, computer-generated official portrait of Bolívar – now looking more like a regular Venezuelan than an olive-skinned Spanish-American aristocrat – based on measurements of the Liberator's skull.

History – the saying goes – is written by the victors. Nowhere is the cliché truer than in South America. Its pre-Columbian polities boasted sophisticated state-builders, engineers, artists and agronomists. But none developed a system of writing with which to tell their own story – at least not one that we have yet deciphered. The lust of Europeans for silver and sugar, and the diseases they brought with them, caused many native societies to collapse. Few of the millions of Africans brought to the continent in chains were ever permitted to put pen to parchment. The oral histories passed down by Afrodescendant and Indigenous survivors have often been dismissed as myth. The region's Cold War despots even made the bodies of dissidents disappear, kidnapped their children, and sold them into adoption abroad. Up until the present day, populists and dictators have tightly controlled the narrative: shuttering newspapers, pumping out propaganda on the airwaves, and spreading disinformation on social media.

The defeat can seem total, the diagnosis unchanged since Eduardo Galeano outlined it more than fifty years ago in *Open Veins of Latin America: Five Centuries of the Pillage of a Continent*. In Galeano's hugely influential broadside, Latin America's story is a drumbeat of raw materials ripped out of mountainsides and flattening forests: gold, silver, tin, rubber, sugar, coffee, bananas, beef. Indigenous and popular resistance hardly stood a chance against 'the caravelled conquistadors and the jet-propelled technocrats; Hernán Cortés and the Marines; the agents of the Spanish Crown and the International Monetary Fund missions; the dividends from the slave trade and the profits of General Motors'. The region's underdevelopment 'is a consequence of development elsewhere', he later emphasised: 'we Latin Americans are poor because the ground we tread is rich.' While North America developed a strong internal economy and relatively robust institutions, 'the south developed outwardly and blew into fragments like a grenade'.

Bombarded by the winners' version, we are used to seeing history 'from the eye of the invader, from the perspective of conquest', writes the Peruvian-American author Marie Arana. 'The rest scatters into the haze.' We divide the Latin American past into victors and vanquished: Pizarro and the Incas. Spain and her colonies. 'The tinpot dictator *and* his unfortunate casualties. The Roman Catholic Church *and* the pagans. The vast world economy *and* the coveted veins that lie dormant in the earth.' But the 'ands', Arana argues, remain 'deeply imprinted' in the very psyche of the continent. And 'until we understand the "*ands*" of history – the ghosts in the machinery, the victims of our collective amnesia – we cannot hope to understand the region as it is now'.

In a decade covering the region, I have often heard a similar refrain. On the far outskirts of Rio, where the city blends into jungle-covered mountains, an instructor of *capoeira* – a martial art brought to Brazil and honed in secret by the enslaved – had traced his suburb's history to those who escaped. 'This is a story of people who fought, died, suffered, who built this country,' he argued. 'They tried to cover up this history, but now we're working to remember it.' 'It's not like we were taught at school,' said a young Indigenous guide, showing me around the ruins of a pre-Columbian metropolis in north-west Argentina. 'Our people weren't wiped out.' I visited a Harakbut village in the Peruvian Amazon, clinging on amid the devastation caused by illegal gold mining. The first thing my host told me was their creation story: defying the idea that the world's largest rainforest is a wilderness devoid of history. The spate of statue-toppling in Chile was hardly mindless vandalism, the Mapuche writer Pedro Cayuqueo told me: 'There's something far deeper going on.'

Turn on the TV, scroll through a news app – or even buy a paper – and you can guess the headlines. Bombs dropped on innocents in Eastern Europe and the Middle East. The protracted crack-up of the United States. Symptoms of China and India's inexorable rise. Perhaps even a report on a military coup or conservation initiative will have made it out of Africa. Meanwhile, the 650 million souls between the southern US border and the tip of Patagonia have to fight for the world's attention. If Latin America is a 'forgotten continent' – rendered invisible to outsiders – especially myopic is Britain, whose colonial footprint pressed heavier on the rest of the globe. The quarter of a million people of Latin American descent who live in the UK can't even identify as such on official forms. Instead, they have to tick the box marked 'Other'.

Mexico, Central America and the Caribbean are slightly more familiar to the English-speaking world. Partly a legacy of Washington's invasions of and interventions in its southern neighbours, a fifth of the US population is Latino. But when it comes to South America, we turn up more of a blank. The world's southernmost continent save Antarctica, it is cut off from the rest of the Americas by a mountainous jungle called the Darién, and given a distinct cultural identity by the Amazon rainforest, the vast lowland plains and the Andes: the great mountain chain that curves for 5,000 miles down its western flank like an arched spinal column. Yet our understanding of the ancient history of this quarter of the planet begins and ends with the Incas: a late Andean empire contemporary with the Tudors.

Most are then dimly aware of a Spanish and Portuguese 'conquest', of those who fought back being easily bested by European 'guns, germs and steel'. Some might be able to name Bolívar. The Venezuelan revolutionary freed his homeland then pressed onwards, seeking to forge a united continent – an ephemeral yet powerful dream, later referred to as the *patria grande*, which lingers to this day. In 1982, Argentina's invasion of the Falkland Islands, which Buenos Aires still claims as Las Malvinas, briefly put the region's juntas and autocrats on Westminster's radar. Earlier this millennium, a wave of left-wing leaders such as Chávez made headlines – distributing oil wealth to the people, lambasting the warmongering and imperialism of the United States – only for the world's interest to wane as the commodity boom went bust and the 'Pink Tide' ebbed.

This strange, continent-sized gap in our memory leaves us far the poorer. To begin with, Latin American history is also our history. For over five centuries, Latin America has been entwined with the making of the modern world. It was the place where European imperialism overseas was first trialled and tested. Indigenous cultures, philosophies, political systems – and resistance – moulded debates about the nature of humanity. Many of the foods we eat, the stimulants we consume, and the words we use originated on the far side of the Atlantic. For centuries, the global economy and even the world's climate has hinged on events in the New World.

People once walked into the Americas. Ten thousand years ago, the ice caps melted and the land bridge connecting Siberia and Alaska sank beneath a rising sea. The western hemisphere was not as entirely cut off as was once thought. Viking seafarers established a foothold on the tip of Newfoundland around AD 1000. Polynesian navigators undertook epic odysseys to South American shores. Siberian traders paddled across the Bering Strait bearing bronze and obsidian artefacts. But such fleeting encounters aside, millennia passed without sustained contact between the hemispheres. Their animals, plants, societies, technologies – and pathogens – developed in isolation.

In 1492, these worlds collided when Cristoforo Colombo – a

Genoese navigator in the service of the Spanish monarchy, known to us as Columbus – stumbled upon the Caribbean while looking for a short-cut to Asia. Europeans introduced plants like bananas and sugarcane to the Americas. Their cows, horses, pigs and rats multiplied unchecked, forming vast, marauding herds. In the other direction, the fruits and crops of the New World – painstakingly improved from wild varieties by Indigenous Americans over millennia – supplemented the meagre fare of the Old. Potatoes, tomatoes, maize, beans, cassava, peanuts, pumpkins, squashes and chili peppers – each with dozens or hundreds of varieties – transformed rural landscapes, defined national palates and powered demographic explosions from Ireland to Romania, Italy to West Africa, and Indonesia to China.

The most fateful exchange took place at the microbial level. Indigen-ous Americans had no immunity to Eurasian diseases like influenza, measles, typhus and pneumonia. Smallpox exploded among the Taíno people of Hispaniola – present-day Haiti and the Dominican Republic – and hopped from island to island. Of the million people living on Hispaniola in 1492 – by one count – just 500 were left in 1548. The renegade Spanish conquistador Hernán Cortés did not defeat the Mexica – better known to us as the Aztecs – alone. His victory was delivered by the armies of Indigenous allies like the Tlaxcalans – and the smallpox that raced through Tenochtitlan, the awe-inspiring Mexica capital, in 1521. At least a dozen epidemics ravaged the Mexica in the eighty years to 1600. Their population plunged from twenty-five mil-lion to barely a million.

It was probably smallpox that struck the Maya – whose great stone cities punctured the jungles of the Yucatán peninsula in Central America – in the late 1520s. 'Great pustules rotted their bodies with a great stench,' wrote one missionary; 'so that the limbs fell to pieces in four or five days.' Maya chroniclers vividly described the winnowing of generation after generation. 'People threw themselves into the ravines, and the dogs and foxes lived on the bodies of the men.' Perhaps as many as fifty-five million Indigenous Americans – ninety per cent of the pre-Columbian population – perished in this Great Dying: a cataclysm in human history rivalled only by the Black Death. So much of their aban-doned farmland was reclaimed by forest – some scientists have suggested – that it contributed to the global cooling of the early 1600s, seeding harsh winters, famine, and civil war across Asia, Europe and Britain.

The British Isles in particular have a far longer and deeper entanglement with Latin America than many realise. An Englishman and an Irishman sailed with Columbus' first voyage into the unknown. They never came back: left on Hispaniola, they quarrelled with the Taíno, who wiped the European garrison out. In 1698, Scottish aristocrats bet the house on a disastrous attempt to colonise the Darién. Most of the 2,500 settlers – who named their ill-fated outpost Caledonia, and its capital New Edinburgh – perished from fever. A bankrupted Scotland was driven into Union with England nine years later. By 1796, an impecunious Irish farmer had risen in Spain's service to become viceroy of Peru. Two decades later, rogue British admirals and volunteer riflemen, kicking their heels after Waterloo, joined his bastard son in the revolutions that overthrew colonial rule.

Bolívar plotted his patria grande from exile in Jamaica, a British colony in the Caribbean. The Royal Navy plucked Portugal's royal family from Napoleon's clutches, deposited them in Rio de Janeiro, and stamped out the transport of enslaved Africans to Brazil. Still, Britain's industrialists, banks and middle classes continued to profit from South American mines and plantations whose labourers suffered conditions little different to slavery. Meanwhile, English and Scottish surgeons, railwaymen, engineers and sailors propped up Paraguay's war effort. Welsh nationalists and nonconformists settled in Patagonia, where their language is still spoken. The soldiers and settlers of Victorian empire were fed thanks to centuries' worth of pre-Columbian bird muck, scraped off the Peruvian shoreline by refugees from Britain's opium-pushing wars in China.

As most South American countries mark their 200th birthday as independent nations, they also hold the key to the present. Eight of them share the Amazon rainforest: the world's largest tropical ecosystem, with an indispensable role in cooling the global climate. It is also home to the greatest numbers of Indigenous peoples living in voluntary isolation: put another way, avoiding all contact with us. But the Amazon and other biomes like the Great South American Chaco – also roamed by some of earth's last 'uncontacted' hunter-gatherers – are fast succumbing to an onslaught of loggers, ranchers, farmers and miners. Latin America as a whole contains around half the world's plant and animal species. But since 1970, its monitored wildlife populations have plunged by ninety-four per cent – the steepest decline of any region globally. As agribusiness engulfs the remaining shreds of green, and fleets of illegal Chinese trawlers scour its seabeds, Latin America is the world's biggest net exporter of food, sustaining the diets of hundreds of millions around the planet – while over forty million of its own people go hungry.

As fresh arteries are tapped, Galeano's litany of looting needs an update for the twenty-first century. While a quarter of Paraguayans cook with firewood, their country's abundant hydroelectricity powers Canadian-owned Bitcoin mines. Google, Microsoft and Amazon are cooling their global data centres with the freshwater supply of Chile and Uruguay – even amid a thirty-year drought in Santiago, and as brine trickles out of the taps in Montevideo. The extraction of South American metals is simultaneously undergirding the global 'green' transition and erasing ultra-rare ecosystems on the ground. The shimmering salt flats where Argentina, Chile and Bolivia meet contain two-thirds of the world's lithium: essential to the rechargeable batteries in iPhones, Teslas and data centres. But around two million litres of water are sucked to the surface and evaporated for every tonne of the so-called miracle mineral. In the meantime, the recent discovery of billions of barrels' worth of oil and gas off Guyana – joining huge reserves in Argentina, Venezuela, Bolivia and Brazil – will make South America a fossil fuel player to rival Saudi Arabia by 2030.

Synthetic drugs and smuggled guns are also big business in today's Latin America. It's producing more cocaine than ever before, matching surging demand in Africa and Asia: though Europe and the United States still smoke and snort the lion's share. An iron river of more than 200,000 firearms flows south across the US border, and over from Europe, in the opposite direction every year. The predictable consequence: criminal groups with military-grade firepower – more private armies than petty drug gangs – are fighting over lucrative shipping routes, corrupting and assassinating politicians, and transforming once-tranquil countries such as Ecuador into violent narcostates. Today, Latin America and the Caribbean is the world's homicide hotspot. The region encompasses eight per cent of the planet's population, but one in three of its murders.

Where a century ago South America took in tens of millions of the Old World's poor and huddled masses, she now exports her own people in bulk. Whether refugees from violence, political exiles or economic migrants, the Latin diaspora can be found cleaning offices and performing surgery, giving lectures and delivering takeaways, launching startups and scoring penalties from Brisbane to Brooklyn, Burgos to Brighton FC. In 2023, Border Patrol apprehended a record 2.4 million people trying to cross from Mexico into the United States – no longer just

Cubans, Haitians or Central Americans but record numbers of South Americans, especially from Venezuela and Ecuador. The backlash is likely to fuel the journey of would-be authoritarians to the White House well beyond the 2024 election.

But there are ways around walls. By 2050, a quarter of the US population will be Hispanic. The United States increasingly resembles its southern neighbour *Ñamérica*, to use the term coined by Argentine journalist Martín Caparrós: that vast, searingly unequal land of megacities split into gated communities and sprawling shantytowns; of restless, resourceful Spanglish-speakers; a continent on the move, soundtracked by the stuttering dembow beat of reggaeton. 'Ñamérica and her inhabitants have changed a lot in the last few decades,' Caparrós writes. 'We are no longer what we were: what many people, looking the other way, suppose that we still are.'

For one thing, South America's twelve sovereign states and 450 million people – roughly equal to the population of the United States, Canada, Britain and Australia – increasingly act as an assertive bloc on issues of trade, foreign policy, the climate crisis, the legalisation of drugs, and war and peace. This is to say nothing of the Latin American contributions to art, architecture, music, fiction, poetry, cinema, science – and sport, especially (but not only) football. Penetrating beyond the clichés and understanding the backstory of this distant land is not only an academic endeavour, but essential to grasping our interconnected and fragile planet.

Forty-two years ago, as Colombia's greatest writer accepted the Nobel Prize for literature, Gabriel García Márquez issued such an invitation to the world. From its very inception, Latin America has often seemed stranger than fiction, he conceded. Florentine navigators brought back tales of Patagonian giants and hogs with navels on their haunches. El Dorado, 'our so fervently coveted and illusory country, appeared on numerous maps for many a long year, shifting its location and form to suit the fantasy of cartographers'. Mexico's president held a funeral with full military honours for his right leg, mangled by a French cannon in the Pastry War: sparked by the looting of a patisserie on the outskirts of Mexico City.

But the condescension of the global north – forgetting how turbulent and violent its own rise had been – 'serves only to make us ever more unknown, ever less free, ever more alone'. And as new technologies shrank the distance between continents, García Márquez predicted, Latin America's enormous solitude would soon come to an end. Those who share in the dream 'of a more just and humane patria grande could help us better' – he suggested – 'if they changed their way of seeing us'.

That long-overdue paradigm shift is already upon us. The future of South American history has never looked more exciting. Cutting-edge technologies are turning up new archaeological, genetic and paleobotanical clues. Archivists and historians are rediscovering and reassessing old manuscript evidence. Pioneering scholars – Latin American, Indigenous and from overseas – are deploying fresh perspectives and frameworks, dramatically changing how we understand the continent's past. New generations are reconstructing their own history, challenging outdated discourses to do with race and Indigeneity. As statues to cutthroat conquistadors and genocidal generals tumble from Colombia to Chile, hoary national myths and stale hagiographies are also being dismantled, along with grand narratives that render everyday people helpless victims or two-dimensional martyrs.

A new, continent-crossing history from below is starting to take their place. It's one of complexity, coexistence, resistance and revolution, where ancient Amazonian agriculturalists mould the world's largest rainforest; Inca noblemen press the flesh with Mexica princes in Habsburg palaces; Muslim master-engineers build fortresses against Dutch mercenaries in the forests of Brazil; a transgender Basque nun trades his habit for armour, seducing and murdering his way through the Andes; Angolan revolutionaries cut down Spanish royalists on Chilean battlefields; Bolivian silver – mined by Andeans, minted by Congolese artisans and shipped in Mexican galleons to Manila – fills the coffers of Turkish, Iranian and Chinese emperors; and the mounted armies of an Indigenous Patagonian power are wined and dined by British diplomats, rescue shipwrecked Royal Navy sailors and their pet sheep, and elect a penniless French penpusher their king.

To tell some of this story, and to de-familiarise us with what we think we know, this book doesn't begin with existing lines on the map, taking modern South American states and explaining how they got there. Instead, it uses as stepping stones places that can't be found in an atlas but still shaped the continent, and sometimes the world, as much as any present-day nation. This is a history of some of those 'ands': not the mythical realms of outsiders' fantasies like El Dorado, but real-life kingdoms, nations, territories and peoples, whose legacy both material and upon the imagination – like the lost *patria* of López – can still be felt. In many cases, they have not disappeared as entirely as once believed.

There is more evidence than there might seem at first glance. Stretching along miles of shelves inside a palace in Seville sit thousands of bundles of fragile, yellowing manuscripts bound by ribbons and labelled after far-off places: Guadalajara, Cuzco, Cuba, the Philippines. Spain's Archivo General de Indias contains the nervous system of the world's first global empire fossilised on parchment. The authors of these reports – viceroys, judges, ambassadors and inquisitors – were rarely impartial observers of the Indigenous realms that defied them. But other voices sometimes break through the spidery handwriting, or can be perceived against its grain. National archives, private collections and museums across South America also contain countless other pieces of the puzzle.

Reams of documents are being digitised and declassified – from Portuguese governors plotting the downfall of Palmares to US Secretaries of State trying to keep Stroessner on side. Messages from those long gone can sometimes reach us in unexpected forms. Among the pointers that would aid my search for South America's lost countries were a mysterious carved slab buried beneath a dungheap and long mislaid in the vaults of the British Museum; a painting on a shattered pot unearthed from a lost Inca city in the jungle; and a cardboard box of dusty tapes in a wooden shack. My backpack, mosquito net and borrowed machete would prove as essential as a notepad and pen.

Some of these vanished realms are ancient civilisations whose mutually beneficial relationship with the natural world holds lessons for us today. We tend to think of the Amazon as a pristine wilderness, untouched by human hands. But new aerial technologies – along with old-fashioned trowel work – are uncovering vast complexes of roads, pyramids, earthworks and interconnected settlements beneath the canopy. Such discoveries point to the existence of flourishing Amazonian societies that enhanced the ecosystem around them: and to a future, say their present-day inheritors, in which the rainforest can be preserved for the benefit of all.

Others were hybrid realms that straddled the pre-Columbian, colonial and modern eras, adopting every new tool available – swords, horses, writing, guns – to withstand European invasion. After Cuzco, the Inca capital, fell to the conquistadors, the survivors retreated to the mountains behind Machu Picchu. Here, they founded a rump Inca state known as Vilcabamba. It endured for a generation, inspiring rebellions far beyond their cloud forest refuge. Palmares – the rebel kingdom of African and native fugitives – has had a similarly subversive afterlife throughout Brazilian history.

By contrast, few in Argentina today recall how a warlike Indigenous confederation resisted Spanish rule for a century and a half. Yet the Diaguita people have recently re-emerged, challenging the official history that their ancestors were wiped out during their last great uprising. On the other side of the Andes, the Mapuche are Chile's largest pre-existing nation, whose southern homeland of lakes and valleys some call Wallmapu. In recent years, a radical constitutional experiment briefly promised to restore their autonomy and self-determination. But it hasn't proved enough for the armed Mapuche revolutionaries who demand nothing less than Wallmapu's liberation.

The past two centuries have seen a flowering of more chimerical countries: whether nationalist reveries of lost greatness, the fearful hallucinations of the powerful, or the utopian visions of revolutionaries. Fired up by memories of Inca and Mapuche resistance, patriot leaders laid the blueprint for a United States of South America, ruled by a descendant of the Incas enthroned in Cuzco. Many Bolivians, from the president downwards, insist that their nation will not be whole until it recovers the coastline it lost to Chile in a nineteenth-century war. Until then, their landlocked navy putters around Lake Titicaca and practises in a simulator for its return to the high seas.

In 1964, Colombian troops bombarded Marquetalia – a remote refugee commune that officials in Bogotá and Washington feared was forming a breakaway socialist republic. In response, the survivors founded the Marxist-Leninist guerrilla army known as the FARC. It was the beginning of the world's longest civil war, leaving 450,000 people dead and counting. In the past decade in next-door Venezuela, the Bolivarian dream of reviving the patria grande turned into a nightmare of hyperinflation, hunger, corruption and repression. Protesters have destroyed statues of the late Chávez and even Bolívar. The crisis has triggered the planet's largest exodus of refugees outside of a war zone: nearly eight million Venezuelans have fled. I would later join some of the hundreds of thousands now risking their lives in a desperate attempt to reach a better life on US soil.

'We find a little of everything in our memory,' runs a line from Proust's *In Search of Lost Time*. 'It is a sort of pharmacy, or chemical laboratory, in which our groping hand comes to rest now upon a sedative drug, now upon a dangerous poison.' As for individuals, so for nations. Paraguay's nostalgia for the lost patria of López has shored up one-party rule for generations. It's a kind of state religion, an opiate that distracts the people while their rulers embezzle public funds, bulldoze the forests and get into bed with organised crime. Like the choking fumes that swirled around me in the jungle at Cerro Corá – damp sacks of weed bursting into flame, mingling with gasoline, mildewed bedding and molten plastic – it's one hell of a drug.

In his study of Europe's vanished kingdoms, Norman Davies dwells on the theme of transience, the 'pitiless passage of time'. His ancient Britannic monarchies, patchwork medieval duchies and ephemeral Carpathian republics are today 'poorly remembered or half-forgotten, or completely derelict'. The historian of such deceased and friendless polities is forced to become 'a beachcomber and treasure-seeker, a collector of flotsam and jetsam, a raiser of wrecks, a diver of the deep, scouring the seabed to recover what was lost'. My experience was to be very different. At times, the trail went cold, leaving only fragments and guesswork. But nearly everywhere I travelled, these supposedly dead and gone societies were live issues.

And in most places I visited – among smouldering Brazilian rainforest; climbing up to melting glaciers; traversing the world's driest desert, now turning wetter and warmer – the evidence of natural breakdown was unmistakable. As man-made forest fires incinerate the Amazonian orchards planted by ancient hands, and rain disinters mummified bodies buried in the sand seven millennia ago, the accelerating climate crisis across South America is disturbing the dead as well as the living.

It was to the coastal desert of Peru that I headed first of all: the seat of a pre-Columbian kingdom that rivalled the Incas in affluence and might. But, pummelled by invasion, civil war, lethal epidemics and ecosystem collapse, their civilisation crumbled overnight, leaving little trace. Centuries later, their riches would be siphoned off by British capitalists amid an early commodity rush that changed the world forever – and depended entirely on the bowels of Peruvian seabirds.

PART ONE

Resistance

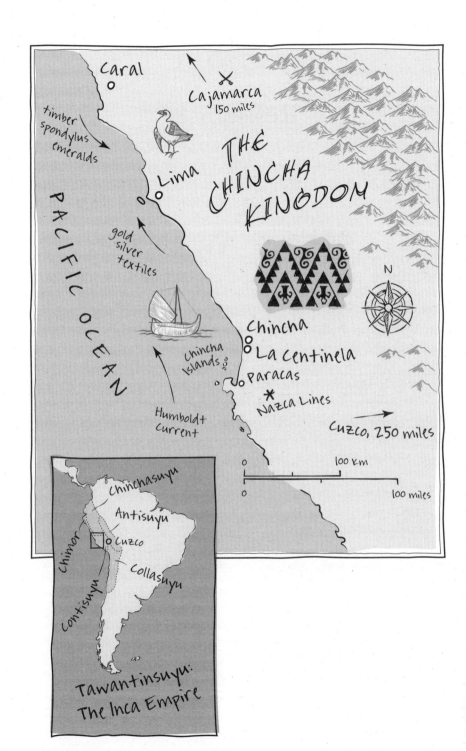

Caral

timber
spondylus
emeralds

PACIFIC OCEAN

gold
silver
textiles

Chincha
Islands

Humboldt
Current

Cajamarca
150 miles

THE
CHINCHA
KINGDOM

N

Chincha
La Centinela
Paracas
Nazca Lines

Cuzco, 250 miles

100 Km

100 miles

Lima

Chinchasuyu
Antisuyu
Chimor
Cuzco
Collasuyu
Contisuyu

Tawantinsuyu:
The Inca Empire

I

The Feathered King

The Chincha Kingdom, AD 1400–1532

ESTEEMED, FAMOUS AND FEARED

We cast off around 4 a.m. The air is thick with the greasy smell of fishmeal and gasoline, shouting men and thudding motors, bilious floodlights shining on a dark, freezing sea. *Jehovah is King*, her turquoise planks spattered with white, weaves through the trawlers. They haul bulging nets of anchovies into the air, the glistening globes appearing as from under a conjurer's cloth.

We emerge alone in the fishing boat – me, a grizzled scallop diver called Rodolfo Soto and Nick Ballon, a photographer – under a vast streak of stars. We steer north-west towards a faint, flashing speck. Muted by the wheezing outboard motor, Soto wordlessly shines a torch onto leaping shoals of kingfish. I settle on a damp foam pad. The boat lurches through the waves, my skull reverberates with the swell.

When I wake, three grey smears with silvery-white crests are rising out of an ashen dawn. As the trio of islets loom higher, I make out dark cliffs, inlets where waves crash and boil. Crumbling concrete walls, collapsed piers, wooden cranes garrisoned by feathered sentries. An eerie, high-frequency hum, growing in volume, and an acrid, ammoniac smell become installed in the senses.

As we come to a halt in the strait off the central island, a figure appears on the veranda of a dilapidated house. It sprints down a flight of rickety stairs, shoves a dinghy into the surf, and leaps in. The man plunges a paddle tied to a plank into the breakers and pulls up alongside us. Augusto is six feet tall, in his late forties, with a mop of black hair that makes him look younger. He wears a ragged, sun-bleached T-shirt, his toes poke out of his tattered trainers, and he is beaming from ear to ear.

We hop into his craft, now with a few jerry cans of water brought by Soto bobbing on a line, and Augusto steers back to land. We drag the inflatable ashore and haul in the containers. Soto moseys off to do some fishing. We are left with our host and half a million non-human residents – screeching and dive-bombing around our heads – on a rock barely a mile long and half a mile wide on the edge of the South Pacific.

Augusto, who has spent much of the past two years here on the Chincha Islands alone, is buzzing in the presence of visitors. He is part of a peculiar Peruvian tribe, the *guardaislas*: biologists, watchmen, climate scientists, gamekeepers, steeped in the lore and solitude of a lighthouse keeper. 'You have to be content with birds,' he warns us. 'If you don't like birds, you're going to suffer.'

16 November 1532. Hidden in the buildings around the square in Cajamarca, northern Peru, they wait, sunken-eyed and shaking. Sweating in their armour, fiddling with their sword-hilts, checking their harquebuses – better at producing putrid smoke and a deafening bang than killing a man – one final time. Shadows lengthening, they hear Mass, beg for divine assistance: please, Lord, anything but a night attack. Then word arrives: they are coming. Many piss themselves – one will later remember – 'out of pure terror'.

They are right to be afraid. The 180 Spaniards and a handful of Indigenous allies have marched right into the largest empire in the New World. Tawantinsuyu, the realm of four parts, stretches 2,500 miles between Colombia and Chile: the width of the United States, or the length of London to Timbuktu. Commanded by Francisco Pizarro – a poor, illegitimate soldier made good in the Caribbean – they are the first Europeans to tread so deep into this unfamiliar land. And on their gruelling journey, down from Panama in ships, along the Ecuadorian coast on foot and up into the Andes, they have been dumbfounded by the wealth and power of what is better known today as the Inca Empire.

They have passed storehouses stacked with years' worth of supplies: bulbous ears of white, golden and purple maize, the dried llama meat called *charqui* and dozens of kinds of tubers. Paved roads that snaked along even the most vertiginous ridge. Squadrons of soldiers surveilling them from forts of impeccable, mortar-less masonry in whose joins not even a needle could be inserted. Convents full of the fairest young women, destined to serve the Sun as priestesses or as concubines to his living descendant, the emperor, or Sapa Inca. Haughty local chieftains who trembled in the presence of imperial messengers. Towns razed to cinders, trees hung with corpses: the losing side of a pitiless civil war.

Yesterday, at the hot baths east of Cajamarca, they had a chilly audience with the victor. The emperor Atahualpa had not even deigned to look at them – even when the nostrils of a Spanish officer's horse, a beast none of the Inca's court had ever seen before, came close enough to disturb the thick scarlet tassel covering his forehead. The Spaniards' protestations of love, and their offer to conquer his enemies, had met only with a wan smile. He agreed to return the visit, however. That night, the sleepless Spaniards gazed up at his army's campfires, stretching across the hillsides 'like a brilliantly star-studded sky'.

And now, that vast constellation of warriors is descending: 40,000 of them, 80,000. They come singing, sweeping wisps of straw off the road, dressed for a party rather than a battle, with glittering discs of gold and silver encircling their heads, and tunics chequered like a multi-coloured chessboard. The Inca emperor, wearing his crimson-fringed crown and a collar of giant emeralds, travels in a silver-tipped litter lined with golden plates and Amazonian macaw feathers, borne aloft by eighty noblemen in livery of ocean blue. They have left their spears, shields and clubs behind, bearing only slings and ceremonial axes. Although only Atahualpa's honour guard enter the plaza of Cajamarca, they still outnumber the Spanish by forty to one. The invaders have one shot at seizing control of this empire and its untold riches: by capturing Atahualpa alive.

First, there are some formalities to get over with. A Spanish priest emerges and presents the young emperor with a prayer book: the new faith he will submit to, freely or by force. Atahualpa fumbles it open, leafs through the pages, and – turning red with rage – hurls it to the ground. Pizarro gives the signal. The hidden Spanish cannons belch flame and iron into the dense ranks of the Incas. To the blare of trumpets, armoured horsemen charge into the square, hacking at bare heads and hands, calling on Santiago, St James the Moorslayer. Panicking at the noise and the strange, braying beasts, slipping on slicks of gore, the Inca's retainers trample each other. Mounds form of the dead and dying. Swordsmen block the exits, cutting down those who flee.

Atahualpa's followers heroically put their bodies between their ruler and the Spaniards' steel. When their hands are cut off, they support his litter with their shoulders. Pizarro parries a Spanish sword-thrust away from the emperor. 'Nobody hurt the Indian,' he yells, 'on pain of death!' Another nobleman – the only other afforded the privilege of being carried about – is not so lucky. Finely dressed, swathed in feathers, he is easily mistaken for Atahualpa. Pizarro, struggling to tell them apart, orders detachments to make for both when the killing begins. Juan, the general's hot-headed half-brother, leaps up and stabs the prince in the plumage where he sits.

Finally, the riders grab hold of the emperor's platform and heave. He topples to the ground and is captured. The survivors break through a wall and scatter through the fields, hunted by the Spanish cavalry. Atahualpa's men went unarmed – his nephew later wrote – 'because they thought little of the Spaniards'. It was a fatal mistake. They were slaughtered, Titu Cusi Yupanqui lamented, 'as one kills sheep, with none resisting. Of more than ten thousand, only two hundred escaped.'

The prisoners pile up the bodies and shoo away the llamas that have wandered, unattended, into the town. Atahualpa, unaware that his ultra-violent kidnapping is the prelude to conquest, orders his armies to stand down. To buy his freedom, he offers to pour golden treasures into a long, wide chamber to a line halfway up the wall, and to fill it twice again with silver to the ceiling. He sends his followers to strip Qorikancha – the Temple of the Sun in Cuzco – of its adornments: goblets and serving vessels, a great golden image of the Sun 'set with many precious stones', animal figurines made of precious metals, the glittering sheets that clad the roof and walls, even a garden whose clods of earth and stalks of corn are made of gold.

To while away the time, the hostage learns chess from his captors. Atahualpa realises – with visible disdain – that Pizarro is illiterate, and has to have letters read to him. The Inca reminisces about the flamboyantly feathered retainer they had killed: his steward, a 'dear friend' and master of the Chincha Kingdom, which Atahualpa's great-grandfather had conquered. It was a 'great province, esteemed in ancient times', 'famous throughout Peru and feared by many'.

The Chincha had somehow turned a coastal desert in southern Peru into a fertile paradise. Their capital, Chincha Alta – a great complex of a dozen earthen pyramids – centred on an oracle called Chinchaycamac, which attracted offerings of gold, silver and livestock from across the Andean world. A wide central avenue stretched for miles, thronged with men, women and children, 'all content and joyful, for when not at sea their only care was to drink and dance'. Some 12,000 manual workers built earthquake-resistant palaces out of huge adobe blocks. Ten thousand fishermen plied the rich waters nearby, 'each one with their raft and nets, going in and out of ports well known to them, without rivalry among themselves, because in this (as in all things) they had great order and harmony'.

The Chincha lord, Atahualpa claimed, commanded 100,000 ocean vessels: a navy without parallel in the pre-Columbian world. Plying the Pacific seaboard hundreds of miles north, Chincha mariners exported luxury goods and imported precious commodities, including a sacred, spiky oyster plucked from the warm waters of the equator. The shiny, reddish shell of *Spondylus* was prized as jewellery, while its flesh – which, eaten out of season, can trigger euphoria, a feeling of flight, paralysis and death – may have been used in Inca religious ceremonies. It was perhaps a Chincha merchant ship that Spanish sailors encountered off Ecuador in 1525: a thirty-tonne craft with cotton sails, laden with golden crowns, daggers, armour, tweezers, birds, fish and trees; burnished silver mirrors; sheets of fabric and clothes dyed burgundy, crimson and yellow; weights to measure gold and necklaces slung with precious gems.

In the early 1400s, the emperor Pachacuti – a bold strategist who kick-started the Incas' expansion out of the valleys around Cuzco – turned his sights on the maritime power at his doorstep. What followed is related by Inca Garcilaso de la Vega – the son of a conquistador and an Inca princess – in his historical epic *Royal Commentaries of the Incas*. The Chincha, he wrote, refused to either 'receive the Sun for their God, nor the Inca for their King'. Instead, they insisted 'that the Sea was the Deity, which they had most reason to Adore, in regard it supplied them with Fish for their nourishment, and was in other particulars and instances the most usefull and beneficial'. Months of pitched battles and complex negotiations followed. Finally, the Incas cut off the Chincha irrigation channels. Their crops withered and the Chincha submitted.

The Inca usually razed the shrines of vanquished enemies, erecting their own eminences of perfectly joined stone atop the ashes. But on this occasion, the Inca palace – relatively small, and made of local adobe blocks – was built in the shadow of the Chinchaycamac oracle's towering ziggurat. Special treatment was also given to the Chincha king, Guavia Rucana, and his descendants. He remained the chief justice of his people, with Inca officials only judging offences against the emperor. At Cajamarca, Pedro Pizarro – the teenage cousin and squire of the Spanish commander – marvelled at how the Chincha ruler was carried on a litter behind the Inca, 'for no Indian, no matter how great a lord, could appear before him if not barefoot and with a burden on their shoulders'. Atahualpa even told him over a game of chess that Tawantinsuyu's northern quarter – its richest and most populous – had been named Chinchaysuyu in honour of the coastal kingdom it encompassed.

For Garcilaso, his Inca ancestors had shown habitual 'gentleness and moderation' when they could have wiped out the 'puffed-up' Chincha rabble. Reading between the lines, other considerations were probably at work. The Inca were highlanders, landlubbers: annexing intact a client state of seafarers could double their reach and influence overnight. The Chincha perhaps remained an entrepreneurial enclave within the regimented Inca system, tasked with ranging beyond imperial frontiers to cut deals for exotic, dangerous goods like *Spondylus*.

But another reason why the Chincha were afforded such prestige may lie in the epic and unforgiving landscape of Peru. The country is split by chains of snowbound Andean peaks, climbing to 5,000 metres above sea level, occasionally falling to highland plateaus where little grows but spiky grass. To the east, sweltering jungle. To the west, a bone-dry strip of sand, the mountains and cold oceanic currents blocking moisture on either side. As if that weren't enough, Peru is regularly battered by earthquakes, floods and the violently see-sawing Pacific climate pattern known as El Niño. How to feed an empire from the little land available, much of it sandy grit or a few inches of dirt? The Chincha Kingdom, it seems, was guardian of a secret weapon that could transform barren Andean slopes and blasted deserts alike into flourishing granaries. Speakers of Quechua, the language of the Incas, called it *huanu*, hence the Spanish *guano*. In plain English: birdshit.

The frigid Humboldt Current sweeps up from Antarctica and along South America's western coastline, drawing nutrients to the ocean's surface. Phytoplankton feast on this floating banquet, supporting vast populations of fish like the Peruvian *anchoveta*. These billion-strong shoals in turn sustain the cormorants, pelicans and gannets that nest on rocky Peruvian islets in their millions. Over thousands of years, their droppings – rich in phosphate, potassium and nitrogen, scarcely disturbed by a drop of rain – formed towering, compacted mounds. The white-breasted cormorant or *guanay* even evolved to fashion nests out of its own guano to stop its eggs from rolling into the sea. And this providential resource lay in its greatest concentrations on the Chincha Islands – just fifteen miles across the water from Chincha Alta.

The Inca were manure connoisseurs, carefully applying fish heads and alpaca muck to their terraces. Human excrement was especially prized. In Garcilaso's *Royal Commentaries*, the words 'dung' and 'manure' appear nearly fifty times. But the product the Chincha were sitting on, he conceded, was without compare: 'this sort of Birds dung was esteemed precious, being the best improvement and manure for Land in the World.' The 'incredible flocks' of birds that nested on Peru's coastal islands, he added, created 'such heaps of Dung, that at a distance they seem to be Hills of Snow'. After Pachacuti brought the Chincha to heel in the fifteenth century, their guano deposits were shared between his subjects, and 'all People enjoyed sufficient for their support, never any scarcity or famine having been known in that Land'. Proud nations submitted to the Inca without a fight: in exchange for tribute, they need never go hungry again.

Archaeologists have uncovered huge quantities of woven cotton and llama dung at Chincha Alta: perhaps caravans laden with sacks of the malodorous commodity set out from here up into the mountains. In Cuzco, a garden at the Qorikancha was planted with earth brought from the Chincha Valley: a test bed for recreating their blooming orchards. On the eve of Pizarro's invasion in 1532, the Chincha armada were not necessarily all fishers or traders, but bird-handlers and guano-haulers: paddling the choppy waters around the islands, carefully gathering the manure in exchange for offerings without disturbing the guanay, knowing which areas to leave fallow so the guano might accumulate afresh. This unique skillset – master kayakers, agronomists and ornithologists – may best explain why the Inca treated their conquered rival with kid gloves.

Peruvian guano not only fuelled the rise of the strongest power in pre-Columbian America. It also forged the modern world. In the mid-1800s, the Chincha Islands became the epicentre of one of the first global commodity rushes. The forlorn archipelago and its miracle fertiliser attracted international merchant fleets, sparked imperial conflicts and forever transformed the way our species farms, eats and lives. Few patches of terrain have had such an outsized influence on the history of the planet.

Tracing the rise and fall of the Chincha Kingdom – and the island jewels in its crown – helps us return South America and its Pacific seaboard to the centre of global history where they belong. It also offers a premonition, or perhaps a warning. Our own civilisation is hardly less fragile than if it hinged on cold water, some fish, some pathogens, the digestive tract of a pelican.

THE AGE OF MANURE

The three of us climb the few steps from the beach. Abandoned, rusty anchors, splintered warehouses. Railway tracks connect a ruined pier to a custard-yellow cliff. Birds whirl overhead and crowd every surface.

Augusto, a *guardaisla* of nine years' service, appears oblivious, but apologises for the few hundred sea lions half a mile away on the southerly island. 'They make a scandalous noise,' he tuts. We climb a gap-toothed staircase up to his house. A wooden plank, cut and painted to resemble the outline of a rifle, hangs on a nail. 'This is to frighten the enemies,' he giggles.

Over watery porridge, Augusto explains that most of Peru's guano islands are protected reserves, watched over by guardaislas like him. Every few years – taking care not to scare the birds away – the agriculture ministry sends workers to harvest the guano by hand. The modern Peruvian state, much like the ancient one, then distributes it to poor Andean farmers. This marvellous manure is valuable. A subsidised fifty-kilo sack worth fifty *soles* – around thirteen US dollars – earns double that on the black market. That's a lot of cash in a country where a third of people live on less than four dollars a day.

For some, the islands' natural riches are too tempting. 'If they don't rob the guano, they kill the birds,' Augusto adds, frowning. Then there are illegal fishermen who drop dynamite among shoals of anchovies, spooking the guanay. 'On other islands there have been hand-to-hand confrontations. Since our weapons were taken from us the poachers have been less afraid.' A few years back, the guardaislas had their real rifles withdrawn: there were 'problems' involving solitary, cabin-feverish colleagues. Augusto's back-up plan is to wave his wooden prop at night-time intruders, hoping its silhouette will scare them off. I don't ask what happens if they call his bluff.

We exit through a back door into a cleft that bisects the island. No vegetation nor running water: just two undulating flanks of formless yellow-grey. Photographs taken here in 1860, two decades into the global guano rush, show a lofty mound still largely intact. Nearly forty-five metres tall, it contained an age's worth of densely compacted huanu. Today, a couple of years since the latest harvest, there is a relatively light dusting. Still, everywhere you look, the surface is pockmarked by millions of craters of excrement and grubby feathers: the nests of the guanay. An anaemic sun slips through the mist, rendering them a gritty white and gold, reminiscent of halogen-lit slush at the roadside after a blizzard.

The nests crumble beneath our feet as we trudge to the island's northern edge. The bulk of its residents are nesting here in deafening swarms of tens of thousands, an indecipherable air-traffic pattern of take-offs and landings. Though impossible to follow a single bird, you can piece together their action from the whole: they wheel out to sea, plunge underwater, return with food for the scrappy balls of fluff protected by their mates. 'The hum of wings is like the effect of an overdose of quinine upon the ears,' wrote Robert Cushman Murphy, a visiting ornithologist who walked here a century earlier, 'and the combined voices seem like mutterings of the twelve tribes of Israel. It reminds one of all sorts of strange, oppressive roarings, such as the noise of railroad trains in river tunnels.' Sudden movements of the hand, he noted, produced pandemonium among the birds, as did brandishing a rifle, but firing a lowered gun did nothing. At the sound of human speech, 'their mumbles and grunts die away, and they listen for a while as if in amazement'.

We pad in respectful silence past caved-in sheds, decades of droppings engulfing their splintered timbers like stalactites. The panorama seems desolate. But Augusto finds beauty in the endlessly unfolding ritual of birth, life and death around him. Over time, you get to know the birds' different characters. The undersized head of the penguin-like guanay pokes out of a dress shirt and tails. The Inca tern or *zarcillo* has a feline, mewling call, his rubbery white whiskers curling around butter-smeared cheeks. The yolk of their eggs 'is very yellow', Augusto adds. 'It's pure anchovy. Very calorific.' An ungainly pelican, the *alcatraz* scoops up fish from the surface with her bucket-like bill. Belying his black mask and fighter-jet wings, the *piquero* engages in a coy courtship ritual. He shyly presents would-be partners with a sprat, clamped in his beak like a silver rose. Augusto discourages us from getting too close, showing a paternal concern for his feathery charges, anxious to avoid a mass flight that would leave their eggs untended.

The keepers of the guano birds, ancient or modern, demonstrate the same complex of affection and reverence. Under the Inca, wrote Garcilaso, landing on the islands during breeding season carried the death penalty. Pedro Cieza de León, another sixteenth-century chronicler, recorded how coastal peoples crossed to the islands to make sacrifices: 'It is presumed that great treasure is buried on them.' When the guano began to be scraped off by the tonne in the 1840s, this presumption was proved right. Most of the artefacts went unrecorded, stolen by the captains of foreign ships and disappearing forever into private collections. The findings that we know about include black Inca pottery; a golden female figurine; ceramic statues of bound captives; ten silver fishes found beside a mummified woman, her head metres from her body, covered in golden sheets; and a heavy, engraved slab. Around 1560, the stone was placed atop the guano by one of the very last of the Chincha people.

*

At the end of the 1700s, Europe and North America were haunted by the spectre of starvation. For centuries, they had fed their people by simply creating more and bigger farms. They cut down forests, drained swamps, stole land from Indigenous nations, forced their own peasants off the commons. But as life expectancy grew, humans were multiplying at a worrying rate.

Farmers were running out of land. The fields under cultivation were tilled to exhaustion, their lifeless soil producing meagre yields: the world seemed headed for mass starvation, war and disaster. 'I do not know that any writer has supposed,' mused the economist Thomas Malthus, 'that on this earth man will ultimately be able to live without food.' If humans did not succeed in wiping each other out, then 'gigantic inevitable famine stalks in the rear, and with one mighty blow, levels the population'.

Desperate to revive the depleted dirt, growers sprinkled their fields with whatever they could get their hands on: feathers, seaweed, dried blood from slaughterhouses, skeletons of the exterminated bison that littered North American prairies. British agents ransacked European catacombs, looted ancient Egyptian cat cemeteries and scoured Napoleonic battlefields – including Waterloo – for remains to grind up as fertiliser. One journal branded England the world's 'greatest trafficker in human bones'.

But there was one substance – still used by a few sugarcane haciendas along the Peruvian coast – that was rumoured to make a Lazarus of any moribund furrow. When the young Prussian naturalist Alexander von Humboldt came across barges outside Lima heaped with huanu from the Chinchas, he erupted in a sneezing fit. In 1802, he took a sample back to Berlin. European chemists – aided by Peruvian scientists like Mariano de Rivero – gradually caught up with what the Chincha, the Inca and their ancient predecessors had figured out many centuries before.

'In a soil that consists entirely of sand and clay,' a radical young journalist called Karl Marx scribbled in his notebook, 'it is enough to mix in a small quantity of guano to get the richest harvests of maize.' The Malthusian Trap had been broken, he believed. With mankind released from eking a subsistence from the grudging earth, the potential for building a freer, fairer society was unbounded. Nothing matched the awesome power of Peruvian guano. It proved twenty-five times more effective than farmyard manure, growers in the United States marvelled. One County Kerry farmer applied a dusting of the off-white powder: his apple trees and raspberry bushes flowered twice in a year, while his potato, wheat and turnip yields tripled. British warships scoured the oceans for other major deposits in vain: Peru was blessed with the strongest, most abundant fertiliser on the planet. 'It is the thing most worthy of admiration,' the government minister Mariano Paz Soldán reflected in 1862: 'it is as though Providence created guano for Peru alone.'

Peru had won nature's lottery. But everybody else wanted a slice. In March 1841, a ship called the *Bonanza* docked in Liverpool with the first stinking consignment. The guano rush had begun. Forty years later, nearly thirteen million tonnes of guano had been shovelled off Peruvian shores. It went to France, the United States, Spain, China, Cuba, Costa Rica – but above all to Britain and her colonies. In 1850 alone, the mother country imported 200,000 tonnes.

This near-monopoly was the work of the Gibbs family. Having turned a profit from Caribbean plantations toiled by enslaved Africans, in 1843 the trading house won the right to export Peruvian guano to Britain, and to Europe, Africa and Australia soon after. William Gibbs, a former clerk in the family firm, became England's wealthiest commoner. He built a neo-Gothic pile near Bristol called Tyntesfield, its stained-glass windows graced by guanay. The public could tolerate fortunes made from captive-harvested sugar, but reserved their mockery for the huanu parvenu: 'The House of Gibbs made their dibs,' went one ditty, 'selling the turds of foreign birds.'

Peru also turned its guano into gold. Between 1840 and 1878, it earned US$750 million – an untold fortune for a bankrupt former colony. In 1862, while totting up the income derived from guano exports so far, Paz Soldán bookended his figures with doubled exclamation marks: 'Two hundred million pesos!!' The proceeds paid for boulevards, parks, railways, schools, hospitals and soldiers. Peru's finance minister wrote 'without exaggeration' that guano 'underwrites the state's subsistence, the maintenance of its credit, its future enlargement, and the conservation of public order'.

Between 1823 and 1830, Peru had cycled through six different constitutions, and it went through eight rulers in the decade to 1836. The mainlining of guano to the body politic did little to straighten it out. Peru's government was 'as unstable as water', wrote one British visitor in 1877. 'It would be difficult to reckon up the number of revolutions which have taken place in the Age of Manure.' Other industries fell by the wayside. Peru was forfeiting annual business worth £20 million, thought A. J. Duffield, an English mining engineer and camelid enthusiast, by sending its alpaca and llama wool 'to England to be made into things which the growers of the staple never see'. The fees paid up-front by contractors like Gibbs mainly went to cronies and creditors. The resulting system of guano extraction was so inefficient, and demand so great, that ships idled for months off the Chincha Islands in their hundreds.

Luckily, entertainment was on hand. In 1866, a census recorded that the archipelago, with a free resident population of barely 1,100 people, hosted twenty-three taverns, nineteen diners, fifteen stores, four billiard halls and cafes, two hotels – and one school. Imports for the year included 882 'crates of different liquors', 533 bottles of *pisco* and *aguardiente* brandy, 300 barrels of Peruvian rum, 162 kegs of beer and sixty vats of Bordeaux. The crews contributed their own contraband. Customs agents seized thirty-five 'crates of diverse liquors', eight barrels of beer, four butts of French wine and a revolver wrapped in a bundle of clothes.

Smuggling, gambling, prostitution and theft flourished. Crime lords lurked. Murders went unpunished. What had been hallowed, strictly legislated territory under the Incas became a byword for lawlessness and vice. 'Small though the Chinchas are, their name is known in the farthest seaports of the world,' wrote Robert Cushman Murphy a few decades later. 'Their share in making fortunes and abetting calamities, in debauching men and demoralizing administrations, and in serving as the inanimate cause of greed, cruelty, extravagance, economic ruin and war has given them a historic place quite out of proportion to their size.'

Guano addiction fuelled not just violent crime but international aggression. The 'guano question' – how to secure a reliable supply of the stuff for US farmers – was hotly debated in congress and featured in four presidential addresses. In 1852, President Millard Fillmore backed an armed merchant fleet bound for the guano-laden Lobos Islands. Their owner, Peru, readied itself for a fight. One newspaper called on its readers to 'exterminate' the hated North American race. Fillmore only called off the expedition in exchange for promises of the chalky Peruvian powder.

Washington also chased its fix elsewhere. Between 1857 and 1902, it annexed ninety-four lesser guano islands, clustered like pimples in the Pacific and the Caribbean, and peopled them with captive workers from Hawaii. The occupied atolls would later come in handy: as airbases for US bombers and test sites for its nuclear weapons.

HEAT, STINK AND DAMNATION

It was known as the Pantheon. Dozens of hands and feet wrapped in rags poked out from the grit. Exposed faces, taut and parched like papyrus. Birds nesting in gaping mouths, some with coins still on their tongues. In 1925, a young Indigenous Peruvian called Pizarro guided Murphy, the bird scientist from New York, to this spot: the 'hottest and ugliest part' of the northern Chincha Island. Decades since the industry had collapsed, a patina of guano had mummified these human remains. It was, Murphy believed, a mass grave of suicides.

Using the proceeds of the first decade of guano fever, Peru had freed its enslaved African and Indigenous workers in 1854. But all that bird-crap wasn't going to shovel itself. There were only so many convicts. And attracting workers with a decent wage would eat into the profits. So Peru looked across the Pacific, where a punitive imperial war was creating a starving, desperate population.

Britain had been haemorrhaging a fortune in silver buying tea from China. Instead, it wanted to trade one addictive substance for another: Bengal-grown opium for Chinese tea leaves. The Qing dynasty refused. But the East India Company flooded the country with the narcotic anyway. Millions became hooked. Then, Britain invaded – twice – to force China to legalise the trade. The redcoats seized Hong Kong, looted the Summer Palace and burned it to the ground. What's more, Marx wrote to the *New York Tribune* in 1857, British imperial officials were selling Chinese refugees into 'worse than slavery on the coast of Peru'. Britons back home, meanwhile, looked 'no further than the grocer's where they buy their tea'.

Some of those who embarked were promised food, a wage and their freedom after several years' labour. Others were simply kidnapped. And it soon became apparent that the Chinese labourers had been consigned to a fate hardly preferable to death. They were transported in 'slave ships', said eyewitnesses, forced to crouch or lie flat for weeks on end. Most of the vessels were English, noted one observer in 1853. Another argued that this Pacific passage 'reproduced all the horrors' of 'the old African slave trade'.

And once disembarked on the islands, their cargo of men and boys entered 'the worst and most cruel slavery', outdoing even the planta-tions of the US South: 'it was universally said to be so by captains who had visited every quarter of the globe.' The refugees laboured from 5

a.m. to sunset, six days a week, in choking, blinding, miasmic dust. With
nothing but picks and shovels, they each had to fill eighty sacks a day –
four tonnes of guano – and haul them to the waiting boats. They were
paid eight pesos a month, while the prisoners labouring alongside them
earned twelve.

Exhausted, many fell down the loading chutes, smashed into the
ships below and drowned. Overseers whipped those who flagged. The
rebellious were lashed to a leaky raft and pushed out to sea. Some
100,000 indentured Chinese workers entered Peru between 1847 and
1874. By one count in 1860, of the 4,000 consigned so far to the guano
islands, none had survived. Far from liberating the proletariat as Marx
had imagined, guano entailed appalling new forms of exploitation. 'No
hell has ever been conceived,' wrote A. J. Duffield, 'that can be equalled
in the fierceness of its heat, the horror of its stink, and the damnation of
those compelled to labour there.'

Little testimony by the press-ganged workers survives. But they
weren't resigned to their fate. They staged mutinies on at least sixty-
eight ships between 1847 and 1874, and revolted against their bosses
on the central Chincha island in 1866 and 1877. But escape was nearly
impossible. Exercising what little freedom they had, many took their
own lives, some believing that they would be reincarnated at home. 'No
single day passes,' wrote one administrator, 'without someone hanging
themselves or throwing themselves upon the rocks.'

These tragedies reverberate in the ghost stories swapped by guardaislas. Augusto has glimpsed an apparition scraping his shackles along the
corridor, and felt a figure at his side while visiting the bathroom. Another
colleague has heard a child weeping on his evening rounds. We meet
Mauro – at sixty-seven, the oldest island-keeper in service – on leave on
the mainland. 'Sometimes at night you hear someone yanking on a
chain,' he says. 'You don't need to be scared or pay it any mind. Because
if you get nervous, hell . . .' Mauro has come across corpses embalmed
in the guano on Chincha Norte: 'Although you might not believe me,
the bodies are still intact. Even their nails grow, their moustaches.'
Augusto has also learned to treat the phantasms as old friends, even
chiding them for disturbing his beauty sleep. 'If you're afraid, it's worse,'
he agrees.

Suicide would recur in the history of the islands. In 1862, Spain dispatched a fleet to its former South American colonies, supposedly for
scientific research. A deadly brawl broke out involving Spanish citizens
in Peru. Madrid then demanded payment for debts dating back to the

wars of independence. When Peru refused, Spanish marines disembarked in the Chincha Islands, seizing over half the country's annual revenue without even firing a shot. In a fleeting moment of unity, Bolivia, Ecuador, Peru and Chile resolved to fight off this neo-colonial outrage. A pair of young lieutenants – Miguel Grau, a Peruvian, and Arturo Prat, from Chile – fought side by side. Two Spanish ships were sent to the bottom. As if infected by the islands' melancholy, the invading admiral donned his dress uniform, lay down in his bunk, and shot himself in the head.

British diplomats meanwhile howled in protest at this last gasp of Spanish imperialism in South America. Of the $30 million of foreign goods Peru had imported the previous year, two-thirds were from England, half paid for in guano. Lima was on the hook for $100 million in investment and loans in London. Swathes of British manufacturing, shipping and banking – to say nothing of the food on British tables – depended on birdshit leaving the Chincha Islands as smoothly as possible.

Soto fetches us in his skiff, and we bob across the strait to the southernmost island, Chincha Sur. Penguins and sealions bask in the spray, whipped up by a hot breeze from the mainland. A basket is lowered from a pier for our bags. We jump from the pitching prow of the *Jehovah* onto a swaying rope ladder. At the top, we are greeted by Jhon, the twenty-eight-year-old resident guardaisla, and another expanse of white. I ask Jhon what brings him to the island. 'It's a long story,' he sighs. 'You could fill a book with it. Sometimes it's good to get a change of air, you know?'

Every few years, hundreds of workers descend on each island to harvest the guano. Their field kitchens produce tonnes of waste. Jhon is comparing this man-made fertiliser with the huanu. If his findings are favourable, they could be scaled up nationally. 'If the quality is as good or much better,' he enthuses, 'why throw it away?' Used on the islands, it could help the guardaislas grow fresh fruit and vegetables to supplement their crackers, rice and fish. Innovations even bolder than compost are coming to Peru's guano islands. Mobile reception has reached some, and the internet and solar panels are next. The ascetic existence of the guardaisla will change forever.

We had spent hours in Lima negotiating our access to the islands. The agricultural ministry had given us grudging permission to visit during daylight – but forbidden us from watching the harvest on

Chincha Norte. The work is tough, an official tells us defensively, but well-paid. Machinery is shunned not out of stinginess but for fear of frightening the birds. The labourers, mainly down from the mountains, are not forced to do it, he insists. We say our farewells to Jhon and Augusto, and ask Soto if we can circle the north island. From a short distance, we see the sacks of guano piled high. Sunbeaten Andean workers, T-shirts wrapped around their heads, form a queue for lunch. Others shower in concrete cubicles open to the sea.

When Duffield, the English engineer, first saw the Chincha Islands in the 1850s, 'they were bold, brown heads, tall and erect, standing out of the sea like living things, reflecting the light of heaven, or forming soft and tender shadows of the tropical sun on a blue sea'. Returning in 1877, they 'looked like creatures whose heads had been cut off, or like vast sarcophagi, like anything in short that reminds one of death and the grave'. In barely thirty years, the guano deposits of millennia had vanished, scattered to the four corners of the globe. The islands, their governor reported, were 'not even the shadow' of their former glory. Passing ships only called in for the saloons. The surviving workers were shipped to guano deposits far to the north. The town and cemetery on the north island were flattened, the last yellowy residue scraped from among the shrunken corpses.

Nor would the guano stacks recover any time soon. A popular 'guano song' in Germany had once imagined the guanay as unflappable philosophers: 'ever pondering pious questions / They labour right faithfully / For blessed are their digestions / And flowing like poetry.' Now, nearly all of the birds – painstakingly preserved by the Chincha and the Inca for centuries – had disappeared.

Not twenty years since lieutenants Grau and Prat had joined forces against Spain, they found themselves enemies. One historian calls it Guano War II. Vast guano deposits had been uncovered in the Atacama Desert spanning northern Chile, southern Peru and south-west Bolivia, along with rich fields of nitrate – also known as saltpetre, prized as a fertiliser and in explosives. Having long claimed all the desert as its own, Chile wanted control of these riches. In 1879, it went to war.

Chilean artillery cut Bolivia's army to ribbons and occupied Lima. Prat, captaining a Chilean corvette, was shot down in an attempt to board Peru's flagship. Months later, Grau was blown to pieces by a Chilean shell, leaving only his feet and a few teeth. Chile still keeps his ship – the *Huáscar*, built in Birkenhead – as a floating museum. Chile also kept a chunk of southern Peru, as well as Bolivia's entire coastline, including its nitrate mines and deposits of guano, silver, copper and lithium.

In the early 1900s, Peru closed the Chincha Islands to foreign companies. Peruvian workers, under better conditions, harvested the guano sparingly for domestic use. But if the authorities planned to replenish stocks enough to compete with Chile's nitrates, their hopes were dashed by another astounding discovery. In 1909, the German chemist Fritz Haber found a way of plucking nitrogen from the air with hydrogen to produce ammonia: a highly reactive compound used to make fertiliser. Carl Bosch standardised the procedure in 1913. In the following year alone, the Haber-Bosch process created as much reactive nitrogen as Peru's guano islands.

This was a historic breakthrough, even greater than the West's rediscovery of guano seventy years before. Ammonium nitrate fertiliser would revolutionise agriculture, eliminating the limits posed to the growth of humanity by soil exhaustion, land shortages and the finite supply of natural fertilisers. Today, without synthetic nitrogen – a road embarked upon by the guano trade – up to half of the world's population would starve.

But our reliance on artificial fertilisers comes with a sting in the tail. Our chemical-dependent monoculture crops can easily be wiped out by disease. Run-off from fields is sterilising rivers and creating vast dead zones in the world's oceans. Ammonia production emits 500 million tonnes of carbon dioxide every year: almost twice as much as Britain's greenhouse gas emissions.

Today, Latin America imports eighty per cent of its fertilisers. When prices tripled after Russia invaded Ukraine in 2022, Peru's rice, maize and potato harvests were forecast to halve. The president suggested that the guanay could fly to the rescue. But barely 100,000 tonnes of guano could be scraped together that year: not even a tenth of the 1.8 million tonnes of fertiliser Peru imported in 2021. Amid a political crisis, unrest erupted in 2023. Its epicentre – where police killed dozens of protesters – was in the poor Andean south, where drought and spiking prices for fertiliser had led to shortages of food.

OF WOLVES, BIRDS AND MEN

Barely a generation since the Chincha ruler had been killed in the massacre at Cajamarca, his kingdom had collapsed entirely. A hot, dusty wind whipped through the empty avenue. Boats splintered into flotsam on the shore. The temples lay looted and abandoned; the Oracle of Chinchaycamac had departed forever. The once-verdant valley was nothing more than a 'great expanse of empty and forsaken farmland'.

In 1532, 30,000 households lived here. In 1570, there were just 300, concentrated in a mission ruled by Dominican monks. Some still furtively paid obeisance to their *huacas*, holy places in the hills. Others, broken by the trauma of conquest, drank themselves to death. The near-annihilation of the Chincha, one Spaniard cruelly suggested, was punishment for such sins: part and parcel of the 'secret judgements of God'.

The reality was no less harsh. Pizarro had Atahualpa garrotted after his ransom of gold and silver was delivered. The conquistadors marched into Cuzco but soon fell into a vicious civil war, replicating age-old rivalries between the coast and the highlands. The Chincha were drawn into the carnage. Their careful cultivation of the guano birds and scarce water resources probably faltered, triggering famine. And above all, they were extremely vulnerable to an invisible enemy that had already brought dozens of Indigenous American nations to their knees.

The great Mesoamerican empires and the Inca realm thousands of miles south likely had no direct knowledge of each other. But passed from person to person – from a warrior paddling an Orinoco tributary, via a messenger traversing the Inca road network, or a Chincha vessel navigating down the coastline – European illnesses ranged far ahead of Pizarro's forays into Tawantinsuyu. Those inhabiting the Inca Empire's core fell from 4.6 million to 1.3 million people in the fifty years to 1571. The coastal population of Peru meanwhile plunged from 7.5 million to scarcely 130,000: the worst mortality rate of anywhere in the Americas. A densely urbanised population, in contact with cultures along the Pacific seaboard, the Chincha were probably among the first to succumb.

Peruvians today have greater insight than most into their ancestors' ordeal. Their country experienced the world's worst death toll per million from Covid-19. Hospitals were short on oxygen, beds and masks; with most people working in the informal economy, obeying lockdowns meant going hungry. Four presidents took office in one year. The authorities in Iquitos, an Amazonian city, piled hundreds of bodies into a secret mass grave. Over 185,000 Peruvians died: one in every 200 people. Officials said it was the most devastating epidemic to hit the country since 1492.

*

Dusty lanes through banana plantations, barking dogs, concrete houses. I speed in a rickshaw *mototaxi* through the outskirts of the town of Chincha Alta. Today, there is not much left of its ancient predecessor. An archipelago of terracotta mounds rises out of the green valley floor, a wooden cross planted atop the nearest peak. Cracked and lop-sided, this was La Centinela, the pyramid at the heart of the Chincha realm, containing quarters for Chincha nobles, a palace for Inca administrators, and the Chinchaycamac oracle's temple.

I climb up crumbling pathways to the summit. Rusty trawlers bob a mile away through the mist. An 8.0-magnitude earthquake struck off the coast here in 2007, killing 500 people and levelling nearby cities. Considering her age, La Centinela didn't come off too badly. Outer layers of the pyramid have sheared away, revealing a zig-zag pattern on interior walls: leaping fish and diving birds, like the décor of the Gibbs family pile in Somerset. The mud, straw and sand isn't as fancy as Inca stonework, but has withstood time and tremors.

The caretaker, Tony, huffs his way to the top. We walk along ruined corridors, patios, staircases and ramps. Excavations, and efforts to prop up the Chincha temples, began in 2004. But then, says Tony, 'the earthquake came and destroyed everything'. At the site museum, he shows me an unlocked storage cupboard, stacked with golden foil spears used in local school plays. He unfurls the contents of one of dozens of cardboard tubes. Inside, wrapped in brown paper, is a desiccated 700-year-old Chincha textile.

I had seen similar examples in Lima. One, using cotton and camelid fibres, popping with the crimson dye obtained from the cactus-dwelling cochineal insect, mixes geometric shapes – half an Andean cross, a modern directional arrow – with the outline of a llama train. With 398 threads per inch, curators at the Museo Larco say it is the finest textile in existence. Another consists of snapping parrots, vultures and gulls. Other woven depictions are more puzzling, like a snarling, four-armed, purple jaguar, a third eye staring from its chest: perhaps a feline deity borrowed from the Andes. These intricate weavings likewise seem best appreciated after snorting a hallucinogen or chewing *Spondylus*. 'There were hundreds rolled up in here a few years ago,' says Tony. 'Now there are only a handful. Robbers, some of them. Then there are the international collectors.' The once-esteemed Chincha kingdom, it seems, is now so unloved that its custodians can't even afford a padlock.

Think of ancient South America, and you probably think of Machu Picchu, the Inca summer residence similar in function and age to

Hampton Court Palace. We follow the lead of early chroniclers like
Garcilaso, who claimed that the Incas were the pinnacle of pre-
Columbian civilisation, an Andean Rome surrounded by lowland
barbarians of the shoreline and jungle. 'In comparison with the spell of
the interior, which affects very nearly all minds,' Robert Cushman
Murphy reflected in 1925, 'the appeal of the long, shining coast of Peru
seems to have been felt by few.' But the Incas were only the latest power
to arise in the Andes. The Chincha rivalled the interlopers from Cuzco –
hard-headed builders, warriors and administrators – in artistic
achievement.

And both were striplings compared to coastal civilisations like Caral.
Only uncovered in the 1940s, this complex of cities emerged in the
desert north of Lima around 5,000 years ago: perhaps the oldest urban
centre in the Americas. No weapons, fortifications or mutilated remains
have been found among its ruins: it may have been entirely pacifistic. In
2014, archaeologists reported the discovery of a sprawling astronomical complex: dozens of ceremonial mounds and seventy-one giant lines
etched into the Chincha Valley. Created by the Paracas culture around
300 BC, they align with solstice sunsets. And like the nearby Nazca
lines – monumental geoglyphs, some in the shape of a hummingbird,
monkey and spider – they are more easily discerned from high up. They
are the ancient equivalent of neon signs, said one researcher: the Paracas enticing trading partners down from the Andes to the riches of the
coast.

One reason why the Chincha fail to attract our magpie gaze is that
few of their golden artefacts have survived. Burials belonging to the
Chimú – builders of monumental palaces in northern Peru around
1,000 years ago – have been found with golden headdresses, golden
armour, golden jewellery and golden weapons. The labyrinth-like walls
of their cities are also flecked with birds, waves and pilchards in Pac-
Man-like procession; their tapestries emblazoned with full-bellied,
super-sized pelicans borne aloft on litters by lesser feathered beings.
From Lima to Cuzco, Chimú goldwork is invariably the star exhibit in
pre-Columbian art museums.

But practically anything that glittered in Chincha temples and tombs
was looted by Hernando Pizarro, a younger brother of Francisco. He
asked for the Chincha Valley as his fiefdom, judging it to be the 'richest
and best' territory on offer. His men melted down 'one hundred thousand marks of silver in huge and small vessels and insects and snakes
and small dogs and deer all in gold and silver . . . and there is much

more to find, god willing, for the natives of that land say they have not found even the tenth part of what is missing.'

Maybe the rest was hidden where it could never be found. In recent years, archaeologists have found hundreds of examples where Chincha grave bundles – possibly ransacked by Hernando's henchmen – were reassembled. Not long afterwards, the vertebrae of the dead were threaded onto reed posts: exactly as the Chinchorro, a pre-historic coastal people far to the south in the Atacama, had done 6,000 years before. In a time of catastrophe, the Chincha may have revived ancient traditions lying dormant in the desert to remain close to their perished loved ones. In pre-Columbian Peru and long afterwards, the deceased were part of everyday life. Mummified Inca nobles, given pride of place at banquets and ceremonies, enjoyed richer social lives than many of the living. The dead were never past: they weren't even dead.

Although Atahualpa had been killed and his armies were in disarray, the fight for Peru – to say nothing of the rest of South America – was far from over. Some of the Chincha elite carved out spaces of autonomy in the colonial system. In the early 1600s, two Chincha noblewomen even took abusive Spaniards to the highest court in Lima. Juana Curilla sued for the return of her land, as did Magdalena Chimaca, who also denounced her husband for domestic violence. Others seem to have maintained their sacred link with the seabirds. In 2006, curators unearthed a strange slab in a British Museum warehouse, dug out of the guano on the Chincha Islands in 1847. An inscription was squeezed around four carved images:

> Dom   pedro gu
>
>   anu   SI
>   que ma
>   yor
>   delvalle
>   de
>   [c]hincha

Don Pedro Guanuque, lord of the Chincha Valley, was an Indigenous chief or *cacique* who owned rich coastal lagoons north of La Centinela in the 1560s. The tablet's quadrants broadcast hidden meanings to his different audiences.

A bell tower and cross, still daubed with red pigment, suggest Pedro's fealty to Spain and the Church. Despite the terrible cost in lives, some coastal peoples were proud of having allied with the Spanish to overthrow the Inca imperialists. Below, an arm clutches an Indigenous staff of authority tipped with feathers. A puffed-up guanay occupies the upper right. Beneath it, the Chincha Islands appear as three mounds rising out of the waves. Bulbous with thick crests of ordure, and marked with a horseshoe-shaped nest, an ancient coastal name for the Moon goddess, Si, floats above them.

Pedro, whose surname itself encompasses huanu, may have overseen its careful harvesting, just as his ancestors had done. The slab bears the coat of arms of a Chincha survivor who had not forgotten his origins. He was a native knight in Spanish service, a post-conquest guardian of the guano.

Sprinkled over fields, farms and plantations across Europe, Asia, Africa and the Americas, Peruvian guano produced the surpluses that unlocked the final phase of the industrial revolution. The global population surged, along with demand for the synthetic fertilisers and carbon that kept the show on the road, long after the guano – the gateway drug to modernity – was all gone.

The aftershocks are now beating their way back to the islands. The seabird colonies are slowly recovering. But warming oceans and overfishing are depleting the marine life that they depend on. And in 2023, over half a million seabirds perished along the Peruvian shoreline – including almost 30,000 on the Chincha Islands. They were the latest victims of the worst eruption of avian influenza ever recorded. It had already swept through Europe and North America, leading to the cull of over 140 million farmed birds.

The livestock industry – and the scrambling of bird migration routes by climate change – are making such outbreaks more common and deadly. Bird flu is spreading to mammals and, occasionally, people. While two per cent of those with Covid-19 died before vaccines were produced, the H5N1 strain of bird flu has killed half of the people it has infected. If it mutates to spread easily between humans, scientists warn, the world could soon face a far more lethal pandemic.

Nobody alive today, as far as I can find out, claims to be a descendant of the Chincha. But their spiritual inheritors are, perhaps, the guardaislas. We catch up with Mauro – spritely, weathered by sun and spray – on a rare weekend off. His concrete bungalow is about as close to the islands as you can be on the mainland. When he first came down from

Ayacucho to work on Chincha Norte forty-five years ago, he felt estranged. The loneliness, the strain of being always alert for intruders. 'We suffered quite a lot: robberies of guano, slaughters of birds.'

But caring for the seabirds soon became his life – stopping the bomb-wielding fishermen from frightening them away, keeping pilfering gulls from the eggs of the guanay. 'We have to give them tranquillity: more tranquillity means more reproduction, more eggs, and more guano. It seems like the birds know us, that we're their friends. You walk among them, they see you, and let you pass.' He talks wistfully of luminescent nights among the guano. 'There are little anchovy bones and fish scales in the nests,' he explains. 'When the moon shines, they light up like metal.' An uncanny trick of lunar multiplication: a million silver crescents across the land.

But in two years, once his youngest son finishes studying, 'it's bye to the island for Mauro'. Leaping onto rope ladders, clambering down a cliff to inspect a nest, facing off against bandits: the Chinchas are no country for old men. I ask him if exile will be hard after decades spent more in the company of birds – their endless song, their delving into mackerel-crowded seas, their wooing ceremonies, birth and death – than his own kind.

'That's what I'm afraid of. Once I leave and return here, I can never go back. But I have to get used to here, to family life. I'll still be thinking about the islands. There won't be that huge colony of birds, fussing, reproducing . . . how they give each other food, it's beautiful to see when they're in heat.' His voice falls to a whisper. 'The birds, like humans, also fall in love, you know. They caress and hug each other, lift up their wings . . .'

He suddenly rises from his plastic chair, imitating an angular, feathery embrace, arms rising at the elbows. A strange flash of bird in the man; an image of the befeathered Chincha prince of centuries past. The avian inhabitants of the isles, he says, 'show more affection than a human being. And I'll no longer see that.'

Sirens, growling buses, thudding music from a passing car. His granddaughter kicking a ball around, tugging at his sleeve, desperate to play outside. The bittersweet business of life on land intrudes. Mauro brightens. 'One of my sons is also a guardaisla, up at Trujillo, on Isla Guañape. Loads of birds there. Maybe he'll take his old man to visit.' He chuckles. 'Even if I'm leaning on a walking stick.'

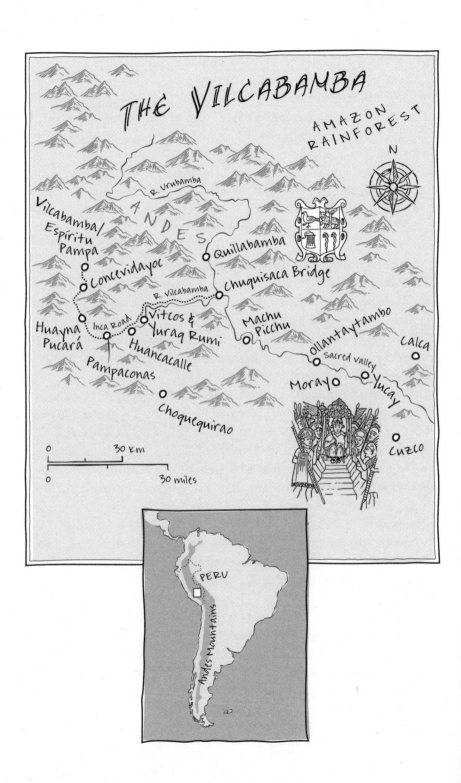

2

The Last Stand of the Inca

Vilcabamba, AD 1537–1572

PLAIN OF GHOSTS

Take the bus out from Cuzco through the Sacred Valley. When the road forks left to Machu Picchu – the soaring mountain-top citadel, wreathed in mist and clogged with tourists – keep going straight. At Quillabamba, the passengers unload bundles of reeds and lower lambs on ropes from the roof. Climb into the back of a pickup, perching among schoolchildren, drainpipes and a cardboard box of puppies. Cross the bridge over the foaming Urubamba River, and ride a mud track high above the river through a lush valley, forest sprouting from sheer cliff-faces.

Bang on the roof and jump down in Huancacalle. The Cobos family – expert guides and muleteers – live here. Rex, their Alsatian, takes you up to Vitcos, an Inca palace glinting in a shaft of sunlight. Crossing a grassy plaza where an Inca was murdered, you pass through trapezoidal doorways of smooth white granite, framing glacial peaks in the distance. The army base below is a reminder of how the remnants of Shining Path, a Maoist insurgency, still linger in the region.

Nearby lies the Inca answer to the Parthenon friezes, showcasing their skill at making stone seem alive. At the centre of this shrine crossed with a sculpture garden, in a valley filled with birdsong, buttercups and the sound of rushing water, sits Yuraq Rumi: a monumental, silvery rock the size of a battle tank. It bulges with steps, shelves and channels that once guided the blood of sacrificial guinea pigs into the earth.

You jump in a truck with Jorge Cobos and his cousin, Alvaro, to the top of the next valley, and set out downwards on foot along a winding Inca road. An elderly woman in a cardigan, knitted skirt and sandals ascends in the opposite direction. Another relation of Jorge, she reaches into her multicoloured bundle to trade a handful of tiny potatoes, their violet skin flaking off under a thumbnail to reveal golden, butter-flavoured flesh.

You follow the mossy cobbles down through dense cloud forest, splashing through streams and crossing swaying plank bridges. Where landslides have swept away the trail, you scrabble on all fours. The spiky grass of the uplands gives way to bromeliads and creepers; the thin air of the mountains is replaced by mosquitoes and sticky heat. Luckily, there are cold, deep pools in which to plunge. Alvaro casts a line with a stick, soon breaking into a crooked grin. He has the *tilapia* sizzling over the campfire within minutes. Rounding a hillside, the valley below flattens; the forest thickens. Here, where the Andes crumple into the Amazon, lies the last capital of the Incas.

The caretaker, Ángel Chilla, swings a strimmer to keep the foliage from a labyrinth of cobwebbed chambers, temples and tombs. Doorways are crowned by towering strangler figs, *matapalo*, their roots entwined around fallen lintels like boa constrictors. The electronic honk of yellow-rumped *paucar* birds rings out from dangling nests; armies of leaf-cutter ants carve trails below. Curved roof tiles slumber amid the weeds. You ask Ángel how many visitors he gets in the average week. He stops to think. 'Between one,' he finally says, 'and zero.'

Five centuries ago, the inhabitants of this place called it Vilcabamba. Today, locals know it as Espíritu Pampa: the plain of ghosts. The ruins were unknown to the outside world for centuries. The Cobos family, who once lived here, helped explorers and archaeologists identify them anew. But only part of the city has been reclaimed from the jungle – let alone excavated. 'Just imagine,' says Jorge, having donned a spotless, lime-green tracksuit in honour of his return. 'There are lots of buildings left to discover in the forest. And beyond, in the mountains: who knows?'

There's a genre of painting, copied time and again to hang in churches along the colonial Andes, that looks like a comic strip. The fourteen rulers of Tawantinsuyu sit in boxes, august and serene. In the top left is Manco Capac, the semi-mythical Inca founding father. A dozen emperors follow until Atahualpa – who passes his sceptre to Charles V, Holy Roman Emperor and King of Spain. The succession rolls on, from Habsburg dynasts in armour to periwigged Bourbons. The message is clear: the legitimate rule of Peru had passed seamlessly to Spain, from a native royal dynasty to a European one. With the death of Atahualpa in 1533, the Incas had disappeared.

But a back room in a palace in Lima contains a family portrait that contradicts the official narrative. Painted in 1718, it shows the marriage of an Inca princess, Beatriz Clara Coya. Behind sit her uncle, Túpac Amaru, and her father, Sayri Túpac. The three are dripping in gold: crowns, axe-heads, earrings, cloak-pins, bracelets, even the buckles on their sandals. An attendant hovers with a parasol of parrot feathers. Another holds a sign that labels Sayri Túpac 'the last King of Peru'.

Four of these forgotten Incas – airbrushed out of history by the conquistadors, disowned even by the liberators who later won Peruvian independence – held out for a generation after Pizarro executed Atahualpa. They ruled a remote mountain realm known – like their jungle capital – as Vilcabamba. In a world upended by European invasion, it could hardly have been an untouched idyll. In fact, the Vilcabamba Incas were quick to adopt outside technologies – swords, steeds, gunpowder, the written word – to defend themselves. They welcomed priests, diplomats and renegade conquistadors to their court, exchanged missives with European royalty, and flaunted Old World commodities: mirrors, silks, scissors and racehorses.

But in other ways, the rebel principality was a Tawantinsuyu in miniature. Its rulers jealously enforced their sovereignty over a dozen neighbouring tribes. They preserved their ancestral faith, worshipping the Sun, maintaining the cult of their mummified ancestors, and – much to the annoyance of missionaries – keeping multiple wives. They bickered and backstabbed over the succession. They fought off armies of Spaniards and rival Andeans, conducted a game of cat-and-mouse with colonial authorities, and inspired resistance far beyond their refugee kingdom.

The last Incas embodied the dilemma facing Indigenous South Americans in the decades after Europeans erupted onto their shores. 'They debated whether to collaborate or confront,' wrote the Peruvian historian Alberto Flores Galindo: torn between going down fighting or capitulating and preserving their position under a 'Spanish protectorate'. Yet for a while, they seemed to be the match of the invaders. This 'residual separatist state of the Incas' – another scholar has suggested – 'might have continued as a formal entity in the colonial and modern history of South America'.

The epic of Vilcabamba deserves to be retold. Little-known written sources have been published and translated only recently, including a remarkable native account of the Spanish invasion of Peru dictated by Titu Cusi, its penultimate ruler. Shifts in our understanding of the early modern Andes are putting Vilcabamba's diplomatic tightrope walk in context. A cooling in the many-sided violence between the Peruvian state, Shining Path and other armed groups has made remarkable archaeological discoveries possible: like an artwork created by Vilcabamba artisans themselves.

Excavated near a doorway at Espíritu Pampa – enveloped by massive matapalo trees – lay a painted serving vessel, perhaps shattered in the final evacuation of the city in 1572. Andean and Amazonian warriors leap at a pair of mounted conquistadors with spears, clubs and bows. Snarling, super-sized jaguars face off against the Spanish horses. One of the riders, Bible in hand, fumbles for his rapier; the other raises his hand in terror or surrender.

It distils the call to resistance made by Manco Inca Yupanqui, who ordered the retreat into the mountains. 'Believe nothing that these bearded men say,' he told those who remained behind. His people could 'make a show on the outside' of cooperating: handing over tribute, pretending to worship the Christian God. 'But do not forget our ceremonies,' he commanded, nor the holy spirits or huacas in the hills; the Sun and Moon; how Viracocha, the creator, can turn mountains into plains and rivers into dust. 'Be ready for when I send for you,' Manco urged them. 'If these people attack you or try to take your lands, defend yourselves – if need be, with your very lives.'

'I am the rich Potosí, treasure of the world; king of mountains and envy of kings.' So went the coat of arms granted in 1547 to the mining boomtown that had sprung up, almost overnight, beneath this lonely Andean eminence the colour of dried blood. Those who enter the tunnels that honeycomb its entrails have long known it by another name: 'the mountain that eats men'.

Two years earlier, a native prospector called Diego Gualpa was hurrying across a desolate hillside when a gust of wind blew him off his feet. He hit the dirt. It glittered. Word spread: the mountain beneath Gualpa's nose was marbled with the richest veins of silver anywhere on earth. Chancers, desperadoes and flunkies flocked. Within a century, Potosí was the source of half the silver circulating on the planet, and her population had rocketed from a few hundred to 160,000. The ramshackle metropolis rivalled London, Seville and Milan in size, with more dive bars and bordellos per capita than anywhere in the Iberian world. By 1810 – through many a tech boom, financial bust, gangland killing and hyperinflationary episode – almost a billion pesos of metal had been hacked out of the bowels of the mountain, stamped into coins and loaded onto Spanish galleons.

The pieces of eight slipped through the palms of many: Flemish traders, English and Moroccan pirates, Ottoman caliphs, African kings, Mughal princes, Chinese emperors. But the biggest spender by far was Spain. Gualpa's paydirt underwrote the credit of the world's first superpower, made its monarchs, merchants and muleteers filthy rich, and entered the Spanish lexicon: something valuable beyond words is still said to be worth a Potosí, worth a Peru. As early as 1561, a grateful Philip II sent the Imperial City another ornamental shield that outlined his ambitions. 'For a powerful emperor or a wise king,' it read, 'this lofty mountain of silver could conquer the whole world.'

Few Spaniards did any mining. For that, they turned to Indigenous Andeans. Some showed up willingly, hoping to score a nugget of their own. Most had to be forced. Colonial officials ratcheted up the *mita* – an Inca system of corvée labour – casting a dragnet of thousands of miles across the Andes that scooped up almost one in five healthy men. Their pitiful wage was far outstripped by the funds they burned through to reach – and survive – Potosí.

Some worked the refineries filled with choking mercury vapours, or scoured the freezing hillsides for firewood. Others, nearly 5,000 at a time on four-month shifts, were sent ever-deeper into the earth. They descended a chain of rickety ladders with rungs made of hide. They remained in the stifling darkness for a week, hacking at the rockface by candlelight, chewing coca for sustenance, climbing the same ladders with sacks of ore weighing forty-five kilos on their backs. Boulders tumbled down the mineshaft, turning limbs to pulp. Cave-ins buried fathers and sons alive. Some said that half the *mitayos* emerged crippled. Nobody kept count of how many died.

Even today, the Bolivian miners picking through the tailings for tin, zinc and lead don't expect to live long past forty. Those venturing inside the sagging mountain first offer dried llama foetuses, coca leaves and neat alcohol to El Tío – a horned statue of the underworld deity – or tuck cigarettes in his maw. If they survive the collapses triggered by cheap dynamite and careless drilling, they soon contract silicosis – known as *mal de mina*, miner's evil – from years of inhaling mineral dust. Their lungs blacken and harden. Their skin turns blue. They die young, wheezing and withered.

The *cerro rico* or rich hill towering above Potosí, one visiting friar concluded in 1551, was nothing less than 'a mouth of hell, into which a great mass of people enter every year and are sacrificed by the greed of the Spaniards to their god'. But not everyone took such atrocities lying down.

For a while after the massacre at Cajamarca in 1532, Pizarro had it easy. Epidemics had wiped out most of the Inca elite – including Huayna Capac, a domineering emperor who had expanded into Ecuador. His death soon led to the civil war between his sons Atahualpa – whose supporters hailed from the empire's northern possessions – and Huáscar, whose powerbase was in Cuzco. Merciless in victory, Atahualpa liquidated his captive rivals. Even as a prisoner, he had Huáscar murdered.

The Spanish invaders now styled themselves as liberators, parading Huáscar's son, Túpac Huallpa, as a puppet emperor. As they marched south in August 1533, crossing chasms on Inca bridges of woven grass, locals cheered. Atahualpa's Ecuadorian forces, led by a general called Quisquis, ambushed Pizarro's dismounted vanguard, hanging their horses' heads on flowery spikes. Few disputed that nimble Andean warriors – genetically adapted to the altitude – outclassed lumbering European infantry one-on-one. But Spanish cavalry were near-invincible on the open field. In November, as the temples and towers of Cuzco came into view, the armies of Quisquis melted away.

Túpac Huallpa had died. But a replacement appeared on the hillside before the Spanish, wearing a commonplace tunic and yellow cloak. Manco Inca, another son of Huayna Capac, had been on the run from Atahualpa's assassins for most of his adolescence. Now, Pizarro promised to 'free the people of Cuzco from this tyranny' and install the twenty-year-old as Tawantinsuyu's rightful ruler. The young prince embraced him. Together, they marched into the Inca capital, whose name in Quechua, qosqo, means 'the navel of the world'. The fourth Inca in eighteen months was crowned among his embalmed ancestors. The boozy celebrations lasted a month.

But relations soon broke down. The conquistadors ransacked Cuzco for its remaining treasures, gambling them away in a night. The Spanish nicknamed Inca nobles orejónes – big-ears – for their elongated lobes plugged with precious gems. The coming-of-age piercing ceremony was the most important event in the Inca social calendar. But the Europeans crashed it with drawn swords, snatching the golden sceptres carried by the debutants. Their greed was insatiable. Pizarro's younger brothers, Gonzalo and Juan, shackled Manco, burnt him with candles, and urinated on him when he refused to hand over more riches. Gonzalo raped

Cura Occlo: the Inca's beloved sister, wife and *coya*, or queen. It was now clear beyond doubt: the outsiders meant not to restore Tawantin-suyu, but only to enslave its people and strip it for parts.

Manco secretly mustered weapons and men from the four corners of his realm. He made contact with Huayna Capac's loyal lieutenants, still holding out in the mountains. In April 1536, Manco left Cuzco for the last time, promising to bring back a golden image of his father. In the hills at Calca, the Inca's council of war plotted their great rebellion against the hated occupiers. 'We will finish them off, leaving none alive,' Manco vowed. 'We shall rid ourselves of this nightmare and rejoice.'

It was like a cloak had shrouded the hills above Cuzco. Nobody knew how many warriors there were: 50,000, 400,000. Against them stood just 190 Spaniards with eighty horses. They tried to charge out but were swamped. The mayor was dragged from the saddle. Moments later, the gore-spattered head of his white charger was raised above the jeering throng alongside his own.

Slingers flung red-hot stones, setting the thatch ablaze. The coughing Spaniards were trapped in their palaces as a hailstorm of projectiles pinged off the plaza. Finally, in May, Manco's army surged down the narrow alleyways, taking the city block by block. Some ran along the bare, fire-blackened walls, trussing up the Spanish riders with weighted cords of llama tendons. At night, raiding parties set fire to the conquistadors' tents.

Villac Umu, Manco's high priest, directed the assault from Sacsayhuaman: a fortress of giant blocks – some weighing hundreds of tons – whose zigzagging ruins still lour over the city. The Spanish spent a fearful night at prayer. In the morning, they dug their spurs into their horses, burst through the Inca barricades, and made for the castle. Juan Pizarro had his skull stoved in by a stone thrown from the ramparts, and took two weeks to die. The warrior-priest sallied out to fetch reinforcements from Manco, coordinating the nationwide uprising from Calca.

But they came too late. Buttressed by Chachapoya and Cañari warriors – conquered by the Incas only decades before – the Europeans stormed Sacsayhuaman with ladders. An *orejón* captain in European armour stalked the battlements, cleaving Spanish heads with an axe, ignoring the arrows that pierced him. But seeing his men flee, he wrapped himself in his cloak and leaped over the edge. His remaining soldiers followed, the dead cushioning the fall of those who jumped last. As August came around, Manco's demoralised levies thinned out for the sowing season. Spanish back-up arrived from Lima, Mexico and the Caribbean. After ten months, the siege was broken.

The fighting spread to the valley west of Cuzco. At a steep mountain-side bastion called Ollantaytambo, Manco charged on horseback, lance in hand, driving the invaders back. Many of his men now wielded captured swords, harquebuses and cannons. Cura Occlo led an ambush where two dozen Spanish horsemen were slaughtered. But every dead European seemed to take ten Andeans with them. Spanish raids captured Villac Umu, Manco's infant son Titu Cusi, thousands of his unarmed followers and the vast herds of llamas that provided his mobile kingdom with sustenance. Manco's half-brother Paullu defected, receiving the royal fringe as the new Inca. 'The Christians', he pleaded in his defence, 'were so valiant that they could never fail to be victorious.'

Manco's armies needed somewhere to lick their wounds. He alighted on Vilcabamba, a remote mountain region of shrines and sanctuaries settled a few generations before. He made Vitcos his capital, and built another settlement at Espíritu Pampa on the edge of the Amazon. In 1539, Gonzalo Pizarro and Paullu attacked. Jungle archers harried the invaders. Rolling boulders swept many to their death. Manco dived into a river to escape, appearing on the far side. 'I am Manco Inca!' he shouted, promising to reconquer his birthright. 'I am Manco Inca!'

Denied their target, the Spanish torched the city and retreated. They had captured Cura Occlo, who smeared herself with dung, determined not to endure Spanish outrages again. Francisco Pizarro sent fine silks, a pony, emissaries and a Black attendant to tempt Manco out. The Inca killed them all, even the pony. Enraged, Pizarro had the pregnant coya stripped, tied to a stake, and shot full of arrows. She died still defiant, without uttering a sound. The Spanish governor then burned Villac Umu and sixteen Inca generals alive. Heartbroken, bereft of counsel, Manco and his men were reduced to little more than bandits.

In June 1541, disgruntled conquistadors burst into Pizarro's palace in Lima and stabbed him to death. Civil wars roiled the colony. Paullu – now baptised as Cristóbal – flitted from one camp to the other. Manco's forces watched the carnage from the hills. In 1542, a group of Pizarro's assassins sought asylum at his court. Over his captains' protests, the Inca took them in, ordering his wives to serve them and feasting with them as brothers. The refugees came with valuable weapons, horses and intelligence, and drilled his men with swords and guns. They also gave cosmopolitan cachet to Manco's court-in-exile, allowing him to indulge his passion for fencing, riding, chess and dominoes.

But Pizarro's murderers were desperate, dangerous men. A few years later, in 1545, the Inca was relaxing in the main square at Vitcos. This afternoon's diversion was *herrón*, a throwing game with horseshoes. Titu Cusi – now almost a teenager, having been stolen back from Cuzco by his father's spies – looked on as the Spaniards joked and jostled. The Inca, by now around thirty, let his guard down. His armies had been sent away to subdue a rebellious chief. And as he turned his back, the Spaniards fell upon him with concealed daggers, knives and scissors.

Manco, though unarmed, defended himself 'with the fury of death'. Titu Cusi rushed to his aid, but the Spaniards turned on him, flinging a spear and grazing his leg. 'If their aim were any better,' he would later write to Philip II, 'they would have killed me as well.' The wounded, terrified boy blundered into the forest beneath Vitcos. The assassins galloped out of the palace, bound for a hero's welcome in Cuzco. 'We have killed the Inca,' they shouted to Manco's stunned servants. 'Be not afraid!'

But if the regicides expected to be hailed as saviours, they were sorely mistaken. Runners were sent to Manco's soldiers, who headed off one group. 'They pulled them off their horses and dragged them away to be sacrificed. They were all given cruel deaths,' Titu Cusi recalled, with grim satisfaction. The pursuers cornered the rest of the Spaniards in a thatched building and set it ablaze. Those not burned alive were speared as they stumbled out of the conflagration.

Manco clung on to life for three days. 'You see how well my trust in these Spanish people has turned out,' he told his captains. 'I don't think I'll escape from this one.' The instructions issued by the dying Inca – or put in the father's mouth by his son twenty-five years later – have all the authenticity of bitter experience: 'My beloved son,' the Inca whispered, drawing Titu Cusi close. 'Listen to me: I command that you never, ever have honest dealings with such people as these . . . do not let them enter your lands, however persistently they entreat you. For I was fooled by their honeyed words, and the same will happen to you if you believe them.'

Manco finally entrusted Titu Cusi the care of their subjects, 'for they have followed, protected and supported me in my every hour of need, leaving behind their lands and homes out of love for me'. In return – said Manco, with his last, ragged breath – they would follow his heirs to the very end.

I WILL KILL THEM ALL

For a while, the rebel Inca state seemed fragile. Though Titu Cusi was Manco's eldest child, his mother was not of royal blood. Manco's chosen heir – Sayri Túpac, his son with Cura Occlo – was only five. Chaperoned by a regent named Atoc-Sopa, the new Inca's court permanently relocated to the town of Vilcabamba. It was further away from assassins, but hot, humid and insalubrious: not an ideal setting for an Andean prince.

Nor did Sayri Túpac appear cut out to rule. His orejón courtiers seemed poised to give him up to a gilded early retirement among the Spanish. One went ahead to fix up Huayna Capac's old houses in Cuzco. Embassies and gifts were exchanged: pumas and parrots for wine and gold. In 1549, Paullu – Sayri Túpac's uncle – set out to fetch him but sickened and died, spooking the Inca's advisors. The deal was off, for now.

The Spaniards spent another decade shooting and garrotting each other. And a fierce controversy unfolding thousands of miles away gave the Inca *infante* further breathing room. In 1550, Charles V ordered all Spanish campaigns in the New World to be paused, calling an urgent legal debate in Valladolid. At issue was the moral justification – or lack thereof – for his fast-expanding empire over the Atlantic. In one corner was Juan Ginés de Sepúlveda, a mediocre theologian beloved of Spanish colonists. Cherry-picking from Aristotle and Aquinas, he argued that Indigenous Americans were 'natural slaves'. Catholic Europeans were entitled to conquer and civilise them: in fact, it was their duty.

Bartolomé de las Casas disagreed. The Dominican friar had been appalled by Spanish atrocities against the Taíno peoples of the Caribbean. As a chaplain to conquistadors in Cuba, he saw 'cruelty on a scale no living being has ever seen'. He now contested that Native Americans were thinking, feeling humans like any other. They should be converted – of course – but only with their free consent.

The friar knew of Manco's resistance, writing that the killing of Cura Occlo was 'against all justice and reason'. Vilcabamba's example of organised resistance shaped his arguments in defence of native sovereignty. Las Casas even proposed that Spain hand over the entire rule of Peru to the Incas in the hills. For a while, the king seemed inclined to agree. The debate had no formal winner. Attacks against ordinary Indigenous Americans soon resumed. But the priest-turned-whistleblower had pricked the crown's conscience, guiding Spanish tactics in the Andes for twenty years to come. The Incas holed up in the mountains were Peru's legitimate sovereigns: they should not be subdued by force, but persuaded to submit.

Philip II, Spain's new monarch, wrote to Sayri Túpac with a blanket amnesty. Manco's rebellion had been justified, he conceded. Sayri Túpac's priests rummaged through the entrails of guinea pigs for omens, and peered at clouds scudding past the sun. The Inca came of age. Finally, in October 1557, Sayri Túpac was escorted out of the mountains. Villagers lined the road in silence as he passed in a litter carried by 300 warriors. Banquets and bullfights were thrown in his honour. He was granted rich estates at Yucay, nestled in the sunny Sacred Valley, now dotted with boutique hotels and yoga retreats. Sayri Túpac's new properties included a sprawling pleasure palace built by Huayna Capac. Quispiguanca came with parkland stocked with deer, allotments of exotic Amazonian produce, a dovecote for his queen – and a sacred rock of its own, today marooned between a cemetery and a welder's workshop. Sayri Túpac had been put out to pasture in style.

While the Inca was visiting Cuzco, Garcilaso – the future historian – went to pay his respects. The seventeen-year-old parted with a traditional Inca obeisance. Sayri Túpac's ethereal demeanour relaxed, and he smiled and embraced his cousin. Garcilaso had grown up listening to his mother – a ñusta, or princess, named Chimpu Ocllo – swapping tales of Tawantinsuyu with his aunts and uncles. 'As my mother lived in Cuzco, her patria, she was visited every week by her few relatives who had survived the cruelties and tyrannies of Atahualpa,' he later recalled. He bunked off his studies in Latin and Spanish letters to eavesdrop: 'as a young boy, I loved to hear them speak.' They laughed and smiled, their faces lighting up with glories past. 'They usually recounted the origins of their Kings, their majesty, the greatness of their Empire, their bold deeds and conquests, their government under war and peace, the laws they made to the great benefit of their vassals.'

Yet so fresh and powerful was 'the memory of those lost, happy times, that their conversations always ended in tears'. The Incas left behind in occupied Cuzco – hostages, collaborators, survivors – 'wept for their slain kings, their stolen empire and the end of their country . . . they lamented, "Now it falls to us to reign as vassals."' Two years later, in 1560, Garcilaso's father was dead. The conquistador's bastard, mixed-race son was sent to Spain to sue for his inheritance in vain. He never saw his mother, or Peru, his 'beloved patria', again.

But later in life – as Garcilaso, now a captain in the army of Don John of Austria, fought Moorish rebels in the snowy mountains near Granada; as he walked the torch-lit alleyways and patios of Córdoba, strangely like those of his native Cuzco; as he prayed among the Islamic arches of the great mosque-cathedral, reminiscent of the Santo Domingo church now enveloping the bare andesite walls of Qorikancha – a jumble of memories and his relatives' stories came to him unbidden.

Provincial chiefs wearing party gear – grotesque carved masks, condor wings on their backs, and puma skins like Hercules – blowing kisses to the Sun as His first rays touched the Cussipata plaza on the winter solstice. The menageries of insects, vipers, jaguars, poisonous tree frogs and spectacled bears they brought to Cuzco to delight the Inca from beyond the furthest confines of the empire. Reaching out on the eve of his departure to touch the finger, stiff as oak, of his embalmed great-grandfather Huayna Capac: still with his eyebrows and eyelashes intact, as though he might wake up and speak.

The mummified Incas had since been consumed by fire. The living scions of their royal house had been vanquished by the sword. He bitterly reproached himself for not paying closer attention as a teenager. He had never thought to write anything down. But maybe his pen could keep his ancestors and their patria alive, snatching them a kind of victory from the oblivion of defeat. 'I will tell of the marvellous things I have guarded in my memory,' he resolved, 'and endure the pain of those memories that I have lost.'

Sayri Túpac had meanwhile become a model Spanish subject. His marriage to his sister, Cusi Huarcay, was consecrated in a church by papal dispensation; they had already given birth to a daughter, Beatriz. He was baptised, taking the name Diego. He prayed in the Santo Domingo church.

Yet some whispered that he was secretly worshipping the solar deity, and his mummified ancestors who had once been kept there. There were other signs that Sayri Túpac's capitulation was for show. He had left his tasselled crown in Vilcabamba. Titu Cusi – his older half-brother – would later claim that Sayri Túpac had been sent out as a spy. It seemed a dangerous gamble, the Inca had told his people. 'But you must consider that the Sun wishes I should leave, so that my domain should be increased – and because out there I could be the salvation of my family and of you all.'

He died suddenly in 1561. Most suspected poison. But it soon became clear that his realm remained unbowed. Titu Cusi took control, shunting aside Túpac Amaru, his sixteen-year-old half-brother whom Sayri Túpac had named as heir. There would be no more weak, underage rulers. Spanish embassies returned empty-handed. Titu Cusi even poached Martín Pando, a mixed-race or *mestizo* secretary who accompanied one diplomatic mission, to remain as his interpreter, scribe and advisor. Raids on outlying villages resumed, bringing back hundreds of Andean captives.

Vilcabamba's new leadership, it seemed, had revived Manco's ambition to cast out the invaders from Tawantinsuyu. In 1564, the viceroy suspected Titu Cusi of being behind insurrections a thousand miles away in modern-day Argentina and Chile. Colonial authorities in Peru busted clandestine workshops churning out thousands of iron-tipped pikes and jagged clubs. The plan, an informant revealed, was to fall on the invaders as they processed through the streets on Holy Thursday. A map found in the rebels' possession suggested that they then planned to slip away into Vilcabamba.

A strange, apocalyptic movement was meanwhile sweeping the Andes. Its adherents abjured Spanish food, clothing, names and religion, and began to sacrifice once more to secret huacas in the hills. The huacas spoke through select intermediaries, who thrashed around in the dirt, trembling uncontrollably. Many suspected the mysterious religious revival – known as the *taki onqoy*, dancing disease – was sparked by the semi-divine rulers of Vilcabamba. 'It has always been understood' – the Spanish viceroy wrote to the king in 1565 – 'that the Inca hidden in the Andes has been the cause of all these disturbances among the natives.'

Early in the same year, a Spanish ambassador arrived at the border of Vilcabamba. Diego Rodríguez de Figueroa had been deserted his porters. The people he was about to parley with, they warned him, were 'not men, but devils'. The marauders had ransacked their villages a dozen times, kidnapped their wives and children, and burned their churches to the ground. The raiders had even used a stolen cross to barbecue a llama, and destroyed the bridge over the Urubamba River. Rodríguez tied a handkerchief to a tree as a flag of truce, and waited.

His feet swelled with mosquito bites. He threw letters back and forth with the suspicious border guards. Eventually they hauled him over in a basket. Warriors in feathered armour surrounded him: 'It was very bold to plant a flag next to the land of the Inca.' The emissary smoothed his way with gifts of figs, jam, scissors, knives, needles, feathered hats, coral necklaces, packs of cards and bundles of paper. The skulls of Manco's murderers leered down from the ramparts of Vitcos.

The summit was held outside a fort at Pampaconas, a misty moor halfway to the town of Vilcabamba. Inca squadrons, armed to the teeth, sealed off the perimeter. Finally, Titu Cusi arrived and made a gesture of reverence to the Sun. He wore a silver breastplate, a crown of feathers, a red mask, and carried a golden shield, spear and dagger. His face was serious, and scarred by smallpox. He handed Rodríguez a goblet of *chicha* – a potent maize beer – laughing as the Spaniard spluttered and dabbed at his beard.

Over the next few days, the emissary conferred with Pando, the mestizo secretary in a tattered cloak. He preached to a group of baptised nobles, moving them to tears. He dined at the Inca's table – roasted parrot and monkey on silver platters, twenty to thirty 'rather decent-looking women' seated behind their spouse and sovereign. The atmosphere was tense. Titu Cusi said Spanish visitors were invariably liars. As if to prove the point, he showed Rodríguez the scar on his leg inflicted by Manco's assassins. He denied destroying churches or murdering Spaniards. As for his captives, 'they had more freedom in his land', and were rightfully his subjects anyway. Yet he hinted that he might come quietly, for the right price.

But after Rodríguez suggested that Titu Cusi was not Manco's legitimate heir, negotiations seemed to break down. He watched all afternoon from a hillside as the Inca's soldiers caroused themselves into a frenzy, performing a drill with their spears that left several bleeding. Eventually, Titu Cusi angrily called the emissary back. It was in his power to order an uprising 'of all the Indians in Peru', he proclaimed. He called for his jungle allies. It was time to move against the invaders. He would personally take down fifty Spaniards. In fact, he shouted, 'I will kill them all!'

Seven hundred Amazonian warriors bearing bows, clubs and axes trooped into the plaza. They begged their Inca's permission to eat the Spaniard on the spot. Two orejón captains sprinted forward and prodded their spears against his ribs. 'Bearded men,' they shouted, 'Our enemies!' Rodríguez slipped away and hid. When he reappeared the next morning, Titu Cusi and his captains fell about laughing. Had he enjoyed yesterday's party, the Inca asked?

The talks ground on. Titu Cusi sent for twenty-five harquebuses, handing them out to trained musketeers. He drew Rodríguez close: 'He told me that, since I was his friend, he wanted to show me a secret.' Retainers brought out 300 bloodstained tunics and trousers: the clothes of those slain by his warriors. The Inca boasted – the emissary reported – that 'even if the power of the king was great and he held as many nations subject as I claimed, including black or Moorish, in those mountains he would be able to defend himself, just as Manco Inca, his father, had done'.

With such threats delivered, in 1566 Titu Cusi signed an advantageous peace deal. Quispe Titu, his young son, would be baptised and marry Beatriz, the daughter of Sayri Túpac. The Inca would receive a hefty income, accept priests in Vilcabamba, and pledge allegiance to the kings of Castile. 'If we had to bring him out by war, it could not have been done for 40,000 pesos,' one triumphant official trilled. 'It is well done,' Philip II scribbled in the margins of his report. But nowhere did their agreement stipulate that Titu Cusi had to leave Vilcabamba.

Titu Cusi was baptised, but still worshipped at Yuraq Rumi, threw heavy-drinking festivals, and kept all his wives. In 1570, the Inca took the missionaries – two friars called Marcos García and Diego Ortiz – down to his jungle capital at Espíritu Pampa. Yet when his guests arrived – having waded through swamps while the Inca was carried on his litter – they were confined to the outskirts and subjected to an unusual form of hazing. Local women tried day and night to seduce them, 'employing the greatest wiles known to sensuality', until the flustered priests fled back to Vitcos, mustering a mob of converts. They burned down the temple of Yuraq Rumi, but the White Rock itself was unscathed by the flames. The Inca expelled García, but forgave Ortiz, keeping the more easy-going friar as a confidant.

Espíritu Pampa remained a 'university of idolatry, with shaman instructors who are masters in abominations', one cleric claimed. Titu Cusi 'was recognised as king of this land by the natives, and they hoped he would bring them back to their old idolatry and pagan ways', a Spanish lawyer in Peru wrote to a colleague in 1575. And not only among Indigenous communities, but the mixed-race descendants of Europeans, Africans and Andeans – as well as restive Spaniards – 'always went about in the hope that, in case of some rebellion or uprising, they would treacherously receive a warm welcome in that remote stronghold of the Inca captain'.

WE LEAVE THINGS BEHIND

By now, the court of Vilcabamba had been ensconced in its jungle capital at Espíritu Pampa for twenty years. The town was over a mile wide and several long, mirroring the layout of Cuzco, wrote Martín de Murúa – a priest who lived on the southern edge of the rebel province. Most of its houses were simple dwellings of stone and thatch. But the palace of the Inca was spread across two levels, its doors and gables made of fragrant cedar, and roofed with curved, Iberian-style tiles. 'The Incas', Murúa reported, 'did not miss the pleasures, grandeur, and opulence of Cuzco in that distant land of exile.'

The Incas and their predecessors criss-crossed the Andes with a network of gravity-powered, mountain-filtered aqueducts called *amunas* – as well as a million hectares of terraces that turned near-vertical slopes into productive plantations. Their genius is still on display at Moray in the Sacred Valley. Nestled in the cleft of a mountain, some twenty stone terraces stretch upwards in concentric circles like an amphitheatre. This was, archaeologists think, an agricultural laboratory, allowing Inca agronomists to experiment with how crops fare at different altitudes. With the chaos unleashed across the Andes by European invasion, the canals were clogged up and dried out, and untended terraces collapsed, causing thousands upon thousands to starve to death.

But at Espíritu Pampa, Inca irrigation techniques were still intact: yielding three harvests of maize per year. Its farmers cultivated chili peppers 'in great abundance', along with sugarcane, coca, yucca, sweet potatoes, cotton and *chuño* – a tough, chewy tuber, naturally freeze-dried by Andean frosts. The streets were lined with guavas, papayas, avocados, pineapples and lucuma – whose intensely sweet, yellow flesh is Peru's favourite ice cream flavour. European diseases had winnowed Tawantinsuyu's vast herds of llamas and alpacas. But Vilcabamba boasted a mix of European, Andean and Amazonian livestock: cows, pigs, sheep, chickens and ducks, the ubiquitous guinea pig, llamas, vicuñas, turkeys, pheasants, curassows, guans, parrots, macaws, 'and a thousand other types of birds of diverse and beautiful plumages'. The great central plaza could hold huge crowds for horse races and festivals. Honeybees built their hives under the eaves.

As well as Manco's mummified body – dutifully attended by the Virgins of the Sun – the city guarded the holiest object in Tawantinsuyu. Legend told how, on the eve of a fateful battle against the Chanca over a century earlier, the Inca prince Pachacuti had a vision. 'Be not afraid,' it said, 'for I am the Sun, your father, and I know that thou shall conquer many nations.' With victory secured, Cuzco's finest smiths recreated the Inca's dream in solid gold: a seated boy wearing a diadem and flanked by pumas and serpents, his earlobes studded with precious stones. Polished sheets of gold fanned out like the rays of the sun. 'When the light caught them' – wrote one Spaniard who beheld it – 'they shone in such a way that the idol could not be seen, but only their blazing radiance.' It was known as the Punchao, or dawn. A cavity contained the ashes of the hearts of Incas past in a dark, spongy mass. Manco had rescued the reliquary from the Qorikancha and taken it with him into Vilcabamba. The Punchao offered his people a kind of consolation: it was their divinely ordained destiny to rule the world.

Others watched over them from beyond the grave. The Wari culture dominated swathes of Peru for five centuries from AD 500. Javier Fonseca, an archaeologist with the Peruvian Ministry of Culture, has recently identified a Wari burial complex at Espíritu Pampa. One occupant, dubbed the Lord of Wari, was interred with a silver mask, breastplate and axe blades, golden bracelets and dozens of finely crafted vessels. The finds have redrawn the map of pre-Columbian Peru – Javier tells me, as we sit on the balcony of a bar in Cuzco – revealing how the Wari also expanded to the jungle.

The character of Indiana Jones was loosely based on Hiram Bingham III: the explorer who made Machu Picchu famous, and took some 40,000 artefacts and human remains back to the United States. I reckon Javier better fits the bill of swashbuckling archaeologist. A few years ago, while excavating at Espíritu Pampa, a group of Shining Path guerrillas stepped out of the jungle. They accused him of bad-mouthing their political allies: the penalty was death. Fonseca convinced the firing squad to let his colleagues go. Then he talked himself out of danger. They even parted with vows of friendship. He jumped on a truck down to Quillabamba and strolled into a bar: 'I need a drink.'

Around AD 1000, the Wari culture imploded: there was a drought that lasted decades, a frenzied civil war. They abandoned their cities and stopped up their doorways, as if intending to return. Yet the Wari community seems to have clung on at Espíritu Pampa, coexisting with the Incas. In 2017, the archaeologist identified a Wari temple containing both Inca and Wari metalwork: a silver crown, the ornate cloak pins known as *tupus*. The rigid academic distinctions between the two cultures are breaking down. It's a paradigm shift for Peruvian archaeology,

Fonseca argues. 'With all this new information, we're going to have to reconfigure its DNA.'

'A society doesn't collapse or disappear overnight,' he continues, sipping from his bottle of Cusqueña. 'Then come the grandchildren, the great-grandchildren; they persist.' He gestures to the crowds below in the square, the teenagers shooting pool in the pub behind us. Not so long ago, this city was a village. Most of the population are migrants down from tiny highland communities. 'We're from different places than Cuzco, but we always leave a print of where we're from. We leave things behind.' It brings to mind the 1753 painting of the Last Supper that hangs in the cathedral next door: typical, except for the roasted guinea pig. Or the seamless Inca stonework that lines Cuzco's passageways. In 1950, an earthquake levelled the city's houses and churches. But among the wreckage, their pre-Columbian foundations stood firm.

The vestiges of Wari occupation may have influenced Manco's decision to take refuge in Vilcabamba. Here, like Briton kings falling back to Iron Age hillforts to resist Saxon invaders, they could draw strength from its buried lords and half-forgotten gods. And the painted bowl Fonseca unearthed at Espíritu Pampa in 2010 also hints that the Vilcabamba Incas envisioned themselves as leading a pan-Andean resistance. It is more than a simple battle scene, he argues, mentioning the rainbows and spiders – linked in Inca symbology to upheaval and divination – and how the warriors wear the different clothing of Antisuyu, Contisuyu, Collasuyu and Chinchaysuyu.

The painting may represent a prophecy: the four quarters of the shattered Inca realm are knitted back together to overthrow the Spanish and restore order to the world. Perhaps Manco or Titu Cusi used this four-handled vessel to toast their future victory, sending copies of it far and wide, commanding chiefs like the Chincha lord Don Pedro Guanuque to join their rebellion.

The Inca meanwhile sought to capture more distant hearts and minds. In 1570, Titu Cusi dictated his history – of the Spanish arrival in Peru, his father's retreat to Vilcabamba, and his own negotiations with the invaders – and sent it with the departing viceroy to the king of Spain. Still preserved in the library of El Escorial – Philip II's imposing palace in the mountains near Madrid – the manuscript remains a unique eyewitness account of the European assault on Tawantinsuyu, told by a leading protagonist in the resistance.

Titu Cusi vividly captures the astonishment felt by those who first laid eyes on the Spaniards. The interlopers claimed – and appeared – to be emissaries of the gods. They arrived on the wind. They rode giant llamas with glittering silver shoes. They communed with white cloths, 'which is how the Indians perceived the reading of books and letters'. They seemed to cast *llapas*, thunderbolts, against their enemies, for observers 'thought that the thunder made by their guns came from the sky'. But a generation later, any such notions had been thoroughly disabused. The Incas had lost their wives, children and lands, forced even to clean the filth from the Spaniards' horses with their cloaks. 'I was mistaken. For you must know, my brothers, that they are the sons not of Viracocha but of the Devil,' Manco tells his subjects. 'I admitted such people to this country, and thus put the noose around my own neck.' It was a lament deftly calculated by Titu Cusi to needle Spanish scruples.

Not only did a tsunami of such letters, petitions and exposés flow back to the royal court. In the centuries from 1492, tens of thousands of Indigenous Americans – diplomats, interpreters, enslaved people, even royalty – also undertook the perilous reverse journey to the Old World. Decades before Walter Raleigh brought Virginian tobacco to England, the wharves of Seville were filled with the second-hand cigar smoke of Mesoamerican travellers, fragrant with spices, rose petals and mushrooms. A cottage industry of native translators and fixers set up shop in the Spanish capital, drawing up family trees and interpreting between Náhuatl and Castilian. In 1602, Don Melchor Carlos Inca travelled to Madrid to confirm his privileges as the great-grandson of Huayna Capac. He likely crossed paths with Don Diego Luis Moctezuma – a grandson of the last Mexica emperor – who held lands in Spain. Native petitioners nimbly exploited a legal loophole: as the king claimed to be their protector, those who set foot in court could not be refused an audience. Manco had swiftly learned to ride and use cold steel. Born in the shadow of conquest, his sons' generation became equally adept at wielding proofs of merit, tax receipts and genealogies.

While the Mexica painted pictograms and the Maya covered their temples with glyphs, the Incas are often said to be the only great ancient civilisation that didn't develop writing. The closest thing they had were the *quipu* – colourful knotted strings, often used to tally tribute, a thousand of which still survive. Garcilaso noted how his ancestors not only 'recorded on knots everything that could be counted', but also 'battles and fights, all the embassies that had come to visit the Inca, and all the speeches and arguments they had uttered'. It's a passage often chalked up as exaggeration, but the most intricate quipu seem to be more than simple abacuses. Some bear a hundred combinations of dyed and natural colours, wool and cotton fibres, and different directions of ply. These may be three-dimensional Inca historical texts akin to braille: legible to the eye and by touch, intelligible to subject nations across Tawantinsuyu. By cross-referencing colonial-era quipu with contemporary documents, scholars are starting to decipher them, potentially unlocking a trove of information about the pre-Columbian world. To Andeans used to unspooling ancient memories encoded in the quipu, navigating the parchment bureaucracy of the Spanish royal court may have even felt like child's play.

Today, Vilcabamba still seems poised between two worlds. As I journey with Jorge and Alvaro down to Espíritu Pampa, the trail has been freshly cleared of foliage. We catch up with a group of government workers with machetes and clipboards. They are surveying the Inca path, they explain, to avoid damaging it with a new road that will – for the first time – make this remote valley accessible to motor vehicles. It will inevitably bring enormous change, further exposing young people to the lure of the outside world.

Halfway through our journey, we camp at the remote farmstead belonging to the Cabrera family, growers of bananas and breadfruit who have lived in Vilcabamba for generations. Guinea pigs roam the earthen floor of their one-room home, munching on vegetable peel. The family hope the road will make it easier to scrape a living. 'As it is, we have to walk two days in either direction to get to market,' the father explains, as Jorge translates into Spanish. They have a small solar panel, but no internet or phone reception. News still travels – like sacks of potatoes and coffee – by mule. 'This is a place of extreme poverty,' the teacher in the nearby hamlet of Concevidayoc tells me. 'The kids come to school in the same clothes day after day.'

As night falls, we pitch our tents on the playing field, sloping at a forty-five-degree angle. The outside world is on Jorge's mind. Archaeologists sometimes ask him: 'You're the Cobos family? Your grandparents lived at Espíritu Pampa, right? Surely they must have looted it?' The accusation annoys him, but he laughs it off. 'I say: "If they'd found gold and things like that, do you think we'd be living in Huancacalle? We'd be in the United States, Europe or England."'

Early 1571 found Titu Cusi at Vitcos, mourning at the spot where Manco was killed twenty-five years before. Although Vilcabamba's centre of gravity had shifted down towards Espíritu Pampa, the shrine of the White Rock – and the site of Manco's death – still held an irresistible pull. Worship of one's semi-divine ancestors was at the core of the Inca state religion. But Titu Cusi idolised his father in the way common to those who lose a parent young. Manco's murder before his eyes was the defining event of his life.

After a day of prayer and ceremony, he practised fencing with Martín Pando. Heavy-set from years of relative indolence, he sweated profusely. And as the sun retreated behind the mountains, he caught a chill. The Inca self-medicated with wine washed down by chicha. His condition worsened overnight. His tongue swelled up, he vomited, blood streamed from his nose and mouth. In the morning, Pando and a trusted Inca courtier gave him a remedy of egg white with sulphur. Titu Cusi Yupanqui gulped it down and died.

His followers were distraught. His wife, Angelina Quilaco, set them on the outsiders at court. Pando was killed on the spot. Suspicion of poisoning the Inca also fell on Diego Ortiz, known for his knowledge of herbs. The mob roughed up the friar, and forced him to say Mass in a desperate attempt to resurrect Titu Cusi. At Espíritu Pampa, the Inca captains had chosen Túpac Amaru – the blue-blooded son of Manco – to succeed his half-brother. They had Ortiz killed, ritually trampled, and buried upside down. Titu Cusi's Hispanophile tendencies – whether a matter of taste or diplomacy – had been deeply unpopular. The missionaries' chapels were burned to the ground. Raiders went forth again. There would be no more talk of surrender.

Hawks were also in charge on the Spanish side. In 1569, a new viceroy stepped ashore in Peru. A veteran of Habsburg wars against Protestants and the Ottomans, Francisco de Toledo forced native communities into new towns, *reducciones*, where they could be more easily taxed, converted and controlled. Toledo was unsentimental about the Incas, and sceptical of their claim to have ruled the Andes since time immemorial. His inquiries indicated they had marched out from Cuzco barely a century before Pizarro arrived. And his efforts to bring order would be in vain unless the Vilcabamba Incas were reined in, he urged his sovereign: 'This affair must be terminated once and for all.'

The problem was bigger than petty banditry. A generation after the conquest, the exiled Incas still maintained a deep psychological hold over their former subjects. It mattered little who wore the royal fringe: their mere presence in Vilcabamba was fissile material. 'It was impossible to keep the Indians quiet, and within terms of peace, while the Inca was so near them, and daily in their eye,' Garcilaso concluded. The last remnant of Tawantinsuyu could not be allowed to survive.

The pretext came in March 1572. A Spanish emissary, Atilano de Anaya, was killed on the border by the Inca's jumpy sentries. Túpac Amaru was dozens of miles away, and could not have given the order. But the viceroy seized his opportunity. Toledo declared the young Inca an 'apostate, turncoat, murderer, rebel and tyrant'. The most powerful man in the New World now vowed to wage a war of 'fire and blood' until Vilcabamba was destroyed.

PACHACUTI

The army Toledo formed for the mission was far more native than European. Its backbone was formed of 1,500 warriors from the highlands around Cuzco. With them, led by Francisco Chilche, marched 500 Cañari: an Ecuadorian people brutally subdued by Huayna Capac. The Andean game of thrones had rolled on through the centuries, new Spanish overlords providing fresh opportunities to settle old scores. The task force was completed by 250 conquistadors' sons, expensively equipped but green. A trio of greying old soldiers – veterans of Pizarro's ambush at Cajamarca, forty years earlier – were on hand to advise on how to catch an Inca.

Out in front was Martín García Óñez de Loyola: a young, glory-hungry captain who normally commanded the viceroy's bodyguard. On 1 June 1572, edging south along a narrow trail high above the roaring Vilcabamba River, he led the expedition into a trap. Barricades of thorns blocked their way; vines tripped them up; archers peppered them with arrows. Inca warriors thundered down the slope, wielding maces and lances with as much determination 'as the most skilful, brave, and experienced soldiers of Flanders'. A captain named Hualpa – 'a man of such great size and strength that he seemed a half-giant' – enveloped Loyola in a crushing bear hug, wrestling him towards the cliff edge. Only his native page, Corrillo, could scramble close enough to take down the Inca champion by hacking at his legs.

The melee lasted for nearly three hours. But the Spanish harquebuses eventually found their mark, killing six Inca commanders. The defenders rolled boulders downhill, crushing three Spaniards, to cover their retreat. The invaders seized Manco's palace at Vitcos. The valley before it was carpeted with maize, alpacas and llamas ready for the taking. The

Spanish quartermaster was in such a hurry to purloin the plump live-stock grazing near Pampaconas that he toppled off his horse into a bog.

The expedition paused for two weeks as an outbreak of measles ran its course. The army continued through winding, claustrophobic ravines. The Inca road was strewn with wartime sacrifices: the tiny, bloodied corpses of guinea pigs. At one critical moment, a Portuguese soldier inched around a cliff with a small cannon slung over his shoulder, loaded and primed it, and blasted the path free of enemies.

Túpac Amaru's forces tracked them closely, heckling them from the undergrowth. The Cañari skirmishers returned from the treeline blood-ied and bested. Worse lay ahead: Huayna Pucará, a fearsome fort of thick, crenellated walls and towers, whose narrow causeway prickled with poison-tipped stakes. The Spanish had taken heavy losses here in 1537. Unknown to Toledo's men, a heap of stones was poised atop levers above the only approach, ready to smash the attackers into the void. Half a thousand Amazonian archers waited to pick off the survi-vors. 'Not a single soul of the entire army would have been left alive,' Murúa believed.

Yet Puma Inca, one of Túpac Amaru's captains, switched sides. He told the Spanish that the Inca wanted to surrender. But a trio of Inca nobles – Curi Paucar, Colla Topa and Paucar Inca – had insisted on fighting to the bloody end. Whether acting on Túpac Amaru's orders, or seeking to save his sovereign, Puma Inca's next act all but doomed him. He sketched out the fort's defences, showing how it could be taken. At dawn, Loyola took a few hundred men sideways through the dripping, vine-strangled forest. In the afternoon, they resurfaced above the boul-der field. Cover blown, the would-be ambushers fell back to Huayna Pucará. Colla Topa and the garrison resisted the Spaniards' gunfire bravely with slings and bows, but slipped away once the enemy artillery opened up.

Chilche scouted ahead and into another ambush. The harquebusiers panicked, scrabbling to light their fuses. Jerónimo, a nephew of Toledo, set his padded armour on fire, only saving himself by leaping into a creek. But all resistance seemed to melt away. Another fort, Machu Pucará, was abandoned. The famished interlopers fell upon plots full of guavas, yucca, plantains and sugarcane.

On the morning of 24 June, the army marched into the last capital of the Incas. Pedro Sarmiento de Gamboa, the expedition's secretary, unfurled the royal standard in the main square. 'Vilcabamba for King Philip of Castile and León!' he proclaimed. Nobody responded.

Nothing moved. The city had already been ransacked, its temples and sundry storehouses little more than smoking ruins. Túpac Amaru, or his generals, had resolved on a policy of scorched earth, hoping to force their enemies to retreat.

But the invaders stayed put for two months. A few locals returned with critical information. The Inca had fled north-west into the jungle. The Spaniards set out in hot pursuit, dodging rattlesnakes and crossing rivers on rafts. Túpac Amaru's captains and relatives – living and dead – were tracked down one by one. The Indigenous-Iberian bounty hunters seized the mummified bodies of Manco and Titu Cusi, the Punchao – and an Inca's ransom in gold, silver, jewels and silk and velvet from Holland and Rouen. But as long as their owner remained at large, Vilcabamba could recover, and the embers of resistance might burst aflame once more.

Loyola picked out forty men experienced in jungle expeditions. They journeyed 200 miles north on Túpac Amaru's trail, hurtling down raging rapids and cajoling intelligence out of local chiefs. The Inca was moving slowly, because his wife, Juana Quispe – heavily pregnant – refused to travel any further by canoe. Loyola's crack company, by now barefoot and hungry after multiple capsizes, pressed on. They finally came upon the royal couple warming themselves by a campfire. Weakened by their desperate flight through the rainforest, escape seemed impossible. Promised fair treatment, Túpac Amaru surrendered.

Vilcabamba had been quashed in a matter of months. Viceroy Toledo had brought overwhelming force to bear: a corps of conquistadors who stood to gain prestige, wealth and security from its destruction, and Indigenous allies who craved loot and revenge. Yet they used extreme violence sparingly. The sons of Spaniards and Inca princesses marched with Loyola, helping to persuade their cousin to come in from the cold. And though 'eloquent and intelligent', Túpac Amaru was no warrior in his father's mould. He had spent decades confined to the Convent of the Sun at Espíritu Pampa, maintaining the cult of Manco's mummified body. The inexperienced acolyte struggled to control his frontier garrisons, let alone his orejón generals, who were fatally divided on strategy.

The captive Inca was marched back into Cuzco, and to his doom. A Spanish captain carried the Punchao out in front. Loyola brought up the rear, holding a golden chain looped around the Inca's neck. Passing the viceroy's palace, Loyola buffeted his prisoner for refusing to doff his crimson royal fringe. With Toledo determined to score a moral victory as well as a military one, Túpac Amaru was subjected to round-the-clock indoctrination by shifts of Jesuits, Mercedarians and Dominicans. Curi Paucar and the orejón captains were sentenced to the gallows.

The Inca – though now baptised as Felipe, after the king – was evidently headed the same way. Toledo charged him with a litany of robberies, kidnaps and murders. Most saw the show trial for what it was. Rectors, friars, bishops and priests protested the Inca's innocence, begging the viceroy on their knees to spare him. Túpac Amaru offered to plead his own case before Philip II. Toledo moved before popular opinion could turn against him. The Inca was sentenced to die.

On 24 September 1572, Don Felipe Túpac Amaru was led through the streets of Cuzco atop a mule clad in black velvet, his hands bound and his neck now encircled by a noose. Twenty thousand of his grandfather's subjects from across Tawantinsuyu squeezed into the plaza. Others perched on balconies, walls and rooftops; when the city was full, they spilled over the hills. It was said that an orange thrown into the crowd would not have touched the ground. María Cusi Huarcay, Sayri Túpac's widowed sister-wife, cried out, reaching for her brother, 'prince and sole king of the four corners', but the priests held her back.

As the Inca climbed the scaffold, the air shook with such wailing and lamentations that it seemed like Judgement Day. Túpac Amaru raised his right hand, then let it fall to his thigh. 'So great a silence ensued,' wrote Garcilaso, 'it was as if there had not been one soul alive within the whole city.' The Inca announced that he would die a Christian. 'And I must die. All that I and my ancestors the Incas have told you up to now – that you should worship the Sun, Punchao, and the huacas,' he said, 'is completely false.' He and Titu Cusi had only pretended to commune with the Punchao: 'It did not speak, we alone did.'

So complete a renunciation surprised even Toledo, monitoring proceedings from a window. Perhaps the Inca's capture and enforced catechism had shattered his faith. Maybe he hoped to secure clemency for himself or his children. But none was forthcoming. Túpac Amaru said farewell to his people and placed his neck on the block. A Cañari swordsman stepped forward, blindfolded the Inca, and gripped his hair in one hand. With the other, he brought down his blade.

The cries of grief in the square were drowned out by the bells of the cathedral, followed by those of Cuzco's convents, monasteries, chapels and churches, the death knell of the last Inca ringing out across the navel of the world. Righteous resolve against the Vilcabamba rebel immediately dissolved, replaced by 'compassion and sorrow'. Mournful Masses were sung as Túpac Amaru's body was buried in the cathedral, built on the site of the Inca Viracocha's palace. His head, impaled on a pike, became the focus of a fervent cult. Crowds gathered around it at night, refusing to disperse. After two days, the Inca's head was hastily interred alongside its owner.

Learning his lesson, the viceroy had the mummies of Manco and Titu Cusi burned to cinders in private. Later, he would take the Punchao back to Philip II, suggesting that such a diabolical object – looted of its golden rays by the Vilcabamba veterans – be sent on to the Pope. It vanished from the royal treasury: perhaps the ashes of the Incas remain hidden in a Spanish monastery or the vaults of the Vatican.

With Vilcabamba's ruling dynasty extirpated, living and dead, Toledo uprooted the Inca nobles 'who preserve their memory'. Even the children of Paullu – the quisling Inca – were bound for exile in Mexico before the king intervened. But the sons of Túpac Amaru and Titu Cusi were left stranded in Lima. Unused to the sea fog and pestilential miasmas of the new colonial capital, they died within a few years.

In the end, Toledo proved overzealous. Like Don Melchor Carlos Inca, many of the rump Inca elite willingly gravitated towards Madrid, where they were bought off with racehorses, knighthoods, African servants and coats of arms with serpents and pumas rampant; their spiralling arrears with tailors, silversmiths, and mistresses hedged against the promise of a pension. Some showed more attachment to their vanquished mountain fastness. In 1586, María Cusi Huarcay promised to reveal the location of gold and silver mines if only she were allowed to return to Vilcabamba. But the last Inca princesses were given only the choice of being confined to a convent or safely married off.

On the day of Túpac Amaru's execution, Toledo approved the betrothal of the Inca's niece, Beatriz – now fifteen years old – to his kidnapper, Loyola. Her inheritance, the rich royal estates at Yucay, passed to her new husband. This was the rosy wedding scene depicted on canvas some 150 years later: the last kings of Peru watching impassively as their independence is ended. The viceroy had meanwhile commissioned his own set of paintings – the line-up of Incas that passes from Atahualpa to Charles V – to erase the rulers of Vilcabamba from the record.

'Thus did this poor prince submit with great courage to death,' concluded Garcilaso, bringing the history of his ancestors to an end after seventeen books and 530 chapters. Manco's sons had always been the underdogs, but their defeat was not inevitable. Had the defenders of the fort at Huayna Pucará sprung their ambush – contemporaries thought – they would have wiped out the invaders. Túpac Amaru could have sued for an advantageous peace, his descendants remaining spiritual leaders in their mountain principality: a cross between Andorra, Vatican City and the exiled Dalai Lama.

But with every Spanish ship that arrived in Peru, any chance of turning the tide shrank even further. If Manco's hosts could not overcome the few dozen defenders of Cuzco – Túpac Amaru had implored his kangaroo court – it was inconceivable for him 'to rebel with such a small number, against such multitudes of Christians, who were now increased and dispersed over all parts of the Empire'.

Vilcabamba holds an ambiguous place in Peruvian history books. Manco's sons were disappointingly amenable to negotiation and conversion. Túpac Amaru's armies folded like a paper tiger. It was a strange, unclassifiable coda to conquest. The rebel capital itself was mislaid for centuries, swallowed up by the forest. Despite being led by locals to Espíritu Pampa in 1911, Hiram Bingham insisted that Machu Picchu was Vilcabamba, the last Inca city to fall in 1572. As a lucrative tourist industry sprang up around the photogenic royal retreat in the clouds, few dared challenge him. Consensus has only shifted decisively towards Espíritu Pampa since the 1960s, when a new generation of explorers hacked their way down to the overgrown ruins.

Garcilaso also struggled to fit the Vilcabamba monarchs, his cousins, into the history of the Incas, 'for though they had a right to the inheritance, yet they never had a possession of the government'. But they were direct heirs via the male line to the legendary founder Manco Capac, he conceded: perhaps the line of kings had continued past Huáscar and Atahualpa to Manco Inca and his sons, only ending with the death of the Vilcabamba princelings in Lima.

Three decades later, in the early 1600s, some distant Inca relatives wrote to the chronicler and old soldier, asking him to help press their claims at court. 'There are more descendants than I thought,' Garcilaso wrote. 'But I have been unable to contribute more beyond writing this history. I hope I have as well done justice to the Spaniards, who have conquered this Empire, as to the Incas, who were the true lords and possessors of it.'

January 1781. Two centuries later, the slopes overlooking Cuzco are carpeted with people once more. This time, they are not mourners. The

40,000 Andean rebels pound drums, blow trumpets and blast pistols
and fireworks into the air. One witness writes that the hillsides bristle
with so many pikes that they seem like a giant porcupine.

Commanding the besieging host is a muleteer, merchant and mixed-
race lesser nobleman called José Gabriel Condorcanqui. A proclamation
later found in his pocket declares him 'Don José the First by the Grace
of God, Inca of Peru, Santa Fe, Quito, Buenos Aires and the Continent
on these South Seas, Duke of the Superlative, Lord of the Caesars and
Amazons, with Dominions in the Great Paititi, Commissary Distributor
of the Divine Piety'. But he is best known – after his great-great-great-
grandfather – as Túpac Amaru II.

A few months earlier, Condorcanqui and his wife, Micaela Bastidas –
a tough, efficient strategist – launch their coup in their hometown of
Tinta. They seize muskets, treasure, and a Spanish official, making him
summon local troops and send for more cash. Then they have him garrotted. Meanwhile, in his letters, Condorcanqui insists on his loyalty to
the crown. A handful of criollos, Spanish-Americans, have even joined
him. Their quarrel is with a new crop of royal officials: gouging prices,
tripling sales duties, snubbing ancestral chiefs and sending thousands
more to an early grave in the mines of Potosí. The weather has been
harsh, people are starving.

But this is clearly about more than bread and taxes. The insurgency
spreads like wildfire. There are pitched battles in mountain passes
clogged with snowdrifts, desperate shootouts in churches, wild reports
of babies being thrown into Lake Titicaca and the rebels drinking blood
from communion chalices. Over 100,000 people perish. Deadlier and
more widespread than the revolution simultaneously unfolding in
North America, it is the greatest anti-imperial revolt to erupt in the New
World since 1492. A descendant of the last Inca – adopting the name
not of Huayna Capac nor Atahualpa, but the final sovereign of
Vilcabamba – has emerged to turn the colonial order upside down.

Condorcanqui – who had spent years peacefully petitioning the
authorities – grows into the role of implacable Andean avenger. His
breeches and silk stockings are now complemented by a golden chain
with an Inca sun, his hair flowing in ringlets down his back. He declares
the freedom of enslaved Africans, and orders Spanish women to chew
coca leaves, go about barefoot, and wear Indigenous skirts. Rebels in
Nueva Granada – modern-day Colombia – proclaim him 'King of
America'. Rumours spread that he is marching on Buenos Aires to be
crowned. In Upper Peru, today's Bolivia, a vast army of Indigenous

Aymara besieges the city of La Paz, twice. Dogs gnaw on cadavers; the survivors eat the dogs. Rebellions spring up in Chile and in Tucumán, now northern Argentina. 'Each and every Indian' – one observer panics – 'declares himself a Túpac Amaru.'

The caciques who had venerated the severed head of Túpac Amaru I in 1572 went home telling how the Inca's visage had grown more beautiful with each passing hour. A prophecy known as the Inkarri was born: when the Inca's living head and body are reunited, the era of darkness brought by Europeans will end, and Tawantinsuyu will be restored. The Inkarri legend fed into the pre-Columbian concept of Pachacuti: history looping back on itself in centuries-long cycles, marked by upheaval in the human and natural world. A veneer of Catholicism had only supercharged this millenarian mindset: many of Condorcanqui's fighters believed that if they fell, they would rise again on the third day.

And their leader would never have rebelled – Spanish officials later concluded – had he not as a schoolboy 'drunk from the poison' of the *Royal Commentaries*. When Garcilaso died in 1616, half of the print run was gathering dust on his shelves. But in the late 1700s his historical masterwork exploded in popularity among those smarting at Spanish abuses. Songs, rituals and popular theatre had also helped to transfigure a repressive, expansionist empire – albeit one where abject poverty and starvation were rare – into a lost paradise.

Condorcanqui's rebellion and its many offshoots fail. The insurgents are divided and outgunned. Many Andeans, including descendants of the Incas, throw in their lot with the royalists. Condorcanqui is betrayed and tortured – a clerk transcribing his every cry of pain – but refuses to incriminate anyone else. In May 1781, Cuzco assembles to witness the killing of another Inca. Condorcanqui and Bastidas are made to watch as their sons are hanged. Her neck proves too thin for the garrotte, so her executioners strangle her with ropes and kick her to death.

They lash Condorcanqui's arms and legs to four charging horses. But though his limbs are dislocated, he is too robust to be torn apart. As he is finally beheaded, the heavens open, sending the crowds scurrying for shelter. In November, Túpac Katari – the co-leader of the Aymara siege of La Paz – is captured and cut into quarters. His last words, according to oral tradition: 'You kill only me. But tomorrow I will return as millions.'

The *Royal Commentaries* was the rare history book that changed history. In the wake of Condorcanqui's abortive revolution, the Spanish authorities burned every copy of Garcilaso's book they found. They prohibited Peruvians from speaking Quechua. They banned the surname 'Inca', 'for this title makes them enter into fanatical thoughts of royal lineage'. They destroyed the paintings and busts of the Incas that decorated Cuzco colleges. Such images made the sons of Andean nobility 'wish to restore those imagined golden centuries', one bishop fumed. 'They have tried to paint our first conquistadors as inhuman pirates.'

Yet the memory of the Incas would endure – and spread. In 1802, Jean-Jacques Dessalines, the commander of the revolutionary Black republic of Haiti, declared his troops to be 'The Army of the Incas' and 'Sons of the Sun'. Around 1820, distant Uruguay echoed with the hoofbeats of gaucho freedom fighters who dubbed themselves, after Condorcanqui, the *Tupamaros*. So did the Marxist guerrillas who kidnapped Britain's ambassador to Montevideo in 1971. In Peru, a leftist army officer had meanwhile seized power, broken up colonial-era estates, and shared out the land among downtrodden campesinos, promising to finish the revolution that Túpac Amaru II had started.

'Justice has at last arrived to the countryside of Peru,' General Juan Velasco Alvarado told the packed central plaza of Cuzco in September 1971. 'And it comes under the aegis of that heroic figure, the great rebel that this land gave to Peru, América, and the world. It comes two hundred years since the martyrdom, since the blood, since the savage crime that failed to finish off the great Túpac Amaru.' He promised that Peru, 'the patria of Túpac Amaru', would 'become the home of real social justice built by Peruvians themselves'.

At another rally held by Velasco in 1974, a twenty-year-old Venezuelan cadet called Hugo Rafael Chávez Frías looked on. The general gave him a booklet of his speeches. The spectacle – a historical revolutionary resurrected to serve the struggle in the present – made a lasting impression. Meanwhile, in New York, a Black Panther activist gave her son a Quechua name meaning 'Shining Serpent'. For Afeni Shakur, the struggles for Black and Indigenous liberation were one and the same. And like his namesake, the legend of the rapper Túpac Amaru Shakur only grew after his untimely killing in a drive-by shooting in 1996.

The patria of Túpac Amaru – the Andean utopia whose shimmering outline began to take form the moment Vilcabamba fell – has proved elusive. Sometimes the yearning for it has metastasised into chilling forms. Shining Path and the Túpac Amaru Revolutionary Movement sowed terror across Peru in the 1980s, triggering brutal repression by Alberto Fujimori, the president-turned-dictator. In the wake of the conflict, government doctors sterilised 300,000 Peruvians – mostly rural, Indigenous women, many without their consent. Survivors are still fighting for justice, some leaving searing testimony online via an anonymous phone line called The Quipu Project.

Since the turn of the millennium, exports of Peruvian minerals have inflated GDP and slashed poverty. But the foreign-owned open-pit mines have scarred the countryside, poisoned locals, and left yawning inequalities – between the coast and the sierra, Cuzco and Lima, the capital and its outskirts – largely untouched. Nor has the age of copper proved more calming than the age of manure. As of mid-2024, Peru had ploughed through seven presidents in eight years: outstripping even Britain's six prime ministers in the same span. Political careers invariably end in congressional coup or corruption scandal. The country has created a special jail for disgraced heads of state.

Meanwhile, Andean communities face a new existential threat. On a highland plateau to the west of Cuzco, I visited Hilaria Supa Huamán: Peru's first parliamentarian to take the oath of office in Quechua. It was winter, but she wore her jumpers, woven skirt and knitted socks within her re-soled sandals more from habit. 'It shouldn't be this warm, and there shouldn't be all these clouds,' Hilaria muttered, as we sat down to a potato and quinoa stew in the fields. The rituals of her childhood sixty years ago were breaking down. 'We don't know when to sow, when to plant, like our ancestors did. When I was a girl, the mountains were all white. You could see them shining at night.' Most of the surrounding peaks were now dark grey, with a patchy comb-over of translucent ice. 'Without the snows, where will our water come from?'

Yet Peru's pre-Columbian inheritance is still palpable. Quechua is spoken by some ten million people worldwide. Peru's cornucopia of fruits, flavours and thousands of varieties of tubers, improved by Andeans and Amazonians down the ages, have cemented its status as a gastronomic powerhouse. In 2023, Lima boasted four eateries among the world's fifty best restaurants, including the top spot.

Offshoots of Tawantinsuyu's aristocracy still exist. In Cuzco, I called in on Alfredo Inca Roca: a silver-haired agronomist with an aquiline nose and patrician manners who descends from the Inca Viracocha. He has donned a golden costume to play the Inca in Inti Raymi – the midwinter Festival of the Sun, revived in 1944 – eight times. When Alfredo was selected for the role, local thespians were up in arms. 'How can he play the Inca,' they demanded, 'if he's never trod the boards?' Alfredo replied: 'You can learn to be Inca. I'm Inca every day of my life.'

In Lima, I had visited a shanty town on the doorstep of the capital's wealthiest districts. Forty years ago, this was desert. Then over half a million people fled the torture and massacres in the mountains. Edwin Rojas' mother was among them. The conflict followed her to the capital. As a child, Edwin remembers bombings and blackouts, bodies on the sand. Aid agencies dropped crates of tinned food into the slums. The farmers had to learn how to fish. But the refugees reinforced their new hill-top homes like their Andean ancestors had always done: with sturdy, tremor-absorbing terraces of earth and stone, built without mortar. 'People are still building as the Incas did,' says Edwin, an athletic community activist.

As we climb higher, he points out repeated rows of mortarless masonry. 'It's considered a high-tech construction: not my words, but those of *National Geographic*. Obviously, people are not as perfectionist as the Incas,' he admits. These look more like the dry stone walls of the Yorkshire Dales than the smoothly rippling ashlar of Sacsayhuaman. 'But the idea is to move with the earthquakes. Concrete breaks. But when the city shakes, we live through it.' And even on this steep, gritty soil, his neighbours rear ducks and guinea pigs, spreading their muck on shared vegetable patches. Locals pool resources, and care for each other when they fall ill. It's the Andean principle of reciprocity, or *ayni*, Edwin explains: 'Today for you, tomorrow for me.' He's encouraging the older generation to pass on such ancient common sense.

We summit a staircase. To the left, green foothills beginning their ascent to the sierra; straight ahead, the slumped pyramids of the Pachacamac oracle, many millennia old; the Pacific blending into mist. 'I don't call myself a Peruvian,' says Edwin. 'Not because I don't like Peruvians,' he clarifies. 'My mum says it's a bit pretentious: that I couldn't build Machu Picchu or the Inca Trail. But I checked my anthropology books. And it's my decision, a decision to respect our traditions. If someone asks me what I am, I say I'm Inca.'

I step outside into the sunshine at Espíritu Pampa. Jorge is stretched out in a wheelbarrow, sipping coffee. Only now, I notice the sacks piled in the garden of his relatives' farmhouse. Guano: maybe even from the harvest I had seen on the Chinchas a few weeks before.

We climb into the back of a truck, then another, clinging on to the roof as we rattle down dirt switchbacks and campesino families pile aboard. After our week in the mountains, Quillabamba – restaurants, nightclubs, karaoke bars – feels like a metropolis. A waft of aftershave in the hotel lobby announces Jorge's reappearance, wearing an impeccable dress shirt plucked from the bottom of his pack. It's his fortieth birthday.

The night unfolds in a blur of Mexican rum, Cusqueña lager and Puerto Rican reggaeton. Alvaro shouts a prediction in my ear. 'I think, in the future, America will be like a single place.' I'm taking the bus back to Cuzco in the morning, then heading down into the Amazon. But Jorge makes me promise to return to Vilcabamba soon: 'We could take the back route over from Choquequirao.' There's lots more to explore, he says, places only locals know about. 'Next time, we'll bring some mules.'

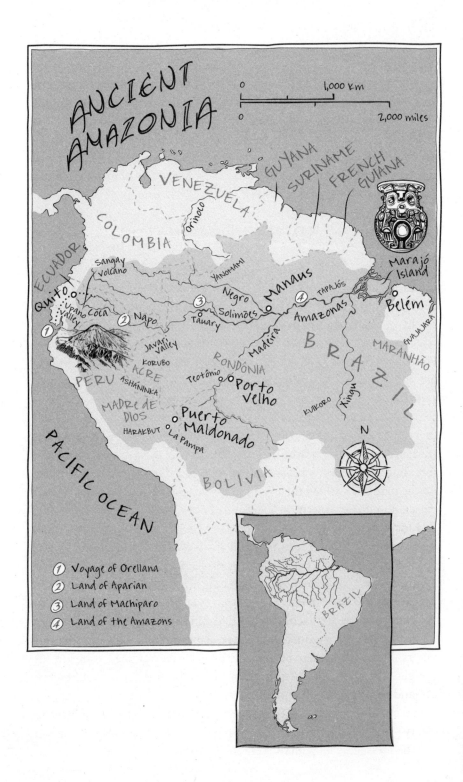

3

Dark Earth

Ancient Amazonia, 20,000 BC–AD 1542

A LAND WITHOUT HISTORY

As the truck jolts along a rutted track, swerving between illegal gold mines in the Peruvian Amazon, Yesica Patiachi is telling me how the earth was created. She first heard it around the campfire as a child, told by the last Harakbut to be brought out of the forest.

A long time ago, the world was in chaos. The animals were dying. Food and water tasted bitter. The forest was ablaze. Enemy tribes, including the Harakbut, put aside their differences. Even jaguars and serpents, suddenly meek, sought refuge among them. Still, the mud boiled, the smoke thickened. 'No one,' says Yesica, 'had an answer to the tongues of fire.' Suddenly, a parrot circled overhead bearing a sacred seed, seeking a virginal host. Mothers shoved their daughters to the fore. But Wehweh only brushed them with his wings and flapped higher. As the matrons scolded their red-faced youngsters, and the flames raced closer, an outcast elderly woman and her teenage granddaughter shuffled forward.

Wehweh placed the seed between the girl's legs. In an instant, there grew an immense tree called A'nämëi. In the nick of time, the Harakbut climbed into his branches. Capybaras, anteaters, boa constrictors, peccaries – a kind of pungent, bristly pig – and bullet ants raced them to the canopy. A great anaconda curled around the trunk, forming a pool for fish to shelter. A'nämëi gave yucca, papaya and bananas to the survivors. He covered their noses with damp leaves, pooled water in his boughs, and stretched out beds of branches. But he threw back thieves, philanderers, witches and gossips. A man claimed to have been bitten by a snake and cast it into the air. The tree of life plucked the serpent to safety – and swatted the liar into the conflagration below. The Harakbut got the message: the animals were their brothers.

When they clambered down, they had forgotten everything: even where babies come from. They cradled shells like newborns. A family of monkeys took pity on them and gave them a demonstration. The Harakbut watched carefully, paired off – even the elders – and went into the trees. 'Some say A'nämëi will return when the world is destroying itself,' says Yesica. 'But he left us this world, he left us the forest, for us to look after it.'

The truck grinds to a halt on a rise of parched earth. We look out over a scarred moonscape. Cobalt water, glassy and lifeless, pools between heaps of rocks, grubby sand and splintered trunks. Tubes disgorge wet earth onto rusty conveyor belts. Grime-smeared figures shelter under tarpaulins from the midday sun. 'All of this used to be forest. We used to fish and hunt,' says Yesica. 'There are no fish or animals anymore.'

This is just one clearing. From the air, you see waterlogged craters gouged out of the forest in clusters twenty miles long and three miles wide. Toxic run-off tinges them aquamarine, salmon-pink, custard-yellow or a gangrenous grey: the Western Front shelled by a Dulux colour chart. In barely a decade, unregulated mining has turned 270 square miles of rainforest into a ravaged wasteland. When the global economy crashed in 2008, the international gold price soared. A few years later, a highway into Brazil was rammed through the Madre de Dios region, its riverbeds speckled with gold washed down from the mountains. Some 50,000 miners have since poured in.

In Delta 1, a camp of clapboard houses, two men with wispy moustaches enter a store wearing white rubber boots and shorts, their calves caked in orange mud. One produces a few shiny flakes wrapped in newspaper. A woman weighs them, punches a sum into a calculator, and counts out banknotes. They pocket the cash and leave. I ask the shopkeeper about today's price, but she quickly clams up. Yesica suggests we keep moving. There are no police here, she says. Reporters have their cameras smashed to bits.

I had travelled out that morning from Puerto Maldonado, the regional capital: two shared cars, a motorised canoe, standing on the bed of a truck, then hiring another and its driver with Yesica. I passed through La Pampa, a strip of clapboard bars, brothels and hardware shops lining the highway. Its 25,000 residents live in thrall to a murderous mafia who force children into sexual slavery.

Pavel Martiarena makes a living photographing weddings and *quinceañeras*. In his spare time, he chronicles the pillage of the province.

Some miners, he says, believe if they go to bed with an underage girl, they'll strike gold. 'I have friends, girls I went to school with, who I'm never going to see again, because they tried to escape from La Pampa. They were shot by the guards and their bodies were burned.' Most of the gold-hunters are dirt-poor, Pavel adds. Mining seems like their only way out. But sifting through the soil quickly becomes 'a madness, a sickness. Then their kids grow up in that world and it seems normal. Where the only authority is death.'

We pass the last of the mining pits, separated by a narrow strand of forest from the Harakbut village of San José. Chickens peck around huts and a concrete evangelical chapel. Here, we can talk more freely. A linguist and historian, Yesica has translated and compiled the stories of Harakbut elders. Petite and round-faced, she is also the most outspoken opponent of the criminal industry ransacking their home.

Outsiders have invaded before: the Incas, would-be conquistadors. Carlos Fermín Fitzcarrald – a Peruvian businessman of Irish-American descent – enslaved thousands of native Amazonians to extract rubber from the forest, slaughtering those who resisted. Fitzcarrald even forced them to haul a dismantled steamship for miles through mountainous jungle: the inspiration for the Werner Herzog film *Fitzcarraldo*. The King of Rubber was sucked under by rapids and drowned in 1897. Fifty years later came the missionaries, and more epidemics.

But the latest resource rush is more insidious, says Yesica. The Harakbut are sickening inside and out, their bond with nature being broken. Some have become pit workers and mining bosses themselves. 'The spirit of Fitzcarrald is here,' she says, 'in every miner, in every narcotrafficker, in every logger attacking the lives of Indigenous people and life itself.' She gazes across to the thick vegetation on the far bank of the river. 'If they don't fix this, in fifty years, all of this will disappear. I'd like for my grandchildren to see the forest.'

The miners add mercury to the slurry of sediment and river water. The liquid metal binds with the particles of gold and sinks. Then they burn it off with blowtorches. Two hundred tonnes of the substance settle in the rivers and soil every year, says César Ascorra, the director of CINCIA, a research institute in Puerto Maldonado. 'It also enters the food chain,' he explains, including the fish that locals eat daily. Once ingested, 'it enters your molecular makeup. It becomes your flesh.' Mercury poisoning deforms foetuses in the womb. It makes it hard for children and adults to breathe, to walk, and to remember. Over time, it can kill.

On a map, the scientist indicates a native Machiguenga village sixty miles north-west in a protected reserve. 'They don't know anything about gold, or how to mine it. But we had to tell them to stop eating their fish.' Indigenous peoples trying their best to avoid the outside world – with no use for bullion reserves, smartphones or aerospace components – are probably being poisoned too.

It wasn't timber, rubber, oil or gold that first drew Europeans deep into the world's largest rainforest, but cinnamon. Hearing rumours of a country rich in the precious spice to the east, Gonzalo Pizarro marched over the Andes from Quito late in 1541. When the Inca roads ran out and his army's horses perished, they built a makeshift boat and followed the Coca and Napo rivers. Their supplies ran low. Their Andean allies became sick, the Spaniards mutinous.

Francisco de Orellana – a one-eyed, thirty-year-old veteran – volunteered to scout ahead. He took a few canoes and fifty-seven men, including a Dominican chaplain called Gaspar de Carvajal. Yet after a few days' bumpy voyage, it was clear there was no going back. The current was too fierce to return upriver; none dared go by land. They voted to carry on, Carvajal later recorded, 'to follow the river, and see what lay along it, or die'.

Fainting with hunger, they boiled their belts and shoes with herbs, and crawled into the hills to grub around for roots. Some became 'mad and witless' after eating strange plants. Seven starved to death. On New Year's Day, 1542, they thought they heard drumming. Days later, they came across a settlement. The Spaniards fell upon everything edible, swords tucked under their armpits. 'There, they gave us news of the Amazons and the wealth that lies downriver.'

A little further on, at the town of a lord called Aparian, they gorged on roasted monkeys, ocelots, and turtles the size of shields. Between mouthfuls of manatee, Orellana took possession of the land in the name of Charles, Emperor of the Christians, and pronounced the Spaniards to be 'sons of the Sun'. Aparian and his courtiers were politely enthusiastic, but seemingly unconvinced that the barefoot, emaciated foreigners with matted hair and beards were gods. 'They said that if we were going to see the Amazons,' Carvajal recorded, 'whom in their tongue they call *coniu puyara*, great noblewomen, we should be careful: for we were few and they many, and they would kill us.'

Undeterred, the Spaniards went into the forest to fell timber, plagued by swarms of biting insects. They melted down their buckles and blades to make nails. They built another vessel, a pint-sized warship caulked with cotton and fish scales. News of their presence spread. Emissaries from a great ruler arrived, a hand higher than the tallest Christian, wearing golden ornaments and their hair down to their waist. They took a message to their sovereign, but never returned.

On 24 April 1542, the expedition embarked once more, Carvajal preaching on Sundays, the men shooting iguanas out of the trees with crossbows. On 12 May, they entered the lands of Machiparo. His towns stretched for 200 miles along the banks of the river; in one of them, each dwelling squeezed against the next for thirteen miles. In another, the Spaniards scooped up hundreds of turtles from half-submerged corrals. But mainly they went hungry, as Machiparo's armies – reportedly 55,000 men strong – fought them tooth and nail.

They were no longer received as a curiosity, but as hostile invaders of a powerful civilisation; a people Orellana called the Omagua. On the water, they were intercepted by fleets of warriors bearing shields of turtle carapace and tapir hide, pounding drums, playing pipes, and threatening – the Spanish believed – to eat them. Shamans, caked in white pigment from head to toe, huffed clouds of smoke and cast incantations with their staffs. By land, troops mustered in great plazas and battled the interlopers house-by-house, constantly relieved by fresh squadrons. With their gunpowder often drenched by showers, the Spaniards fell back on swords and daggers. They wrapped their wounded in bundles so enemy spies wouldn't see them limping aboard the boats.

On one day, they counted twenty towns, 'and this only on the bank by which we passed, for we could not see the other because the river was so wide'. They saw hilltop forts with stout wooden walls; farmland managed carefully by fire; avenues lined with fruit trees – what looked like avocados, plums, guavas, pineapples and pears. They captured the residence of a wealthy lord. It contained figures made of feathers – with mechanisms that moved their arms and legs – and ceramic pitchers, plates and candlesticks 'of the best craftsmanship seen in the world', glazed and painted 'so brightly in every colour that they were astonishing'.

They passed another great river on their left, 'whose water was black as ink, and which ran with such volume and ferocity that for more than twenty leagues it ran alongside the other water without the two mixing'. They constantly heard tales of the coniu puyara. Eventually, they came to grips with the mysterious warrior-women. Their armies danced amid musket balls. It seemed to rain arrows. One buried itself in Carvajal's

side to the bone. His companions waded ashore and into the fray. A
dozen bow-wielding Amazons fought out in front, pummelling to death
those who dared retreat. Tall and strong, with braided hair and strips of
hide covering their modesty, each 'made war like ten men'.

The Amazons wore golden crowns the thickness of two fingers – a
hostage later told the Spaniards – thatched their homes with the plumage of parrots, and stacked their temples with silver. They dwelled in
fortified cities, connected by roads behind high walls, where only women
were permitted past sundown. They abducted men in war, keeping them
'as long as they pleased'. If they gave birth to a boy, he was killed; if a
daughter, 'they train her in the ways of war'. After taking out seven or
eight of these fearsome commanders, the Spanish managed to escape,
their vessels studded with so many arrows 'that they looked like
porcupines'.

Great cities glimmered off in the interior. A chief called Nurandaluguaburabara sent so many men after them that the river was jammed
with canoes. Orellana hanged his prisoners as a warning, and threw
trinkets behind him in floating gourds, but the men hunting them – now
painted black, with shaven heads – only jeered. One Spaniard after
another sustained flesh-wounds, became paralysed, and was dead within
a day. Carvajal heard confessions and lost an eye to an arrow.

Too exhausted to row, too terrified to steal food, the survivors drifted
downriver, picking snails off rocks. In August, the crashing of waves
revived them. The river spat them out into the mid-Atlantic. Another
two weeks' hard sailing took them to safety in the Caribbean. Yet their
eight-month, 2,000-mile odyssey – the first recorded voyage down the
world's longest river after the Nile – had not put them off the jungle.

Three years later, Orellana would come back with a fleet, his wife,
and the title of governor of this coveted new province of Nueva Andalucía: only to perish amid a flurry of poison-tipped darts. These forest
realms were too well-governed, their mastery of their environment too
complete, their love of liberty too great for them to readily yield to outsiders. Even the great Orellana River the captain supposedly discovered
would become known as the *Amazonas*, after the warlike sorority –
originally named in Greek mythology – that nearly wiped out his first
expedition.

'All those we have passed along this river,' Carvajal had concluded,
'are people of much intelligence and ingenuity.' The proof was in their
industrious towns, the thoroughfares lined with bounteous orchards,
their storehouses bursting with produce, their battalions of disciplined

fighters, their complex social arrangements of religion, lordship, languages, inverted (to European eyes) gender hierarchies, and their astoundingly vivid artworks in ceramics, feathers and precious metal. It had all been – the fighting friar reflected – 'a marvel to behold'.

Forty years earlier, the Florentine explorer Amerigo Vespucci reached a similar conclusion. In the years either side of 1500, he skirted the coastline of the Amazon and southern Brazil. Ancient authors maintained that the planet's southern half was an endless expanse of ocean – or that if any landmass existed beneath the equator, it was uninhabitable.

'But their opinion is false and utterly opposed to the truth,' Vespucci reported. 'In those southern parts I have found a continent more densely peopled and abounding in animals than our Europe or Asia or Africa, and, in addition, a climate milder and more delightful than in any other region.' Columbus died in 1506 insisting that he had found another part of Asia. But Vespucci was quicker to the mark. His name, not that of his Genoese rival, was soon adopted for the New World he claimed to have discovered: America.

Yet for centuries, tales of an urbanised Amazon were relegated to the realm of legend. In fairness, the survivors of Orellana's impromptu river cruise were hardly the most reliable narrators. When they weren't tripping on hallucinogenic herbs and tree frog toxins, they barely dared peek above the gunwales. Orellana and Carvajal may not have seen eye-to-eye on everything – the chaplain wanted souls, the captain servants – but both had motive to embellish their exploits. Locals also had a strong incentive to fob off the pillaging foreigners with tales of cities dripping in gold, ruled by powerfully-built femmes fatales – just a few days further from their own humble circle of huts.

By the time that Portuguese soldiers and slavers sailed up the Amazon in the 1600s, little trace remained of these jungle civilisations. Vegetation, not dwellings, now pressed upon the riverbanks. Brazil's Indigenous peoples, one chronicler concluded, 'lived in disorder'. They were godless, lawless, leaderless: '*não têm Fé, nem Lei, nem Rei*.' As explorers and rubber tappers steamed further upriver two centuries later, native Amazonians fled deeper into the trees. Geographers breezily drew undeviating borders through the backlands, splitting isolated tribes into fractions. Civilisation was impossible in the sweltering tropics, concluded Euclides da Cunha, who hashed out Brazil's frontier with Peru in 1904. The Amazon, he believed, was a 'land without history'.

Until recently, many archaeologists – especially dominant figures in the discipline from the United States – also dismissed the idea that the Amazon could sustain large populations. The soil, constantly sluiced away by tropical downpours, was too poor to grow enough food; there were few big animals to hunt; there was little stone for buildings and no metal for tools. Amazonians were probably later offshoots from the great Andean empires: small bands of nomads roving a virgin wilderness, eking out a frugal existence within the limits imposed by the forest.

The idea of an empty Amazon stuck. In the 1970s, Brazil's military dictatorship – fearing that its rivals would seize this blank space and its resources – carved highways through the forest and encouraged poor farmers from the north-east to settle. Amazonia, the slogan went, was a 'land without men for men without land'. Prospectors rushed into the jungle's northern stretches and tore up the earth for gold. At least 8,300 Indigenous people were killed amid massacres, illnesses, evictions and torture; few doubt the true figure is much higher.

Over the following decade, the Yanomami – hunters, foragers and gardeners, straddling the Venezuela–Brazil border – were ravaged by malaria, measles and tuberculosis. They perished 'like poisoned fish in a dry pond', recalled Davi Kopenawa, a Yanomami spiritual leader. 'After their death, I remained alone with my anger . . . I always feel sad when I see the emptiness of the forest that my elders travelled.' Soon, he predicted, the orphan spirits of the last Yanomami shamans would chop down the sky, smashing the sun and crushing the earth. 'We will perish before we even notice. Then the sky will remain dark for all time.'

The peoples of the Amazon fought back. Brazil returned to democracy in 1985, and recognised native ownership over country-sized tracts of rainforest. The ranchers and miners were held in check for a while. Yet even well-meaning conservationists, working the heartstrings and purse strings of donors, still describe the rainforest as a 'vast, untamed wilderness'. The notion of Amazonia as a backwater and its inhabitants as backwards remains alive and kicking in the twenty-first century.

'The Indians don't speak our language, they have no money, they have no culture. How did they manage to get thirteen per cent of the national territory?' demanded an ultraconservative congressman called Jair Bolsonaro – himself the son of a former wildcat miner – in 2015. The country's Indigenous reserves were squatting atop precious metals, he griped, and 'suffocating' the advance of agribusiness. 'It's a shame' – he had previously mused – 'that the Brazilian cavalry wasn't as efficient as the Americans, who exterminated the Indians.'

*

How we think about the Amazon and its history has real-world consequences. Spanning eight countries and 2.5 million square miles – the
size of Western Europe – it is critical to the earth's climate. It contains
one in ten of all the world's known species, despite making up just one
per cent of the planet's surface. It is home to over 350 distinct native
peoples, including at least sixty avoiding contact with outsiders. And,
gnawed all around the edges and deep from within, the rainforest's
existence is threatened like never before.

Agribusiness is the major driver of illegal deforestation. Someone
takes a chainsaw to the ancient hardwoods, sells the shorn trunks, and
bulldozes and burns the wreckage. The land is sold time and again until
the paper trail goes cold. In Brazil, the landgrabbers are known as *grilei-
ros*, cricketeers: they sometimes leave forged property titles in a drawer
full of insects to artificially age them. The cows move in, fatten up on
the pasture, and their meat is exported to the United States, China and
Europe.

The farmers demand highways, ports and power. More colossal
hydroelectric dams are planned across Amazonian rivers in Brazil and
Bolivia, fracturing ecosystems and submerging tracts of forest. Oil drilling in Ecuador has brought contamination and clear-cuts. Colombian
and Peruvian drug cartels are branching out into wildlife poaching, and
laundering their profits through land speculation, logging and mining –
a phenomenon the UN calls narco-deforestation.

Illicit mining for precious metals is perhaps the most sinister threat.
In 2021, dystopian images went viral of a floating city of 400 barges
and 3,000 miners advancing up the Madeira River, dredging for gold
and spewing mercury fumes into the air. Chinese companies are churning up Bolivia's national parks for gold. Mining gangs in Venezuela
have carved an arc of devastation along the Orinoco River, enslaving
hundreds of Indigenous children. Defying police crackdowns, miners
are spreading from La Pampa to other remote corners of Amazonian
Peru. 'It's not a regional problem anymore,' Ascorra, the scientist in
Puerto Maldonado, told me. 'It's national.'

As the threats to isolated forest peoples multiply, some have advanced
a deeply controversial argument: for 'controlled contact' to be made –
with doctors and interpreters – before others reach them first. And while
the planet heats up and the forest shrinks, some scientists warn that the
Amazon is nearing a tipping point, where it will irreversibly transform
into dry savannah. Its great flying rivers of rainfall will vanish, seeding
drought across South America. The earth's climate will warm by 0.25

degrees Celsius as the lungs of the earth exhale over a hundred billion tonnes of carbon: equivalent to a decade of global fossil-fuel emissions. Roughly seventeen per cent of the rainforest has already been razed. Most put the point of no return at between twenty and twenty-five per cent.

An array of solutions is being touted. CINCIA is using drones and satellite imaging to explore how the pockmarked landscape around La Pampa can be restored. Eco-tourism is providing some with an alternative to mining. Colombia has banned new oil projects. Nations like Norway – made rich from fossil fuels – and figures like Leonardo DiCaprio and Jeff Bezos are paying Brazil billions to keep the forest intact. But buried deep in the soil, and in the very trees themselves, lies a glimmer of hope that doesn't depend on tourists' wallets or celebrity chequebooks.

It is the fast-accumulating evidence that the rainforest has supported many millions before: not just 'simple' hunter-gatherers, but also prosperous, urban realms. They were pioneering, bioengineering farmers, artists, explorers and builders. They experimented with socio-political systems to safeguard against tyrants. And most intriguingly, it now seems that ancient Amazonians shaped the forest around them into a rolling orchard, plantation and apothecary to live sustainably for millennia.

Across the Americas, wherever archaeologists look – or look again – they are finding that pre-Columbian societies were more populous, more sophisticated, and thrived thousands of years earlier than they once were willing to believe. 'Indigenous peoples were here far longer than previously thought' – Charles C. Mann has summarised – 'and in much greater numbers. And they were so successful at imposing their will on the landscape that in 1492 Columbus set foot in a hemisphere thoroughly marked by humankind.' But nowhere has the paradigm shift been more profound than the Amazon. It vindicates Carvajal and other chroniclers long written off as fabulists. More importantly, it buttresses what native communities have long been telling us: they, like their ancestors, know how to flourish within and with the rainforest.

It's now dark at Delta 1, the mining camp in Peru. I say goodbye to Yesica at the river. Figures with headlamps unload generators, fuel tanks, crates of beer and bundles of tools. Over the next few weeks, I'm headed along the highway into Brazil, and down the Amazon to find out how our understanding of the rainforest's deep past is shifting, and how this might hold the key to its future. Yesica holds on to hope that her people and their home can recover. 'They can cut your branches,' she says, 'but not your roots.'

AMAZONIAN ROME

In February 1978, while traversing a misty jungle valley in eastern Ecuador, the priest-turned-archaeologist Pedro Porras stumbled across a tall mound of earth rising from the forest floor. 'It was a stroke of luck,' he later recalled. As he investigated and excavated, more and more hummocks appeared – 180, by his count – along with pitchers, pottery and sunken pathways. But the dense vegetation either side of the Upano River made it impossible to gauge the relationship between these seemingly small, isolated villages – until almost fifty years later, when researchers brought a powerful new tool to bear.

Lidar – light detection and ranging – involves shooting laser pulses out of an aeroplane towards the ground and measuring how long it takes them to rebound. Like a bat scanning a cave with sonar squeaks, it generates a picture of the topography hidden beneath the forest canopy: hills, depressions – and man-made structures. In little more than a decade, the technology has unveiled a vast cityscape around the temples of Angkor in Cambodia, a sprawling Maya metropolis in the Central American jungle, and pre-Hispanic pyramids some twenty-two metres tall in the Bolivian Amazon. Applied to the Upano Valley, in a survey funded by Ecuador's government, the results were just as extraordinary.

Lidar surveys revealed more than 6,000 mounds and platforms – some 140 metres long and forty metres wide – densely clustered in fifteen settlements across 115 square miles. The hillocks encountered by Father Porras were the foundations of temples and houses. Their occupants, a society of at least 30,000 people, carved fields and terraces into the hillsides, made fertile by past eruptions of the still-smouldering Sangay Volcano. And what most excited researchers was the network of wide, straight thoroughfares running for miles through rugged terrain – and seemingly over rivers – to connect towns, neighbourhoods and houses. These were the streets and trunk roads of an organised, urbanised culture with serious resources and manpower.

The discovery – announced to a major media storm in January 2024 – has pushed back the advent of Amazonian urbanism by a thousand years. Radiocarbon dating suggests the Upano garden cities were inhabited from around 500 BC until roughly AD 450: contemporary with the height of classical antiquity in the Mediterranean. Stéphen Rostain, one of the archaeologists leading the investigation, has likened them to an Amazonian Rome. And with even larger areas nearby yet to be surveyed, the Upano Valley civilisation may end up in the same league as those of Mesoamerica. What has been found so far – the Ecuadorian archaeologist Fernando Mejía told *Science* magazine – 'is just the tip of the iceberg'.

Few ancient Amazonians could rely on a ready-made resource like the volcanic soil of early Ecuadorians or the Chincha guano deposits of pre-conquest Peru. Instead – many scientists now believe – they engineered a humble yet remarkable substance of their own that laid the foundations for thriving, long-lasting kingdoms in the depths of the rainforest.

Squeezing into shared taxis with Bolivian tourists and Brazilian businessmen, I cross the Peruvian border and traverse the far-western Brazilian state of Acre. The treeline always stands a mile or more away from the highway. It's a red-eyed blur of truck stops and diners, the fried plantains and chicken stews of Amazonian Peru giving way to Brazilian *feijoada* – black bean and pork-trotter stew – and *farofa*, the toasted yucca sprinkled liberally over stringy stewed beef. At night, as we cross the Madeira River on a pontoon, the lights of mining dredgers blink in the dark like deep-sea anglerfish.

Porto Velho – the capital of Rondônia, the next state along – is a shabby grid-plan on the banks of the chocolate-milk Madeira. Beyond the rusting locomotives and water towers, a hydroelectric dam stretches two miles across. I meet up with Eduardo Bespalez and Silvana Zuse, archaeologists at the local university, UNIR. Sadly, they don't have the budget for a lidar flight. But they offer to show me some of their research at ground level. We drive out through duelling polygons of farmland and forest, parking up at a fishing village of brick bungalows called Teotônio. I follow them down a narrow trail towards the shore. Eduardo's waist-length ponytail – he plays in a death metal band back home in the southern state of Paraná – disappears between the foliage.

I push through the branches and leaves, finding myself in a cool, sunken pathway like the ancient holloways of south-west England. Banks of closely-packed soil, two metres deep and studded with fist-sized chunks of pottery, rise on either side. It's nothing like the sandy loam I'd seen torn up by the miners at Delta 1. This is a deep brown, nearly black: the colour of a forest gâteau, and similarly spongy to the touch. In Brazil, it's known as *terra preta do índio*, or Amazonian dark earth, and farmers treat the ancient trash like treasure.

A fertile, carbon-dense compost of manure, animal bones, mollusc shells, potsherds and charcoal, terra preta is packed with calcium, zinc, phosphorus, nitrogen and potassium. Though spread throughout the Amazon, it's concentrated atop riverside bluffs at the rainforest's core – the same sorts of places that Carvajal glimpsed settlements crammed cheek-by-jowl. Some scientists have argued that the dark earth is merely refuse and rubbish – the accidental by-product of prehistoric cookfires and latrines. Others suggest it's natural in origin, mainly consisting of nutrient-rich river sediment. But a growing body of research suggests that terra preta was generated on purpose, deliberately enhancing Amazonian dirt to sustain long-term habitation.

In 2023, a landmark study compared ancient terra preta with soils artificially improved by a present-day native people of south-eastern Amazonia. The Kuikuro settled along the Upper Xingu River at least a century before 1492, in towns of a thousand people ringed by paths and palisades. Today numbering just over 800, the Kuikuro still live in circular villages of thatched longhouses and pile their waste – ash, manioc peel, fish bones, broken pots and charcoal from slash-and-char farming – into heaps known as middens. After leaving it to stew for a few years, they spread the darkened humus on their garden plots to grow crops – sweet potatoes, beans, papaya, cotton, tobacco and more – in abundance. When left fallow, the modified soil sprouts fresh forest within weeks.

The modern Kuikuro dark earth is just as rich in organic matter as the pre-Columbian kind, and similarly clumped near plazas, roads and houses. The paper's authors – including seven Kuikuro researchers – conclude that much of the rainforest's terra preta was 'intentionally created in ancient times'. This was advanced agricultural technology, locking carbon into the soil rather than unleashing it into the atmosphere, while producing food for millions. And as we seek to create a climate-friendly food system to feed a planet of nine billion by 2050 – over half of whom will live in the tropics – we can 'draw on traditional methods practiced to this day by Indigenous Amazonians'.

Teotônio, says Eduardo, boasts some of the Amazon's deepest, most fertile, and most ancient terra preta deposits, roughly 6,000 years old. It's probably no coincidence that this sleepy riverbank was one of the longest continually inhabited places on the planet: or that Rondônia was a crucible of American civilisation. Ancestors of the Arawak, Tupí-Guaraní and Panoan linguistic groups overlapped here. They hunted, fished and farmed, domesticated wild vegetables, developed new languages, and went on the move. The Arawak were especially bold navigators, paddling the rainforest's riverine highways and settling as far away as the Chaco forest of northern Paraguay, the Orinoco basin, Guyana and the Bahamas. It was their Taíno descendants who encountered Columbus on Hispaniola in 1492, giving us words like barbecue, canoe, hammock, hurricane, maize, potato and tobacco. 'The cultural diversity here is one of the greatest in the Amazon,' Silvana explains, lifting up a tarp to inspect an excavation trench. 'There are plant materials dating back 9,000 years.'

Ancient Rondônians also churned out prodigious quantities of pottery. Back in Porto Velho, the couple had unlocked a storage facility stuffed with tens of thousands of prehistoric ceramics, scattered across tables in fragments and stacked in plastic crates to the ceiling. The reassembled objects range bewilderingly across shape, colour and category: grey, red, white and tan; Saladoid, Barrancoid, Pocó-Açutuba, Jatuarana, Jamari, Dionísio and Morro dos Macacos. There are cauldrons for brewing, vessels for cooking, urns for interring the dead. Geometric monkeys and serpents writhe around bulbous pots; bowls still shine from hours of polishing.

Many were deliberately shattered to bulk out deposits of terra preta – or maybe smashed in ritual celebration, like partying Greeks breaking plates. Their makers were hardly seasonal fishermen, scratching a living, frozen in time. These were sedentary, cosmopolitan societies with enough food, fuel and material to support a prolific assembly line of artists and artisans. What's more, Eduardo explains, all this is only what could be excavated before the floodwaters of the Santo Antônio megadam – completed in 2012 – submerged most of the Teotônio site and dozens more like it.

This sustained pottery production is further proof for what scholars of early humanity call complexity. In a nutshell, this means people living in populous, permanent settlements with specialised roles, like the priests, musicians, farmers, potters and potentates encountered by Orellana's expedition. Such societies can't be classified as mere tribes: they bear the hallmarks of cities, kingdoms – even nascent states. The textbooks that insisted South American civilisation originated in the highlands also need a rewrite. 'Agriculture is older here in the Amazon than in the Andes,' says Eduardo. In recent decades, he adds, archaeologists have found the oldest ceramics in the Americas – made some 7,000 years ago – in great shell middens in the eastern Amazon.

They have also identified the hemisphere's earliest artworks, daubed in red pigment in high-up places across the biome. Most impressive are those adorning the *serranías* of Chiribiquete and La Lindosa: table-top

mountains amid lush jungle in southern Colombia. The paintings –
75,000 and counting – depict crowded, kinetic dances, battles and hunts.
And alongside hand-prints, turtles, rays, caimans, deer, porcupines and
jaguars, the cliff-faces are prowled by extinct megafauna from the Ice
Age. There is an ancient relative of the elephant; a giant sloth shielding
its baby; a three-toed creature with a dangly proboscis; and an ungainly
camelid called the Palaeolama. Declared a World Heritage site in 2018,
the Chiribiquete range remains strictly off-limits to tourists: uncontacted
people are still adding to the sacred rock canvases. They are a late Pleis-
tocene work-in-progress, begun as many as 20,000 years ago by the first
South Americans. Carlos Castaño – who has been deciphering the picto-
graphs for decades – calls them the Sistine Chapel of the Amazon.

'The time has come to change the interpretations,' says Eduardo, as
we stand among the terra preta of ages past at Teotônio. 'Amazonia is a
huge region, with many environmental and ecological niches. It can't be
considered an inhospitable place.' With the sheer number of discoveries
with every survey, and mounting evidence of bustling townscapes amid
the forest, a growing consensus holds that between ten and twenty
million people lived across Amazonia on the eve of 1492. Vespucci's
guesstimate that the New World was more populous than Europe – then
home to around 70 million people – was possibly not far off the mark.

We sit at an outdoor restaurant, looking over a flock of swan-shaped
pedalos. Over plates of fried *pirarucu* – a man-sized river fish with
armour-like scales – Silvana and Eduardo report a disorienting mix of
emotions: exhilaration at how their field is transforming, but deep trepi-
dation at the future. The previous fifteen years were a golden age for
Brazilian archaeology. Presided over by Luiz Inácio Lula da Silva – a
gravel-voiced former factory worker, union leader and organiser against
the dictatorship – Brazil got rich selling minerals, foodstuffs and oil to
China. Social programmes rolled out by Lula and his Workers' Party,
the PT, lifted tens of millions of Brazilians into the middle class.

'This is my man, right here,' said Barack Obama in 2009, stretching
across the table of the G20 summit in London to wring his Brazilian
counterpart's hand. 'I love this guy: the most popular politician on
earth.' New public universities were flush with cash for research and
enthusiastic first-gen students. Deforestation slowed. Even Lula's controversial development projects – roads, pipelines, dams and power
lines – advanced the study of the ancient Amazon by leaps and bounds.
Well-funded archaeological surveys salvaged reams of material before
the dynamite was planted and the concrete was poured.

But as I pass through in late 2018, Brazil is shifting on its axis. The economy is stuttering, corruption scandals are abounding, and violent crime is spiking. Radical conservative forces are on the march. President Michel Temer has slashed the science and education budget. Bolsonaro – who thinks the generals didn't exterminate nearly enough 'Indians' and subversives – is leading the polls. Lula, who was also in the running for a third term, has been jailed for corruption and money-laundering by a flawed trial. The next day, Bolsonaro wins the first round of the presidential election by a landslide.

The looming crisis – environmental, humanitarian and for Brazil's very democracy – is scary enough in itself. But it could also close off the next line of enquiry into the deep history of the rainforest: closer collaboration with its longest-standing inhabitants. 'We still don't know anything about the Amazon,' Eduardo reflects. 'We archaeologists still haven't explored the knowledge of Indigenous cultures – their history, culture and oral traditions – that could help us understand the past.'

THE PARIS OF THE TROPICS

The Teatro Amazonas puffs up like a pink marshmallow above downtown Manaus, the Brazilian metropolis of two million souls in the middle of the rainforest. The neo-Renaissance edifice took $10 million and thirteen years to finish. Most of its materials and Louis XV furnishings had to be shipped across the Atlantic and 900 miles upriver: dozens of Tuscan marble columns topped with theatrical masks paying homage to Molière, Mozart, Goethe and Aristophanes; 198 chandeliers, including thirty-two of Venetian glass; acoustic steel beams from Glasgow; a geometric parquet floor of 12,000 planks in dark and tan wood, tessellating like the keys of a gargantuan grand piano.

Money was no object. 'When the growth of our city demands it,' the governor boasted, 'we'll pull down this opera house and build another.' Native dryads and naiads stood sentry beside the gubernatorial box and fluttered on the fire curtain. Frescoes of cherubs, cumulonimbi and an upskirt angle of the Eiffel Tower unfurled across the ceiling. Thirty-six thousand ceramic tiles in emerald, azure and gold were imported from Alsace. They formed a glittering cupola in the colours of the Brazilian republic, founded eight years before the theatre's inaugural performance – *La Gioconda* – in 1897. To muffle hooves and carriage wheels, the cobblestones were smothered with rubber.

Rubber made Manaus rebound: from humdrum frontier fort to 'Paris of the Tropics'. The city boasted more cinemas than Rio and more playhouses than Lisbon. It fizzed with electricity while the nation was still groping around by candlelight. In the decades either side of 1900, skyrocketing European demand for the vulcanised sap of the *Hevea* tree – used in tyres, wires, galoshes and gaskets – made a few men wealthier than Croesus and Crassus combined. Fitzcarrald's peers and associates blew their ill-gotten fortunes here, unlocking levels of seedy opulence not seen until Pablo Escobar imported hippos from Dallas for his Colombian hacienda. Tales abounded of these moustachioed latex barons wrestling with pet lions in their palazzos and filling their horses' troughs with Veuve Clicquot.

Roger Casement – a sensitive, saturnine Anglo-Irish diplomat – had already exposed the evils of the rubber trade in the Belgian Congo. But the way the industry treated native Amazonians plumbed new depths of horror. 'The search was never for rubber, or trees, or commodities, but for men – men and women, boys and girls,' he recorded in 1910. Armed thugs 'surrounded a house, set fire to it, shot down the old, and captured the young'. If they failed to meet their quotas, press-ganged workers were 'murdered, flogged, chained up like wild beasts, hunted far and wide and their dwellings burnt, their wives raped, their children dragged away to slavery and outrage'.

Cruelty was an end in itself. 'Here are lots and lots of gentlemen I meet daily at dinner who not only kill their wives, but burn other people's wives alive – or cut their arms and legs off and pull the babies from their breasts to throw in the river or leave to starve in the forest – or dash their brains out against trees.' And the business was carried out with British shareholders, directors and subjects: many of the henchmen were brutalised Barbadian hostages. Casement's eyewitness reports earned him a knighthood. But the experience confirmed his calling as a revolutionary. In 1916, a German U-boat put him ashore in County Kerry days before the Easter Rising. Weak and malarial, he was captured and shot for treason. Meanwhile, the British government leaked Casement's purported diaries, in which the humanitarian investigator cruised the Manaus waterfront to pick up teenage boys.

I'm in no state to sample the nightlife. The day after I step off the twelve-hour speedboat ride downriver and poke around the opera house, a sudden fever leaves me shivering and hallucinating under the covers. The owners of the guesthouse, a kindly pair of middle-aged men, bring me platters of sliced fruits and sugary milk. They insist on taking

me for a blood test. I roll up my sleeve. The nurse looks at me and gestures to turn around and drop my trousers.

With the chills subsided and malaria ruled out, I take an Uber along
corkscrewing highways to the National Institute of Amazonian
Research, nestled inside a finger of jungle nearly subsumed by factories
and suburbs. Waiting for me is Charles Clement, a white-bearded
scholar of pre-Columbian trees. 'Archaeobotany is extremely new in the
Amazon,' he admits. But his field is quietly changing the shape of early
world history.

Clement and his colleagues have identified at least eighty-three Amazonian species – manioc, sweet potato, Brazil nuts, peppers, fruits,
palms, tobacco – domesticated by pre-Columbian peoples, and a further
5,000 that were exploited by them. This process was well underway by
6000 BC, making the Amazon one of the major centres where agriculture emerged: up there with the Fertile Crescent, the Yangtze basin and
the highlands of the Americas. In fact, several quintessentially Andean
or Mesoamerican crops now seem to have originated in north-western
Amazonia. New research has shown that cacao beans – used by the
Maya and Mexica as currency, and imbibed as a sacred, bitter drink
called *xocoatl* – were first consumed in lowland Ecuador some 5,300
years ago.

Pre-Hispanic forest-dwellers interacted with wild plants in myriad
ways: from cultivating and pruning to modifying their genetics through
breeding for taste, size, hardiness or yields. They selected the likeliest-
looking specimens and propagated them in garden plots and orchards – a
trial-and-error process that probably unfolded over dozens of lifetimes.
One example is *açaí*, a palm that grows twenty metres tall in floodplains
across the forest. Its leaves are perfect for baskets, brooms and thatch;
its white heart is nutritious. But it's the purplish-black fruit – harvested
in clusters of a thousand berries per branch twice a year – that gets all
the hype.

The pulp is packed with carbohydrates, fat, protein, fibre, calcium,
iron and anti-oxidants. And it's deliciously moreish – a mix of dark
chocolate, raspberry, cherry and blueberry, perfect frozen or in a
smoothie. While Amazonians have relied on açaí as a cheap staple for a
millennium or more, North American health shops now sell it at a major
markup. In 2021 alone, Brazil exported nearly 15,000 tonnes of the
purple gold: a business worth over $1 billion. Ancient Brazilians, of
course, couldn't refrigerate açaí to the point of inducing brain freeze –
unless they transported it to the Andean snowpack. But it seems that

they painstakingly improved and propagated the fruit until they had a calorie-dense superfood always on hand. They lived among abundance, not scarcity, with caches of ready-made sustenance in nearly every corner of the rainforest.

Clement swivels his monitor to show me a map of the ancient human presence across the Amazon. Over 6,000 black dots mark sites where surveys and excavations have revealed ceramics, terra preta, human remains, mounds and causeways, rock art, or the consumption of domesticated plants. Inky splodges blur along the biome's edges, crowd the banks of the Madeira, Xingu and Amazon, and spread outwards along their tributaries like red blood cells rushing through capillaries. The blank spaces that remain lie in the furthest-flung corners of Brazil and the Guyanas: and bandit country in southern Colombia and Venezuela where few archaeologists have dared to tread. One new study, based on Amazonia's largest lidar survey to date, estimates that as many as 24,000 pre-Hispanic earthworks – ponds, ditches, paths and geoglyphs – remain hidden under the forest. 'Imagine this map in another ten years,' Clement reflects. 'There's not going to be many green areas left.'

'The myth of the pristine has a strong hold,' he adds. The popular understanding of the Amazon lags way behind the science. But it can't be long until the rest of the world catches up to the growing consensus: humans have long lived in large numbers in the rainforest and tinkered with it according to their needs. There's a risk, he concedes, that this plays into the hands of the agro lobby. 'They'll probably use it to say, "Oh, we can cut the whole place down and get on with planting soybeans."' But it's not like they need an excuse: what scientists say, he comments drily, 'is seldom considered by the majority of the world's population'.

And properly understood, the evidence for pre-European stewardship of the Amazon bolsters the cause of conservation. Clement and his colleagues are working with Indigenous peoples to map domesticated species in their territory: another way of proving that it isn't unproductive or abandoned land. What's more, fossilised pollen suggests that Amazonian civilisations – the low-density sprawl of the Upano Valley, the built-up Moxos plains of northern Bolivia, or the riverbank populations that chased Orellana out of town – didn't cut down swathes of the forest. Instead, these green-thumbed suburbanites added useful species along forage trails that extended twenty-five miles into the jungle. This wasn't tree-hugging for the sake of it, but common sense. It takes all day to bash through a hardwood trunk with a stone axe. You'd starve before you could clear a field. It was easier to thin out the undergrowth sparingly and plant a living larder that restocked itself.

'Think about the English countryside,' Clement continues. Though seriously deforested, it remains a jumbled landscape of gardens, fields, parkland and copse, each component on a sliding scale between wild and man-made. Foraging, coppicing, making hedgerows, gathering firewood, hunting: it's only a few centuries ago that most Europeans moulded and were moulded by the woods. The jury is still out on how extensive this process was in the Amazon. The rainforest today consists of an estimated 400 billion trees. The cautious estimate: a little over ten per cent are there because of humans. Clement would put the figure far higher: 'We're talking about a domesticated forest.'

One of the most commonly cultivated plants – spread in a belt across Amazonia from Ecuador to the Atlantic – was known to the Omagua. When the French explorer Charles Marie de La Condamine retraced Orellana's journey in 1745, he found that the Omagua had been decimated. But they still bled a certain kind of tree to extract a milky fluid, coagulating it over flames to make shoes, gourds and bouncy balls for their children. It was called *heve*.

As the ferry leaves the cranes and containers at the port of Manaus behind, the dark waters of the Río Negro meet the coffee-coloured Río Solimões, officially forming the River Amazon. The tributaries cling to their respective banks for miles, neatly dividing in the middle of the river. The fins of dolphins break the boiling white water along the seam. Eventually, the silty current on the right wins out and the black dissolves into blotches. The journey from here to the Atlantic took Orellana three months. I find a place to hang my hammock, say hello to my neighbours for the next five days, and take a look around.

The stiff breeze up top is a welcome change from the stifling air below. Miles away to starboard, a pillar of dirty smoke rises into the sky. I pull up Google Maps: the forest there is being steadily mulched into agrobelt in an arc off the BR-319 highway. A rake-thin man summits the staircase and approaches me unsteadily. Arnaldo has roamed the Amazon for work, from Acre to Guyana, but won't tell me what he does. 'Temer poverty, PT poverty,' he mutters. He knocks back the dregs of his Itaipava, flings the can over my head into the river, and cracks another. 'Bolsonaro will be the first good president this country ever had.'

An orange moon slowly emerges out of the water ahead. With the distant riverbanks lost in the darkness, it feels like we're drifting amid open ocean. Downstairs, passengers rock in their hammocks, doing biblical word searches, playing poker and arguing about politics. Every few hours, an anaemic bar of 3G appears and the space dings with notifications like a pinball arcade. The second round of the election is just days away, and WhatsApp is alight with fake news funded by Bolsonaro's allies in big business.

The doctored images, videos and audio clips range from crude to downright weird. George Soros is meddling with the elections. Venezuela has hacked the voting machines. Lula is trying to assassinate Bolsonaro. The PT candidate, a centre-left economist called Fernando Haddad, is plotting to turn children gay. As mayor of São Paulo, Haddad issued schools with penis-shaped milk bottles. The torrent of misinformation is stoking the evangelical conservatism and anti-globalist paranoia that have lately made inroads among Brazilians.

Nearing the ocean, the river splits into a mosaic of islands dotted with wooden houses and Pentecostal chapels on stilts. Children paddle out to meet us. Those with outboard motors speed alongside, latch on with grappling hooks, climb onto the fenders and pass up plastic bags of shrimp. There are violent downpours, then rainbows. Herds of water buffalo, an imported species, splosh around in waterlogged meadows. The tower blocks of Belém do Para, a city of 1.5 million people, come into view on the right. To the left, sitting like a cork in the mouth of the river, lies Marajó Island.

The western side of the Switzerland-sized landmass would be the obvious place to settle. The Amazon constantly replenishes the shore with sediment as fertile as that of the Nile or the Ganges. Meanwhile, the island's eastern half is all but submerged during the rainy season between January and June. Yet it's there that the rainforest's longest-lasting civilisation emerged. In the late 1800s, Brazilian scholars noted how Marajó wasn't all swamp. Dozens of hillocks rose above the floodplain. They rooted through the mounds and found painted burial urns, ceramic stools and female figurines.

But when archaeologists from the Smithsonian Institution dug deeper in the 1950s, they concluded that the story of the Marajoara culture was one of terminal decline. Later burials were simpler, their pottery less accomplished. These were – the prevailing theory posited – the descendants of an Andean migration around a thousand years ago, who shed their civilised highland ways as they swatted bugs and sweated amid the marshy equatorial thicket.

Recent surveys, bringing new technologies to bear, found reason to believe otherwise. They registered hundreds of platforms, scattered across 7,700 square miles. They contained clay floors, cemeteries and hearths that had burned for centuries. While the first signs of habitation stretch back to 3500 BC, these were places of sustained feasting, worshipping and mourning for over a millennium from AD 300. The skeletons of the Marajoara suggest they were healthier and stronger – resembling modern-day Graeco-Roman wrestlers – than the average Brazilian today. Feminine divine imagery proliferated on the ceramic sculptures; female graves were richer in goods. Maybe, like the Amazons of Carvajal's chronicle, Marajoara women ruled the roost and took their pick of muscle-bound admirers.

And they were exceptional in other ways, ignoring the standard checklist for early societies. Step one: develop agriculture. Step two: kowtow to an upper crust of priests and kings, who force you to build pyramids while they scoff the surplus. So far, there's no firm evidence that the Marajoara engaged in farming beyond some light agroforestry. Instead, their civilisation seems to have been fish-fuelled. By digging ponds and dams, they could harvest at leisure the teeming aquatic resources of the Amazonian delta – piranhas, turtles, catfish – once the seasonal floodwaters receded. And while they piled up earth on which to build their halls and houses, and some ate better others, there's no proof that they tolerated a single overbearing chief. Travel back to Marajó a century before Orellana's voyage and you might see an archipelago of towns, connected by bridges and walkways, populated by industrious, egalitarian fish-farmers and potters.

Stepping ashore in Belém, I walk through the *ver-o-peso* fish market – passing purple-stained baskets of açaí and drooping 200-pound pirarucu on ice – and come to a museum inside a seventeenth-century fort. Inside are a procession of Marajoara burial urns. The circumference of two outstretched arms, they're lavishly decorated with protuberances and swirling red and black paint. The largest wears a haughty, owlish expression: hooded eyes, puckered fish lips, monkey-like ears, chin protruding like the fake beards on Egyptian pharaohs. Anna Roosevelt, a leading archaeologist of early Amazonia, thinks their makers may have numbered well over 100,000 people – and that their signature polychrome style originated here before spreading to the eastern foothills of Tawantinsuyu. Their culture, she argues, 'was hardly a flash in the pan Andean invasion that succumbed in the terrible tropics'.

Roosevelt's findings have been hotly contested – as with most things in Amazonian archaeology. As the date for human settlement in the Americas gets pushed ever earlier, and ancient Amazonian societies appear ever more advanced, some scholars are fighting a fierce rear-guard action to defend the bounds of their discipline. Many of these settlements – low-density, seasonal, devoid of a single urban core – can't be classified as cities, they argue: still less the basis of pre-Columbian states. But when the evidence defies classification, perhaps the classification needs reconsidering. We may need to change our understanding of what a city, what a country, is.

The day our ferry pulls into Belém, Bolsonaro wins a crushing victory: fifty-eight million votes to forty-seven million for Haddad. The ex-paratrooper cleans up in southern agrobelt states and mining towns in the forest. The PT contender fields a weaker crescent of red between the Afrodescendant north-east and the intact parts of the Amazon.

That night, there's a victory rally either side of a fetid creek running between shopping malls. Meat sizzles on shopping-trolley grills; fireworks explode. LED speakers pump out *baile funk* from the back of trucks. Mixed-race teenagers pose for selfies flicking Bolsonaro's trademark double gun-sign: first fingers extended, thumbs cocked. Others stand watching the celebrations in a daze. Down in Rio, supporters in the yellow-and-green national football shirt swamp the road outside Bolsonaro's beachfront apartment, chanting his nickname – *Mito, Mito!* – meaning 'legend'.

In a stump speech a week earlier, Bolsonaro promised a 'clean-up of red bandits the likes of which has never been seen in Brazilian history'. His victory sermon, streamed via Facebook Live, is now a milder form of menacing. 'You will know the truth, and the truth will set you free,' he says. 'We can no longer keep flirting with socialism, communism, populism and leftist extremism. We are going to unleash Brazil. Brazil above everything, God above everyone!'

URBAN TRASH

What was the fate of these thriving Amazonian realms, undeniably present in the archaeological record and accounts of early eyewitnesses? Why – by the time the colonisation of the rainforest began in earnest centuries later – did little trace of them remain?

Climate change may have seeded the downfall of many. In the

millennium prior to 1492, lowland South Americans migrated great distances, as if fleeing turmoil and disaster. The Sangay volcano – whose
name in Quechua means 'the frightener' – may have catastrophically
erupted, spelling the doom of the Upano Valley civilisation that flourished in its shadow. Far-off cultures would have been destabilised by the
fallout. Across the Amazon, the production of terra preta falls off
sharply around AD 1000, and earthen walls and wooden palisades
spring up. Two centuries later, the Marajó mounds were abandoned as
the rains dried up and their fishponds turned brackish. As Amazonian
societies became more complex, they grew more vulnerable. Sudden
shortages of a particular plant, fish or commodity could trigger a
domino effect that led to their collapse.

Then as now, droughts could wreak havoc with transport, trade and
harvests. In late 2023, the Río Negro beside Manaus shrank to its lowest
level since records began. Ferries were marooned on mudflats. Villages
were cut off. Thousands of fish and dozens of river dolphins perished.
Children fell sick after drinking from stagnant pools. And the receding
waters revealed eerie petroglyphs, scored into the rocky riverbank
roughly 1,500 years ago, alongside grooves for sharpening weapons.
The faces look like the ghostly figure from Munch's *The Scream*. Perhaps they are a warning or cry of despair, like the *Hungersteine*: carved
boulders on European riverbeds uncovered by recent parched summers.
One such etching, usually submerged beneath the Elbe, reads: 'If you see
me, weep.'

The prosperous villages Orellana passed through in 1542 were perhaps only the shadow of once-great Amazonian powers. Yet their busy
settlements and far-ranging traders and travellers were perfect vectors
for the lethal illnesses brought by Europeans. Epidemics raced through
the rainforest – smallpox, measles, influenza, bubonic plague, malaria,
diphtheria, typhus, cholera. The survivors fled. Their vegetable plots
and houses were reclaimed by thickening jungle. Scientists have estimated that fifty-six million hectares of abandoned pre-Columbian
farmland – an area the size of France – were smothered by vegetation
across the Americas. The expanding forests sucked gigatonnes of carbon
from the atmosphere: perhaps contributing to the Little Ice Age, when
bull-baiting and horse-and-coach races were held on the frozen River
Thames. The primeval rainforest of the popular imagination was more
like a carefully-tended garden grown wild.

Yet the decision to return to the forest wasn't necessarily a step backwards. Later anthropologists living among Amazonian tribes made a

DARK EARTH   103

surprising discovery. Their chiefs, though fine speakers, were the poorest, hardest-working members of the community. They regularly gave
away their belongings, and their wives could choose other lovers. These
may have been, in one famous formulation, societies against the state:
people who had consciously designed their affairs to prevent hierarchies
from emerging.

The transition from regimented city-dwellers to fleet-footed, anar-
chistic hunter-gatherers wasn't permanent or simultaneous. Some
perhaps drew lessons from the Inca despots up in Cuzco, or the Portuguese slaveocracy creeping along the coast. Or maybe their forebears
had sampled urban living, and decided the juice simply wasn't worth
the squeeze. The biome was planted with so many life-giving species
that there was no need to submit to emperors, theocrats, capitalists or
kings. Far from Stone Age holdouts, many isolated Amazonians today
are probably descended from sedentary peoples who ran from the
rubber trade just outside of living memory.

Others mixed with European settlers and Africans, forming *caboclo*
or mixed-race populations, today often known as *ribeirinhos* – river
people – and *quilombolas*, or Afrodescendants. Many retain a deep
understanding of how to thrive within their given ecological niche to
this day. Upriver from Manaus, I had visited the Mamirauá Institute – a
research station deep in dense rainforest – to meet the archaeologists
Eduardo Kazuo and Márjorie Lima. We took a speedboat to the tiny
ribeirinho village of Tauary, where they had recently excavated nine
ancient burial urns: perfectly intact and painted in the bold, branching
colours of polychrome style.

Francisco Dias, a local fisherman, took us along a winding trail.
Within barely twenty minutes, he pointed out a dozen trees whose bark,
fruit, wood, sap and roots locals use in food, medicine, ceramics, as
glue – and to stupefy fish so they can be scooped from the river. 'This
region was occupied by many groups of Indians for centuries,' said
Francisco. There may be no genetic link, but he felt an affinity with the
people who enhanced this plot of forest. 'They were Amazonians just
like us.' Such crucial knowledge was transmitted through the generations. As late as the 1760s, the caboclo inhabitants of Marajó were still
keeping the city of Belém supplied with crabs, manatees, turtle-egg
butter and 200 tonnes of mullet every month.

In November 2025, Belém will host COP30, the world's most
important climate summit. Lula – now back at the helm of Brazil – bills
it as a chance for the world to learn from the rainforest's inhabitants.

'When we talk about preservation, we have to preserve the fifty million people who live in the Amazon,' the president said, announcing the news in late 2023. 'People who want to live in dignity; to drink coffee, to eat lunch and dinner; to go for a walk; to dress up. To take care of the environment, we have to start by taking care of the poor people who live in these regions.' There's a long tradition in Brazil of ecology practised by and for the downtrodden. Chico Mendes, a poor rubber tapper turned union leader and conservationist who was shot dead by a rancher in 1988, summed it up: 'Environmentalism without class struggle is gardening.'

Later, I drop by the University of São Paulo, a rare green space amid endless white skyscrapers. Jennifer Watling is a specialist in interactions between plants and prehistoric Brazilians. Eduardo Neves is the godfather of modern Amazonian archaeology. 'There are river valleys as large as the Rhine with virtually no work done on them,' he says. 'Really anything could happen. The question is: what now?'

The ancient Amazon, they argue, contradicts accepted truths about humankind: that we are hard-wired towards inequality; that our gain is nature's loss. And it offers a different perspective to the warring visions of the rainforest – pristine wilderness versus blank space for development – that are really two sides of the same coin. The biome has been developed for thousands of years, Watling argues, by ancient applied botanists who increased rather than depleted its biodiversity. 'What you end up with is a transformed forest. And Indigenous people, ribeirinhos and quilombolas are still doing it today.'

'The Amazon has to be protected, not only because it's natural, but because it represents very sophisticated systems of knowledge that have been developed over the millennia,' Neves agrees. 'We don't have any idea what we might learn.'

José Urutau Guajajara was leading his community in a maraca-shaking ceremony when he saw the night sky turn red. He sprinted across to the gardens that house the National Museum in Rio de Janeiro. He took the same route most days to study the museum's archival holdings, including the earliest dictionary of the Tupí-Guaraní language – compiled in 1595 by the Jesuit priest José de Anchieta – spoken by his ancestors. But on 2 September 2018, José faced a different kind of salvage mission: to try and save something, anything, from the fire engulfing one of the largest collections of pre-Columbian and Indigenous artefacts anywhere in the world.

He pushed through the police cordon and the fire crews. Their hoses lay limp: the nearby hydrants were dry. He tried to enter the museum, but flames were shooting out of the nineteenth-century palace, the roof was collapsing, and the doorhandles were red-hot. A few things were rescued or resisted the inferno: half a dozen fire-blackened meteorites; a couple of thousand molluscs; the skull of Luzia, over 11,000 years old and the earliest human remains found in South America. But by the time the blaze was contained, over ninety per cent of the museum's collections – nearly nineteen million items – had been lost.

'It had five thousand years of world history,' laments José, a fast-talking doctoral student of linguistics with a long grey ponytail and black markings on his cheeks and arms. Many of the incinerated relics reflected the antiquarian hobbies of the Brazilian imperial family, who lived in the mansion like dragons atop a hoard. There was a Pompeiian fresco that had survived the eruption of Vesuvius; the curved wooden throne of Adandozan, King of Dahomey; Maxakalisaurus, a giant herbivore from the Late Cretaceous; and five Egyptian mummies, including the sarcophagus of Sha-Amun-en-su, a priestess who lived and died in eighth-century BC Thebes.

But perhaps the most irreplaceable treasures belonged to the great civilisations of South America. There were Nazca textiles, Moche gold-work, mummified remains from Minas Gerais and the Atacama Desert, and several quipu – the knotted Inca memory cords. The Brazilian collections included flint arrowheads from the Neolithic; phallus-shaped female figurines made by the Marajoara; the fantastical, branching vessels of the Tapajós, like art deco candelabra; Karajá headdresses and capes of multicoloured feathers; and multiple *muiraquitãs*, the green gemstone amulets, often shaped like frogs, that recur across Amazonian archaeological sites.

For José, a particularly painful loss were centuries-old ethno-linguistic maps and glossaries – of the Kamaiurá, the Kuikuro, the Guarani-Kaiowá, the Mbya Guarani, the Guajajara – that were a Rosetta Stone to the deep history of Brazil's native peoples. Also incinerated were hours of recordings of Amazonian tongues no longer spoken by anyone, photo negatives of tribes that no longer exist, and tens of thousands of printed academic theses on Indigenous history, languages and archae-ology from across the continent: including his own. It was like the British Museum, the Bodleian Library and the Louvre had simultan-eously gone up in smoke.

The curators had long warned that governments of all stripes had left

them perilously underfunded. Their annual budget amounted to one
cent per item. The walls were peeling, infested by termites and sprouting
with wires. There was no sprinkler system. The police would later find
that a faulty circuit had sparked the blaze. But José suspects that only
organised sabotage by powerful interests could have so thoroughly
erased millennia of Brazil's non-European heritage. 'It wasn't only gold
that was lost there, but memory,' he says. 'It's a snuffing out, a smothering of Indigenous peoples and the memory of the Brazilian people.
Whoever burned it had that in mind.'

Coming just weeks before the elections, the Museu Nacional's immolation seemed like an ominous prelude to the Bolsonaro era. Fire and
destruction defined the following four years. Within weeks of taking
office in January 2019, Brazil's new far-right management gutted the
government bodies responsible for protecting the rainforest and defending its original inhabitants. The inevitable result: the deforestation rate
shot up by over fifty per cent, reaching a fifteen-year high in 2021.
Record numbers of forest fires raged through the understorey, mostly
set by loggers, ranchers and farmers. Vast banks of smoke turned the
afternoon sky black 1,200 miles away in São Paulo.

Over 17,000 square miles of the Brazilian Amazon – an area larger
than Denmark – was razed on Bolsonaro's watch between 2019 and
2022. Tens of thousands of wildcat miners rampaged through Indigenous lands once more, contaminating rivers and wildlife, sowing
malnutrition and spreading malaria. Nearly 600 Yanomami children
died from easily preventable illnesses. Dário Kopenawa – the son of
Davi Kopenawa, who had denounced the assault on his homeland a
generation before – called it *onokãe*: a genocide.

The place where I meet José – a nineteenth-century palace in downtown Rio – was the launchpad for many such incursions into the interior.
From 1910, it housed the Indian Protection Service. The government
agency demarcated reserves for Indigenous peoples, but soon became
complicit in the enslavement and massacre of thousands: some bombed
with dynamite from planes, others poisoned with arsenic-laced sugar. In
1950, the Rio mansion became the Museum of the Indian, exhibiting
the curios left behind by an ongoing extermination. The building fell
into disrepair. Trees sprouted from the neoclassical facade. It was destined for demolition: slated to be replaced by a metro station, a car park
for the Maracanã Stadium next door, a mall, a museum of the 2016
Olympics and – most recently – a laser tag arena.

But since 2006, the site has been occupied by a community of native peoples from across the country. The Marak'anà Village serves as a kind of Indigenous embassy in the nation's historic capital. It's also a symbolic reminder that they belong in the metropolis as much as in the backwoods: they've been living in towns since before Brazil – colony or country – was even thought of. Residents have planted native fruit trees in cracks in the asphalt and a medicinal herb garden. They host teach-ins for Indigenous groups from across the Americas, and are setting up their own university to pass on native knowledge.

It's hardly romantic, says José, showing me around the dilapidated interior: basements overflowing with rubbish; empty, echoing staircases; tents on hard dirt. They have no power and only patchy running water. City authorities have branded them 'urban trash', and constantly threaten to kick them out. After the full-time whistle blows across the road, they brace for hundreds of tanked-up fans kicking in their fences and pissing on the perimeter. 'Staying here, resisting, it's fucked up,' José laughs. 'Only a madman would do it. But why does the state want to kick us out at all cost? Because here is where our memory is.'

'My ancestors, my umbilical cord are up in Maranhão,' he continues: the state on the Amazon's north-eastern fringe where most of the Guajajara live. Some of his people, known as the Guardians of the Forest, have taken up guns to defend their territory from illegal loggers and miners. Dozens have been killed. When José returns to visit, they ask him to stay. But Brazil's first peoples need an observation post in the urban jungle. 'The decisions aren't being taken inside the forest, but here, by the bigwigs: judges, magistrates, businessmen, governors, the president, deputies, senators, the Beef, Bible and Bullet benches,' he explains: meaning congressmen in league with big agro, evangelicals and the gun lobby. 'Knowing how our enemy thinks – the dominant culture – is very difficult. I want to give my people that understanding.'

In the ruined entrance hall, a short, bare-chested man in flip-flops and a headdress of emerald feathers coaxes a campfire into life. També identifies himself as a member of the Korubo, a remote tribe of the Javari Valley, most of whom avoid contact with outsiders. Though tucked away in the westernmost quarter of Brazil, they're being invaded by loggers, miners and poachers. It was in the Javari in 2022 that British journalist Dom Phillips – and Bruno Pereira, a veteran advocate for isolated Amazonian peoples – were shot dead after receiving threats by illegal fishing gangs. Bolsonaro suggested they had it coming.

'The Amazon is much less protected and pristine than most people think' – Dom wrote a year before his murder – 'and much more threatened than people realise.' Though swathes of the canopy look intact, nearly half of the forest below has been thinned out, and few of its ancient hardwoods remain. Dom was researching a book on how Indigenous and traditional communities hold the key to restoring the rainforest. The manuscript – now being completed by his friends and colleagues – is titled *How to Save the Amazon: Ask the People Who Know*.

'It wasn't you that chose to come here,' També tells me. 'You were called. The spirits of this place brought you here.' He stares into the flames, now addressing them directly. 'The fire of resistance from five hundred years ago is still strong. Send more warriors to help our struggle.' The cynic in me wonders whether it's a regular performance to convert gullible gringos to the cause. But as the twigs crackle, and shadows flicker over the vines that snake up the walls like veins, the moment feels uncanny.

A lithe, long-haired figure with a fang hanging from his neck and a wooden piercing through his septum beckons me over. I perch by his sleeping mat, next to a bow and a handful of jagged-tipped arrows. He gives his name as Ash Asháninka, after the native people in western Amazonia. A federation of Indigenous peoples should rule the Amazon once more, he argues, with their own government, laws and currency. Study after study has proved it beyond doubt: they are the best guardians of the rainforest – and with it, the future of us all.

'International organisations should take note,' Ash continues, lighting a clay pipe on an ember and blowing smoke into the gloom. 'If they want to preserve the planet, leave forested land to native peoples. Because we know how to protect it and live there without destroying, poisoning or burning it. We know how to live well.'

PART TWO

Rebellion

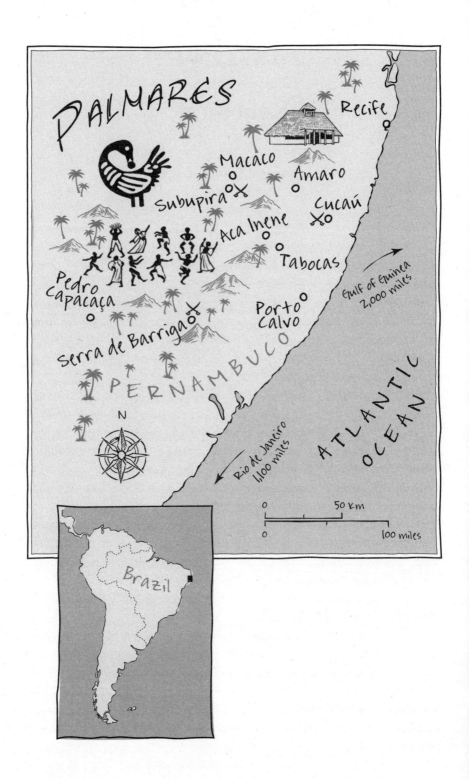

4

Black Rebel Kingdom

Palmares, 1588–1694

ANGOLA JANGA

The hill known as Serra de Barriga rises out of the sugarcane fields of Alagoas, where north-east Brazil bulges out into the middle Atlantic towards Africa. It's a cross between a village, an archaeological dig, a theme park and a shrine. The top is fringed with palm trees, and a stout wall of wooden stakes. There are a handful of huts, and an imposing temple – like almost everything here, a reconstruction – with a watch-tower rising out of its thatched roof.

Plaques mark the visits of presidents, ministers and mayors. Floral offerings are nestled in the crook of a sinuous *gameleira-branca* tree. Signs describe how *eguns* – spirits of the dead – roam this place, made restless by the blood spilled here. Dandara Thaty is showing me around. A member of a local Afro-Brazilian dance group, she wears a purple T-shirt with Rosa Luxemburg's image. We wave to a few local women hanging their laundry between banana groves and brick bungalows.

Forest encircles a dark green pond. At its shore lies a jumble of mossy boulders, scored with deep incisions where – legend has it – warriors once sharpened their swords. The soil is studded with pottery dating back 800 years. Dandara stoops to pick up a curved fragment. It turns out to be the rim of a buried pitcher, and breaks off in her hand. 'Oops,' she says, gingerly putting it back.

Serra de Barriga – Belly Ridge – was scene to one of the great sagas of world history. This was the last capital of Palmares: a nation of enslaved Africans who escaped their chains in the colonial province of Pernambuco sometime before the year 1600. They joined forces with local native peoples to hold out in the jungle for a century, facing down dozens of invasions by two global empires. Palmarian armourers hammered out blades and arrows. Traders bartered for cutting-edge firepower. Ruled by a priestly sovereign known as Ganga Zumba – and its warriors commanded by a wily captain called Zumbi – Palmares staged lightning strikes on nearby plantations, freeing the enslaved, stealing weapons and supplies, and springing captives from jail.

At its peak, this sweep of Atlantic rainforest, similar in size to Portugal, swelled to a population of 20,000 or more – while barely 7,000 people inhabited Rio de Janeiro. Contemporaries referred to the constellation of fortified towns as a 'republic'; some scholars today describe Palmares as a 'state within a state'. Fearing that his prized New World colony would be overrun, the king of Portugal, Pedro II, pleaded with Palmares to sign a peace treaty. Ganga Zumba struck a deal. But Zumbi kept the resistance alive, defending Barriga against enemy cannons in a dramatic final siege in 1694.

We look out from the Barriga's northern edge: a steep, forested slope tumbles into empty air. 'Hundreds threw themselves to their deaths rather than surrender,' Dandara whispers. Among them, she says, was her namesake: Zumbi's spouse, a dauntless captain of an elite all-female guard. In 1996, Zumbi became the second hero to be inscribed in the Panteão da Pátria: Brazil's national pantheon in Brasília, the capital. In 2019, Dandara – the Palmarian queen, not the dancer – joined him.

Powerful matriarchs are reported to have ruled Palmarian towns. They probably fought to defend them. But there's no firm evidence that Dandara, whose name first appears in a 1962 novel, ever lived. No remains from the supposed mass suicide have been uncovered. The manuscripts said to flesh out Zumbi's origins have mysteriously disappeared. That's probably not even his real name. Many free settlements existed in the *palmares*, the palm forests of Pernambuco. But that's about the only thing we know for sure. The kingdom of Palmares has been lost twice over. First when it was destroyed and its people returned to slavery. And once more when colonial chroniclers – and later writers – rewrote its story, blurring fact and fiction to suit their own purposes.

In Brazil – the saying goes – even the past is unpredictable. And few other topics have changed so frequently in the public imagination. Those who peer into the lake at Barriga see their own times reflected back at them. Palmares shape-shifts: nest of brigands; multicultural paradise; African monarchy; revolutionary stronghold. In recent years, it again became a lightning rod for disputes over Brazilian identity. Activists fighting racial injustice drew inspiration from the unbowed rebel realm – a kind of seventeenth-century, South American Wakanda, defying slavery with advanced technology. Meanwhile, right-wing officials branded Zumbi a 'fake hero'. Bolsonaro even denied that Portuguese slavers set foot in Africa.

Every text that mentions Palmares was penned by its sworn enemies. We only know the exact location of one Palmarian settlement, at Barriga. Few archaeologists have been permitted to disturb its sacred soil. A trove of artefacts was probably destroyed when diggers scraped the summit flat to build the memorial site in the 1990s. Films, novels, artworks, songs and legends have filled in the blanks, fusing inextricably with popular memory.

Yet there are ways we can get at something like the truth. Historians are combing archives on several continents, compiling new evidence in Portuguese, Dutch and Latin. The experiences of Afrodescendant communities across the Americas – as well as African nations themselves – offer insights into what Palmares may have really been like, and what it might have become in time. New generations of Brazilian scholars have challenged the traditional version: of an isolated, monolithic and unchanging stronghold in the wilderness. Ganga Zumba and Zumbi are now coming into focus neither as traitors nor martyrs, but as leaders of their time: trying to save their people from a fate worse than death.

Palmares, like Brazil itself, was born out of two addictions. First was rocketing demand for an exotic delicacy which, by 1650, was sweetening the palates of the European masses. The second was lust for the riches yielded by this labour-intensive cash crop. One contemporary succinctly encapsulated this bitter intercontinental entanglement. 'Say sugar, and you say Brazil. Say Brazil, and you say Angola.'

Sugarcane, native to South-east Asia, was first brought to Europe by crusaders and Venetian merchants. Slavery, often more akin to serfdom, was widespread in the ancient Mediterranean – and early modern Africa, many of whose rulers cooperated with the Atlantic trade. But it was European empires in the Americas that ratcheted up sugar production and slavery to an untold scale and intensity. Portuguese traders and slavers began dabbling in both in the late 1400s on the mid-Atlantic islands of Madeira, Cabo Verde and São Tomé. Europeans became hooked on the crumbling, crystalline blocks, sprinkled into medicines, baked into cakes, or stirred into other outlandish commodities such as coffee, chocolate and tea.

The Portuguese crown was desperate to defend its South American toehold: and turn a profit in the process. The solution was sugar. Mills and plantations proliferated from the 1530s, 'clutching the shoreline' – one contemporary remarked – 'like crabs'. As their native workforce perished, or fled into the unconquered interior, Portuguese Brazil looked across the ocean to sustain its deadly sugar rush. Over nearly four centuries from 1520, some five million enslaved Africans were transported to Brazil – out of twelve million taken to the Americas in total. Brazil today has the largest Black population of any country other than Nigeria: just one legacy of the greatest forced migration in history.

Enslaved Africans, especially Bantu peoples from modern-day Angola, could be found as coachmen, streetsellers, blacksmiths, wet nurses, and in a hundred other occupations throughout colonial Brazil. But it was in Pernambuco and the neighbouring province of Bahia that the slavery and sugar industries reached their apogee. In the decade from 1580, 6,000 enslaved Africans were imported to Pernambuco; by the 1620s, 4,000 were arriving every year. 'Without Angola, there are no blacks' – wrote one Jesuit priest in 1648 – 'and without blacks there is no Pernambuco.'

A persistent myth holds that slavery in Brazil was somehow a picnic – 'almost angelic' in the words of one influential historian – compared to the United States or the British Caribbean. This notion implodes in contact with the evidence. Portuguese and Dutch slavers branded captive Africans with red-hot irons. They were chained and forced to crouch or lie flat for the months-long Atlantic passage. Starvation, shipwrecks, dysentery, smallpox and yellow fever – and murder at the hands of their enslavers – killed nearly 700,000 of those bound to Brazil alone. Their ordeal changed little over the centuries. Mahommah Gardo Baquaqua was abducted from Benin and sold into slavery in Pernambuco in the 1820s, later escaping aboard a ship to New York. 'Day and night were the same to us, sleep being denied us from the confined position of our bodies, and we became desperate through suffering and fatigue,' he recalled. 'The loathsomeness and filth of that horrible place will never be effaced from my memory.'

Survivors of the journey had a life expectancy of twenty-five: ten years fewer than in the United States. On the sugar plantations, they slept on the dirt in stifling, windowless barracks. At the slightest excuse, their overseers applied torture instruments 'of such severity that they are not even used upon brute animals'. Padlocked into spiked iron collars, or with muzzles clamped over their face, some were flogged bloody before salt and boiling pitch were rubbed into their wounds. Their enslavers, wrote one eyewitness, placed 'more value upon a horse than half a dozen slaves'.

The work was exhausting and dangerous: felling trees, harvesting the cane and feeding it into the crushers that could snap an arm like a twig, an axe kept nearby for impromptu amputations. Shackled captives fed furnaces with cartloads of firewood, scorched and scalded by broiling vats of molasses. One spectator likened the scene to 'mouths swallowing up entire forests; prisons of perpetual flame and fume; living images of volcanoes, Vesuviuses and Etnas, and – one might almost say – of Purgatory or of Hell'.

Meanwhile, in his *casa-grande* scarcely metres away, the lord of the manor draped his wife and horses in jewels and Genoese silks, sipped from English tea-sets, quaffed Portuguese wines and slumbered beneath Indian bedspreads. Those that weren't aristocrats soon gained enough wealth to buy a title or three: 'many rich men come from this land,' wrote one Portuguese official in 1587, 'that went to it very poor.' They feasted off silverware, including forks – an affectation only recently catching on among European royalty – serenaded by enslaved musicians and Chinese fireworks. 'In summary,' huffed one visiting priest, 'there is more vanity in Pernambuco than in Lisbon.'

Thousands of miles away, fashionable Europeans supped on gingerbread, sweetmeats and marshmallow syrup. Banquet tables groaned under so-called *subtleties*: sugar sculptures of pigeons, rabbits, Roman deities and St George. Most of the sugar stocked by the grocers of Tudor England came from Brazil, much of it stolen mid-Atlantic by English privateers. 'In these days' – wrote one Londoner in 1596 – 'there is nothing accounted either dainty or delicate' without its 'due proportion of sugar'.

Perhaps the most eloquent proof of the dehumanising horrors of slavery is the courage shown by the many who resisted. Rebellion could take the form of small – even subtle – acts of sabotage: dropping a slice of lemon into the cauldrons to spoil the batch, downing tools or working slowly to demand the right to rest, socialise and sing. Or it could be violent: breaking machinery, committing suicide, or rising up and wreaking revenge.

And there was another course of action, though desperately risky, that hurt the enslaver's profits and regained the enslaved person's liberty. To somehow escape their shackles and sprint headlong for the hills. They would have to dodge the armed posses sent in hot pursuit, led by the notorious bounty hunters known as *capitães-do-mato*.

Thousands of these free Black communities emerged across the Americas, ranging from a few families on the run to permanent, industrious towns. In the British Caribbean and North America, their inhabitants were called maroons; in Spanish colonies, *cimarrones*. In Brazil, such settlements were first known as *mocambos*, and later, *quilombos*. The quilombo of Palmares probably started out like any other: a handful of people stealing away from a sugar plantation, and making for the forests just a few dozen miles inland.

This was perhaps around 1588, when royal orders referred to 'three thousand Indians' raiding plantations in southern Pernambuco 'with all the blacks of Guinea that have risen up'. Or maybe decades earlier: 'Some say that Palmares began to have inhabitants', one chronicler recorded in 1678, 'from the moment there were black captives in these provinces.'

Yet before long, the mocambos of Pernambuco had grown to an unusual size, strength and audacity. Partly this was down to quirks of geography. The palm trees, like those in Africa, provided coconuts, timber, clothing, rope, oil, wine, and 'a very clear and white butter'. The seeds smuggled by the refugees, planted into rich alluvial soil, sprang into blooming plots of sweet potatoes, beans, corn and manioc: a striking contrast to the barren sugar monoculture along the coast.

The dense forest, wide rivers and steep terrain frustrated pursuit, allowing the people of the palmares to settle near to outlying farms and plantations: a ready source of tools, food and weapons. In 1603, the Portuguese governor of Pernambuco complained of the 'many robberies' and 'constant assaults' perpetrated by the forest-dwelling fugitives. He killed and captured many, 'leaving this captaincy free for now from the insolence of those rebels'. But Palmarians also showed a remarkable ability to bounce back – and to knit dozens of mocambos together in a new society.

Called *Angola Janga* by its people – outsiders took it to mean 'little Angola' – Palmares replicated Central African institutions such as the *kilombo*. Originally an initiation camp for warriors, the kilombo had evolved amid the dislocation triggered by Portuguese slavers. It became a flexible, agile community, able to regroup diverse peoples on a permanent war footing. This model of African statebuilding was now exported to Brazil. Palmarians called each other *malungos*: shipmates, united not by blood but by the shared ordeal of the Atlantic passage.

Yet the mocambos in the forest depended on neighbouring Portuguese settlements for resources, recruits and intelligence. Many, not just enslaved Africans, seem to have preferred the hard-won freedoms of

Palmares to the pecking orders and persecutions of colonial society. They weren't just running away from slavery, but towards something better. For one archaeologist, the pottery excavated at Serra de Barriga reflects African, native and European styles. Eyewitnesses spoke of mixed-race and Indigenous residents – probably those labouring alongside captive Africans in the plantations, as well as from free native societies in the Brazilian outback known as the *sertão*. At least two Palmarian settlements, Subupira and Tabocas, bore Tupí-Guaraní names. While Kimbundu and other Bantu languages predominated, Palmarian leaders were likely conversant in *língua geral*, a mish-mash of Guaraní, Spanish and Portuguese widely spoken across colonial Brazil.

Rival empires also took Portugal's attention away from Palmares. In 1630, the Dutch West India Company conquered Pernambuco. While ramping up the business of sugar and slavery, Johan Maurits of Nassau found time to redesign Recife, the provincial capital, fill a pleasure garden with peacocks, tortoises, monkeys and jaguars, collect native bows, arrows and headdresses, and invite artists and botanists to study this strange Nieuw-Holland. Meanwhile, his spies obtained the first detailed intelligence concerning Palmares.

In the early 1640s, Bartolomeu Lintz infiltrated the rebel nation, perhaps blending in with Dutch and Portuguese fugitives. Palmarian settlements, he reported, had a combined population of 11,000, were well-armed and boasted ample food, fish and game. Palmares practised a form of slavery: but they were hostages, not chattel, and given a fair chance to win their freedom. 'Any slave that brings a black captive from another place is freed,' Lintz noted, 'but all those who willingly wish to join their society are considered free.' The ranks of Palmarian farmer-fighters swelled, and bonds of solidarity were forged, by the shared experience of flight and rescue from the plantations.

Though ever-vigilant, they led a vibrant social and cultural life. The inhabitants of Great Palmares lived 'in scattered houses built at the very entrance of the forests', Lintz reported, with hidden entrances that 'offer a path cut through the undergrowth to run and hide. Wary and suspicious, their spies watch out for the enemy's approach. They pass the day hunting, and when it gets dark, return home and worry about the missing. After posting sentries, they dance until midnight, their feet beating the ground with such force that it can be heard from far away.'

Time and again, this network of lookouts and informants paid dividends. In 1645, the Dutch resolved to put an end to the rebel nation. A band of hard-bitten mercenaries struck out for Palmares. Cutting their way through the forest, wading through rivers, drenched by torrential showers, they were only kept alive by the wild pigs and fowl caught by their native porters. They passed ruined sugar mills and freshly abandoned mocambos, ringed by fertile banana plantations, fields of sugar cane and flocks of chickens.

Finally, they reached the capital. It was defended by two high palisades, and trenches filled with wooden caltrops. Inside were some 220 dwellings, four forges, dozens of workshops, a church and a large council house. The town was normally home to some 1,500 people. But it was deserted: they captured only one family. 'They said that their king knew of our coming,' the expedition's chaplain recorded, 'having been tipped off from Alagoas.'

This Palmarian monarch – by the name of Dambij, in the Dutch rendering – governed them with an iron fist, executing those who fled his domain. And well in advance of the invasion, he had withdrawn his people, their stores and valuables to a safe distance. A Dutch bugler, enraged after stumbling into a spike-filled trench, cut off the captive woman's head. His comrades set fire to what they could and retreated, starving, sick and empty-handed. 'This was the Great Palmares that is spoken of so widely in Brazil.'

GOD OF WAR

By 1654, the Portuguese – or rather their Black and Indigenous regiments led by Captain Henrique Dias, the son of enslaved Africans, and Filipe Camarão, a native Potiguara commander made knight of Portugal – had kicked the Dutch out of Pernambuco. They could now turn their sights on the enemy within.

Yet in the following two decades, twenty-five further expeditions – undertaken by 'the best minds of this colony' and its 'most experienced soldiers' – straggled out of the Palmarian thickets half-dead, leaving the wounded for the jaguars. The trails through the undergrowth were impassable by cart; every soldier had to stumble under their weapons, gunpowder, ammo, water, food, cloak and hammock. All the while, wrote a local priest, Palmarian guerrillas flitted between the trunks, showering the invaders with arrows and bullets. These invasions had only served to make them 'skilled at arms', 'forewarned' and 'battle-hardened'.

Britain's Caribbean plantations had begun to undercut Brazilian sugar. By the 1660s, the sugar produced in Barbados alone was more valuable than all the precious metals exported by Spain's New World colonies. It was doubtful whether trying to subdue Palmares was worth the cost; colonists clamoured for a permanent peace. In the same period, Maroon warriors in Jamaica and Suriname forced the British and Dutch empires to formally recognise their freedom. Not long afterwards, in the early 1800s, Haiti's enslaved population rose up and won their own independent republic. Palmares could also have survived to this day, argues one recent author, 'radically altering Latin American history'.

Wide-eyed visitors unfailingly recorded its flourishing orchards, vegetable gardens and broods of plump, pecking hens. Palmarians used this surplus to barter with nearby cattlemen, settlers and officials for meat, milk, salt, tools, gunpowder – and muskets. In 1670, the Portuguese prince regent worried that locals might even sell them cannons. Even if this commerce were stopped – Pernambuco's governor fretted – the nearby sertão was rich in ore and saltpetre, and Palmares possessed skilled blacksmiths and forges 'where they can manufacture weapons'. As with Vilcabamba, the mere 'example and permanence' of Palmares prompted others to flock there. Or worse, to lie in wait in the 'very houses and plantations' of their enslavers. They were poised to rise up, massacre the whites, and become 'masters of the country'.

By now, over 20,000 Palmarians were reportedly spread across ten fortified towns and countless outlying farmsteads: the largest quilombo or maroon nation to ever arise in the New World. Perhaps Palmares could have even become a maritime power. A local bureaucrat would later praise her forests as the 'most fertile' in the country. They boasted *pau amarello* trees of 'extraordinary greatness' – prized by builders of Portuguese warships, he noted – and rivers suitable for transporting lumber. In the same era, Indigenous Algonquian seafarers, having replicated British sailboats, extracted protection money from Massachusetts to Nova Scotia. Algerian pirates ranged the mid-Atlantic as far as northeast Brazil. In time, Palmarian sailors might too have plied the coast, intercepting slavers' ships – or taking passage across the ocean to the mother continent, as free Black Brazilians and Jamaican maroons would do throughout the 1800s.

The names – or more likely the titles – of Palmarian leaders suggest that memories of African ancestors remained strong. The king was known as Ganga Zumba, recalling the *nganga a zumbi*: leaders of Angolan kilombos who interceded with the dead. He ruled from

Macaco, a fortified 'metropolis' of 1,500 dwellings, according to one
chronicler. Attended by judges and ministers – who knelt and clapped
their hands when entering his presence – Ganga Zumba's court boasted
'all the regalia of any republic'. A chapel contained images of the infant
Jesus, the Virgin Mary and St Brás. An ancient martyr who took refuge
from persecution in the hills, befriended lions and wolves, and was later
flayed alive, he was an apt patron for a society that – guarded by nature
itself – offered resurrection to those suffering under the lash.

The king's family governed lesser Palmarian strongholds: his mother,
Aca Inene; Gana Zona, his brother; Anajubá and Tuculo, Ganga Zumba's sons; Andalaquituxe, their cousin. But foremost among them was
another nephew: Zumbi. Letters in a Portuguese archive – described by
Décio Freitas, an influential mid-century historian of Palmares, but
never located since – fill in his backstory. The infant Zumbi was supposedly captured in a raid on Palmares and raised by a Jesuit priest,
who baptised him as Francisco and taught him to sing the Latin Mass.
Fifteen years later, he ran away to his people, rising to command their
armies. His name, according to one Portuguese scribe, meant 'God of
War'.

Whatever his origins, Zumbi stalked the colonial imagination. He
seemed a kind of avenging spirit, descending upon sugar plantations,
setting fires and breaking chains before vanishing once more. Although
slight in stature, he showed 'singular bravery, great spirit and uncom-
mon steadfastness', admitted a contemporary. 'He was the most
intelligent of all, for his industry, judgement and strength served to
embarrass us and to inspire his followers.' Whether Zumbi and Ganga
Zumba descended from a royal African lineage, or their authority rested
on ability alone, under their leadership Palmares had grown intolerably
powerful. The seed of a more egalitarian patria, it was a dangerous challenge to the colonial order.

Without enslaved Africans, a common refrain held, it was 'impossible
to do anything in Brazil'. This was how society had to be structured:
with a tiny elite reaping the wealth generated by those who lived and
died in chains. Palmares, while no utopia, presented an alternative. Here
was a flourishing, mixed-race society of smallholders, craftsmen and
warriors – albeit living under military discipline – where all could earn
their freedom.

For one Jesuit priest, this inversion of the divine will had grown too
much to bear. The Black rebel kingdom threatened to make a laughing
stock of the Portuguese crown as 'two abominations' became known

around the world. 'The first was for captive blacks to rise up and seize the best provinces of Pernambuco. The second was for masters to be dominated by their very slaves.'

Royal officials got serious. They wanted Palmares burned to the ground, leaving nothing but 'the memory of its destruction' to terrify all the enslaved across Brazil into submission.

The sugar economy recovered in the second half of the 1600s, replenishing the colony's war chest. Seasoned veterans of Portuguese wars in Africa were sent to occupy Palmarian principalities, resupplied and reinforced until local resistance was broken. A 1672 incursion killed and captured many: 'the first loss felt by those countries'. An expedition in November 1675 – complete with priests and surgeons – saw fierce fighting at a 'great city of more than 2,000 houses', its defenders armed to the teeth 'with every kind of weapon'. The attackers only conquered the town by setting it aflame. Zumbi took a bullet to the leg but managed to limp away.

Two years later, it was the turn of Captain Fernão Carrilho, who had crushed rebel mocambos in nearby Bahia. He consulted survivors of previous campaigns against Palmares, and promised his troops captives, land and honour. They were outnumbered, he told them, but their adversaries 'were a crowd of slaves, who nature created to obey rather than resist'. This time, Ganga Zumba torched his stone-clad fortress at Subupira rather than let it fall into enemy hands. Carrilho's forces managed to capture or kill the commander of the king's guard, two 'famous captains' called João Tapuya and Ambrosio, and Tuculo, 'a son of the king and a great corsair'. In all, twenty of Ganga Zumba's wives, children and relatives were seized. The monarch himself was wounded by an arrow and fled 'in such a hurry that he left behind a golden pistol and his sword'.

In January 1678, Carrilho marched back into Pernambuco in triumph. He promised Ganga Zumba lands and liberty if he surrendered. Palmares was on the ropes. Left undisturbed for a generation, the prosperous forest realm had registered a baby boom. Its children, pregnant women and senior citizens could hardly take off into the wilderness like the warrior-founders of old. Their ruler struck the best terms he could.

In June, Ganga Zumba's sons led an embassy down to Recife. The city burghers jostled for a glimpse of the princes who had haunted their nightmares – and done a brisk trade with their neighbours – for generations. The Palmarians played up to their fearsome image. They paraded through the streets bearing bows, arrows and a single musket, a few wearing jaguar skins, 'some with their beards braided, others long and flowing, others clean-shaven, all well-built and tough'. Ganga Zumba's eldest son, wounded in the fighting, rode in on horseback.

They kneeled before the governor, Ayres de Sousa de Castro, and beat their palms together. 'There, they asked for peace with the whites.' They demanded the right to trade with the Portuguese colony, lands at a place called Cucaú, and freedom for all those born in Palmares. Ganga Zumba's wives and children, bound for Lisbon, would be recalled. In return, they would abandon their jungle refuge, accept priests among them – and hand over any fugitives. Delighted, Castro garlanded the king's sons with ribbons, baptised them, and sent two Black soldiers with a copy of the pact to Ganga Zumba for further negotiations.

Historians have usually argued that Ganga Zumba was duped. But Portugal signed similar treaties with Central African rulers such as Queen Nzinga of Ndongo: another warrior-monarch and master diplomat. So did Spanish, British and Dutch authorities with Black rebel towns across the Americas. Palenque, Colombia – founded by a Mandinka king called Benkos Biohó – formally secured its freedom in 1691. Like Ganga Zumba, the *palenqueros* agreed to return new escapees, but mostly reneged on the deal. They still retain their own language, and a distinct identity: much like today's Afro-Ecuadorians, the Saramaka of Suriname, and Jamaica's maroon communities.

Palmares likewise could have survived, somewhere between buffer territory and client state. Castro sent supplies and priests to Cucaú, telling officials that the Palmarians should build their houses 'as if they were to live there forever'. Yet both sides feared a double-cross. Barely a thousand Palmarians followed their king out of the forest. Rather than join his uncle, Zumbi withdrew with a diehard band of fighters deeper into the hills.

Cucaú was fatally caught in the middle. Ganga Zumba died suddenly; suspicion fell on Zumbi. Cucaú fell into civil war. In 1680, colonial forces destroyed the settlement after a three-month siege and decapitated its leaders. Most of the survivors were enslaved, although two of Ganga Zumba's youngest sons – Pedro and Brás – were honoured members of Pernambuco high society decades later.

The sole leadership of Palmares passed to Zumbi. His nation was fragmented and divided, occupying settlements far from those destroyed in 1677, and constantly on the move. But Palmares was still armed and dangerous. Zumbi's raiding parties even stormed a jail in the town of

Alagoas and freed its Palmarian inmates. In an extraordinary letter of February 1685, Pedro II pleaded with the corsair-king to come quietly. 'I, the King, make it known to you, Captain Zumbi of Palmares, that I pardon you of all the excesses that you have carried out,' he wrote. 'I also make it known that your rebellion was justified by the evils practised by several evil lords, in disobedience of my royal orders. I invite you to live in any place you wish, with your wife and sons, and all your captains, free from any imprisonment or servitude, as my faithful and loyal subjects, under my royal protection.'

Zumbi feigned interest. But whether unwilling to betray his people, or suspecting that surrender would spell his death, the offer was a non-starter. Hardliners won out on the Portuguese side, too. Leaving the rebels in peace – an influential diplomat and priest called António Vieira argued – would spell 'the total destruction of Brazil, for when the other blacks hear that they have won their freedom this way, every city, every town, every place, every plantation, would become many other Palmares, fleeing for the forest'. Besides, Palmarians were 'living in sin', and could only be absolved if returned to the 'obedience of their masters'. To spearhead this righteous crusade, the authorities turned to a murderous paramilitary force.

NO SLAVES, NO KINGS

Today a skyscraper-studded metropolis of over twenty million people, São Paulo started out as a rural market for human traffickers. The *paulistas* – later known as *bandeirantes* – were part-Portuguese, part-Indigenous slavers who ranged deep into South America, snatching up gold, diamonds and entire native communities.

An especially sanguinary paulista named Domingos Jorge Velho was summoned to Pernambuco. With him marched a thousand Indigenous warriors 'so brave, reckless and steadfast in battle' – he boasted – 'that no other nation on earth is their equal'. Velho would receive a cash reward for every Palmarian taken alive, who would then be packed off to Rio de Janeiro and Buenos Aires. Only their children were deemed safe to remain in Pernambuco as captives. In December 1693, a motley force of thousands mustered on the coast: the Black soldiers of the Henrique Dias Regiment, a company of Potiguara warriors, the private militias of local sugar barons, Velho's barefoot soldiers of fortune.

In January, they encircled Zumbi at the Serra da Barriga, seemingly taking him by surprise. But the Palmarian general had prepared for a siege. The clifftop citadel, rumoured to have been designed by a fugitive North African, seemed 'almost impregnable'. A triple ring of wooden walls bulged with towers. Protruding bastions turned the steep, thorny ground – riddled with pits filled with stakes at foot, neck and groin height – into a killing zone. Inside, 232 dwellings of 'admirable perfection and order' hunkered against the walls with ample firebreaks. A clump of trees provided timber; a deep, clear pond contained 'abundant water'. Meanwhile, forty workshops manufactured shields and arrowheads. 'Each man showed such care and vigilance at his post' – one report noted – 'that they seemed more like soldiers than barbarians.'

For three weeks, Velho's ragtag forces failed to take the city. Officers forced their men at sword-point into a storm of bullets, spears and rocks. The few that made it to the walls were stabbed through gaps in the stockade. Messengers were picked off by Palmarian sharpshooters. Slinking back to their lines after dark, gnawing on roots to stave off hunger, the invaders heard drumming, revelry and virtuoso trumpet solos coming from the city, its ramparts lined with watchfires 'that shone so brightly it seemed like day'. Velho's enslaved porters were suspected of passing intelligence to Zumbi and their malungo comrades inside the walls.

An artillery piece was hauled up from the coast. Grenadiers mustered to storm the breach. There was a deafening explosion. Velho sounded the charge. But when the smoke cleared, no one had moved. It was a miss. The Palmarians loosed a hail of musketry and arrows, sending their besiegers scrambling for cover. A jittery sergeant overshot Barriga seven more times, managing only to knock some planks off a watchtower – and to hit the Portuguese camp on the far side – before he ran out of ammunition.

In February, more cannons arrived. Sappers extended a counter-wall to a lightly fortified clifftop overnight. Making his rounds the next morning, Zumbi stopped short. Now just metres away, the enemy could punch a hole in the defences and pour into the city. He grabbed the nearest sentry: 'You let the whites build this wall? Tomorrow we will be overrun and killed, and our women and children made captives!' They were out of gunpowder. To stand and fight was futile. The general had one last card to play. The strategy that had, for a century, saved his people from annihilation. The same choice – the story goes – that allowed a captive choirboy called Francisco to be reborn in the forest as Zumbi, God of War, and to defy the Portuguese Empire. To run.

That night, the Palmarians abandoned Barriga, creeping through a gap in the enemy lines. Zumbi brought up the rear, his son clinging to his back, his wives holding on to each other's waists. But Velho had been tipped off, his patrols put on alert. Two sentries' shots rang out. Chaos ensued. The Palmarians fled in all directions: some back into the fort, some into the forest, where the paulistas tracked the bloodstains left by the wounded. Zumbi fell in the fighting. Trapped and panicking, hundreds hurtled over the cliff, smashing onto the trees and rocks below. Velho's men ransacked Barriga. A handful of warriors staged a last stand in a cave, accompanying their desperate gunfight with flutes. Over 500 Palmarians 'of all sexes and ages' were marched away; just 350 made it alive to Recife. Zumbi 'means demon', trilled one priest from the pulpit; 'to defeat an armed demon in the field is the triumph only of God.'

Except Zumbi – perhaps bundled away by his lieutenants – had once more cheated death. Over the following months, colonial forces hunted the Palmarian refugees to remote mocambos, toppling their leaders like dominoes: Pedro Capacaça, Quiloange, Quissama. In November 1695, an informant led them to Zumbi's hiding-place, a dugout by a river. His remaining family had been sent to safety; he had just twenty men left. Cornered, they fought tooth-and-nail until all but one was dead. The Portuguese cut Zumbi's head from his battle-scarred body, displaying it on a spike in Recife 'to terrify the blacks who superstitiously believe him to be immortal'.

Mentions of Palmarian kings disappear with Zumbi's death. With its great towns in ruins and occupied, its tutelary forests felled and burned by ranchers and settlers, its ruling dynasty extirpated and its last soldier-sovereign slain, the danger posed by Palmares had seemingly vanished forever. With Zumbi's death, Pernambuco's governor insisted to Pedro II early in 1696, there could be no doubt: 'Palmares, and everything to do with it, is finished.'

Since 1931, Cristo Redentor has gazed down upon Rio de Janeiro. The open-armed, soap-stone statue is Brazil's most iconic monument. But his perch atop Mount Corcovado was originally intended for another.

Isabel Cristina Leopoldina Augusta Micaela Gabriela Rafaela Gonzaga was an unlikely saviour. Her father, Emperor Pedro II of Brazil, couldn't imagine a woman as ruler. He cosseted her from birth, never showing her state papers. But on 13 May 1888, acting as regent – while Pedro was laid flat in the Grand Hotel et de Milan, receiving caffeine injections and sulphate of strychnine for nerve damage caused by diabetes – Isabel signed the fourteen-word law that finally ended slavery in Brazil.

The eyebrowless scion of the House of Braganza was hailed as a heroine. Twenty thousand people squeezed into her presence at an open-air thanksgiving Mass. The Pope sent her a golden rose. She refused a colossal mountain-top statue in her image: Jesus, she insisted, was the true redeemer of men. But conservatives have kept the cult of *Isabelismo* alive. In 2022, Bolsonaro created a new human rights award, the Princess Isabel Order of Merit. Among the first recipients: the president himself and his wife.

Few dispute that Isabel was sympathetic to the plight of the enslaved. But her hand was forced, new research has emphasised, by mounting pressure from below. For a century or more, uprisings, revolts and rebellions had laid bare slavery's shaky foundations. The spectre of the quilombo continued to haunt Brazilian elites long after Barriga was razed to the ground.

Camuanga, described by the paulista captain Velho as 'Zumbi's successor', held out in the north-east until 1704. In 1746, officials reported that Indigenous runaways had joined with 'soldiers of Palmar' in a fort in the 'deepest part of the forest'. They raided nearby plantations and towns, remaining 'the best refuge and bolthole for loafers and malefactors of every caste; of Indians, Blacks and even some whites'. There are references to quilombos in the region of Palmares as late as 1829.

The Palmarians captured by Velho and transported to Rio de Janeiro, a thousand miles south, weren't beaten either. They agitated among the enslaved of local households, soon founding new quilombos in the forested mountains around the city. In 1792, with the colonial capital fast becoming encircled, the authorities feared that such free communities would soon coalesce into a 'new Palmares'.

Brutal methods were employed to prevent and punish flight. Officials in Minas Gerais mooted slashing the Achilles' tendons of captured fugitives: they could still hobble around the fields, but would no longer be able to run for it. Repression only fuelled resistance. Countless quilombos thrived across Brazil – from the depths of the Amazon, via the far north-east, to the mountains and mining towns of the south – right up until abolition. Whether mobile camps, de facto urban suburbs, or booby-trapped fortresses like Barriga, some would have heard of Zumbi's example. But most needed no outside inspiration to rise up and claim their freedom.

In 1808, it was the turn of the Portuguese to run away. As Napole-on's armies advanced into Portugal, Dom João VI and some 10,000 family members and frantic hangers-on piled onto British ships. The monarchy's arrival in Brazil, and the opening of her ports to foreign ships, turbocharged the transatlantic trade in humans. Between 1801 and 1850, more than 1.8 million enslaved Africans arrived on Brazilian shores. By the 1820s, the court itself held title to 38,000 enslaved people.

A liberal revolution in Portugal in 1820 recalled Dom João; he left his feckless son, Dom Pedro I, in charge. But two years later, with local elites angered by domineering politicians in Lisbon, Pedro declared an independent Kingdom of Brazil. Unlike the revolutions that were sweep-ing Spanish America, this was no radical citizen uprising, but the coronation of an autocratic emperor in a cloak of toucan feathers, a third of whose 2.5 million subjects had no rights whatsoever. But Black Brazilians were still ready to fight the colonial power. In 1823, the islanders of Itaparica, Bahia, fended off a Portuguese fleet. Local oral histories tell how Maria Felipa, a formerly enslaved fisherwoman, pad-dled out to the enemy warships and set them ablaze.

As the century wore on, resistance to slavery gathered unstoppable momentum. Breakaway countries – the Pernambuco Republic, the Con-federation of the Equator, the Riograndense Republic – formed and fell within a matter of years: symptoms of Brazil's stumbling search for a new political order, where the majority would no longer be treated as disposable. Brazil outlawed the trafficking of enslaved Africans to Brazil in 1831. But the law was universally acknowledged as *para inglês ver*: to fob off the English. A further 700,000 Africans were taken to Brazil over the following two decades. And even as the Royal Navy sought to eradicate the trade, London's banks profited from enslaved labour in Brazil's coffee plantations for sixty years to come.

Enslaved Malês – Yoruba Muslims – meanwhile plotted in clandes-tine mosques in Salvador, Bahia. They rose up during Ramadan in 1835, the ringleaders quickly executed or deported to West Africa. In 1837, a separatist revolt known as the Sabinada erupted in the same city, its ranks swelled by freedmen, runaways and disgruntled militia officers like José de Santa Eufrásia, who said 'it should be blacks who govern the Republic'. Legend holds that Luísa Mahin, a shopkeeper from the Gulf of Guinea, fought on the front lines of both rebellions. Slavers tightened their grip. But the conspiracies made it plain that Brazil would always face turmoil as long as slavery existed.

Thirty years later, the bravery of Black Brazilians in the war against

Paraguay turned their comrades and commanders against slavery. André Rebouças, a mixed-race military engineer, used his favour with the imperial family to push for abolition. He later travelled to fight slavery in Africa, but was overwhelmed by the scale of the task. The self-described 'miserable African Ulysses' was found dead at the foot of a cliff in Madeira in 1898.

Others widened the gaps in the slaveocracy's armour with their pens. Maria Firmina dos Reis, a poor primary school teacher, pioneered a new genre – the abolitionist romance – in her 1859 novel *Úrsula*. The sympathetic portrayal of Suzana, her enslaved heroine, was quietly revolutionary. A grandson of enslaved Africans, the novelist Machado de Assis skewered Brazil's elite, his characters toasting Napoleon's defeat and to liberty while chattering of the latest consignment of humans from Luanda. Contemporary photographs of Brazil's greatest writer were whitened, probably by his publishers. Now, a century later, he is being reclaimed. Zumbi dos Palmares University in São Paulo has colourised a more faithful portrait, an inscrutable expression behind his pince-nez and greying moustaches. High school students have pasted it into their copies of his books.

Quilombos and revolts among the enslaved proliferated from the 1870s. In 1881, Black sailors went on strike, refusing to disembark captives off slavers' ships. Chico da Matilde – their leader from the fishing village of Aracati – became an overnight celebrity. Crowds paraded the Sea Dragon and his raft through the streets of Rio. But perhaps the most remarkable abolitionist biography belongs to Luís Gama. The son of Luísa Mahin, his father – a white aristocrat – sold him into slavery aged ten to settle a gambling debt. Gama sued for his freedom, taught himself the law, and crusaded against slavery in landmark court cases, freeing 500 people. He died in 1882, not long before his dream was realised: a Brazil 'with no kings and with no slaves'.

Yet emancipation in 1888 hardly ensured equality at a stroke. The abolitionist Joaquim Nabuco made a prescient prediction: 'Slavery will long remain Brazil's defining feature.' Today, roughly half of Brazilians identify as Black or mixed-race. But they make up two-thirds of prisoners, and three-quarters of the extremely poor. Bolsonaro dismissed Covid-19 as a 'little flu' and suggested the vaccine would turn people into alligators. The pandemic would claim the lives over 700,000 Brazilians, with Afrodescendants far more likely to die. In Rio, eighty per cent of those killed by police are Black, despite making up just half the city's population. 'Although slavery is no longer practised in Brazil, its legacy casts a long shadow,' two Brazilian historians have recently written. 'The experience of violence and pain is repeated, dispersed, and persists.'

One night in Rio, I drop by Mangueira – Brazil's most storied samba school – to catch an open rehearsal for their Carnaval parade. Titled *Bedtime Stories for Grown-Ups*, it's a riposte to the conservative version of Brazilian history, where elites bestowed rights on their inferiors out of the goodness of their hearts. As I arrive, a green curtain falls away to reveal a battery of drummers. A rapid-fire rhythm ricochets around the hall as dancers in electric pink and emerald costumes sashay into the swaying crowd.

The lyrics are a roll-call of Afro-Brazilian heroes – and especially heroines – from the queens of Palmares to Marielle Franco, a socialist Rio councillor and strident critic of police violence assassinated in 2018. 'It didn't fall from the sky / nor from Isabel's decree / freedom is a Dragon on the Aracati sea', sings the room, a churn of top hats, tambourines, tinsel epaulettes, translucent tights and sloshed cups of lager.

The stanzas merge, rising and falling like the passing of generations. 'Brazil, your name is Dandara / now has come the day / to listen to the Marias, Mahins, Marielles, Malês.'

A HUGE PAST AHEAD

The memory of Palmares proved versatile. Where colonial accounts branded Palmares a den of bandits, nineteenth-century romantics rendered it a Black Troy, a 'barbarian' republic whose fall to the forces of civilisation provided a new nation with its own *Iliad*. The hero of the story was not Zumbi but the bloodthirsty paulista Velho, transformed into a flag-carrying pioneer.

The revolutionary currents of the twentieth century stirred fresh interest in the lost rebel realm of the north-east. Historians scoured foreign archives for scattered evidence on Palmares – and maybe made some up – reconstructing it as a proletarian plantation revolt. Of the 'authentic class struggle that has filled centuries of our history', wrote Astrojildo Pereira – a founder of the Brazilian Communist Party – in 1930, 'its culminating episode of heroism and greatness came with the formation of the Republic of Palmares, headed by the epic figure of Zumbi, our black Spartacus'. It's an epithet Zumbi shares with Toussaint Louverture: the formerly enslaved Haitian general and statesman, and other great revolutionary figure of the Black Atlantic.

After tanks rolled onto the streets in 1964, Palmares was held up as a beacon of democracy against the generals who ruled Brazil – backed by the United States – until 1985. The Palmares Revolutionary Armed Vanguard, a guerrilla group, hijacked airliners and carried off a safe containing $2.5 million from a governor's mansion. In 1971, a Black resistance organisation, the Grupo Palmares, argued against commemorating abolition on 13 May. Instead, they proposed that Zumbi's death on 20 November be marked in remembrance of Palmares: 'the most glorious moment in the history of Black people in Brazil.'

Two films directed by Carlos Diegues – *Ganga Zumba* (1972) and *Quilombo* (1984) – popularised the image of a proud African monarchy in the forest and the character of Dandara, Zumbi's consort. In modern folklore, Zumbi became the once-and-future king who would soon return to deliver justice. 'The masters are seated, watching black hands harvest white cotton,' sang Jorge Ben Jor in 1974. 'I want to see what will happen when Zumbi comes.'

Black artists and intellectuals made pilgrimages to Barriga, getting married and having their ashes scattered there. The Palmares Foundation, a government agency, was created in 1988 to support modern-day quilombo communities and promote Afro-Brazilian culture. In 2003, Black Brazilian history was made compulsory in schools. And since 2011, 20 November has been formally inscribed as Black Consciousness Day, officially celebrated in five states and a thousand towns across Brazil.

Archaeologists had a brief window in the 1990s to dig at the hilltop in Alagoas before the bulldozers moved in and the access road and toilet block went up. What they found – European-style wares, evidence of previous Indigenous occupation – could comfortably be absorbed into the Palmarian canon. As Brazil joined the BRICS and prepared to host the greatest sporting events on earth, scholars spoke of Indigenous, European, Muslim and Jewish Palmarians, with a sprinkling of heretics and witches and presided over by a queer Zumbi. Here was a prototype of the harmonious, multicultural society that many hoped their country was becoming.

But as the economy crashed and the far right surged, Bolsonaro appointed Sérgio Camargo – a journalist and self-described 'right-wing, anti-victimist, Black' – to lead the Palmares Foundation. Camargo sought to purge it of 'Marxist' history books, and mooted swapping its name for that of Princess Isabel. Homages to Afro-Brazilian leaders were scrubbed from the website, including Zumbi: for Camargo, 'a son of a bitch who enslaved blacks'. He called structural racism in Brazil a myth. 'Slavery was terrible,' he conceded, 'but beneficial for the descendants' of the enslaved.

Palmares continues to reflect Brazil back at itself, fleeing a settled interpretation. Interest in quilombos in general has never been greater, says Ana Carolina Lourenço, a postgraduate historian of the long afterlife of Palmares. She has worked on a recent documentary about Brazil's largest runaway settlement. A graphic novel about Palmares by Marcelo d'Salete, *Angola Janga*, has been taught in schools nationwide and translated internationally. Abroad, there are podcasts, video games, novels. The Kentucky-born writer Gayl Jones published an eponymous epic of Palmares, forty years in the writing, in 2021. 'They destroy one Palmares, we scatter, we form another one,' says one character. 'Generations of destroyed villages, new villages and new destructions. I know the cycle by heart.'

'Dandara is now the most common name among Black activists of my generation, for example. And she didn't exist,' Lourenço laughs. Some creative licence can be forgiven, she thinks, to fill in deliberate silences in the historical record. The men who destroyed Barriga and other Palmarian mocambos would hardly admit to being bested for so long by warrior-queens. But though she's made two pilgrimages to Barriga, she's not a fan of the reconstruction. 'For me, it was better as a ruin.'

'Palmares never disappears,' she adds. Fresh excavations, new finds in the archives and future swings of the political pendulum may produce radical new interpretations. Brazil, as another saying goes, has a huge past ahead.

Thousands of quilombos still exist across Brazil: communities descended from runaways, rebels and survivors of slavery. I take the metro to the end of the line out west, then a taxi down the long, golden strand at Barra de Tijuca. Outside Bolsonaro's gated community, fans strain for a glimpse of the *mito* himself.

The road runs upwards into the forest to a neighbourhood clustered around a plantation house and a colonial chapel. I'm met outside by a lithe forty-nine-year-old in a baggy T-shirt and tracksuit, his hair bunched in braids past each shoulder. Adilson Almeida leads the community association here in Camorim, one of Brazil's oldest quilombos. We perch atop a pair of logs in the vegetable garden.

Adilson was always curious about his origins. His grandmother, whose parents had been enslaved, used to take him into the trees to look for medicinal plants. They walked past grottoes, former hideouts for fugitives; the ruins of an old plantation building smothered in vines. He learned the cartwheeling, free-flowing movements of capoeira. But the older generation were dying. As Rio's apartment blocks crept up the mountainside, it looked like the quilombo and its history would vanish under the concrete.

Then, twenty years ago, 'one day, I went into the forest,' says Adilson. 'I stop at a waterfall and sit on a rock. And I ask myself the question: where do I come from? Who am I? And where do I want to go? And I made a journey in time. I closed my eyes, I travelled, I saw many Black people. And I woke up, and found myself in Africa and I found such a good and strong energy there. And that's when I began the work.'

He gathered oral histories, tracked down colonial documents, and invited archaeologists to dig. Gradually, entangled with Brazilian history itself, the story of the plantation and quilombo emerged. The sugar mill, built in 1622, was worked by native Paraguayans and enslaved Guineans in their thousands. Mixed in with the Portuguese porcelain that came out of the soil were ceramic pipes incised with geometric Guaraní patterns. One fragment was carved with a BaKongo cosmogram, depicting the circular journey of humans through the lands of the living and the dead. As a teenager, Adilson remembers rains unearthing skeletons. The condominiums that housed the world's media for the Olympics were built atop his ancestors' cemetery.

Today, Camorim's volunteers teach capoeira to local children, guide visitors along forest trails, replant trees and tend the community's allotment. They host a rite-of-passage ritual from Ghana, called Sankofa: 'go back and fetch it'. Only by reckoning with the past, the belief goes, can we progress towards the future. The quilombo also hosts an annual feijoada cookout in honour of Dandara and Zumbi – although Adilson thinks the Palmarian general is overrated. 'Zumbi didn't win a single battle. The first thing he did was go to the front and die.' If Ganga Zumba's hot-headed nephew hadn't declared all-out war on the Portuguese, he thinks, Palmares might still be around today. There's a lesson there: 'The struggle has to have a strategy. If not, you'll be decimated.'

Quilombos across the country are still under attack, he explains. Soybean barons, ranchers and urban developers want their land. Locals are smeared as lazy squatters to justify their forced eviction. Bolsonaro once branded quilombo residents obese and 'unfit even to breed'. When these communities recover their history, it isn't navel-gazing. It helps them secure their territory and way of life – and provides inspiration to resist.

Finally, in 2014, the Camorim quilombo achieved official recognition. Adilson takes me into the trees, over a gurgling stream, past the ruins slowly being absorbed by the earth, parakeets flitting overhead. 'We're teaching our kids that they don't have to lower their heads to anyone: they can walk upright. In this territory, there's a quilombo, there's ancestry, and there's a people who deserve respect,' he explains. 'What's written can be wiped away. But memory renews itself.'

In June 2022, the heart of Pedro I – floating in formaldehyde inside a golden urn, flown over from Portugal and escorted through South American airspace by a pair of fighter jets – was driven in the presidential Rolls-Royce to the Planalto Palace in Brasília. A hundred metres from where Zumbi and Dandara are inscribed in the Pantheon, Bolsonaro was there to receive it. 'Two countries, united by history, joined by the heart. Two hundred years of independence. Ahead, an eternity of freedom,' he barked. 'God, patria, family! Long live Portugal, long live Brazil!'

In Brazil's bicentenary year, the war between rival visions of the nation's past came to a head. The one patrician, European, conservative, where freedom was graciously granted by the ruling class to their non-white compatriots. The other a centuries-long struggle, still incomplete, for freedom and justice. Lula, his corruption conviction overturned, squeaked a victory in the election that November: fifty-one per cent of votes to Bolsonaro's forty-nine per cent. 'I will govern for 215 million Brazilians and not just for those who voted for me,' Lula croaked. 'There are not two Brazils. We are one country, one people, and one great nation.'

Lula appoints Sonia Guajajara, an Indigenous activist from the Amazon, to head a new ministry to defend Brazil's native peoples. He renames the Princess Isabel medal after Luís Gama. Deforestation slows sharply. But Bolsonaro's supporters claim the election has been stolen, and storm the seat of government in Brasília. Waved on by the cops, they smash the doors into congress, the supreme court, and the Planalto palace. They trash furniture, scrawl graffiti, carry off armfuls of documents, urinate on artworks and defecate on the floor. It's Brazil's own January insurrection, with rumblings of support from the military. A congressional inquiry later accuses Bolsonaro of a 'wilful and premeditated coup attempt'.

The moment of danger passes. Hundreds of the rioters are sent to jail; a judge bars Bolsonaro from office for eight years. On Lula's orders, the army expels some 20,000 wildcat miners from Yanomami territory in the Amazon. But right-wingers in congress defang the Indigenous and environmental ministries. One NGO calls it the 'kiss of death' for Brazil's native peoples and their forest home. To bring jobs and development to the north, Lula now mulls destructive new mega-projects: repaved highways, a vast railway for agribusiness, even oil drilling at the very mouth of the Amazon.

Far from being finished, Palmares proved immortal. Zumbi has been reborn in different guises: a champion of freedom, of democracy, of Black power, of co-existence. Perhaps he will next be enlisted in his fiercest struggle yet: as an eco-warrior in defence of the world's greatest rainforest. It would be a natural fit for the lord of a jungle realm that was clothed, fed and sheltered by the natural world.

Up in the Amazon, I had visited a small quilombo of single-storey houses hugging a bend in the river. Tucked behind ancient mounds of shells harvested six millennia ago by pre-Columbian foragers, the territory of Tiningu is an island of green holding out amid the expanding farmbelt around Santarém. Here, Palmares is not only history, but a source of hope. Joanice Mata de Oliveira teaches at the local school, daubed with the names of African nations. 'Zumbi was the beginning of everything,' she tells me. 'He was the one who began our fight.'

THE DIAGUITA CONFEDERATION

Salta

Cachi

San Bernardo

R. Calchaqui

Tacuil

Angastaco

Mt. Llullaillaco
100 miles

N

Jesuit Missions

Tolombón

Buenos Aires
900 miles

Quilmes

0   50 km
0   100 miles

San Miguel
de Tucumán

Tafi

Argentina

5

Inca, Tailor, Soldier, Spy

The Diaguita and the Lost Realm of Paititi,
1450–1666

THE RICHEST PROVINCE IN
THE UNIVERSE

We saddle up soon after dawn, and ride a few hours under a harsh sun among tough, gnarled trees: *quebracho*, the axe-breaker; *algarrobo*, white carob; and *brea*, a starburst of yellow tendrils. A monumental dog-tooth ridge, blue-grey against a cloudless sky, encloses the valley. Then up a dry river bed, hooves scraping on pebbles, thorns snagging skin.

Back at the ranch, Martin Pekarek, a winemaker and anthropologist by training, had offered me a refresher on horsemanship. At a twitch of the reins, his *criollo* mare turned figures-of-eight on the spot. Mine now ignores me, picking her own path under green spikes at chest-height. Eventually we come to a gorge, shallow caves in a high rock face. I sling my camera over my shoulder and climb upwards. Martin calls up. 'You see the markings?'

I shimmy along a ledge and crane my head beneath an overhang. Llamas and alpacas process among jagged thunderbolts of scarlet pigment. Beneath them, a cryptic series of black and white dots and dashes, monochrome Morse code. Over 500 years ago, the artists – herders descending from the parched Andean plateau to greener grazing lands – watered their flocks below. They also carved the handful of smooth bowls into a rock at the entrance to the valley: probably mortars for preparing food, drink and medicine.

Martin's efforts to protect the pre-Colombian cemeteries, settlements and cave paintings here in the province of Salta, north-west Argentina, have met with little government enthusiasm. There is no interest in them anymore, he tells me, once I'm back on the ground. He whittles some sticks with his *facón*, the double-edged knife favoured by gauchos, spearing strips of beef over a fire kindled in seconds.

Woodsmoke drifts through the gully; the hum of cicadas penetrates the sleepy midday heat. Martin hands me a roll and continues. The powerful would rather his compatriots forgot those that came before them. 'A people without identity is like a flock of sheep. You can lead them anywhere.'

Think of Argentina: you might imagine a tangoing couple; a chanting sea of football fanatics letting off flares; a waiter pouring Malbec in a leafy Buenos Aires boulevard. Chances are, they all look European.

If Mexicans descend from 'Indians', and Brazilians came from the jungle, said President Alberto Fernández in 2021, 'we Argentines arrived on boats. They were boats that came from Europe.' His predecessor, the conservative plutocrat Mauricio Macri, agreed. A trade deal between Argentina and the European Union is only natural, he told the Davos conference in 2018, 'because in South America we are all descendants of Europeans'. There are no Black people in Argentina, another president, Carlos Menem, famously opined: 'that's a Brazilian problem.'

Census data tell a different story. Fifty-eight Indigenous groups inhabit Argentina: from the highland Andean culture of the Kolla, to the peoples of the arid Chaco such as the Wichí, Toba and Mocovi, several branches of the Guaraní, and nations like the Mapuche and Tehuelche of the pampas and Patagonia. Those claiming native ancestry have more than doubled in twenty years, reaching 1.3 million in 2022: three per cent of the population. In fact, there are almost as many Indigenous people in Argentina as in Brazil, home to 1.7 million native people. Factor in the Afro-Argentine population – both recent migrants and descendants of enslaved Africans – and the picture looks even more complex. 'Yet in the popular imagination,' two leading Argentine anthropologists have argued, Brazil is typically seen 'as a land full of tribes and Argentina as a semi-European territory.'

Like all myths, it has a grain of truth. While Portugal colonised Brazil from 1500, Spanish expeditions sought a shortcut to the fabled riches of the Andes. They rowed up the great arterial waterway that empties into the South Atlantic and winds its way up to the heart of South America. In an act of wishful thinking, they called it the Río de la Plata: River of Silver. Yet as the local Querandí people rained flaming arrows on a precarious fort called Buenos Aires, the Europeans were reduced to gnawing on rats, snakes, insects, shoe leather and the flesh of men they had hanged for stealing. And when they finally reached Upper Peru, they froze to the spot: locals cheerfully hailed them in Spanish, and explained that Pizarro had already conquered the Incas. Orders came from the viceroy in Lima to turn back on pain of death.

With few precious metals or settled Indigenous peoples to exploit, the Río de la Plata remained a comparative backwater, receiving only a trickle of Iberian settlers. Then, between 1881 and 1914 alone, Argentina opened its doors to four million poor immigrants from the Old World. Half were Italians – who imparted their cuisine, radical politics, lilting accent and expressive gestures – but there were also Poles, Russians, Germans, Greeks, Britons, Jews, Arabs and Scandinavians. The country's population doubled. With its polyglot café chatter, tramcars, literary salons and psychoanalysts, Buenos Aires became known as the Paris of the South. On the eve of the First World War, around half of those living in the capital were born in Europe.

Not long before this great migration, a provincial intellectual – and future president – despaired of the other half. Argentina was cloven down the middle, Domingo Faustino Sarmiento lamented in 1845, divided into 'two distinct societies, rival and incompatible; two different civilisations: the one Spanish, European, civilised, the other barbarous, American, almost indigenous'. Above all, he was referring to the gauchos: tough, taciturn cowboys who wielded horses, knives and lassoes like extensions of their own bodies. Subsisting on beef and brandy, moonlighting as mercenaries for regional warlords, they looked and acted like the native peoples supposedly assimilated long ago. Sarmiento might have shown the gauchos some gratitude: in the early 1800s, they fought like madmen against Spain to liberate the nation.

But theirs was not the first independence struggle to be waged in what is now Argentina. The Diaguita – an Indigenous confederation of the Andean north-west – held European rule at arm's length for 130 years until 1666, erupting in three great rebellions that some feared could drive Spain from South America. In their final breakout, they allied with an eccentric Andalusian conman, Pedro Bohórquez. Then, the traditional version goes, they were annihilated.

This curious, tragic epic complicates the narrative of Argentine history beginning and ending at the Atlantic. It further disproves the trope of Indigenous resistance melting away before European guns, germs and steel. Yet the tale of Bohórquez and the Diaguita is hardly known in the rest of Argentina, still less beyond. The evidence is fragmentary:

folk tales, carved and painted rocks, terse Spanish dispatches, mass graves piled with jewellery and shells.

My search for the Diaguita was one of dead ends and retraced steps, cold nights camped in the desert, bumpy journeys in the back of pickup trucks. I often felt one step behind Bohórquez, as if the shape-shifting adventurer were pulling off another disappearing act. I began to wonder why this desperate figure, hounded by delusions, had ensnared me, and where his trail might lead.

I poke around the crumbling school and a cemetery of rusted iron crosses that have seen generations of gauchos come and go. I spend a night leafing through Martín's library by candlelight. He drops me off in Chicoana, the nearby town, with words of encouragement. 'Come back whenever you like,' he says. 'You can help with the harvest.'

For now, I'm taking the bus upwards, juddering for hours along the switchbacks of a mountain pass. Ruined farmhouses, dried-up river beds, Martian rock formations. The slopes stubbled with *cardón* cacti: the pronged, hands-up kind from cowboy movies. On the radio, 'Hotel California', sung in Spanish to synthesised drumbeats. The top of the gorge is invisible, wreathed in cold fog. But within minutes we are traversing an arrow-straight highway through a shimmering desert. The bus sucks in dust, and spits me out in Cachi. The adobe and cactus-wood village is hemmed in by snowy mountains, glinting in the perpendicular light of the austral winter.

This is the only northern route into the Calchaquí Valleys: the stronghold of the Diaguita. Polygamous, gifted metalworkers and fearsome warriors, they straddled the Andean desert between today's Chile and Argentina in twenty distinct clans. They built channels and terraces that made the arid mountainsides bloom, cultivating maize, squash and quinoa, rearing llamas and alpacas. Their language, Kakán, was too 'guttural' – one missionary complained – for anyone to learn 'who had not imbibed it with their mother's milk'. Disciplined even in death, they held that the souls of their chiefs departed life for other planets, while commoners and animals made do with the stars.

The Diaguita were quick to unite against the invaders from Tawantinsuyu, who dubbed them the *calchaquí* – the angry ones. Around 1480, the Incas finally prevailed, demanding that Diaguita chiefs send their fairest, strongest children to Cuzco. The infant hostages were wined and dined and ritually married to Inca nobility.

Drugged with chicha and coca, the children were taken to the top of sacred peaks, where Inca priests buried them alive amid the snow. Thirty of these mountain-top human sacrifices have been found across the Andes, buried with *Spondylus* shell necklaces, golden camelids, cactus-spine combs and Amazonian feathers. Three such victims – two girls and a boy – were unearthed in 1999 from the snows of Llullaillaco, 6,715 metres above sea level. Today, they are on display in a climate-controlled museum in the nearby city of Salta. Their ritual killing is supposed to have been a great honour. But the boy's arms are bound to his side by coarse ropes.

The Diaguita retained an independent streak, rising up against the Spanish for three years from 1560 under the leadership of Juan Cal-chaquí. The Diaguita were 'very rebellious', wrote the terrified council of one nearby town, 'warlike, bellicose and used to killing and wiping out cities'. Spain had hardly sent its finest. The province of Tucumán was a dumping ground for washed-up conquistadors and crooks. The settlers cohabited with Diaguita women, their children running off to live with their relatives in the mountains. Around 1600, a Dutch map-maker inked 'Val de Calchaquí' and 'Diaguitas' at the colony's outer limits, floating in formless space: this was truly a liminal state.

An uneasy truce prevailed. The Diaguita agreed to send labourers to nearby Spanish towns, and to drive cattle north to Peru, when it suited them. They also accepted two Jesuit missions. Yet when the Bishop of Tucumán and his bodyguards reconnoitred the Calchaquí Valleys in 1622, he arrived at a speedy conclusion: 'more or less all' of their 15,000 souls were 'going straight to hell'. As he journeyed deep into the desert, 'the Indians rose up and went to the hills with all their families, cutting off our supply of water, such that if not for the mercy of God' – they stumbled across a spring – 'we would have all perished of thirst'.

Eight years later, the Diaguita surged down from the mountains once more, pillaging and burning. The Spanish captured their commander – a cacique called Chelemín – and tore him to pieces with horses. Like Vil-cabamba and Palmares, this free enclave harboured deserters and fomented resistance to European rule. Diaguita independence risked 'the total ruin of the entire kingdom of Peru', wrote a provincial gov-ernor in 1633: 'It is known that all of the natives desire their freedom.'

European settlers meanwhile fantasised about the gold, silver and jewels sustaining Diaguita resistance. If they could secure just a handful of this secret wealth, one friar wrote, 'ours would be the richest prov-ince in the universe'.

NO SPANIARD WILL BE LEFT

In early 1657, an outlandish figure appeared in the Calchaquí Valleys.
He was shabbily dressed, with fair skin and blond hair. With him travelled a Mapuche woman, defiantly sporting the silver jewellery and
long, dark plaits of her people. They had just tramped over the Andes
from Chile, carrying a map to the mythical lost kingdom of Paititi, and
a portrait of the man's grandfather: 'The Inca Don Cristóbal, whose last
name he could not remember.' He was no vagrant, he said, but a descendant of the emperors of Tawantinsuyu, raised in Spain and now
returned to take his rightful place among his subjects.

Pedro Bohórquez – alias Pedro Chamijo, alias Pedro Huallpa – was
born near Granada, Andalucía, in 1602. It's unlikely that he was a
descendent of the Incas, but not impossible: Paullu, the puppet emperor
baptised as Cristóbal, had fathered some thirty-two children. At least
one of them, Melchor Carlos Inca, journeyed to Spain. As a child,
Bohórquez fled his father's beatings and wandered. In Cádiz, the Jesuits
taught him to read and write. He turned up in Peru in 1620, marrying
into a mestizo ranching family and learning Quechua.

But Bohórquez was not content to remain a cowboy. He seduced
upper-crust women, adopted false identities and faked his own death,
ricocheting from the viceroy's court to the fringes of the Amazon. The
silver-tongued Spaniard persuaded officials to bankroll three expeditions in search of Paititi – an El Dorado myth with as many variants as
spellings, blending Spanish greed, an Andean tradition that Inca explorers had settled deep in the jungle, and the Guaraní belief in a Land
Without Evil, somewhere to the west. Bohórquez's telling rendered it a
realm of fabulously rich cities with gentle, biddable inhabitants.

Even as Paititi evaded him, Bohórquez handed out made-up titles
and unconquered territories to his followers. In 1651, he was banished
to a dungeon in Valdivia, a drizzly Patagonian fortress burned to the
ground by the Mapuche fifty years before. Within six years, he had
talked his way out of jail. Bohórquez continued to fail upwards, cultivating wealthy patrons, before scandal forced him to flee once more.
Now in Tucumán, he used his treasure map to cajole money from Spanish villagers, and his Inca portrait to curry favour with Diaguita chiefs.

Bohórquez also ingratiated himself with the local Jesuits: including
Hernando de Torreblanca, who soon became the go-between for
Bohórquez and the Spanish governor. 'With all the fathers who served

in the Calchaquí mission having died, and with none having set down in writing what happened there,' Torreblanca wrote forty years later, 'there grows within me the need to do so, for the closeness with which these events that I witnessed passed through my hands.'

In May 1657, a letter reached the local governor, Alonso Mercado y Villacorta, a thirty-something Catalonian soldier. Bohórquez offered to be Spain's eyes and ears behind enemy lines. He claimed that his return – the Inca's return – had provoked mass ecstasy among the Diaguita. 'God wanted to make himself present to this province of Calchaquí,' he wrote. 'Its inhabitants are today prostrated and humble ... they adore me as their Inca and obey me, whatever I order them to do, and with much love. They have promised all peace and quietude and that they will show me all the mines that this land hides.'

Mercado met Bohórquez on the edge of Diaguita territory. The ersatz Inca passed through an arch of flowers and Spanish muskets. The pair held a long, private conversation. The governor eventually emerged, chastising the Diaguita for not showing their Inca enough respect. A fortnight of feasting followed. The Diaguita kneeled and kissed Bohórquez's hands. Spanish bards spelled out the deal in song. The 'barbarous Calchaquí' would 'humbly throw away their bows and arrows' and forget 'their idolatrous desires'. Bohórquez was to 'rule with rightful place' over them. They would lead the Spanish to 'the inestimable prize we desire'.

Many caciques saw through Bohórquez. Some plotted his murder. He clearly planned to use them. But they could use him too: an advisor on European tactics; a figurehead to unite the clans and stall the Spanish invasion they knew must one day come. As the foreigners caroused, the Diaguita chiefs passed around an arrow, brokering a new alliance.

Bohórquez returned with them into the mountains, having been proclaimed Inca and lieutenant governor and captain general of the Calchaquí Valleys, with authority stretching across the Andes to the Atacama. He was laden with a silver sun and crown, *Spondylus* and emerald necklaces, bracelets of pearl, and flamboyant robes of his own design. Inca, tailor, soldier and spy: it was the high point of Bohórquez's career, a double-bluff of spectacular proportions. True to the epic romances that had warped his imagination, a dramatic fall from grace was soon to follow.

A few miles south of Cachi, I walk up a gravel track under a hand-painted banner: 'Diaguita Territory'. I approach a timbered farmhouse.

Inside is Julio Octavio Ruiz Moreno, the unofficial resident historian of the Calchaquí Valleys. He is in his mid-eighties, slumped in a chair by the hearth. 'Where are you from?' he demands. 'I had friends in the war of Las Malvinas in '82. They fought and died bloody hard.'

A former local mayor, Ruiz Moreno has little time for the murmurings of a Diaguita revival, the claim that some survived Bohórquez's rebellion. People pretend to be Indigenous to get handouts, he argues. So his neighbours aren't Diaguita? 'No. They're just an invention of Cristina,' he says flatly, referring to one recent left-wing president.

Virginia, his daughter, accompanies me down the track to La Paya. We walk amid piles of stones, thickets of cacti and craters left by graverobbers. 'I used to play here with my sister,' she says. 'Loads of arrowheads were always turning up.' This was a Diaguita settlement, later an Inca waystation. Juan Bautista Ambrosetti, the father of Argentine archaeology, excavated the site in 1907, marvelling at its petroglyphs and stout stone walls. He exhumed fragile skeletons, laden with bracelets of gold, silver and bronze by 'the most ancient, faithful hands'.

But he was disparaging of his local workforce and their 'prevailing superstitions, inherited from centuries ago'. If they profaned the graves, they feared, illness, drought and frosts would follow. Only cash could convince them to start digging – along with coca leaves and alcohol. These they used to make an offering before opening a tomb, 'so that the ancient one is appeased and submits without later wreaking vengeance'. The bones they unearthed, Ambrosetti believed, were the only link 'with this strange people whose very name has been lost'.

Those claiming to be Diaguita today are waging an 'anachronistic struggle', says Virginia. 'The Incas came and they moved everyone around. So how far back are you going to go?' The various Diaguita clans were called different names at different times by different people. After their last rebellion, the Spanish uprooted them. Nobody, she argues, can trace their bloodline back. Self-declared Diaguita are occupying other people's property, Virginia claims, dodging rent by declaring it Indigenous land, pitting neighbour against neighbour.

Up at the farmhouse, I had taken a volume off Ruiz Moreno's shelves. Wearing white shirts, sandals and broad-brimmed hats, Ambrosetti's reluctant tomb-robbers stared sullenly into his camera and off the page. Just a century ago, these locals had venerated the Inca and Diaguita remains. Perhaps the valley's pre-colonial inhabitants had not vanished as thoroughly as the archaeologist, and my hosts, supposed.

*

A year of subterfuge and skullduggery followed Bohórquez's dual
coronation as Inca and colonial plenipotentiary in 1657. His spies
intercepted Mercado's letters and infiltrated the governor's retinue,
spurring rumours that the pretend Inca possessed diabolical powers.
He sent men to the Chaco forest to make bows, and manufactured
gimcrack wooden cannons wrapped in cowhide. Carried about in a
hammock from sacrifice to harem to Mass, he cemented his alliance
with Diaguita caciques by marrying their daughters.

Bohórquez realised that he had fatally overpromised. The Diaguita
would never lead him to a lost city of gold. But whether he had come to
identify with his adoptive subjects, or merely wanted to save his own
skin, their cause was now the same. The false Inca tried to persuade
local chiefs to flood the silver refineries of Potosí, thus crippling the
finances of Spanish empire. A Diaguita spy was even intercepted some
400 miles south: sent, she reportedly confessed, to stir up rebellion
among the Pehuenche and Puelche nomads of northern Patagonia. If
they were all to attack at the same time, the authorities panicked, 'all
will unfailingly be lost'.

The Calchaquí had no secret mines nor shrines dripping in gold, the
Bishop of Tucumán warned. They did not really venerate Bohórquez as
their Inca, and 'the only riches they give us are arrows'. Governor Mercado and Bohórquez were on a collision course. In December 1657,
they met in the village of Tafí. The governor asked Bohórquez to supply
warriors to garrison Buenos Aires, some 1,000 miles away. The Andalusian humbly agreed: on the condition he was given supplies and weapons
for an army of thousands. His movements became evasive, his letters
erratic. In March 1658, orders arrived from the viceroy in Lima. Bohórquez
had gone rogue – and worse, gone native. He was to be brought in dead
or alive.

Bohórquez received a pair of Mercado's assassins, pretending to be
emissaries, with ironic magnanimity. One night, the two Spaniards padded
past the Inca's sleeping guards. They entered his chambers, daggers
drawn – only to be foiled by the barking of a huge dog by his bedside.
The pair crept back to their beds, undetected. Before they sloped off
home, Bohórquez let them witness his vast stockpiles of arrows, spears,
horses, and his well-drilled troops.

Mercado wrote with an ultimatum. Bohórquez was given eight days
to 'leave those Indians in the state that you found them', confess to them
his real identity, and turn himself in. It wasn't only Spanish patience that
had worn thin. As the rebel ranks swelled, the Calchaquí Valleys were

running out of food. More disgruntled Diaguita caciques plotted to eliminate him: they could carry on their struggle without this cowardly chancer. Bohórquez had no choice but to roll the dice. He unleashed the third and final Calchaquí War.

'The King of Spain has usurped the crown of these kingdoms that is mine by inheritance from the Incas,' Bohórquez harangued his troops. 'But if they want war, I will make them sick of it,' he vowed. 'I will defend us, even if it means destroying churches, convents and every last city. No Spaniard will be left in the entire Indies, for it is all my kingdom.' Once more, he invoked the shining vision of Paititi. 'I have come to liberate you from slavery, my children,' he concluded. 'It is time to recover what is ours, and enjoy it in peace!'

Bohórquez's only chance of survival was to inflict so damaging a defeat that the Spanish could never come after him. The Diaguita ransacked nearby villages, rustled thousands of cattle, and razed the Jesuit chapels. One priest took an arrow to the leg and had the spectacles punched off his face; another fended off his attackers with a pair of spurs. Their ruthless commander, Bohórquez's Mapuche consort, delighted in the chaos. 'Look how their God or their king helps them,' she reportedly cried. '*Viva el Inca!*' The clerics were only saved by a little white dog who led them to safety, flinching at the moonlit silhouettes of cacti. The rebels diverted a river to wash away the mission's smouldering ruins. The threat to flood Potosí had not been idle.

'The Calchaquí uprising caused by the tyrant Don Pedro Bohórquez is heading towards not only the perdition of this valley', one Spanish officer reported, 'but all the Republics of this kingdom.' And even if he could be defeated, Bohórquez was only the frontman for a much deeper animosity. The Diaguita posed an ever-present danger that could only be diminished, the soldier recommended, by 'denaturalising half or more' of them – and scattering them to the four winds. The blueprint was laid down for an act of ethnic cleansing that would shape Argentine history to this day.

THIS IS ONLY THE BEGINNING

The bumpy road south through the valley follows the Calchaquí River. The passengers of the dilapidated bus doff broad-brimmed fedoras trimmed with rope as they board. Looms strung with alpaca wool sit idle in the shade. Horses flick their tails in corrals made of thorn bushes.

I stay a few days in Angastaco, a sandy village dotted with desert blooms. Busloads of weekenders from Córdoba leave globs of spilled yerba mate in the streets. At night, truckers enter the diner, carrying a dry cold in the folds of their leather jackets. They set about demolishing pork schnitzels that droop over the plate, washed down with litre-bottles of Quilmes. Sonia, the hamlet's hotelier, doubles up as its police officer. She shakes her head when I ask her about Bohórquez. A faded plaque in the town square suggested his stronghold was nearby, but she is fuzzy about the history. 'Maybe you mean the *antigal*,' she suggests, an ancient site above the town.

I walk through a vineyard and up the hill. A half-finished hotel has destroyed most of the pre-Columbian fortification. I duck under the exposed girders and dangling wires of the abandoned building, its walls designed to look like Inca masonry. Hidden down a nearby alleyway, a patio is hung with scythes, sickles, sausage grinders and a Motorola flip-phone. It belongs to Leonardo Gutiérrez, a guitar-strumming bard and fixture at local weddings.

Now approaching eighty, the Calchaquí Soloist apologises for his wheezing cough. 'My great-grandmother was an Indian and my great-grandfather a Basque, so the story goes.' The mention of Bohórquez again draws a blank. 'You mean Juan Calchaquí. He was the chief from here. He was a strong warrior who commanded all the tribes before the Incas came from Peru. They couldn't defeat him.' I ask about the Diaguita and he sighs. 'Round here, there's no monuments, and little respect, for the Indian.' His parrot screeches from a corner. In a swell of strength, Leonardo straightens up and dictates:

> My name is Leonardo Gutiérrez.
> This is the place, if someone asks for me.
> I'm Diaguita, I am Calchaquí,
> The hills my home, that Pachamama blesses.
> She's here – in the gullies, the flowers, high and low.
> I grew, and I grew old, in Angastaco.

Mercado cobbled together eighty men and marched into the northern valley. Finding ashes in place of the missions, he retreated to a ruined Inca fortress at San Bernardo. For a month, the raw recruits, greybeards and few Indigenous allies endured the dust and heat. Mercado sent out riders to scout for the enemy.

Then, on 21 September 1658, over a thousand Calchaquí warriors descended the ravine into Spanish territory, led by Bohórquez and his mestizo lieutenant, Luis Enríquez. Their victory would mean the ruin of nearby cities, and fan the flames of rebellion well beyond the province. The governor gave Father Torreblanca his papers and the keys to his desk, ordering him to flee to Salta if the battle seemed lost. The Jesuit heard confessions in a chapel made of branches.

As night fell, the Diaguita approached in silence. A branch snapped, and the Spaniards fired blindly into the darkness. Then, a nasty shock: a handful of Diaguita commanded by Enríquez, armed with muskets, shot back. Stabs of flame illuminated the massed ranks of the attackers, now sprinting to encircle the fort, making the ground shake. At first light, the Diaguita launched their assault, yelling war cries, blowing shrill whistles and loosing flaming arrows. They attacked in waves, 'some coming forward and others retreating, in a continuous movement', Torreblanca later recalled.

A year of migraine-inducing negotiations with Bohórquez finally over, Mercado was in his military element. The mission was now simple: win or die. Atop his white horse, in a fine cloak and a scarlet cap, he marshalled his men to a desperate defence on all sides. The veterans stood to at loopholes, thinning the Diaguita ranks with gunfire; the cavalry cut down anyone who got too close. The novice soldiers overstuffed the cannons with powder, missing the enemy altogether. But as the shot sailed past Bohórquez's head, he fell back to the rear.

A stray spark ignited a barrel of gunpowder. Far behind the front lines, Bohórquez was convinced that the Spaniards' ammunition had gone up in smoke. He launched an all-out attack. The Diaguita unleashed their arrows in droves, ignoring his earlier advice to aim each shot carefully. They soon ran low and pulled back. The battleground fell silent. The Spanish plucked broken shafts from the walls and ground to kindle fires. They sipped their morning yerba mate amid the dead and the dying.

Bohórquez ordered a desperate final assault. A Diaguita cacique, hewing his way towards Mercado, was abruptly beheaded. A mestizo soldier hoisted the grisly trophy on a spear, sowing panic among the Diaguita, who sensed divine disfavour. At that moment, the Spanish scouts reappeared on a hill to the west and fired a salvo. Believing himself surrounded, Bohórquez ordered the retreat. After four hours of fighting, the Spanish had triumphed with just three wounded, including Mercado's secretary, limping from a slash to the foot.

In a wheedling, raging missive, Bohórquez excoriated the Spanish for executing the wounded he had left behind. He denied having sacked the missions, and branded the Bishop of Salta a fraud and a womaniser. More attacks would come, he promised. 'In conclusion, gentlemen,' he wrote, 'this is only the beginning.' In reality, it was over. With his army depleted, mutinous and starving, Bohórquez surrendered in April 1659. The caciques laid their bows and arrows at the governor's feet.

Bohórquez was promised a pardon but still tried to escape, trusting the word of Spanish authorities no more than his own. He languished in a Lima dungeon for years while the lawyers wrangled: after all, almost everything he had done was on Spanish orders. But in 1664, a rebellion led by his son, Francisco, back in the Calchaquí Valleys – and rumblings of revolt in the hills around Lima in late 1666 – stiffened official resolve.

On 5 January 1667, Bohórquez was garrotted. His severed head was impaled on the bridge between the plaza mayor and the native neighbourhood of San Lázaro: halfway between one culture and another. Bohórquez insisted on his innocence of any crime to the end, even asking to be rewarded for bringing Christianity to the Diaguita. Perhaps he offered to lead one final quest for Paititi.

The Third Calchaquí War was long treated as a footnote, and Bohórquez as a sad joke. 'So ended the obstinacy of this man, who ambitiously aspired to nothing greater than to crown himself king of the Indies. He obtained this end by his strange wits and entangled relations, all with the aim to be worth more, be more, but he erred,' wrote one Jesuit historian, 'by pretending to be an Indian when the Indians in the Indies are the ones worth the least.'

It's hard to feel much pity for Bohórquez. Many paid with their lives for his delusions of grandeur. But he lived painfully torn between dreams of Indigenous liberation and European domination, a tension made incarnate in the tantalising vision of Paititi. He was, in the words of the bemused Spanish viceroy, 'a man without a place in the world'.

Cafayate, halfway down the Calchaquí Valleys, is a strange oasis of vineyards, patisseries and beret-clad cyclists. I ring the bell at the local museum. Black jugs, marked with hundreds of miniature impressions made by Diaguita fingernails, line the shelves. Dozens of wooden club-heads hang from the ceiling. Copper pectoral plates, blackened by age, sit in a case like a dinner service. A woman in her mid-seventies, all of five feet tall with a sweep of golden-grey hair, glides in. 'Step back from those pots,' she rasps, tossing a mantle around her shoulders. 'You're too close.'

Helga Mazzoni, a writer, is the widow of local archaeologist Rodolfo

Bravo. It's quite a collection, I remark. Why did her husband start excavating? 'Out of a great Americanist vocation,' is the gnomic response.
How did he find them? 'You're a journalist? So you studied journalism,
history, politics, to prepare. He also made the necessary preparations.'
Bravo looks down over his mustachios at us from the wall. He started
reading archaeological reports, Mazzoni says, at the age of seven. At
twelve he opened his first museum in his grandfather's house. Aged thirteen, he was sharing his findings with other archaeologists who thought
they were corresponding with an adult.

'Whenever he went out into the field at the weekends, I'd prepare
everything perfectly – with special pockets and cases for his instruments
and whatever he found,' Mazzoni chuckles. 'He'd come back with artefacts secreted in rolled up sleeves, wrapped up in his scarf.' Bravo had
often gone to Buenos Aires to give conferences in a mismatched suit. On
the wall is a letter from Jorge Luis Borges – as director of the National
Library – thanking him for 'a fascinating talk on the Diaguita, called the
Calchaquí by the Spanish'.

Mazzoni recalls her childhood in the era of Juan Domingo Perón, the
army officer whose bombastic, pro-worker presidencies still define and
divide Argentina. Some still pray to his First Lady as Saint Evita. 'I love
my country, I love its people,' she says, 'but we're like a pendulum, we
oscillate from one extreme to another. Peronism, fascism, populism . . .
Of course, the Spanish were only able to defeat the Incas because they
were divided,' Mazzoni sighs. 'It's always the same. We never learn.'

A glass case across the hallway case holds bows, arrows and quivers,
malachite necklaces, and bracelets made of *Spondylus*. These were excavated from the nearby grave of fifteen adult males. The Diaguita rarely
buried their dead with so many items. The prevailing hypothesis, says
Mazzoni, is that these belonged to chiefs captured during the Third
Calchaquí War. The Spanish executed them and threw them in a pit,
possessions and all. Bravo had found evidence of a massacre.

Night has fallen quickly, and the air is sharp with cold. I step outside
into the dark. The custodian of Cafayate's Calchaquí relics bids me safe
travels and locks herself in.

Such atrocities are corroborated by a report from Mercado penned at
Tolombón, Bohórquez's hideout a few miles south of Cafayate. In June
1659, two months after the false Inca turned himself in, the war was far
from over.

Diaguita chiefs had 'faked friendship' and peace offerings, the governor wrote, only to withdraw to the hills and ambush the Spanish column, guerrilla-style. His men found themselves in the desert, parched and pinned down behind circled wagons. 'We spent all night with our weapons in our hands, having in sight around us the fires of the enemy, who were determined to fight the following day to break us or block us from reaching water.' In the morning, they broke out, charging entrenched Diaguita positions. Mercado's victorious soldiers cut the throats of fifty captured caciques. The survivors 'fled to the depths of the mountains, leaving no trace or sign at all'.

I walk up to the hillfort at Tolombón. Its waist-height walls wind up a scraggly hillside, a labyrinth of scree and spines. The fighting would have been fierce here: corridor to chamber, boulder to barricade. Fist-sized lumps of fool's gold roll underfoot. Nothing else moves apart from the vultures, drifting overhead under a hot noonday sun. I reach a dead end and haul myself upwards instead, buffeted by a hot wind. I crawl over a ledge to a commanding view. Dark mountains float above a blue haze on the far side of the valley. Here are the tell-tale stones with mortars ground into them, and ashes from campfires. It's like I've missed the Diaguita council of war by minutes.

Bohórquez proved expendable. The revolt simmered on for years under Enríquez, his notional second-in-command. But cracks emerged in the Diaguita alliance. Mercado turned several clans to his side, and crushed the remainder in 1666, resolving to end their resistance once and for all. Those who gave up early on were resettled nearby in reducciones – the model towns pioneered by viceroy Toledo – where the Spanish could keep tabs on them.

A worse fate was reserved for the Quilmes. A warlike Diaguita people and mainstay of many an insurgency, their eponymous city guarded the southern entrance of the valleys. Unwilling to risk a direct assault, Mercado's troops simply cut off its water supply and waited for their surrender. Thousands of captive Quilmes – men, women and children – were sent on a forced march of 900 miles to Buenos Aires, then a fleapit village on the edge of a vast, unfamiliar ocean.

It was colonial Argentina's own Trail of Tears. Only a few hundred souls failed to succumb to exhaustion and starvation. The survivors were put to work fortifying the future metropolis, building the port as more and more boats from Europe arrived. As the centuries passed, little but their name survived: in the satellite city that subsumed the plantation where the Quilmes were confined, its football club, and Argentina's national lager, brewed in the same suburb of the capital.

Like the Quilmes, the Diaguita as a whole, it seemed, had been expunged from the earth. By the late 1700s, scarcely a thousand Indigenous people were living in the Calchaquí Valleys: a population collapse of over ninety per cent in barely a century. Even the Diaguita language was doomed to disappear. A Kakán dictionary compiled by the Jesuits was probably lost in the fire and flood that Bohórquez brought down upon on the missions. A royal decree in 1770 obliged all Indigenous peoples to use Spanish, further erasing any lingering memories of the Diaguita tongue.

After the genocide, a pact of silence reigned. 'I have wandered on foot and on horseback through the region which, according to the historian Herrera, was populated by the Diaguita,' the Bishop of Tucumán reflected in 1768 after six years in his post. 'Although I have talked about that place with many who are familiar with it, no one has spoken to me of the Diaguita. What has been done, Lord, with all those Indians? I ask around, I read, I investigate, yet I can find nothing but their names.'

WE WERE ALWAYS HERE

I walk for an hour up a gravel track off the highway. At the entrance to the ancient city of Quilmes, I step over eleven mortars in a flagstone, polished smooth by centuries of footsteps. Nearby, fluttering in the breeze is the Wiphala, the banner of multi-coloured pixels that represents the Indigenous peoples of the Andes. Narrow pathways lead between bulging walls and under huge boulders up to a ruined tower. The valley is filled with mist. Llamas pick their way through the hectares of scrub and rubble yet to be excavated.

With 3,000 residents on the eve of its apocalypse, Quilmes was the largest pre-Columbian city in present-day Argentina. It dated back to at least AD 800 – six centuries before Machu Picchu. But unlike the palaces and servants' quarters of Inca cities, the dwellings of the Quilmes were all the same shape and size. It seems they were a more horizontal society, one harder to divide and conquer.

Here's what really happened, says Moises González, a young local guide with high cheekbones and jet-black hair. After the climactic siege in 1666, 'some small groups were able to escape and flee to high areas. Later, they were forced to work in haciendas and ranches, and with time they mixed with the Spanish population,' he tells me. 'That means that today the local population is still indirectly descended from those people.'

Tomorrow, 1 August, is the Day of Pachamama, Moises adds. Locals gather to offer the Andean Mother Earth part of what they produce. 'The tradition was prohibited for a long time by the Church and by landowners – it was considered diabolical and pagan,' says Moises. 'But among some hidden circles they were able to maintain it, and nowadays we can spread it.'

The next morning, I pack up my tent and walk back down the track to a village hall, daubed with a Diaguita warrior stomping on a con-quistador's helmeted head. A circle forms in the pre-dawn chill: teenagers in tracksuits, elders in knitted shawls and bowler hats. A stout, grey-haired man, his poncho draped over a T-shirt bearing the Quilmes lager logo, kicks off proceedings. He is Francisco Chaile, the community's elected chief.

He instructs us to bow before the rising sun and each compass point, and make our offerings. I watch as locals approach a small cairn in turn. They pour wine into the earth, crumble in coca leaves, leave jars of *dulce de leche*, blow cigarette smoke towards the ground. 'You've got to get up close,' Chaile fusses, as an awkward teenage girl throws a hand-ful of walnuts from a distance. 'Don't just chuck it in.' Sergio Condori, a community leader with a dark ponytail and a stern expression, steps forward. 'Two years ago we were asking for the freedom of our cacique – and now he is with us!' The circle whoops and whistles; Chaile grins and shakes his staff. 'We won't surrender another metre,' Condori vows. 'This land is ours!'

The serious part over, the microphone is passed around. Old-timers trade rhyming couplets to a steady drumbeat: folk wisdom, ribald jokes, lines from the gaucho epic *Martín Fierro*. Lunch is served on long trestle tables in the shade. I take the chance to speak with the cacique. 'There are versions that when the Spanish took the Quilmes to Buenos Aires, they killed the rest and no one was left,' says Chaile. 'But, clearly, that's not true. People stayed here, hidden from sight, they escaped to the hills and the forests.' In time, he says, they returned to populate the valley. The lands and title of the cacique of Quilmes were officially recognised in a Royal Charter of 1716.

The murderous military junta that ruled Argentina between 1976 and 1983 tried to turn Quilmes into a tourist trap to rival Machu Picchu. Swathes of the Diaguita metropolis were damaged in a botched restoration job. Private companies later built a pool, hotel and museum – now all disused – atop a chunk of the site. Quilmes is not an archaeological ruin, I realise, but the rubble of an ongoing conflict. Locals have fought back with roadblocks and occupations. Landowners and the local government have sent mounted police to evict them. Chaile spent months behind bars. 'History is repeating itself,' Condori argues. 'The descendants of the Spanish are still persecuting us.'

The battle for Quilmes, and the dramatic comeback of its people, is replicated across Argentina. Several Indigenous groups supposed to have disappeared have re-emerged in recent decades: from the Ranquel of La Pampa in the north, via the Huarpes of Cuyo, to the Selk'nam of Tierra del Fuego. In the 2022 census, over 86,000 people identified as Diaguita. Over in Chile, surveys report another 90,000 Diaguita descendants. Some chalk it up to cynical identity politics: a phenomenon known in North America as 'pretendianism'. Local anthropologists offer a different explanation. Conflicts over land and water are causing rural, working-class Argentines to embrace an Indigenous heritage that has never been entirely forgotten. And few first nations set much store by DNA tests: what matters is recognition by the community, and continuity of culture and place.

After lunch, a duo of young musicians from Quilmes – the Buenos Aires suburb – take the floor. Takiri Folklore have collaborated with Diaguita elders to develop their album, *Sumamao Quilmes*. Inspired by the forced march made by the founders of their hometown, it hops across musical styles: *chacarera, zamba, vidala, huayno*. It's a bridge between the two Quilmes; between the Argentina of the mountains and the Argentina of the boats.

'Little by little, the links between these two peoples are starting to emerge,' says Gimena Pacheco, Takiri's singer. 'They're starting to bring it into classrooms. It's very little and very recent, and, you know, all change is slow,' she reflects. 'There's a lot of work to do yet, but the seed is there.'

Tacuil, the remotest part of the Calchaquí Valleys. The last of the Diaguita, survivors from the siege of Quilmes, stage a desperate last stand on a tabletop mountain that is impossible to storm. So the Spanish surround the outcrop, starve them of food and water, and wait. After a few days, the Diaguita send their children down the track to the waiting arms of Jesuit negotiators.

But the men and women do not follow. They walk to the precipice. Their drums and whistles fall silent. They embrace each other and leap into empty space. The Spanish, denied a rich haul of captives, howl in frustration. A solitary runner breaks through the enemy lines. He sprints north, bearing the arrow of resistance, and the message: 'Better to die free than live as slaves.'

This, at least, is the story you'll find in bookshops in Salta: the final embers of Diaguita resistance stamped out with a cry of defiance that echoes down the ages. So, as a last stop, I'm headed back north through the valleys to pull on this melancholic loose thread. I hitch a lift in the cab of a petrol tanker, then jump into a 4x4 driven by a group of Italian tourists. They're only headed as far as Colomé, a vineyard, luxury hotel and art museum up in the mountains, owned by a Swiss billionaire. I walk out into the desert, pitch my tent at twilight in the ruins of a stone hut, and light a fire, algarrobo wood producing a sweet, soporific smoke.

The following morning, I come to a fertile, vine-filled valley. Its owners, the Dávalos cousins – descendants of Salta's last colonial governor – are politely perplexed to have me turn up out of nowhere. But they pour me a glass of Malbec and we chat about the recent elections. 'We were at the edge of a precipice,' Diego says darkly, his gold-rimmed spectacles glinting in the gloom of the manor house. 'Argentina is recovering now, but in a few more years we could have been like Venezuela.' In November 2023, the pendulum swung again. Voters in Salta turned out in droves to elect Argentina's new president, Javier Milei – a messy-haired libertarian economist and former tantric sex coach who communes with his dead mastiff for guidance.

I'm here to find out about the Holocaust of Tacuil, I explain. 'Listen,' Raúl replies. 'I don't want you to go up there with the wrong idea. There is a *pucará*, a hillfort here at the other end of the estate. But the siege is a legend. It was made up by an artist our father invited here many decades ago. I guess he wanted to give his watercolours some glamour.' Archaeologists had dug all around the hilltop, but found no Diaguita remains. There had been one fatality: one of the excavators had stumbled backwards and over the edge. 'You can see how the myth stuck,' says Raúl. 'But it is a myth.'

Having come all this way, I might as well take a look. We buzz past the Juan Calchaquí Primary and Secondary School on Diego's quadbike, and he leaves me at the foot of a winding track. I ask a woman putting out her washing about the pucará. She says she doesn't know much. Despite living just down the hill, she's only been once. Perhaps she is wary about chatting to an associate of the boss. Maybe she has better things to do than worry about ruins.

I squeeze through a gorge and climb up between two huge pink cliffs. If the pucará is here, I can't see it. I try to scale one of the large outcrops but the wind nearly knocks me off balance. A second broken neck in search of phantoms would look like carelessness. Sunburnt, tired and hungry, I turn back, still rueing not finding any trace of the Diaguita.

On my way down, I trip over a flat rock. I scrape the earth off: two bowl-shaped depressions, carved right at the entrance to the ancient settlement of Tacuil, looking out over the country that the Diaguita once ruled. It isn't as dramatic as the last survivor running to spread the flame of rebellion. But it is still a message of sorts, hiding in plain sight.

It brings to mind something Francisco Chaile, the sturdy Diaguita cacique at Quilmes, had told me after rattling off the documents, laws and customs that anchored his people to their territory. 'I tell you this just to show you,' he had argued, 'we were always here.'

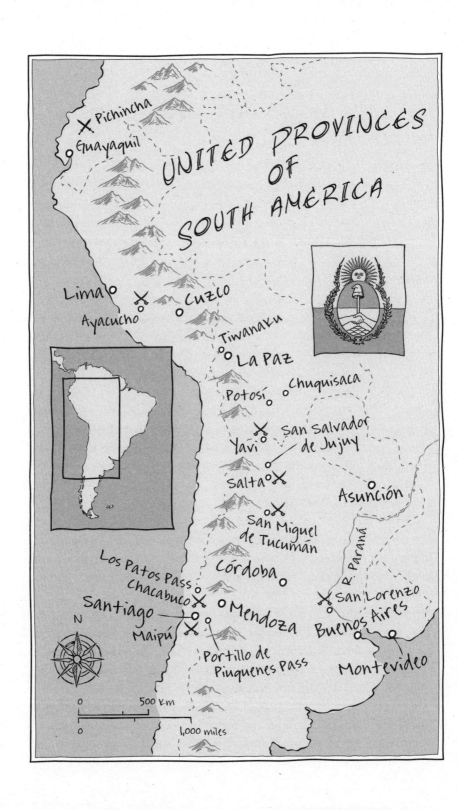

6

The African Army of the Andes

The United States of South America, 1816–1820

SOON YOU WILL HAVE YOUR INCA

An hour's drive west of La Paz, the endless russet plains of Bolivia's highland *altiplano* are punctured by a great city of reddish pyramids. Among them sits a solitary doorway, made from a single block of smooth volcanic rock. Carved into the apex of the Gate of the Sun stands an inscrutable, staff-bearing deity in a feathered headdress, flanked by a phalanx of bird-headed men.

Tiwanaku was the monumental capital of an Andean empire that arose around AD 1000, predating Tawantinsuyu by centuries. But when Juan José Castelli visited in May 1811, he jumped to a different conclusion. The rabble-rousing, chain-smoking Jacobin commanded the revolutionary Army of the North, dispatched from distant Buenos Aires. Tiwanaku, he believed, was evidently 'the sumptuous Palace, Castle, and Garden of the Inca Monarchs'.

Castelli leads a radical triumvirate. One member is Bernardo de Monteagudo, a wiry public defender from Tucumán of Black and Indigenous parentage. The year before, he had authored an incendiary pamphlet. It imagined Atahualpa rising from the grave to reprimand the king of Spain – and inviting other pre-Columbian kings to shake off their chains and 'enjoy the delicious enchantments of independence'. The other is Andrés Jiménez de León Mancocapac, a burly cathedral canon of impeccable Inca lineage. In 1809, both had led an uprising in Chuquisaca, Upper Peru, calling on the 'real Indians' and the 'white-skinned Indians' to join forces against the Spanish.

And now that alliance is sealed by an unusual ceremony at Tiwanaku. Castelli's army of criollo and mestizo soldiers forms up, flanked by hundreds of Andean communities at arms. To the retort of muskets and cannons, the general summits the great Kalasasaya temple to pay homage to the 'magnificence of our ancestors'. Monteagudo reads out a revolutionary proclamation, later published in Spanish, Quechua, Guaraní and Aymara. All native peoples would enjoy the same rights as whites. Land would be divided equally, onerous taxes and tributes abolished, and the abuses of colonial overseers ended. The militiamen from Buenos Aires and their ecstatic Andean hosts mingle in an open-ended fiesta. Gourds of chicha and bottles of brandy are passed around; native flutes and cymbals duel with regimental pipes and drums.

The trio's quixotic revolution falters. Spanish forces push the Army of the North out of Upper Peru and inflict gruesome reprisals. Castelli dies from tongue cancer while facing court-martial. Monteagudo is assassinated before he can realise his dream of uniting all Spanish America in a single patria. Yet for years after the summit at Tiwanaku, a carnival of apocalyptic insurrections sweeps the Andes. The Inca will soon return atop a white horse with golden reins – the prophecy goes – to share out the land, kill all the Spaniards, and free his people.

Mancocapac, the cleric, manages to escape to Tucumán. In 1814, he pens a proclamation to 'all the peoples of Peru'. The 'legitimate kings are their majesties the Incas; there is a descendant', he insists. 'Keep asking God for the speedy arrival of the troops of Buenos Aires, and soon you will have your Inca among you once more.'

Latin America in the early 1800s was scene to one of the most dramatic revolutionary experiments in world history. Sixteen independent nations burst into existence in barely thirty years, supplanting at a stroke the European powers that had held sway over much of the continent since 1500. What's more – with the notable exceptions of Mexico and Brazil – most started life as republics of notionally equal citizens, when swathes of the planet were still cowed by empires and absolute monarchies.

Seeking to explain this explosion of patriotic sentiment, historians have traditionally focused on Latin America's upper classes, the European-descended criollos. Lawyers, landowners, slavers and bureaucrats, they imagined a sense of national identity out of nowhere, we are told, frustrated at being second-class subjects to Spanish officials. It was supposedly the criollos, especially Simón Bolívar – the brilliant commander, ruthless politician and romantic visionary from modern-day Venezuela – who delivered South America's independence.

Second billing is sometimes afforded to José de San Martín. In the Argentine history books he bears the epithet of '*el hombre necesario*':

the taciturn soldier who unfussily liberated the bottom half of South America, before ceding the limelight to Bolívar and vanishing into exile. There is no denying that both men inspired their followers to incredible feats. But the resulting narrative of the years between 1800 and 1825 ends up seeming strangely flat: 'Bolívar here, Bolívar there,' as one later writer puts it, 'bloodshed, death-scenes, and long pauses in the action for fine speeches.'

This picture of independence dreamed up and delivered by elites is fast collapsing. Not only did those at the lower end of the colonial hierarchy shape the intellectual underpinnings of independence: they fought and died for it. And not as expendable bodies, but often as articulate believers in the cause of the patria – a free, united American homeland – whose bravery turned the tide of many campaigns. In doing so, they fatally weakened the institution of African and Indigenous slavery and secured their place as equal citizens. Restoring them to their leading role in liberating South America is not just a matter of correcting the record. It has revolutionary implications for how the region sees itself today.

San Martín's remains were repatriated to Argentina in 1880, placed atop a marble slab in the cathedral of Buenos Aires, and guarded by a pair of elite grenadiers ever since. But in life, he was clear that the true credit for the continent's emancipation should not fall to him, nor any white, whiskered founding father. 'The rich and the landowners refuse to fight, they don't want to send their sons to battle ... they say they care little if they remain a colony,' he observed. 'One day it will be known that the patria was freed by the poor and their children,' he predicted, the 'blacks and Indians, who will now no longer be anyone's slaves.'

In 1776, Spain carved out the new viceroyalty of the Río de la Plata from that of Lima. Buenos Aires was named the capital of the new province: a vast territory encompassing modern-day Bolivia, Argentina, Uruguay and Paraguay. Exports of Potosí silver were re-routed via the city, and its merchants could now trade with other Spanish ports.

South America's centre of gravity had shifted eastwards. The backwater to which the Quilmes had been banished 150 years previously was now a cosmopolitan jewel in Spain's imperial domains. Along with Montevideo across the wide, muddy river, Buenos Aires was becoming ever wealthier, shipping out cowhides and precious metals and sucking in foreign merchandise – as well as trafficked human beings.

Buenos Aires was a bustling slavers' port. Between 1585 and 1835, at least 203,000 enslaved Africans and their descendants were disembarked to labour in the households, ranches, mines and workshops of the Río de la Plata: including 72,000 in the years 1777 to 1812 alone. Most were baptised, their names replaced with Spanish ones, although a few reclaimed their identity. The surname of Antonio Porobio – who fought throughout the wars of independence, won his freedom, and rose to become a captain – seems to refer to the Quisamá region of Angola where he was born around 1780.

Those who secured their freedom formed fraternities known as nations, each with their own king, queen, president and treasurer. Around 1800, Africans and Afrodescendants made up a third of the population of Buenos Aires, and half in Salta, Córdoba, Tucumán and Asunción. As well as farmers, cowherds and servants, they were cooks, builders, barbers, cobblers and coachmen. They sold cakes, removed ants' nests, collected scrap metal and rubbish, and were prized as wet nurses and piano teachers. 'They had an excellent ear,' one diarist recalled. Black *porteños*, Buenos Aireans, could be heard at all hours whistling 'snatches of opera' in the street.

The washerwomen of many African nations could be found smoking, sipping mate, dancing and gossiping along the banks of the Plata. Joining them in the urban melting pot were a small but significant Indigenous community: Andeans down from the north-west and Upper Peru; the Guaraní of the disbanded missions straddling the provincial border with Paraguay; and the Pehuenche of the pampas, whose trading stalls filled the streets for five blocks from Plaza Lorea, selling ponchos, lassoes, feathers of the ostrich-like ñandú, and capes of fox, hare and deer skin.

Spain had neither men nor money to garrison the Río de la Plata. 'In all its provinces,' Paraguay's last colonial governor complained, 'there is not to be found a single military man.' So its defence fell to the local population: criollo, Indigenous, mestizo and Black, forging a collective identity. The viceroyalty's free Black soldiers had served with distinction against Portuguese raiders and Guaraní rebels. Militia officers like Bentura Patrón, 'overseer of the nation of Ethiopia', journeyed to Spain to secure promotion.

And when a British invasion force appeared off Buenos Aires in 1806 – and the viceroy fled with the treasury – regular porteños stood their ground. As the Connaught Rangers marched through the streets under heavy fire, it felt like the 'entire population' had taken up arms. Native militiamen showered them with grapeshot. Women tossed grenades from the rooftops. Enslaved Africans hacked down the invaders with pikes. Gauchos lassoed sentries around the neck and dragged them off to be butchered.

Boys gathered musket balls and dragged cannons into position. Women, too: María de los Remedios del Valle, enslaved in a local lady's household, was later awarded twelve pesos for valour. Pablo Jiménez, an enslaved volunteer, vanquished two enemies with a pick before carrying his wounded brother out of danger. Manuel Macedonio Barbarín – a free militia sergeant born in Calibali, Angola – was given a medal for 'martial conduct' and would go on to become a lieutenant colonel.

When the smoke cleared, some 2,500 British and Irish soldiers had been killed, captured or wounded. Britain was defeated twice in as many years; a humiliation that ended Whitehall's dreams of dominating South America, at least by force. Captured British standards still hang in the city's museums and churches. In November 1807, nearly 700 enslaved heroes were nominated for freedom. Criollo regiments pooled cash to liberate their comrades. A lottery was held, the 130 winners carried forward by the Black militia companies, 'in whose ranks they already mixed as if they belonged'. The rowdy celebration ended 'in acclamations of *viva* to the king and the patria'.

The ovations hinted at why Jiménez, Remedios and Barbarín had been willing to lay down their lives. They professed loyalty to the king of Spain, but not to Spain per se. Their love was for the patria: a nebulous idea to which all on South American soil could stake a claim. Though fighting under Spanish flags, theirs was an anti-colonial insurrection. Manuel Belgrano – a young criollo lawyer, militia captain and revolutionary – encapsulated this ambiguity when asked to swear loyalty to the British occupiers: we want 'the old master', he retorted, 'or none at all'.

Anger at Spanish rule and Spanish taxes was simmering across Spanish America. Her seventeen million people were lorded over by scarcely 30,000 *peninsulares*: a hated caste of Spanish-born generals, judges and viceroys. With Potosí's silver snatched away by Buenos Aires, Peru was broke and mutinous. Túpac Amaru II fired the starting pistol in 1780, his neo-Inca revolution ricocheting down the Andes. The Thirteen Colonies were king-free by 1783, France by 1789.

Events unfolding on Saint-Domingue, a French outpost in the Caribbean, between 1791 and 1804 sent shockwaves around the Atlantic world. Black revolutionaries had broken their chains in the sugar plantations, wreaked revenge on their captors, and seen off French and

British fleets. Later, they would arm and shelter South American freedom fighters, and push for emancipation across the continent. The world's first free Black republic, they adopted the native Taíno name for the island: Haiti.

Now, the invasion of Buenos Aires had acted like a 'flash of lightning' upon people's minds. Not only were the population now united, armed and dangerous, one British captive noted. If the Duke of Wellington's finest could be bested, they began to wonder, why not Spain? South Americans had begun 'to feel their strength': their 'rising spirit' must soon 'create a new independent power in this quarter of the new world'.

If a British invasion primed the Río de la Plata for revolution, a French invasion pulled the trigger. In 1808, Napoleon's armies marched into Iberia. 'My beloved vassals,' the Spanish king Carlos IV proclaimed; 'Breathe easy; know the army of my dear ally the Emperor of the French crosses my kingdom with ideas of peace and friendship.'

A day later, an anti-French mob forced the king to abdicate. Not content with occupying Portugal, French troops turned their attention on Spain. Napoleon locked up Carlos and his young successor, Fernando VII. The emperor's brother, Joseph Bonaparte, was proclaimed King of Spain. Her colonies were plunged into crisis. They could hardly remain obedient to a French puppet, and wait to be carved up – one Buenos Aires patriot panicked – 'like the turkey at a wedding'. Maybe, some felt, their loyalties lay closer to home.

José de San Martín was an unlikely convert to the cause of independence. Born in 1778 on the Río de la Plata's sweltering northern frontier, his family moved back to Spain six years later. Aged thirteen, he followed his father into the army, crossing swords with Algerian pirates, the Portuguese, the British and, from 1808, the French. But as a criollo, born in the Americas, Lieutenant Colonel San Martín could only climb so far. His birth in a subtropical backwater and dark complexion earned him sneers from his superiors. He rubbed shoulders with British officers, read Thomas Paine, Voltaire and Rousseau, and crossed paths with other disgruntled expatriates in a secret Masonic lodge.

His countrymen had meanwhile taken matters into their own hands. In 1809, uprisings erupted in La Paz and Chuquisaca but were soon suffocated. In May 1810, more bad news arrived in Buenos Aires. The French had trounced Spain's armies. Now under siege in the port city of Cádiz, Spain's liberal caretaker government had been sidelined by an authoritarian council. Fearing equally a French takeover or a Spanish crackdown, a militia-backed mob overthrew the viceroy in Buenos Aires, forming a junta still loyal – the rebels insisted – to Fernando VII.

'The Spaniards of Spain have lost their land,' said Castelli, their cigar-chewing spokesperson. 'The Spaniards of America are trying to save theirs.' Castelli, Belgrano and other criollo intellectuals were the face of the May Revolution. But their muscle in the streets came from the lower classes. The city's enslaved population, wrote the ousted viceroy, were 'the staunchest supporters of independence'.

In September 1811, San Martín slipped aboard a British ship from Spain to London, telling his superiors that he was bound for Lima. At the Mayfair house of Venezuelan founding father Francisco de Miranda, San Martín narrowly missed Bolívar. And it was aboard a British frigate that the thirty-four-year-old anchored off Buenos Aires in March 1812. Absent from South America for three decades, wearing a curved English sabre, San Martín was rumoured to be a spy. But his only objective, he insisted, was 'to work for the independence of my native land'.

He created a company of mounted grenadiers, a revolutionary guard that installed a new, more radical government. The trade in African captives was banned. No one else would be born into slavery. The Inquisition was sent packing. Indigenous peoples would enjoy 'equal rights to all other citizens'. In February 1813, the grenadiers earned their military stripes, ambushing Spanish marines upriver at San Lorenzo. San Martín's horse was shot from under him. Juan Bautista Cabral, a Black grenadier and the son of enslaved farmhands, hauled the future liberator out of danger but was fatally wounded. San Martín installed a plaque above the barrack gates in his memory.

The mixed-race militias of Buenos Aires had meanwhile marched hundreds of miles north-west to link up with revolutionaries in Upper Peru. But in November, on a dusty highland plain called Ayohuma, patriot forces under Belgrano were encircled by the royalists as they heard Mass. As Spanish guns blasted holes in their ranks, María Remedios del Valle – the Black maidservant and veteran of the battle for Buenos Aires – was seen patching up the wounded on the front line. But del Valle was more than just a nurse, as later schoolbooks would claim. Contemporaries described her as a courageous combat medic who earned the rank of *capitana*. In the rout at Ayohuma, she took a bullet, was captured, and later flogged for helping other prisoners to escape.

By the end of 1813, Portugal, British redcoats and Spanish partisans had pushed Napoleon's legions out of Iberia. Fernando VII returned to the throne as an absolutist, tearing up the freedoms afforded Spain's colonies in his absence. Seasoned Spanish regiments steamrollered through South America. By 1816, they were bearing down on the Río de la Plata. San Martín's compatriots needed to be steeled: they needed something to fight for, not just an enemy to fight against. And rather than turning to Europe and Enlightenment philosophy, they directed their gaze to the Andes and backwards: to a pre-Columbian dynasty that was supposed to have vanished centuries before.

THE BLACK KING AND THE
INDIAN KING

With the revolution in peril, an urgent congress was called in San Miguel de Tucumán, far from the intrigues of the capital on the southern edge of the Calchaquí Valleys. The strange fiction that South American patriots had so far observed – claiming loyalty to the king of Spain while killing his soldiers – had run out of road. The people were clamouring for an outright declaration of independence. Without one, they were little better than common outlaws.

On 9 July 1816, as jubilant crowds crammed into the streets outside, the Rioplatense delegates pronounced into existence a 'free and independent nation'. Their country was to be the United Provinces of South America; some later called it the United States. Emissaries were dispatched to foreign powers and the Papacy. The invitation to join them would be printed in Indigenous languages and sent far and wide; including to Paraguay and Uruguay, provinces of the former viceroyalty that had broken with Buenos Aires. That was the easy part. But how should this embryonic, expanding nation be governed?

According to Captain Johan Adam Graaner, a Swedish spy, the debate began as a three-way tussle. Politics junkies bandied about 'The Social Contract, the Spirit of the Laws, the English Constitution and other works'. Solon, Lycurgus and Plato were name-dropped by classicists. Cassocked clerics 'condemned the ancient philosophers as blind pagans and the modern writers as impious, apostate heretics'. The compromise option seemed to be a constitutional monarchy. But then, Belgrano entered the ring with a gobsmacking proposal. Nothing less than the 'restoration of the empire of the Incas' would do if this continent-sized country were to stick together and stand up to the world.

A secret session was called for General Belgrano to lay out his arguments. Crowning an Inca descendant in Cuzco would be in keeping with conservative, post-Waterloo Europe: restoring a royal house 'so unjustly despoiled of its Throne' by the 'bloody revolution' of Pizarro's conquistadors. This enlightened Inca sovereign would be checked by 'a constitution drawn from the best that can be taken from those that govern England, the new Prussia, and Norway'. What's more, the 'very news of such an agreeable step' would excite the 'general enthusiasm of the inhabitants of the interior'. This Inca-king would be all things to all people: sufficiently respectable for foreign powers, thrillingly radical for the masses. 'In a word,' said another of the scheme's supporters, 'it is the only way of overcoming our misfortunes, restoring order, and speedily concluding the revolution.' San Martín weighed in: he thought the idea 'admirable' and with 'many-sided advantages'.

The Europhile politicians from Buenos Aires were 'stunned by this ridiculous and extravagant idea'. Some thought it was a hare-brained British scheme put in Belgrano's head while he visited London. The Argentine president Bartolomé Mitre would later scoff that it was entirely against public opinion. But there is ample evidence to suggest the opposite: that the Inca plan tapped into Indigenous and popular demands for self-rule, ideas that had percolated upwards over centuries to criollo elites.

Even as the congress deliberated, Graaner recorded, 'all the Indians are grieving for their reigning House'. They had slaughtered their white llamas, 'so their wool may not be made into white thread and contradict their mourning dress'. Every year, he explained, Andean communities staged 'macabre' re-enactments of Atahualpa's execution. One traveller in 1820 found they generated 'such a sense of distress that I never witnessed it without mingling my tears with theirs'.

The crackdown that followed Túpac Amaru's rebellion in 1780 had done little to dampen Inca-mania. When Humboldt, the Prussian scientist, toured Peru in 1802, he observed how 'expectations of the return of the Inca' existed wherever Quechua was spoken. Like a backpacker toting a dog-eared *Lonely Planet*, he used Garcilaso's history of Tawantinsuyu as his travel guide. In 1814, convalescing from his wounds sustained at San Lorenzo – and heavily self-medicating with laudanum, a tincture of opium – San Martín planned a reprint of the *Royal Commentaries of the Incas*: a 'Little Red Book' for Rioplatense revolutionaries. The United Provinces' new anthem described the Inca rising from his tomb as his sons renewed 'his patria's ancient splendour'. The country's coins and battle standards were stamped with an Inca sun: it still flutters on the flags of Argentina and Uruguay.

Emphasising the grandeur of lost pre-Columbian kingdoms provided ballast to the struggle for independence. It counteracted European prejudices that the New World was made to be dominated by the Old. Across Spanish America, criollos invoked the pre-conquest era – in songs, plays and poems, and in the names of warships, territories and newspapers – as the foundation of their national identity. They even sometimes identified as Indigenous. Revolutionary North America had seen a similar trend: the rioters who dumped crates of tea in Boston Harbor in 1773 wore Mohawk-style headdresses.

Such cosplaying may have also found sympathisers among the viceroyalty's Black population. Many were born in African monarchies assailed, like the Incas, by rapacious Europeans. When royalists attempted a coup in 1812, Valerio, an enslaved porteño, declared himself for the patriots: 'because the Indian king and the Black king are the same thing.'

In July 1816, a celebration of independence was held on the plains outside Tucumán. A host of 5,000 Indigenous and mestizo militiamen bristled with spears, swords and muskets. There were 'tears of joy' and 'rhapsodies of enthusiasm', the Swedish captain recorded, as those present 'swore over the very tomb of their comrades in arms to defend with their blood, their fortunes, and all that they held most dear the independence of the patria'. Belgrano then put his plan to the people, announcing 'the establishment of a great empire in South America, governed by the descendants of the imperial family of the Incas'.

According to Graaner, it was music to the crowd's ears: 'the Indians are as if electrified by this new proposal and flock to the flag of the sun. They arm themselves, believing that soon an army will be formed in Upper Peru, from Quito to Potosí, Lima and Cuzco.' A few days later, General Belgrano wrote another proclamation to the 'Peoples of Peru', selling his plan as a done deal: the congress had decided 'to revive and reclaim the blood of our Incas, drawn from their sons, to rule over us as our King'.

An all-out struggle was meanwhile unfolding around Chuquisaca, some 400 miles north. Almost every mountain valley was transformed into a *republiqueta* – a mobile, rebel statelet with its own patriot chieftain, flag and army. Ambushing Spanish patrols and plundering their estates, they were dozens of thorns in Fernando VII's side, drawing a steady trickle of royalist blood. Reports reached Tucumán of a 'beautiful lady' leading a mounted host of Indigenous warriors. She had hacked her way to the middle of a Spanish battalion, seized its standard at sabre-point, and captured 400 men.

This was Juana Azurduy. She learned to ride on her father's ranch, and picked up Quechua from her mother. Orphaned young, she was packed off to a Chuquisaca convent. She liked the warrior saints – Joan of Arc, Ignatius of Loyola – but little else about the monastic life. Kicked out at seventeen, she married her childhood sweetheart, Manuel Padilla. And when the revolution sweeping Upper Peru was crushed, the couple took to the hills, waging a war of resistance for twelve long years at the head of the Lagunas republiqueta. Legend would later tell that Azurduy had once given birth on the battlefield before returning to the fray; that she rode with a gaudily-dressed, all-female bodyguard known as the Amazons.

The reality was less glamorous. Padilla was captured and beheaded. Four of their children died while camped out in the freezing desert highlands. Just nine out of 102 republiqueta leaders survived. Belgrano named Azurduy a lieutenant colonel, while remarking that such valour was 'most unusual to her sex'. Novelists have imagined how she responded to such condescension. 'Is a woman's lot only to bear children, lose them, and sit back while so many others join forces to free us? What kind of justice do you all preach if you still enslave women and bar us from all ideals?'

The patriarchy remained intact. But the proclamation of Tawantinsuyu's rebirth fed into rumblings of class war. In August 1816, a band of gaucho irregulars in Jujuy proclaimed their loyalty to the 'dynasty of the Incas'. They were commanded by Martín Miguel de Güemes, a well-off criollo from Salta known for capturing a British frigate grounded off Buenos Aires with a cavalry charge in 1806. But his soldiers were of more humble station: Antonio Visaura, a Black cobbler who rose to become a gaucho colonel; an unruly, mixed-race sergeant, Vicente 'Panana' Martínez, who was stirring up the masses in the countryside. In some versions, María Remedios del Valle rode with them, having sprung herself from a Spanish prison camp after Ayohuma. In September, they were joined by Azurduy, who had fled Upper Peru to fight on, unwilling to 'witness the humiliation of my patria'.

Further north, the summons to the Inca's banners was repeated by an unlikely figure. Juan José Feliciano Fernández Campero was the marquis of a vast Andean fiefdom at Yavi, straddling the border with Upper Peru. The aristocrat had outfitted a force of Quechua-speaking warriors dubbed the Peruvian Regiment. Diego Cala – his Indigenous second-in-command – intercepted and annihilated royalist posses, tipped off by local llama herders. Campero and his band now swore to the continent's liberation. 'To arms, Americans! You will see the empire of our Incas reborn, and the Court of Cuzco flourish,' he vowed. 'Viva South America! Viva our beloved patria! Viva the Peruvian empire and her sons in union!'

For seven years, these gun-toting gauchos and poncho-clad guerrillas held the Quebrada de Humahuaca – a winding valley that was the only road to Upper Peru, Cuzco and Lima – against all comers. A Spanish general marvelled at their 'confidence, self-assurance, and cold-bloodedness'. They were 'better horsemen than the Cossacks', shooting from the saddle and reloading as fast as line infantry. San Martín was astounded by the 'intrepidness and enthusiasm' with which they threw themselves at heavily armed royalist regiments. His superior in Buenos Aires praised the 'bold peasant patriots' of the north. But they were no ordinary cowboys or campesinos, but great-grandchildren of the Diaguita, fighting to avenge their ancestors and transform the present.

In November 1817, the royalists ambushed the Peruvian Regiment as they heard Mass at Yavi. Cala was executed on the spot. Campero died in chains. Güemes was killed in 1821, just weeks before his men pushed the last royalist soldiers out of the Río de la Plata. The papers in Buenos Aires celebrated the death of an 'abominable' strongman: 'That's one cacique less.' Azurduy died in poverty aged eighty-two, and was buried in a common grave. Once the shared dangers and freedoms of revolution had passed, women were 'once more relegated to family life', writes Carmen de Mora, 'and the heroines of Independence condemned to oblivion'.

The gaucho and republiqueta wars of the highlands have likewise been treated as a footnote in Latin America's liberation. Yet even Bolívar conceded that their contribution had been crucial. When he strolled into Upper Peru in 1824 without firing a shot, the upper classes named their new nation after him. The Venezuelan liberator responded with rare humility: 'this country should not be called Bolivia in my honour, but Padilla or Azurduy, for it was they who made it free.'

MADMEN, ONIONS AND OPIUM

While the gauchos held the royalists at bay in the north-west, San Martín was a long way from the action. He had been made governor of Cuyo, a backwater province of vineyards and cows in the south. It seemed like a voluntary demotion. But his secretive designs soon became clear.

From September 1814, San Martín transformed Cuyo's capital, Mendoza – a sleepy town in the shadow of the Andes – into a hive of activity. He set up forges and factories, amassed a legion of pack animals, sent guerrillas into the mountains, put women to work stitching uniforms, and purloined their jewellery. His objective: a total war economy to equip an army created from scratch. This force would march over the Andean passes to the west into royalist-occupied Chile – the country that would determine 'the fate of the revolution'.

Merchants and messengers sometimes braved the scorching sun, suffocating altitudes and snowstorms of the cordillera. But never before had an army of thousands made this journey. If they arrived in one piece, they would have to defeat the crack troops of imperial Spain, fresh from routing Napoleon's armies. And a fleet would then have to be cobbled together to ferry the survivors – circumventing the deserts of northern Chile – to even stiffer fighting against 'the fortress of tyranny' in Lima. For some, 'el Rey José', cooped up in his Mendocino kingdom, had gone mad.

The plan was in place. But the men were not. San Martín's mounted grenadiers were reinforced by gaucho riders and a volunteer company of English, Scottish and Irish riflemen, prisoners from the battle for Buenos Aires who had settled in Mendoza. The remnants of Chile's patriot forces straggled over the mountains, eating their mules to survive, led by Bernardo O'Higgins – the bastard son of a poor Irishman turned viceroy of Peru. But the numbers still fell short. 'There is no alternative,' San Martín wrote. 'We can survive only by putting every slave under arms. I have studied our soldiers and I know that only the blacks are really good infantry.'

Mendoza hadn't been isolated from the currents of revolution. A third of the province's population was Black and mixed-race. In 1812, a plot had been hatched in the town's taverns, churchyards and fraternities. Led by Joaquín Fretes – a twenty-four-year-old music teacher from Guinea – dozens of Black residents planned to storm the barracks and demand their freedom to join the patriot armies. Some, citing Haiti's example, also wanted to shoot their enslavers. The conspiracy was foiled. But the defendants were granted their first wish, and enlisted in a Buenos Aires battalion.

So when San Martín ordered Cuyo's households and monasteries to donate two-thirds of their able-bodied, enslaved workers to the cause in 1815, many would have jumped at the chance. These new recruits, combined with freedmen and runaways in the local militia, added up to around 2,500 Black soldiers. Most were enrolled into the 7th and 8th Battalions: a backbone of shock troops that would prove decisive. In total, half of the soldiers in this new Army of the Andes were born in Angola, the Gulf of Guinea, the Congo and even distant Mozambique, or descended from Africans transported to South America.

It is a strange irony: people enslaved by the Old World taking up arms to free the New. Many are forced recruits. But some are idealistic volunteers, or veterans blooded in a decade of battles from Buenos Aires to the future Bolivia, who see in the struggle against Spain a chance to win their own liberty and forge a new society of equals. Men like Francisco Estrada, who fled enslavement and joined the patriot advance on Montevideo in 1811, pledging to fight 'under the flags of freedom'. Or like Antonio Castro, who had reported for duty in Buenos Aires in 1815, ready to 'sacrifice himself for the just cause of his patria'.

In stark contrast to his contemporaries, San Martín values the service of Black freedmen and the formerly enslaved. They are more than just grunts, cheap manpower. As well as making the 'best infantry', he writes, many are officer material. He has decreed that they can serve as corporals and sergeants, and in distinguished navy-blue jackets with scarlet collars, green piping and gold braid. Meanwhile, the general's pains are attended to by Juan Isidro Zapata, a Black medical expert from Lima and the army's senior doctor. His meals are served by a Black servant, María Demetria Escalada de Soler. His trusted aide is Andrés Ibañez, a West African prince enslaved at the age of fifteen. The band of the 11th Battalion is made up of Bantu farmhands: overheard singing in the fields of Mendoza, trained in the Academy of Buenos Aires, and equipped with Belgian instruments.

News of the unlikely force being assembled in Mendoza reached Spanish ears. In 1816, San Martín sent a messenger to Casimiro Marcó del Pont – the royalist governor of Chile – bearing the United Provinces' declaration of independence. The blue-blooded Galician dandy had it burnt in the main square of Santiago. He replied with an ugly swipe: 'I sign with a white hand, unlike that of your general, which is black.' Meanwhile, Vicente San Bruno, del Pont's sadistic chief of police, stripped and mutilated patriot prisoners and any civilians found out after curfew.

San Martín scoured the United Provinces for tents, bugles and uniforms, and drilled his soldiers with the sabre. Most of Mendoza's church bells were melted down for cannons and bayonets; a quartermaster manufactured cartridges, grenades, horseshoes and packs. After three years of preparations, by January 1817, with the snows in the passes thawing, the Army of the Andes was ready to march: 10,600 mules, 1,600 horses, 700 cattle and 5,000 men and women.

San Martín outlines their objectives: the liberation of Spanish America from three centuries of tyranny, and the forging of 'one single nation' in the place of half-a-dozen isolated Iberian colonies. 'The continent will become unified,' he proclaims. 'Nothing must occupy our minds but the larger objective of universal freedom.' It is these soldiers 'that will carry this task to completion'.

His troops could have dismissed it as a drug addict's delirium. But many share in their general's zeal. An exuberant fiesta sends them off. They march through arches of artificial flowers; peals of bells explode from steeples; salvoes fill the streets with smoke. San Martín produces a sheaf of paper: intercepted letters, he says. The Spanish plan to enslave any Black POWs in the plantations, or sell them for their worth in sugar. Their flag is unfurled: a mountain, a red revolutionaries' cap, an Inca sun. 'This is the first flag to have been raised in America,' San Martín tells them. 'Do you swear to uphold it, and die in its defence, as I do?' The answer is deafening: 'We swear.'

Then, there are bullfights: flamboyant gauchos, chieftains from the Pampas and African soldiers driving lances and sabres into the thundering mass of muscle. The dripping genitals of a slaughtered bull are offered to the general's young wife, Remedios, who gingerly accepts. Few could miss the meaning: the very symbol of haughty Spanishness, unmanned by these subaltern insurgents. San Martín allows himself a chuckle. Their bravery bodes well for what lies ahead. 'The patria', he remarks to a nearby officer, 'has need of these madmen.'

A strange and fearful sensation of biting cold and painful pressure at your temples. Your breathing feels ragged and shallow, like slowly drowning on land. The piercing summer sun – over 4,000 metres closer than normal – refracts off snow whipped by the wind into frozen waves, dazzling your eyes. Your throat and nose dry out and fill with dust. Your lips become bleeding scabs.

There is little end in sight: trudging for weeks, deeper and higher into banks of jagged purple teeth. You, or your parents, have crossed one ocean in chains in the deathly dark of a ship's hull to come here. Now, you are journeying rifle in hand over another, a former seabed 200 million years old. White ammonite fossils speckle the scree. You move among petrified trees, smothered by prehistoric cascades of lava.

Single-file along sheer precipices, you edge past the frozen corpses of your comrades. Pack mules lie broken-limbed and screaming in the abyss. Thirty-degree heat during the day, ten below freezing at night. And little firewood to stave off the cold that stabs through ponchos and blankets, before even these precious embers – and pipes and cigarillos – are smothered to evade the eyes of enemy spies. Crosses dot the trail, the graves of previous travellers struck down by the *puna*: altitude sickness. This unnerving disease lingers like a miasma at these altitudes and slowly suffocates its victims. The cure, to chew raw onions and garlic, is cold comfort.

The Army of the Andes has split up. The Black freedmen of the 11th battle royalist detachments, leaving the Uspallata pass awash with blood and scattered with the dead. Securing the plains north of Santiago on 8 February, they are by now all 'on foot and tired, but say what you will, and we'll march', their commander reports.

But the main force faces an even tougher crossing via Los Patos, forty miles further north. Battered numb by hail, they trudge deeper into the cordillera, now mere specks at the bottom of ravines. As they climb to 4,500 metres above sea level, O'Higgins fears the men 'in peril from the intense cold'. The expedition's commander sags atop his mule, asthmatic, old wounds aching, coughing up blood and swigging laudanum. One night, he huddles under his cloak by a guttering campfire. 'What keeps me awake is not the resistance of the enemy,' San Martín broods, 'but the crossing of these enormous mountains.'

Yet in the morning, he emerges from a cave with studied self-assurance, knocking back aguardiente and smoking a cigar. He calls for music. The band of the 8th strike up the anthem of their new nation, the strident notes bouncing around the desolate crags. The Black liberators rise from under their cloaks, as if birthed from the very mountain. They shoulder their weapons, mount weary mules, and move upwards towards the distant pass.

San Martín would later try to describe their collective ordeal: 'an army travelling with the cumbersome baggage of subsistence for almost a month, weapons, munitions, and other camp followers, along a path of 100 leagues, bisected by steep slopes, gorges, crossings, deep abysses, sliced by four mountain ranges; in sum, where the toughness of the ground is matched only by the harshness of the elements.'

Yet precisely what happened on their long march is still enveloped in mystery. And when it comes to what the rank-and-file of the Army of the Andes would have seen and thought – marching ever upwards into an alien environment in sandals stuffed with rags, preparing to die in the service of an imagined nation – the silence of the archive is even more profound. In such contexts, all that is left is speculation.

To aid this speculation, I plan a similar journey with a group of friends. To traverse Los Patos would take weeks, and some serious survival skills. So we walk in the footsteps of a smaller column under Captain José León Lemos, who went over the Portillo pass south of Mendoza to draw away the royalist army. Charles Darwin made the same journey during his voyage with the *Beagle* in 1834. Compared to the Uspallata, it is 'rather more lofty', he wrote, and 'more dangerous during a snow-storm. For these reasons it is but little used, especially late in the seasons.'

The night before our departure is nearly as raucous as that of the Army of the Andes. We nurse hangovers on the bus that drops us in the foothills. Sweet-smelling wildflowers push through the grassy slopes, rushing water sounds in the air. Argentine gendarmes stamp our passports, share our whisky and let us bed down in a stable. We will need help to ford rivers, they tell me: look out for Walter Martínez. 'He's the trustworthy man round these parts.'

The next day we walk up a narrowing swathe of green munched by cattle. Gauchos in berets with neckerchiefs and knives lounge about at a lean-to of wood and stones. Heavy, grey skies, rumbling thunder. Seb, normally irrepressible, slows down. His face turns crimson and puffy. It's clearly the dreaded puna. The Malbec back in Mendoza probably hasn't helped.

We pitch our tents, taking the following day to acclimatise in an eerie, silent valley called Las Yaretas. The elongated skulls of mules leer at us, scraps of hide preserved by the rarefied air. Dark banks of cloud sail up the pass and settle. As Matthew uses our satellite phone to text his girlfriend, I read Darwin's notes from the same spot: 'The great mountains, bright with the full moon, seemed impending over us on all sides, as if we had been buried at the bottom of some deep crevice.'

Next morning, we follow winding switchbacks through the snow-line. The green Tunuyán valley sprawls out below. I peer inside a sturdy refuge, formerly an Argentine military base, and make myself known to the gauchos. Walter is there, drinking with the others; strangely dapper in a pink flannel shirt and black, baggy *bombachas*. He offers to help us cross the nearby river the following day.

Sundown is spectacular at this altitude, with a pink glow on white peaks and a blue aurora overhead. Then, neon-lit nebulae, bright white smudges against a coal sky. Seb sprawls by the fire, sipping a concoction of whisky, lemon juice and water straight off the glacier. 'I call it the Lemos,' he grins. Nightfall brings a curtain of cold; I turn down another nightcap in favour of my sleeping bag.

Walter silently clops past in the mid-morning and we fall in step. We take it in turns to splash though the churning, murky Tunuyán atop a muscular white mare and lithe piebald, roped to the gaucho's own mount. The horses place their hooves surely among slippery, submerged boulders. Walter fords one final time and calls out behind him: 'Good luck, Don Lorenzo.' We grin at our brief encounter with such an unruffled character. The gauchos who dwelled in these passes in 1817 perhaps watched the Army of the Andes troop past with as little outward emotion.

The next day, we splash barefoot through another freezing river unfolding off a lick of ice, traversing grey, shifting scree onto the slope of the Piuquenes range. Even the *Beagle* expedition's pack animals halted here every fifty yards. My legs feel leaden and I start to do the same. As their mounts perished, most of the Army of the Andes likewise found themselves struggling upwards on foot. Tom eventually hoists my pack alongside his own and steadily brings up the rear, as dogged as one of Darwin's mules.

Then we reach the top of the pass. The only thing marking the border is a rusted iron frame inscribed with CHILE-ARGENTINA. Thrown about by sixty-mile-per-hour gusts, we unfurl the flags we have carried for the different nations of the 1817 march: Irish, British, Argentine, Chilean, a Pehuenche symbol for the expedition's native guides and mestizo militiamen; a pan-African emblem for its Black revolutionary patriots.

Downwards again: through sheets of grubby snow, sliding down a dark gravelly pumice that jolts our joints and kicks up plumes of filmy dust. Reaching the trailhead, we strip and lower ourselves, sun-burned and brown with filth, into a sulphurous hot spring. A pair of startled tourists soon jump out and back into their 4x4. We trudge on for a few more hours and hitch a lift down to Santiago the following day.

After nearly a week's walking, we are only fit for a shower, a five-hour siesta, and a stiff-legged shamble around the dive bars of Providencia. This has been a comparatively short stroll over the mountains in hiking boots, with nutritious rations, warm clothing and unusually fine weather. But I still feel drained, my feet are blistered and my muscles are painfully cramped.

The Army of the Andes had no such respite as it crossed into Chile. The advance guard surprised royalist outposts, and hot on the heels of the fleeing enemy, the army reunited on 9 February. The two-week march, San Martín wrote, 'has been a triumph'. But his men were exhausted, many of his cannons had yet to arrive, and the serious fighting still lay ahead.

Around 2,500 hardened Spanish troops are amassed nearby, at a hill-top estate north-west of Santiago called Chacabuco. The patriot army creeps close under cover of darkness. At dawn on 12 February 1817, a heavily dosed-up San Martín orders the attack. The headstrong O'Higgins hurls himself at the enemy with his Black battalions: 'Soldiers! Live with honour or die with glory! The brave, follow me! Columns, charge!'

Taking heavy casualties, they are forced backwards. But San Martín races to the rescue with his mounted grenadiers, smashing into the Spanish flank. O'Higgins and his men return to the fray with a fierce charge of cold steel that breaks the enemy squares. There is time for score-settling amid the carnage. An African soldier fells a trooper of the elite Talavera Regiment with his bayonet. He shoots him for good measure, before cutting off his lip and moustache. 'You want sugar?' he shouts: 'Here's your sugar!'

It is a stunning victory. Six hundred Spaniards are killed. The 500 prisoners include San Bruno, the merciless police chief. The 8th Battalion protect him from a vengeful mob who pelt him with filth as he rides, backwards atop a mule, into Santiago. Within a few days he is tried and sent 'crying like a child' to the noose.

San Martín's scouts chase down del Pont – trembling, flimsily disguised in a poncho and sombrero – before he can board a ship for Lima. Humbled by the Black infantry of the Army of the Andes, the Spanish aristocrat is brought before their commander. San Martín can't resist a wisecrack: 'General! Give me that white hand.'

The army's Black musicians provide the soundtrack to the celebrations that follow. A pair of trumpeters play the United Provinces' anthem as the guests toast their victory and smash their glasses on the floor. When O'Higgins is sworn in as Supreme Director of Chile a few days later, upon hearing the music played by the band of the 8th, the crowd 'believed themselves in heaven'.

Yet San Martín soon found himself depressed, trapped in 'a continuous ill-humour, which corrodes my sad existence'. Despite the efforts of friends to intervene, he was now gulping down a cocktail of opiates every morning. Royalists were still at large in the south. December 1817 brings worse news: some 6,000 Spanish reinforcements have landed, headed for Santiago. In late March, near Talca, they attack by night, putting the patriot army to flight. San Martín is rumoured to have shot himself. Santiago is pitched into panic. Looters smash up shops; women faint in the street; the upper classes flee into the mountains.

San Martín and O'Higgins finally appear and rally their forces. They meet the Spanish at Maipú, two miles south-west of the city, on Sunday, 5 April 1818. The men are given wine and aguardiente to stiffen their resolve. Deserters will be shot. 'This battle is going to decide the fate of all America,' San Martín tells them: better 'to die on the field of honour than at the hands of our executioners'. There is birdsong, the perfume of orange blossom, distant church bells. O'Higgins, badly wounded in the royalist ambush, directs workers digging trenches in the streets. The Black patriots showed a 'silent and gloomy ferocity', wrote Samuel Haigh, a British merchant on San Martín's staff. They 'declared that they would neither give nor ask quarter'.

Outgunned and outnumbered, San Martín decides to attack the enemy head-on. It is a suicidal gamble: one aide declares him insane and flees. The general sends his Black battalions against the formidable Burgos Regiment, trusting that – while their zeal will stop them from breaking – the royalists will push them backwards. As the crackle of gunfire crescendos, the enemy fall into San Martín's trap: their line becomes skewed and overstretched. His cavalry wheel around them in a pincer movement with the 7th and 8th, who hurtle into the action once more. 'The shock was tremendous,' wrote Haigh. 'The firing almost instantly ceased, and the two parties crossed bayonets.' No time, now, amid choking clouds of dust and smoke, to load muskets: only a desperate struggle of blade against blade, body against body.

Eventually, the shouts of 'Viva el Rey!' give way to 'Viva la patria!' and 'Viva la libertad!' Falucho, a soldier of the 8th, slices through the mass of men to seize a royalist standard. The Spanish army breaks and scatters, 'pursued and butchered by their merciless foe'. Veterans of the Napoleonic wars say they have never seen a gorier sight. A farm where the retreating royalists stage an ambush is left clogged with corpses, its every surface 'clotted and sprinkled with brains and blood'. Two thousand royalists have been killed and 3,000 captured. 'We have just obtained a complete victory,' San Martín scribbles to O'Higgins. 'The country is free.' As priests let off fireworks from the steeples, the

Chilean Supreme Director rides out, his arm in a sling, and embraces the Rioplatense liberator amid the carnage.

The Black patriots had 'borne the brunt of the action against the finest Spanish regiment, and had lost the principal part of their forces', wrote Haigh. He saw an old veteran 'crying with rage' when prevented from shooting captive Spanish officers. Many were doubtless traumatised after surviving a second bloodbath in scarcely a year. Francisco Fierro – a formerly enslaved twenty-eight-year-old from Guinea, forcibly recruited in Buenos Aires in 1813 – was wounded as he fought bravely at Maipú. Anaesthetising himself with alcohol, he tried to desert soon afterwards; his death sentence was commuted for service at sea until the war was over.

The valour of Fierro and his comrades was the linchpin of the dazzling victory, vindicating San Martín's audacious Andean campaign. It does them an injustice to assert, like one Chilean writer, that they were 'cannon fodder in a global contest that was too distant for them to understand'. The evidence suggests otherwise: that many formerly enslaved fighters saw a close parallel between the continent's liberation and their own. Contemporaries were struck by their revolutionary fervour: 'the blacks who have served in our armies', wrote William Miller, another British comrade of San Martín, 'deserve the highest praise' for their 'constancy, valour, and patriotism'.

The foreign stranglehold on South America could finally be broken. Nearly fifteen years later, Haigh thought that without the victory at Maipú, Peru and Chile might have 'remained under the crown of Spain to this day'. Thousands of miles north, news of the battle reached Bolívar, still holed up in the swamps of eastern Venezuela. 'The day of America', he rejoiced, 'has arrived.'

Dispiriting years of drift were to follow. Civil war erupted. The United Provinces, a state that once had designs of encompassing all of Spanish America, was no more. Yet in 1820, San Martín's troops still embarked for Peru. 'The world waits to declare us rebels if we are defeated,' the general told his men, 'or to recognise our rights if we triumph.'

San Martín captured Lima, declared Peru's independence and was named its Protector, modelling himself on Oliver Cromwell. He abolished Indigenous servitude and the trade in enslaved Africans, and scoured the sugar plantations of the coast for new recruits. Support for the Inca plan had cooled, but he still cast around for a spare European prince to serve as emperor of Peru, even inviting George IV to send a relative. After all, Walter Raleigh had returned from the New World in 1596 with a beguiling legend – that 'Inglatierra' was fated to rescue the 'Ingas' from Spanish rule. The prophecy had circulated ever since on both sides of the Atlantic, and even been found scrawled on temple walls in Cuzco.

San Martín came up with an unusual way of emphasising Peru's ancient credentials and scientific potential to would-be royal signings. In 1822, he sent an 'Inca mummy' to the Hanoverian-British monarch in London. But rather than donate the desiccated corpse – an anonymous Andean from a cave near Lima – to the British Museum, the king palmed it off to the Royal College of Surgeons. Here, it was exhibited alongside a woman who had been embalmed by her husband, a dentist.

There was another obstacle in the way of restoring the throne of the Incas. Their ancient capital had become the last redoubt of Spanish rule in South America. Some 20,000 royalists – backed by Indigenous Andean troops – were entrenched in Cuzco. San Martín's expedition sustained heavy losses as it tried to dislodge them. He needed backup.

Bolívar had meanwhile raced to match San Martín's achievements. His ranks swelled by British and German volunteers, as well as hardy cowboys from the plains of the Orinoco, he freed his home country. Then he staged his own march over the Andes – far more desperate, improvised and deadly – to liberate Colombia. In July 1822, the two liberators met at the port of Guayaquil, Ecuador. What exactly transpired will forever remain a secret, but their political and personal differences were clear. San Martín felt that only a constitutional monarch could restrain Peru's warring factions; Bolívar preferred to found another republic. Bolívar wanted the glory of conquering Peru to himself: he would not even accept San Martín's offer to serve under him.

That evening, there was a ball in the Protector of Peru's honour, Bolívar pirouetting as his guest ruminated. At two in the morning, the victor of Maipú slipped away to catch the tide. Within eighteen months, he had left South America, never to return. Bolívar's parting gift, as 'a memento of his sincere friendship': a portrait of himself.

Abandoned by Buenos Aires, distrusted by their new Venezuelan–Colombian commanders, the remainder of the Army of the Andes were left in limbo. Now garrisoning El Callao, a fortress outside Lima, and subsisting on worm-ridden jerky, they hadn't been paid for year. The new recruits lacked the esprit de corps of the Andes veterans. And on the night of 5 February 1824, the rank-and-file seized control of the fort, led by a drummer sergeant named Dámaso Moyano. The son of enslaved servants to a wealthy Mendoza household, he was 'marked' – one contemporary recalled – 'with the stamp of Judas, in the form of a horrific scar that crossed half of his face'.

The mutineers simply demand their back pay, and to return home as free citizens. The patriot commanders seem to acquiesce. But the rebel ringleaders learn they're to be executed. So Moyano escalates, springing royalist officers from the dungeons, who promote the conspirators and hoist the Spanish flag. Many of the Andes veterans are shot as they try to fight back or flee. One hides their flag in a trunk. In the following months, Colonel Moyano leads his men in stiff fighting around Lima – on the orders of the king of Spain.

He would later claim to have been a royalist sleeper cell waiting to strike. 'Inspired', his service record reads, 'perhaps by a divine impulse,' he tried 'to prove his faithfulness to the sovereign even at the cost of his life.' More plausible is that the Black veterans had little choice. They had fought and bled to liberate lands thousands of miles from their own, but their generals had backed them into a corner: it was disloyalty or death.

In December 1824, Bolívar's legions delivered the knockout blow to Spanish rule at the Battle of Ayacucho, halfway between Lima and Cuzco. They were supported by only 'the mere skeleton' of the mounted grenadiers who had fought all the way with San Martín since the skirmish at San Lorenzo in 1813. Haigh watched them embark for home, thin horses and thinner men. Ground down by attrition and desertion, 'ill paid, ill fed, and in a most undisciplined state', the Army of the Andes had ceased to exist.

With it died the best chance for realising the vision of a united continent. Writing from exile in 1815, Bolívar had also fantasised of 'forming the entire New World into a single nation'. Given that Spanish America, at least, shared 'a language, many customs, and a religion, it ought therefore to have a single federal government over its different states'. His dream never materialised further than Gran Colombia, an awkward conjoining of Venezuela, Colombia and Ecuador that survived just a year after Bolívar died – on his way to exile once more – in 1830.

'All those who have served the revolution,' Bolívar famously lamented, 'have ploughed the sea.' Distinct national identities had already taken root. The distances were too great, topographies too confounding, local powerbrokers too parochial. Latin America was divided,

Bolívar admitted, by 'distant climes, diverse circumstances, opposed interests' and 'dissimilar characters'. But San Martín allowed himself a flicker of nostalgia for the romantic ideal that had blossomed under his protection.

In 1822, a solitary figure on a mule picked his way over the Piuquenes pass on his way to exile. He wore a Chilean poncho and a broad-brimmed Guayaquil sombrero; a royal standard borne to Peru by Pizarro was stowed in his luggage. Met halfway by an old comrade, he paused to rest. 'We had better descend from this height,' José de San Martín finally exhaled, 'where in other times I gazed upon America.'

SOVEREIGNS IN BLACK TAILCOATS

In 1848, a visitor from Argentina encountered an elderly African pedlar selling candles on the street in Lima. He had been recruited in Buenos Aires, he said, and fought with the 8th Battalion all the way through Chile and Peru, dodging the mutiny at Callao because he was sick in hospital. From his pocket, he produced a paper containing a grisly proof: the Spaniard's moustache he had sliced off thirty years before at Chacabuco.

San Martín made it back over the Andes, but most of his men did not. Of some 2,500 Black soldiers who marched over the mountains, as few as 143 returned. Most had died in battle, perished from illness and the elements, or had been executed by one side or another. Yet whether through valour, shrewdness or sheer luck, some had survived.

Andrés Ibañez, the West African prince, retired to run a tavern in Buenos Aires, having earned the rank of captain and five medals for his valour under fire. Perhaps he sometimes visited María Demetria, cook and fellow member of San Martín's staff, to reminisce about their journey over the mountains. In 1880, she was living a block from the Iglesia Mater Misericordiae, the church that served the city's burgeoning Italian population: the old Buenos Aires clinging on in the shadow of the new. Though aged 105, a diarist recorded, she was still finding servants for wealthy households in exchange for a meagre pension. Falucho, the hero of Maipú, was living in Peru in 1830 and recalled his general fondly.

Many other Black veterans were left disabled and destitute. Some were even forced to return to their former masters. In 1826, María Remedios del Valle – battlefield nurse, prison breaker, guerrilla – was discovered begging on the streets of the Argentine capital. Her husband and sons had perished in the wars of independence. Her former comrades, from 'the foremost general to the lowest officer of the army', intervened. 'She is singular in her patriotism,' they insisted; 'There was no battle in Peru in which she could not be found.' The infirm old soldier was given a salary and the honorary rank of sergeant major – although not before having to present 'her body full of bullet wounds, and covered moreover with the stripes of lashes', as searing proof of her service.

Moyano secured safe passage to Spain for seventy-six of the Callao mutineers. But the rest were captured and sent before a patriot firing squad; only their ringleader made it out alive. A few years later, a Spanish frigate arrived in Cuba with a Black brigadier on board, 'decorated with this rank for services to the King in Peru'. A serial survivor, Brigadier Dámaso Moyano died sometime after 1845, leaving behind his young Spanish wife and their son.

Taking up arms, as well as securing many their own freedom, also weakened the institution of slavery. Emancipation was painfully slow and came with small print: the children of the enslaved had to remain low-paid workers of their 'patron' into adulthood. Yet through saving up money, suing their captors, or demonstrating incredible bravery on the battlefield, many won their liberty against the odds. 'They weren't given their freedom,' the Afrodescendant Argentine historian Magdalena Candioti emphasises: 'they conquered it.'

And then, the conventional story goes, they faded away. Common explanations for this vanishing act include war, fever and mass migration to Uruguay. More importantly, those of African descent were encouraged to ditch the 'label of Africanness' and 'blend into the dominant mass'. Argentina's 1853 constitution enshrined the state's duty – which still remains in the charter – to 'foster European immigration'.

As millions of migrants from the Old World disembarked, one memoirist keenly felt the washerwomen, street hawkers and piano teachers of his youth 'slipping past our eyes like figures in a magic lantern'. Across the river in Uruguay, in 1880, the papers reported the passing of Mariana Artigas, queen of the Banguela nation, at the incredible age of 130. 'Day by day they disappear,' wrote El Siglo, 'the few remaining representatives of the African race who stepped foot on this soil under the chains of slavery.'

Yet by marrying whites and Indigenous elites, changing their dress, and defending their status in court, Afro-Argentine women and their children could swerve the rigid hierarchies of the day. Military prowess could also confer this whitening on paper: Antonio Porobio, the Angolan veteran of the independence wars, was described as white in an 1838 census. Today, nearly one in ten Argentines is descended from Africans, according to a recent study. Their legacy also lives on in tango, in soul food, in slang. Since 2013, Argentina has celebrated Black History Day on 8 November: in memory of María Remedios del Valle, who died on that date in 1847.

Chileans have likewise tended to think of their country as largely European. But enslaved and free Africans made up twelve per cent of the population by 1800. And in the past decade, hundreds of thousands of people have abandoned Haiti and South America's Caribbean-facing countries for one of the region's steadier nations.

Walking around Santiago after a few years away, the change is obvious. Teenagers, sporting sharp fades and bantering in *kreyòl*, crowd around the buskers and clowns in the Plaza de Armas. A Haitian jazz band, snazzy in suits and dresses, pose for photos on the Santa Lucía hill. In search of calories after our amble over the Andes, rather than a traditional *completo* – a hot dog smothered in avocado and mayo – the go-to late-night snack now seems to be a starchy maize pancake bulging with cheese: the Venezuelan–Colombian *arepa*.

Some have found these changes hard to stomach. In late 2021, a blond, far-right populist called José Antonio Kast was nearly elected president, promising to dig a trench along the border to keep foreign criminals out. He plans to run again in 2025. Many migrants believe that 'Chile is a country where you can make the American dream come true,' says Leandro Cortés, who works for a Jesuit charity in Antofagasta, a major migrant hub. 'When they get here, they find that the reality is not quite as lovely. The Chileans are a bit like the English in Europe,' he smiles. 'They think they're better than the others.' Leandro comes from Arica, on the border with Peru, where Spain transported many enslaved Africans. 'I'm an Afro-descendant,' he explains. 'Black people are part of our history.'

In Santiago, I leave behind the crowds in the plaza and enter the quiet of the National History Museum. Upstairs is a small watercolour of the Battle of Chacabuco, painted around forty years later. Almost all of those depicted, marching steadily into royalist gunfire with levelled bayonets in scarlet-trimmed caps, are Black. Along with San Martín, other officers of the Army of the Andes felt that their sacrifice should not be forgotten.

'It matters little that few of you remain who saw the days of victory,' Enrique Martínez told them in 1823. Remains of their comrades, holy relics of these 'heroic defenders of America', lay scattered on battle-fields from the Atlantic shores of Argentina, via the plains of Chile and deserts of Peru, to the snowy slopes of Ecuadorian volcanoes. 'Four great republics of the New World', he said, 'owe you gratitude and remembrance.'

In 1822, a baleful octogenarian was ferried ashore to Buenos Aires. Juan Bautista Túpac Amaru had been captured when his half-brother's rebellion was crushed in Peru in 1781. After a horrific voyage across the Atlantic – chained to the mainmast with his relatives' corpses, scram-bling for bones thrown by the crew – he had spent four decades in prison and poverty in North Africa and Spain. Now, he was billed as the leading pretender to resurrect the long-vacant Inca throne. The local press fell about laughing at the idea: a king 'in Indian sandals', an emperor 'with dirty shoes'. If such a descendant truly existed, one critic snorted, 'we would probably have to drag him, drunk and covered in rags, from an alehouse'.

In fact, there were several suitable candidates. Belgrano, unveiling his Inca plan at the Congress of Tucumán in 1816, may have had Dionisio Inca Yupanqui in mind. A Cuzco-born noble, he had served with distinction in Spain as a lieutenant colonel of dragoons. At an emer-gency pan-Hispanic congress amid Napoleon's invasion, Yupanqui denounced centuries of abuses against his countrymen as an 'Inca, Indian and American'. Equality between the nations of the empire, he insisted – as French bombs rained upon Cádiz – would reconcile Span-ish America and save Spain itself: 'A people that oppresses another cannot be free.'

But in the end, the merchants of Buenos Aires knew that a constitu-tional monarch in Cuzco would dilute their power. In 1817, they relocated the congress to their own city, where they kicked the Inca plan into the long grass. The so-called 'republicans and democrats' of the capital, one contemporary from Tucumán pointed out acidly, 'admit to being content with their country's destiny depending on half a dozen sovereigns in black tailcoats'.

Güemes, Belgrano and San Martín – the plan's most prominent backers – were all dead or in exile. San Martín refused to take part in the civil wars tearing his patria apart. Now widowed, he departed for Europe in 1823 with his daughter, Mercedes. He never set foot in South

America again, ending his days in Boulogne-sur-Mer in 1850, wracked
by old wounds, addiction and illness. Juan Bautista Túpac Amaru died
in 1827, having never returned to Peru, whose politicians had also settled on a republic. Spanish and criollo authorities alike censored all
mention of Túpac Amaru II, writing the Andean rebels who took up his
mantle out of the Age of Revolutions. As the streets of Lima were gilded
by guano, Peru dropped the reference to the Incas from its national
anthem.

Across Spanish America, as the nineteenth century wore on, Indigenous heroes were ditched in favour of the criollo generals of independence,
those gallant white men with the luxurious sideburns. Indigenism had
galvanised the masses and polite society alike for the fight, but could
now be discarded. By the 1840s, Argentines had forgotten how wildly
popular the promised Inca utopia had proved in Tucumán, Jujuy and
Chuquisaca: it was, they now guffawed, a 'truly crazy idea', 'theatrical
nonsense', a 'burlesque'. Their nation's essence was European, not
Andean: they came from the boats, not the mountains.

Truth be told, most criollos had always preferred vanished pre-
Columbians to their living descendants. One patriot leader in Upper
Peru tellingly complained that trying to win over captured Indigenous
royalists was 'like speaking to thin air, as though it were a foreign country which we had to reconquer. They did not know what their patria
was,' or whether 'it was a man or a woman. As for the king, they knew
him, his government was well established, his laws were respected and
duly observed. So they were put to death, all eleven of them.'

In light of what came after, the failure of the transnational, egalitarian project sketched out at Tucumán in 1816 is one of the great tragedies
of Latin American history. It might in time have produced 'a great
Republic of the United States of South America'. Union and liberty are
no guarantee of fraternity and equality. The USSA, like the USA, likely
would have failed to live up to its ideals. But the merciless wars that
followed – between South American nations, and within them – might
have been avoided.

O'Higgins was toppled by Chile's oligarchs in 1823. He headed into
exile in Peru, never to see his patria again. San Martín, the Argentine
Liberator, wrote to his Chilean counterpart to commiserate. And to
make a grim prophecy: 'They will miss us before long.' The republics that
the Black and Indigenous patriots had died to forge, grappling to realise
the principle of popular sovereignty, became a byword for instability. Elite
fears of their Indigenous, Afrodescendant and mixed-race compatriots

fuelled dispossession, civil wars and dictatorships well into the twenti-eth century.

But such strife was not unfamiliar to the United States – which in the 1860s fought the western hemisphere's bloodiest conflict to date, over the issue of slavery – or to war-torn, autocratic Europe. The 'early pages' of South America's republics 'may be disfigured by accounts of civil broils', conceded Haigh, the British aide to San Martín. But 'the spirit of independence is now too deeply rooted', he believed, for them to ever submit again 'to any foreign yoke'.

Today, the Incas have largely been stripped of their radical connota-tions, instead being subsumed into new-age mysticism. Yavi, the former seat of the Incaphile aristocrat Campero, is a huddle of adobe houses in the desert. The owner of the hostel, a retired union activist with grey curls under a brown trilby, has visited Machu Picchu four times. 'I'm part of a circle that is open to receiving solar knowledge,' she confides, peering through bottle-bottom glasses. 'We all have a third eye, the pineal gland, which we activate only rarely.'

Hers was activated in an ayahuasca ceremony in the Peruvian jungle with her son and daughter. 'I dreamed I was on a slab, my hair down to my waist and being combed by a crowd of people in white. Each knot they combed out contained a secret I mustn't forget,' she says. 'The Inca wasn't like the historians say, like a European nobleman. He was an incredibly solar, wise and serene being.'

I slip out into an inky night. The agrotechnical school is hosting a beauty pageant. Teenagers in sparkly dresses parade on the stage among plastic cacti and a yellow papier-mâché Minion. Speakers pump out Bad Bunny. It could be almost anywhere in the Americas. But there is a flicker of fealty to an ancient Andean lineage. 'We have a winner,' the MC booms: 'Queen Carolina Inca!'

PART THREE

Revolution

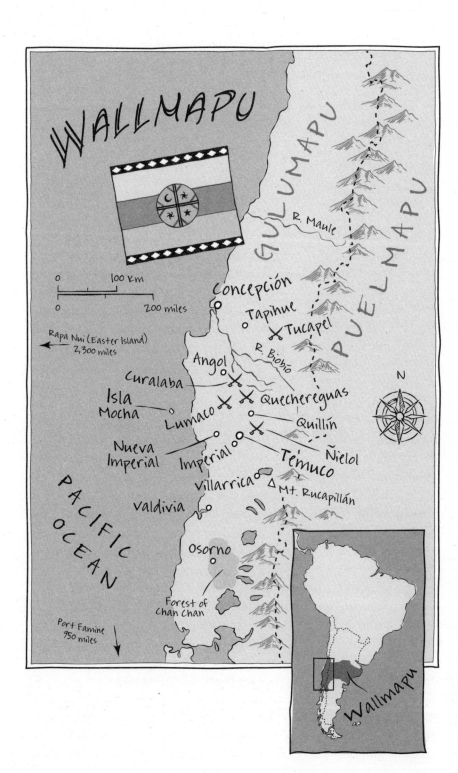

7

Lords of the Ends of the Earth

Wallmapu, 1350–1883

WE WILL WIN A THOUSAND TIMES

It was a time of earthquakes, volcanic eruptions, tsunamis – and giant, duelling Godzillas. In the depths of the ocean dwelled a great serpent named Caicai. Angered because the people turned their back on the sea, he smote the surface with his tail. The waters churned and surged, covering the earth, transforming humans into fish, birds, boulder fields and forests. But another powerful being, Tenten, ruled the land, and made it rise.

The people make for high ground, wearing pots on their heads to shelter from the snow and rain. The peaks outpace the floods. As the exhausted monsters slink back to their lairs, the waters recede. The survivors come down to a long, thin land of lakes and rivers, enclosed by Andean glaciers to the east, the driest desert on earth, the Atacama, to the north, and the cold waters of the South Pacific to the west. Once known as the *reche*, the true people, they have since gone by several names. But their descendants today call themselves and their ancestors the Mapuche. And some refer to their country, past and present, as Wallmapu.

Mapuche tradition holds that their story begins with Caicai and Tenten, incarnations of the elemental forces that shape their land to this day. The warring serpents still hiss and snap at each other in the basement of the Museum of Pre-Columbian Art in Santiago, trapped for now on a carved stone mace-head or *toki*. Just a block away, a different national origin myth is crystallised in another artwork.

The neoclassical chamber that once held congress is dominated by a vast watercolour, painted in 1913. At its centre, the conquistador Diego de Almagro sits atop an impetuous white charger. At his feet are Andean guides, weary from the long march south from Peru. And before him, a figure in a Mapuche poncho gestures to a fertile valley beneath a snow-capped mountain, as if transferring wholesale dominion of the land. The fifty-square-metre canvas is titled *The Discovery of Chile*.

But Chile was not discovered by the Spanish. The Mapuche and their ancestors, along with over a dozen other Indigenous nations, had already lived there for at least 15,000 years. And far from the swooning fantasia of native submission painted by Pedro Subercaseaux, Spain – and later Chile – had to fight for every inch of it. The Mapuche faced down the Inca Empire, then imperial Spain, killing two famous conquistador captains on the field. The Habsburg crown then recognised Wallmapu's sovereignty in treaties that held for nearly 250 years. The Mapuche extended their domain on the far side of the mountains as far as the Atlantic: a vast new territory known as Puelmapu.

In the late 1800s, Argentina and Chile invaded, killed and forced the Mapuche off their land. Yet the memory of a free Wallmapu never died. And in recent years, shadowy revolutionaries have waged a violent campaign of resistance: staging blazing shootouts with the police and firebombing corporations. As fears of a full-blown insurgency grow, coming to terms with this history has never been more urgent.

The distortions of Spanish chroniclers and Chilean colonists make it difficult. The Mapuche committed few words to paper until their subjugation was well underway. Yet in recent decades, scholars and writers – especially from among the Mapuche themselves – have gathered invaluable oral histories, flipped Santiago-centric perspectives, and challenged the notion that their people were destined to be conquered. And if Chile were to better understand the nation that its southern border crossed just a few generations ago – the Mapuche historian Sergio Caniuqueo suggests – it might discover itself.

The Mapuche hadn't been preserved in aspic since the time of the flood. They mixed with their neighbours – and those from further away, possibly undertaking vast voyages across the ocean.

Archaeologists think that remains found on Isla Mocha, a few miles off the Mapuche heartland, belong to ancient Polynesian seafarers. Chicken bones with Polynesian DNA, dating to around AD 1350, have been found at a Mapuche settlement nearby on the mainland. New genetic evidence from Rapa Nui – also known as Easter Island – suggests that South Americans travelled there with trans-Pacific seafarers nearly 900 years ago. Toki – like the one featuring Caicai and Tenten – take the same shape and name as far away as China. In the 1830s, one British sailor noted how the Patagonian term for canoe, *kialu*, was mirrored in Hawaiian: *kialoa*.

But those who arrived in Wallmapu planning on conquest and plunder faced a rude awakening. Diego de Almagro's expedition, in 1536, found no gold but plenty of Mapuche arrows. His replacement, Pedro de Valdivia – a wily conquistador who had fought all over Europe – set out for Chile in 1540. He shared out native peoples to serve his companions, laying the foundations of an oligarchic society for centuries to come. But as he probed further south to the Biobío River, the Spaniards encountered fierce resistance.

In February 1550, they were charged 'with such impetus and yelling that they seemed to make the earth sink', Valdivia reported. The attackers only retreated once their arrows had run out, leaving the Spanish and their horses bruised and bleeding. 'I swear, in the thirty years I have served Your Majesty and fought with many nations,' Valdivia marvelled, 'I have never seen such tenacious people in a fight.'

The Mapuche weren't full-time soldiers. They farmed garden plots, fished in coastal waters, and reared a fluffy cousin of the alpaca, now extinct, called the *chiliweke*. Spread between different groups, albeit with a common language, Mapudungun, their clans dwelled in thatched homesteads known as *rukas*. They made decisions by consensus, venerated mountains and rivers, bathed and depilated assiduously. But if outsiders judged them to be pushovers, it was a fatal mistake.

The Mapuche had already stopped Tawantinsuyu in its tracks. In the 1490s, the armies of Túpac Inca Yupanqui conquered as far as the site of Santiago, then pushed south into Mapuche country. The fighting lasted for three days. Of some 20,000 warriors on the battlefield, Garcilaso de la Vega claimed, 'more than half were killed, and almost all the living were wounded'.

The Inca retreated. The clash was left imprinted in language. The Mapuche still call outsiders *winka*. Those collaborating with the winka are branded *yanacona*, a Quechua term for the conquistadors' native allies. Meanwhile, the Spanish name for the Mapuche – *Araucanos* – probably drew on Inca warnings that they were *auca*: savage, indomitable.

Pedro de Valdivia treated the Mapuche with a savagery all of his own. His soldiers cut off their captives' hands and feet. Those he spared were enslaved and made to grub around for gold. All the while, tradition holds, he was being observed up close by a Mapuche teenager.

Lautaro, 'hawk' in Mapudungun, had been captured at the age of eleven, and made to serve as the governor's page for six years. His own parents are said to have been mutilated. Fired with righteous rage, he stole away and joined his people's resistance.

Like Manco Inca and Zumbi of Palmares, Lautaro turned what he'd gleaned about European tactics against his former subjugators. The Mapuche's ritualistic manoeuvres would have to adapt to the straight-for-the-jugular combat of the conquistadors. They would need to hold ground with fortifications, to wield swords and daggers, to tip their tall pikes with iron, to dig ditches filled with spikes to skewer Spanish horse-men. Above all, they would need to master these strange new beasts which – at least for the uninitiated – gave their riders a terrifying phys-ical and psychological edge.

When Querandí warriors forced the conquistador Pedro de Men-doza to abandon Buenos Aires in 1541, he set loose five mares and two stallions. Their descendants multiplied like mad, roaming the pampas 'in such enormous troops', wrote one Spanish naturalist, 'that it is no exaggeration to say that they often amount to ten thousand'. Fast and fiery, they were soon herded over the Andes. As early as 1601, a priest in Santiago moped about the 'most unhappy' stalemate on Chile's southern frontier: 'there is not an Indian but who can mount his horse, and dare encounter with his lance the best Spanish soldier there is, and though we send soldiers there every year, none of them return.'

Lautaro provided the brains. The brawn was courtesy of Caupolicán, a Mapuche *toqui* or elected war chief, famed for handling tree trunks like twigs. Together, they staged a lightning strike against Valdivia's forces at a Spanish fort at Tucapel on 25 December 1553. There were no European survivors. Rumours reached Peru that the 150 men had simply been swallowed up by the ground. The conquistador captain was beheaded, his skull used as a drinking vessel. In some versions, Lautaro's men generously bestow on Valdivia the precious metal he so desires – in molten form, poured down his throat. 'If you are such a friend to gold,' they tell him, 'have your fill.'

A few years later, typhus stalked Lautaro's ranks. His warriors were said to vomit and keel over mid-melee. The Mapuche population plunged, from half a million in 1550 to just 100,000 fifty years later. Still their victories stacked up. Lautaro even came close to razing San-tiago. He was ultimately betrayed by the local Picunche people, ambushed, and beheaded in 1557. Caupolicán, too, was captured and impaled. Yet authority among the Mapuche was more dispersed than the centralised Inca hierarchy. New leaders soon sprang up.

The Mapuche were meanwhile transformed by decades of frontier skirmishing. The clans coalesced. Fighting and plunder became a way of life. In the late 1800s, an elder encapsulated the way of war laid down by Lautaro's generation. Mapuche captains, he recalled, 'taught the young men how to make war as you train a racehorse. They taught them how to fight with lances, on foot and on horseback,' and 'to truss up the winka with *boleadores*.' This fiendish throwing weapon of weighted cords could topple a Spaniard or his horse just as easily as the flightless ñandú.

Warriors learned how to spring an ambush, retreat along hidden trails, and escape across raging rivers. They learned to hurl a spear at a gallop with pinpoint accuracy; to canter in zig-zags and duck behind their horse's flank, clinging to its mane, to dodge musket volleys – before thundering home with a blood-curdling yell. 'If things went well, they chased down the enemy, spearing whoever they pleased and seizing horses, saddles, sabres, guns and cloaks. A good war gave more than one harvest.'

By the 1590s, command of the Mapuche warbands had fallen to Pelantaro, a charismatic toqui from Purén. There was a reshuffle on the Spanish side as well. Twenty years on from his conquest of Vilcabamba, Martín García Óñez de Loyola – a man experienced in subduing independent Indigenous realms – was called out of gilded retirement in Peru. Wallmapu had to be occupied, or Patagonia would be left wide open as a base for Dutch and English pirates to plunder the Spanish Pacific. But when Loyola took up his post in 1592, things went from bad to worse.

Soldiers venturing out from their stockades were found with their throats slit. Friendly Mapuche scouts, interpreters and warriors were defecting. 'They fled from us every day, taking the best horses we had to ford the rivers,' Chile's new governor wrote to the king. 'One by one, their loss was sorely felt.' His enemies only used peace, Loyola complained, to prepare for war.

The Mapuche, one contemporary wrote, had 'sown the valleys with Spaniards' bones'. Their reputation was cemented by *La Araucana*, a verse epic finished in 1589. The 'Araucanian state', wrote Alonso de Ercilla, was famed the world over: 'the people there are proud and quick to war / they serve no king, nor any foreign law.' The Basque soldier-poet wrote from experience, having drafted his stanzas on scraps of cowhide by the campfire while chasing after Caupolicán.

Late in 1598, Loyola received an urgent request for backup from deep in hostile territory. The governor charged south with fifty Spaniards and 200 native reinforcements. He wrote a letter detailing his movements; an allied Mapuche named Nabalburi offered to deliver it. Instead, he promptly took the missive to Pelantaro. The governor's path wound through the marshes of Lumaco. Making camp at a riverbank called Curalaba, cloven rock, he neglected to place sentries.

Pelantaro seizes his moment. At first light on 23 December, horns blaring around the valley, Mapuche horsemen descend from all sides. They trample the Spanish tents, spearing their drowsing occupants 'like sparrows in a net'. Just one soldier, fumbling with match and powder, manages to fire his harquebus before being clubbed to death. Others throw themselves into the Lumaco River, smashing onto rocks and drowning in the rapids. The grey-bearded governor emerges from his pavilion in doublet and britches, swinging his rapier wildly. Loyola, Knight of the Order of Calatrava, captor of Túpac Amaru I, captain-general and chief justice of the kingdom and province of Chile, is pierced by so many spearpoints that the Mapuche later argue over who had killed him.

Chilean historians have termed it the Disaster of Curalaba. Just two Spaniards lived to tell the tale. Pelantaro sends trophies to the four corners of Wallmapu to invite his fellow chiefs, or *lonkos*, to join the uprising: a gore-stained arrow, captured treasure, and the heads of Spanish captains, or all but one of them. The Mapuche lonkos toast their new alliance by chugging chicha from Loyola's cranium. The slain governor's skull, like a Catholic relic, will inaugurate Mapuche war parties and feasts for years to come: part battle standard, part novelty mug.

Between 1598 and 1604, Pelantaro's warriors burned every Spanish town on the mainland south of the Biobío to the ground, killing 3,000 men and carrying off 500 women. The setback was permanent. A map sketched in the Spanish court in 1610 shows Angol, Villarrica, Osorno, Valdivia and Nueva Imperial struck through with penstrokes. Indigenous people fled servitude in Chile for the free Mapuche territory, further impoverishing the isolated Spanish colony north of Wallmapu. The southern frontier of European rule in the Americas had been pushed back for centuries.

The comparison later made by Diego de Rosales, who served as a chaplain on the front line, was apposite. To the south of Chile, Spain had stumbled into an 'Indian Flanders', he wrote, meeting 'a daring resistance among the natives of this land'. It was a nod to the Dutch War of Independence, which had ended in an embarrassing Habsburg defeat in 1648 after eighty enervating years. Several grizzled Spanish commanders had even been transferred from the Low Countries to Wallmapu, trading one doomed counterinsurgency for another.

For the triumph at Curalaba was no mere act of banditry, Rosales explained. Rather, the Mapuche were waging a revolutionary war, a struggle for national liberation. Pelantaro and the rebels of 1598 had a clear objective: 'to put an end to the Spanish, to restore the patria, and to seize their freedom.'

A parched field, a monolith, an empty flagpole. I walk across the site of the Battle of Curalaba, on the outskirts of the town of Lumaco. A military helicopter thuds overhead, a machine-gunner sitting in the doorway. Four centuries on, this is still a conflict zone.

Churches in flames. Truckers and police shot dead. A local politician made to watch at gunpoint in her pyjamas as her house is burned to the ground. A group called Mapuche Territorial Resistance posts a Facebook video in flak jackets and black hoodies, brandishing sub-machine guns and pump-action shotguns, demanding a free Wallmapu. Sebastián Piñera, Chile's billionaire former president, says drug gangs and terrorists are behind the violence. In 2021, he declares a state of emergency and sends in the troops.

Rebellion is in the soil here. In December 1997, unknown perpetrators firebombed three lumber-laden trucks outside Lumaco. The region, known as the Araucanía, has smouldered with unrest ever since. More than fifty people have been killed. On one side, paramilitary organisations like the Coordinadora Arauco-Malleco (CAM). They say they are *weichafes*, warriors pursuing self-defence, territorial autonomy and Mapuche independence from Santiago. Their enemies: the cops, winka-owned farming estates and the corporations smothering the land with forestry plantations for pulp and wood. Those deemed yanaconas aren't safe either. And for the authorities, it seems like Mapuche lives don't matter. In 2018, police shot Camilo Catrillanca, a farmer and former student activist, in the back of the head – and destroyed the video evidence.

Lumaco has 'always been a centre of resistance. Not just in terms of conflict, but in terms of keeping culture alive,' says Gonzalo Garcés, a young anthropologist who works for the local council. Every 19 January at dusk, locals gather around a nine-foot-tall boulder near the battlefield of Curalaba. 'The rock used to be on the other side of the river,' says Gonzalo. 'And it walked over here. Well, rolled.' It contains the spirit of a Mapuche girl. 'She grants you whatever you want: a better job, a new house, a girlfriend.' A peeved Catholic priest once tried to dynamite the shrine into smithereens. When the smoke cleared, the story goes, blood welled up from the stone.

We watch as devotees pour libations of homebrew over the candle-lit megalith. They tuck entreaties in a letterbox, presided over by the grandmotherly shamans called *machis* who wear robes of turquoise and crimson. One starts pounding a *cultrun*, a drum divided into quadrants containing symbols for the sun, moon and stars. Another produces a slender branch – *canelo*, winter's bark. Blowing on stone flutes, the revellers shuffle, stamp and jig around the bough, faster and faster. At the end of each revolution, they wail and clash together their wooden staffs, used in an ancestral game similar to hockey. Eventually, breath steaming and red in the face, the scrum dissolves to knock back hooch around campfires, before dispersing to bootleg raves around the valley.

Lumaco contains the causes of the Mapuche conflict in microcosm. In South America's richest nation, half the district's inhabitants live in poverty. Some ninety per cent of its native forests have been felled since 1870. Even the *luma* tree that gives the area its name is vanishing. The non-native eucalyptus and pine that have replaced them are sucking the water out of the earth. One in four families lack reliable drinkable water. As forestry executives reap the profits, locals get chainsaw work: seasonal, poorly paid and dangerous.

In the morning, I get talking with Ana Alcamán Curín, whose family own the land around the sacred rock. 'Do you think the Mapuche are violent?' she asks, serving up a fresh batch of *sopaipillas* – fluffy, oil-fried pastries – to unsteady cowboys in spurs. 'You saw for yourself, nobody had guns last night. We don't have the money to spend on weapons. We're working families; people have wives, kids to look after.' Nor are they country bumpkins, frozen in time, says Ana. Most of the two million Mapuche across Argentina and Chile today live in towns and cities. She's a teaching assistant; her sister, María Josefa, is about to qualify as a lawyer.

Ana dislikes being lumped in with a radical minority. But she shares their anger with the forestry firms. A stream used to gush past the sacred rock. Now, it's barely a trickle. The family depends on rationed water deliveries by truck. Something more than climate change seems to be at work. 'No es sequía, es saqueo,' interjects María Josefa, pouring wine for the punters who are still standing. 'It's not drought, it's looting.'

Temuco, the capital of the Araucanía, is three hours' drive from Lumaco. The Andes a dark smudge on your left, you pass hillsides stubbled with felled eucalyptus, military checkpoints, a Korean-owned sawmill and toll booths on the privately-owned highway. Armoured personnel carriers roll around town. Butchers sell horse meat, a traditional delicacy. A bronze Caupolicán monitors the traffic, brandishing his tree trunk. A plinth holds the broken feet of Pedro de Valdivia.

I wait with a small crowd outside the penitentiary. After a few hours, a pale figure with a scrappy goatee steps into the sunshine, carrying a bundle of possessions. He wears a grey poncho and a blue-and-gold headband. Facundo Jones Huala, co-founder of the Resistencia Ancestral Mapuche (RAM) movement, is wanted in his native Argentina on terrorism charges, and has just completed several years behind bars here in Chile for arson and firearms offences.

Now, he pledges to continue his campaign of 'sabotage' and 'self-defence'. 'The enemy is not the poor winka or the small landowners,' Jones Huala tells the handful of reporters and sympathisers. 'The enemy is the forestry, mining, petroleum and hydroelectric companies. And we have to keep advancing on that path until we liberate the Mapuche nation.'

Since he was jailed, Chile's normally placid politics have been turned upside down. In late 2019, millions thronged the streets to protest against inequality, many bearing the Wenufoye – a Mapuche flag of blue, green and yellow stripes with a cultrun at its centre. Some demonstrators battled the tear gas and rubber bullets of the Carabineros, Chile's military police, with bricks and firebombs. More than thirty people were killed, thousands were wounded.

Gabriel Boric, a thirty-something congressman and former student leader, came up with a way out of the crisis. The country's ills, he argued, were rooted in the dictatorship of Augusto Pinochet. On 11 September 1973, Pinochet overthrew the man who had appointed him army commander-in-chief – Salvador Allende, the world's first democratically elected socialist leader – in a coup backed by the United States. As British-made fighter jets strafed the burning presidential palace, rather than surrender, Allende shot himself using an AK-47 gifted to him by Fidel Castro. Having murdered and exiled nearly all opposition, General Pinochet made Chile the lab rat of a new economic doctrine called neoliberalism. His regime imposed a constitution where the market is king, the nation is indivisible, and Indigenous peoples don't exist.

An elected convention, including Mapuche lawyers and academics, set about rewriting it in 2021. Their most striking proposal: Chile's first nations would henceforth govern themselves, according to their own laws. Boric has since been elected president, vowing to bury neoliberalism, fight climate change, and pull the troops out of Wallmapu. But for some, these promises are not to be trusted. 'We're not with the constitutional process, nor with the election of Boric, nor any of those sell-outs to the system of capitalist oppression,' Jones Huala insists, raising a fist. 'Forward, without any negotiating, until national liberation!' His supporters whisk him into a car and away. 'Marichiweu!' they yell: We will win a thousand times.

Jones Huala's words echo those of other hardliners. Weichan Auka Mapu, a paramilitary group, puts out a video vowing to fight the state of emergency. Thirty figures in ski masks, draped in coils of ammo, file through the undergrowth brandishing Uzis, rifles and shotguns. 'With our ancestors who fought the Inca and Spanish invaders and the Chilean state,' a distorted voice intones, 'we call on this new police and military force, guard dogs of the rich, to abandon our territory, because they will be defeated by the force of the Mapuche people in arms.' The WAM spokesperson saves some scorn for the 'feeble and servile centre-left'. Then, fumbling with magazines and safety catches, they blast the foliage with a ragged salvo. 'Pigs and squaddies out of Wallmapu!'

After Jones Huala departs, three young men with long hair and heavy metal T-shirts appear around the corner and push me up against a gate. 'A fucking cop, are you?' one of them hisses. My explanation does little to calm things. 'Journalist for who?' grunts another, shoving me in the chest. 'You're going to call us terrorists, right? Violent?' Their friend, seemingly more sober, pulls them back and tells me to walk away.

A few minutes later, I'm picked up by Francisco Alanis, a construction boss of Italian-Lebanese descent with a thick black beard down to his chest. He heads the Association for Peace and Reconciliation in the Araucanía (APRA), a lobby group for victims of radical Mapuche organisations. We sit on a patio outside a petrol station.

To my surprise, Alanis takes a long-term view of the conflict. He situates its origins in Chile's nineteenth-century conquest of the Mapuche, its theft of their land, and Pinochet's efforts to stamp out native identity. 'Indigenous groups have been held back. You can't deny it, you'd be mad to. They've been made invisible, discriminated against. There's no doubt.'

But for Alanis, the CAM, RAM and WAM 'cloak themselves in the noble cause' of the Mapuche to traffic drugs, guns and stolen timber. Back in 2013, his road-building company had twelve teams of diggers, tractors and trucks. 'They burned nine of them. I had to start from scratch. The damage is not only material. It's escalating; people are dying.' That morning, two forestry workers had been killed in a drive-by shooting nearby. The violence 'still hasn't reached its peak', Alanis predicts. 'This will take two generations to solve.'

The courts have censured APRA for using racist language online. The organisation has incited its followers to confront Mapuche demonstrators. It's a short step to armed vigilantes taking matters into their own hands. A TikTok video is circulating of a man in camouflage claiming to speak for a militia of local farmers: 'We're coming for the heads of many,' he warns.

'APRA is looking for reconciliation,' Alanis insists. 'We're trapped in a conflict that emerged 140 years ago. But there have been societies that resolved their problems,' he adds, mentioning the Balkans and post-war France and Germany. 'No European today wants to change their borders.' The lakes, ski slopes and hot springs of the Araucanía still attract more tourists than any other Chilean region, he concludes. 'We have a problem with violence, but we're working on it.'

I'm not entirely convinced by his faith in the fixity of European frontiers. As we speak, Russian tanks are massing on the border with Ukraine. Corsicans are clashing with French gendarmes. Spain has stifled secessionist revolt in Catalonia, for now. An independent Scotland seems possible and a united Ireland likely within my lifetime. Older constructions than the Chilean nation-state are being remoulded. Recognition of Mapuche autonomy would not be inconceivable. In fact, it's happened dozens of times before.

A FOREIGN POWER

Philip III – Spain's henpecked, strawberry-blond monarch – responded to the 1598 Mapuche revolution with an iron fist. POWs over the age of ten were to be enslaved. Those younger could also be abducted from 'the rebel provinces' to be 'indoctrinated and instructed in the ways of my Holy Catholic Faith'. Mapuche resistance would be weakened, Spanish enslavers would get rich, and the crown could congratulate itself on its Christian charity.

In 1625, a council of advisors in Madrid checked in on how this genius strategy was going. By now, Spain had wasted eight decades and untold blood and treasure trying to annex Wallmapu. But rather than tasting victory, Spanish soldiers were 'greatly demoralised, seeing that the war never ends'. Amputating the limbs of Mapuche warriors, assaulting their women, seizing their lands and kidnapping their children had – somehow – failed to win hearts and minds, the courtiers noted acidly: 'It is no wonder they rebel.'

Yet generations of close-quarters combat – skirmishes, sieges, duels – had bred a grudging mutual respect. Hidebound binaries of race, sexuality and even gender seemed to dissolve in the fluid frontier society on the empire's southernmost limit. Francisco Núñez de Pineda y Bascuñán, a captain of pikemen, was taken prisoner in 1629, spending six months in 'happy captivity'. The Mapuche 'are not as barbarous, cruel nor mean-spirited as they are made out to be', he reported, but hospitable, charitable and more deeply attached to 'their beloved patria than any other nation in the world'. With captive Spanish women, the Mapuche had sired a fair-haired generation who were the equal of their peers: unlike half-Mapuche children born into slavery under Spanish rule. And Núñez observed how a respected class of shamans known as the *weyes* – seemingly male, but long-haired and long-nailed, in skirts, necklaces 'and other womanly adornments' – 'performed with women the office of men, and with men the role of women'.

The Catholic colonisers lacked the language to describe two-spirit and trans people. But they could still be mugged and murdered by them. In the early 1610s, the Chile–Wallmapu border was worked by a Basque highwayman straight out of a convent. Antonio de Erauso had been baptised in 1592 under the name Catalina. Raised by nuns, he escaped to live as a man, working as a merchant, a royal page in Madrid, and a cabin boy – before jumping ship in Panama. Brawling, duelling and seducing his way down to Chile, he enlisted against the Mapuche. Too bloodthirsty even for the conquistadors, Lieutenant Erauso turned to banditry, later only dodging a death sentence by confessing his biological sex. Back in Spain, he posed for a portrait wearing a soldier's steel neckplate and a lugubrious scowl, ending his days as a muleteer in Mexico.

Antonio de Meneses made the opposite journey. He was an 'Indian born of Arauco in the Kingdom of Chile' – a Mapuche – around 1628, he guessed. Not long afterwards, Antonio had been kidnapped by Alonso Perez de Salazar and taken to Madrid. But in 1648, Antonio escaped and went to ground for months. Then he took his enslaver to court. 'By my aspect, I am around twenty years old. He has deprived me of my liberty for more than twelve years,' he noted. 'When they captured me, I would have been seven or eight.' But by that point, the legal age for enslaving Mapuche – for any purpose – had been raised to fourteen. Perez had clearly broken the law. 'I am no slave,' Antonio insisted. 'I declare myself a free man and subject to no kind of servitude whatsoever.' The mass kidnap of Mapuche children had failed to turn them into model Spanish servants. Their love of their 'native liberty' was too strong. And Antonio vowed to keep petitioning, 'in any way that may be useful and necessary', for his freedom and that of his compatriots: 'I ask for justice.'

The Spanish weren't only in legal jeopardy. Their technological and biological edge had been dulled. The Mapuche population had gained immunity to Old World diseases and started to recover. Gunpowder often proved a damp squib in the Araucanian mizzle. Their adversaries now came at them swinging swords and steel-tipped lances. Above all, the Mapuche were mounted and mobile. They lassoed wild cattle and horses in Puelmapu – or rustled them from Spanish caravans – before selling them back to Spaniards in Chile at a hefty mark-up. Then they spent the silver on more weapons.

And in 1640, Madrid had to contain two more independence revolutions. Catalonian peasants turned their sickles on Spanish troops. Portuguese nobles threw Philip IV's chief minister out of a window. The Mapuche were also reeling. Rucapillán – the sacred, snow-shrouded volcano that loomed above the Spanish ruins of Villarrica – dramatically blew its top. Spanish forts nearly 200 miles away heard the explosion. Not only was the eruption an ominous portent. The pyroclastic slurry flattened Mapuche villages, boiled the fish in rivers, and carbonised their crops. So, early in 1641, the foremost empire of the age and the Patagonian power that defied it signed a treaty of 'perpetual peace'.

The agreed location was Quillín, deep in no-man's-land. At dawn on 6 January, thousands of Mapuche warriors strolled into the Spanish camp, laughing and jostling. Among them were sixty-five of the most powerful lonkos, in sumptuous cloaks and finely worked collars of silver, some brandishing Spanish broadswords. The Spanish, warned of a double-cross, surrounded them with pikes. The chiefs hardly flinched. The two sides heard Mass, then entered a ruka to negotiate. Musketeers lingered outside, their match cords lit.

Spain's chief interpreter sought to kick things off, but a lonko named

Antuwenu interrupted. This wasn't his first rodeo. The Mapuche were master negotiators, with a rich repertoire of diplomatic rituals – like the *koyang*, or parliament – to defuse conflicts and reinforce alliances. First, Antuwenu said, they would cut out the hearts of twenty-eight chiliweke, whose meek submission would imbue their dealings with the same trusting mildness.

With the camelids duly dispatched, Antuwenu lamented the enslavement suffered by his people, 'their fathers, sons, ancestors and relatives cut into bits, or exiled, and uprooted to strange Kingdoms, losing all faith of seeing them ever again'. He decried 'the hardships that they have lived through, passing nights among the mountains and days with weapons in their hands, unable to put them down, when they should have been working their fields'. Lienkura – a sage, battle-scarred chief – spoke movingly of the horrors of war, provoking 'such emotion that everyone rose to their feet, and called out aloud for peace'.

The principal Mapuche demands: freedom from Spanish slavery and the right to return to their occupied lands. They, in turn, would formally come under the 'protection' of the king. They would abandon their forts, accept missionaries, and release any captives who wanted to go back to Chile – in return for cold hard cash. If the Dutch, French or English disembarked in Wallmapu, or rebel lonkos rose up against the crown, they would fight them 'with weapons and horses'. And – as a sweetener – they would hand back Loyola's skull.

It was a deal. The lonkos embraced the Spanish lieutenants. They gave and accepted gifts, and handed out chunks of chiliweke. The governor – Francisco López de Zúñiga, a Flanders veteran – received a gore-smeared bough of canelo 'with great shows of esteem and courtesy'. The negotiations had proceeded 'with such trust and familiarity', the Jesuit Alonso de Ovalle remarked, one could hardly tell that 'we would have only yesterday soaked the fields with their blood, and they with ours'. López de Zúñiga proceeded through Wallmapu, repeating the parliament twice, before marching home. Over 150 chiefs and some 120,000 Mapuche were now, at a stroke, allies of Spain.

The fine print agreed in 1641 is fiercely debated. But the parliament would be remembered a century later as a triumph of Mapuche diplomacy. Colonial Chile had recognised them as a 'free people', with the Biobío forming the 'limit of both nations'. Spain had dealt 'power to power with the Indians' and 'guaranteed them their beloved liberty'. The agreement was published in a compendium of Spanish treaties: the only one signed with an Indigenous nation. In 1816, a Rioplatense revolutionary wrote that Madrid had capitulated to a 'shameful peace' at the hands of the 'valiant Araucanians'.

Dozens more parliaments in the centuries following 1641 confirmed the nagging sense that the Mapuche had the upper hand. Not only did the royal treasury have to fork out 1,500 pesos every time for food, drink, gifts and flashy martial parades. Coughing up this protection money, one colonial governor complained, was an insult to 'the honour of your Majesty's arms'. Spain, another soldier grumbled, signed treaties with the Mapuche 'as with a foreign power'.

Europeans failed dismally to conquer the New World. The job was half-finished, at best. Through shrewd diplomacy, hard fighting and sheer geography, independent Indigenous and Afrodescendant peoples in their millions still held sway over most of Latin America by the early 1800s. From the frozen confines of Patagonia to the deserts of northern Mexico, via the steppes and prairies of Puelmapu, the bountiful forests of the Amazon and the Chaco, and the mangrove swamps of Central America: these were wildernesses for outsiders, but havens for their light-footed possessors. 'To conquer them by force' – wrote one viceroy of Peru of such peoples – 'has always been impossible.'

Wallmapu was not a country in the sense that most Europeans would recognise – no cities, no capital, no court nor king – and this was its salvation. Rather than collapse under Spanish pressure, the Mapuche maintained their independence for some 250 years after Quillín, spreading their culture, language and trading empire from sea to shining sea. It was the beginning, writes Pedro Cayuqueo, of a 'Mapuche golden age'.

THE STEEL CROWN

Ambrós Bearnárd Ó hUiginn knew how to parley. By the time the postal engineer settled in Chile in the 1760s, Spanish-Mapuche summits almost ran like clockwork. Once terms were reached, the lonkos broke their lances and the Spanish sergeant major his musket, casting them onto a bonfire. Cannon fire, 'vivas' to the king, etcetera, etcetera, cavaliers of both nations trotting past the royal standards. Then the fire was put out with wine – for extra ostentation – and the burned fragments placed in the strongbox of the council in Santiago.

The Irishman – now going by Ambrosio O'Higgins – followed the recipe to the letter. He fought the Mapuche when necessary, but was generous in peace. In the quarter-century to 1796, he was promoted from a frontier captain of dragoons, to commander of the border, governor of Chile and viceroy of Peru. Resumé burnished by his deft handling of the crown's relations with Wallmapu, the tenant farmer from Sligo became the most powerful man in South America.

Bernardo, the red-haired bastard he left behind on the border, was schooled alongside the sons of Mapuche lonkos, picking up a smattering of Mapudungun. He inherited Ambrosio's ranch a few miles from the Biobío, often hosting his former classmates. And later, as Supreme Director of the newborn Chilean republic, O'Higgins junior penned a series of extraordinary diplomatic overtures to the Mapuche.

In August 1817, fresh from the march over the Andes, he promised 'an eternal and lasting peace between this government and its subjects with all nations that dwell from the far bank of the Biobío to the ends of the Earth'. In March 1819, still giddy with the victory at Maipú a year earlier, he went further. Chileans had 'bought with our blood that same Independence which you have known to guard at the same price', he wrote, in a proclamation to 'our brothers the inhabitants of the southern border'.

'Araucanians, Cuncos, Huilliches and all the southern indigenous tribes,' O'Higgins continued. 'There no longer addresses you a President who, as a mere servant of the king of Spain, affects an unlimited superiority over you. There speaks to you the chief of a free and sovereign people who recognises your independence.' He offered to sign with them 'a great Charter of our alliance, presenting it to the world as the impregnable wall of the freedom of our States'. O'Higgins even put an eight-pointed asterisk, the Mapuche *Wünelfe* or morning star, on the flag of his new nation.

In her final years as a colony and her first as an independent country, Chile was gripped by Mapuche fever. Leaf through the Santiago newspapers and you'd begin to spot a theme: 'Araucanian Enlightenment', 'Araucanian Insurgent', 'Araucanian Decade', 'Araucanian Alert'. Not to be outdone, the *Aurora de Chile* had a suggestion: 'henceforth let us call ourselves "Indians", so that our brothers should know the worthy esteem in which we hold them.'

Just as Inca Garcilaso's *Royal Commentaries* lit the fuse on Andean revolutions centuries later, patriots in the plains were radicalised by an improbable bestseller. *La Araucana*, Ercilla's 1589 ode to Mapuche resistance, 'began to awake in our hearts love of our patria, warlike

sentiments, thirst for glory, and a vague yearning for independence',
recalled Francisco Antonio Pinto, Chile's second president. It wasn't for
the baroque rhyme scheme, 'but because of the heroic deeds of the
Araucanians and the Spaniards, which we considered to be our own, as
we were compatriots of the former and descendants of the latter'.

Chile's patriots would surely overthrow the Spanish, Bolívar believed,
because 'the free and indomitable *araucanos* are their neighbors and
compatriots. Their sublime example is proof to those fighting in Chile
that a people who love independence will eventually achieve it.' And
when the Army of the Andes marched into Lima in 1821, one Chilean
official imagined the ghosts of Atahualpa, Caupolicán and Lautaro
reviving to congratulate 'their sons' upon seeing 'their patria independent and the wrongs they suffered avenged'.

Meanwhile – in Wallmapu – Mapuche chiefs in Spanish uniforms
were busy slaughtering the patriot comrades of O'Higgins. Between
1815 and 1827, lonkos led by Mañilwenu – a faithful ally of Spain –
waged a vicious guerrilla war in alliance with royalist bandits. The roles
had seemingly been switched: as Spanish Americans lionised Lautaro in
their literary salons, his descendants fought and bled for Spain. Native
friendship with the crown extended over the other side of the Andes.
When British warships anchored off Buenos Aires in late 1806, a group
of Rankülche and Puelche chiefs pledged 20,000 warriors to the city's
defence: 'We want them to be the first to charge these "redcoats" that
bother you.'

One hundred and fifty years after Quillín, the Mapuche still took
their treaties deadly seriously. Some did so for tradition's sake, for prestige, to keep the gifts coming, or to retain their lands and trading
partners. Others thought a distant king in Madrid a more comfortable
patron than a power-hungry president in Santiago. It took another eye-
wateringly expensive parliament in 1825 for most of the lonkos – led by
Francisco Mariluán, a wily nonagenarian and serial defector – to recognise Chilean independence and cut ties with Spain.

The resulting deal, the Treaty of Tapihue, once more fixed the Biobío
as 'the dividing line between these new allied brothers'. The Mapuche
would be treated as part of the 'great Chilean family'. They could send
their children to Chilean schools and deal with intruders according to
their own law. Chile would pull its troops out, forbid its citizens from
dwelling in Mapuche lands, and even provide boats so the Mapuche
could freely cross the river to trade. And though Chile's negotiators
cavilled about 'the cost to the treasury', Mariluán insisted that the

entertainments laid on for his fellow lonkos when visiting would continue, as befitted their rank as leaders of a friendly nation.

European powers were also eager to curry favour with the Mapuche. When their merchants were wrecked along Wallmapu's shores, the survivors were often robbed, enslaved or killed: partly for profit, partly out of residual friendship with Madrid. Soon after arriving in 1825, London's first consul to Santiago set out for the southern border bearing gifts. His mission: to stifle a 'malign' rumour that Britain was an enemy of the Mapuche. Instead, he assured them, his country 'desired no more than an eternal interchange of amity and good-will with the Araucanians'. A great assembly in 1837 of French, British, Chilean and Mapuche authorities further hashed out terms.

Ever amenable to honest diplomacy, many in Wallmapu cooperated. In 1835, HMS *Challenger* ran aground near Isla Mocha. A group of Mapuche spurred their horses into the surf to save the crew – and Jack, their pet sheep – from 'the appalling prospect of a watery grave'. The followers of Cheuquante and Pinoleo bartered supplies with the sailors for cash, clothes and snuff. The warriors of Colissi, another Mapuche chief, even fended off 2,000 men under a lonko called Cadin intent on plundering the twenty-eight-gun wreck.

Yet scarcely fifteen years after Bernardo O'Higgins had promised 'eternal' peace, and the broadsheets had competed to demonstrate their pro-Mapuche credentials, this brief blooming of Araucophilia had wilted. While camped out ashore awaiting rescue, the officers of the *Challenger* perceived how Chilean authorities sought the 'forcible possession of the whole country south of their present frontier'. Their plan, it now seemed, was 'to exterminate the race of Indians'.

News of the power that held sway over the bottom of the hemisphere also reached the emerging one in the north. In 1832, the US Secretary of State remarked that the 'Araucanians' of the South Pacific, and their Puelche and Tehuelche cousins on the Atlantic seaboard, were 'perfectly independent'.

But the new republics on Wallmapu's doorstep were growing in strength. Buenos Aires cemented its control over the provinces of Argentina. In 1830, authoritarian conservatives triumphed in a civil war in Chile. The fleeting dream of a free association of nations, where the Mapuche would enjoy equal confederation with their Chilean brothers, was no more.

Meanwhile, the fratricidal war of independence had left the Mapuche bitterly divided. It was hard enough to get the lonkos to agree in times of peace, Mariluán wrote in 1824, and now nearly impossible given that Wallmapu had been 'so entangled in a living fire'. Where O'Higgins senior had convened over 2,600 Mapuche chiefs and their lieutenants in 1793, Mariluán struggled to muster 300 at Tapihue in 1825.

The reports of scientists, journalists and explorers stirred up Chilean covetousness towards their prosperous neighbours. 'The Araucanian Indians are not savages,' wrote the Polish-Lithuanian geologist Ignacio Domeyko after his 1845 journey through Wallmapu, passing rich farm-steads ringed by fat cows and ripe orchards, and stuffed with creature comforts: palaces compared to the shacks of Chilean campesinos. 'Per-haps they are more civilised,' he remarked, 'than many of their civilisers on the border.'

Chilean forts and missions leap-frogged south of the Biobío. State-backed settlers encircled Mapuche land in a drive to 'improve' the nation. In particular, thought Vicente Pérez Rosales – Chile's local agent of colonisation – 'the German race' was 'the most apt for mixing with the Chilean'. These imported Hessian Protestants and Catholics from Württemberg needed farmland. Pérez knew just the spot: Chan Chan, an 'immense and virgin forest' that tumbled down from the Andes to the south of Wallmapu. So in 1851, he ordered Pichi Juan, his Huilliche helper, to burn it down.

Today, little remains of these temperate Valdivian rainforests that once covered Wallmapu. But a protected reserve on Isla Mocha offers a glimpse of their former majesty. You tramp through thickets of *boldo*, heady with an aroma of camphor. Slender, silver-dappled *olivillo* trees twenty metres tall sway in the breeze, their trunks caressing and creak-ing. Vines knit a dense understorey between the rust-coloured *arrayán*, Chilean wineberry; the pink ballerina skirts of *Fuchsia magellanica*; bamboo-like *quila*. The moss known as old man's beard trails down the bark, along with *Luzuriaga radicans* – a white Inca-lily with an orange fruit, also known as forest coral.

The dense, dripping vegetation of Chan Chan took three months to succumb. In Valdivia, eighty miles away, a shroud of black smoke blot-ted out the sun. The ritual bonfire of the Spanish–Mapuche parliaments had now become a conflagration that dragged Wallmapu into the Anthropocene. When Chile's first ecocide was consummated, all 800 square miles of the forest had gone up in smoke. Or almost all. Inspect-ing his handiwork, Pérez found the flames had spared a few trees, 'which it seemed as though the divine hand had intentionally reserved so that the colonists might have, as well as the clean and clear soil, lumber for their work and needs'.

Another disaster – the shipwreck of the *Joven Daniel* in July 1849 – stoked anti-Mapuche hatred. Wild reports circulated that the coastal Lafkenche had slaughtered the survivors in an orgy of rum-fuelled violence. Little matter that witnesses said that local Mapuche had, in fact, rescued as many as they could from the waves. Paintings depicted a Chilean damsel in captivity. Columnists frothed over Mapuche terrorism: 'This stain on humanity must be wiped out, and if possible not even the memory of such an execrable race should be left.' The alleged murderers had 'no rights before God nor civilisation', fumed another. 'Let Arauco one day be Chile, let there be no other language, religion, or race.'

Above all, there was an economic motive for this creeping annexation. As miners rushed to California in search of gold from 1848, Chilean farmers were ideally placed to provide the wheat that kept the United States marching westwards. The value of land south of the Biobío skyrocketed. In 1852, despite the protests of Mapuche chiefs, Santiago began parcelling it out to the highest bidder. The Mapuche were sucked into a Chilean civil war in 1851 and a revolution in 1859, burning farms and destroying forts. Cornelio Saavedra, a soldier with estates along the border, launched a punitive foray into Wallmapu in response.

In the early 1850s, the travel writer Edmond Reuel Smith called on Mañilwenu at his ruka in a verdant Andean valley. Thirty years since the Chilean war of independence, the astute, ageing lonko still sometimes donned a tattered Spanish uniform with fraying gold braid. He grilled his visitor on international politics, even asking whether Madrid might reconquer Chile, 'for, strange to say, these people cherish a strong love for the Spaniards'. Most Mapuche were hazy about Lautaro and Pelantaro, Smith observed, but remembered Spain's respectful negotiations across subsequent generations. 'Under the republic an opposite system is pursued; the Indians are generally treated with ill-disguised contempt, and they do not fail to perceive the difference.'

Reeling from Saavedra's assault, Mañilwenu called for reinforcements. In a letter to Argentina's president, Justo José de Urquiza, he said he was 'defending our territory and our independence' as established 'in the peace treaties that my ancestors made with the King of Spain'. Along with Argentine troops, he asked Urquiza to entreat a legendary Mapuche warlord, statesman and diplomat to come to Wallmapu's defence:

Calfucurá, who had crossed into Puelmapu around 1830, establishing a vast, multi-ethnic confederation, and who possessed a precious blue stone that was said to make him invincible. Instead, back-up came from an unlikely quarter.

In 1860, a strange figure with an aquiline nose, bushy beard, and dark ringlets to his shoulders appeared in Wallmapu. He wore a woollen poncho and the woven headband of a Mapuche lonko. A sixth son and country lawyer, Orélie-Antoine de Tounens was another fanboy of *La Araucana*. And that November, a council of Mapuche chiefs convened by Kilapán proclaimed the thirty-something Frenchman King of the Araucanía and Patagonia.

They drafted a lengthy constitution: the monarchy would be guided by an elected parliament, a council of nobles and a cabinet. Kilapán – Mañilwenu's son, and a seasoned warrior – was to be minister of war. Letters were penned to Queen Victoria and other potentates. But, barely two years later, de Tounens was betrayed and captured.

Accused of fomenting rebellion, he riposted that the government in Santiago was plotting to invade his realm. 'Would it think of conquering it if it was already in its power? It speaks of borders between Chile and the Araucanía; does this not mean that Chile ends there?' He was destined for a lunatic asylum before the French consul stowed him on a warship bound for home.

Chilean and foreign writers alike have long shared the same verdict: de Tounens was a fantasist who hoodwinked a desperate people. But some Mapuche writers have recently argued otherwise. As with the Diaguita and Bohórquez, the Mapuche used a European pretender – however self-interested – as a figurehead to defend their freedom. Chile may have thought twice about invading a constitutional monarchy with a plausible French agent at its head.

The exiled king of the Araucanía also defended his coronation. 'I may be reproached for not having founded a republic rather than a monarchy in a country surrounded by republics,' he conceded in his memoirs. But 'this form of government would have been rejected by the Araucanians, who have fond memories of royalist Spain, a scrupulous observant of treaties concluded with their fathers, and for whom the word republic has been rendered synonymous with disloyalty by the deeds of Chile'. The Mapuche had every right to decide what kind of government to put themselves under, he added. 'Are their parliaments any the lesser for being held on horseback in the open air?'

Back in Paris, de Tounens drummed up support in high places via his newspaper, *The Steel Crown*. He met with Napoleon III and returned to South America in 1870. France was meanwhile annexing swathes of Africa, South-east Asia and Polynesia – and even invaded Mexico to impose a short-lived puppet ruler, Maximilian I. If de Tounens' return was supported by the French emperor, writes Pedro Cayuqueo, it would be 'totally coherent with French colonial policy of the time'.

Setting out west from Argentina, de Tounens' journey was bumpier than before. The Mapuche of Puelmapu imprisoned him as a spy before a young warrior called Lemunao remembered him. He rode for months over the pampas to join up with Kilapán, reportedly offering him guns and cannons. A French gunship lingered off the coast.

But Chile's thrust into Wallmapu was now well underway. Saavedra, who had interrogated de Tounens eight years previously, put a price on his head. 'King Aurelio was afraid,' Lemunao's son recalled in 1913. The Frenchman fled back over the Andes, where Calfucurá – occupied with directing an all-out assault on Argentine border posts – packed him off to Buenos Aires.

De Tounens' court-in-exile set up shop in a Parisian garret. He minted his own copper coinage stamped with the words 'New France'. As his 'appetite for rule swelled to megalomaniac proportions', the travel writer Bruce Chatwin later imagined, 'his career followed that of other dislocated monarchs; the picaresque attempts to return; the solemn ceremonial in shabby hotels; the bestowal of titles as the price of a meal ticket'. Aurelio I died without issue in 1878, once more a municipal bureaucrat in the Dordogne.

The latest pretender to the throne – a Toulouse aristocrat going by the name of Prince Frédéric I – was elected in 2018. The monarchy's defenders in the Mapuche diaspora say it serves as an overseas embassy for their cause. In Wallmapu, while some today dimly recall de Tounens as a friend, others call Frédéric a nonentity. 'No one wants him in Mapuche territory,' Juana Calfunao Paillaléf, a Mapuche lonko, tells me flatly. In fact, she adds, 'people are just waiting for him to come so we can batter the crown off his head. No one knows him here, he's never done anything. They're made-up kings.'

The exploits of de Tounens ratcheted up Chilean paranoia about their southern neighbour becoming a springboard for foreign invasion. Saavedra, now a congressman, masterminded Chile's assault on Wallmapu.

'There is no other way of forcing them to the submission that we seek,' he insisted, 'save taking from them all their resources.'

Kilapán had promised Mañilwenu on his deathbed not to cede one metre more of Mapuche territory. But he saw the situation spiralling out of control. Settlers had pushed twenty-five miles south of the Biobío, robbing and murdering as they went. Convening the Mapuche chiefs, Kilapán described the impossible situation they faced: when the Chilean government marched right behind the killers, he asked, 'How can justice be done?'

The only option left was war. The trusted former lieutenant to Calfucurá and de Tounens was proclaimed toqui. After stealing the horses of a grenadier regiment, Kilapán ambushed his Chilean pursuers in a stunning combined action of slingers, spearmen and cavalry at Quechereguas in April 1868. The Chilean commander barely escaped alive. Kilapán's army, a binding of scarlet wool adorning their spears, rampaged across Wallmapu's northern borders, appearing like 'sparks of flame, unexpectedly, at any place and at any time'.

Saavedra responded with a vicious policy of scorched earth. In early 1869, Chilean soldiers swept through Wallmapu, burning down houses, tearing up crops, slaughtering livestock and stealing over 20,000 cattle. They kidnapped Mapuche children to be servants for Santiago households: a crude reversion to the child slavery denounced by Antonio two centuries before. The starving survivors begged outside Chilean forts, bartering their silver for crusts of bread. Even the *Mercurio* pondered why Chile was waging a 'war of savages' against the Mapuche.

In January 1871, Kilapán's forces had a Chilean fort at Collipulli surrounded. Then, dozens of his warriors fell dead from the saddle in an instant: shot down by enemy cavalry wielding Spencer repeating carbines. Rapid-firing, breech-loading firearms now gave Chile a decisive edge over the Mapuche, who – other than the odd captured rifle – relied on weapons barely changed since the time of Lautaro. Railways meanwhile shortened the weeks-long journey between Santiago's barracks and the frontier with Wallmapu to scarcely a day.

Now nearing one hundred years of age, Calfucurá died in 1873, soon after plundering within a day's ride of Buenos Aires and returning to Puelmapu with hundreds of captives. The Emperor of the Pampas and Napoleon of the Desert was buried alongside his two long sabres. Kilapán, too, perished suddenly around 1875. His followers placed him a dug-out canoe, as his people had done for at least a thousand years.

Then they interred him alongside his father Mañilwenu in a secret spot, never to be found.

With the leading Mapuche statesmen out of the picture, the assault on their lands proceeded with a vengeance. Argentina and Chile, suspicious of each other's designs, raced to snap up territory either side of the Andes. In 1879, 7,000 Argentine soldiers drove their nation's border some 800 miles south-west into Puelmapu almost overnight. 'Our self-respect as a virile people,' said General Julio Roca, 'obliges us to put down as soon as possible this handful of savages.'

His campaign of extermination – killing at least a thousand Mapuche men and enslaving 15,000 women and children – is often called the 'Conquest of the Desert'. In reality, Argentina had conquered Puelmapu's rich grazing grounds and flogged them to foreign sheep and cattle barons, displacing the Indigenous cultures who had thrived there for centuries. Some 8.5 million hectares, an area larger than Ireland, ended up in the hands of just 381 men. Meanwhile, Roca's soldiers sent Calfucurá's skull to Argentina's Natural Sciences Museum. It remains in their collections: along with body parts of a further 3,000 Indigenous people from across what is today Argentina.

Chile's soldiers were just as pitiless. In September 1880, they murdered a lonko called Melín and his relatives on the roadside. When Alejo – a primary school teacher who had studied in Santiago – went to retrieve his father's body, he was also shot dead. Provoked by such brutality, in late 1881, the Mapuche rose up in a desperate last stand.

Chilean forts exchanged terrified telegrams. 'November 3rd. 9pm. Imminent danger, Indian attack, surrounded several thousands, reinforcements urgent.' The garrison at Imperial was left a 'pile of cadavers and ruins'. Laying siege to Ñielol, the Mapuche wore animal skins and screened their advance among herds of cattle. Others charged their vast flocks of sheep into the ditches surrounding enemy walls. 'The dumb animals pile up to the height of the parapet,' wrote one quivering eye-witness, 'forming a ramp atop which the daring horsemen can charge with their lances.' Only outright victory could preserve their independence. But 'how can you win with slings, *boleadores* and spears,' asked Jerónimo Melillan, who refused to join the insurgents, 'against those with rifles and cannons?'

On 5 November, warriors from across Wallmapu gathered at Lumaco, metres from where Pelantaro had slain Loyola three centuries before. Again and again they charged the fort, their long lances glittering in the dawn. But the Chileans were prepared. Locals still talk of the river run-ning red with blood. The few surviving Mapuche retreated. In 1882, Colonel Gregorio Urrutia continued south to finish the job.

Villarrica represented the last enclave of Mapuche sovereignty. The lakeside site controlled a strategic mountain pass over to Puelmapu, and held an important propaganda value: in 1602, Pelantaro's forces had razed the Spanish outpost to the ground after a desperate siege. Now, Chilean soldiers hacked down the forest covering the ruins. Treasure-hunters with lanterns flitted around like spirits.

Urrutia spun a shamelessly back-to-front tale for Epulef, the local Mapuche lonko. As the ruins had 'belonged to our ancestors', said the colonel, 'it was a great work of justice and reparation that their descend-ants should take possession of them to begin the great task of their reconstruction'. A peaceful man who strummed a guitar and doted on his daughter, the Mapuche paterfamilias – at least in the Chilean telling – seemed to consent.

But the hazy memory of Lautaro and Pelantaro resurfaced overnight. The next morning, Epulef came to Urrutia's quarters, a ruined patio under a dense canopy of Patagonian oak, to protest. His forefathers, 'owners of the city, had been the most exalted patriots, and fought for their land until defeating the winkas', he recalled. Their deeds had been written in a great tome that had vanished in a fire. In their names, the colonel's troops must withdraw. Urrutia lost patience. Chile was now the 'absolute owner of these territories', he snapped, and its 'soldiers would go where they please'. The Mapuche would be protected like brothers, he added: 'they had nothing to fear.'

Epulef's leg trembled; conflicting emotions passed like storms over his face. Perhaps he was weighing up the shame of his ancestors, the terrible wages of resistance. 'It is well,' he reportedly grunted. He turned on his heel and left in silence. Mapuche 'barbarism' was finished, Urru-tia told his soldiers. The Chilean anthem sounded among the ancient trunks. A telegram of congratulations was sent to the president. It was New Year's Day, 1883.

The victors shared out Mapuche land among thousands of settlers. Its former possessors were corralled into fragmented reservations. Between 1884 and 1930, Santiago recognised Mapuche ownership over 500,000 hectares of territory: barely five per cent of the domain acknow-ledged by nearly fifty parliaments over the centuries. In a euphemism to match Chile's ultra-violent 'pacification' of the Araucanía, these piece-meal property titles were called *títulos de merced*: deeds of grace. In the sixty years to 1990, a further 200,000 hectares were lost. 'We were right to rise up, because they were going to take our lands,' reflected a Mapuche elder named Taita Cuyupi, twenty years after the war of 1881. 'That's how it turned out. I barely have a place to live.'

Chile not only planned to absorb the Mapuche as second-class citizens but to remould their environment: Wallmapu's woodlands, swamps and ridges. Engineers felled forests, built roads and sought to drain Lumaco's wetlands. Lieutenant Ambrosio Letelier wrote that his men would 'civilise the Indians' by the spade, the saw, and the rifle. Barracks, telegraph lines and railroads sprang up under his soldiers' tools. A steel railway bridge, soaring 100 metres over the Malleco River, extended Chile's grasp deep into the Mapuche heartland in 1890. 'This wonderful monument', chirped the president, would forever mark the moment when Chileans 'shook off their traditional shyness and apathy' and undertook the 'solid enlargement' of their country.

By the close of the nineteenth century, the former colonial backwater had expanded by more than two-thirds at the expense of its neighbours. The conquest of Wallmapu – alongside Chile's simultaneous invasion of Peru and Bolivia, and Argentina and Brazil's defeat of Paraguay a decade earlier – was the third great South American conflict of the late 1800s. Each redrew the continent's borders, relegated the conquered territories to the status of extraction zones, and bequeathed a deep psychological trauma to this day.

The transformation of Wallmapu's forests, orchards and pastures into lucrative agricultural plantations was the key motive driving Chile's invasion. The monoculture that resulted also gave ready analogies to the conquered. 'After our independence was ended, all we have achieved with this civilisation that they say they have given us' – reflected Lorenzo Koliman in 1913 – 'is to live like wheat crushed into a sack.'

The Mapuche's fight would now take place within the Chilean state. On 25 December 1931 – the anniversary of Lautaro's victory over Pedro de Valdivia – a rowdy assembly took place in the shadow of Rucapillán, the slumbering volcano near Villarrica.

Convened by Manuel Aburto Panguilef, the eleventh Araucanian Congress was packed with thousands of Mapuche lonkos, Indigenous societies and Chilean feminists and workers. The Mapuche called for funding for schools and training for Indigenous teachers, support for small farmers, and identity cards. And, after passionate deliberation, they demanded an Indigenous Republic: one 'in which the Araucanian people governs itself' and, 'in accordance with its psychology, customs and rituals, can be owner of its land'.

Chile, entirely dependent on copper and nitrate exports and up to its eyeballs in debt, had been pulverised by the Wall Street Crash. While world trade fell by twenty-six per cent between 1929 and 1932, Chile's exports plummeted by three-quarters. The jobless millions swelled breadlines and slums. Gun-toting, grudge-bearing groups proliferated. The homeless moved into caves around Santiago. Amid the chaos, many Mapuche saw their chance for revolution.

Their Republic would form part of a federal Chile, in a great 'alliance of the indigenous, campesinos, and workers, once the united Chilean proletariat fraternally seizes power and makes its just demands a reality'. The old cause of Antuwenu, Bernardo O'Higgins and Mariluán – a union of equals between Chile and Wallmapu – had been revived.

The following year, in June 1932, Chilean military officers staged a coup to realise this dream. Among the ringleaders was an eccentric air force colonel named Marmaduke Grove. They sought to recognise the Soviet Union, hike taxes on the rich, and sign new treaties with the country's native peoples. But the Socialist Republic of Chile lasted just twelve days before suffering a reactionary counter-putsch. Grove was banished to Rapa Nui aboard a gunship called the *Araucano*.

TODAY, TOMORROW, ALWAYS

They march through Temuco, led by machis banging cultruns and young men dancing and blowing flutes. They take down the Chilean tricolour outside city hall, and hoist the Wenufoye. Another group throws a rope around Pedro de Valdivia's neck. With scarcely a tug, the conquistador snaps off at the ankles and crumples on the pavement. They stamp on his lifeless body and bludgeon it with clubs.

Across town, the demonstrators decapitate a figure they take to be Diego Portales, the authoritarian chief minister who crushed the cause of a federal Chile in the 1830s. The blameless head of the aviator Dagoberto Godoy is slung from Caupolicán's outstretched arm. In Nueva Imperial, another effigy of Pedro de Valdivia is smashed to bits. A nearby statue of Bernardo O'Higgins is left intact, with a message sprayed on its base: 'Your nice letter saved you.'

A few months later. Mid-winter, August 2020. The bridge over the Lumaco River, where Mapuche independence was restored in 1592 and lost in 1881. A steady drumbeat. Cornelio Saavedra, butcher of the Araucanía and architect of Wallmapu's annexation, his face ashen-grey, is manhandled forward. With little ceremony, Saavedra is heaved over the edge. The statue disappears under the freezing current with a heavy, satisfying splash. The crowd whoops, claps and yells: 'Marichiweu!'

'Good evening, Chile!' The shaggy hair from his student protest leader days has been trimmed, the beard clipped, the forearm tattoo of a Patagonian lighthouse hidden under a crisp white shirt. But as Gabriel Boric takes to the stage in Santiago, on the warm election night of 19 December 2021, his words are implicitly radical. To deafening cheers, he grins and repeats his greeting in Rapa Nui, Aymara and Mapudungun. 'Pō nui, suma aruma, pün may!'

Boric's path to the presidency was paved by the protests that erupted in Santiago in October 2019. Hundreds of miles south, Mapuche protesters toppled statues of conquistadors and colonisers. Up north, protesters in La Serena burned a bust of the conquistador Francisco de Aguirre, replacing it with an effigy of Milanka, a Diaguita woman. The Wenufoye, fluttering from statues around Santiago, became the protests' defining symbol.

As a congressman, Boric helped channel the messy, conflicting demands in the street towards a peaceful outlet: the redrafting of Pinochet's constitution. His plan was backed by a landslide in a referendum. For the first time in history, the very blueprint of the state would be determined not in smoky rooms by men in uniforms and ties, but by an elected assembly with over half its seats reserved for women and Indigenous people.

Diego de Almagro still presides over the old congress chamber in Santiago. But the scene below the painting now tells a different story. Among the suits are people wearing shorts, flowery shirts, wide Andean skirts, straw hats, long, dark plaits and tinkling Mapuche silverwork. Empty seats are slung with the Wenufoye, the Wiphala, and the Wünelfe. In January 2022, the 155 delegates were halfway through writing the new constitution, presided over by Elisa Loncón, a Mapuche academic. After centuries of discrimination, she says, Chile's native peoples have proved that 'our country, in all its differences, can hold dialogue and live together democratically'.

In the end, the draft contains 388 articles: the longest such document in the world. It enshrines the protection of animals, mandates a fifty-fifty gender split in all government jobs, and guarantees the right to food, healthcare and education. More momentously, it declares Chile 'a regional, plurinational and intercultural state'. The country will henceforth be made up of autonomous provinces, districts and Indigenous territories – although they will be prohibited from seceding. Native peoples will have a separate court system according to their traditions.

Outside, on the steps beneath the Doric portico, I talk with Rosa Catrileo, a Mapuche lawyer and delegate. 'First, we need recognition that the state is plurinational, of our existence within the boundaries of the state as people who are holders of certain rights,' she says. She wants Wallmapu to be formally treated as an autonomous nation, in line with the 1825 Treaty of Tapihue.

Other Indigenous peoples are seeking the same. Tiare Aguilera is the delegate from Rapa Nui. The Polynesian island – famous for its blocky, half-buried statues known as *moai*, two of which were stolen and are still kept in the British Museum – lies 2,300 miles west of Chile. Annexed in 1888, its people only became citizens in 1966. But the biggest challenge, Aguilera cautions, is making sure the new constitution speaks to everyday priorities. 'If the public don't feel part of this process, it won't be successful.'

An hour's drive east of Temuco, I call in on Juana Calfunao Paillaléf, a firebrand advocate of Mapuche sovereignty. By her count, she has been arrested dozens of times and spent four and a half years in jail. When I visit, she is facing four trials. Her alleged offences include assaulting a policeman and a government official.

Calfunao wears a black smock with pink tassels, an ornate necklace of silver, and her sable-and-grey hair in a long plait down to her waist. Her house, standing next to a thatched ruka, is set behind a gate made from sticks and twisted barbed wire. If I plan to ask her about Chilean politics, Calfunao tells me, I've made the journey for nothing: I'm no longer in Chile.

We sit down to a lunch of boiled potatoes in cheese sauce and pickled vegetables. The constitutional convention, she argues, is just the latest manoeuvre by Chile and its yanacona lackeys 'to perpetrate looting and invasion. They've been doing it for 450 years.' Figures like Loncón and Catrileo, she says, 'are not representatives of the Mapuche people'.

In 1860, a Prussian traveller visited one of Calfunao's relatives. The ruka of Ambrosio Paillaléf was stuffed with sacks of gold coins, silver riding spurs, guns, the skins of pumas and sea lions, and 'a great number of Chilean and Argentine uniforms, which he had acquired from deserters or looted in his raids'. The territory that now makes up Chile was already plurinational back then, says Calfunao. 'It's the Mapuche people who recognised *their* independence. So how are they going to grant it to *us*? The Chilean state is an enemy; nefarious, terrorist, genocidal, thieving, lying, usurping. I can't negotiate with a state like that.'

Her stance is understandable. Soon after Pinochet's coup in 1973, when she was a young woman, police arrested her mother, tore down their ruka, and beat Calfunao mercilessly. Tears come to her eyes, her voice wavers. She recalls blood mixing with the earth as she dragged herself along the ground, praying to the principal Mapuche deity. 'I remember asking Ngenechén to spare my mother, and I would spend my life fighting for this land.' At Isla Teja, a detention centre near Valdivia, the dictator's agents threw Calfunao off a bridge. She only escaped worse, she says, by hiding underwater and breathing through a reed: something she had learned as a child.

Many other families were separated. Thousands of Mapuche babies were adopted overseas, their parents sometimes told that their newborns had died. Only recently have they started to be reunited. Calfunao proudly shows me a photo of an emotional re-encounter that she helped organise. The regime meanwhile carved up the former Wallmapu among forestry firms run by its cronies. Many Mapuche were forced off land they had tenaciously recovered in preceding decades.

Since Pinochet stepped down in 1990, Chile has returned about $1.5 billion worth of land to Mapuche communities. But this remains a drop in the ocean. And other abuses continued. Not content with crossing the Biobío, Chile stopped it up. Between 1997 and 2004, a US$700 million hydroelectric dam was built across the river's upper reaches. Despite fierce resistance by Pehuenche communities, their ancestral cemeteries disappeared underwater forever, the Chilean leviathan accomplishing what Caicai could not.

'I'm never going to change. The restitution of territory, today, tomorrow, always,' Calfunao continues, slapping the tablecloth with a hand broken by a baton and never fully healed. I ask her if she thinks the offer of plurinational status in the draft constitution could calm the conflict. She scoffs. 'On the contrary. We will reject it entirely; we won't sign it. The Mapuche people will never be free that way, if they folkloricise us even more, so they can market us to the tourists.'

The Mapuche are a minority in their homeland. Most people in southern Chile descend from European settlers. What would happen to them, I ask, in a hypothetical, newly-independent Wallmapu? The winka are welcome to stay, Calfunao says, but 'they will have to live under our legal, social and political rules, speak our language, respect our land . . . They have to change their way of life to live with nature.' Besides, Calfunao is known for lambasting young Mapuche men for not fathering more children. If they do their duty, the ratio could one day be reversed.

We walk through the trees by a stream where Calfunao learned to swim. After some initial suspicion, she has been welcoming and open to the point of bluntness. But even the mention of Chile seems painful to her. As a survival mechanism, as an article of faith, she lives not in that hated nation, but in Wallmapu. 'I'm Mapuche first, second, third and fourth; I was born to defend my territory,' she concludes. 'I will live that life until I die. And after that, my words will remain in the earth.'

Villarrica, or Mapu Mülewma Zugu, is a tourist town with Bavarian coffee houses, burger joints and a replica ruka where tourists clad in athleisure wear slurp hearty Mapuche stews. A grassy corner down by the lake contains the many-layered ruins of occupations past: the pre-Columbian settlement, the Spanish fort of 1552, the Mapuche restoration of 1602, the Chilean garrison town founded by Urrutia on the first day of 1883.

There are BMX trails over the earthworks, broken bottles in the long grass, a couple of teenagers necking beers. A young man meditates in the dying summer sunlight, his face turned towards the dark mountain on the far side of the lake, streaked with snow, a thick clump of cumulonimbus mingling with its grey breath. That's where I'm headed finally, the volcano that Spanish-speakers call Villarrica, place of wealth, and the Mapuche call Rucapillán: House of the Great Spirit.

The next day, the road around the lake is clogged with timber trucks. As the new-build condos thin out, it turns into a bumpy gravel track. I drive through a tunnel of trees into the hills, as far as the car can manage, then walk ever higher amid a fragrant forest. There are cold, fast-flowing streams, bleached and broken trunks, monkey puzzle trees with knotted whorls on their trunks the size of dinner plates. Approaching the shining slopes of Rucapillán, the land is bare. Petrified lava gives way to crunching pumice.

Pichillancahue, the largest glacier to descend from the volcano, is nowhere to be found. Even past the signs announcing it, and further out onto the boulder-strewn moraine. Rucapillán's glaciated surface has retreated by nearly two-thirds since 1961. A few years ago, hikers filmed the moment when a thin frozen arch imploded. It seems to expire, bleeding black slush, before crashing to the earth. As my trainers fill with volcanic shingle, I round a hillock. It turns out to be an abandoned calf of ancient ice, cloaked in grit, sweating steadily into an ashy puddle.

When it was finally unveiled in July 2022, Chile's new draft constitution was perhaps the most progressive of any country in the world. It heralded sweeping advances for human rights, Indigenous autonomy and the environment. But the world had changed since the radical days of late 2019. Buffeted by Covid-19, gangland shootings and Russia's war in Ukraine, Chileans were now more worried about inflation and violent crime than giving rights to animals, first nations and glaciers.

The press made hay with the constitutional convention's cock-ups. Some delegates mused about replicating Soviet workers' councils in the army. One admitted he had lied about the cancer diagnosis that got him elected. Another voted via video-call from the shower. The spectre of King Aurelio stirred: conservatives alleged that the constitutional protections afforded Chile's first nations would amount to an 'indigenist monarchy'.

That September, a striking sixty-four per cent of voters rejected the document. Rejection rates were even higher in majority-Mapuche districts down south. For Sergio Caniuqueo, a Mapuche academic, an Indigenous 'elite' centred on Santiago have lost touch with working-class Mapuche – who saw the new constitution as bewilderingly radical.

In 2023, after Chile's driest decade on record, forest fires raged through Wallmapu, killing dozens and displacing hundreds. The eucalyptus and pine plantations blazed like torches. Vast plumes of smoke billowed over the continent. President Boric failed to deliver his breakthrough on the Mapuche conflict. Shots were fired near his interior minister's motorcade. He sent in the army to patrol highways and protect the timber trucks. The state of emergency rolled into its third year.

Dispersed, outnumbered and divided, the Mapuche are unlikely to see the restoration of their lost country any time soon. Even strident believers often speak of autonomy rather than independence. Given a free choice, and looking at the turbulence that lies ahead in this century, most Mapuche might opt to stick with Chile and Argentina. Yet others note that 2025 will mark 200 years since the newborn Chilean republic and the ancient Mapuche realm recognised each other as brothers. If the spirit of the great parliaments of Tapihue and Quillín can be recovered, perhaps the relationship between Chile and its greatest pre-existing nation can yet be refounded.

A billboard rises above the ruins of Villarrica, where Epulef, the last free lord of Wallmapu, struggled to recall what was written in the lost book of Mapuche heroes. 'This is a memory that has been silenced,' it reads. 'We must awaken it.'

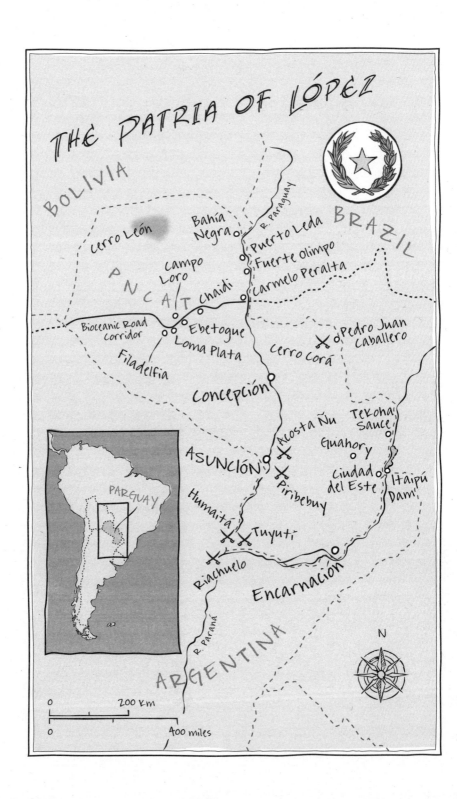

THE PATRIA OF LÓPEZ

BOLIVIA

BRAZIL

R. Paraguay

Cerro León

Bahía Negra

Puerto Leda

Fuerte Olimpo

Campo Loro

Carmelo Peralta

P N C A T   Chaidi

Bioceanic Road Corridor

Ebetogue

Loma Plata

Pedro Juan Caballero

Filadelfia

Cerro Corá

Concepción

Tekoha Sauce

Acosta Ñu

Guahory

ASUNCIÓN

Ciudad del Este

Itaipú Dam

Piribebuy

PARGUAY

Humaitá

Tuyutí

Riachuelo

Encarnación

R. Paraná

ARGENTINA

N

0   200 km

0   400 miles

8

I Die With My Country

Paraguay and the Patria of López, 1870–

MARKED IN FIRE AND ASH

I've just returned to Paraguay when congress goes up in flames. Horacio Cartes, the president, is secretly trying to change the constitution so he can be re-elected. He is later alleged to have offered a million dollars in bribes to senators – from his Colorado Party and the opposition – to wave it through.

But word has got out. Demonstrators wearing Paraguay's red-and-white striped football shirt descend on the plaza outside. Piles of trash smoulder. Fireworks explode around our ears. The cops blast rubber pellets and canisters of tear gas, forcing the crowds back. My retinas prickling, I lend my water to a spluttering, red-faced man, who sluices his eyeballs clean and returns to the fray.

As night falls, half-naked protesters, T-shirts wrapped around their faces, break through the thin security cordon. They use wooden planks and metal barriers to smash through the glass into the lobby. Flames gut the ground floor, smoke blackening the modernist edifice. It's like Carnaval and a Copa Libertadores win in one. The rioters emerge from the inferno with sheaves of parliamentary resolutions, throwing them like confetti over the pogoing crowds. They chant the words of Paraguay's unofficial anthem: 'beloved patria, we are your hope / the creed of valour the Paraguayan race must follow / is triumph or die.'

The police regroup, now on horseback and wielding long batons and shotguns. Silhouetted against the flickering flames, they charge in a line among tangled roots, broken paving slabs and statues of conquistadors and liberators. I weave through the skirmish to the cathedral on the far side of the square, where student doctors are carrying unconscious, bloodied bodies to an ambulance. Then the vehicle pings with pellets as the paramedics also come under attack.

Skirmishes spread to the nearby streets. Across town, inside the head-quarters of the main opposition party, there is a crowd of ashen-faced young people. On the floor, shell casings and a pool of crimson. The CCTV shows the police bursting in, shooting a twenty-five-year-old activist in the back, and stepping on him as he died.

The Church and the US Embassy call for calm. Cartes – a cigarette-manufacturing mogul partial to Scotch and skinny jeans, most of whose merchandise is smuggled into Brazil and Argentina – backs down. Soporific normality returns to the streets of central Asunción. Mangoes gently spoil in the gutter. Taxi drivers play checkers with bottle-tops beneath purple-blossomed jacarandas. Shoeshine boys, and Indigenous Maka matrons selling wooden jaguars, mingle with lost-looking back-packers and baby-faced Mormon missionaries. A pedlar dangles goldfish in plastic bottles from a stick.

I slip back into the routine of barbecues and power cuts. The in-crowd down litres of ice-cold pilsner to electronica in crumbling fin-de-siècle palazzos, bantering in porteño dialect and Guaraní slang. Hens peck among the shacks squeezed behind the bubblegum-pink presidential palace. Their inhabitants hang hammocks in the steam locomotives from Glasgow that finally ground to a halt in 2012.

A few weeks later, with the bloodstains scrubbed off the plaza, flag-waving crowds gather again. Women in swishing dresses with bottles stacked on their heads dance to polkas played on the harp. A short, bespectacled man with a grey beard takes to the stage. It's Independence Day, celebrating the bloodless revolution through which Paraguay shrugged off Spanish rule in 1811.

But Fernando Griffith – a motivational speaker turned minister of culture – has the events of fifty years later on his mind: the War of the Triple Alliance, a 'horrendous crime that marked us in fire and ash'. Contemporaries, he says, described Paraguayans as the happiest, healthiest, strongest, most law-abiding, best-educated people in the world. So imperial powers in league with Argentina, Brazil and Uruguay sought to 'extinguish Paraguay as a nation, because of the fear that Paraguay provoked, because of its independence, its fortitude'.

It wasn't only allied bullets and bayonets that destroyed the country, Griffith continues, his voice falling to a husky squeak. 'It is an honour, a God-given privilege, to be Paraguayan. But this nation has forgotten its greatness. Because after every crime there always comes the forgetting, the lie. There was so much pain, the nation remained in silence for decades.'

'Paraguay is today a country under reconstruction. You are standing among the ashes and the rubble of a great nation. But a better time is coming, a time when we recover our memory,' he vows, cadences rising to match his peroration, bemused silence turning into applause, turning into cheers. 'Una patria nueva' – a new fatherland – 'is being made. As with any birth, there is always pain and discomfort. But Paraguay will rise again.'

In late 1869, Richard Francis Burton stepped ashore in Southampton, fresh from a sightseeing tour of bone-strewn South American battlefields. The most lethal conflict ever fought on the continent was still stumbling to its gory conclusion. But if the celebrity adventurer expected to be mobbed with reporters, he was disappointed.

Burton was 'mortified' to perceive how oblivious his fellow Britons were to 'perhaps the most remarkable campaign fought during the present century'. Tales of Dr Francia – Paraguay's dour, iron-willed dictator for almost thirty years – had once piqued the public's curiosity. But the country had since 'dropped clean out of vision. Many, indeed, were uncertain whether it formed part of North or of South America.' He found 'blankness of face' whenever Paraguay was mentioned, 'and a general confession of utter ignorance and hopeless lack of interest'.

Over 150 years later, the amnesia persists. If South America is a forgotten continent, Paraguay has fallen off the map altogether. Foreigners often confuse it with Uruguay, in many ways – a secular, liberal, World Cup-winner – Paraguay's opposite. The world takes Paraguay's drugs, beef, soybeans, migrant labourers, cleaners and midfielders, but has blanked out their distant source. In London, Madrid or New York, this might be understandable. But Paraguayans have long felt isolated and ignored even by their neighbours. In an aphorism so often repeated it has taken on the character of a curse, Augusto Roa Bastos – the country's most famous novelist – described his nation as 'an island surrounded by land'.

But Paraguay's invisibility – and its profound inequality – are no accident. They are rooted in two calamities that befell it within a century, double hammer-blows that changed its course forever. The 1864–70 War of the Triple Alliance is the central tragedy in Paraguay's history, and Marshal López its main character. Yet half-truths still dominate the public understanding of the *guerra guazú* – the Great War – while the blame for it remains bitterly disputed. For liberals, the conflict was a senseless slaughter provoked by the megalomania of López: a 'brutal and sybaritic satrap' of Hitlerian proportions. For conservative *Lopiztas* as well as many on the left, it was a genocide concocted by British bankers to destroy the emerging Paraguayan superpower, resisted by a strategic genius whose immolation – along with half of his people – represents an eternal moral triumph snatched from the jaws of annihilation.

This view of López was championed by Alfredo Stroessner, whose 1954–89 dictatorship was the second great catastrophe to befall the nation. The conventional accounting – over 400 opponents, imagined or otherwise, murdered and 'disappeared', some 17,000 tortured and tens of thousands exiled – can barely convey the bitter legacy of authoritarian rule. The regime – an unholy trinity of Stroessner, the army, and the scarlet-shirted Colorados – enslaved and slaughtered Indigenous peoples. Some 30,000 square miles of public land were stolen by Stroessner's cronies.

Meanwhile, the dictator claimed to be the 'rebuilder' of the patria, the inheritor of the marshal's mantle. He issued stamps with López's image alongside his own, and the slogan 'Peace and Progress': also blinking in neon lettering above the national bank. While mass movements brought down Stroessner's fellow Cold War despots, the Paraguayan dictator was toppled by his generals, living out his days by the beach in Brazil. Stroessner's functionaries still serve as cabinet ministers; presidents hail the general's birthday, widely celebrated with fireworks and polka music, as the *fecha feliz*: the 'happy date'. By the next election in 2028, the Colorado Party – of which Stroessner remains honorary president – will have ruled Paraguay for seventy-five of the previous eighty years.

Reflecting on these twin calamities – one dictator's ruinous war, another dictator's murderous peace – Roa Bastos was unequivocal. Together, they had all but caused his nation to vanish. 'At several moments in our history we have been on the verge of disappearance: historical, biological, physical,' the writer told an interviewer. Yet 'the damage done by Stroessner's dictatorship has been worse than the war of 1864–70. Because the Great War wiped out the country's population, but Stroessner finished off the country.'

The seeds of the guerra guazú were sown four centuries earlier, when the New World was divided up by the Old. While the Portuguese scuttled up the Brazilian coast, Spanish, German and English conquistadors rowed 700 miles inland in search of silver. A town rose above a bend in the Paraguay River, protected by two sturdy wooden stockades and a labyrinth of stake-filled pits.

The settlement belonged to a branch of the Guaraní, a far-flung Indigenous nation whose pathways criss-crossed the continent from the Amazon to the Atlantic. Their encounter, in 1537, was not exactly the love-in of popular legend. 'They didn't listen to us,' wrote Ulrich Schmidel – a Bavarian soldier-of-fortune – 'because they hadn't yet had the measure of our armour and harquebuses.' In Schmidel's telling, it took a three-day siege, with sixteen Europeans spitted by Guaraní arrows, before the defenders shared their maize, manioc, chickens and daughters. A new stockade was built, and named after Nuestra Señora de la Asunción.

Nor did the Guaraní women meekly accept their new role doing the conquistadors' laundry and bearing their mixed-race heirs. In 1542, the governor executed one of them – known as Juliana – after she poisoned her Spanish enslaver and encouraged others to do the same. When not revolting, the Guaraní enlisted the invaders in their wars against the nomadic peoples who ranged the Chaco: the vast, thorny outback across the river. Schmidel's company spent months tramping across it through waist-high water, cutting burrowing insects from their toes, enslaving thousands who resisted and paying off others with Nuremberg scissors and knives.

Back in Asunción, hierarchies crumbled amid the perils, privations and polygamy of frontier life. Formerly dirt-poor Spaniards, now attended by ten or twenty wives and bartering in Guaraní with their in-laws, became the equals of their aristocrat commanders. Guaraní women, who had traditionally done most of the farmwork, now shared in the hardships of the Chaco expeditions. The few Spaniards' wives who made the long journey upriver also had no choice but to muck in. Their husbands 'were so frail that we poor women took on all the work: washing their clothes, healing them, cleaning them up, cooking them what little food there was, standing watch, lighting the fires, shouldering the crossbows when the Indians came to make war', wrote Isabel de Guevara. 'Were it not for us, they would have been wiped out.'

Most of the Guaraní still lived amid the plunging waterfalls and dense Atlantic forest far to the east of Asunción. The Spanish crown sent Jesuit missionaries to convert and control them. The missions they established, clustered along the riverine frontier with Brazil, were no utopias. Discipline was harsh; epidemics killed thousands. But in between choir practice and tending the yerba mate harvest – and playing keepie-uppies with rubber footballs – the Guaraní novices drilled with pikes, horses and muskets, defeating marauding Portuguese paulistas in battle in 1641 and preserving their relative freedom.

At their height in 1732, the missions were a wealthy, quasi-independent republic of over 140,000 people. They became so rich and powerful that the crown expelled the Jesuits in 1767, leaving the missions to fall into ruin. Thousands of enslaved Africans were also transported to Asunción: by 1800, half the city's population was Black or mixed-race. Free Afrodescendant women attended Mass 'sporting silks and golden braid', upper-crust contemporaries sniped. Black soldiers trotted through the streets with silver spurs and reins, and could be found 'forgetting their condition' in militia companies officially reserved for whites.

After slipping Spain's clutches in 1811, Paraguayan society was further consolidated along martial, racially mixed lines. Popular congresses gave absolute power to José Rodríguez de Francia, a radical and austere public defender. He ruled as Supreme and Perpetual Dictator until his death in 1840, cementing the nation's independence against Madrid, Brazil – and Buenos Aires, which viewed his domain as rightly belonging with the ex-viceroyalty. Dr Francia forbade Spanish families from intermarrying, tightly controlled trade and immigration, turned monasteries into barracks and banished dissidents to a frontier gulag. *El Supremo* transformed Paraguay into 'a military state, able to make itself respected by its neighbours', conceded a Swiss doctor, one of the few foreigners permitted an audience. 'Bullets' – the sallow Jacobin was known to say – 'are the best saints to guard our borders.'

Rule passed to his nephew, Carlos Antonio López, a jowly, scowling patriarch who named his beefy teenage son, Francisco, commander-in-chief. Together, they splurged the state coffers on schools, railways, telegraph lines, weapons and battleships. Some 200 British surgeons, builders and machinists were hired to supervise Paraguay's pell-mell modernisation. This was not the warp-speed industrialisation that revisionist historians would later claim. Lacking coal, the iron foundry's output faltered; warships were still launched with wooden hulls. As a regional conflagration loomed, rather than produce rifled cannons, the ironworks were swamped with commissions from the ruling family: like reinforcing a buckled bedframe belonging to Francisco's mother.

But unlike Paraguay's fissile neighbours, Dr Francia and López senior bequeathed a stable, unified nation: one of state-owned munitions workshops, tobacco farms, cattle ranches and yerba mate forests worked by prosperous campesinos and the enslaved, who were gradually being emancipated. A satisfactory future awaited this landlocked, agrarian, middling power that could punch above its weight against the giants that surrounded it. 'The sun does not shine upon a country richer than Paraguay in natural resources,' wrote a US diplomat in 1853. He hoped 'that its policy may enable it to realize a destiny worthy of its natural endowments'.

Still, the region's jumbled constellation of warlords, factions and squabbles over river navigation required a shrewd statesman to chart a path to peace. López junior wasn't it. On his deathbed in 1862, his father exhorted him to resolve Paraguay's pending border disputes not 'by the sword but with the pen'. Francisco had only glowered in silence. His troops surrounded the congress called to decide the succession. The two delegates who demurred were sent to reconsider in a dungeon. For George Frederick Masterman, who served as Paraguay's chief military apothecary, the marshal's early promise had been dashed by a diplomatic visit to Paris in 1854. There, López was 'dazzled by the parade and glitter, the false glory and proud memories of wars and warriors'.

Along with French uniforms for his officers, Francisco Solano López brought back an unusual choice of consort. Eliza Lynch was a married Irishwoman whose parents had fled the famine in Cork. Statuesque, imperious, able to quaff more champagne than any high-society soak, she 'virtually was the ruler of Paraguay', Masterman thought. Determined to play Joséphine to the Napoleon of the New World, Madame Lynch convinced López he was the greatest soldier of the age, destined to make Paraguay 'the dominant power of South America'. Her 'evil counsels', the English doctor believed, were 'the remote cause of the terrible war' which 'utterly depopulated' her adoptive country.

The trigger came in October 1864. Defying López's warnings, Brazil intervened in a civil war in Uruguay and installed a puppet government. Seeing his future writ large, López sent troops to capture Brazil's forts upriver of Asunción and seized a Brazilian steamship. He had its flag stitched into a carpet for his half-finished presidential palace where he could stomp over it every day. López could have pressed his advantage against Brazil. Instead, he asked Argentina's permission to send troops marching 700 miles across its territory to Uruguay's aid. When Buenos Aires refused, he invaded.

It caused the nightmare scenario – Paraguay's larger rivals teaming up against it – to come true. On 1 May 1865, Argentina, Brazil and occupied Uruguay signed a treaty in Buenos Aires sealing their alliance. 'The peace, security, and well-being of their respective nations is impossible while the actual Government of Paraguay exists,' the signatories concluded. 'It is an imperious necessity, called for by the greatest interest, to cause that Government to disappear.' Students flocked to enlist, wearing armbands bearing the promise made by the Argentine president, Bartolomé Mitre: 'Asunción in three months.'

AMERICAN ATTILA

The years that follow – a gruelling slog of trenches, cholera, hunger, torpedoes, shells, thousands of lives thrown into the grinder to gain metres of mud – are a grim presage of the mechanised mass slaughter of the twentieth century.

Paraguay's forces in Argentina, micromanaged by López from far behind the lines, are quickly beaten back. The next best hope to win the war lies on the water. In June 1865, López orders his ad hoc flotilla – mainly civilian steamers, barges and canoes – downriver for a dawn attack. They set off late and chug alongside the allied navy mid-morning at the mouth of an inlet called the Riachuelo. With no grappling hooks, the Paraguayan boats bounce harmlessly off. Shot pierces their boilers, scalding the British engineers to death. One sailor boards a Brazilian vessel, cleaves an officer's head with his cutlass and – finding himself alone – dives through the porthole opposite. The ships that aren't beached or destroyed limp back in heavy fog, decks covered with dying men.

Peace talks fail. The slugging match shrinks to the swamps around Humaitá – a Paraguayan fortress of earthworks dominating a horse-shoe bend in the river, with seven heavy chains twisted across it to block enemy ships. The ladies of Asunción drill with lances and pawn their jewellery for the war effort. The men forge a supersized field gun from church bells – the Christian Cannon – melt down machinery for ammo, and wrap bundles of shrapnel in cowhide and creepers. Curious caimans are periodically sent sky-high by floating mines. Madame Lynch's col-lection of eau de parfum is rattled as stray cannonballs glance off López's bunker. The damage is quickly plastered and painted over to preserve his aura of invincibility.

In May 1866, López attacks the enemy's fortified camp at Tuyutí. The backbone of Paraguay's army are piled onto pyres a hundred corpses high, 'so lean that they would not burn'. Four months later, the invaders return the favour, marching across boggy ground, through thorns and sharpened stakes, into a ditch, up a steep escarpment and level with the Paraguayan guns at Curupayty. 'To die for one's patria

gives our name a lustre that will never be dulled,' scribbles Domingo
Fidel Sarmiento, a twenty-one-year-old Argentine captain. 'But let us
leave off with these lines, for this is starting to look like a posthumous
letter. Today is September 22nd, 1866. It is ten in the morning. The
shells are starting to explode over the battalion. Goodbye, my mother!'

'The bombs, cannonballs and shrapnel vomited by our cannons
carved holes in their columns. Entire companies fell to the ground,'
recalls Juan Crisóstomo Centurión, a Paraguayan colonel. 'Weapons,
clothes, and men torn to bits were thrown in the air in total confusion.'
It is the deadliest battle in modern South American history. Some 5,000
attackers perish, including Sarmiento. Cándido López, a cobbler and
photographer from Buenos Aires, has one arm mangled by a grenade.
With the other, he later paints the aftermath as a Boschian hellscape.
Half-dead men crawl through pools of blood and smouldering brush
fires under a leaden sky. Not ones to waste scarce meat, barefoot Paraguayan troopers carve flesh from disembowelled horses with their
bayonets. They strip dead officers of their dress uniforms, shoot the
wounded, and dump the bodies in the river, where they float past the
morose allied camp the next morning. Had López counter-attacked, he
might have driven the invaders back to the Atlantic. Instead, he hardly
budges for a year.

A young career soldier from humble origins, José Eduvigis Díaz had
risen through the ranks to mastermind the victory at Curupayty. But
López is careless with his star general. In January 1867, Díaz paddles
downriver to surveil the enemy fleet. A Brazilian shell explodes near his
canoe, shattering his right leg. The limb is amputated, embalmed and
placed in a tailor-made coffin by his bedside. Díaz dies from sepsis two
weeks later. His absence is sorely felt. In November, the Paraguayans
finally go on the offensive again, charging the allied lines at Tuyutí and
catching them by surprise. The Uruguayan contingent is left with barely
twenty men and a general. But on the marshal's orders, his troops disperse to pillage the camp, stuffing their pockets with artichokes and
swallowing fistfuls of sugar amid exploding powder magazines. As they
stagger back to Humaitá – carrying parasols, crinolines and a telescope –
the allies rally, cutting down 2,500 veterans whom López can hardly
afford to lose.

British diplomats try to broker a deal: if López goes into exile, the
allies will withdraw. He refuses. *Seminario*, an official broadsheet,
makes his thinking plain: the marshal would only quit the patria once
every last Paraguayan was dead. Time and again, Paraguayan units fight

to the last man. Some of those patched up by the allies tear off their bandages, preferring to bleed to death than be forced to fight their comrades. Others gratefully receive new weapons from their captors, march forwards – and defect as soon as they see the Paraguayan flag. Eyewitnesses reached for facile explanations. The rank-and-file were obviously terrified of 'the American Attila'. López must have brainwashed his peasant conscripts: or maybe they didn't speak enough Spanish to ask for quarter. Others thought Paraguayans worshipped their marshal like a messiah. 'It is a devotion that surpasses anything' – said a sympathetic US diplomat – 'I have ever witnessed before.'

The bearded, barrel-chested chieftain in the poncho and straw sombrero, giving fine speeches a safe distance from the shooting, was a serviceable figurehead. But in reality, his people needed little exhortation to defend themselves tooth-and-nail. They had closed ranks for centuries against all contenders: Portuguese slavers, raiders from the Chaco, scheming European monarchs and frock-coated despots in Buenos Aires seeking to swallow their province whole. This was just the latest existential threat: a clash over the control of Montevideo city hall that had spiralled out of control, becoming a civilisational struggle with ugly racial overtones.

In the pages of *Cabichuí*, a Paraguayan propaganda sheet printed in the trenches, Pedro II of Brazil became 'his majesty of the monkeys', plotting to 'extend the chains of black slavery'. The invaders were depicted as donkeys, apes and winged demons, drinkers of Paraguayan blood, 'barbarous and faithless, lawless, godless and without Christ'. On the other side, Buenos Aires had long looked down on Paraguay as a 'semi-barbarous, almost "Indian" power'. At the imperial court in Rio de Janeiro, López's ultimatums had met with 'shouts of laughter'. His opponents in Uruguay suggested he focus on 'the squabbles of his half-naked squaws at home'.

Nobody was laughing anymore. The Triple Alliance seemed 'determined not to leave a Paraguayan of any age or sex alive'. This was now, thought Masterman, a 'war of extermination'.

State-of-the-art ironclad warships arrive from Brazil. They steam past the guns of Humaitá in February 1868 – helped by heavy rain, which lets them glide past the submerged chains – with barely a dent to their plates. A brief bombardment knocks a pinnacle off López's palace in Asunción and splatters stray dogs across the marketplace. The capital's residents are evacuated to the outskirts, where they shiver, sicken and starve. The diplomatic corps hole up in the American legation, besieged by ravening cats, until neutral gunships come upriver to rescue them.

By night, boarding parties paddle alongside the Brazilian ironclads and drop grenades down the funnels. A storm of shrapnel sweeps them from the decks. The allies now control the Paraguay River, and encircle Humaitá by land. On 24 July – López's birthday – bands with battered instruments play waltzes as the Sevastopol of the South and its skeleton garrison are surreptitiously abandoned. In their penultimate issue, the editors of *Cabichuí* delve further into science fiction. López rides out in front of his armies, sunbeams arcing off his sabre to smite the Brazilian emperor and put his terrified hordes to flight.

Over the following six months, with the enemy inching closer to his makeshift camp at San Fernando, López executes hundreds of alleged conspirators and cowards: foreign merchants, his two brothers and two brothers-in-law, the bishop, an early unrequited crush, and the wife of the officer who dared to surrender Humaitá. To save bullets, and to make an example, most are bayoneted or impaled. López even has his mother and sisters flogged. The blameless and the deserving alike are caught up in the paranoid marshal's dragnet. An officer from the defeated Confederate army called James Manlove – with an acute sense for picking the losing side – had offered to plunder Brazilian ports with a 'fleet of corsairs' under the Paraguayan tricolour and Dixie flag. López sends Major Manlove before a firing squad as well.

In December, at the Battle of Lomas Valentinas, the remnants of Paraguay's army are destroyed. The marshal's escort, dragoons with monkey tails swinging from their helmets, drop from the saddle under heavy fire. He orders his aides to fight with lances. Those who return, saluting with shattered limbs, are given a swig of rum and sent forward again. Ramona Martínez, a nurse enslaved in the marshal's household, picks up a sabre and charges into the fray, rallying the wavering survivors. López is allowed to escape into the hills. The allies seem to want him to scrape together what's left of his people for the slaughter. Burton and assorted rubberneckers pitch up. They're here to see 'the end of the struggle', one tells a Paraguayan prisoner. 'Then,' he replies softly, 'you'll be waiting for many years.'

The conflict had mutated: from cross-country Napoleonic marches in Argentina, via a Trafalgar-esque engagement at the Riachuelo, to Somme-style trench warfare around Humaitá. It evolves once more, spawning a plucky civilian resistance against the merciless counterinsurgency waged by the allies. In March 1869, López sends a train mounted with a cannon hurtling down the tracks towards occupied Asunción. Its crew gun down forty Brazilians before steaming to safety, picking up Madame Lynch from a tea party at her country house along the way. In August, as the marshal sets out on a winding, gruelling retreat north, a garrison of old men, women and schoolboys are left to defend the village of Piribebuy, his temporary capital. Though outnumbered twenty to one, they refuse to surrender, packing their mismatched guns with potsherds and palm shells.

The handful of adolescents who survive the allied bombardment and cavalry charges mount a last stand at the church. 'It was no fun fighting against children,' the Brazilian squaddies later reflected. A house used as a Paraguayan field hospital burns to the ground with scores of casualties inside. Among them is Nimia Candía, a twice-wounded veteran whose company of riflewomen had sworn to never be taken alive. Today, the soot-blackened beams are propped up in the town's museum. People are still unearthing bullets from beneath their patios, says Miguel Ángel Romero, its custodian. A glass case contains long auburn tresses, exhumed from a mass grave.

Meanwhile, the victors ransack López and Lynch's quarters at Piribebuy. As a lieutenant plays the piano beside the headless corpse of a Paraguayan defender, Brazilian soldiers carry off tablecloths full of Spanish silver, Jesuit relics, cases of champagne, a well-thumbed copy of *Don Quixote* – and centuries of official correspondence. Some 50,000 manuscripts were returned in the 1980s. But Paraguayan historians and presidents alike still accuse Brazil of holding back an incriminating secret archive – along with trophies like the Christian Cannon, displayed in the patio of the National History Museum in Rio. 'They handed back eighty-five per cent of the documents,' an archivist in Asunción tells me. 'But they kept all the ones to do with land and jewels.'

Atrocities multiply as the conflict staggers towards its end. An Argentine surgeon pulls up short on a country track, 'covered with the bodies of women, especially girls, dead from weariness and weakness, and others by lance and knife'. A few days after Piribebuy, the allies close with López's rearguard at a plain known as Acosta Ñu. Though mainly invalids and minors, they 'fight like lions', a Brazilian officer concedes. But the Paraguayans are armed with colonial-era muskets, blunderbusses 'and other pieces you only see in archaeological museums'. As the allied cavalry close in for the kill, he claims, the pubescent defenders throw away their weapons and stretch out their necks, 'anxious to have it all over with'. Over 2,000 perish to just sixty-two allied casualties.

Bernardino Caballero, their commander, sets fire to the pasture to cover his retreat, incinerating the dying. As the flames flicker closer, a mortally wounded boy begs his comrade to shoot him.

By 1 March 1870, the marshal and the last dregs of his haggard Home Guard have been cornered at Cerro Corá. López's men vote to make a last stand. He gives them all a medal. The Brazilian lancers quickly make mincemeat of the senior citizens and boys in rags. López canters into the trees, bleeding heavily. His men abandon him; Brazilian soldiers surround him. While the Triple Alliance's generals fought and sometimes died alongside their men over five long years, the marshal rarely risked his skin. Yet little in López's life becomes him like the leaving of it. As the American Attila feels his life force dissolving into the Aquidabán-Niguí, he seems to discover some inner store of stubborn bravery. He knows what posterity requires of him; how to play the role of the heroic martyr.

His infamous last words – 'I die with my country' – prove paradoxical. They mark the moment when Paraguay's half-century of independence and relative prosperity has been utterly annihilated. But they plant the seed of the imagined patria of López: a distorted memory of greatness far more enduring than the Potemkin power the marshal ruled in life. His hagiographers would later claim that López had time to pronounce his own extended obituary. 'The victor is not he who is left alive on the battlefield, but he who dies for a beautiful cause. We shall be vilified by the generation born of the disaster, who will bear the defeat in their soul, and carry the hate of the victor in their blood like poison,' runs the novelistic speech: repeated as if verbatim at official events today.

'But future generations shall do us justice, proclaiming the greatness of our immolation ... I shall rise from the abyss of ignominy, growing in the eyes of posterity, until I become what I must in the pages of History.'

A LAND OF SUNSHINE AND BUTTERFLIES

Deep in eastern Paraguay, among an island of trees surrounded by an endless expanse of soybean, a wiry, weather-worn man steps forward. He lifts up his ragged pinstriped shirt to reveal a torso pockmarked with dozens of dark circles.

A year earlier, the police burst into his clapboard house and broke his ten-year-old son's hand. When Milciades tried to stop them, they sprayed him with twenty-six rubber pellets at point-blank range. 'They almost killed me,' he says, choked by angry tears at his remembered powerlessness. It wasn't the first time that hundreds of cops have stormed the village, tearing up crops, slaughtering their animals and tearing down their homes. 'We're hearing rumours there's going to be another eviction,' says Milciades. 'I'd rather die than let them torture my kids again. If they come back,' he vows quietly, 'Guahory will be left a cemetery.'

'The river was beautiful before. There were lots of birds,' says a young woman called Elva. A baby girl with a whorl of black hair clutches with pudgy fingers at the sequins on her top. Now, crop-dusting planes buzz overhead, spraying the edges of the village with pesticide. The forest is quietening, bleached white. Chemical tendrils sometimes drift through the village while they are eating breakfast, Elva adds. 'Who knows how many people will die from this?'

'It's not right. Because we're in our country.' Government institutions offer landless campesino communities a few hectares of earth – and only after a grudging, glacial process. Meanwhile, Stroessner and his successors doled out estates to Brazilian soybean barons for a song. Not content with farmsteads larger than some European principalities, these foreign landlords are now circling around Guahory and hundreds more places like it. 'It's not just the land,' Elva continues. 'We need tools. Working in the fields is a big hardship, especially for the kids. I see that my children are barefoot, they barely have enough to eat. But the government is nowhere to be seen.'

With the community meeting over, our group of journalists and Amnesty International investigators sit on a porch exploding with yellow flowers. It belongs to Doña Silvia, a spritely smallholder with skeins of grey in her dark, loose hair. She recently inspected their neighbours' chemical-doused farms. 'The earth there was pitiful. The maize only grew so high,' she frowns, drawing a hand level with the tablecloth. 'But here, our land produces.' The spread she has just served, despite the monoculture advancing on all sides, is proof: the rich broth of a chicken that was pecking around out back a few hours ago, plates piled high with boiled manioc, and a golden, fluffy *chipa guazú* that is the tastiest version of the cheesy corncake I have ever sampled.

She is only sorry to host us in these circumstances, she adds, her voice cracking. Her son, Andrés, is facing trumped-up charges for resisting the latest expulsion. Her grandchildren are visiting him in jail. 'They want to isolate us, to discredit us and remove us, and give the land to the big businessmen.' The rest of the country doesn't know, or doesn't care. 'This is the problem of the Paraguayans. We forget very easily. It's not that we're poor, exactly, but that we lack a place where we can work in peace.'

'This land doesn't belong to foreigners,' Pedro, the village's teacher, chips in from the end of the table. 'It belongs to Paraguayans. Our grandfathers fought for this land in the War of the Triple Alliance, in the War of the Chaco. And we as a community are part of that, too.'

On 2 March 1870 – the day after the marshal bled out into the Aquidabán-Nigüí – one Buenos Aires newspaper despaired for the future of the country López left behind. 'I can compare Paraguay to nothing save a tree withered, scorched, blighted by a flash of lightning,' *The Weekly Standard*'s correspondent filed. 'The land is cursed, and its future is a blank.'

The true death toll has long been fiercely debated. Perhaps as many as 250,000 Paraguayans – more than half the pre-war population – were killed by bombs, bullets, epidemics and hunger, or taken back to Brazil in irons. Of the men, little more than toothless elders, toddlers and a handful of legionaries – Paraguayan émigrés who fought to over-throw López – were left. Photographers developed ghostly images of corpse-covered battlefields. Victims of massacres lay unburied. Forest swallowed up entire villages. Jaguars padded through abandoned, over-grown suburbs and snatched up feral dogs.

In Asunción, Brazilian cavalrymen and their mounts were billeted in the marshal's half-finished palace. Rampaging soldiers turned the city upside down in search of buried treasure, leaving 'not a pane of glass, nor mirror, nor lock untouched'. The National Theatre – where women had stitched uniforms for the war – became an industrial-scale bordello, where hundreds of widows in rags went to bed with the invaders for a crust of bread. The allies would occupy the country for another seven years, propping up a puppet government that rubber-stamped the asset-stripping of the nation.

Brazil and Argentina wrenched chunks of territory out of Paraguay's northern and southern flanks, shrinking the nation's claimed extension by nearly half. Only the mutual distrust of South America's two great powers stopped the buffer state between them from being partitioned. Instead, the victors saddled the vanquished with an unpayable war debt that was only forgiven in the 1940s. Two colossal British loans were taken out to finance reconstruction. Most of the money was creamed off by bankers in London and home-grown crooks. It was still being repaid until 1964.

Bernardino Caballero survived Cerro Corá: he was off rustling cattle on López's orders. In 1887, he founded the Asociación Nacional Republicana, better known as the Colorado Party. The 'heroic but unfortunate' war had left Paraguay 'a corpse', the Colorados would later proclaim. But their movement had managed 'to bring about its resurrection'.

Caballero's life-giving elixir was little more than a fire sale of public goods. Pre-war Paraguay possessed 100,000 square miles of state-owned natural resources: vast tracts of quebracho hardwoods rich in tannins used for dye, great forests of yerba mate trees. But as president between 1880 and 1886, López's chief lieutenant parcelled off eighty per cent of them. Foreign corporations moved in to take control of Paraguay's most lucrative export industries. President Caballero saw no reason not to snatch up shares in them, either. And he pulled the strings even out of power. In 1902, he toppled President Emilio Aceval: a rare survivor of the child soldiers he had left to be crunched up by Brazilian cavalry at Acosta Ñu thirty years before.

Rafael Barrett, a Spanish essayist with anarchist sympathies, reported on how Paraguay's famished peons suffered under the whips of their new bosses in the yerba mate forests. They were eaten alive by insects, enslaved in all but name in conditions akin to the Congo. 'On you weighs the memory of the nameless disaster,' he wrote in 1907. 'You waste away in the shadow of a horror. You are the survivors of the catastrophe, the wandering spectres of the night after the battle. What are thirty years to heal such wounds as these?' Meanwhile, financiers and their friends in office promised that the latest wave of privatisations would finally restore the nation's vital energies. Barrett likened them to 'pharmacists preparing to sell the dying man the final injections of morphine'.

Many Paraguayans still insist that Britain was the 'fourth ally' in the war – puppeteering the invaders to destroy Paraguay's surging economy, plant it with cotton for Lancastrian textile mills, and flood it with their manufactures. Queen Victoria is on the hook for genocide, some politicians argue. The theory is seductive, soothing the ego of the vanquished and salving the conscience of the victors. Foreign loans, mainly from London banks, made up a fifth of allied spending on the war; with Paraguay blockaded, Brazil snapped up her orders of British weapons, parts and ironclads. 'Brazil fights with English capital,' one indignant

Londoner wrote to *The Times* in May 1868. 'It is unfair to present her also with English ships.' But this was private profiteering, not state policy. Unless some smoking gun emerges from the archives, the guerra guazú will remain of South America's own doing: a rare bloodbath in the age of imperialism where European powers were bystanders.

Still, once the rubble had been cleared away, British stockholders readily snapped up the land and labour made available by Caballero's economic shock therapy. The average Briton 'really knows a great deal more of the heart of Africa than the untrodden wilds of Central South America', wrote a regular visitor in 1911. 'Nevertheless,' he added approvingly, 'it is a fact that a considerable part of Paraguay is owned by British capitalists.' They were drawn by the image of a subtropical Eden, 'a land of sunshine and butterflies where there are neither unemployed nor "Suffragettes", nor very rich nor extremely poor'.

The country's new elites even argued that the allies had done Paraguayans a favour. They had overthrown a tyrant and prepared the ground for development: mission accomplished. Paraguay is 'the paradise of South America', insisted one industrialist from Philadelphia: a fertile land of barefoot, cigar-smoking Amazons and industrious, docile men. 'No such war would be possible again,' he reassured would-be investors and immigrants. 'The new constitution of Paraguay does away forever with dictators.'

He was wrong on both counts. Despotism festered in the wounded body politic for generations. The symptoms were putsches, counter-coups, rigged elections, anarcho-syndicalist uprisings that lasted a few hours. And though the oligarchic Liberal Party held power between 1904 and 1936, the blueprint laid down by the Colorados – savage capitalism, dysfunctional politics – went unchanged. Paraguay's former conquerors kicked the man on the ground. 'Are your fans any good?' asks a customer in a Buenos Aires cartoon of 1915. 'They do fifteen hundred revolutions per minute,' comes the reply: 'like in Paraguay.'

Post-war governments sought to erase the very memory of López. It was made illegal to praise the alleged architect of Paraguay's ruin. Intellectuals theorised that the Guaraní language, the tyrannical legacy of the López dynasty, and the impenetrable Chaco and Atlantic forests posed a 'triple barrier' to civilisation. Paraguayans were demoralised, corrupted and 'cretinised'. His countrymen, argued one thinker, were 'the poorest, the most ignorant, and the most incapable of democratic life'.

New generations kicked back against the prevailing pessimism. In

1924, a group of students made a pilgrimage to Cerro Corá. Waking up in their tents after a chilly night, they were moved to tears by a small bronze cross: erected by locals near López's resting place in the depths of the jungle. In an extended but heartfelt metaphor, one later imagined a bandage, 'in the profound solitude of the centuries, extended in distance like a silver hair'. It was a 'bandage that is waiting for its removal by the Paraguayan youth', and, once lifted, 'will allow history to bathe in light'.

More than any other, Juan O'Leary – the teacher and lifelong Colorado apparatchik – tore off the bandage. For a while, his pen deified the common soldier. On an excursion to Curupayty in 1912, he imagined the crumbling ramparts 'springing up like a miracle under the divine hands of General Díaz'. He praised the 'anonymous heroism' of Paraguay's fallen, 'sublime Christs of a martyrdom crueller than that suffered by the son of Bethlehem'.

O'Leary was an unlikely champion of López: during the war, his mother had been banished to a prison camp. But his energies soon lasered in on the besmirched figure of the marshal. 'Half a century of persecution continues, the war to the death is prolonged,' he wrote in 1930. Paraguay's internal enemies sought to 'bring about a new, definitive Cerro Corá'. López's only error was not winning the war, O'Leary insisted; his only crime, loving the patria too much. 'The dilemma is simple: *either we are with him, or with the Triple Alliance.*'

The glowing embers of nationalism burst into flame. In 1932, Paraguay went to war with Bolivia over the Chaco, a conflict that lasted three years and left a further 200,000 people dead. As many are said to have perished from thirst – driven half-mad, sucking on brackish mud and draining drops from truck radiators – as from enemy bullets. Between bombardments, biplanes dropped giant blocks of ice amid the trees. On paper, Paraguay came out on top, with most of the disputed territory. But Bolivia's remaining slice of the Chaco was later found to contain all its accessible oil.

Before the war, Lopizmo had mainly been an affectation of elites. But in the Guaraní songs that circulated in the trenches, Paraguay's campesino veterans came to identify as the 'grandchildren of López', fighting for their patria's survival against another invader. In 1936, they installed a charismatic colonel called Rafael Franco as dictator. One of the February Revolution's first acts was to proclaim the marshal 'national hero without exemplar' and expunge from the national archives the decrees that blackened his name. Franco then had López's bones dug up from

Cerro Corá – at least, locals reckoned they were his – and brought back to Asunción. Schoolchildren singing a hymn penned by O'Leary lined the way. The marshal's remains were enshrined in a chapel – re-christened the Pantheon of Heroes – where a pair of bayonet-wielding guards stand vigil to this day.

But López's apotheosis did little to bring stability to his patria. A vicious civil war in 1947 killed a further 30,000 Paraguayans and pushed a million into exile, leaving the Colorados holding the whip hand once more. Defeat and humiliation, some argued, had poisoned Paraguay's very psyche. 'There is an infinite, rending sorrow that weighs heavily upon the heart of our people; there is bitterness for the injustice consummated with such impunity on the live embers of suffering and misery,' wrote Arturo Bray – an Anglo-Paraguayan veteran of the Chaco War – the decade after López's disinterment. 'The Paraguayan people are tired and sad; night has fallen on their destiny after a magnificent sunset of glorious crimsons; and that weariness and that sorrow, which are not dissipated with the first convulsions of a skin-deep democracy, explain and define much of the sickly process of our political develop-ment from then until now.'

The ground was prepared for a radical treatment for this self-diagnosed ailment. When Alfredo Stroessner – an artillery general, Chaco veteran and the son of a Bavarian brewer – seized control in 1954, he became the country's thirty-fifth ruler since the turn of the century: an average of one president every eighteen months.

Stroessner had his opponents dismembered by chainsaw as he lis-tened on the phone. His regime fomented a genocide of the Aché, a Guaraní people of eastern Paraguay. The dictator gave asylum to fugi-tive Nazis: including Dr Josef Mengele, the Auschwitz 'Angel of Death'. Gay people were rounded up and tortured; girls from poor families were abducted and raped by the general and his officers. The top brass – allowed to traffic drugs, cars, whisky and under-age women as 'the price of peace'; building replicas of Versailles to launder their loot – lined up in the broiling heat to wish Stroessner a happy birthday.

Not that they had any real fighting to do. Instead, Stroessner's Para-guay was the keystone of Operation Condor, a club of South American tyrants who murdered each other's enemies – students, trade-unionists, intellectuals – underneath the fig-leaf of anti-communism: trained and financed by the United States. The drugged or dead bodies were dumped into rivers, forests, deserts and oceans.

By way of thanks, Stroessner's regime received a billion dollars in aid and guns courtesy of Washington. When his regime misbehaved – for example, by sheltering and doing business with a heroin kingpin and former Nazi collaborator named Auguste Ricord – the embassy mulled cancelling its 4 July garden party as punishment. In 1974, the dictator gifted half an Asunción neighbourhood to his coke-addled son. It took until 2016 for city hall to demolish the property Freddy had left half-finished when he overdosed in 1993: a collapsing clone of the White House.

Few of those disappeared by Stroessner have ever been found, still less identified. Such progress, however piecemeal, is largely thanks to Rogelio Goiburú. He heads the tiny, underfunded government agency tasked with searching for the disappeared. 'We're fighting against time,' says Rogelio, when I meet him in an Asunción café. He has dark brown eyes, a firm handshake, a goatee and a tonsure of unruly grey hair. Para-guay's red earth is highly acidic, he explains. 'It consumes bones very quickly. Once the DNA disappears, it's much harder to obtain a genetic profile. And many of the *Stronistas* are betting on this.' Forced disap-pearance is a crime against humanity. Without a body, grieving cannot truly begin or ever really end. 'All human beings have the right to mourn,' Rogelio says. 'And I include myself.'

Agustín Goiburú, a doctor and dissident Colorado, was the regime's number-one enemy. He tunnelled out of jail and almost blew up the dictator's motorcade. The second time Stroessner's spooks abducted him, in 1977, he vanished. 'People are very scared to talk about Dad's case,' Rogelio exhales. 'It's all kept in a very tight circle. I know that there are people who know. But there's so much fear in this country to tell the truth. And it's logical.'

Sometimes, guilt proves more powerful. A retired major once came to Rogelio. 'He says, "Doctor, I want to tell you. I myself buried eight in a common grave. They were still warm." But the remains had been moved.' Years ago, Rogelio's brother was at a rally, watching the stage. Someone grips him: don't turn around, the voice in his ear says, but I'll tell you where your dad is buried. They excavate the tip-off and find bodies, but none are Agustín.

People often ask him how he can spend all day with bones. Firstly, Rogelio always replies, skeletons aren't alive. They're not going to do anything to you, he chuckles. He's been around bodies since he was a seventeen-year-old medical student. 'You have to be afraid of those who are alive,' he says pointedly, 'not the dead.' What's more, 'so many

compatriots have been disappeared because they fought for their ideals
in this country. In the last moments of their life, I'm almost certain they
would have wanted to be found.'

When his excavations turn up remains, Rogelio is struck by sadness.
The last shred of possibility vanishes, however implausible, that this
person escaped an inhuman end. 'But on the other hand I feel an
immense joy, because I found him. And – if there's any kind of energy
around us that we're not physically conscious of in this world – he's
probably happy that I've found him.'

Rogelio doesn't plan to retire. On holiday, he counts down the days
until he can get back to work. 'I'm searching for Dad, but I'm searching
for everyone. While my strength lasts and blood runs through my veins
I'll keep doing it. It's like a duty. And in this duty, always seeking justice,
I found a reason to live.'

The dictator invoked the memory of López to cloak his grand larceny,
rapine and murder. Banknotes and schoolbooks anointed Stroessner the
'second reconstructor' of the patria after Caballero. He branded the
tiny guerrilla groups that defied him 'legionaries', after the exiles who
had taken up arms against López.

Franco, the Chaco War hero turned revolutionary president, had
already stolen a march by fetching the marshal's remains from Cerro Corá.
The next best thing was his empress. In 1970, Stroessner had Madame
Lynch's remains scooped from a jumbled Parisian plot and shipped
back to the country that had chased her out – luggage full of purloined
silver – exactly a century earlier. Even O'Leary, the marshal's hagiog-
rapher, got a bust and a square named after him outside the Pantheon.

The dictator also imitated López, Lynch and Caballero when it came
to public goods. His party converted dozens of parks and plazas into
Colorado Party offices where handouts, threats and favours are still
dispensed for votes. Between 1954 and 2003, Stroessner and his heirs
parcelled out nearly 30,000 square miles of state land to their cronies:
an area the size of Panama. The plunder of Paraguay's countryside, and
the dispossession of its people, was entrenched. Today, just two per cent
of the population own eighty-five per cent of Paraguay's crop fields and
cattle pastures: the greatest concentration of farmland in the fewest
hands anywhere in the world.

Stroessner, despite his macho bluster, was easily intimidated. In 1965,
Brazilian troops crossed the border and occupied the Guairá Falls – a
series of eighteen cascades twice the height of Niagara. Paraguay's venal

and paranoid despot quickly capitulated to Brasília's demands. Over two decades, a gargantuan hydroelectric dam was built downriver, designed to be shared equally between the two countries. The falls were submerged forever. Thousands of the Guaraní peoples that lived along the Paraná River were forced off their land.

The Itaipú dam was dubbed a wonder of the modern world. Philip Glass composed a choral work in Guaraní in its honour. In 2016, it generated enough electricity to power all of Paraguay for seven years, or to keep the lights on across Latin America for a month. But as billions in kickbacks were siphoned off by Brazil's generals and Paraguay's kleptocrats, its final cost ballooned to US$79 billion: the most expensive infrastructure project in human history. The Paraguayan people were saddled with another colossal debt.

To repay it, in 1973 Stroessner agreed to sell Paraguay's enormous surplus of power back to Brazil at cents on the dollar for fifty years. His countrymen remained poor, forfeiting US$77 billion in potential income, while their natural resources powered Brazil's rise to South American superpower. Some 250,000 Brazilian farmers poured over the Paraná to colonise eastern Paraguay, fanning out from a new city in the shadow of the dam: Puerto Presidente Stroessner.

Several hours north, a clutch of huts – made of branches and tarpaulins – are sandwiched between fields of soybean and a polluted tendril of the Paraná. They lack clean water, medical attention – and electricity. Chemical run-off from the fields has given their children weeping sores. This is Tekoha Sauce, a community of forty Ava Guaraní families. Like many other Indigenous villages, the dam's floodwaters swallowed their homes and ancestral cemeteries. They returned here to the edge of the reservoir ten years ago, to pressure Itaipú – itself a major landowner – to return part of their territory. Soon after, a police raid flattened their crops and burned their houses, school and church.

'If there's another eviction we'll stay and die,' Amada Martínez, a steely community leader, tells me. 'Because we have nowhere else to go. People think Itaipú is a marvel. But the damage it caused to our people . . .' Martínez trails off. 'Behind the story, there's suffering.'

Today, Paraguay is what political scientists call a 'hybrid regime'. Puerto Stroessner has been rebranded. The smuggler's paradise on the triple border with Brazil and Argentina now goes by the bland epithet of Ciudad del Este. The products have changed too. It's no longer just TVs, drugs and smokes. On the outskirts of the city, shotgun-toting guards

patrol giant warehouses. Inside is a tangle of wiring, LEDs and dismantled CPUs, resembling a thicket of Christmas trees, cooled by industrial
fans and sheets of damp cardboard.

Paraguay's latest big business is Bitcoin mining: a hardly regulated
industry burning through the same amount of cheap power as a city of
hundreds of thousands, the profits largely landing in the digital wallets
of Europeans, North Americans, Argentines and Brazilians. The domination by outsiders denounced by Barrett in the wake of the guerra
guazú remains intact. Horacio Cartes – the tobacco mogul alleged to
have bribed his way to the presidency in 2013 – put it best. 'Paraguay is
like a pretty and easy woman,' he winked at foreign investors. 'You can
do what you like with her.'

He later rammed the invitation home to a soiree of Brazilian industrialists at López's palace: 'Use and abuse Paraguay.' In 2023, a protégé
of Cartes called Santiago Peña, a former IMF economist, was elected
president. But it's clear who's really in charge. Paraguay's new head of
state calls his patron *papá guazú*: big daddy. On Cartes's birthday,
crowds of sycophants queue around the block.

In his inaugural speech in the palace gardens, Peña blames Paraguay's
underdevelopment not on seventy years of rule by his party, the Colorados, but the War of the Triple Alliance. 'One hundred and fifty-three years
later, we are still recovering,' he says. But now, thanks to a new highway
across the sprawling outback on its doorstep, 'Paraguay is determined to
leave behind its former image as an island surrounded by land.'

'Paraguay was once great, and today we are decided to be so once
again,' he vows. 'The world shall bear witness to the revival of a giant.'

THE CHACO CONNECTS US

Mateo shuffles into the gloom of his home – a jumble of compacted
earth, fence posts and corrugated iron – and emerges with a tattered
cardboard box. Inside is a muddle of plastic bags, each filled with dozens
of plastic cases, all of them coated with a film of sandy dirt. 'Here in my
house,' he says, 'I have more than 1,000 tapes of Ayoreo stories and
songs.'

The midday sun beats down on Campo Loro: a dust-blown settlement of wooden shacks, rubbish snagged in bushes, a disembowelled
tractor and a brick-built evangelical chapel. Mateo adjusts his cap
against the glare and slots a cassette into his portable tape player. The

voice of an elderly woman issues forth, shrill and defiant, intoning a shamanic incantation along two keening notes.

'I'm an old man now,' Mateo explains, a rueful smile stretching his copper-and-silver stubble and deepening the creases around his eyes. 'I don't know how many more years I will live.' He pushes the stop button down with a thumb. 'The work I'm doing is for our children, our grand-children. So they can find the tapes, and the messages of the Ayoreo who died many years ago.'

Rewind six decades. Mateo, then a boy called Sobode Chiqueno, lived deep in the northern reaches of the Great South American Chaco: a tap-estry of swamp, savannah and dry, spiky forest the size of Afghanistan. Maps had long shown the Chaco stretching across the borders of Bolivia, Paraguay, Argentina and Brazil. They deemed it a hostile wil-derness, a 'Green Hell' populated only by snakes and warlike tribes.

Yet its name probably derives from *chaku*, the Quechua word for hunting-ground. And Mateo remembers it as teeming with plenty. 'Before, in the forest, there was everything. There was abundance, there was always something to eat. Honey, tortoises, giant anteaters. Those little golden birds. Even the roots, the fruits. You didn't need money to find things to eat. We didn't think to use clothes, or to buy hats. The life of the Ayoreo in the forest was better. Because they didn't know colds, tuberculosis, none of that.'

The Ayoreo were hunters and nomads. Wielding tall, powerful bows, the toughest warriors wearing conical caps of jaguar pelt, they ranged the Chaco in search of game and water, traversing the invisible frontier between Bolivia and Paraguay, sometimes pausing to tend pumpkin patches. Sobode's group always remained in sight of Cerro León, a sacred range of russet-coloured hills that rippled above the scrub. Sobode was happy living in the forest. Soon, when he became a teen-ager, he would be allowed to climb the tallest trees – like the bottle-shaped *samu'u* – to gather honey. It was an important rite of passage. The Ayoreo worshipped Gedé, the Sun. They felt closer to him in the canopy, looking out across the ocean of gnarled branches flowering with puffs of silken floss.

But their world was already being turned upside down. Outsiders were cutting trails through the forest, building great earthen houses, laying iron tracks. Ayoreo shamans foresaw a great illness that would kill many. A man called Pupude dreamed of the trees collapsing, screech-ing as they fell. Twenty years or so before Sobode's birth, terrifying sounds – staccato *ratatat* bursts; deep, gut-shaking booms – reverberated through the understorey. Soldiers hollowed out the samu'u, turning them into machine-gun nests. When they weren't killing each other, they wiped out entire Ayoreo clans with artillery. The survivors glimpsed great four-winged birds swooping and spitting fire. When the Ayoreo heard distant shells exploding, they thought they were stars falling to earth.

Alongside the Chaco War, there came hide-hunters, oil prospectors – and settlers. From the 1920s onwards, thousands of Mennonites from Canada and Russia journeyed upriver, driving ox-carts through lakes of mud and griping about the mosquitoes in Plautdietsch, a medieval Prussian dialect. Paraguay's government sold the persecuted Anabaptists cheap land in the middle of the forest, leaving them alone to build an autonomous, ultra-traditionalist nation of pacifists. The native peoples already living there were not consulted.

Ranchers enslaved their children. Iquebi, an Ayoreo boy, was captured and displayed in a cage in Asunción. Mormons, Anglicans, Lutherans, Latvian Baptists, Franciscans and Salesians came in search of their souls. Aided by Stroessner's regime, the New Tribes Mission sent native converts to capture the 'uncontacted' groups, pastors from Florida directing the manhunt from helicopters and planes overhead. At the turn of the millennium, Sun Myung Moon – a Korean tax fraudster who claimed to be the messiah – bought up 2,300 square miles of the Chaco, entire villages included. Reverend Moon dispatched a handful of Japanese acolytes to till the briny clay, rear a vegetarian piranha called *pacú*, and build a 'heavenly settlement' where 'God and humanity would cooperate to restart the world in accord to the Original Ideal of Creation'.

Those native peoples closer to the river and the capital – Enxet, Qom, Nivaclé, Yshir – gradually succumbed to the outsiders' bullets, Bible classes and poverty wages. The Ayoreo resisted for longer. Some are still holding out in the forest: the last 'uncontacted' people in the Americas outside of the Amazon. Taking their cue from the Spanish, the new crop of colonisers called the Ayoreo *moros*: Moors. The Ayoreo, in turn, refer to the interlopers as *Cojñone*: the senseless ones.

In 1961, the missionaries made contact with Sobode's group through his older half-brother. He brought a sling to hunt birds, fine words about life among the Cojñone, and some crackers. Mateo's parents spat them out, but agreed to go with him. 'After those encounters and re-encounters came the illnesses,' says Mateo. 'It was a very difficult process.' Nearly all of his group of eighty-five people perished. His father tried to walk back to Cerro León but died, convulsing, at the roadside. His mother seemed to expire from a broken spirit.

In the mission settlements, the survivors realised that clothes and food were not free: they had to work for money. The orphaned Sobode was baptised and renamed after the Apostle Matthew. Mateo felt lost. Maybe, he thought, helping the missionaries was the right thing to do. He was sent to the seminary at Fuerte Olimpo to learn Spanish and look for the Ayoreo still in the forest.

But Mateo earned a reputation as a rebel. He snuck out with his fellow novices to search for honey in the trees. The priests blamed him, 'the stubborn Ayoreo among us', and he had to leave. He met his future wife, Dona, and they returned to her parents' community, where they planted squash and beans and started a family. The village was called Campo Loro, or Camp Parrot, by its missionary founders: mocking how their flock chattered and repeated fragments of psalms.

When the evangelicals captured another group of Ayoreo in 1979, Mateo saw how they fell ill and suffered. It reminded him of his own family's ordeal; of painful memories he had tried to forget. He resolved to no longer help with such searches. And, seeing how the Cojñone used tape recorders, an idea began to germinate.

Mateo interviewed his newly contacted relatives. He recorded songs telling of encounters with spirits in the forest. He preserved Ayoreo wisdom: how the roots of the *chicoi* plant store water, how to track animals through the undergrowth, how the jaguar, armadillo and deer have souls and deserve respect. He had to overcome the fear and shame the missionaries instilled among their Ayoreo charges. 'It's like it was a muzzle,' he says. 'Every people has their history. But it's as if by remembering, I was teaching my people stories of the devil.'

The preachers switched up their tactics. They recorded Gospel readings onto cassettes and MP3 players, sending them with converts into the bush. In 1986, a group in the forest killed five Ayoreo working for the New Tribes Mission. One of their tape machines fell to the ground but kept recording. It was later recovered. Today, as the tape rolls, Mateo translates, his steady voice a strange contrast with the hoarse shouting coming from his hand: 'We don't want to accept what you say to us. You should flee, run away to your area, leave us here in peace.'

Nowadays, many of Mateo's recordings are peaceful snapshots of Ayoreo life: community meetings, conversations with old friends, football matches. The deadly rivalry between clans in the forest has mapped onto the Paraguayan Primera División. Like most in Campo Loro, Mateo supports Cerro Porteño. His neighbour's bungalow is painted in *cerrista* red and blue. The village next door, meanwhile, have daubed the bark of a samu'u in the black and white of Club Olimpia, Paraguay's other football giant.

Mateo has recently branched out into filmmaking, shooting a short documentary: *Ujirei*, meaning 'Regrowth'. 'We must not give up our lives,' he tells a handheld camera, balanced on a bucket. 'I am not yet dead, neither is my mind. Now the Cojñone think we are like worthless debris. As if we did not have a big country before.' His driving purpose, Mateo now explains, is to remind coming generations that they have a history; that their existence did not begin – or end – with the cataclysm of contact. 'I'm doing this work for my people,' he says, 'for the future of the Ayoreo.'

That future has never looked more uncertain. South America's largest ecosystem after the Amazon, the Chaco as a whole is home to some twenty Indigenous peoples. But this uniquely biodiverse carbon bomb is rapidly going up in smoke. By some measures, it's the fastest-vanishing forest on the planet.

Pupude's vision of the toppling trees many decades ago has come to pass, Mateo reflects. 'It was of the bulldozers today that have cut down all the forest where the Ayoreo live. I can't say that it's false. It was true.'

The Chaco has long been a symbol for Paraguay's isolation. One of the world's last great frontiers, it lies barely a hundred metres over the river from the capital. It takes up two-thirds of the country, but just four per cent of the population live there. Occupying the Chaco, in turn, has long been a yardstick by which the country will be judged to have escaped its long, post-López lethargy.

In 1924, a die-hard Lopizta mused on the theme. 'The incorporation of the Chaco into civilisation' would require heroic effort, wrote Justo Pastor Benítez: 'the cunning Indian, fever, serpents, innumerable wild beasts: all inhabit the trail marched by the conquistadors in search of El Dorado.' But riches were being sought once again in the Chaco, he noted: 'no longer the fabled Patiti, but its lucrative, real-life forests, its beautiful pastures, and its fertile soil. The railway and the automobile will soon reduce the months-long journey of the conquistadors to a few hours.'

It took a century, but Pastor Benítez's prediction is coming true. By the end of 2025, four years of construction work will finish on a bridge – the only one for hundreds of miles – stretching for a mile across the Paraguay River to Brazil. On the Paraguayan side, it will connect with a new highway carving a swathe of asphalt for 350 miles east to west through the Chaco. Together, they form the keystone of the Bioceanic Road Corridor: a massive infrastructure project bisecting the continent, connecting the Brazilian mega-port of Santos, via a shortcut across the Chaco and northern Argentina, to Chile's Pacific coastline.

The highway's backers say it will slash the time and cost for South America's soybeans and beef to get to Asia. Once the road is complete in 2025, the Chaco will finally be integrated into the nation, and hundreds of jobs will be created, says Arnoldo Wiens – Paraguay's public works minister, and a former pastor of Mennonite descent – in an interview. Space is being left alongside for a freight railway, he adds: the project 'exemplifies the win-win concept for everyone'.

Its critics say it will spur deforestation, accelerate global climate change, and pile deadly pressure on vulnerable native communities. 'For us the building of big highways is very dangerous, because they cause loss of biodiversity, animals – even human beings,' Mateo warns. Miguel Lovera, director of an NGO called Iniciativa Amotocodie, puts it even more bluntly. 'It's the final nail in the coffin for the Chaco and all its peoples,' he tells me. 'With this, the Chaco is finished.'

In December 2021, I travel the 400 miles from Asunción to Carmelo Peralta, where the president is unveiling the bridge's foundation stone. As our bus-load of dishevelled reporters arrives after a gruelling overnight journey, dignitaries are exchanging bear hugs and waving Brazilian flags inside a stuffy awning. Mario Abdo Benítez – Paraguay's president between 2018 and 2023 – pulls up in a jeep, fresh from the nearby airstrip.

'This will be the great Panama Canal of our region,' he says. 'This is a historic day for our country, and for Brazil.' The governor of Mato Grosso do Sul – the Brazilian agro-belt state on the far side of the river – agrees. 'We're going to integrate our two peoples. This is the realisation of a dream.' For the Indigenous locals I speak to afterwards – standing on the other side of a fence manned by gun-toting soldiers – the Bioceanic Road sounds more like a nightmare.

The project has brought some positives, says Oscar Posoraja, a community leader. Until 2019, the surrounding region of Alto Paraguay – the size of Austria, with 1.8 million cows to just 11,000 people – had no asphalted roads at all. Buses got stuck for days in the mud; their passengers had to be airlifted to safety. A trucker tells me he brings a shotgun to hunt caimans and peccaries when he gets stranded. Some Ayoreo have taken jobs on the roadworks.

But 'the building of a highway always brings negative things with it,' Posoraja adds. The bridge and motorway have triggered a property rush. Foreigners, mainly Brazilians, now own two-thirds of land within thirty miles of the border. Like the notorious BR-319 in the Brazilian Amazon, lines of destruction are fish-boning out from the newly paved road into the trees.

A few weeks before – says Enrique Pebi, another Ayoreo elder – a Brazilian landowner bulldozed a track deep into Ayoreo territory for timber. 'We want to keep it as our reserve to go hunting, to fetch honey, to get home-made remedies,' he explains, showing me photos of the devastation. But Ayoreo villagers are now too afraid of being shot by the 'invaders', Pebi says, to visit the area alone.

Their communities are poor and hungry. So they consented to the Bioceanic highway in exchange for fishing boats and tractors. 'The things they've given us will wear out in five or six years. The road will stay. I don't know how many hectares we've lost forever.'

A few months later, Tagüide Picanerei is speeding down the *bioceánico* at eighty miles per hour. He juggles the steering wheel, Instagram, his *tereré* gourd and Cerro Porteño thermos – and twiddles with the dashboard, the build-up to tonight's match crackling through the radio. With us are Santi Carneri and Mayeli Villalba, photojournalists who cover the Chaco. We pass construction camps and workers in orange overalls. Steamrollers flatten smoking tarmac in an arrow-straight streak that vanishes into the horizon. The first half of the highway is nearly complete.

Smoke-darkened palms line the roadside. Sometimes, the flames set by cattlemen to clear pasture have consumed the green fronds altogether, leaving just a slender trunk tapering absurdly into the sky. In places, it can seem like the forest is infinite, an impression of endless green outside the window, punctuated only by chained wooden gates and 'Private Property' signs. But fly over the Chaco and you see how the vast rectangular clear-cuts begin just metres from the road, stretching as far as the eye can see between a thin latticework of trees.

Tagüide was born in Campo Loro to Ayoreo parents a little over thirty years ago. Today, he spends most of his time in Asunción, lobbying politicians in defence of his people. Powerfully built, softly-spoken and dry-humoured, Tagüide is unsentimental about life in the forest: it could be nasty, brutish and short. 'The Ayoreo were an empire, between the Incas and the Guaraní,' he says. 'They decided to expand.' Spears glinting in the light of the full moon, they fell upon Yshir villagers – men, women and children. 'There was no mercy.' As soldiers and settlers began to encroach on the Chaco a century ago, such bloodletting spiralled out of control. But Tagüide is adamant that those Ayoreo still living among the trees should be allowed to remain there.

There are around a hundred of them, flitting between fragmented islets of forest in at least ten small bands. It's no paradise. Tired and hungry, sometimes wearing scraps of discarded tyres on their feet, they flee from the bulldozers and chainsaws – and trigger-happy truckers and ranch hands. On the last day of 2023, a man's body was found by the roadside near the Bolivian border. He had been mauled post-mortem. But from his splayed toes, and the black pigment covering his arms and legs, Ayoreo leaders knew he was one of their uncontacted relatives. 'The people still in the forest are suffering,' Basui Picanerei Etacore, an Ayoreo leader from Ebetogue, tells us. 'They're running from danger. We heard rumours that ranchers killed one of them, but we don't know if it's true.'

Ayoreo construction workers have spotted such groups loping across the new highway. Others have heard them singing, lamenting the destruction of their home. A group of Ayoreo women recently visited the PNCAT – a forested reserve that the Ayoreo fought to have recognised as their own – to forage. When they looked up, they were being watched by a tall, near-naked figure. They ran for it, blundering through the thorns, weeping inconsolably until they reached their village. Such 're-encounters', Tagüide explains, trigger a powerful mixture of shock and nostalgia. He likens it to running into a former lover – only more disorienting. Even though it's over, 'you still feel something. It's a feeling of profound estrangement.'

A sixty-mile stretch of the Bioceanic Road Corridor runs alongside the PNCAT. A tenth of it has been destroyed for pasture since 2005. And as the new motorway puts more farmers, hunters and missionaries within striking distance of their territory, the risk of violent contacts increases. 'If the Ayoreo that still live in the forest are taken out by force, they will suffer like we did back then,' Mateo had warned us. 'The government should respect them, and let them live how they want to live. Because they are humans, too.'

As night falls, we drop by Chaidi. A village on the edge of the reserve founded by Ayoreo who abandoned the mission settlements, its name means 'refuge'. Barefoot children tear around with puppies. Young men play kick-ups over a volleyball net. Tagüide's mother weaves a bag out of coarse *dajudie* fibre, a torch balanced in the crook of her neck. The women respond to our conversation starters with bashful smiles.

Eight blackened paws, two long snouts, and a pair of bushy tails poke out of a campfire. They had to walk for hours to find the anteaters, says one of the hunters, wearing flip-flops, an Argentina jersey and FC Barcelona shorts. He scrapes off the singed fur with a stick. Few Ayoreo can afford the prime cuts of cow packaged for export by the Mennonites. Their protein – tortoises, tapirs – still trundles through the shrinking undergrowth. But more roads means that more endangered creatures, including jaguars, will end up as roadkill and trophies – or vanish with the forest.

Demetrio Picanerei, Chaidi's primary-school teacher, approaches. 'You're asking people about the highway? I see both sides, positive and negative.' Before he was born, he explains, his parents fled Ayoreo communities on the fringes of Bolivian cities, ravaged by alcohol and crack. Paraguay was a haven by comparison. Now, he worries that the new motorway will spread the same vices as truck-stops, diners and motels proliferate.

The Chaco is already a major staging post for drug cartels. At night, it lights up with clandestine airstrips and cocaine-laden Cessnas coming in to land. The highway linking the world's two great oceans will make things even easier. Vulnerable locals will probably end up using. Prostitution carries little stigma in Ayoreo culture. Women have long gone with men – Mennonite, Paraguayan or Indigenous – in exchange for gifts. 'That's their right,' shrugs Demetrio. 'We don't judge them for it.' But he worries about the vastly expanded pool of fly-by-night boyfriends.

'The roads were very bad before,' Demetrio concedes. The paved highway, he says, has slashed the time it takes to get to hospital from four hours to eighty minutes: in an emergency, the difference between life and death. Few of the Indigenous people we speak to are against road projects per se. But they are keenly aware of the trade-offs: and that the highways are planned with other beneficiaries in mind.

The next day, we wake up in Filadelfia: the largest of the Mennonite towns in the central Chaco. It's like fast-forwarding to the region's future. There are street signs in Plautdietsch, a Chinese restaurant, austere chapels and retirement homes with manicured gardens. Mixed-race teenagers on dirt bikes rattle down Avenida Hindenburg in a cloud of dust and cologne. In the museum, stuffed wildcats goggle with glass eyes at a Holy Roman emperor on a corroded copper coin, probably dropped by Schmidel's company five centuries ago.

In the nearby settlement of Loma Plata, groups of Enlhet men – once far-ranging nomads like the Ayoreo – cluster on street corners waiting for work. A gleaming new petrol station at the centre point of the bioceánico sells jars of sauerkraut and twenty varieties of truck lubricant. We meet with Patrick Friesen, who works for Chortitzer, the town's Mennonite cooperative. They emigrated here from Canada in 1925 to live in self-sufficient isolation, he says. 'For the first two generations, nature was the enemy. They had to fight for survival, for every cow, every grain. The state was completely absent.' Until the 1970s, sports and singing in harmony were considered sinful.

Things have changed a bit since then, he says. Most have traded their horse-and-traps for John Deere combines and Hiluxes. No straw hat in sight, Patrick wears the Paraguayan farmer's uniform: plaid shirt, jeans, Timberlands. He shows us around the cooperative's dairy factory: the tallest building in the Paraguayan Chaco, it produces a hundred million litres every year. 'We're capitalists in the positive sense. We believe that if you get something, someone else worked for it,' Patrick says. The world wants meat and milk; this is where it comes from. His community welcomes the Bioceanic Corridor as a means of reaching new markets worldwide. 'You could see it as a threat, or as an opportunity.'

This prosperity has come at a cost: the Mennonites have flattened an astounding amount of Chaco forest. According to Earthsight, an NGO, one of Chortitzer's suppliers has been illegally cutting down chunks of the PNCAT reserve, along with two Brazilian companies. Leather sourced from the area lines luxury European cars. Chortitzer's manager insists that they have permits to bulldoze the trees. 'We're totally against illegal deforestation,' he adds.

Foreign charities and development agencies come and go, Patrick tells us. They dig wells, the wells dry up. Meanwhile, Chortitzer spends around $1.5 million every year on clinics, schools and sports projects benefiting thousands of Indigenous families. 'Our objective is to try to live together. We need more union, less division. We've learned that we're not going to change them. And they're not going to change us.'

Later, near the village of Ebetogue, we drive past a battered bulldozer in a fresh clearing, an iron cage shielding the cabin. Sunburned Mennonite workers sip tereré amid the wreckage. To see the tangle of roots and churned-up earth is to hear the screaming, once prophesied by Pupude, as the stubborn trees crash to the ground.

Summer is fire season in the Chaco. Livestock farmers set the felled trunks alight, flames racing through the brushwood. Hundreds of miles away in Asunción, you taste a sickly mixture of sap and cinders in the air. Towering, ash-bearing storms turn the afternoon sky dark as night, filling the streets with choking smog.

Lush rainforests like the Amazon have long hogged the limelight. As the world looks the other way, a fifth of the entire Gran Chaco – 54,000 square miles – has been felled since 1985. In Paraguay's stretch of the Chaco alone, an average of 1,200 football fields' worth of forest have been razed every day for the past fifteen years. The EU and UK are among the top final consumers of the soya and meat produced atop the destruction.

Scientists say that the Chaco still sequesters huge reserves of carbon. Trees like the *palo santo* and *quebracho blanco*, found nowhere else on earth, can stand for centuries. One recent study found that the ecosystem holds fourteen times more biomass above ground than commonly thought: half on the territory of communities like the Ayoreo. If the forest, their forest, continues to burn, it will heat up the entire planet.

Paraguay has always been sweltering. But temperatures now climb towards forty degrees Celsius in the winter. Water runs hot from the tap. You break out in a sweat as you brush your teeth. To cap it all, the soybean and lithium frontiers are now expanding from Argentina to the Paraguayan Chaco. And as governments clamp down on deforestation in the Amazon, even more ranchers may pile across the new bridge into the unloved, unprotected ecosystem on their doorstep.

Nostalgia for the lost patria of López has mutated into its latest deadly incarnation: as a smokescreen for an unfolding ecocide. And once seen as isolating Paraguay, the Chaco is now viewed as its way out. Near Loma Plata, a billboard advertises the Bioceanic road: 'The Chaco CONNECTS US to the World'.

I had put the slogan to people in Carmelo Peralta. Another Ayoreo leader called Juan de la Cruz had smiled wearily. The new highway 'connects all the sufferings of many, and the good of a few, the businessmen', he countered. 'And us, we'll be left at the roadside watching them pass by.'

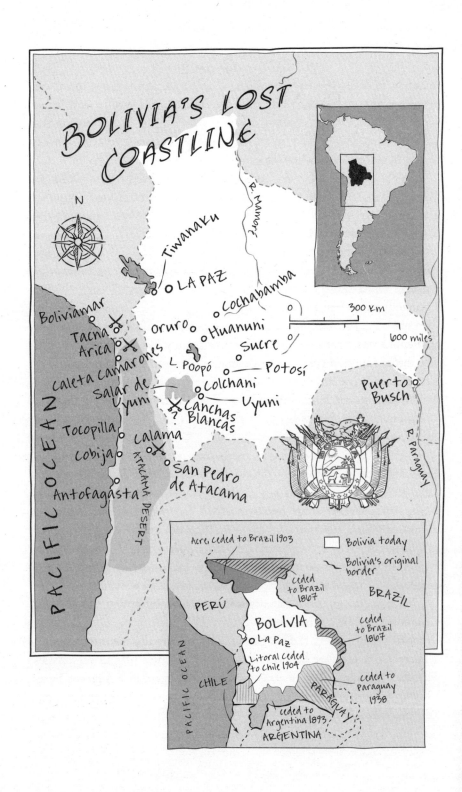

BOLIVIA'S LOST COASTLINE

N

Tiwanaku

○ LA PAZ

Cochabamba

R. Mamoré

Boliviamar

Tacna ✕

Arica ✕ ○

Oruro ○

○ Huanuni

Sucre

300 Km

600 miles

Caleta Camarones ○

Salar de Uyuni ○

L. Poopó

○ — Potosí

Puerto Busch

Colchani ○

○ — Uyuni

✕ Canchas Blancas

Tocopilla ○

Cobija ○

Calama ○ ✕

San Pedro de Atacama ○

Antofagasta ○

PACIFIC OCEAN

ATACAMA DESERT

R. Paraguay

Acre, ceded to Brazil 1903

☐ Bolivia today

〰️ Bolivia's original border

PERÚ

ceded to Brazil 1867

BRAZIL

ceded to Brazil 1867

BOLIVIA

○ La Paz

Litoral ceded to Chile 1904

CHILE

PACIFIC OCEAN

ceded to Paraguay 1938

PARAGUAY

ceded to Argentina 1893

ARGENTINA

9
The Map of Catastrophe
Bolivia's Lost Coastline, 1879–

A HISTORY OF SADNESS

Every Tuesday for forty-four years, a two-deck ship with warped white planks and a salvaged truck engine has set out from the town of Concepción for the upper reaches of the Paraguay River. The *Aquidaban* brings food, fuel and medicines to villages whose roads become sludge when it rains, or have no roads at all. But the vessel is another casualty of the Bioceanic Highway. Since asphalt reached the larger towns, the cargo business has collapsed, says Alan, the boat's owner, leaning on the rail in a thrash-metal T-shirt. The hold is half-empty, the boat falling to bits. He can barely pay his sailors and stevedores, he sighs: 'This is possibly our last year.'

As if delaying the inevitable, the *Aquidaban* travels slowly: mooring at tiny settlements to unload bananas, sacks of fish food, a wardrobe and a pink tricycle over three languid days. Her decks are crowded with all 200 members of the Tomaraho tribe returning from the elections. The state governor handed them 200,000 guaraníes each – a little over £20 – as they went into the polling station. Most say they would have voted for him anyway: the Colorados are the only show in town. And highway or no, the *Aquidaban* is their only way to get home.

We rock in the wake of barges flagged to Liberia and the Marshall Islands carrying lumber and livestock. The passengers snooze in hammocks, sprawl out in the gangways, or perch amid crates and chickens. There's a sushi chef headed to Reverend Moon's utopia of Japanese hermits at Puerto Leda, and a red-eyed policeman transporting a prisoner, who holds his cow-horn of tereré between cuffed wrists. Upstairs, two brothers from Utah with perfect teeth and Indiana Jones fedoras are mopping up bowls of stew. Former Mormon missionaries, they are now influencers, hoping to pay the Tomaraho to perform their rain dance – complete with ankle castanets made from Coke cans – so they can film it for their Facebook followers.

The boat turns around at the two-street town of Bahía Negra. Nervous about pitching up at a Bolivian military base unannounced and empty-handed, I spend the last of my guaraníes on rum and cigarettes. Another adolescent with an outboard motor takes me the final half-hour to my destination. As we cross the unmarked border, we pass abandoned, overgrown ranches and caimans lurking in knots of pink waterlilies. The skipper leaves me on the bank and buzzes off round the bend. I come to a Spartan building on concrete stilts where a group of shirtless young men are playing keepie-uppies. Unfazed by my arrival out of nowhere, the oldest gives his name – Nicolás Espejo, second lieutenant – and dives into the water to freshen up.

This is Puerto Busch: an isolated naval outpost on a sliver of Bolivian territory in the middle of South America. Espejo, twenty-two, is the ranking officer. I slide the smokes onto his desk, pass him a light, and ask him what he's doing here in the Pantanal, a sweaty tropical wetland the size of Belarus. The Atlantic Ocean is 1,250 miles downriver; the Pacific, 620 miles overland to the west. Espejo's unit – him, a sergeant and six teenagers on national service – are all city boys from the highlands. The cadets are freckled with white scars among their spots. 'We're mosquito food,' the lieutenant puffs, as a rainstorm rolls in across the river.

There are some consolations. The sailors' new quarters are luxurious compared with their former accommodation: a pontoon now housing only broken bunks and a bat colony. They have plentiful downtime for hunting and angling. Espejo swipes through recent prizes on his phone: piranhas, huge spotted catfish, and capybaras. He has taught one of the seventeen-year-olds how to swim. And at night, encased in malaria nets, they dream of the sea.

At the time of my visit, their dreams – and those of a nation that lost its only shoreline to Chile in the War of the Pacific nearly 150 years ago – seem to be edging closer to reality. The International Court of Justice has just agreed to hear a claim brought by Bolivia. The lawsuit aims to compel Chile into talks about restoring Bolivia's access to the Pacific: possibly by handing back a slice of its former coastal territory. The news from The Hague has prompted wild celebrations across the landlocked nation of eleven million.

And if that fails, there's a back-up plan. A stone's throw down the riverbank, Bolivia is building an international seaport out of the mud.

One of the largest iron deposits in the world sits nearby. A $7 billion loan from China will pay for a railway to span the swamp, connecting Puerto Busch with the mine. And Puerto Busch will connect Bolivia with the world.

'This is an exit to the Atlantic Ocean,' says Espejo, as we squelch over to the construction site. 'The best way right now to get out to the sea, to abroad, is via the Paraguay River. It's the most sovereign access that we Bolivians have.' The port is eagerly awaited by the country's navy: currently confined to patrolling jungle waterways and ferrying dentists around Lake Titicaca. 'We're not a country without a naval presence,' Espejo continues, slightly defensively. 'It's not like you'd give us big boats and we wouldn't know what to do with them.' Work will be finished soon, says the chief engineer, Jesús Ampuero, as his workers down tools to eat lunch and drink peanut chicha. 'Although it's small, this is very important for the country: it's our first port.'

This master plan is counterintuitive. Bolivia's south-western quarter, home to the bulk of its population and natural resources, is barely eight hours' drive from the harbours of northern Chile – which reserve space for Bolivian exports bound for Asia, the United States and beyond. But the Puerto Busch project will require ships to steam for a week down the drought-prone Paraguay River just to reach the south Atlantic. From there, the nearest large trading partners are in Europe, or back in the Pacific around Cape Horn.

But this pharaonic port complex rising from the mire, and Bolivia's parallel quest to return to the Pacific, respond to something beyond economic logic. There's a clue in the motto daubed on bases like this one across the country. 'The sea is ours by right. To recover it is a duty.'

In La Paz – Bolivia's political capital, 930 miles to the west, 3,500 metres higher, and twenty degrees cooler – you can get around with the Coastal Bus Line, drop by the Coastal Shopping Centre, and party at the Coastal Nightclub. You might catch FC Coastal in the final for the city-wide title. If you prefer to attend a beauty competition, you'll get to meet Miss Seaside, representing Bolivia's lost coastal province.

Visit on 23 March – the Day of the Sea – and the streets will be lined by grandmothers waving miniature blue flags. Regimental bands, rifle-women in white skirts with fixed bayonets and guardsmen in lampshade hats goose-step past, intoning the Naval March: 'Let us sing the song / of the sea, the sea, the sea / which soon will make us all / happy and carefree.'

You can also walk down a narrow alleyway to pay your respects at the Coastal Museum: a colonial house, painted ocean-blue. I come across its manager sweeping up after a throng of primary school pupils. 'We want to perpetuate the memory in all our visitors,' says Dante Vera, showing me rifles, uniforms and faded flags from the War of the Pacific. 'We encourage them not to renounce their right to the sea.'

Many countries draw on a golden age of expansion, a glorious independence struggle or a heroic defence of the patria to furnish a shared foundational myth. Not so with Bolivia. Instead, a series of embarrassing defeats is imprinted in the nation's psyche from an early age. An unusual atlas of despoliation hangs in classrooms across the country. The Map of Catastrophe shows Bolivia at the moment of its independence in 1825, inheriting the limits of colonial Upper Peru. The newborn country looks like a continental power, thrusting deep into the Amazon, the Chaco, over the Andes and down to the ocean. And within it lies a shrunken husk – today's Bolivia – resembling a plucked chicken whose extremities have been hacked off.

First went the comb and a sliver of the right flank, vast Amazonian territories granted by a dictator to Brazil in 1867 – the urban legend goes – for a briefcase of jewels and a thoroughbred white stallion. Then a mortal blow: the left wing, the Atacama Desert and adjoining seacoast invaded by Chile in 1879. A leg is thrown to Argentina in 1899 to keep Buenos Aires at bay. Then the beak, another swathe of northern jungle known as the Acre, annexed by Brazil in 1903. Finally, the tail feathers: Bolivia's pretensions as far south as Asunción were ceded to Paraguay in 1938, after another war as disastrous for Bolivia as for the native peoples of the Chaco caught in the crossfire.

Nostalgia bubbled forth for the super-sized landmass even while it was still being cut down to size. In 1903, Bolivia's envoy in London invited his compatriots to take a hard look at the country's former limits. 'What remains to us of that vast empire?' asked Félix Avelino Aramayo. 'According to certain Bolivian writers, everything ... they maintain it in their imagination as sacred patrimony, integral and inalienable.' A century later, the Map of Catastrophe – also known as the Map of Mourning – is still 'effectively the first history lesson that Bolivian students receive, and it's the hardest to overcome', argues Jorge Abastoflor, a member of the Bolivian Academy of Military History. 'It makes even optimists automatically link the history of Bolivia with territorial losses for the rest of their lives.'

Only the most ardent revanchists demand the restitution of all

million square miles of these lost lands. It is the leftmost appendage on
the map, Bolivia's former Pacific coastline, which gets the parades, pageants and poems. It would be easy to dismiss as garden-variety
nationalism – or play it for laughs, as visiting correspondents often do.
But the enduring significance of the absent ocean is both material and
acutely emotional. Unlike the other tracts of jungle, forest and mountain, Bolivia's coastal region, the Litoral, contained untold natural
resources: guano, nitrates, copper and lithium. Meanwhile, its ports
gave the country a tenuous link to the global flows of commerce, immigration and capital that would soon enrich its neighbours. The loss of
the Litoral cut Bolivia off from a different future.

This foreclosing of possibility – the denial of a fighting chance to a
hard-pressed nation – is encapsulated by *enclaustramiento*, the word
Bolivians use to describe their cloistering, their confinement, their land-
locking-in. 'It was a particularly great loss because with the Atacama we
had access to the sea,' explains Vera, the curator of the Coastal Museum.
'So once this was taken, we've lost our connection with other countries,
with the rest of the world.'

Bolivia, its naval officers are fond of saying, was born with the ocean.
But the connective tissue between capital and coast was gossamer-thin.
La Paz, the seat of government, lay a month's hard march from its por-
tion of the Pacific, with the small matter of the Andes and the Atacama
lying in between.

Francis Burdett O'Connor had marched with Bolívar's armies all the
way south from Venezuela. The Liberator had even promised him a
regiment of hussars to help fight for Irish independence once the struggle for South America was won. But O'Connor stuck around in Bolivia,
encouraging his countrymen to settle this New Erin, where a bright
future surely beckoned. In 1827, he was sent to reconnoitre the newborn republic's coastline for a suitable place for a harbour.

Cobija didn't look like much. The rocky cove was home to a village of
Chono fishermen, who sheltered from the sun in whale-bone huts and
paddled out on inflated sea lion hides to haggle with smugglers. But before
long, the capital of the Litoral was one of the Pacific's major ports of call.
By 1862, it boasted 5,000 residents and a US consul, whose residence – he
complained to the Bolivian government – had been bottled during Carnaval. And although Bolivia's merchant vessels could be counted on one
hand, Cobija proved a handy base for the prospectors who struck out into
the desert, stumbling across vast fields of guano and nitrates.

But Bolivia had competition. The border between the Litoral and Chile, falling somewhere in the endless wastes of the Atacama, had always been hazy. Now, with natural resources worth a Potosí up for grabs, talk of parallels suddenly took on life-or-death significance. Thousands of Chilean settlers steamed up the coastline, agitating for Santiago's sovereignty to catch up. 'Of every twenty inhabitants, seventeen are Chilean, one a Peruvian, one a European, and one a Bolivian colonel,' a French visitor to the Litoral in the 1870s reported. The Chileans worked, the Europeans traded, and the Bolivians barked orders.

An uneasy truce prevailed: Bolivia promised not to raise taxes on Anglo-Chilean mining conglomerates, and Chile parked its territorial claims. Battered by earthquakes, yellow fever and tsunamis that deposited ships miles into the desert, Cobija was gradually abandoned. Antofagasta, eighty miles closer to the nitrate fields, took its place. In May 1878, residents marked the centenary of Voltaire's death with gun salutes, civic processions, Chinese firecrackers and Bengal rockets. This was, some hoped, a beach-head for the Enlightenment to sweep the Tibet of America. 'Bolivia, represented by the port of Antofagasta,' a pamphleteer wrote, 'will be no longer the savage Nation hidden between the folds of the poncho and the cassock.'

Meanwhile, over the Andes, a former petty thief and presidential bodyguard called Hilarión Daza had wrested control of the nation's highest office. As thousands of Bolivians dropped dead amid drought and famine, the president in the plumed hat and golden epaulettes threw bullfights and banquets to mark his birthday. The celebrations were compulsory. Every house in Antofagasta, and every ship in its harbour, was festooned with flags. The port's prefect hosted a tea party for 'all the civil and military corporations, the consular corps, and the innumerable friends that his liberal and honest administration has captured'.

Bolivia urgently required a railway to the sea. More importantly, Daza's battalion of praetorians had to be kept sweet. In 1878, he raised export taxes on the nitrate mines by ten cents per hundred-pound sack, and expropriated those who didn't cough up. It was the final straw for Chile's mining barons, their political allies, and an irate public. On Valentine's Day, 1879, Chilean soldiers strolled ashore at Antofagasta. Bolivia's innumerable friends were conspicuously silent. Enemy ironclads appeared off Cobija and bombarded the unfortunate harbour with verbiage. 'I see myself possessed of the indispensable necessity of taking transitory possession of the Litoral,' wrote Chile's admiral. 'I trust you will not want to force a resistance that I judge to be useless, and whose consequences will be your exclusive responsibility.'

Bolivia's shoreline had been captured without a shot fired. To secure the riches of the desert, Chile marched on the crossroads of Calama. A handful of Bolivian locals in trench coats with bandoliers and mismatched revolvers volunteered for the town's defence. Among them was Eduardo Abaroa: a thirty-nine-year-old accountant, father of five, and purveyor of jerky, watermelon and Danish pale ale to the mines. He made an unlikely Rambo. But as the invaders approached, Abaroa charged out of his ditch, guns blazing. He was soon pinned down on a hillock. Chile's colonel implored him to see sense. 'Me, surrender?' came the reply. 'Surrender your grandmother, dammit!'

Abaroa went out in a hail of bullets. His defiant last stand earned him a statue in La Paz. On paper, Daza still had the advantage. Bolivia had signed a secret defensive alliance with Peru in 1873. Their troops outnumbered the enemy three-to-one. But Chile's armies had decades of combat experience against the Mapuche, and packed state-of-the-art artillery. Bolivia's few cannons were 'only good for salutes', one minister admitted. Her forces were heavy on marching bands and over-promoted officers but short on actual soldiers. When they reached the front in Peru – a local society lady recorded – they gawped at passing trains and stared slack-jawed at the sea. They had been 'torn from their huts, analphabetic, naïve and pacifistic', she sniffed, and 'went to war without knowing what it meant, with no concept of patria, of home nor duty'.

Disproving such snobbery, Bolivia's rank-and-file fought bravely, often to the last handful of men. With little more than toasted corn and undercooked alpaca for sustenance, the soldiers were kept alive only by the *rabonas* – wives, sisters and mothers who followed the army, foraging their meals, carting around their children in slings on their backs, bandaging the wounded, 'and fighting at times at the side of the men, with rifles ripped from the stiff hands of the dead'. Daza showed no such courage. He marched over the Andes, was promptly overthrown, U-turned before he reached the fighting and fled to Paris with half the national treasury.

At the Battle of Tacna in May 1880, Bolivia's newly-formed medical corps watched their country crash out of the war. Bullets shattered their medical instruments. Bombs buried themselves in the sand. A weeping drummer boy picked up a rifle and wandered into the fog of gunsmoke. An aide lowered his ashen-faced colonel onto a stretcher. 'Now I go calmly to die with our comrades,' he said, and galloped off. Narciso

Campero, Bolivia's new commander-in-chief, was meanwhile gripped by thoughts 'of the delirium of men and nations'. He felt his blood freeze in his veins as his battalions broke and scattered.

Chile's warships chased down the enemy fleet. Admiral Grau and Captain Prat, erstwhile defenders of Peruvian guano and South American honour, were reunited in death. Santiago's soldiers looted Lima. Andean guerrillas held out for three more years, picking off enemy sorties with slings and boulders just like Manco Inca. By 1884, the war was clearly lost. Over 25,000 people lay dead. Chile had not only annexed Bolivia's Litoral, but Tarapacá – Peru's southernmost province, carpeted with nitrates.

A 'current of riches' was flowing to the victors at a 'prodigious rate', noted a French engineer, André Bresson. With the opening of the Panama Canal, he predicted, all the western republics of America 'will occupy a place at this grand banquet' of commerce. But 'Bolivia without any port is a country reduced to slavery, without commercial independence, with no link that joins it to the rest of the world.' Ultimately, 'Bolivia will be Chileanised', he feared, 'and entombed among the arms of Chile like a lifeless, bloodless corpse'.

Yet as long as their coastline were occupied, Bresson predicted, 'this quivering of hearts at the memory of the past will be the hope of the future, the moral force of which will inevitably lead Bolivians to a Second Independence, more glorious than the first'. 'Bolivia', he fervently hoped, 'will soon come out of her long isolation and slumber in the heart of the South American continent.'

In July 1899, the USS *Wilmington* docked at Belem do Pará, Brazil, after a 4,000-mile voyage up and down the Amazon. Monkeys, macaws and cockatoos perched among its armour-piercing cannons. Cantankerous llamas squeezed between bulkheads. 'It is safe to say,' reported the Colorado *Chronicle*, 'the vessel was the queerest man-of-war that ever touched at any port.' And as well as a menagerie bound for the National Zoo in Washington, DC, Captain Chapman Todd was bringing back a top-secret treaty signed with Bolivia.

In the twenty years since the War of the Pacific, Bolivia had discovered an unlikely substitute for the Litoral in the northern jungle known as the Acre. Bolivian entrepreneurs founded a commercial empire shipping the latex of the *Hevea brasiliensis* tree down Amazonian rivers and overseas to make golf balls, condoms, velocipede tyres, car parts, telegraph wires and electrical cables. By 1900, the Amazon was producing ninety-five per cent of the world's rubber, with Acre's annual exports of the hardened sap worth half a billion dollars.

One Bolivian rubber baron, Nicolás Suárez, had a Packard automobile shipped upriver from Detroit to chauffeur him around his model town at Cachuela Esperanza: complete with pint-sized steam train, illuminated tennis courts, a Japanese-run hotel and cocktail bar, stores selling Russian caviar, and Bolivia's first X-ray machine. A ruthless patriarch with sweeping silver mustachios, Suárez cashed cheques in dollars, francs and yen, paid his bills in sterling, summered in Monte Carlo, and put his children through finishing schools in London, Heidelberg and Geneva. He lived to eighty-eight but only ever visited La Paz once. 'I feel I am nearer to England,' he often said.

Here was a cash cow to rival the Atacama. And, in a satisfying twist of fate, the only country in South America excluded from the riches of both the Amazon and the Atlantic was Chile. Yet as Indigenous Caripúna workers fled Suárez's murderous enforcers for the safety of the forest, poor Brazilian rubber tappers took up the slack. The new settlers amassed guns and grievances against Bolivian customs officials and police prefects.

Sensing that the Acre was slipping through her fingers, Bolivia entreated foreign powers to defend her vast northern territories: in exchange for a hefty cut of their resources on a fifty-year lease. 'The whole of Bolivia' was on offer, wrote a surveyor from the US: 'animal, mining, financial, and almost spiritual – exclusive rights of international communication and river navigation – Bolivia inside and out, present and future, Bolivia down to the base of the Andes.' As the scramble for the Amazon heated up, the United States seemed poised to establish a colony at the rainforest's very core.

But before the Marines could arrive, in 1899, the Brazilian settlers rose up. Rather than be 'handed over like vile slaves to foreign adventurers', they declared an Independent State of Acre, styling themselves after the Boer guerrillas defying the British Empire in South Africa. Bolivia's ragtag forces – armed and led by Suárez – won the following exchanges of Winchester rifle rounds and flaming arrows. But Brazil's diplomats paid off US investors, its ships blockaded the rivers, and its armies mustered nearby.

Bolivia, fatally outmanoeuvred, ceded Acre to Brazil in 1903 in exchange for £2 million – barely 50 pence per square mile – and a railway to circumvent the rapids of the Madeira River. Most locals shrugged at the latest swap of sovereignty. One Bolivian latex magnate said 'it mattered little to him that these territories should belong to Japan or any other country: the main thing was to earn lots of pounds'.

Thirty thousand labourers from Greece, Portugal, Italy, India and the Caribbean perished from typhoid, dysentery and malaria while laying the 250 miles of track through the jungle. But by the time the railway was finished in 1912, the bottom had fallen out of the Amazonian rubber business. In 1875, a British spy called Henry Wickham had smuggled *Hevea* seeds from Brazil to Kew. Within a few decades, the seedlings were transplanted to Ceylon and Malaysia, where intensive rubber plantations flourished, free of the leaf blight that ravaged similar attempts in South America.

The railway, and Suárez's latex emporium, fell into ruin. The northern route to the Atlantic was closed off. In 1904, Bolivia formally surrendered the Litoral to Chile in the Treaty of Peace and Friendship. In return, Chile built its former enemy a railway to its ports. But it felt like 'a noose at our throat, rationing us out barely enough air for our lungs'. Thirty years later, the Chaco War left Bolivia with only a toehold on the Paraguay River. Whether north, south, east or west, all escapes from 'the asphyxiating pressure of our granitic tomb have been amputated', lamented one Bolivian diplomat. 'The only way left to us is space.' The history of Bolivia was 'one of sadness', the historian Alcides Arguedas agreed in 1922, 'for it is the history of a poor people without culture'.

Yet the Pacific remained tantalisingly close: an escape from the maze, a silver bullet for Bolivia's woes. José Aguirre Achá, a Bolivian survivor of the Acre campaign, took the long way home: down the Amazon, along the coast to Buenos Aires, across into Chile via train, and up its expanded coastline. He felt despondent: nearly half of the 700 young volunteers he had set out with from La Paz three years earlier had perished. He found Chile's fishing villages and mining docks 'sad and uninteresting'.

But his spirits lifted as Antofagasta, Bolivia's erstwhile harbour-in-chief, hoved into view. 'I will not try to describe the impression that the sight of that port makes on the soul of every Bolivian. The memory, and the hope, are still there!'

WE HAVE RETURNED

Tiwanaku, January 2006. Two centuries after Castelli, Monteagudo and Mancocapac, another avowed revolutionary climbs the steps of the

ancient Andean metropolis. This one wears sandals, a red poncho and a
wreath of coca leaves. His dark, springy hair is tucked into a pointed
cap stitched with an Andean cross. 'We will finish off the colonial state
and the neoliberal model,' he tells the sea of supporters, shamans, international press and foreign presidents. 'Five hundred years of resistance
by the Indigenous peoples of America are over.'

When Evo Morales was born in 1959, native peoples like his family –
Aymara smallholders and llama herders – were second-class citizens.
They were doused with pesticides upon entering government buildings,
and barred from the square outside the presidential palace. Most lived
in grinding poverty. Five of Morales' siblings died in childhood. After a
spell selling ice cream in northern Argentina as a six-year-old – and
organising football tournaments back home as an adolescent – his
family traded the drought-stricken highlands for the Chapare jungle.
Here, he organised his fellow coca-growers against efforts by the US
Drug Enforcement Administration to eradicate the sacred leaf.

He overcame arrests, beatings and factional infighting to lead MAS,
the Movement Toward Socialism: an alliance of miners and farmers,
Indigenous Andeans and urban intellectuals, trade unionists and former
guerrillas. Elected a congressman, in 2003 he headed a rebellion against
moves to sell Bolivia's natural gas cheaply via Chile to the US. The
authorities – drawn from the same white minority that had dominated
the country for five centuries – sent troops onto the streets, massacring
more than sixty men, women and children. The president fled, his
replacement resigned. Morales swept to power in December 2005 with
over half the vote, becoming Bolivia's first Indigenous head of state
since Atahualpa.

Now, at his symbolic inauguration, he vows to carry on the ancestral
struggle of Manco Inca and the eighteenth-century rebel Túpac Katari;
of 'Simón Bolívar who fought for the patria grande', of Ernesto 'Che'
Guevara 'who struggled for a new world of equality'. He also promises
to 'fix that pending historical issue' with Chile: the two countries haven't
exchanged ambassadors since 1978.

But the triumph is not his alone, nor can he realise his promised
Democratic and Cultural Revolution by himself. 'We are presidents,
brothers and sisters, not just Evo,' he says. 'Scrutinise me, push me if I
fail to advance, correct me always. I might get things wrong, we might
make mistakes, but we will never betray the fight of the Bolivian people,
nor the battle to liberate the peoples of Latin America.'

*

Head thumping from the altitude, still blinking from the sideways ultra-violet rays of El Alto, I step inside the Salón de Eventos Príncipe Alexander. Polystyrene leaks from a lintel. Upended chairs flash their legs in the gloom. Then, after some fumbling with a fuse box, Alejandro Chino Quispe flicks the ballroom into life.

'Forty chandeliers imported from China,' boasts the pinstriped fifty-eight-year-old. 'They make it stand out from any other place in Bolivia.' The globular, squid-like shapes, flashing scarlet, now turquoise, aren't Chino's only calling card. 'There are other big venues, perhaps,' he continues, 'but they don't have the finishing on the columns, the bridal bedroom, the three-phase, high-ampere current, multiple bathrooms, the anti-slip ceramic floor of Spanish manufacture, the imported marble ...'

The showman's spiel echoes up and around a psychedelic collision of the Alhambra, the Forbidden City and Santa's workshop. The cavernous ceiling is flecked with LEDs set into candy-striped protuberances. Lime-green pillars are enveloped by diamond-shaped mirrors the size of small cars. A mezzanine decorated with Andean and Asiatic landscapes undulates around the dance floor, known to cater to a thousand revellers at once. Then there's the shopping mall below; the indoor football pitch one floor above; Chino's luxury living quarters up top. 'This venue, to be sincere, doesn't have competition,' the self-made entrepreneur concludes, flashing the golden grill that ornaments his front teeth.

A decade into MAS rule, Bolivia is booming. Morales has nationalised half the country's natural gas industry and hiked taxes on the rest, plunging the proceeds into hospitals, schools, highways, fuel subsidies and sports pitches. The poverty is tumbling, GDP growth is humming at an annual average of five per cent – the fastest in South America – and the black market in coca leaves and used Japanese cars is burgeoning. Call it Keynesianism with Andean characteristics: newly minted Aymara impresarios are splashing billions of bolivianos on extravagant carnival costumes, weddings that last all weekend, and quinceañeras of Dionysian proportions. 'These people have money,' Chino chuckles, 'and they want to throw parties.'

El Alto, a satellite city perched along the clifftop above La Paz, feels like the epicentre of this sea-change in Bolivia's fortunes. The world's largest Indigenous-majority city – with around a million residents – it's also the country's fastest-growing conurbation. Thousands of people turn up here every month from the countryside, hoping to join the ranks of the emerging Alteño bourgeoisie. The most emblematic signs of Bolivia's renaissance are here: a crop of high-rises like the Príncipe Alexander.

Their exteriors alone – darkened glass, polished chrome and lurid red-and-green acrylics – look like the offspring of a Transformer and a Tyrolean ski lodge. It's quite a statement in a city whose predominant palette is brick dust, garage-door grey and the sun-bleached blue of market-stall tarps. Some dismiss the garish buildings as *cholets*: a play on *cholo*, or mixed-race. But Freddy Mamani, a local bricklayer turned master designer, prefers 'The New Andean Architecture': a revival of the Indigenous and ancestral after centuries of discrimination. Until now, Bolivian society 'hasn't been reflected by architects', he says, taking my call from Potosí, the site of his latest masterwork. 'But for me, it's very important to centre our culture and our roots.'

In late 2023, he unveiled his tallest, most expensive creation yet: an imposing El Alto skyscraper clad in gleaming turquoise panelling. Downstairs, a bank, a ballroom, a boutique hotel and gym. On the eleventh floor, The Cruise Ship of the Andes: a multi-level penthouse in the shape of an ocean liner, complete with a wooden wheel and navigational instruments, its prow jutting out over a busy thoroughfare. 'This is a ship that set off from the Atlantic, crossed the mountains' – Mamani told reporters – 'and got stuck in El Alto, facing the Pacific.'

On El Alto's southern edge lies the Bolivian Space Agency, or ABE. Stray dogs skip around a replica of Tiwanaku's Gate of the Sun. *Cholitas*, Andean women in flouncy knitted skirts, pull up weeds. The ABE controls Túpac Katari I: Bolivia's first satellite, beaming television, radio, telephone and internet connectivity nationwide from 22,300 miles above the earth. The unmanned antenna was launched in 2013 from Beijing, and paid for by a $300 million loan from the People's Republic.

Inside, there are models of future spacecraft Bolivia hopes to put into orbit. Posters of Morales and Túpac Katari are emblazoned with the rebel's last words: 'We will return as millions.' I drop by the control room, surprising a Chinese technician taking a siesta. Williams Balladares, ABE's press director, says Bolivia's foray into outer space has doubled the available TV channels and multiplied radio frequencies several times over. It's also cheaper than foreign satellites, he laughs: 'It helps with economic sovereignty and it saves cash.' By 2025, ABE plans to give internet access to every Bolivian: 'It's a huge change in people's quality of life.'

Until recently, the only way to get down to La Paz, El Alto's older sister-city, was to take a crammed minibus via vehicle-choked switchbacks down the hillside. But in the decade since 2014, a multicoloured network of cable cars has steadily connected nearly every valley and suburb of the metropolis.

The teenagers sharing my gondola fall silent as we slide out of the station and sag over the plummeting drop. An ocean of corrugated rooftops falls away under our feet, the white chocolate fancy of Huayna Potosí unfolds to our left, and the majestic tricorne of Mount Illimani rears up ahead. It's the continent's most jaw-dropping commute: and just thirty pence a ride.

A few minutes later, I step off in downtown La Paz, also undergoing a transformation. A new government palace towers over the old one – in fact, over the entire city. Unveiled to significant controversy in 2018, the glass-fronted Casa Grande del Pueblo features exterior Tiwanaku motifs, interior murals of heroes like Juana Azurduy, and a luxury presidential suite and a helipad. The $34 million build cost will apparently be offset by saving on renting offices elsewhere.

Across the square, the clock set into the facade of congress has undergone a more subtle reinvention. Its numbers now run backwards, its hands counter-clockwise, the way the shadow moves around a sundial in the southern hemisphere. 'Who says that the clock always has to turn one way?' asked David Choquehanca, the MAS foreign minister, unveiling the change in 2014. 'Why do we always have to obey? Why can't we be creative?'

And inside the parliamentary chamber – now watched over by floor-to-ceiling portraits of Túpac Katari and Bartolina Sisa, his wife and co-commander – politics has similarly been turned on its head. Over half the members of the Plurinational Assembly are women. A fifth are Indigenous, proudly sporting ponchos, jaguar-skin caps and the traditional cholita dress of petticoats, skirts and brown bowler hats. 'From being a republic of classes, castes, and skin colours, Bolivia today is a country that has to be inclusive by law,' says Valeria Silva Guzmán. At twenty-seven, she is Bolivia's youngest congresswoman and an emerging figure within the MAS.

Bolivia is a country-sized conundrum, according to the thinker René Zavaleta: a 'hodge-podge society' of cultures with diametrically different worldviews. But the MAS has sought to make this dizzying diversity into a strength. In 2009, the country was formally refounded as the Plurinational State of Bolivia, with official status given to thirty-six Indigenous peoples and their languages. Respect for Pachamama – the Andean Mother Earth – has been enshrined in the new constitution.

'The history of our country will no longer be told without the Indigenous,' says Silva, 'without social movements, without women, without young people, and their struggle for dignity.'

Abroad, Morales appeared at summits with Chávez, Lula and other Pink Tide leaders to foster South American unity and lambast North American imperialism. At home, he kicked out the DEA and the US ambassador, legalised coca cultivation, and quashed a separatist revolt by lowland provinces. In a country notorious for putsches, assassinations and revolutions, whose presidents cling on for an average of three years, he was re-elected in 2009 and 2014 with even greater majorities, twice repeating his symbolic investiture at Tiwanaku. 'We are living in a time of Pachacuti. It means return to balance, return to equality,' Morales told the crowd in January 2015, now in a glittering golden tunic. 'We have returned,' he added, recalling Túpac Katari's prophecy in 1781. 'They couldn't make us disappear. We're here to govern ourselves.'

Yet Silva describes Morales as humble, honest and unguarded. His party trick: identifying isolated hamlets from the presidential jet, reciting how his government has helped out – a clinic, football ground or primary school down there, clean drinking water soon to be piped in over there. 'It's difficult for us to call him president because he's our comrade, he's our brother.'

The plurinational constitution meant Morales could run for his third term: this was a new country, after all. To endorse his fourth attempt, Morales asked Bolivians to tweak the constitution once more in a referendum in 2016. Forty-nine per cent said yes, fifty-one per cent said no. Undeterred, judges friendly to Morales ruled that term limits would violate his human rights. The president joined Twitter with the handle @evoespueblo: Evo is the People. Placard-waving supporters demand he stays in power until 2050. Even supporters of the revolution worry that Bolivia is backsliding into one-man rule.

Silva blames the backlash on 'post-truth' peddled by 'hegemonic media'. Strongmen who refuse to tiptoe around liberal sensibilities get an unfair rap: 'It is caudillos that have changed history in this part of the world,' she argues, mentioning Túpac Katari and General Perón. 'Men like Evo Morales, who fight for the majority, aren't born every two or three years.' There's also a generational issue, Silva admits. 'Kids today that are leaving school at sixteen and seventeen have practically lived all of their lives with Evo as president. They don't know the country that existed before.'

Not everyone shares the same affection for Morales, or his Litoral fixation. I meet with Roger Chambi at the student cafeteria of UMSA, the top public university in La Paz. Chambi forms part of Colectivo Curva, a group of young Aymara thinkers from El Alto with a popular radio show. Politics is the new rock and roll in plurinational Bolivia: he is dressed all in black, chunky sunglasses resting atop his gelled-up hair. 'It's an outrage against the decision of the people,' he says of the court decision to ignore the referendum and allow the president to run again. 'You see where politics and justice has got to in Bolivia. The worst thing is that we saw this coming, but could only watch.'

Chambi and his comrades are disciples of an anti-colonial tendency named after Túpac Katari with its roots in highland campesino organising. *Katarismo* rejects Western values, looking back beyond the Bolivian state to the pre-Columbian past for inspiration. Yet despite the indigenist rhetoric of Morales, many Kataristas feel deeply disappointed by his leadership, Chambi says. Felipe Quispe, a former ally of the president, has branded the MAS a corrupt, 'soulless, stinking corpse'.

'The government uses the maritime demand against Chile as a political tool,' Chambi continues, sipping his orange juice. 'But we Kataristas – and many others – still feel part of the broader Aymara people that is also found in northern Chile. So we don't feel the loss of access to sea,' he smiles, 'which was only a loss for the post-colonial Bolivian state.'

It sounds academic, but it's a daily reality for many. Tens of thousands of Bolivian migrants work in diners, markets, mines and docks across northern Chile. Smugglers known as *chuteros* drive second-hand Toyotas over passes taken by their great-grandfathers' mules to get to Cobija. To ignore this ebb and flow from the highlands to the sea, age-old and ongoing, is to buy into the fiction of Bolivia's modern borders.

Beneath the artifice of Bolivia, die-hard Kataristas maintain, lies another lost country waiting to re-emerge: the eastern quarter of the Inca Empire. 'We say with pride that we are of the nation of Kollasuyo, of the greater Tawantinsuyo,' Quispe told one newspaper in 2020, as his followers blockaded the highway into La Paz. 'Just as one plant smothers another, so Kollasuyo has to liquidate Bolivia. Are you getting it?'

In the south-east quarter of La Paz sits an office block: nondescript, except for the guardhouse in front decked out in rigging. This is the headquarters of Bolivia's navy. I follow a sailor in a crisp cream uniform along red carpets, past telescopes, portholes and ship's wheels. Cadets in kung-fu robes grapple on mats. A novice rower wobbles in a swimming pool, plastic bottles strapped to his craft for added buoyancy. Somewhere, a brass band plays 'We Will Rock You'.

We enter the office of Renán Winsor Guardia Ramírez. The colonel in charge of social media looks stressed. He is fighting on two fronts, he explains: convincing the world that Bolivia needs the ocean, and reminding Bolivians that they have a navy. Ramírez gives me a potted history of the institution, from its creation in 1826 to its refoundation as a separate entity in the 1960s. 'People still have the idea that we're part of the army,' he tuts. 'We've grown so much in the past few decades that we're the envy of the other armed forces.' They now have 3,500 sailors.

Much of their mission involves firing off social media broadsides. Bolivia has just been swept by the Blue Tide: a nationwide demonstration of flag-waving workers, campesinos and schoolchildren. It coincided with the delivery of Bolivia's latest arguments before the International Court: that because Chilean presidents and diplomats have previously mooted giving Bolivia a corridor to the coast, they have to follow through. Ramírez and his keyboard warriors meanwhile summoned up a Tweetstorm under the slogans #SeaForBolivia and #TheSeaUnitesUs.

They also operate through analogue media. A year earlier, the navy distributed 15,000 textbooks to the nation's schoolchildren. *My First Book of the Sea* features pop-up drawings of copper ingots, Evo Morales, and the palace in The Hague where the country's claim will be decided. A labyrinth coils inside Bolivia with the instruction: 'Find the way to the Ocean.' A decade ago, pupils were instructed to raise the issue with the UN. The result, according to the *Guinness Book of Records*, was the longest letter in the world: over sixty miles of hand-written missives, wrapped in bales weighing over two tonnes. I had flipped through some in the military museum in Sucre: faded felt-tip drawings of boats and waves, heartfelt pleas to the secretary-general.

Ramírez fishes out a miniature naval ensign from his jacket. A lonely gold star representing the Litoral, Bolivia's lost coastal province, drifts in a sea of deep azure. Since 2017, it has been flown on government buildings during March, the Month of the Sea. 'This flag has been refounded as the third flag of state,' Ramírez explains. There's the national tricolour; the kaleidoscopic Andean chessboard known as the Wiphala – and now the Flag of Maritime Revindication, signalling that Bolivia will not be complete unless the outcome of the War of the Pacific is reversed.

Until then, the navy is not sitting on its hands, the colonel explains. There are speedboat patrols against drug lords in the jungle, responding to floods in the Pantanal, bringing vaccines to the one-llama towns around Lake Titicaca. They send personnel for training with China and Venezuela, and are having an ocean-going vessel built in a French dockyard. Morales, Ramírez says, 'wants it to have sails, so it's more striking.' Another diplomatic triumph is Boliviamar, the deserted Peruvian beach on loan to Bolivia until 2091. 'The rallying call is still trying to return to the sea. It has always been. And we can't stop thinking that way.'

I try to phrase it delicately. If the Court rules in Bolivia's favour, does it know what it wants with the ocean? If the navy were to wake up tomorrow with a seacoast, how would it make use of it? This line of questioning provokes a frosty silence. Then a dressing-down by a heavy-set major, who has sat on the sofa opposite in silence until now. 'Of course we do. But that is something we absolutely cannot tell you. No military in the world would divulge that kind of operational intelligence.'

I reassure them that I'm not digging for state secrets. But it seems our conversation has come to an end. It is not far-fetched to imagine Bolivian ships on the high seas a few years from now, Ramírez argues, his fatigue briefly wiped away by the zeal of the faithful. 'We were born with the ocean, so Bolivia can't be described as a landlocked country,' he adds, gripping my hand as I get up to leave. 'We are a country temporarily deprived of the sea.'

THE EGO MUSEUM

I take the overnight train from Tupiza, waking up at 6 a.m. a few miles south of Oruro to Rod Stewart music videos on the TV and a mug of sweet black coffee. I pull up my reclining seat and push back the curtains: a white expanse of salt stretches to the horizon in the pale dawn.

This ancient sea at the centre of the Andes is fast becoming a memory. It was once South America's greatest highland lake after Titicaca. But when I alight at Llapallapani, a near-deserted thatched village, and ask for directions to Lake Poopó, Arminda Choque corrects me: 'You mean the ex-lake; the salt flat.' The twenty-three-year-old waits outside a mobile dental clinic with her two toddlers. They belong to the Uru-Murato people who have lived off the lake for millennia. 'I want my children to leave and go to college,' she says. 'There's no future for them here.'

Lake Poopó had always shrunk and swelled with the rain. At its full-est extent, it covered 920 square miles: one and a half times the size of Greater London. But since the turn of the millennium, the droughts became steadily longer. Showers added a few centimetres to the shallows, only to evaporate. In 2014, millions of birds and fish suddenly perished, rotting where they lay. In 2016, the authorities declared an environmental disaster. And now the lake has dried up altogether.

Boats rust and splinter out on the burning salt. Desiccated fishing nets and grubby flamingo feathers mark the ghostly outline of the former shore. In Villa Ñeque, stranded inland years ago, Vicente Valero doubts it's worth repairing his canoe. 'The water used to come up to here,' he says, squinting from beneath a straw hat. He recalls sleeping under the stars on week-long voyages, casting sweets into the lake at Lent to thank her for her bounty. Now he's rearing llamas and sowing quinoa. The first few harvests have been bad, he admits.

The Uru-Muratos aren't natural farmers. They bartered their catch for whatever else they needed. Those now trying to grow food are often shouldered out by their Aymara and Quechua neighbours, the majority ethnic groups in western Bolivia. Faced with starvation, many have migrated to towns and cities to work as day-labourers. With just a few hundred left scratching a living around the vanished lake, it seems like one of the oldest societies in the Americas will disappear with it.

A hundred miles south, on the dazzling Uyuni salt flat, a few dozen Uru-Murato migrants hack grey-white bricks out of the ground. Inside a shed, Aureliano Mauricio, his wife and pre-teen daughter scoop the gritty salt into cellophane bags and seal them with a flame. 'We can do 5,000 bags a day,' Mauricio says. That earns them 125 bolivianos: around £14. He took on the occasional job here during the lake's previous dry spells. But when they returned two months ago, it was for good. He remembers hauling in bulging nets of kingfish through the night as a boy. 'With Lake Poopó dried up,' he says, 'we're like orphans.'

The global North shares in the blame. Highland regions like this one are heating up even faster than the rest of the planet. But Bolivia's leaders – including Morales – have made things even worse. The Desa-guadero River flows down from Lake Titicaca to top up Lake Poopó. But Peru takes its fill first. Then Bolivia diverts most of the rest for Aymara farmers. Over 300 nearby mines also use huge amounts of water, and produce catastrophic contamination: cadmium, zinc, arsenic, lead. Fish are born malformed in the toxic puddles that remain. Locals are falling sick.

I climb aboard a minibus into the mountains. It leaves me in a town square dominated by a metal pagoda in the shape of a miner's helmet. Huanuni is home to Bolivia's largest tin mine: a ramshackle, state-run operation that employs 3,000 people. A warren of rusting sheds, pipes and chutes tumbles down the mountainside, dumping waste directly into the Huanuni River. The stream – here a sickly orange, then a gun-metal grey – trickles through town and down to Lake Poopó. Tighter regulations would hurt the miners: a fickle friend to the MAS. The shock troops of revolutions past, they're known to block roads with dynamite. In 2016, they beat a minister to death.

It's the same story for nature across the country. Lake Titicaca is also drying out. In 2023, Bolivia ranked third on the planet for deforestation – behind only Brazil and the DRC – for the third year in a row. Poor Andean settlers are slashing and burning the Amazon for beef, soy and gold. The government wants to double the cattle herd to eighteen mil-lion: nearly two cows for every Bolivian. Rich countries have spewed out carbon for centuries, Congresswoman Silva had told me: now it's Bolivia's turn to develop. But this defence is at odds with Evo's promises to respect Pachamama.

The European Union has spent fourteen million euros trying to get Lake Poopó off life support. I find the programme's former director, an engineer called Eduardo Ortiz, in Oruro city hall. He says the funding probably won't be renewed. When I ask what measures they took, he takes off his glasses and starts to cry. 'We didn't have the resources or the remit to make a difference,' he sobs. 'Now even my friends blame me for not saving the lake.'

The inaction of Morales is all the stranger because Lake Poopó lies within sight of Orinoca, his childhood home. The tiny, windswept vil-lage is home to the Museum of the Democratic and Cultural Revolution. A $7 million complex – housed in a trio of Mamani-esque edifices shaped like the heads of a llama, jaguar and armadillo – the museum is officially dedicated to the refoundation of Bolivia as a many-nationed, classless society. There's an exhibit on Indigenous history, a library with computers and *Das Kapital* in Mandarin, and an auditorium.

But today, the only people here are a guide and the receptionists. And most people call it the Museum of Evo. One of the animal heads is given over to busts of Morales, an image of him made of coca leaves, scores of gifts from his foreign tours, his school shoes, the trumpet he played during national service, and his golden glad-rags from the latest

Tiwanaku ceremony. There's also a gallery of his football shirts, including the number 10 he donned for FC Litoral as a middle-aged head of state. Some disgruntled netizen has dropped a pin nearby on Google Maps labelled 'The Museum to the Ego'.

A short way outside the village is Pampa Aullagas: an ancient hilltop site overlooking the ex-lake. I take a path to the summit. Tiny ceramic fragments crunch underfoot like gravel. I look out across the erstwhile ocean that once stretched between here and Tiwanaku: now with nothing but a rusty smear of moisture at its southern edge. It's a bitter irony. While promising to lead his people back to the sea, Morales is letting the closest thing Bolivia has disappear on his watch.

Meanwhile, international gas prices have plunged. The money is running out. Bolivia's maritime dispute has taken on the tone of a life-or-death crusade. At the president's third inauguration, the band strikes up with the Naval March. Chilean diplomats look uncomfortable as MAS senators namecheck their northern cities: 'Bolivia soon will be / reunited with the Sea / Cobija, Calama, Antofagasta / shall return to the Patria.' Morales blames demonstrations in Potosí on Chilean spies.

Some of the Uru-Muratos cling on to hope. They gather to pray to Pachamama that the rains will return, the rivers might run free again, that the lake and its wildlife may be replenished. 'We're fishermen,' says Mauricio, in Uyuni. 'And when there's fish, there's work.' For now, his family turn back to their new existence shovelling salt.

DREAMS OF THE SEA

The Litoral is still hard to get to. At the office of Bolivia's railway in La Paz, they had sworn blind I could catch the train to Chile. But here at the station in Uyuni, they tell me the service has been freight-only for years. They call the station-master up in Oruro: he says no tourists. Maybe it's the Old West scenery, but for a few wild moments, I imagine hiding in a shed and sprinting alongside as the carriages pull out. But Chilean border patrol, I reason, probably don't look kindly on stowaways.

I queue up for the 4 a.m. bus with a group of cholitas lugging sacks of second-hand clothes. We gaze blearily out of the window at the widescreen scenery: a graveyard for old locomotives, purple volcanoes streaked with snow, flamboyances of flamingos in red lagoons. A gritty football pitch spans the unmarked border. The cops in the customs shed take hours to stamp us through. My plan is to travel west to the ocean, to find out how Bolivia's lost coastal province has fared under Chilean rule: and what locals make of Bolivia's claim to their home.

At first, there's no difference from one stretch of sand to the other: whitewashed adobe churches; rusting rail depots; wandering llamas and solitary vizcachas, a kangaroo-faced rabbit that slumps on rocks with its belly to the sun. But it gradually becomes apparent: the otherworldly landscape here is scarred by two centuries of intensive resource extraction. The desert preserves everything: the ancient past, painfully fresh memories, and glimpses of the future. And while Bolivia is fixated on what has happened here, many Chileans would rather forget.

In the middle of *la pampa*, an undulating plain in the central Atacama, I come to Calama. The mining town squats in the shadow of Chuquicamata, a gargantuan open-pit copper mine. I seek out the riverbank where Abaroa's company were shot down and buried by the Chilean invaders in 1879. An enclosure of mud and straw contains a monolith dedicated by Bolivia's consul in 2002: 'may the passions of the living never disturb the calm of the dead.' Small crosses dot the sand, hung with dog collars and squeaky toys. The first casualties of the War of the Pacific now share their resting place with a pet cemetery.

The hills close by were scene to one of the worst atrocities in Chilean history. In September 1973, not long after the armed forces overthrew Salvador Allende, a radio summons went out for twenty-six students, union leaders, miners and leftists. Most turned themselves in. Previous regimes had rounded up and released suspected subversives. It was almost routine. But in October, a helicopter landed in Calama, bearing a death squad ordered north by Pinochet.

One of those detained was Mario Arguelles Toro, a baby-faced thirty-four-year-old taxi driver and Socialist Party activist. I meet with his widow, Violeta Berríos, at her small wooden bungalow in central Calama, cast into shadow on three sides by a three-storey construction painted salmon pink. Now eighty-six, she has silvery hair, deep creases beneath her cheeks, and brown eyes magnified by thick glasses. I perch on the edge of the sofa as her dog wriggles and yaps behind me. Violeta lights a cigarette.

On that October day fifty years ago, the prisoners were told they would soon be transferred to a Patagonian prison camp. Violeta brought Mario warm clothes, and said she'd follow on the bus. She was at the butchers when they told her the prisoners were being moved. She rushed to the jail but was stonewalled. The same at the police station, the barracks, the courthouse, the town hall. Later, the governor claimed the men had, regrettably, been shot en route to Antofagasta: they had risen up and attacked their guards. 'I said, "With what? Breadsticks?"' He didn't reply, but promised to return the bodies soon.

A year became three, became ten, fifteen. The authorities offered to show the families sealed caskets. The official story kept on changing, as if to test their sanity. 'They lied to us for so many years. They said they'd run off with other women, or moved abroad.' Neighbours swung their gates shut on her. Even Mario's comrades crossed the street. 'It's like we wore a sign reading "Spouse of an Executionee". There were no friends. You're left completely alone.'

Violeta undertook the search herself. Every weekend, a small group of mothers, sisters and wives scoured la pampa for signs of their loved ones, inch by inch. They walked through desolate valleys, swept the roadsides, probed ditches with poles. 'We found lots of ancient bones, loads. Everywhere we looked. I mean, remains that are lying there in the open air. No one bothers to bury them.' They found the half-frozen corpse of a missing North American businessman, a mass grave of fifteen nitrate workers a century old. But none of the bodies were the twenty-six.

In June 1990, a tip-off pointed them to a grey, windswept slope barely ten miles south-east of town. They dug for a month, expecting to find their men whole. But some time after the killings – a volley of machine-gun fire at dusk, the grunts chugging pisco and slicing off wedding rings – the remains had been removed with a digger. The largest of the broken fragments left behind was a femur. But they were enough to run DNA tests. Of Mario, they identified a rib, a scrap of tendon and a finger bone. 'Some people got more bones,' says Violeta. 'But that's what fell to me.'

She disputes the accepted version: that the bodies were dumped in the ocean. 'Why would they go all that way? I've never believed that story about the sea. If you ask me, they're here in the hills.' In 2020, eight members of the firing squad were jailed. Violeta worries the rest will die without paying for their crimes, like Pinochet. 'It looks like they've got friends at the Supreme Court. Or maybe it hasn't got the trousers to sentence them. There'll be no justice for us,' she says, more resigned than angry. 'I lost faith in politics many years ago. They've tried to cover us with earth and forget.'

I ask her what was Mario was like. She replies instantly: 'Sexist. Very *machista*.' He didn't let her receive visitors, even watched her as she went to the corner shop. They first met in Santiago: he asked her the time, they went for tea. 'He was a free bird. He didn't like to be tied down.' He'd stay up with friends until dawn, putting the world to rights. The soldiers took him, she thinks, because he served on Allende's security detail when he visited Calama the year before.

She knows the desert better than most, I suggest. How would she describe it? 'Look, I love la pampa, but I hate her. Because she hid from us something so beloved, only to give us back something so small.' I ask if she ever thought of going back home down south. 'Never. I just wanted to find him. And not just Mario, all of them. We've found twenty-four of the twenty-six they shot. We're still missing two.'

The pampa west of Calama is ex-nitrate country. The vista is speckled with the white heaps of tailings known as *tortas*, or cakes, resembling spilled sugar on a dun tablecloth. The ruins of *oficinas* – the saltpetre company towns where generations lived and died in the decades either side of 1900 – slide past the window. One of them, Chacabuco, was reactivated by the Pinochet regime as a ready-made prison camp for musicians, artists and left-wing organisers. Attempting to escape was futile. If they somehow scaled the wire and walls without being gunned down by the guard-towers, they would find themselves in a minefield in the middle of the desert.

With Patric Canales, a local history buff, I poke around the next set of ruins along: once the Atacama's biggest oficina, home to 15,000 men, women and children. Today, the empty streets of Pampa Union – mud-brick skeletons of warehouses, shops and homes – are mainly occupied by fly-tipped fridges. Patric's grandfather was press-ganged here at the age of fourteen, he says. Back then, Pampa Union 'was a town of vice and prostitution. There was no church, and unlike the other nitrate mines, alcohol was allowed.' Migrants flocked from around the world. But there was no way out.

Their wages were paid in scrip that could only be spent in company stores, which duly gouged their customers. Diseases, venereal and otherwise, shrank lifespans. Yellow fever wiped out entire classrooms. Patric's grandmother told him stories of workers – impossibly indebted or driven mad by monotony – leaping into boiling vats of saltpetre or blowing themselves up with dynamite. In 1912 alone, 400 nitrate workers in the province of Tarapacá took their own lives. 'We northerners are moulded by these realities,' Patric reflects: dizzying booms and harrowing busts, lifetimes spent among the debris of ecological collapse.

'Calama today is one of the cities with the highest rates of suicide in Chile.'

He tucks his dirty-blond hair into his hoodie, leans back, and poses for a photo amid the rubble. Patric is part of Guerrilleros de La Pampa: an Atacama autonomist rap group. They reject the sabre-rattling of Chilean elites, he explains, instead imagining an intercommunal utopia. 'There's a media war. They invade us with misinformation and nationalism every day. But we want to return to how we were. Before the War of the Pacific, we all lived together: Chileans, Bolivians, Peruvians. There was no need to fight.' Protestors, he says, sometimes raise the Bolivian flag, arguing Chile's neglected north would be better off ruled by La Paz.

'We could be a separate country,' he continues, mentioning the Atacama's abundant copper, wind energy, solar power – and Alexis Sánchez, the local kid turned FC Barcelona forward and Chile's all-time top goal-scorer. 'We have it all.' The highland desert region where Argentina, Bolivia and Chile meet also contains an estimated trillion dollars of lithium: the battery metal essential for smartphones, laptops and electric vehicles. With the global EV fleet forecast to multiply tenfold to reach 250 million by 2030, the Atacama is the centre of a new commodity rush. But not everyone has been seduced by the so-called white gold.

In San Pedro de Atacama – an oasis of white-washed houses, hotels and water gurgling through tree-shaded lanes – I had called in on Sonia Ramos, a healer belonging to the Lickanantay people. The Salar de Atacama, a briny salt flat that stretches for sixty miles south of San Pedro, 'has been our little ocean for thousands of years', she tells me. Her grandmother, a llama herder, taught her that – if you looked closely – the desert was thrumming with life. 'It was a way of educating me, preparing me. Perhaps she could already see what was coming.' Today, giant emerald pools – used to evaporate lithium-rich water sucked up from underground – are spreading across the Salar.

'In the rest of Chile, lithium is seen as wealth with no downside,' says Sonia, whose grey hair flows loose past her shoulders. 'That it has to be exploited, because it's the best thing that could have happened to the country.' But nearby lakes are vanishing. Hardy, drought-proof grasses are wilting. The copper mines have already drunk rivers dry and displaced entire villages. Calama is running out of water. Lithium, Sonia fears, is causing history to repeat itself. 'It used to be the sword, then the rifle. Now, they're uprooting us with money.' Many of her people have sold up, she explains, driving big trucks and buying city apartments.

'But it's a present without a vision of the future, leaving the next generation totally helpless. Tell me that's not corruption.'

The damage to the *salares* is also destroying clues to the origins of life on earth – and its existence on other planets. The salt lagoons of northern Chile contain an alphabet soup of the elements, the microbiologist Cristina Dorador tells me. 'You can find most of the periodic table here.' And these chemical brines teem with microscopic organisms – known as extremophiles – that take this impossibly harsh environment as an invitation to thrive. Some consume molecules of arsenic and sulphur, producing pigments that tinge the lakes yellow-green and dye flamingos pink. It's a close analogue of the primordial soup that we come from – and which may have spawned life-forms elsewhere in the universe.

Swathes of the territory wrested from Bolivia and Chile in the War of the Pacific are now officially designated 'sacrifice zones' for industrial contamination. Every year, some 40,000 tonnes of used clothes from around the world – the cast-offs of fast fashion – are dumped in the desert. Darwin once branded the Atacama a place 'where nothing can exist'. Yet its salt flats and rocky plains are actually biodiversity hotspots, Cristina says. Every few years, when it rains, the desert blooms with flowers from long-dormant seeds. Among the trash and grit live tiny creatures that could clean up oil spills, grow crops, and make medicines and eco-plastics. 'There is life there, but it's invisible,' she adds. 'And if it ceases to exist, there'll be nothing else.'

The debris of the nitrate industry offers a reminder that even the most lucrative resource rush never lasts for long. With Patric, I walk over to the cemetery outside Pampa Union, a thicket of crude wooden crosses. Salt crystals glimmer like snowfall over graves disturbed by treasure-hunters. Smashed-up family vaults bear the surnames of Croatian migrants. 'The number of kids always hits me,' says Patric. Out of the corner of my eye, I glimpse shards of bone in splintered two-foot coffins.

Heat and distance blur the icy palisade of the cordillera. The ground cracks underfoot. The last resident of a nearby ghost town has decorated the lonely plots with yellow paper flowers. 'Here lie the profaned remains of my ancestors,' reads an engraved slab outside a ransacked crypt. 'There are only bones. Let us leave them to rest in peace.'

I link up with Nick Ballon, the photographer who had shared the journey to the Chincha Islands. We drive past the twelve-foot carbon-fibre penguin that lours over the motels and refineries of La Negra. In the middle of a sun-baked turning circle, an elderly man reads the news-paper atop a cool-box in a tiny wooden booth, doling out gooey pink ice-cream to passing truckers. It's been his job for thirty-one years. 'It's a bit solitary,' he grunts. 'But you get used to it.' The craggy landscape south of Antofagasta is earth's most extra-terrestrial surface. NASA test-drive their Mars rovers here. And the night skies – freezing cold and astonishingly clear – are ideal for peering into space.

We wind our way up to Paranal, a mountain-top observatory where astronomers from around the world keep vigil over the cosmos. Using instruments as intricate and expensive as gargantuan Fabergé eggs, they have already found bright green galaxies, a brown dwarf star the tem-perature of a cup of tea, and a gas giant named WASP-76b: half of which is always 2,000 Celsius, while a rain of iron droplets falls in per-petual darkness on the other. But merely discovering distant interstellar bodies is old hat, says Roberto Castillo, an engineer in a hairnet polish-ing the gold-plated arms of the K-band Multi Object Spectrograph. 'Now we're thinking: why don't we try to study their atmosphere, the exoplanet itself, the air, the components, maybe even discover life?'

His latest gadget is the Extremely Large Telescope: an apparatus bigger than the Coliseum with a 1.2 billion euro price tag, a thirty-nine-metre main mirror, and forty million bolts holding it together. When it comes to life in 2028, the ELT will transform our understanding of everything. It will enable us to see thirteen billion years back in time, before the first stars: the era astronomers call the Dark Ages. Answers may be in reach to ancient questions: How was the universe formed? Are we alone? Forty years ago, Roberto was squinting at the ice caps of Ganymede, many-cratered Callisto, and the rings of Saturn through spyglasses made of reclaimed portholes. 'For an amateur astronomer,' he grins, 'this is a very special place to be.'

We head down to the scientists' residence, an elongated structure of copper cubes blown up by James Bond in *Quantum of Solace*. Palms and banana trees maintain a humid microclimate. We wash away the talc-like dust of the desert with custard-apple juice and cheesecake. The son of a Bolivian father and English mother, Nick shares my fascination with Bolivia's maritime nostalgia. He has also visited Bolivian naval bases for his photography project *The Bitter Sea*, taking portraits of an all-female scuba unit on Lake Titicaca. We discover something else in common.

Nick's father died suddenly when he was young, he explains, and he feels increasingly distant from his heritage. But his study of Bolivia's landlocked condition, and the spectral landscapes of its former seacoast, helps him feel closer to his dad. I've got no such family connection to Bolivia, or South America as a whole. But maybe early bereavement has inducted me into the language of loss, mourning and remembrance, whether for a lost father or a lost fatherland. Death, as a playwright once put it, is also an undiscovered country, one from which no traveller returns.

I follow Jannina Campos along a hillside in Arica, a port city on the Atacama's northern edge. The sand is dotted with dozens of orange markers, fluttering in the breeze. Each indicates skeletal fragments uncovered a few weeks before. Chilean soldiers stormed this clifftop during the War of the Pacific in a maelstrom of mines and shells, executing hundreds of prisoners. But these remains are far older.

'Every time a body appears we place a flag, and we bury it again,' says Campos, a young archaeologist. 'They've been preserved there for 7,000 years.' At a museum a hundred metres away, she points through a glass floor to dozens of exposed skeletons, the sand around them speckled with white: 'That's the bones turning to dust.' Older residents recall playing with skulls in their backyards, she adds. The neighbourhood sits atop one of the oldest cemeteries in the world.

It belongs to an ancient culture – known to us as the Chinchorro – who painstakingly spruced up their dead. After stripping their loved ones of their skin and organs, they swaddled their skeletons in elaborate confections of reeds, clay, sea lion skins, alpaca wool and wigs of human hair, trusting in the arid desert climate to preserve them for eternity. They are among the earliest examples of deliberate mummification in the world: dating back five millennia before ancient Egyptians first embalmed their great and good.

But the Chinchorro didn't reckon on the climate crisis. Their gravesites are increasingly being disturbed by abnormal weather. Harsh winds are scooping up the sand. Rain is rotting the reed mats that envelop the bodies. Archaeologists face a dilemma. Try to rescue everything – or simply cover up the cadavers and focus on those already excavated.

'The museums are a bit overwhelmed with all this material,' Bernardo Arriaza tells me, showing me around his lab at the University of Tarapacá, a short walk away. Growing humidity is damaging the mummies in collections. Some are sprouting with mould; others are succumbing to dry rot or being nibbled by insects. Their eclectic mix of materials – animal, vegetable, mineral, human – makes it hard to get storage conditions exactly right, Arriaza explains, as one of his students pulls up a microscopic image of a prehistoric mite latched onto a Chinchorro hairpiece. 'There's no magic solution.'

Peering in near-darkness into the display cases of a nearby museum, I'm struck by how small the mortuary bundles are. These aren't the bandaged walkers of Hammer horror films. But they are strikingly expressive, almost modernist, adorned by sparingly carved masks of black manganese. And they have a poignant human resonance. The Chinchorro cast no pottery, raised no permanent dwellings, made no golden artefacts nor etched any geoglyphs. Instead, they poured all their creativity into beautifying the dead. And the trigger for this flowering of artistic feeling, it seems, was grief.

I drive two hours south through a barren massif of shimmering, empty desert, shrines to car-crash victims the only way to gauge distance. It's a relief to descend to Caleta Camarones, a cove of clapboard houses at the mouth of a verdant valley. The fresh drinking water probably enticed the first Chinchorro to settle here. But it had hidden dangers. On its journey down through the mountains, the Camarones River picks up traces of arsenic. With every sip of water – analysis of hair samples by Arriaza's lab has shown – the Chinchorro were poisoning themselves.

The earliest Chinchorro mummies come from here: tiny babies and stillborn foetuses, their fragile forms bolstered by sticks. Perhaps keeping them close helped their parents come to terms with their inexplicable loss. And over nearly 4,000 years, Chinchorro mummification evolved, spreading to adults and other clans along the shoreline and inland. The assemblages became more elaborate, the bodies now stuffed with feathers and wrapped in pelican skin. The tradition seems to have held its power as a mourning ritual long after the Chinchorro were gone: witness the Chincha survivors of the sixteenth century reassembling skeletons vandalised by the conquistadors.

In Caleta Camarones, I'm met by Jorge Ardiles – sun-beaten, stooped and gregarious, the unofficial local custodian of the Chinchorro. His community only occupied the inlet thirty years ago, but also feel an affinity with their ancient predecessors. 'They were fishermen,' he explains, 'so are we.' We rattle along the shoreline in Jorge's truck. Ribcages and pelvises jut out of the scree amid desiccated bundles of reeds. 'All this hillside is full of bodies,' he says, with a note of pride. 'Right there is where they found the oldest mummies in the world.'

A short way down the track, we run into Cristian Zavala, the local mayor. Tourism initiatives have petered out, he says. Visitors were disappointed not to find pristine cadavers in Inca-style palaces. 'If you go to Machu Picchu, it's obvious. But here, the history is below the ground.' In 2021, the Chinchorro mummies were inscribed on the UNESCO World Heritage list: he hopes it might make the authorities in Santiago take notice of them. 'Look how many bodies are turning up,' Mayor Zavala adds, gesturing to the bone-studded slope. 'If we don't look after the Chinchorro, they'll vanish.'

The living are also suffering from ecological upheaval. The coastal waters off the Atacama are warming and emptying of marine life. The younger generation are giving up on the ocean and going down the mines. 'I can't see the fishermen continuing here,' Jorge reflects. 'We're going to disappear, like the Chinchorro.'

The Bolivian battleship cruises through a sparkling stretch of placid ocean. In a second, the weather worsens. Rain lashes the bridge. Breakers crash over the prow. A tall cadet from Venezuela wrestles with the wheel; two Bolivian sailors, their hair scraped into buns, shout coordinates. A huge red shape looms into view. Despite myself, I brace for collision. Then, the pixelated buoy emerges from the other side of the ship, with both unscathed. A robotic voice comes through the speakers: 'Your exercise has been interrupted by the instructor.'

The lights turn on, a door opens, and an officer explains how the simulator works. Recruits can practise sailing the Atlantic, the Panama Canal, and Fictitious Area River Thames. They can test their navigating skills in a range of craft – Container Ship, Aircraft Carrier, Pirate Skiff – and conditions: from the choppy waters of Cape Horn to a starlit sky off the Chilean coast. The navy is thinking about paying for an upgrade to equip their virtual vessels with missiles. 'It needs to be extremely lifelike,' says the major. 'Everything is possible in the simulator.'

For now, this state-of-the-art facility near Cochabamba, central Bolivia, is the closest its sailors will get to the open ocean. In October 2018, crowds gathered before big screens across the country to watch the International Court of Justice deliver its ruling. Their hopes were dashed. The judges voted twelve to three against them. Chile might choose to talk about bettering Bolivia's access to the ocean in 'a spirit of good neighbourliness'. But it had no obligation to do so. The 1904 treaty wherein Bolivia ceded its occupied coastal territory 'absolutely and in perpetuity' remained in force.

Morales tries to spin it as a draw. But the disappointing setback – and the sense that the president has overpromised – feed growing disquiet. Without the glue of the maritime cause, the Plurinational State starts to come unstuck. Criticism grows of the revolution's personalist turn, and its loosening of protections for Pachamama. Forest fires set by ranchers and settlers devour millions of hectares of forest and savannah. The MAS remains Bolivia's most popular party. But in a run-off election, its leftist, centrist and right-wing rivals might rally behind a single candidate and win.

On election day in October 2019, the preliminary vote count suddenly halts. When the tallying resumes twenty-four hours later, Morales has surpassed the ten-percentage-point lead needed to win in the first round. Election monitors from the Organization of American States cry foul, citing 'clear manipulation' of voting data, a hidden server, forged scrutineers' signatures and phantom votes. Sympathetic observers point to late-returning rural votes to explain the incongruities – and accuse the OAS of fomenting a coup.

Protests and counter-protests spread across the country, from the eastern city of Santa Cruz to the conurbations of the western highlands. Morales accepts an audit of the vote, then agrees to fresh elections. But as demonstrations rage, the police mutiny. A powerful union of miners and workers calls on Morales to consider his position. Guards abandon the Casa Grande del Pueblo. MAS leading lights resign. Generals appointed by Morales appear on television to suggest he step down.

As the president flees northwards in a Mexican jet, the country he ruled for nearly fourteen years plunges into uncertainty. Police tear the Wiphala from their uniforms, burning the Andean flag in the street. Triumphant right-wing leaders burst into congress holding a Bible aloft. Crowds jog through the streets of El Alto, chanting of guns, dynamite and civil war.

Jeanine Áñez – an evangelical senator who has described Aymara beliefs as 'satanic' – is installed as a caretaker president. She authorises the army to use deadly force. Troops massacre dozens of pro-MAS demonstrators. Áñez stalls holding fresh elections for a year, citing the pandemic. The economy crashes. When a fresh vote is finally held in October 2020, the MAS sweep back to power in a landslide.

Morales returns to Bolivia a diminished figure. He tours fish farms and plays five-a-side with youth squads in the Chapare, his political career having come full circle. A bitter rift emerges with Luis Arce, his former finance minister and now president. MAS supporters kick Arce out of the party and choose Morales as their candidate for 2025. But the judges now block him from running. Without the prospect of the ocean to entice voters, the party may lose its first election in decades.

As of 2024, the Museum of the Democratic and Cultural Revolution in Orinoca was shuttered and starting to collapse. Locals reportedly told government inspectors they want it to reopen – but with the exhibits dedicated to Morales removed.

My arrival at Cobija, Bolivia's prized Pacific possession, feels anticlimactic. The air is parched and silent. The tidal waves and seismic events of centuries past have left only doorposts and corners standing. The rubble is flecked with shell, corroded tin cans, shards of ochre glass, perfume vials and mouldering leather soles. Vultures in black robes, grave-robbers turned sentinels, huddle atop the gate of the derelict cemetery. A white cross sticks out from a pile of mud bricks, bearing a hand-written sign:

> In this Place
> was the Church
> Saint Mary Magdal
> en of Cobija.

The shells of Bolivia's barracks and customs office are occupied by wooden lean-tos, owned by a few dozen fishermen who hunt octopus with spears. They recently called a meeting – says an elderly woman sitting on her porch – to discuss the foreign claim on their coastline. 'I said that the Bolivians can have the alleyway running past my house here, right down to the sea – as long as they give us running water and electricity in return.' Judging by the Chilean flags adorning her neighbours' houses, she was in the minority.

When I crawl out of my tent on the beach in the morning, locals are piling mounds of kelp onto pickups for export to China. I walk waist-deep into the surf, flinching at the cold. I dive, surface, and swim out into the sheltered cove. I turn to look backwards at the russet cliffs rising into sea mist. That's the way I've come, a stop-and-start, years-long journey through South America that has brought me back to the Pacific.

Bolivia is unlikely to return to the same ocean any time soon. Chilean public opinion has hardened to match the rhetoric coming from La Paz. The country's tricolour now flies from even the most tumbledown shack across the former Litoral. The redrafting of the Chilean constitution raised the prospect of an autonomous north, one conceivably able to cut some kind of deal with its Andean neighbour, only to fizzle out. If it ever came to a fight, Chile would probably win, again.

But strange things are happening in geopolitics. Well beyond South America, from Cornwall to Kurdistan, countries, identities and territories long thought to be subsumed by modern states have resurfaced, like bones pressing against skin. 'The traces are there, despite the time. Deep within the territory, one breathes Bolivia, one feels Bolivia, one sees Bolivia in the faces of the people,' a descendant of Abaroa has written of the Atacama. 'The drama is not yet over . . . history has paused, and is waiting.'

Back in Antofagasta, in a diner called El Gran Pacífico, I had met Juan Arauz, a carpenter who sent money back to his wife and four daughters in Bolivia. He had giggled nervously when I asked his thoughts about Bolivia's maritime campaign. 'Personally, I'm in favour of it. But I can't say anything more,' Arauz whispered, leaning forward over a steaming peanut soup. 'One needs to be careful.'

He opened up when I asked him about the time – six years ago, after a two-day bus journey through the mountains and the desert – he had first caught sight of the sea. 'It's engraved in my memory. For the first time, I felt the waves, the freezing cold, the salt water. I didn't like it, but the idea of throwing myself in, it attracted me.'

'I'd always dreamed about the exit to the sea,' he continued. 'Our forefathers, those who were left after the war, dreamed of returning to it. You feel such emotion, I even cried. Because this is the – what's the word? – the yearning of every Bolivian,' he enunciated with reverence. 'To have the ocean, and to know the ocean. That's it.'

Epilogue
Fatherland
The Darién Gap, Colombia

Striking camp on the beach at Necoclí, north-west Colombia, they look like groggy revellers in the wake of a music festival. José – a skinny twenty-year-old in a tracksuit and flip-flops – shoulders a rucksack almost as tall as he is. It's stuffed with nappies and oat milk, and topped with a tent and tarpaulin. Katherin is twenty-two, but seems the younger of the couple. She carries a water bottle, portable speaker and coiled rope at her waist, and straps their seven-month-old baby, Kylean, to her front.

They've been travelling for two and a half months – walking, hitch-hiking, perching in the back of trucks and clinging on to trailers – for thousands of miles through South America. But this isn't a trip to find themselves. Their group of Venezuelans is headed north, says José, 'for a better future for our children. Getting to the United States, American soil, the American dream.'

They come from Petare, a barrio – reputedly Latin America's most dangerous – that spills up the steep hillsides east of Caracas. Life there was 'bad, bad, terrible', José explains. 'Crime is rising, the cost of food is rising, and salaries aren't going up.' He dropped out of high school and they travelled to Chile. He sold fruit on the street. Kylean was born. Then the pandemic came, and the economy nose-dived there, too. Venezuelan gangs took root. Mobs attacked migrant camps, chucking tents and prams on bonfires. They hit the road again.

They have no money, nor any friends or family in the US, only a vague idea of making it to New York. 'We don't know what the jungle is going to be like,' admits Katherin. 'We don't know the route. We could encounter a lot of things. But we have to overcome all of that. To have the opportunity to get ahead, to work, to give the kids a good future. That's the most important thing, right?' I ask if they think the border guards will let them in. José doesn't stop to consider it. 'If God wills it.'

There's more talk of God on the hour-long speedboat ride across the Gulf of Urabá. A shaven-headed man wearing a gold chain stands up, steadying himself on the plastic seats either side of the aisle. 'Our Father, all-powerful Lord, who fills every one of our lives with glory in every moment, take control of this vehicle,' he calls out. 'Place your precious mantle over this boat and the ocean, so we may reach our final destination in peace and safety. May it be a glorious journey, to unite our families, our homes, and may you help us to know the most beautiful landscape that you have put on this earth. Blessed God, powerful God, glorious God, I love you, thank you in the name of Jesus.'

The passengers join in as one: 'Amen.' Ahead of them lies one of the most gruelling and perilous border crossings in the world.

The Pan-American Highway winds for 18,650 miles between Alaska and Patagonia. But there's one sixty-six-mile stretch in the middle where the road runs out.

The Darién Gap is a lawless region of mountainous tropical forest, venomous snakes and spiders, fast-flowing rivers and murderous bandits. Straddling the border between Colombia and Panama, it's the only land bridge connecting South America with the rest of the world. And in the past few years, it's become one of the busiest migration corridors on the planet.

If you're from one of the world's poorer, more war-torn quarters, it can prove impossible to get a visa to Canada, the United States, Mexico or Central America. Instead, your only option is to fly into South America and brave the Darién. The global new normal – war, epidemics, economic turmoil, a haywire climate – is unleashing a permanent flow of vulnerable people through the jungle.

The journey can take anywhere between five days and two weeks. Hundreds have died. Since 2020, a million people have made the dangerous passage, a quarter of them children. 2024 was forecast to break records. 'The numbers could go up very significantly,' one UN official tells me. 'We don't see this abating.'

Conquistadors, pirates, mercenaries, explorers: the slender isthmus conjoining the Americas has always attracted dreamers and the desperate. It was here, in 1698, that Scotland's merchants founded their doomed Darién colony of New Caledonia. Poised athwart the Atlantic and the Pacific, it was meant to be the 'door of the seas, and the key to the universe'. Little remains of it apart from the name of a palm-fringed cove called Puerto Escocés: Scottish Harbour. When the visiting Bolivian philosopher Takir Mamani swapped stories with the local Guna people in 1975, he felt as though 'our hearts were also talking'. In Mamani's telling, the elders revealed that the true name of their territory – and the entire continent – was Abya-Yala: land of rushing, living blood, a land that has reached full maturity.

Simón Bolívar dreamed of Panama as the seat of a united Latin American superpower – the elusive patria grande – or even an empire spanning the planet. 'This magnificent spot between the two great oceans may in time become the emporium of the universe,' he predicted. 'Its canals will shorten the world's distances, stretching out commercial ties to Europe, America, and Asia, bringing this happy region the tributes of the four quarters of the globe. Perhaps only there may one day be founded the capital of the earth, as Constantine hoped Byzantium might be for the Old World!'

Today, the Darién is host to a macabre version of Bolívar's prophecy. I step off the boat onto the pier in Capurganá – a tiny beach town on the jungle's south-east fringe – into a Babel of a dozen languages. More and more people disembark from arriving ferries: twenty-something men, pregnant women, young mothers. Within minutes, we are ushered into the back of moto-taxis and driven to a community centre. Colombian Red Cross workers hand out water and advice: walk in groups, camp away from rivers, don't travel after dark.

I ask one of them about conditions on the trail. 'Everything changes, every day. It's like the weather. Every nationality comes,' he mutters. 'There are inexplicable things, things you'll never understand. I recommend you don't go. It's very dangerous.' What are the risks? 'That you die. There are animals, you can fall, you can drown. Anything you can think of. All your reading won't be enough to save you.' His team are pulling out tomorrow, he says. Their warnings have made them dangerously unpopular with locals.

We pile into the trailers again, and rattle past the airstrip to a compound of breeze blocks on the edge of town. Murals depict the long, looping route through the jungle valleys and peaceful scenes of ramblers between the trees. 'We want to help them,' says Carlos Ballesteros, part of a local cooperative in fluorescent green polo shirts. Their business, he explains, is to get the new arrivals off the boats, out of town, and onto the trail as smoothly as possible. This staging area will soon include a camping ground, a kitchen, a store, and be ready to cater to a thousand people every day, he adds. 'Everyone's earning a little bit of cash.'

The half a million people who crossed the Darién in 2023 represent a cross-section of the world's woes. Asylum seekers came from Afghanistan, persecuted minorities from Uzbekistan, climate refugees from India and Bangladesh. Last year, some 25,000 Chinese citizens journeyed through here – the single largest nationality from outside the Americas. Some said they preferred the dangers of the jungle to a slowing economy and heavy-handed Communist Party rule at home.

I meet a family from Angola waiting to get moving. Simáo had fled his job at a telecoms company after being attacked amid an ethnic conflict. 'They were going to kill me,' he says, lifting up his T-shirt to show me a scar across his stomach. In Brazil, he faced racism and struggled to make a living. Simáo and his wife, Ruth – and their twelve-year-old daughter, Jacira – are now bound for 'any country that receives us and treats us well. We see there are lots of risks,' he says. 'But I can't bear the situation in Africa. There's no future for our kids.' And they have protection, he adds. Slung around his neck is a laminated photo of William M. Branham: a mid-century evangelist from Kentucky and prophet of the second coming.

Ninety per cent of those making the trek are from South America and the Caribbean. One in ten migrants through the Darién is from Ecuador. The normally peaceful Andean nation has become South America's homicide capital as narcotraffickers fight for control of its ports, assassinate politicians, and burst into TV studios to hold news anchors hostage at gunpoint. Haitians also make up ten per cent of Darién footfall – and rising. I meet two families from Haiti, preparing to set off with three toddlers between them. Shiller, fifty, and Herold, forty-one, have worked for three years on construction sites in Santa Catarina, southern Brazil, to earn enough cash to get moving again. They hope to reach Mexico, and maybe the US.

'Haiti is in many crises,' Shiller explains, in a mix of French and Portuguese. 'Economic crisis, a presidential crisis. We don't have work, we can't earn money to eat, to pay for school.' Since Colombian mercenaries assassinated Jovenel Moïse at the presidential residence in 2021, the Caribbean nation has sunk ever-deeper into anarchy. As of 2024, criminal warlords – including a former police officer known as Barbecue for his alleged habit of burning his rivals alive – controlled eighty per cent of the capital, and people were going hungry.

There's a steady trickle from Colombia, many of them displaced by a conflict of sixty years and counting. In 1964, Colombia's army – equipped and directed by the United States – bombed a tiny mountain hamlet into oblivion. The authorities claimed that this remote socialist commune, founded by refugees from violence raging elsewhere, was a dangerous breakaway country: the Marquetalia Republic.

But the military crackdown seeded the longest war in the western hemisphere. The few dozen survivors, now calling themselves the Revolutionary Armed Forces of Colombia – or FARC – launched a mobile armed struggle. Despite their ideals of social justice and self-defence, the FARC soon became a cocaine-trafficking mafia that massacred civilians and put rifles in the hands of children. The conflict claimed at least 450,000 lives – nearly half of them killed by right-wing paramilitaries in league with the army and landowning elites – and forced nearly eight million people from their homes.

In 2016, Colombia's government signed a historic peace deal with the FARC. Some 7,000 fighters handed in their weapons to be melted down. The guerrillas settled in reintegration camps, had babies and started businesses. On the edge of the Colombian Amazon, I had visited Miravalle: a row of bunkhouses perched on a hilltop amid lush jungle. Once part of the FARC's most feared column, its residents now raft with tourists down local rivers. We paddled through a canyon echoing with dripping vines and squawking parrots, swerved around truck-sized boulders, and bounced through foaming rapids. We glided to a halt on a beach where a local family waited with sweet, cloudy *arazá* juice. 'We've swapped our rifles for oars,' grinned the helmsman, who went by the *nom de guerre* of Pato, or Duck. 'You'd have to be mad to prefer war over peace.'

Not everyone feels the same way. Over 400 demobilised FARC fighters have been murdered. The state's promises of rural development – roads, schools, help for poor farmers – have been slow to materialise. Fearing assassination or extradition, many ex-guerrillas have returned to the jungle, preferring to die with their boots on. Among them was El Paisa, a rebel commander notorious for robbing banks and bombing a nightclub. He slipped away from Miravalle in 2018 to join a dissident FARC faction called Segunda Marquetalia. 'I'm never going to be a trophy of the Americans,' he told his comrades. He was reportedly killed in an ambush by a rival drug-trafficking group in Venezuela in 2021.

And since the FARC laid down their arms, dozens more militias have filled the vacuum and fought for the spoils. In 2022, Colombia elected a new left-wing president: Gustavo Petro, a former urban guerrilla and mayor of Bogotá, the capital. Petro promised to honour the armistice with the FARC and bring about a 'total peace'. But only a

handful of the myriad factions still at arms have come to the table. And
in an ugly unintended consequence – as armed groups rush to strengthen
their control of territory and the cocaine trade before signing a
ceasefire – the fighting has only intensified, setting thousands of refugees
on the move once more.

Yet the swelling exodus through the Darién is fundamentally a tragedy involving one country, Colombia's neighbour. Two out of three
people traversing the jungle are from Venezuela.

Entire books are being written to make sense of what has happened to
the Andean-Caribbean nation with the largest proven oil reserves on
earth. But you could summarise it like this. In 1974, a twenty-year-old
military cadet returned home from Peru. The leftist-nationalist revolution of General Velasco – and his resurrection of the historical hero
Túpac Amaru II in service of the cause – had a lasting impact on Hugo
Chávez.

Venezuela was a prosperous, flawed democracy of baseball and
beauty pageants, deep inequality and corruption, stale two-party politics and boom-and-bust economics that tracked the price of petroleum.
Chávez grew up hearing about Machiavelli and Marx, Che Guevara
and Simón Bolívar. His background had little in common with that of
the Liberator: one an upper-class plantation owner with an expensive
European education, the other mixed-race, born in a dirt-floor shack
and raised by his grandmother. But the soldier felt fated to follow in the
general's footsteps.

In 1982, on the anniversary of the Liberator's death, he met three
other army plotters to repeat Bolívar's oath to the fatherland. 'I swear
by my honour and my patria,' they vowed, 'that I will give no rest to my
arm nor my soul until the chains that oppress us are broken.' A decade
later, in February 1992, the Bolivarian Revolutionary Army seized their
moment. Soldiers rose up in barracks around the country. A tank
smashed down the gates of Miraflores, the presidential palace. Lieutenant Colonel Chávez directed operations from the military museum. The
rebels were gradually surrounded.

But the authorities made an extraordinary concession. They agreed
to let Chávez appear on national TV to call off his comrades. He told
Venezuela that he took responsibility for the coup, admitting that they
had failed, 'for now'. The public were electrified by this tall, magnetic,
straight-talking soldier who looked and spoke like them. His fame grew
in his two years in jail. Once released, he courted foreign media and

toured the country, now cutting a moderate figure in a suit and tie, branding Fidel Castro's Cuba a dictatorship, even comparing himself to Tony Blair. In 1999, he was elected president by a landslide.

In his accession speech, he unveiled plans that went beyond New Labour's wildest imaginings. He vowed to found the nation afresh, with a new constitution, a new national assembly, and a new name. Believing that things could only get better, voters backed him to the hilt, giving him wider powers, extending his term in office, and embracing their country's new identity: The Bolivarian Republic of Venezuela. As the honeymoon soured, Chávez's enemies – the media, the Church, big business, army generals – briefly bounced him out of power in 2002, bundling him away to a Caribbean island jail. Their coup was immediately recognised by the White House.

But amid massive counter-demonstrations, Chávez returned to the Miraflores Palace within forty-eight hours, landing in a helicopter amid ecstatic crowds of supporters. The Bolivarian Revolution crystallised along two axes. It was to be militantly anti-Washington – although it would keep selling the United States its oil – and unashamedly pro-Chávez. 'El Comandante' shook up the military, turning lowly lieutenants into top brass loyal only to him. By 2012, Venezuela boasted no fewer than a thousand generals: roughly one for every hundred soldiers.

The ghost of Bolívar – and his mortal remains – were also enlisted to serve the revolution. Chávez peppered his speeches with quotations from the Liberator's letters, and left him an empty seat at cabinet meetings. The president maintained that Bolívar had died not of tuberculosis, but poisoned by his Colombian enemies. In 2010, as the cameras rolled, Chávez and his retinue marched into the National Pantheon, unscrewed Bolívar's coffin, and extracted some teeth and bone for forensic testing. The results were inconclusive. But two years later, Chávez unveiled a digital reconstruction of Bolívar's face, based on a scan of his skull. The Liberator's new look – swarthy, bushy-browed, full-lipped – bears little resemblance to the slender criollo of contemporary portraits. But it has featured ever since in official propaganda, the unlikely face of twenty-first-century socialism.

The public and foreign press indulged such eccentricities while the good times lasted. As global oil prices climbed, Venezuela's GDP per capita more than doubled between 1999 and 2012. In return for 100,000 barrels of Venezuelan crude dispatched daily to Cuba, Havana sent doctors and teachers to serve the roughest barrios – along with spies and soldiers to shore up Chávez's control. For the first time in their lives, millions of Venezuelans felt enfranchised, like active participants in building a new society. As Chávez convened summits with his fellow Pink Tide leaders – Lula, Evo Morales, Rafael Correa in Ecuador, the Kirchners of Argentina – South America seemed to find its voice on the global stage. El Comandante spoke for many around the world when he used the UN General Assembly – and his rambling weekly chat show, *Aló Presidente* – to denounce the War on Terror and to brand George W. Bush a donkey, a drunk, a genocidal murderer, and the devil.

To call Chávez a populist hardly covers it. He tapped into a deep current of leader worship, descending from the same lineage as Manco Inca, Túpac Amaru II, Che Guevara, Evita, Salvador Allende, even Lautaro and Zumbi of Palmares: battlers and martyrs destined for immortality in the cause of liberation. At a party congress the year after his death, one supporter unveiled an adapted version of the Lord's Prayer. 'Our Chávez, who art in heaven, earth, the sea, and within us,' went the new creed, 'hallowed be thy name ... Give us this day your light, which guides us every day, let us not fall into the temptation of capitalism, but free us from the evil of the oligarchy. For ours is the patria, peace and life. For ever and ever, amen. *Viva Chávez!*'

Endowed with such reverence, Chávez handily won re-election four times – even in October 2012, as he was visibly succumbing to cancer. Five months later, grief-stricken Venezuelans filed past the comandante in his open casket, still wearing his trademark red beret. He was only fifty-eight. Some whispered it was Bolívar's curse for profaning his tomb.

Chávez had anointed Nicolás Maduro – a bearish former bus driver, union leader and foreign minister – as his successor. But Maduro lacked his mentor's charisma. Rampant theft had hollowed out the state oil firm, PDVSA. The rest of the economy had withered. Spending was out of control. And when the oil price tumbled in late 2014, the cracks in the Bolivarian Revolution turned into chasms.

The government seized farms and factories in a bid to secure the food supply, tried to fix prices, and printed money. Before long, Venezuela spiralled into hyperinflation. By 2018, prices had risen by a million per cent. Lifetimes of savings were wiped out: if you changed a million US dollars into bolívares in 2013 and left them in a Venezuelan bank account, they would now be worth – with interest – around three cents. The economy shrank by nearly three-quarters between 2014 and 2021. Oil production cratered to pre-war levels. Supermarket shelves were empty. In 2020, one in three Venezuelans didn't know where their next meal was coming from.

The country became a dystopia to rival *Mad Max*. While the new Chavista elite known as the Boliburguesía flaunted luxury cars, handbags and watches from their shopping trips to Miami, students, children and pensioners sifted through rotting piles of rubbish for anything to eat. The *colectivos* – gun-toting enforcers on motorbikes, half Red Guards, half Hells Angels – roared along the highways of Caracas and crushed demonstrations. Police death squads burst into the barrios and liquidated alleged criminals. Beneath *El Helicoide* – a modernist former shopping mall the shape of a ziggurat – political prisoners were tortured with electrodes to their genitals. Meanwhile, Maduro danced salsa on TV and unveiled his own cartoon superhero: SuperBigote, Mr Moustache.

In recent years, Venezuela has stabilised. A clumsy effort led by the US, Colombia and the UK to topple Maduro – and replace him with a little-known politician called Juan Guaidó – petered out in 2023. As with the sixty-four-year embargo on Cuba, Washington's sanctions on Venezuela's decrepit oil industry hurt ordinary people more than the regime. Polls suggest two-thirds of Venezuelans want change. Some have even tired of the Liberator, manhandled into being the mascot of the Bolivarian Revolution. Statues to Chávez and Bolívar have been burned and decapitated. But riled by foreign meddling, a diehard base still backs Maduro. In elections scheduled for July 2024, many expected *chavismo* to fix the results and slide into its second quarter-century in power.

The rolling man-made catastrophe has produced the world's largest refugee crisis outside a war zone. By now, nearly eight million Venezuelans – almost a quarter of the population – have abandoned their country. The vast majority have put down roots elsewhere in Latin America, especially in Colombia and Peru. Roughly half a million each have settled in Brazil, Ecuador and Chile, some travelling south through the Atacama Desert on foot.

This growing pan-American diaspora may inadvertently prove Chávez and Maduro's greatest contribution towards realising the patria grande. But it is heartbreaking for those forced into exile, not knowing if they will ever see their loved ones again. 'Without realising it, during my time away from Venezuela, my parents – who had always been my home – had become my homeland,' the journalist Paula Ramón writes in her recent memoir, *Motherland*. When they passed away, 'my grief was twofold, and it grew into an emotional and geographical void one could call rootlessness'.

The pandemic set many on the move again. Waiting to catch the boat in Necoclí, I had spoken with Yonatan, a butcher from Barquisimeto who left Venezuela four years ago. 'It was a decision made from hunger more than anything,' he explains. 'When you get home, and your kids ask you for food and you realise there's nothing in the corner shop, you have to take a decision: carry on in failure, or leave to look for a future for them.' In Chiclayo, northern Peru, he worked as a taxi driver. 'But sadly socialism has begun there as well.' He's been walking with José and Katherin for a month 'without a single dollar in our pocket'. I notice he's also in beach sandals. 'My shoes wore out and broke a while ago,' he grimaces.

They're the Bolivarian generation, born and raised under Chavista rule. Having never known a free press, they're more likely to trust what they see on their phones than on TV or in the papers. And social media has convinced many that the Darién will be a cakewalk. Facebook pages offer all-inclusive packages across the gulf and through the jungle. Instagram and TikTok are full of step-by-step itineraries and smiling selfies in the rubbish-strewn clearing that marks the border.

Other videos seem to get swallowed by the algorithm. A long line of people lowering themselves down a rocky crevasse. The injured languishing in the mud. A man neck-deep in a churning river, clinging on to a line, bystanders shrieking as dark water surges over the baby on his back. 'We didn't think it would be so ugly,' a young woman repeats through tears.

Yet even beneath a clip where silent, weary travellers crest a mountain pass known as La Llorona – the weeping woman – would-be migrants ask for packing advice and coordinate journeys in the comments. 'I'm going in April. Who else? I want to go with a big group,' writes a young mother. 'I'm also thinking March–April,' reads one reply. 'We're going with my mother-in-law, my niece, and two kids. Write me.'

At the staging camp in Capurganá, the reality is starting to sink in. The group of Venezuelans are subdued, sitting with their arms crossed on the concrete floor. A local organiser tells them to travel light. 'You can't eat clothes,' he says. 'You're not going to the beach, or to a party. In the jungle, you will get to know the dark side of everyone. You have a dream, but you are not obliged to go.'

With this disclaimer delivered, the so-called guides move in to talk prices. Upbeat dance music pumps from somewhere. Bundles of bank-notes pass from palm to palm. They normally charge $120 per person, a guide tells me. But after an hour of haggling and pleading, the Vene-zuelans insist that between eleven adults they can only scrape together 400,000 Colombian pesos: about a hundred bucks. The *venecas* always claim to be broke, grumbles Germán Colina Bolívar, an unsmiling, stocky farmer with a machete at his hip. Some refuse to pay, he says. Then, in the mountains, they run into bad guys who strip them naked for the greenbacks stashed in their pants.

But he grudgingly agrees to take the group to the border with Panama, and deliver them to Guna tribesmen who will lead them out of the forest. 'I'm not harming anyone,' Colina tells me, as we prepare to set out. He's been fleeing poverty and violence all his life: selling coconuts from a cart, waking up at 2 a.m. for work on a ranch. Four of his brothers were murdered by EPL guerrillas. Now he's here, planting cas-sava, rice and bananas, working part-time as a guide to make ends meet. 'We don't rob people. If someone fractures a bone, I run down to fetch people with hammocks or a mule to come and get them.'

Human rights organisations say the likes of Colina are human traf-fickers. The Clan de Golfo – Colombia's richest and most powerful narco militia, also known as Los Gaitanistas – is known to take a cut for each migrant, earning an estimated $60 million in 2023. Survivors talk of systematic rape and corpses lying along the trail. Hundreds of people have been found dead in the past decade; hundreds more were probably never even reported missing. Migrants are sometimes used as drug mules – or human shields. The cartel packs one speedboat with coke, another with people. If the navy appears, they throw the passen-gers overboard and escape with the powder.

The more expensive seaborne route, circumventing the worst of the jungle, has its own risks. The boats travel by night and are dangerously crammed. Shipwrecks and sinkings are common. In Capurganá, an overgrown corner of the cemetery houses the bodies – mutilated by rocks and sharks – that wash ashore. A chef at a local hotel recently sliced open a fish to find a single foot in its belly, says Katiara Mesa, an official in the mayor's office. I'd found her sitting behind a bare desk, acrylic nails tapping at her phone. They've had no reports of sexual assault or robbery, she says. I ask if migrants have any way to report them once in the jungle. 'No,' she concedes. 'They always say, "We will die in the attempt rather than go back." In the end, it's their decision.'

José, Katherin, Yonatan and company shoulder their backpacks, pick up their children, and follow Colina and a guide nicknamed Cartagena – happy-go-lucky, in sunglasses, jeans and black rubber boots – out of the compound. Giant teddy bears dangle from their rucksacks. We pass brick bungalows and a collapsed wall of the dump, overflowing with discarded clothes and bedding.

Then we enter the forest, filing past monumental trunks with buttress-like roots and a tangle of epiphytes. The group starts to shed luggage and spread out almost immediately. Their feet get soaked as we splash through shin-deep streams. I chat to another twentysomething Venezuelan. He was a soldier back home, but didn't receive his pay for six months. When it arrived, it was just 120 bolívares: 'Not even enough to buy some bread and a tube of toothpaste.'

I'd pictured a narrow, leafy trail. But this is a gash three metres wide gouged through the undergrowth, made slippery by thousands of feet, the slopes on either side littered with tin cans and plastic. The middle is a mudslick, so we stick to the edges, finding rocks and roots, clinging on to branches and scrambling upwards. It's sweaty and exhausting. Before long, José's bare feet and tracksuit bottoms are coated in grey slurry. There's probably some journalistic commandment about not getting involved. But the least I can do is carry Katherin's rucksack, so she can focus on looking after Kylean and placing her feet in the quagmire. ·

In the early afternoon, we reach a hilltop clearing known as El Cielo. A blue sky, but darkening with grey cloud; a sharp forested ridge rising ahead. The Venezuelans sit and rest on the ground. I've witnessed only the beginning of their journey through the Darién – and barely a percentage point of their pan-American odyssey. Teams of reporters braver and better organised than me have followed groups of migrants all the way through the jungle to the trailhead in Panama. But Cartagena has only agreed to accompany me this far, and then back into town.

It's a wrench to return Katherin's pack. José slings it onto his front, now resembling a one-man-band. I give them my water, slip them all the cash in my wallet, and tell them to stay in touch. José solemnly fist-bumps me goodbye. They walk around a bend and up into the trees, disappearing from sight. From somewhere above come shouts of encouragement, and laughter. Then, just leaves rustling in the breeze.

Most of those passing through the Darién say their final destination is the United States, some 2,000 miles away. Many don't make it, having been extorted, detained or deported as they travel upwards through

Panama, Costa Rica, Nicaragua, Honduras, Guatemala and Mexico. Some turn back, or stay put when they run out of money or the will to go on. But their ranks are constantly replenished by those escaping violence, destitution and climate change in Central America and Mexico. In 2023, 2.5 million people were intercepted crossing the southern US border: a record high.

The humanitarian crisis is rocket fuel for ultraconservative authoritarians. If re-elected in November 2024, Donald Trump has promised to unleash 'the largest deportation operation in American history', accusing undocumented migrants – in language mirroring *Mein Kampf* – of 'poisoning the blood of our country'.

But so far, nothing has stemmed the flow of desperate people: not the border wall, not the razor wire strung in front of it, not the Texas troopers told to shove them back into the Río Grande, not the ICE raids on restaurants and construction sites, not the Border Patrol agents who pour out stashes of water into the cracked desert earth, nor the threats from Republican also-rans to send troops and missiles into Mexico. If US authorities were serious about getting to grips with the problem, much of the solution lies not along its frontiers but in DC.

Its politicians could follow countries like Colombia and Uruguay in gradually decriminalising drugs – and providing healthcare to help addicts get clean. This would undercut the astronomical profits made by the cartels, and turn the heat down on the turf wars that set whole communities on the move. They could end sanctions that only entrench regimes. They could meaningfully fight climate change, and provide serious cash to support the communities vulnerable to drought, flooding and other disasters who might otherwise migrate.

The countries of the global North could easily provide safer pathways for the young people their ageing societies desperately need. If more people could apply for asylum and temporary work visas in their places of origin, they wouldn't need to make dangerous transcontinental treks, lining the pockets of cartels and coyotes along the way. Above all, the United States should tighten up its gun laws. Hundreds of thousands of firearms manufactured in the US are smuggled into Latin America every year, giving lethal firepower to gangs from Tijuana to Rocinha, Port-au-Prince to Pudahuel, and making Latin America the most murderous region on earth.

A generation since the Cold War, and two centuries since independence, the region's woes can no longer be pinned wholesale on Europe and the United States. But the wounds of colonialism, invasion and foreign-backed dictatorship run deep. Latin America's institutions are still finding their feet. And though some of the old veins have been sutured or run dry, new forms of extractivism are flourishing – lithium and cryptocurrency mining, 'green' hydrogen, carbon-trading – with dubious claims to sustainability.

After a decade reporting on South America, I'm still optimistic. Its countries have learned the hard lessons of wars past and haven't fought a serious conflict in nearly a century. The continent is a long way away from the conflagrations of the present and future in Europe and Asia. The region is perfectly positioned to play China, the US and other powers against each other to secure loans, technology, and a fair price for its strategic resources. Nearly a third of its energy comes from renewables: twice the global average. South America could prove the green, soft-power superpower of the twenty-first century: disdaining bombs and battleships, instead wielding its massive sporting, musical and literary clout, feeding and fuelling the planet while nursing the Amazon and its other great ecosystems back to health.

Latin America's fully-fledged dictatorships are vulnerable, and can be counted on one hand. Young, social-media-savvy generations are quick to call out corruption and boot politicians from office. As of early 2024, opposition candidates had won almost all of the previous twenty-two free elections across Latin America: only the Colorado behemoth in Paraguay resisted the anti-establishment trend. Family, community and social movements, the building blocks of a fairer society, remain far stronger here than in the atomised global North.

The unified patria grande has proved elusive. The cleavages of nation and class seem here to stay. 'What integration can be achieved' – Eduardo Galeano once asked – 'by countries that have not even been able to integrate internally? Each country suffers from deep fissures in its own body, bitter social divisions and unresolved tensions between its great marginal deserts and its urban oases. The drama,' he added, 'is reproduced on the regional level.' The interests of a Paraguayan campesino are opposed to a Brazilian agro baron; small business owners in Peru don't automatically feel sympathy for Venezuelan migrants.

Even the very idea of Latin America is a recent construct, dating back only to resistance against US imperialism in Central America in the 1850s. The alternative concept of Abya-Yala is yet to catch on widely outside academic and activist circles. And as sea levels rise, the islands off Panama where most of the Guna live – their own Abya-Yala, where Mamani once visited – will be submerged by the end of this century.

With their homes starting to sink beneath the waves, many are already evacuating for an uncertain future on the mainland.

As the Bolivarian Revolution descends deeper into the abyss, some argue that South America's fixation on its bloodstained backstory has done it few favours; that its politicians whip up ancient grievances and poke at historical wounds better off left alone. While Asia looks to the future and invests in science and technology – writes one conservative commentator from Argentina – Latin Americans 'live to navel-gaze' and only suffer from their 'obsession with the past'. But either approach – dwelling endlessly on past trauma, or launching in headlong flight to forget – is likely to yield similar results. History can only be endured, and not repeated, once it is reckoned with.

Eurocentric ways of thinking trap us within linear notions of time – argues the Bolivian historian and sociologist Silvia Rivera Cusicanqui – wherein the past is dead and the future lies ahead. But in the Aymara language and cosmovision, it is the future that lies behind, invisible. Meanwhile, the past – *nayrapacha* – 'is ahead of us, it's the only thing we know, because we can see, feel, and remember it'. Rivera likens the here-and-now to a palimpsest: a parchment whose writing has been scraped off to make way for new text, but where vestiges of the old words remain. In the present, 'traces of the most distant past come to light, bursting into view like a constellation and intertwining with other horizons and memories'. We need to think with the heart and the head, she argues, always walking in the present, but with 'the future on our backs and the past in our sight'.

Tracing the outlines of South America's lost countries is like handling a palimpsest, a much-scrawled-upon manuscript where past, present and future collide. It builds towards a history that looks beyond artificial modern borders, hollow nationalisms, and binaries of victim and victor: instead engaging with the continent in its full and flourishing maturity, following the living blood that flows beyond frontiers and through the centuries. It tells us how the region got here, and where it might be headed next. Palmares is a heroic saga-in-miniature of the making of the Atlantic world. The failed dream of a united continent ruled by an Inca monarchy – and the epic of the long-lived Mapuche power that held sway south of the Biobío – explain much about the debt owed by Chile, Peru and Argentina to their first nations. Bolivia's yearning for the sea, and the long shadow cast by the patria of López over Paraguay, illustrate how the siren song of former greatness can be easily exploited. As we push past the limits of the natural world, the bio-technological ingenuity of ancient Amazonians and coastal civilisations like the Chincha holds new resonance.

Taking the pulse of his continent fifty years ago, Galeano argued that understanding its deep-rooted connection between past and present, the living and the dead, was the best antidote for pessimism as its people groped towards a better future. 'Is Latin America a region condemned to humiliation and poverty?' he pointedly asked. 'Condemned by whom? Is God, is Nature, to blame? The oppressive climate, racial inferiority? Religion, customs? Or may not its plight be a product of history, made by human beings and so, unmakeable by human beings?'

A few months later, a photo catches my eye at the top of my Facebook feed. It's José, Katherin and Kylean. The young family had made it through the jungle and kept me updated as they navigated border crossings and overflowing shelters up through Central America. We'd lost contact once they set off northwards from Mexico City. But now they're wearing winter coats and broad grins amid the lights of Times Square, the first chapter of their new lives just beginning.

But here in the Darién, on the threshold of another continent, my journey through South America has reached an end. I'm not sure where is next. After so long on the road I had started to feel, like the false Inca Bohórquez, without a place in the world. Central America beckons: that land of mysterious Maya cities in the jungle and outlandish leaders like Nayib Bukele, El Salvador's authoritarian, Bitcoin-peddling president and self-styled 'philosopher king'. On the other hand, I feel I've got unfinished business in Paraguay.

As I slide down the muddy track back towards Capurganá, the group of Haitians including Shiller, Herold and their children are climbing upwards. 'God bless you,' Shiller says to me, smiling as he passes. It's been years since I had any religious faith. But as they begin the most dangerous journey of their lives, faith is all they have. I reach for the only words that feel halfway adequate: 'You too.'

Acknowledgements

Explorers and archaeologists seldom 'discover' a lost city without locals showing it to them. And writers or historians would struggle to 'unearth' anything from an archive or library without those who have collected, preserved and (sometimes) catalogued it. I owe a debt of gratitude to workers and volunteers past and present at the Archivo Nacional de Asunción, the Biblioteca Nacional del Paraguay, the Biblioteca Municipal Augusto Roa Bastos, the Centro de Documentación at the Fundación Huellas de la Cultura Paraguaya, the Biblioteca Nacional del Perú, the Archivo y Biblioteca Nacionales de Bolivia, the Biblioteca Popular de Yavi, the Biblioteca Nacional de Chile, the Centro de Estudios y Documentación Memoria Mapuche, Documenta Palmares, the British Library, the Bodleian Library, the London Library, and the Archivo General de Indias, Sevilla.

In Peru, Edgar Ramírez at Agro Rural helped to get us onto the Chincha Islands. Nick Ballon had the idea in the first place; Jahel Guerra and Mila Araoz helped plan the trip and our travels in the Atacama and El Alto. In Lima, Dan Collyns was generous with contacts and ceviche tips, and Jack Cole and Daniela Rodríguez were friendly, beautifully made-up faces. Jack was also a welcome wingman when checking out the Chincha Kingdom on the mainland. Jacob Bongers of the University of Sydney, digging into this overlooked pre-Columbian power and what became of it, is doing Viracocha's work. Gregory T. Cushman's *Guano and the Opening of the Pacific World* is peerless on the world-historical ramifications of Peruvian birdshit. Gregorio Alfredo Inca Roca Concha graciously received me twice in modern-day Cusco. Javier Fonseca filled me in about his discoveries at Espíritu Pampa. His untimely passing in 2022 was a major loss to Vilcabamba studies. John Hemming's *The Conquest of the Incas* remains the authoritative tome on the last days of Tawantinsuyu and the rise and fall of Vilcabamba. Two volumes helmed by Brian Bauer – *Vilcabamba and the Archaeology of*

Resistance and *Voices from Vilcabamba* – proved essential in bringing the narrative to life and up to date. The weaving together of travel writing, history and archaeology in *The White Rock* and *Cochineal Red*, Hugh Thomson's brace of modern classics on pre-Columbian Peru, was a big inspiration. They're the perfect introduction for the armchair Hiram Bingham.

Christopher Heaney, Paulo Drinot and Charles Walker kindly responded to open-ended questions with invaluable pointers and contacts. Prof. Walker's *The Tupac Amaru Rebellion*, and his translation of *In Search of an Inca* by Alberto Flores Galindo, are key texts for neo-Inca utopianism and the forgotten Andean revolutions of the early 1780s. *The Peculiar Revolution*, edited by Paulo Drinot and Carlos Aguirre, is a fascinating study of General Velasco, most curious of caudillos. Heaney's *Empires of the Dead*, tracing the post-mortem voyages of Peruvian ancestors, is rightly making waves. *On Savage Shores* by Caroline Dodds Pennock and *Andean Cosmopolitans* by José Carlos de la Puente Luna are eye-opening companions to Indigenous American travellers to early modern Europe. Garcilaso de la Vega Inca – Herodotus of the Andean world, colleague of Cervantes and contemporary of Shakespeare – is little known to English-speakers and often dismissed as a fabulist. A recent exception is *Inca Garcilaso and Contemporary World-Making*, edited by Sara Castro-Klarén and Christian Fernández. A translation of the *Royal Commentaries* by Sir Paul Rycault in 1688 – taking liberties in places, but conveying the Inca's charming Golden Age vernacular – is available in print and for free online. Big thanks for everything are due to Alvaro Salas Montalbo, Percy Cobos, Juvenal Cobos, Benjamin Cobos, Julia Cobos, Americo and Reyna Sacsa Cobos, Jorge Cobos and Danilo. Let's do that Choquequirao trip soon.

In Brazil, Aaron Cathers furnished me with a helpful who's who in contemporary rainforest archaeology. Eduardo and Silvana went out of their way to make me welcome in Porto Velho, as did João Cunha, Márjorie and Eduardo in Tefé, and Anne Rapp Py-Daniel in Santarém. *Sob os tempos do equinócio* by Eduardo Góes Neves is an excellent handbook to the modern study of the ancient Amazon. Charles Mann's *1491: New Revelations of the Americas Before Columbus* is still a paragon of accessible science journalism. I kept returning to it to see how he'd effortlessly summarised some fifty-year academic feud. *The Third Bank of the River: Power and Survival in the Twenty-First-Century Amazon* by Chris Feliciano Arnold is a gripping guide to modern Manaus and the urban jungle. In the run-up to

COP 30 in Belém, the posthumous *How to Save the Amazon* by Dom Phillips will make for essential, urgent reading. I never met Dom in person, but we compared notes on the Chaco and the Amazon, and he offered some much-valued encouragement. Amid an industry that has its fair share of mercenaries, he was a class act.

The *Documenta Palmares* project – realised by Silvia Hunold Lara and the history department of the Universidade Estadual de Campinas, São Paulo – is a one-stop shop for anyone interested in Brazil's greatest quilombo. It enabled me to flick through nearly 2,000 digitised manuscript mentions of Palmares from around the world while under lockdown. Glenn Alan Cheney's *Quilombo dos Palmares* is a fine survey of the rebel realm and the dozens of attempts to destroy it. I found recent scholarship by Silvia Hunold Lara and Felipe Aguiar Damasceno persuasive on the existence of multiple Palmares in time and space, and the need to look past Zumbi and Barriga to Ganga Zumba and Cucaú. Marcelo d'Salete kindly shared some thoughts about Palmares, fact and fiction. His illustrated *Angola Janga: Kingdom of Runaway Slaves* brings the saga to life in all its tragedy and hope. *Brazil: A Biography* by Heloisa Murgel Starling and Lilia Moritz Schwarcz was seriously well-thumbed. Thais Dandara Thaty helped me navigate Serra de Barriga, União dos Palmares, and Muquém, where traces of Angola Janga are all around, not least in the craft of Dona Irinéia. Geraldo Majella in Maceió gave me a solid grounding on post-Palmarian quilombos in Alagoas. Eduardo de Almeida Navarro, Pedro Ka'Aguasu Potiguara, Mark Meuwese, and Nathália Galdino discussed Filipe Camarão and the Dutch-Potiguara-Portuguese conflict. Kiratiana Freelon connected me with interviewees and was a great help at the Aldeia Marak'anà. Sadakne Baroudi and Cosme Felippsen were passionate guides to the hidden Afro-Brazilian history of Providência and downtown Rio. After many months on the road, some cold beers in São Paulo with Brazilian journo dream team Sam Cowie and Thais Carrança were just what the doctor ordered.

In Argentina, I could have asked for no better launchpad for my peregrination through the Diaguita heartland than Martin, Silvana, Bruno and Mora at Condor Valley. They make a decent Malbec, too. Julio and Virginia Ruiz Moreno were receptive and open hosts, as was Patricia 'Pachila' Cabana in Jujuy. It was great to run into Fernando in Tilcara, Humahuaca and Mendoza. Ana María Lorandi's *Spanish King of the Incas*, translated by Ann de León, is the definitive work on the life and times of Pedro Bohórquez. I also relied on *La Rebelión de Pedro*

Bohórquez by Teresa Piossek Prebisch and her edition of Torreblanca's *Relación Histórica de Calchaquí. The Return of the Native* by Rebecca Earle is a fascinating survey of how revolutionaries across Spanish America adopted pre-Columbian symbols and rhetoric only to turn on their Indigenous compatriots within a generation. John Lynch's *San Martín: Argentine Soldier, American Hero*, Robert Harvey's *Liberators*, and Peter Blanchard's *Under the Flags of Freedom* all helped me fall in step with the African Army of the Andes.

In Chile, Paula Huenchumil, and her coverage with *Interferencia*, helped me find my bearings in Wallmapu. Mat Youkee convinced me that *Patria* wouldn't be complete without the estado araucano and its hapless elected monarch. John Bartlett did sterling work editing podcasts and reporting the estallido social. Pedro Cayuqueo took the time to correspond about the crumpled conquistadors. Cayuqueo's *Historia Secreta Mapuche* is a breakneck gallop through four centuries of Wallmapu–Winka relations as seen from south of the Biobío. I often dismounted to José Bengoa's more sedate but magisterial *Historia del Pueblo Mapuche* and the precious oral histories underlying it. I also tried to pay heed to *Escucha, Winka . . . ! Cuatro Ensayos de Historia Nacional Mapuche*, by Pablo Marimán, Sergio Caniuqueo and José Millalén. Up in the Atacama, Cristina Dorador and Chris Harrod provided a welcome oasis of chilled beers, grilled meats, and microbial and marine knowledge. Jorge Montealegre, Katia Chornik and Jorge Ardiles shared a wealth of insider information about Chacabuco and 1973. Gran abrazo to Dan, Tom, Linne, Raimundo, Valerie, Meaghan, Amanda, and all the ST weónes and weónas. Started in the garden – inexplicably barbecuing our pants – now we're here.

In Paraguay, conversations with Andrew Nickson, Eduardo Nakayama, Juan Marcelo Cuenca, Vicenta Miranda, Ricardo Canese, Rogelio Goiburú, Fabián Chamorro, Miguel Ángel Romero, Alfredo da Mota Menezes, María Victoria Barrata, Ana Barreto Vallinoti and President Santiago 'Santi' Peña Palacios threw up interesting perspectives on Stroessner, López, and the causes, conduct and consequences of the guerra guazú. To understand contemporary Paraguay, I invariably turn to El Surtidor and Base Investigaciones Sociales. Lis García and William Costa switched me on to Rafael Barrett. William's deft new translation of *Paraguayan Sorrow* will hopefully bring more readers to Barrett, up there with Casement as a clear-eyed chronicler of early 20th-century capitalism. Thomas Whigham has written the most detailed studies of Latin America's direst conflict in English: see *The Paraguayan War* and *Road* to *Armageddon: Paraguay versus the Triple Alliance, 1866–70*. For the aftermath, I leaned heavily on *Paraguay and the Triple Alliance: The Postwar Decade, 1869–1878* by husband-and-wife historians Warren and Warren. Captain Humberto Duarte and the crew of the *Anabisetia* gave me time to get to grips with Schmidel and the Supremo; Esteban Ortega gamely imparted the rudiments of Guaraní over Zoom. Taguide Picanerei is an unflappable Chaco chauffeur, and Mateo, Isaac and Dona are always welcoming. *Behold the Black Caiman: A Chronicle of Ayoreo Life* by Lucas Bessire is an incisive anthropology of this resilient, resourceful people and us *cojñone* who invariably want something from them. It's a pleasure and an education to work with Santi and Mayeli. Speaking of capos, Jack Nicas and María Magdalena Arréllaga rode the river with me the second time, while Alan, Humberto and team kept the guiso just as tasty and the *Aquidaban* just as afloat. She made her final voyage in December 2023. Just two months later, after heavy rains knocked out the roads, the government began dispatching a gunship full of supplies every week to the isolated communities of the Pantanal.

In Bolivia, I was permitted to ask searching questions of the Plurinational State's landlocked finest in Puerto Busch, Cochabamba, La Paz and the Cuarto Distrito Naval Titicaca. Thank you for your time, and your service. Bill Wroblewksi, fixer and film-maker extraordinaire, set some things up. In addition to advancing Bolivian studies via the Biblioteca Bicentenario, Amaru Villanueva Rance broke down the MAS and the new class of Bolivianaires for me. Outsiders will struggle to understand the proceso de cambio without him on this planet to guide us. Nación Rap Aymara let us hang around El Alto with them. Luis at the Hostal Graciela, Oruro, helped me get around the ex-lake and imparted some fascinating Atlantean theories. Diego Von Vacano, Kathryn Ledebur and Butch fed me some useful morsels. Olivia Arigho-Stiles – the only good OAS – is always a friendly sounding board on Kollasuyu. Nick is great company and wrangles way nicer hotels than I'm used to. I deferred often to *Andean Tragedy: Fighting the War of the Pacific, 1879–1884* by William F. Sater. Some of Silvia Rivera Cusicanqui's thought is available in English as *A Ch'ixi World is Possible: Essays from a Present in Crisis*. Kris Lane's *Potosi: The Silver City That Changed the World* is a comprehensive and readable biography of the villa imperial and the mountain that eats men. I took a lot from the essays of James Dunkerley on modern Bolivian history.

In Colombia, Cristina Noriega hooked me up with some contacts in the FARC and the Darién. Jhonni Giraldo got us to Marquetalia and back, muddy but in one piece, and furnished me with the *Cuadernos de Campaña* of Manuel Marulanda and the *Diario de la Resistencia de Marquetalia* by Jacobo Arenas: important sources on the genesis of the world's longest-running civil war. The folks at Librería Merlín, Bogotá, also tracked down some useful titles. Emy Osorio took me to El Coreano in Cartagena and allowed me to tick 'work with the Fundación Gabo' off the bucket list. 'Cartagena' also got me safely in and out of the jungle. I found Tom Feiling's *Short Walks from Bogotá: Journeys in the New Colombia* a solid refresher, and *Forgotten Peace: Reform, Violence, and the Making of Contemporary Colombia* by Robert Karl a useful correct-ive. The bravest and best reporting from the Darién is by Julie Turkewitz and Federico Ríos for the *New York Times*. It's a source of serious regret that I couldn't squeeze in more material from Colombia – and that limited budget, time and space prevented me from including much on Ecuador, Uruguay, the Guianas and especially Venezuela. Bolívar and Chávez loom so large South America's recent history that it's hard to tackle them head-on. Instead, I drew on the vivid and varying accounts of Chavismo's hopeful advent and painful descent in William Grant's *Populista: The Rise of Latin America's 21st Century Strongman*, *In the Shadow of the Liberator* by Richard Gott, and *Motherland: A Memoir* by Paula Ramón, translated by Julia Sanches and Jennifer Shyue.

In Spain, Soraya showed me round Garcilaso's Montilla residence in a face mask in forty-eight-degree heat. Jesse and James invited me to blow off some steam in Alaró. Tom, Belén, Lucas and Inés are my excuse to fly home via Madrid and eat my body weight in jamón and patatas.

In the UK, Stefania, Victoria, Javie, Ro, Krishmary and Yara told me about Latinx London. Paz did the Liberator Loop with me and is a great friend, as was Giulio Regeni, our much-missed comrade. In Oxford, Al Moreno, David Parrott, Matt Houlbrook and John Nightin-gale trained me up. I also owe particular thanks to Julia, and in Dorset to Messrs Warren, Hudson, Bryson, Ridgeway, Brooke, Storey and Pryor: their teaching and support, and the generosity of the family of William Yates, changed the course of my life.

By sending me back to South America, the judges of the FT/Bodley Head Essay Prize did the same. I'm grateful to Bodley Head/Vintage for taking a punt on a first-time author's travel guide to non-existent coun-tries. Anna Baty was a valued early partisan of what would become *Patria*. Stuart Williams kept the flame alive. Leah Boulton and Rhiannon Roy kept the schedule in hand. Duncan Heath's sharp eye saved me embar-rassment. Bill Donohoe produced the beautiful maps and illustrations.

Alice Skinner saw it all through with great care and patience. The judges at the Royal Society of Literature gave vital financial support and a vote of confidence at the halfway mark: a huge thank you to them and the family of Giles St Aubyn.

I slept easy in my hammock knowing my brilliant agent, Rachel Conway, and the team at Georgina Capel had my back. Editors at the *Guardian, The Economist, Delayed Gratification,* the BBC, *History Today, National Geographic* and the *New York Times* – including Sam Jones, Martin Hodgson, Emma Hogan, Brooke Unger, Fiona Mackie and Rob Orchard – agreed to commissions that helped bankroll or dovetailed with my research. South America aficionado Ollie Balch passed on a gig that proved a lifeline. Christine Mathias, Christopher Heaney, Jacob Bongers, Olivia Arigho-Stiles, Will Costa, Andrew Nickson and Ángeles Picone were kind enough to read parts of the manuscript, and made many helpful comments. The mistakes that remain are all mine.

Karen Jaques, *kuña mbarete* of Holy City, offered a place to hang my poncho. Paddy, Tilly, Gizmo, Maude and Chihiro forced me to look up from the screen once in a while. Rich and the Portland Beach bums, and Dario, Guise, Guada and the CPH crowd kept me relatively sane. Buena onda was purveyed by Sam, Sylvia, Jamie, Kate, Nick, Tilda, Jem, Mimi, William, Suzie, Ana, Sophie, Chris, Sandi, Indie, Wilko, Hannah, Margaret, JF, Lucy, Skelton, Ellie, Alex, Heather, Bella, Romi, Beto, Manu, Lau, Dai, Leila, Rita, James, Cynthia, Emily, Laura, Maybs, Tasha, Roger, Rosie and Jane. Stubbsy, Matthew, Henry and Seb kept me moving in the mountains and found an escape from the labyrinth.

Seb also fished me out of the Río Pato, and shared an electrifying experience at Marquetalia. Dylan Townley critiqued several chapters – improving them and the verses tenfold – and made Mill Cottage a home. Thanks for everything, my brothers. Will encouraged me to get the essay in, and bought the celebratory Nando's. My mum, Louise, never complained about my long periods of absence. Saranna and Stu always have some hard labour ready in case I want to procrastinate. I can't wait to meet Rolandcito's hermanito soon.

Bill Guidery told me of our Atlantic ancestry, and how every field and floorboard hide treasure of one kind or another. Stuart Blair taught me to give the time of day to everyone, but especially the underdog. There are worse principles when trying to write history, or its first draft. I wish they could have held this book in their hands. Ayelen gave me the love and support I needed to finish it. Here's to the next adventure, together.

Notes

INTRODUCTION

2 *only Venezuela is more corrupt*: Transparency International Corruption Perceptions Index, 2022. Available at: https://www.transparency.org/en/cpi/2022.

saw service against the Vietcong: 'Mueren tres militares en tragedia aérea y exigen investigación externa', *Última Hora*, 25 November 2021; https://www.ultimahora.com/mueren-tres-militares-tragedia-aerea-y-exigen-investigacion-externa-n2973654.

San Marino, East Timor and the Vatican: 'El Papa Francisco y la religión en Chile y América Latina', *Latinobarómetro*, January 2018. Available at: https://www.cooperativa.cl/noticias/site/artic/20180112/asocfile/20180112 124342/f00006494_religion_chile_america_latina_2017.pdf.

4 *I die with my country*: López's wounds are detailed in 'Certificado de las heridas causantes de la muerte del Mariscal Francisco Solano López expedido por los cirujanos del ejército Brasilero (en Portugués y Castellano)', Archivo Nacional de Asunción (ANA), Sección Historia V, 356, No. 18, 1870, f.2. For López's last words see Coronel Silvestre Aveiro Delgadillo, 'El Fiscal de Sangre in Eder Acosta Santacruz', *Venció Fatigas y Penurias. Cerro Corá en las memorias de los sobrevivientes*, Volume II, El Lector, Asunción, 2015, pp. 27–8.

'a gap in the family of nations': George Frederick Masterman, *Seven Eventful Years in Paraguay. A narrative of personal experience among the Paraguayans*, Sampson Low, Son & Marston, London, 1869, pp. 342–3.

South American Sparta: such an analogy was made by Eliza Lynch, an Irish courtesan who became the marshal's consort. The 'immortalised' Paraguayan people and her late husband, she wrote, had 'left to international feeling such a lesson as was given by the Spartans of Thermopylae'. Eliza A. Lynch, *Exposición protesta que hace Elisa A. Lynch*, Buenos Aires, Imprenta rural, 1875.

bodyguards in suits and helmeted cavalrymen: footage of Perón's visit is available at: https://twitter.com/ParaguayEterno/status/116197826035340 9026, accessed 15 May 2024.

5 *'was and is Paraguay'*: Juan E. O'Leary, 'Los Legionarios', in *Prosa Polémica. Ensayos de Juan E. O'Leary*, Ediciones Napa, Asunción, 1982, pp. 152–3.

'*from which our lives are moulded*': 'Discurso Pronunciado por El Historiador Paraguayo Juan E. O'Leary', 16 August 1954, in *El Acto de Entrega De Las Reliquias Históricas del Paraguay*, Presidencia de La Nación, Secretaria De Prensa y Difusión, Buenos Aires, 1954, pp. 5–8.

armed and bankrolled ... by the United States: for a new study of the Stroessner dictatorship that draws on the 2008 Truth and Justice commission (CVJ), see *Ventanas Abiertas. Informe de la Comision de Verdad y Justicia sobre la dictadura en Paraguay 1954–89*, Versión esencial, Coordinadora de Derechos Humanos del Paraguay y Fábrica Memética, Asunción, 2023.

6 *hammered it with wooden staffs*: 'Manifestantes derriban busto de Pedro de Valdivia y Diego Portales en Temuco', *24 horas*, 29 October 2019; https://www.24horas.cl/regiones/araucania/manifestantes-derriban-busto-de-pedro-de-valdivia-y-diego-portales-en-temuco-3691905.

7 *the Mapuche chieftain Lautaro*: Yessenia Márquez, 'No fue la estatua pero sí el busto: empalan a Pedro de Valdivia a los pies de Lautaro en Concepción', *Biobiochile.cl*, 30 October 2019; https://www.biobiochile.cl/noticias/nacional/region-del-bio-bio/2019/10/30/no-fue-la-estatua-pero-si-el-busto-empalan-a-pedro-de-valdivia-a-los-pies-de-lautaro-en-concepcion.shtml.

frigid Lumaco River: *Werken Noticias*, 7 August 2020; https://twitter.com/info_werken/status/1291809057897144321.

a sacred pre-Columbian pyramid: 'Indígenas: juicio a Belalcázar y lo hallaron culpable de delitos', *El Tiempo*, 17 September 2020; https://www.eltiempo.com/colombia/cali/misak-derribaron-monumento-de-belalcazar-por-delitos-contra-indigenas-538244.

Borba Gato ... was guilty of genocide: Kleber Tomaz, 'Após 1 ano, três acusados de incendiar estátua do bandeirante Borba Gato são julgados em SP', G1 SP, 9 September 2022; https://g1.globo.com/sp/sao-paulo/noticia/2022/09/08/apos-1-ano-tres-acusados-de-incendiar-estatua-do-bandeirante-borba-gato-sao-julgados-em-sp.ghtml.

Indigenous term for the island: 'El rastro borrado de los vándalos "borikén" que derribaron la estatua de Ponce de León en Puerto Rico', *El Mundo*, 3 February 2022; https://www.elmundo.es/cronica/2022/02/03/61f80057fc6c83d4588b45df.html.

spattered with blood-red paint: Anatoly Kurmanaev and Oscar Lopez, 'Mexico City Replaces a Statue of Columbus With One of an Indigenous Woman', *The New York Times*, 14 October 2021; https://www.nytimes.com/2021/10/14/world/americas/mexico-columbus-statue-indigenous.html; Jairo Vargas, '"Fuego al orden colonial": activistas antirracistas asaltan la estatua de Colón en Madrid', *Público*, 17 July 2020; https://www.publico.es/sociedad/estatua-colon-madrid-pancarta-fuego-orden-colonial-activistas-antirracistas-asaltan-estatua-colon-madrid.html; 'El monumento a Colón en Londres, manchado de pintura roja', Agencia EFE, 12 October 2021; https://www.youtube.com/watch?app=desktop&v=QLtJDQ-ABno&ab_channel=AGENCIAEFE.

meanwhile being dismantled: 'Whose heritage? Public symbols of the Confederacy (Third Edition)', Southern Poverty Law Center, 1 February 2022; https://www.splcenter.org/20220201/whose-heritage-public-symbols-confederacy-third-edition.

8 *computer-generated official portrait*: Nicholas Casey, 'Will the Real Simón Bolívar Please Stand Up?', *The New York Times*, 13 January 2016; https://www.nytimes.com/interactive/projects/cp/reporters-notebook/moving-to-venezuela/simon-bolivar-posters; Agence France Press, 'Chavez unveils 3D portrait of South American hero Bolivar', *Arab News*, 28 July 2012; https://www.arabnews.com/chavez-unveils-3d-portrait-south-american-hero-bolivar.

that we have yet deciphered: one intriguing potential example of a pre-Columbian writing system in South America are the *quipu* used by the Incas and other Andean cultures well into the colonial era. See Sabine Hyland, 'Writing with Twisted Cords: The Inscriptive Capacity of Andean Khipus', *Current Anthropology*, 58:3, 2017, 412–19; and Chapter 2, below.

sold them into adoption abroad: for the 40,000 children kidnapped or coercively parted from their parents in the wake of Guatemala's civil war, see Rachel Nolan, *Until I Find You. Disappeared Children and Coercive Adoptions in Guatemala*, Harvard University Press, 2024.

'into fragments like a grenade': Eduardo Galeano, *Open Veins of Latin America: Five Centuries of the Pillage of a Continent*, trans. Cedric Belfrage [1971], Monthly Review Press, New York, 1997, pp. 8, 265, 261.

9 *'understand the region as it is now'*: Marie Arana, *Silver Sword and Stone. Three Crucibles in the Latin American Story*, Weidenfeld & Nicolson, London, 2019, p. 374.

'something far deeper going on': personal communication, 3 November 2019.

'forgotten continent': the phrase is that of Michael Reid, *Forgotten Continent: A History of the New Latin America*, Yale University Press, 2017.

the box marked 'Other': for the official invisibility of Latin Americans in Britain, see the campaigning work of LatinXcluded, https://www.instagram.com/latinxcluded/?hl=en, and Romano Pizzichini, *More Than Other*, https://romanopizzichini.com/More-Than-Other.

a fifth of the US population is Latino: Cary Funk, Mark Hugo Lopez, 'A brief statistical portrait of U.S. Hispanics', Pew Research Center, 14 June 2022; https://www.pewresearch.org/science/2022/06/14/a-brief-statistical-portrait-of-u-s-hispanics/.

10 *'guns, germs and steel'*: Jared Diamond, *Guns, Germs and Steel: The Fates of Human Societies*, W. W. Norton, 1997.

the 'Pink Tide' ebbed: for accessible recent accounts in English on Chávez and the Pink Tide, see: Rory Carroll, *Comandante: Hugo Chávez's Venezuela*, Penguin Books, 2014; Will Grant, *Populista: The Rise of Latin America's 21st Century Strongman*, Head of Zeus, 2021; Paula Ramón, *Motherland: The Disintegration of a Family in a Collapsed Venezuela. A Memoir*, trans. Julia Sanches and Jennifer Shuye, Amazon Crossing, Seattle, 2023; and

Oliver Balch, *Viva South America! A Journey Through a Surging Continent*, Faber & Faber, 2009.

Viking seafarers: see Valerie Hansen, 'Vikings in America', *Aeon*, 22 September 2020. Available at: https://aeon.co/essays/did-indigenous-americans-and-vikings-trade-in-the-year-1000.

bronze and obsidian artefacts: see Amy Patterson Neubert, 'Old World metals were traded on Alaska coast several hundred years before contact with Europeans', Purdue University, 8 June 2016; https://www.purdue.edu/newsroom/releases/2016/Q2/old-world-metals-were-traded-on-alaska-coast-several-hundred-years-before-contact-with-europeans.html

11 *these worlds collided*: for the below discussion, see Alfred W. Crosby, *The Columbian Exchange: Biological and Cultural Consequences of 1492*, Westport, CT, Praeger, 2003, pp. 38–56.

just 500 were left in 1548: cited in Ibid., pp. 50–53.

At least a dozen epidemics: Linda A. Newson, 'The demographic impact of colonization', in *The Cambridge Economic History of Latin America*, Volume 1, Cambridge University Press, 2006, eds. Victor Bulmer-Thomas, John Coatsworth and Roberto Cortes-Conde, p. 166. The figure is for the highlands and lowlands of Central Mexico, 1532–1608, taken from Sherburne Friend Cook and Woodrow Wilson Borah, *Essays in Population History: Mexico and the Caribbean*, Volume 1, University of California Press, 1971, p. 80.

'Great pustules rotted their bodies': quoted in Crosby, *Columbian Exchange*, p. 49.

'the dogs and foxes': Daniel G. Brinton, *The Annals of the Cakchiquels. The Original Text, with a Translation, Notes and Introduction*, Library of Aboriginal American Literature, No. VI, Philadelphia, 1885, p. 171, Chapter 130; p. 194, Chapter 185.

civil war across Asia, Europe and Britain: A. Koch, C. Brierley, M. M. Maslin and S. L. Lewis, 'Earth system impacts of the European arrival and Great Dying in the Americas after 1492', *Quaternary Science Reviews*, 207, 2019, 13–36.

12 *wiped the European garrison out*: Christopher Columbus, 'First Voyage of Columbus', in *Four Voyages to the New World. Letters and Selected Documents*, Corinth Books, Gloucester, MA, 1978, ed. and trans. R. H. Major, pp. 12, 51.

attempt to colonise the Darién: for the Darién Scheme, see Darién Chest, National Museum of Scotland; https://www.nms.ac.uk/explore-our-collections/stories/scottish-history-and-archaeology/darien-chest/.

that overthrew colonial rule: see Matthew Brown, *Adventuring through Spanish Colonies: Simón Bolívar, Foreign Mercenaries and the Birth of New Nations*, Liverpool University Press, 2006.

conditions little different to slavery: Joseph Mulhern, *British Entanglement with Brazilian Slavery. Masters in Another Empire, c.1822–1888*, Anthem Press, London, 2024.

propped up Paraguay's war effort: Josefina Plá, *Los británicos en el Paraguay 1850–1870*, Arte Nuevo, Asunción, 1984.

steepest decline of any region globally: WWF Living Planet Report, 2022. Cited in 'Wildlife populations plunge 69% since 1970: WWF', *France 24*, 13 October 2022; https://www.france24.com/en/live-news/20221012-wildlife-populations-plunge-69-since-1970-wwf.

13   *forty million of its own people go hungry*: 'New UN report: 43.2 million people suffer from hunger in Latin America and the Caribbean', PAHO, 13 November 2023; https://www.paho.org/en/news/9-11-2023-new-report-432-million-people-suffer-hunger-latin-america-and-caribbean-and-region.

Canadian-owned Bitcoin mines: Eliza Gkritsi, 'Canadian Crypto Miner Pow.re Lands 100 MW Contract in Paraguay', *Coindesk*, 8 March 2023; https://www.coindesk.com/business/2023/03/08/canadian-crypto-miner-powre-lands-100-mw-contract-in-paraguay/. For cooking with firewood in Paraguay, see Viceministerio De Minas Y Energía, Paraguay, *Producción y consumo de biomasa forestal con fines energéticos en el Paraguay*, San Lorenzo, 2019, p. 14.

brine trickles out of the taps: Grace Livingstone, '"It's pillage": thirsty Uruguayans decry Google's plan to exploit water supply', *The Guardian*, 11 July 2023; https://www.theguardian.com/world/2023/jul/11/uruguay-drought-water-google-data-center; Claudia Urquieta and Daniela Dib, 'US tech giants are building dozens of data centers in Chile. Locals are fighting back', *Rest of World*, 31 May 2024; https://restofworld.org/2024/data-centers-environmental-issues/.

the so-called miracle mineral: Maeve Campbell, 'In pictures: South America's "lithium fields" reveal the dark side of our electric future', *Euronews. green*, 1 February 2022; https://www.euronews.com/green/2022/02/01/south-america-s-lithium-fields-reveal-the-dark-side-of-our-electric-future.

to rival Saudi Arabia by 2030: 'South America to become crude powerhouse by 2030 – Rystad', *OilNOW*, 24 August 2023; https://oilnow.gy/featured/brazil-argentina-guyana-leading-south-americas-oil-production-hike-to-9-million-barrels-a-day-by-2030-rystad/.

Europe and the United States still smoke and snort the lion's share: UNODC, *Global Report on Cocaine 2023*; https://www.unodc.org/documents/data-and-analysis/cocaine/Global_cocaine_report_2023.pdf.

more than 200,000 firearms: for the smuggling of weapons to Latin America, see Ioan Grillo, *Blood Gun Money: How America Arms Gangs and Cartels*, Bloomsbury Publishing, 2021; Ieva Jusionyte, *Exit Wounds. How America's Guns Fuel Violence across the Border*, University of California Press, 2024; and Beatriz Vicent Fernández, 'Arms Trafficking Case Puts Europe-Paraguay Pipeline on the Map', *Insight Crime*, 11 January 2024; https://insightcrime.org/news/arms-trafficking-europe-paraguay-pipeline/.

one in three of its murders: Amanda Erickson, 'Latin America is the world's most violent region. A new report investigates why', *Washington Post*, 25

April 2018; https://www.washingtonpost.com/news/worldviews/wp/2018/
04/25/latin-america-is-the-worlds-most-violent-region-a-new-report-
investigates-why/.

14 *especially from Venezuela and Ecuador*: Eileen Sullivan, 'Crossings at the
U.S. Southern Border Are Higher Than Ever', *The New York Times*, 21
October 2023; https://www.nytimes.com/2023/10/21/us/politics/cbp-record-
border-crossings.html.

a quarter of the US population will be Hispanic: Mike Schneider, 'The
Census Bureau sees an older, more diverse America in 2100 in three immigration scenarios', *AP*, 9 November 2023; https://apnews.com/article/
growth-population-demographics-race-hispanic-f563ebc4537f83792f3
f91ba5d7cdade.

'*We are no longer what we were*': Martín Caparrós, *Ñamérica*, 3rd edn,
Literatura Random House, Buenos Aires, 2022, p. 31.

especially (but not only) football: see Matthew Brown, *Sports in South
America: A History*, Yale University Press, 2023.

15 '*changed their way of seeing us*': Gabriel García Márquez, 'La Soledad de
América Latina', 8 December 1982. Available at: https://www.cultura.gob.
cl/agendacultural/la-soledad-de-america-latina-gabriel-garcia-marquez/.

Bolivian silver ... minted by Congolese artisans: for the global reach of
Bolivian silver, see Kris Lane, *Potosí. The Silver City That Changed the
World*, University of California Press, 2021, p. xvi.

16 *Reams of documents are being digitised*: thousands of manuscripts and
published works relating to Quilombo dos Palmares have recently been
digitised by the Universidade Estadual de Campinas, São Paulo. See DOC-
UMENTA Palmares, Campinas, São Paulo, UNICAMP/IFCH/CECULT,
2021. Available at: https://www.palmares.ifch.unicamp.br/. For declassified
documents relating to United States policy in Latin America, see National
Security Archive: https://nsarchive.gwu.edu/.

17 *450,000 people dead and counting*: Colombia's Truth Commission has concluded that at least 450,664 people have been killed in six decades of
fighting. However, Colombia's civil war is widely considered to have continued beyond the signing of a peace deal with the FARC in 2016. See
Cristina Noriega, 'Colombia Truth Commission presents final report on civil
conflict', *Al Jazeera*, 29 June 2022; https://www.aljazeera.com/news/2022/
6/29/colombia-truth-commission-presents-final-report-on-civil-conflict.

nearly eight million Venezuelans have fled: UNHCR Emergency Appeal,
Venezuela situation, August 2023; https://www.unhcr.org/emergencies/
venezuela-situation.

'*now upon a dangerous poison*': Marcel Proust, *The Captive*, trans. Scott
Moncrieff. Cited in R. Chalupa and K. Nesměrák, 'Chemophobia and passion: why chemists should desire Marcel Proust', *Monatshefte für Chemie*,
153, 2002, 697–705; https://doi.org/10.1007/s00706-022-02945-5.

18 *In his study*: Norman Davies, *Vanished Kingdoms. The History of Half-
Forgotten Europe*, Allen Lane, London, 2011, pp. 8–9.

1: THE FEATHERED KING

22 *half a million non-human residents*: Cristina Burga, Daniela Valencia, 'Reporte Mensual de Conservación en Islas y Puntas Guaneras' [online], Programa de Desarrollo Productivo Agrario Rural (AGRORURAL), Año 2, No. 4, 2021.

'*out of pure terror*': Pedro Pizarro, *Relación del descubrimiento y conquista de los reinos del Perú*, Pontificia Universidad Católica del Perú, Fondo Editorial, Lima, 1986, p. 36.

the first Europeans to tread so deep: in 1524, a Portuguese castaway, Aleixo Garcia, accompanied an Indigenous Guaraní army that raided the south-east fringes of the Inca Empire. See Charles E. Nowell, 'Aleixo Garcia and the White King', *The Hispanic American Historical Review*, 26 (4), November 1946.

23 '*like a brilliantly star-studded sky*': cited in John Hemming, *The Conquest of the Incas*, Macmillan, London, 1970, p. 36. For Cajamarca and its aftermath, see Hemming, pp. 30–45.

'*Nobody hurt the Indian*': Pizarro, *Relación*, p. 39.

struggling to tell them apart: Ibid., p. 38.

24 '*they thought little of the Spaniards*': Diego de Castro Titu Cusi Yupanqui, *Relación de la Conquista del Perú y hechos del Inca Manco II*, Impr. y libr. Sanmartín, Lima, 1916 [1570], Chapter 9.

'*set with many precious stones*': Pedro de Cieza de León, cited in María Rostworowski and Craig Morris, 'The Fourfold Domain: Inka Power and Its Social Foundations', in *The Cambridge History of the Native Peoples of the Americas*, Volume III: South America, Part 1, Cambridge University Press, 2000, eds. Frank Salomon, Stuart B. Schwartz, pp. 769–864, p. 787.

'*dear friend*': Pizarro, *Relación*, p. 222.

'*esteemed in ancient times*': Pedro de Cieza de León, *La crónica general del Perú*, IV, Librería e Imprenta Gil, 1924, p. 35.

centred on an oracle: for analysis of the ethnohistorical and archaeological evidence on the Chincha Kingdom, see Ben Nigra, Terrah Jones, Jacob Bongers, Charles Stanish, Henry Tantaleán, Kelita Pérez, 'The Chincha Kingdom: The Archaeology and Ethnohistory of the Late Intermediate Period South Coast, Peru', *Backdirt: Annual Review of the Cotsen Institute of Archaeology at UCLA*, 2014, pp. 36–47.

'*all content and joyful*': *Aviso de el modo que havia en el gobierno de los indios en tiempo del inga y como se repartían las tierras y tributos*, Biblioteca del Palacio Real de Madrid, Miscelánea de Ayala, Volume XXII, f.271r, cited in María Rostworowski, 'Costa Peruana Prehispanica', *Obras Completas III*, IEP, Lima, 2014.

25 *The shiny, reddish shell of* Spondylus: for this discussion on the possible use of *Spondylus* for hallucinogenic–religious purposes, see Mary Glowacki, 'Food of the Gods or mere mortals? Hallucinogenic *Spondylus* and its interpretive implications for early Andean society', *Antiquity*, 79(304), 2005, 257–68.

'*weights to measure gold*': J. De Samano, *Relación de Samano-Xerez*, Editores Técnicos Asociados, Biblioteca Peruana Primera Serie, 1, Lima, 1936, pp. 65–6. See also discussion in Hemming, *Conquest of the Incas*, p. 25.

'*the Sun for their God*': for this account of the Inca subjugation of the Chincha, see Inca Garcilaso de la Vega, *The Royal Commentaries of Peru* [*of the Incas*, 1609], trans. Paul Rycaut, Miles Flesher, London, 1683, Book VI, Chapter XVII, p. 213.

'*barefoot and with a burden*': Pizarro, *Relación*, p. 37.

had been named the Chinchaysuyo: Ibid., p. 222.

26 *an entrepreneurial enclave*: Thomas C. Patterson, 'Merchant Capital and the Formation of the Inca State', *Dialectical Anthropology* 12(2), 1987, pp. 217–27. Cited in Nigra et al., 'The Chincha Kingdom', p. 43.

vast populations of fish: Bill Chappell, 'Along With Humans, Who Else Is In The 7 Billion Club?', *NPR*, 3 November 2011.

'*this sort of Birds dung*': Garcilaso, *Royal Commentaries*, Book V, Chapter III, p. 136.

27 *a test bed*: Juan Carlos Crespo, 'Chincha y el mundo andino en la relación de 1558', *Historica*, Volume II, Number 2, December 1978, p. 198.

not necessarily all fishers or traders: see Crespo, 'Chincha y el mundo andino', pp. 190, 203, for a 1586 document that refers to the essential role played by the remaining Chincha fishermen in loading mercury from Huancavelica into ships bound for Arica, given the dangerous conditions of the port: 'sin los quales es ynposible poderse enbarcar ny beneficiar dicho acoque por ser de tanto riesgo el dicho Puerto.'

with kid gloves: for this thesis, see Marco Curatola Petrocchi, 'Guano: una hipótesis sobre el origen de la riqueza del señorío de Chincha', in *Arqueología, Antropología e Historia en los Andes: Homenaje a María Rostworowski*, Instituto de Estudios Peruanos y Banco Central de Reserva del Perú, Lima, 1997, eds. Rafael Varón Gabai, Javier Flores Espinoza.

forever transformed: see Gregory Cushman, *Guano and the Opening of the Pacific World: A global ecological history*, Cambridge University Press, 2013.

28 *a third of people*: Marco Aquino, 'Peru's poverty rate ticks up for second straight year', Reuters, 9 May 2024; https://www.reuters.com/world/americas/perus-poverty-rate-ticks-up-second-straight-year-2024-05-09/.

Photographs taken here in 1860: see G. Kubler, 'Towards absolute time: guano archaeology', *Memoirs of the Society for American Archaeology*, (4), 1948, 29–50.

29 '*The hum of wings*': Robert Cushman Murphy, *Bird Islands of Peru. The Record of a Sojourn on the West Coast*, G. P. Putnam's Sons, The Knickerbocker Press, New York & London, 1925, pp. 83–4.

'*great treasure is buried*': *The travels of Pedro de Cieza de Léon, A.D. 1532–50, contained in the first part of his Chronicle of Peru*, trans. Clements R. Markham, Burt Franklin, New York, 1864, Chapter V, p. 28.

The findings that we know about: this and the below paragraph are drawn from Kubler, G., 'Towards absolute time: guano archaeology', 1948.

30 *'live without food'*: Thomas Malthus, *An Essay on the Principle of Popula-tion as it Affects the Improvement of Society*, J. Johnson, London, 1798, pp. 12, 140.

'greatest trafficker in human bones': *Cassell's Saturday Journal*, 1896. Cited in Joe Turner, 'The bones of Waterloo', *Medium, Study of History*, 4 March 2015.

Mariano de Rivero: see Gregory T. Cushman, 'Guano', in *New World Objects of Knowledge. A cabinet of curiosities*, University of London Press, 2021, eds. Mark Thurner and Juan Pimentel, pp. 251–7.

'a small quantity of guano': Karl Marx, *Exzerpte und Notizen*, September 1846–December 1847, MEGA2 IV/9, p. 187. Cited in Kati Renner, 'What's that for? A Humboldt penguin and a packet of guano dung', *Deutsches Historisches Museum Blog*, 19 July 2022.

growers in the United States . . . County Kerry: Shawn William Miller, *An Environmental History of Latin America*, Cambridge University Press, 2007, p. 149.

31 *'most worthy of admiration'*: Mariano Paz Soldán, *Geografía Del Perú*, Lib-rería de Fermín Didot Hermanos, Hijos y Ca., Paris, Volume 1, 1862, p. 45.

Britain . . . imported 200,000 tonnes: Miller, *Environmental History*, p. 148.

England's wealthiest commoner: for the Gibbs family and Tyntesfield, see Madge Dresser, 'Slavery and West Country Houses', in *Slavery and the Brit-ish Country House*, English Heritage, Swindon, 2013, eds. Madge Dresser and Andrew Hann, p. 34. For the stained-glass guanay, see National Trust Photolibrary: https://tinyurl.com/2p942zzf, and 'Tyntesfield: the guano palace', The Gardens Trust, 14 November 2015: https://tinyurl.com/58p27jmv.

'The House of Gibbs made their dibs': James Higgins, *Lima: A Cultural History*, New York, 2005, p. 113, cited in Edward D. Melillo, 'The First Green Revolution: Debt Peonage and the Making of the Nitrogen Fertilizer Trade, 1840–1930', *The American Historical Review*, Volume 117, Issue 4, October 2012, pp. 1028–60, p. 1042.

it earned US$750 million: Melillo, 'The First Green Revolution', p. 1042.

'Two hundred million pesos!!': Mario Paz Soldán, *Geografía Del Perú*, 1862, Volume 1, pp. 45–8.

'without exaggeration': Manuel Ortiz de Zevallos, Ministro de Hacienda, 1857, cited in Cecilia Méndez, *Los Trabajadores Guaneros del Perú 1840–1879*, Universidad Nacional Mayor San Marcos, Seminario de Historia Rural Andina, Lima, 1987, preface.

six different constitutions . . . eight rulers: William F. Sater, *Andean Tragedy: Fighting the War of the Pacific, 1879–1884*, University of Nebraska Press, Lincoln, NE and London, 2007, p. 215.

31–2 *'unstable as water . . . growers of the staple'*: A. J. Duffield, *Peru in the Guano Age. Being a short account of a recent visit to the guano deposits*, London, Richard Bentley and Son, 1877, pp. 9–16.

32 *a census recorded*: 'Cuadro estadísticos de las Islas de Chincha en el año de 1866', Biblioteca Nacional del Perú (BNP), D7024.

'*Small though the Chinchas are*': Cushman Murphy, *Bird Islands of Peru*, p. 95.

The 'guano question' . . . ninety-four lesser guano islands: Daniel Immerwahr, *How to Hide an Empire: A Short History of the Great United States*, The Bodley Head, London, 2019, pp. 49–56.

33 '*hottest and ugliest part*': Cushman Murphy, *Bird Islands*, p. 124.

'*worse than slavery*': Karl Marx, 'Whose Atrocities?', *New York Daily Tribune*, 10 April 1857. For the role of British imperial officials in the trade in indentured Chinese workers, see Melillo, 'First Green Revolution', p. 1038.

'*slave ships*': Melillo, 'First Green Revolution', p. 1039.

Most of the vessels were English: 'Coolie', *Encyclopaedia Britannica*, 9th edition, Volume 6, 1877, p. 334.

'*the worst and most cruel slavery*': George Washington Peck, *Melbourne and the Chincha Islands*, cited in Cushman Murphy, *Bird Islands*, p. 111.

34 *They were paid eight pesos*: for working conditions on the Chincha Islands and Peru's other guano islands, see Cecilia Méndez, *Los Trabajadores Guaneros del Perú 1840–1879*, 1987.

Some 100,000 indentured Chinese workers: Melillo, 'First Green Revolution', p. 1029.

one count in 1860: cited in 'Coolie', *Encyclopaedia Britannica*, 1877, p. 334.

'*No hell has ever been conceived*': Duffield, *Peru in the Guano Age*, p. 77.

They staged mutinies: Melillo, 'First Green Revolution', p. 1047.

'*No single day passes*': cited in Méndez, *Trabajadores Guaneros*, p. 65.

35 '*British diplomats*': 'South America: The Peruvian Difficulty', *The New York Times*, 19 May 1864.

36 '*death and the grave*': Duffield, *Peru in the Guano Age*, p. 89.

'*not even the shadow*': cited in Méndez, *Trabajadores Guaneros*, pp. 28–30.

'*ever pondering pious questions*': 'Guano Song', *Gaudeamus. Humorous Poems*, translated from the German of Joseph Victor Scheffel and others by Charles G. Leland, John Childs and Son, London, 1872.

Guano War II: Miller, *Environmental History*, p. 153.

his feet and a few teeth: Sater, *Andean Tragedy*, p. 157.

37 *under better conditions*: G. T. Cushman, '"The most valuable birds in the world": International Conservation Science and the Revival of Peru's Guano Industry, 1909–1965', *Environmental History*, 10(3), 2005, 477–509.

as much reactive nitrogen: Cushman, *Guano and the Opening of the Pacific World*, p. 155.

comes with a sting in the tail: Melillo, 'First Green Revolution', p. 1055.

500 million tonnes of carbon dioxide: see 'Ammonia: zero-carbon fertiliser, fuel and energy store. Policy briefing', The Royal Society, 2020, p. 6; https://royalsociety.org/-/media/policy/projects/green-ammonia/green-ammonia-policy-briefing.pdf; Simon Evans and Verner Viisainen, 'Analysis: UK emissions in 2023 fell to lowest level since 1879', *Carbon Brief*, 11 March 2024; https://www.carbonbrief.org/analysis-uk-emissions-in-2023-fell-to-lowest-level-since-1879/.

eighty per cent of its fertilisers: Nathalia Vargas, 'Colombia es el quinto país con más autosuficiencia en fertilizantes', *La República*, 3 September 2022.

forecast to halve … 1.8 million tonnes: Fiorella Montaño, Matias Jara, 'Escasez y alza global de precios en fertilizantes afecta producción de alimentos en Perú y Chile', *Ojo Público*, 29 May 2022.

barely 100,000 tonnes: 'Perú da 180 toneladas de estiércol a agricultores ante alza de fertilizantes', EFE, 28 May 2022.

38 *'secret judgements of God'*: *Aviso de el modo que havia en el gobierno de los indios*, 272v. For the demographic decline of the Chincha of a ratio of some 95:1, see Hampe Martínez, T., 'Notas sobre la encomienda real de Chincha en el S. XVI (Administración y tributos)', *FENIX*, (32–33), 1987, 80–95, p. 95.

the worst mortality rate: Newson, 'The demographic impact of colonization', p. 166.

since 1492: Christine Amario, 'A pandemic atlas: Peru's death toll leaves a grieving nation', Associated Press, 16 December 2020.

39 *the finest textile in existence*: Museo Larco, ML600065.

snapping parrots, vultures and gulls: Museo Larco, ML600135.

40 *the pinnacle of pre-Columbian civilisation*: see discussion in María Rostworowski, 'Estructuras políticas y económicas de la costa central del Perú precolombino', *Obras Completas XI*, Instituto de Estudios Peruanos, Lima, 2016, pp. 88–9.

'the spell of the interior': Cushman Murphy, *Bird Islands*, p. 27.

entirely pacifistic: R. Shady, J. Haas and W. Creamer, 'Dating Caral, a Pre-ceramic Site in the Supe Valley on the Central Coast of Peru', *Science*, 292, 2001, 723–6; doi:10.1126/science.1059519.

a sprawling astronomical complex: Charles Stanish, Henry Tantaleán, Benjamin T. Nigra, Laura Griffin, 'A 2,300-year-old architectural and astronomical complex in the Chincha Valley, Peru', *PNAS*, 5 May 2014.

the ancient equivalent of neon signs: Stephanie Pappas, 'Older Than Nazca: Mysterious Rock Lines Marked Way to Ancient Peru Fairs', *NBC News*, 5 May 2014; https://www.nbcnews.com/id/wbna55109227.

Burials belonging to the Chimú: Museo Larco, ML100118, ML100856–ML100861.

birds, waves and pilchards: for Chimú art and architecture, see Cecilia Bákula, 'The Art of the Late Intermediate Period', in *The Inca World: The Development of Pre-Columbian Peru, A.D. 1000–1534*, University of Oklahoma Press, 2000, ed. Laura Laurencich Minelli, pp. 111–20.

'one hundred thousand marks of silver': *Aviso de el modo que havia en el gobierno de los indios*, fol. 272v, cited in María Rostworowski, 'Costa Peruana Prehispanica', pp. 228, 247.

41 *vertebrae of the dead*: J. Bongers, J. Mejía, T. Harper and S. Seidensticker, 'Assembling the dead: Human vertebrae-on-posts in the Chincha Valley, Peru', *Antiquity*, 96(386), 2022, 387–405; doi:10.15184/aqy.2021.180.

two Chincha noblewomen: Liliana Pérez Miguel and Renzo Honores, 'Cacicas, Land, and Litigation in Seventeenth-Century Chincha, Peru', in *Cacicas: The Indigenous Women Leaders of Spanish America, 1492–1825*, University of Oklahoma Press, 2021, eds. Margarita R. Ochoa, Sara V. Guengerich.

a strange slab in a British Museum warehouse: the so-called Bollaert Slab seems to have been one of the *mojónes* or markers described by Garcilaso. British Museum, Object 1859,0322.1. A high-resolution image is available at: https://www.britishmuseum.org/collection/object/H_1859-0322-1.

The tablet's quadrants: Cushman, 'Guano', pp. 2–4. My transcription of the slab varies slightly to Cushman's.

42 *proud of having allied*: Ibid., p. 4, citing Noble David Cook, *Demographic Collapse, Indian Peru, 1520–1620*, Cambridge and New York, 1981, pp. 157–8.

over half a million seabirds: https://www.dge.gob.pe/sala-influenza-aviar/ SITUACION-AH5.html#aves, Table: 'Muertas en islas y puntas'; María Gonzales, 'Gripe Aviar ya mató a más de 500 mil aves en el Perú: ¿Las autoridades tienen protocolos ante un próximo brote?', *Infobae*, 10 December 2023; https://www.infobae.com/peru/2023/12/10/gripe-aviar-ya-mato-a-mas-de-500-mil-aves-en-el-peru-las-autoridades-tienen-protocolos-ante-un-proximo-brote/.

140 million farmed birds: Sophie Kevany, 'Avian flu has led to the killing of 140m farmed birds since last October', *The Guardian*, 9 December 2022.

scrambling of bird migration routes: M. Gilbert, J. Slingenbergh and X. Xiao, 'Climate change and avian influenza', *Rev Sci Tech*, 27(2), August 2008, 459–66; PMID: 18819672; PMCID: PMC2709837; Shayan Sharif, Jeffrey J. Wichtel, 'Avian influenza: How bird flu affects domestic and wild flocks, and why a One Health approach matters', *The Conversation*, 25 May 2022; https://theconversation.com/avian-influenza-how-bird-flu-affects-domestic-and-wild-flocks-and-why-a-one-health-approach-matters-182497.

a far more lethal pandemic: 'Will avian flu be the next human pandemic?', *The Economist*, 14 February 2023.

43 *no country for old men … mackerel-crowded seas*: W. B. Yeats, 'Sailing to Byzantium', from *The Poems of W. B. Yeats: A New Edition*, ed. Richard J. Finneran. Copyright 1933 by Macmillan Publishing Company.

2: THE LAST STAND OF THE INCA

46 *like a comic strip*: such paintings are known as *los Reyes del Perú, efigies de los incas*, or *genealogía de los incas*. Some examples are kept in the church of Nuestra Señora de Copacabana, the Museo Pedro de Osma, the Museo de Arte and the Museo Larco, all in Lima.

47 *a family portrait*: Anonymous, 1718, *Matrimonio de Martín de Loyola con doña Beatriz Ñusta, y de Don Juan Borja con Lorenza Ñusta*, Museo Pedro

de Osma, Lima. A high-resolution image is available at: http://tinyurl.com/4rhbth55.

disowned even by the liberators: the vogue for all things Inca among *criollos* on the eve of Spanish-American independence almost always focused on the figure of Atahualpa, rather than Manco Inca or Túpac Amaru I, respectively the founder and final member of the Vilcabamba dynasty-in-exile. See Rebecca Earle, *The Return of the Native: Indians and Myth-Making in Spanish America, 1810–1930*, Duke University Press, Durham, NC and London, 2007, pp. 25–7, 37–41. A painted screen from the early 1800s, kept in the Lima Museo de Arte, shows the Inca line passing from Atahualpa to an equestrian figure labelled the 'Liberator of Peru'.

'collaborate or confront ... Spanish protectorate': Alberto Flores Galindo, *In Search of an Inca: Identity and Utopia in the Andes*, Cambridge University Press, New York, 2010, ed. and trans. Carlos Aguirre, Charles F. Walker, Willie Hiatt, p. 27.

'residual separatist state': George Kubler, 'The Neo-Inca State (1537–1572)', *The Hispanic American Historical Review*, 27.2, 1947, 189–203, p. 203.

a remarkable native account: see Titu Cusi Yupanqui, *An Inca Account of the Conquest of Peru*, University Press of Colorado, Boulder, 2005, trans., introduced and ed. Ralph Bauer.

48 *a painted serving vessel*: this remarkable object was found by Javier Fonseca Santa Cruz in the course of the 2008–9 excavations at Espíritu Pampa. See Brian S. Bauer, Javier Fonseca Santa Cruz, and Miriam Aráoz Silva, *Vilcabamba and the Archaeology of Inca Resistance*, UCLA Cotsen Institute of Archaeology Press, 2015, p. 102. The vessel has the Ministerio de Cultura inventory number CE 2506 JFS ESPA 2010.

'Believe nothing': 'Instrucción del Inca Don Diego de Castro Titu Cusi Yupanqui al Licenciado don Lope García de Castro', *Colección de Libros y Documentos relativos a la Historia del Perú*, Volume II, Imprenta y Librería San Martí y Compañía, Lima, 1916, ed. Horacio H. Urteaga.

a billion pesos: Kris Lane, *Potosí: The Silver City That Changed the World*, University of California Press, 2019, p. 8.

49 *'conquer the whole world' ... 'mouth of hell'*: for conditions at and Spanish views of Potosí, see Hemming, *Conquest of the Incas*, pp. 369–72, 407.

Nobody kept count of how many died: for recent research on Potosí in the Andean world and the global economy, see *Potosí in the Global Silver Age (16th–19th Centuries)*, Brill, Leiden, 2023, eds. Rossana Barragán and Paula C. Zagalsky.

51 *'rid ourselves of this nightmare'*: Titu Cusi, 'Instrucción', p. 65.

52 *little more than bandits*: Hemming, *Conquest of the Incas*, p. 255.

with swords and guns: Ibid., p. 278.

53 *'Be not afraid!'*: for Manco's murder and deathbed speech, see Titu Cusi, 'Instrucción'.

54 *'against all justice and reason'*: cited in Brian S. Bauer, Madeleine Halac-Higashimori and Gabriel E. Cantarutti, *Voices from Vilcabamba: Accounts*

Chronicling the Fall of the Inca Empire, University of Colorado Press, 2016, p. 6.

the king seemed inclined to agree: Hemming, *Conquest of the Incas*, pp. 412–13.

55   *went to pay his respects*: Garcilaso, *Royal Commentaries*, Part 2, Book VIII, Chapter XI.

'it falls to us to reign as vassals': Ibid., Part 1, Book I, Chapter XV.

56   *stiff as oak*: for the festival of the Sun, see Ibid., Part 2, Chapter IX, p. 19, and Part 1, Book VI, Chapter XXI, p. 302. For wild animals in Cuzco, see Part 1, Book V, Chapter X, p. 232. For Huayna Capac's mummy and Garcilaso's self-reproach, see Part 1, Book V, Chapter XXIX, p. 274.

'I will tell of the marvellous things': Ibid., Part 1, Book I, Chapter III, p. 23. For Garcilaso's 'natural love for the patria', see *Proemio*, p.5.

'the Sun wishes I should leave': cited in Hemming, *Conquest of the Incas*, p. 297.

57   *'the cause of all these disturbances'*: for the *taki onqoy* and the suspected role of Titu Cusi in the Andean uprisings of the 1560s, see Hélène Roy, *La résistance néo-inca de Vilcabamba (1537–1572) et son héritage dans le Pérou actuel: étude historique et anthropologique*, doctoral thesis, Poitiers, 2013, pp. 322–40.

tied a handkerchief to a tree: Diego Rodríguez de Figueroa set down an extraordinary eyewitness account of the Vilcabamba court under Titu Cusi in his *Relación del camino e viaje que hizo desde la ciudad de Cuzco a la tierra de guerra de Manco Inca* (1565). This document, held in the Berlin State Library, was first transcribed and published by Richard Pietschmann (1910). Here, I quote from the recent English translation in Bauer, Halac-Higashimori, and Cantarutti, *Voices from Vilcabamba*, pp. 151–75.

59   *the more easy-going friar*: Hemming, *Conquest of the Incas*, pp. 324–6.

'university of idolatry . . . remote stronghold of the Inca captain': cited in Roy, *La résistance néo-inca de Vilcabamba (1537–1572)*, p. 322.

60   *herds of llamas and alpacas*: Hemming, *Conquest of the Incas*, p. 349.

61   *'only their blazing radiance'*: for the Punchao as described by different chroniclers and its journey from Cuzco to Vilcabamba and Europe, see Catherine J. Julien, 'Punchao en España', in *El hombre y los Andes: homenaje a Franklin Pease G.Y.*, Pontificia Universidad Católica del Perú, 2002, eds. Javier Flores Espinoza, Rafael Varón Gabai, Volume 2, pp. 709–15.

human remains back to the United States: for Hiram Bingham and US archaeology in Peru, see Christopher Heaney, *Cradle of Gold: The Story of Hiram Bingham, a Real-Life Indiana Jones, and the Search for Machu Picchu*, New York: Palgrave Macmillan, 2010, and Heaney, *Empires of the Dead: Inca Mummies and the Peruvian Ancestors of American Anthropology*, Oxford University Press, 2023.

62   *more than a simple battle scene*: for this reading of the vessel, see Bat-ami Artzi, Amnon Nir and Javier Fonseca Santa Cruz, 'Los Fragmentos de Vilcabamba, Perú: Un Testimonio Iconográfico Excepcional de La Visión Andina

Sobre El Enfrentamiento Entre Indígenas y Españoles', *Latin American Antiquity*, Volume 30, No. 1, 2019, 158–76.

63 *tens of thousands of Indigenous Americans*: Caroline Dodds Pennock, *On Savage Shores: How Indigenous Americans Discovered Europe*, Orion, London, 2023, pp. 1–2.

64 *second-hand cigar smoke*: for Mexica smokers in early modern Spain, see Caroline Dodds Pennock, 'Aztecs abroad? Uncovering the early Indigenous Atlantic', *American Historical Review*, 125 (3), 2020, pp. 787–814.

exploited a legal loophole: José Carlos de la Puenta Luna, *Andean Cosmopolitans. Seeking Justice and Reward at the Spanish Royal Court*, University of Texas Press, Austin, 2018, p. 13.

'all the speeches and arguments they had uttered': cited in Daniel Cossins, 'We thought the Incas couldn't write. These knots change everything', *New Scientist*, 26 September 2018; https://www.newscientist.com/article/mg239 31972-600-we-thought-the-incas-couldnt-write-these-knots-change-everything/.

starting to decipher them: for recent advances in our understanding of quipu, see Sabine Hyland, 'Writing with Twisted Cords: The Inscriptive Capacity of Andean Khipus', *Current Anthropology*, 58:3, 2017, 412–19.

65 *'terminated once and for all'*: Hemming, *Conquest of the Incas*, p. 421.

'It was impossible to keep the Indians quiet': Garcilaso, *Royal Commentaries*, Part 2, Book VIII, Chapter XVI.

66 *'murderer, rebel and tyrant'*: Antonio Bautista de Salazar, *De virreyes y gobernadores del Perú* [1596], in Bauer, Halac-Higashimori and Cantarutti, *Voices from Vilcabamba*, p. 182.

how to catch an Inca: for the 1572 conquest of Vilcabamba, see Hemming, *Conquest of the Incas*, pp. 425–40.

'experienced soldiers of Flanders': Salazar, *De virreyes*, in Bauer, Halac-Higashimori and Cantarutti, *Voices from Vilcabamba*, p. 184.

67 *'Not a single soul'*: Martín de Murúa, *Historia general del Perú* [c.1616], in Bauer, Halac-Higashimori and Cantarutti, *Voices from Vilcabamba*, p. 79.

68 *A Spanish captain carried the Punchao*: Felipe Guaman Poma de Ayala, *Nueva Corónica y Buen Gobierno* [1616], Volume II, Fondo de Cultura Económica, Lima 2005, ed. Franklin Pease G. Y., trans. Jan Szemínski, p. 346 [f.450].

69 *an orange thrown into the crowd*: Baltasar de Ocampo Conejeros, *Descripción de la provinca de Sant Francisco de la Victoria de Villcapampa*, in Bauer, Halac-Higashimori and Cantarutti, *Voices from Vilcabamba*, p. 129.

70 *the vaults of the Vatican*: Catherine Julien, 'Punchao en España', p. 713.

sea fog and pestilential miasmas: for noxious airs and environmental conquests in Lima, see Kathleen Kole de Peralta, 'Mal Olor and Colonial Latin American History: Smellscapes in Lima, Peru, 1535–1614', *Hispanic American Historical Review* (2019), 99 (1): 1–30.

reveal the location of gold and silver mines: Hemming, *Conquest of the Incas*, p. 459.

passed to her new husband: Bauer, Halac-Higashimori and Cantarutti, *Voices from Vilcabamba*, p. 18.

commissioned his own set of paintings: for Inca genealogies and their political purposes, see Sara González Castrejón, 'Las efigies de los incas en el MS. 1551 de la Biblioteca Angelica (Roma) y los "Cuadernos de mano" de Francisco Fernández de Córdova', in *Élites, representación y redes atlánticas en la hispanoamérica moderna*, El Colegio de Michoacán, 2017, eds. Francisco A. Eissa-Barroso, Ainara Vázquez Varela and Silvia Espelt-Bombín, pp. 57–111.

71 *their defeat was not inevitable*: the councillors of Cuzco thought 'that land was so harsh and rugged' and its leaders so 'audacious' that its conquest 'seemed impossible'. See 'Petición del Cabildo de Cuzco al Virrey Toledo', 24 October 1572, Cuzco, in María Luisa Domínguez Guerrero, *Una oficina de expedición documental indiana: El cabildo de Cuzco en los siglos XVI y XVII*, University of Seville, 2010, p. 217.

'true lords and possessors of it': Garcilaso, *Royal Commentaries*, Part 2, Book VIII, Chapter XXI, p. 1018.

73 *'declares himself a Túpac Amaru'*: for the best account of the uprisings that swept the Andes in the early 1780s, see Charles F. Walker, *The Túpac Amaru Rebellion*, Harvard University Press, 2016.

half of the print run: Flores Galindo, *In search of an Inca*, p. 31.

exploded in popularity: for Garcilaso as the 'undisputed founder' of Andean nationalism, see Sara Castro-Klarén, 'The Nation in Ruins: Archaeology and the Rise of the Nation', in *Beyond Imagined Communities. Reading and Writing the Nation in Nineteenth-Century Latin America*, Woodrow Wilson Center Press, Washington, DC, 2003, eds. Sara Castro-Klarén, John Charles Chasteen, p. 172.

transfigure . . . into a lost paradise: Flores Galindo, *In search of an Inca*, p. 247. For intriguing evidence that the Vilcabamba Incas promoted the Inkarri myth via popular theatre, see Jean-Philippe Husson, 'Génesis de los dramas del fin del inca Atahualpa y los mitos de Incarrí del reino neo-inca de Vilcabamba y de sus aliados del Taqui oncoy', Libros peruanos, Lima, 1950.

74 *'fanatical thoughts . . . golden centuries . . . inhuman pirates'*: Archivo General de Indias [hereafter AGI], Cuzco, 29, N.58, 13 April 1781. Juan Manuel Moscoso y Peralta, Bishop of Cuzco, to Areche, 4v, 6v, 9v.

Haiti . . . Uruguay: Walker, *Túpac Amaru Rebellion*, p. 274.

a leftist army officer: for a recent reassessment of Juan Velasco Alvarado, see *The Peculiar Revolution: Rethinking the Peruvian Experiment under Military Rule*, University of Texas Press, Austin, 2017, eds. Carlos Aguirre and Paulo Drinot.

'Justice has at last arrived': SINAMOS, *Velasco, La Voz de la Revolución. Discursos del General de División Juan Velasco Alvarado, 1969–1972*, Volume 2, pp. 168, 177.

Hugo Rafael Chávez Frías: for Velasco's influence on Chávez and the Bolivarian Revolution, see Richard Gott, *In the Shadow of the Liberator*.

Hugo Chávez and the Transformation of Venezuela, Verso, London, 2000, pp. 37–40.

like his namesake: Charles Walker, 'Tupac Shakur and Tupac Amaru', 26 February 2014; https://charlesfwalker.com/tupac-shakur-tupac-amaru/.

75   *The Quipu Project*: https://interactive.quipu-project.com/#/en/quipu/intro.

jail for disgraced heads of state: Yesenia Vilcapoma, Martín León and Miguel Gutiérrez, 'Barbadillo, La cárcel de los expresidentes', *El Comercio*; https://especiales.elcomercio.pe/?q=especiales-multimedia/barbadillo/index.html.

Lima boasted four eateries: Simeon Tegel, 'How Peru's food culture pushed Lima to "world's best restaurants" fame', *Washington Post*, 8 January 2024; https://www.washingtonpost.com/food/2024/01/08/lima-peru-worlds-50-best-restaurants-central/

3: DARK EARTH

80   *'for us to look after it'*: for this Harakbut creation myth, see Adolfo Ireyo, Víctor Huenco, Pablo Tayori and Juan Mankehue, 'A'nämëi', in *Relatos Orales Harakbut*, Ministerio de Educación, Lima, Peru, 2015, ed. Yesica Patiachi Tayori, pp. 15–31.

82   *'see what lay along it, or die'*: for Francisco de Orellana's journey down the Amazon, see Gaspar de Carvajal, [*c.*1546], *Descubrimiento del rio de las Amazonas*, Impr. de E. Rasco, Seville, 1894, ed. José Toribio Medina.

85   *'In those southern parts'*: Amerigo Vespucci, *Mundus Novus: Letter to Lorenzo Pietro Di Medici*, 1504, in *Vespucci Reprints, Texts and Studies V. The Mundus Novus in Translation*, Princeton University Press, 1916, trans. George Tyler Northup, p. 1.

'não têm Fé, nem Lei, nem Rei': Pero de Magalhães Gandavo, *História da província Santa Cruz* (1576), cap. 10, fl. 33v, cited in Sérgio Alcides, 'F, L e R: Gândavo e o ABC da colonização', *Revista Escritos*, Ano 3, No. 3, 2009, p. 39.

'land without history': Euclides da Cunha, 'À margem da história. Parte I, Terra sem história (Amazônia)', *Jornal do Commercio*, Rio de Janeiro, 20 February 1907.

86   *Amazon could sustain large populations*: the classic account of environmental determinism in the Amazon is Betty J. Meggers, *Amazonia: Man and Culture in a Counterfeit Paradise*, Aldine Atherton, Chicago, 1971.

the true figure is much higher: 'Comissão da Verdade: ao menos 8,3 mil indígenas foram mortos na ditadura militar', *Amazônia Real*, 11 December 2014; https://amazoniareal.com.br/comissao-da-verdade-ao-menos-83-mil-indios-foram-mortos-na-ditadura-militar/.

'sky will remain dark for all time': Davi Kopenawa, Bruce Albert, *The Falling Sky: Words of a Yanomami Shaman*, trans. Nicholas Elliott and Alison Dundy, Harvard University Press, 2013, p. 406.

'vast, untamed wilderness': World Wildlife Fund, 'The Amazon'; https://www.wwf.org.uk/where-we-work/amazon, accessed 20 July 2023.

'*who exterminated the Indians*': 'What Brazil's President, Jair Bolsonaro, has said about Brazil's Indigenous Peoples', *Survival*, 7 November 2018; https://www.survivalinternational.org/articles/3540-Bolsonaro.

87 *the United States, China and Europe*: Dos Santos, Alex Mota, et al., 'Deforestation drivers in the Brazilian Amazon: assessing new spatial predictors', *Journal of Environmental Management*, 294, 2021, 113020.

the UN calls narco-deforestation: Jake Spring and Gabriel Stargardter, '"Narco-deforestation" in focus at upcoming summit of Amazon nations', *Reuters*, 3 August 2023; https://www.reuters.com/sustainability/narco-deforestation-focus-upcoming-summit-amazon-nations-2023-08-03/.

spewing mercury fumes: Edmar Barrios, Silas Laurentino and Diane Jeantet, 'Big flotilla of illegal gold miners splits up in Brazil', *AP*, 21 November 2021; https://apnews.com/article/business-environment-and-nature-caribbean-environment-brazil-61fe580eb23761117331c10e0b7cfde8.

churning up Bolivia's national parks: Sergio Mendoza Reyes, 'El saqueo del oro boliviano: Empresas chinas se esconden tras cooperativas mineras', *Los Tiempos*, 14 November 2022; https://www.lostiempos.com/especial-multimedia/20221114/saqueo-del-oro-boliviano-empresas-chinas-se-esconden-cooperativas.

enslaving hundreds of Indigenous children: Moises Rendon, Linnea Sandin and Claudia Fernandez, 'Illegal Mining in Venezuela: Death and Devastation in the Amazonas and Orinoco Regions', Center for Strategic and International Studies, 16 April 2020; https://www.csis.org/analysis/illegal-mining-venezuela-death-and-devastation-amazonas-and-orinoco-regions.

before others reach them first: Robert S. Walker and Kim R. Hill, 'Protecting isolated tribes', *Science*, 348, 2015, 1061. Others, including Brazilian experts and Indigenous peoples, have rejected the idea of 'controlled contact' as dangerous and contrary to the wishes of isolated peoples. See 'Brazilian experts blast US academics' call for uncontacted tribes to be forcibly contacted', *Survival*, 7 July 2016; https://www.survivalinternational.org/news/11347.

88 *between twenty and twenty-five per cent*: Emma Brice, 'Why Is the Amazon So Important for Climate Change?', *Scientific American*, 20 February 2023; https://www.scientificamerican.com/article/why-is-the-amazon-so-important-for-climate-change1/.

figures like Leonardo DiCaprio and Jeff Bezos: David Mouriquand, 'Leonardo DiCaprio and Jeff Bezos team up to raise $200m to protect Amazon rainforest', *Euronews.culture*, 5 July 2023; https://www.euronews.com/culture/2023/07/05/leonardo-dicaprio-and-jeff-bezos-team-up-to-raise-200m-to-protect-amazon-rainforest.

'*thoroughly marked by humankind*': Charles C. Mann, *1491: New Revelations of the Americas before Columbus*, Knopf Publishing Group, New York, 2006, p. 4.

89 '*It was a stroke of luck*': Pedro Porras, *Investigaciones arqueológicas a las faldas del Sangay*, Artes Gráficas Señal, Quito, 1987, pp. 15, 41. Cited in Janny Mauricio Velasco Albán, '¿Suelos antrópicos en la alta Amazonía

ecuatoriana?: estudios geoarqueológicos en el basural La Lomita, valle del Upano, Morona Santiago Ecuador', *Antropología Cuadernos de Investigación*, No. 24, January–June 2021, pp. 65–79.

In little more than a decade: Tom Clynes, 'Exclusive: Laser Scans Reveal Maya "Megalopolis" Below Guatemalan Jungle', *National Geographic*, 1 February 2018; https://www.nationalgeographic.com/history/article/maya-laser-lidar-guatemala-pacunam; D. H. Evans, R. J. Fletcher, et al., 'Uncovering archaeological landscapes at Angkor using lidar', *PNAS*, 110 (31), 12595–12600, 2013; H. Prümers, C. J. Betancourt, J. Iriarte, et al., 'Lidar reveals pre-Hispanic low-density urbanism in the Bolivian Amazon', *Nature*, 606, 325–8, 2022; https://doi.org/10.1038/s41586-022-04780-4.

resources and manpower: Stéphen Rostain et al., 'Two thousand years of garden urbanism in the Upper Amazon', *Science*, 383, 183–9, 2024; DOI:10.1126/science.adi6317.

90 *an Amazonian Rome*: Eliot Stein, 'The discovery of the Americas' long-lost "Rome"', BBC, 23 January 2024; https://www.bbc.com/travel/article/20240122-the-discovery-of-the-americas-long-lost-rome.

'the tip of the iceberg': Lizzie Wade, 'Laser mapping reveals oldest Amazonian cities, built 2500 years ago', *Science*, 11 January 2024; https://www.science.org/content/article/laser-mapping-reveals-oldest-amazonian-cities-built-2500-years-ago.

91 *nutrient-rich river sediment*: L. C. R. Silva, R. S. Corrêa, J. L. Wright, et al., 'A new hypothesis for the origin of Amazonian Dark Earths', *Nat Commun*, 12, 127, 2021; https://doi.org/10.1038/s41467-020-20184-2.

long-term habitation: U. Lombardo, M. Arroyo-Kalin, M. Schmidt, et al., 'Evidence confirms an anthropic origin of Amazonian Dark Earths', *Nat Commun*, 13, 3444, 2022; https://doi.org/10.1038/s41467-022-31064-2.

ringed by paths and palisades: Bruna Franchetto/Equipe de edição da Enciclopédia Povos Indígenas no Brasil, *Kuikuro*, 26 March 2018; https://pib.socioambiental.org/en/Povo:Kuikuro.

'by Indigenous Amazonians': Morgan J. Schmidt, Kumessi Waura, Yamalui, Huke, Taku Wate, Takumã, Yahila and Afukaka Kuikuro, et al., 'Intentional creation of carbon-rich dark earth soils in the Amazon', *Sci. Adv.*, 9, eadh8499, 2023; DOI: 10.1126/sciadv.adh8499.

went on the move: J. Watling, F. Almeida, T. Kater, S. Zuse, M. P. Shock, G. Mongeló, E. Bespalez, J. R. Santi and E. G. Neves, 'Arqueobotânica de ocupações ceramistas na Cachoeira do Teotônio', *Boletim Do Museu Paraense Emílio Goeldi. Ciências Humanas*, 15(2), e20190075, 2020; https://doi.org/10.1590/2178-2547-BGOELDI-2019-0075.

92 *Guyana and the Bahamas*: Michael Tennesen, 'Letter from Brazil: Uncovering the Arawaks', *Archaeology*, Volume 63, No. 5, September/October 2010; https://archive.archaeology.org/1009/abstracts/letter.html.

potato and tobacco: Constantine Samuel Rafinesque, 'The Haytian or Taino Language', in *The American Nations*, Volume 1, *Generalities and Annals*, F. Turner, Philadelphia, 1836, pp. 229–30.

hours of polishing: for ceramics excavated at Teotônio, see T. Kater, 'A temporalidade das ocupações ceramistas no sítio Teotônio', *Boletim Do Museu Paraense Emílio Goeldi. Ciências Humanas*, 15(2), e20190078, 2020; https://doi.org/10.1590/2178-2547-BGOELDI-2019-0078.

even nascent states: for social complexity being 'associated with ancient cities, states and civilizations', see Robert McAdams, 'Complexity in Archaic States', *Journal of Anthropological Archaeology*, Volume 20, Issue 3, September 2001, pp. 345–60.

the oldest ceramics in the Americas: Anna Roosevelt, Rupert Housley, M. Silveira, S. Maranca, R. Johnson, 'Eighth Millennium Pottery from a Prehistoric Shell Midden in the Brazilian Amazon', *Science*, 254, 1992, 1621–4; 10.1126/science.254.5038.1621.

the hemisphere's earliest artworks: see, for example, Mustafa Michab, James K. Feathers, J.-L. Joron, Norbert Mercier, M. Selo, Helene Valladas, Georges Valladas, J.-L. Reyss and Anna C. Roosevelt, 'Luminescence dates for the Paleoindian site of Pedra Pintada, Brazil', *Quaternary Science Reviews*, Volume 17, No. 11, 1998, 1041–6.

93   *camelid called the Palaeolama*: J. Iriarte, M. J. Ziegler, A. K. Outram, M. Robinson, P. Roberts, F. J. Aceituno, G. Morcote-Ríos, T. M. Keesey, 'Ice Age megafauna rock art in the Colombian Amazon?', *Philos Trans R Soc Lond B Biol Sci*, 377 (1849): 20200496, 25 April 2022; doi: 10.1098/rstb.2020.0496; epub 7 March 2022.

Sistine Chapel of the Amazon: Alejandro Millán Valencia, 'Chiribiquete: cómo es y cómo se descubrió la monumental "Capilla Sixtina" de la arqueología de América', *BBC Mundo*, 6 September 2020; https://www.bbc.com/mundo/noticias-53947778.

on the eve of 1492: for ten million, see E. G. Neves, L. P. Furquim, C. Levis, B. C. Rocha, J. G. Watling, F. O. Almeida, C. J. Betancourt, A. B. Junqueira, C. P. Moraes, G. Morcote-Rios, M. P. Shock, E. K. Tamanaha, 'Chapter 8: Peoples of the Amazon before European colonization', in Nobre et al., *Amazon Assessment Report 2021*, UN, New York, 2021, p. 4. For the twenty million estimate, see discussion in Alexander Koch, Chris Brierley, Mark M. Maslin, Simon L. Lewis, 'Earth system impacts of the European arrival and Great Dying in the Americas after 1492', *Quaternary Science Reviews*, Volume 207, 1 March 2019, p. 16.

'the most popular politician on earth': https://www.facebook.com/institutolula/posts/2162413327872225/.

94   *'and build another'*: cited in Chris Feliciano Arnold, 'World Cup Boom and Bust', *Harper's Magazine*, 8 July 2014; https://harpers.org/2014/07/world-cup-boom-and-bust/.

94–5   *smothered with rubber … more playhouses than Lisbon*: Greg Grandin, *Fordlandia: The Rise and Fall of Henry Ford's Forgotten Jungle City*, Icon, London, 2009, pp. 26–9.

95   *troughs with Veuve Clicquot*: Robin Furneaux, *The Amazon: The Story of a Great River*, Hamish Hamilton, London, 1969, p. 153.

'The search was never ... dash their brains out': The Amazon Journal of *Roger Casement*, Anaconda Editions, London, 1997, ed. Angus Mitchell, pp. 27, 294, 373. For Casement in Manaus, see Grandin, *Fordlandia*, p. 29.

96 *eighty-three Amazonian species*: Carolina Levis et al., 'Persistent effects of pre-Columbian plant domestication on Amazonian forest composition', *Science*, 355.6328, 2017, 925–31.

some 5,300 years ago: Erin Blakemore, 'Chocolate gets its sweet history rewritten', *National Geographic*, 31 October 2018; https://www.nationalgeographic.com/culture/article/chocolate-domestication-cocoa-ecuador.

worth over $1 billion: 'Acai berry craze boosts incomes in the Brazilian Amazon, but at a cost', *Al Jazeera*, 28 August 2023; https://www.aljazeera.com/gallery/2023/8/28/acai-berry-craze-boosts-incomes-in-the-brazilian-amazon-but-at-a-cost.

97 *every corner of the rainforest*: for a critique of the 'domesticated forest' thesis, see Christopher William Dick, 'A critical take on "Persistent effects of pre-Columbian plant domestication on Amazonian forest composition"', 18 March 2017; https://sites.lsa.umich.edu/cwdick-lab/2017/03/18/a-critical-take-on-persistent-effects-of-pre-columbian-plant-domestication-on-amazonian-forest-composition/.

24,000 pre-Hispanic earthworks: Vinicius Peripato et al., 'More than 10,000 pre-Columbian earthworks are still hidden throughout Amazonia', *Science*, 382, 2023, 103–09.

fossilised pollen: S. Y. Maezumi, D. Alves, M. Robinson et al., 'The legacy of 4,500 years of polyculture agroforestry in the eastern Amazon', *Nature Plants*, 4, 2018, 540–47.

98 *a living larder*: see discussion in Mann, *1491*, pp. 361–2.

It was called heve: for pre-Columbian and colonial use of rubber, see R. J. Seibert, 'The Uses of Hevea for Food in Relation to Its Domestication', *Annals of the Missouri Botanical Garden*, Volume 35, 1948, pp. 117–21, and Chris Feliciano Arnold, *The Third Bank of the River: Power and Survival in the Twenty-First-Century Amazon*, Picador, New York, 2018, p. 35.

99 *Bolsonaro's allies in big business*: Tai Nalon, 'Did WhatsApp help Bolsonaro win the Brazilian presidency?', *The Washington Post*, 1 November 2018; https://www.washingtonpost.com/news/theworldpost/wp/2018/11/01/whatsapp-2/.

100 *from AD 300*: Eduardo Góes Neves, *Sob Os Tempos do equinócio: Oito mil anos de história na Amazônia central*, Ubu, São Paulo, 2022, p. 84.

healthier and stronger ... women ruled the roost: Anna C. Roosevelt, *Moundbuilders of the Amazon: Geophysical Archaeology on Marajo Island, Brazil*, Academic Press, San Diego, 1991, pp. 406–11.

digging ponds and dams: for Marajoara aquaculture and the evidence for hierarchy, see Denise Pahl Schaan, 'The Nonagricultural Chiefdoms of Marajó Island', in *The Handbook of South American Archaeology*, Springer, New York, 2008, eds. H. Silverman, W. H. Isbell, pp. 339–57; Roosevelt, *Moundbuilders of the Amazon*, pp. 411–20; and Mann, *1491*, pp. 351–7.

'*succumbed in the terrible tropics*': Anna C. Roosevelt, 'The sequence of Amazon prehistory: a methodology for ethical science', *Tessituras: Revista de Antropologia e Arqueologia*, UFPEL, V10 N1, January–June 2022, p. 32.

102   *as if fleeing turmoil and disaster*: J. G. de Souza, M. Robinson, Y. Maezumi, J. Capriles, J. A. Hoggarth, U. Lombardo, V. F. Novello, J. Apaestegui, B. Whitney, D. Urrego, D. T. Alves, S. Rostain, M. J. Power, F. E. Mayle, F. W. da Cruz Jr, H. Hooghiemstra and J. Iriarte, 'Climate change and cultural resilience in late pre-Columbian Amazonia', *Nature Ecology & Evolution*, 3 (7), 2019, pp. 1007–17.

palisades spring up: Neves, *Sob Os Tempos*, pp. 163–8.

drinking from stagnant pools: Steven Grattan, 'More rare dolphins die in new spot along Brazil's Amazon River – report', *Reuters*, 27 October 2023; https://www.reuters.com/world/americas/more-rare-dolphins-die-new-spot-along-brazils-amazon-river-report-2023-10-27.

for sharpening weapons: Fernando Crispim and Edmar Barros, 'Severe drought in the Amazon reveals millennia-old carvings', *AP*, 28 October 2023; https://apnews.com/article/amazon-drought-negro-river-petroglyphs-19ef695e7c3bed3849735ff00f09ef30.

'*If you see me, weep*': 'Drought reveals ancient "hunger stones" in European river', *AP*, 23 August 2018; https://apnews.com/article/9512be71cc8f40a7b6e22bc991ef2c6c.

frozen River Thames: Koch et al., 'Earth system impacts of the European arrival'. For a critique of this hypothesis, see Alberto Boretti, 'The European colonization of the Americas as an explanation of the Little Ice Age', *Journal of Archaeological Science: Reports*, Volume 29, February 2020.

103   *societies against the state*: the phrase was coined by Pierre Clastres and expounded in English in his *Society Against the State: Essays in Political Anthropology*, 1989. See discussion in David Wengrow and David Graeber, *The Dawn of Everything*, Allen Lane, London, 2021, pp. 112–13.

just outside of living memory: Neves, *Sob Os Tempos*, p. 189.

200 tonnes of mullet: Denise Schaan, 'Long-Term Human Induced Impacts on Marajó Island Landscapes, Amazon Estuary', *Diversity*, 2(2), 2010, 182–206, p. 194; doi:10.3390/d2020182.

105   *earliest human remains*: 'Pesquisadores encontram fóssil de Luzia no Museu Nacional: o que continua desaparecido?', *BBC*, 2 September 2018; https://www.bbc.com/portuguese/brasil-45391771.

the great civilisations of South America: *O Museu Nacional*, Banco Safra, São Paulo, 2007, pp. 264–75.

ethno-linguistic maps: Cira Gonda, 'Folks, there's nothing left …', trans. Diogo Almeida, *All Things Linguistic*, 3 September 2018; https://allthingslinguistic.com/post/177712815507/folks-theres-nothing-left-from-the-linguistics.

106   *one cent per item*: 'Lessons from the destruction of the National Museum of Brazil', *The Economist*, 8 September 2018; https://www.economist.com/

leaders/2018/09/08/lessons-from-the-destruction-of-the-national-museum-of-brazil.

sparked the blaze: 'PF conclui inquérito no Museu Nacional e descarta "conduta omissa" e incêndio criminoso', *G1 Rio, 6* July 2020; https://g1.globo.com/rj/rio-de-janeiro/noticia/2020/07/06/pf-conclui-investigacao-sobre-o-incendio-que-destruiu-o-museu-nacional.ghtml.

1,200 miles away in São Paulo: Ignacio Amigo, 'Amazon rainforest fires leave São Paulo in the dark', *Mongabay*, 21 August 2019; https://news.mongabay.com/2019/08/amazon-rainforest-fires-leave-sao-paulo-in-the-dark/.

on Bolsonaro's watch: Diego Gonzaga, '4 years of Amazon destruction', Greenpeace, 2 December 2022; https://www.greenpeace.org/international/story/57219/brazil-amazon-deforestation-2022-bolsonaro-lula/.

a genocide: Tom Phillips, '"A war society doesn't see": the Brazilian force driving out mining gangs from Indigenous lands', *The Guardian*, 28 February 2023; https://www.theguardian.com/world/2023/feb/28/brazilian-force-driving-out-mining-gangs-indigenous-yanomami-territory-bolsonaro.

arsenic-laced sugar: Norman Lewis, 'Genocide: From fire and sword to arsenic and bullets – civilisation has sent six million Indians to extinction', *The Sunday Times Magazine*, 23 February 1969; available at: https://assets.survivalinternational.org/documents/1094/genocide-norman-lewis-1969.pdf.

107 *'urban trash'*: Paulo Cappelli, '"Aldeia Maracanã é lixo urbano. Quem gosta de índio, vá para a Bolívia", diz Rodrigo Amorim', *O Globo*, 4 January 2019; https://oglobo.globo.com/rio/aldeia-maracana-lixo-urbano-quem-gosta-de-indio-va-para-bolivia-diz-rodrigo-amorim-23345028.

Dozens have been killed: Salomé Gómez-Upegui, 'The Amazon rainforest's most dogged defenders are in peril', *Vox*, 1 September 2021; https://www.vox.com/down-to-earth/22641038/indigenous-forest-guardians-brazil-guajajara.

they had it coming: Cristiane Noberto, 'Bolsonaro diz que "muita gente" não gostava de Dom Phillips: "Malvisto"', *Correio Braziliense*, 15 June 2022; https://www.correiobraziliense.com.br/politica/2022/06/5015490-bolsonaro-diz-que-muita-gente-nao-gostava-de-dom-phillips-mal-visto.html.

108 *ancient hardwoods*: David Biller, 'After writer's murder in the Amazon, can his vision survive?', *AP*, 19 June 2022; https://apnews.com/article/dom-phillips-murder-bruno-pereira-brazil-amazon-826f2a4f1fe7f3fa8ef7aa96947f26d0.

How to Save the Amazon: Ella Creamer, 'Murdered journalist Dom Phillips' unfinished book to be published in 2025', *The Guardian*, 6 December 2023; https://www.theguardian.com/books/2023/dec/06/murdered-journalist-dom-phillips-unfinished-book-to-be-published-in-2025.

the future of us all: https://www.fao.org/in-action/territorios-inteligentes/noticias/detalle/en/c/1392821/.

4: BLACK REBEL KINGDOM

112 *barely 7,000 people*: Lilia Moritz Schwarcz and Heloisa Maria Murgel Starling, *Brazil: A Biography*, Penguin, London, 2018, p. 97.

'state within a state': the words are those of Pedro Paulo Funari, 'Brazil's Palmares: a beacon of freedom', *The Forum*, BBC World Service, 1 September 2022; https://www.bbc.co.uk/programmes/w3ct38st.

a 1962 novel: namely, *Ganga Zumba* by João Felício dos Santos. See Ana Lucia Araujo, 'Dandara e Luisa Mahin são consideradas heroínas do Brasil – o problema é que elas nunca existiram', *The Intercept Brasil*, 3 June 2019; https://www.intercept.com.br/2019/06/03/dandara-luisa-mahin-panteao-patria/.

the past is unpredictable: 'No Brasil, até o passado é imprevisível.' The expression is usually attributed to the Pernambuco-born playwright Nelson Rodrigues (1912–80).

South American Wakanda: see, for example, Lucas Ed, 'Talvez você desconheça que eu nasci em Wakanda, terra de homens valentes, etc e coisa e tal ...', *Medium*, 28 April 2019; https://lucas-ed.medium.com/talvez-voc%C3%AA-desconhe%C3%A7a-que-eu-nasci-em-wakanda-terra-de-homens-valentes-etc-e-coisa-e-tal-c4f88b00fb46.

113 *'fake hero'*: Thomas Molina, 'Sérgio Camargo, polêmicas sem freios na Fundação Palmares', *Veja*, 14 August 2020; https://veja.abril.com.br/podcast/sergio-camargo-polemicas-sem-freios-na-fundacao-palmares; and 'Declarações do novo presidente da Fundação Palmares geram críticas e indignação', *G1 Jornal Nacional*, 28 November 2019; https://g1.globo.com/jornal-nacional/noticia/2019/11/28/declaracoes-do-novo-presidente-da-fundacao-palmares-geram-criticas-e-indignacao.ghtml.

Portuguese slavers set foot: Géssica Brandino Gonçalves, 'Portugueses nem pisaram na África, diz Bolsonaro sobre escravidão', *Folha*, 31 July 2018; https://www1.folha.uol.com.br/poder/2018/07/portugueses-nem-pisaram-na-africa-diz-bolsonaro.shtml.

Every text that mentions Palmares: for a searchable database of over 1,800 manuscripts and printed documents referring or relevant to Palmares between 1595 and 1800, see DOCUMENTA Palmares [hereafter DP], Campinas, São Paulo, UNICAMP/IFCH/CECULT, 2021. Available at: https://www.palmares.ifch.unicamp.br/. Accessed 10 July 2023.

Few archaeologists: for the archaeological evidence at Barriga and the politics surrounding its interpretation, as well as Palmares in popular memory more broadly, see Scott Joseph Allen, '"Zumbi nunca vai morrer": History, the practice of archaeology, and race politics in Brazil', PhD thesis, Brown University, 2001.

new evidence: for recent work drawing on the Dutch archives, see Felipe Aguiar Damasceno, 'A ocupação das terras dos Palmares de Pernambuco (séculos XVII e XVIII)', Thesis (Doutorado em História Social), Universidade Federal do Rio de Janeiro, 2018.

Afrodescendant communities: for example, the Saramaka of Suriname. See Richard Price, 'Palmares como poderia ter sido', presentation at 'Palmares, 300 años' conference, São Paulo, 1994, trans. João José Reis.

New generations of Brazilian scholars: recent and authoritative studies of Palmares and its context include Flávio Gomes, *Palmares: Escravidão e liberdade no Atlântico Sul*, Contexto, São Paulo, 2005; and Silvia Hunold Lara, *Palmares & Cucaú: O Aprendizado da Dominação*, EDUSP, São Paulo, 2022. For a detailed, readable account in English, see Glenn Alan Cheney, *Quilombo dos Palmares: Brazil's Lost Nation of Fugitive Slaves*, New London Librarium, 2014. For an engaging and deeply researched illustrated history, see Marcelo D'Salete, *Angola Janga: Kingdom of Runaway Slaves*, Fantagraphics, Seattle, 2019.

'Say sugar, and you say Brazil': cited in Stuart B. Schwartz, *Sugar Plantations in the Formation of Brazilian Society. Bahia, 1550–1835*, New York: Cambridge University Press, 1985, pp. 280–81.

untold scale and intensity: Howard W. French, *Born in Blackness. Africa, Africans, and the Making of the Modern World, 1471 to the Second World War*, W. W. Norton, 2021, pp. 7–8.

114   *'clutching the shoreline . . . like crabs'*: Frei Vicente Do Salvador, *Historia do Brasil*, 1627, Chapter III, p. 5.

some five million: between 1501 and 1866, an estimated 5,532,119 enslaved Africans were put on ships bound for Brazil by all nationalities – the vast majority under Portuguese and Brazilian flags – of whom 4,864,373 disembarked. See Trans-Atlantic Slave Trade Database: Estimates; https://www.slavevoyages.org/assessment/estimates. Accessed 16 May 2023.

from 1580 . . . by the 1620s: for an overview of slavery and sugar from late medieval Europe to early modern Brazil, see Schwarcz and Starling, *Brazil*, pp. 80–82.

'there is no Pernambuco': letter of Antônio Vieira to marquês de Niza, 12 August 1648. Cited in Leonardo Dantas Silva, *Alguns documentos para história da escravidão*, Fundaj, Editora Massangana, Recife, 1988, p. 8.

'almost angelic': quase de anjo. The phrase is that of Gilberto Freyre in *Vida Social no Brasil nos Meados do Século XIX* [1922], Instituto Joaquim Nabuco de Pesquisas Sociais, Recife, 1964. See citation and discussion in Flávio Rabelo Versiani, 'Escravidão "suave" no Brasil: Gilberto Freyre tinha razão?', *Brazil. J. Polit. Econ.*, 27(2), June 2007.

killed nearly 700,000: between 1501 and 1866, the difference between those embarked for Brazil and those who disembarked is 667,746. See Trans-Atlantic Slave Trade Database: Estimates; https://www.slavevoyages.org/assessment/estimates. Accessed 16 May 2023.

'Day and night': biography of Mahommah G. Baquaqua, in Robert Conrad, *Children of God's Fire. A Documentary History of Black Slavery in Brazil*, Pennsylvania State University Press, 1984, pp. 27–8.

life expectancy of twenty-five: Schwarcz and Starling, *Brazil*, p. 89. Kátia de Queirós Mattoso has estimated the average life expectancy for enslaved

Africans in Brazil at just six years. Cited in Susanna B. Hecht, *The Scramble for the Amazon and the 'Lost Paradise' of Euclides da Cunha*, University of Chicago Press, London, 2013, pp. 23–4.

'such severity': André João Antonil [1711], *Cultura e opulência do Brasil*. Cited in Jean Marcel Carvalho França and Ricardo Alexandre Ferreira, *Três vezes Zumbi: a construção de um herói brasileiro*, Três Estrelas, São Paulo, 2012, pp. 30–34.

115 *'perpetual flame and fume'*: André João Antonil [1711], *Cultura e opulência do Brasil*, 3rd edn (Coleção Reconquista do Brasil), Book II, Chapter VIII, Itatiaia/Edusp, Belo Horizonte, 1982.

jewels and Genoese silks: for conspicuous consumption by Pernambuco plantation owners – probably exaggerated by some observers – see Gilberto Freyre, *Casa-Grande & Senzala: formação da família brasileira sob o regime da economia patriarcal*, 19th edn, Livraria José Olympio editoria, Rio de Janeiro, 1978, pp. 259–61, and de Sousa and Cardim, below.

'many rich men': Gabriel Soares de Sousa, *Tratado descritivo do Brasil em 1587*, Typographia Universal de Laemmert, Rio de Janeiro, 1851, p. 35.

'more vanity in Pernambuco': Fernão Cardim, *Narrativa epistolar de uma viagem e missão jesuítica pela Bahia, Ilhéus, Porto Seguro, Pernambuco, Espírito Santo, Rio de Janeiro, etc., desde o ano de 1583 ao de 1590*, Imprensa Nacional, Lisbon, 1847, p. 75.

'due proportion of sugar': Bethan Davies and Oliver Finnegan, 'Syrups and ships: Early sugar consumption in England', citing Hugh Plat (1552–1608), *The National Archives Blog*, 16 May 2023; https://blog.nationalarchives.gov.uk/early-sugar-consumption-in-england/. For sugar sculptures or 'subtleties', see Bethan Davies, 'Subtlety', *CEMS KCL Blog*, 10 March 2022; https://kingsearlymodern.co.uk/keythings/subtlety.

116 *'three thousand Indians . . . blacks of Guinea'*: DP 12/03/1588. 'Treslado do regimento que levou Francisco Geraldes que sua magestade ora mandou por governador do Estado do Brasil em março de 88', *Revista do Instituto Histórico e Geográfico Brasileiro*, 67 n. 1, 1906, p. 224.

'began to have inhabitants': Padre Antônio da Silva, [*Relação da ruína dos Palmares*, 1678], DP, ANTT, Manuscritos da Livraria, n. 1185, Papéis Vários, fls. 149–155vi. Transcription by Laura Peraza Mendes, Silvia Hunold Lara and Phablo Roberto Marchis Fachin.

'a very clear and white butter': for the multiple uses of palms at Palmares, see *Diário da viagem do capitão João Blaer aos Palmares* [1645], in Gomes, Flávio (org.), *Mocambos de Palmares. Histórias e fontes (séculos XVI–XIX)*, 7 Letras, Rio de Janeiro, 2010, pp. 167–72. See also Padre Antônio da Silva, [*Relação da ruína dos Palmares*, 1678], DP, ANTT.

'the insolence of those rebels': letter of Manuel Mascarenhas, DP 29/06/1603. In Gomes, *Mocambos de Palmares*, pp. 157–8.

'little Angola': Ernesto Ennes, *As Guerras nos Palmares: subsídios para a sua história*, Ed. Nacional, São Paulo, 1938, doc. 54.

NOTES

the kilombo had evolved: see discussion in Robert Nelson Anderson, 'The Quilombo of Palmares: a new overview of a maroon state in seventeenth-century Brazil', *Journal of Latin American Studies*, 28.3, 1996, 545–66, p. 558.

Palmarians called each other malungos: see Stuart Schwartz, 'Rethinking Palmares: Slave Resistance in Colonial Brazil', in Stuart Schwartz, *Slaves, Peasants and Rebels: Reconsidering Brazilian Slavery*, University of Illinois Press, 1996, pp. 103–35, p. 124.

117 *towards something better*: for Palmarian society, see Pedro Paulo Funari, 'Conflict and the interpretation of Palmares, a Brazilian runaway polity', *Historical Archaeology*, 37, 2003, 81–92.

mixed-race and Indigenous residents: see account of the expedition by Rodolfo Bravo/Rudolphus Baro/Roeloff Baro to Palmares in 1644 in Gaspar Barléu [1647], *O Brasil holandês sob o conde João Maurício de Nassau: história dos feitos recentemente praticados durante oito anos no Brasil*, Senado Federal, Conselho Editorial, Brasília, 2005, pp. 330–32.

Subupira and Tabocas: Pedro Paulo Funari and Aline Vieira de Carvalho, *Palmares, Ontem e Hoje*, Zahar, Rio de Janeiro, 2005, pp. 36–44, p. 16.

Kimbundu and other Bantu languages . . . língua geral: in 1691, Vieira suggested that the '[Jesuit] fathers of Angola' should be sent to Palmares to negotiate because they speak the same language. Letter of Antônio Vieira to Roque Monteiro Paim, DP 02/07/1691, cited in Gomes, *Mocambos de Palmares*, pp. 319–21. In 1678, the governor of Pernambuco sent a captain and sergeant of the Henrique Dias Regiment to negotiate with Ganga Zumba 'because they know the language like you'. See DP 22/06/1678, Aires de Sousa de Castro, governador de Pernambuco to Gana Zumba (Gana Zunbâ). AHU_ACL_CU_015, Cx. 011, D. 1116, anexo 01 (Pernambuco) 1. Transcribed in Silvia Hunold Lara and Phablo Roberto Marchis Fachin (orgs.), *Guerra contra Palmares. O manuscrito de 1678*, Chão Editora, São Paulo, 2021, pp. 176–8.

Rival empires: see Schwarcz and Starling, *Brazil*, pp. 45–50.

Palmarian farmer-fighters: see discussion in Schwartz, 'Rethinking Palmares'. For more evidence of slavery as practised in Palmares, see *Diário da viagem do capitão João Blaer aos Palmares* [1645].

'heard from far away': Barléu [1647], *O Brasil holandês sob o conde João Maurício de Nassau*, pp. 278–80.

118 *'their king knew of our coming'*: for the 1645 Dutch expedition, see *Diário da viagem do capitão João Blaer aos Palmares* [1645], 2010. Rodolfo Baro's expedition the previous year corroborates the double palisade. He reported that a thousand families lived within the settlement walls, in addition to the dwellings of single people: a discrepancy that could be explained by multiple families living in one house.

by the name of Dambij: for this early mention of Dambij/Zumbi, which supports the argument that the name is a title that referred to several individuals over time, see 'Journaal gehouden door kapitein Johan Blaer . . .',

NL-HaNA, OWIC, 1.05.01.01, inv. nr. 60, fl. 4v, cited by Damasceno, 'A ocupação das terras dos Palmares', p. 39.

'battle-hardened': da Silva, [*Relação da ruína dos Palmares*, 1678], DP, ANTT.

119 *Spain's New World colonies*: French, *Born in Blackness*, pp. 5–6.

a permanent peace: Anderson, 'The Quilombo of Palmares', p. 552, citing Décio Freitas, *Palmares: A Guerra dos Escravos*, 3rd edn, Editora Graal, 1981, pp. 73–5, 105–6.

Maroon warriors in Jamaica and Suriname: see discussion in Rafael de Bivar Marques, 'The dynamics of slavery in Brazil. Resistance, the slave trade and manumission in the 17th to 19th centuries', *Novos estudos CEBRAP*, Volume 2, São Paulo, 2006, p. 2. For British–Maroon treaty-making from Jamaica and Nova Scotia to Sierra Leone, see Rachel B. Herrmann, 'Consider the Source: An 1800 Maroon Treaty', *Early American Studies: An Interdisciplinary Journal*, Volume 21, No. 1, 2023, pp. 166–99.

'radically altering Latin American history': Cheney, *Quilombo dos Palmares*, p. 156.

tools, gunpowder – and muskets: Ibid., p. 89, citing Freitas, *Palmares*, p. 73.

might even sell them cannons: DP 19/08/1670. Pedro, dom, príncipe regente de Portugal to Fernão de Sousa Coutinho, governador de Pernambuco. In *Informação geral da capitania de Pernambuco. Anais da Biblioteca Nacional*, 28, 1906, 121–7.

'they can manufacture weapons': letter of Fernão de Sousa Coutinho, governador de Pernambuco to Dom Pedro, 1/06/1671. Reproduced in Stuart B. Schwartz (ed.), *Early Brazil. A documentary collection to 1700*, Cambridge University Press, 2010, pp. 264–5.

'masters of the country': DP 18/10/1672. Letter of Coutinho to Antônio Jácome Bezerra. BNRJ-Ms, *Cathalogo das reaes ordens existentes no Archivo da extinta Provedoria de Pernambuco*, Cod. 11,3,1, fls. 407–08, título 64, doc. 2.

the largest . . . in the New World: Pedro Paulo A. Funari, 'Maroon, race and gender: Palmares material culture and social relations in a runaway settlement', in *Historical Archaeology: Back from the Edge*, Routledge, 1999, eds. Pedro Paulo A. Funari, Martin Hall, Sian Jones, p. 310.

'most fertile . . . extraordinary greatness' . . . and rivers suitable for transporting lumber: DP 20/09/1796. Letter of José de Mendonça de Matos Moreira, ouvidor de Alagoas, to Rodrigo de Sousa Coutinho; DP 30/07/1797. Letter of José de Mendonça de Matos Moreira, ouvidor de Alagoas, to Tomás José de Melo. In 'As matas das Alagoas. Providências acerca delas e sua descripção', *Revista do Instituto Histórico e Geográfico Brasileiro*, 22, 1859, 345–56.

Algonquian seafarers: see Matthew R. Bahar, *Storm of the Sea: Indians and Empires in the Atlantic's Age of Sail*, Oxford University Press, New York, 2019, and Jesse Zarley, 'From Borderlands to the Sea: Recent Studies of Indigenous Atlantic Travellers', *Itinerario*, 2023, 1–10.

Algerian pirates: see Edite Alberto, 'Longe de casa: as listas dos resgates de cativos efetuados durante o reinado de D. João V revelam quem eram os "brasileiros" aprisionados por corsários do Norte da África', *Revista de História da Biblioteca Nacional*, A.2 (13), 2006, p. 56; Schwarcz and Starling, *Brazil*, p. 44.

taking passage across the ocean: for transatlantic journeys by Black Brazilians, see Lisa Earl Castillo, 'Entre memória, mito e história: viajantes transatlânticos da Casa Branca', in João José Reis and Elciene Azevedo (org.), *Escravidão e suas sombras*, UFBA, Salvador, 2012, pp. 65–110. For Jamaican maroons in Sierra Leone, see Herrmann, 'Consider the Source: An 1800 Maroon Treaty'.

120 *'the regalia of any republic'*: for this description of Macaco, see da Silva, *Relação*, 1678.

The king's family: see discussion in Damasceno, 'A ocupação das terras dos Palmares', p. 29.

never located since: the details of Zumbi's purported Jesuit upbringing first appeared in Freitas, *Palmares*, 1981. See also Aureliano Biancarelli, 'Arquivo revela que Zumbi sabia latim', *Folha de S. Paulo*, 12 November 1995. Available at https://www1.folha.uol.com.br/fsp/especial/mais/historia/zumbi12.htm. For claims that Freitas invented the missing manuscripts, see França and Ferreira, *Três vezes Zumbi*, p. 122.

'God of War' . . . 'singular bravery': da Silva, *Relação*, 1678.

their authority rested on ability: for an early argument that Zumbi was elected leader for life, see Sebastião da Rocha Pita [1730], *História da América portuguesa*, Itatiaia, Belo Horizonte, 1976, p. 215.

'impossible to do anything': cited in R. Kent, 'Palmares: An African State in Brazil', *The Journal of African History*, 6(2), 1965, 161–75, p. 161. See also 'Información que hizo por mandado de VMg. sobre unos capítulos que Duarte Gomez de Silveira, vezino de Parahiba, embió a la Mesa de Consciencia', AGS, Sec. prov. Libro, 1583, fs. 382–89. Cited in Stuart B. Schwartz and Hal Langfur, 'Tapanhuns, Negros da Terra, and Curibocas: Common Cause and Confrontation between Blacks and Natives in Colonial Brazil', in *Beyond Black and Red: African-Native Relations in Colonial Latin America*, University of New Mexico Press, Albuquerque, 2005, ed. Matthew Restall, pp. 81–114.

lived and died in chains: just one per cent of Brazil's enslaved population – at most – were freed over the course of the sixteenth and seventeenth centuries. Schwarcz and Starling, *Brazil*, p. 90.

120–21 *'two abominations . . . their very slaves'*: da Silva, *Relação*, 1678.

121 *'the memory of its destruction'*: Viceroy Óbidos to Gov. Francisco de Brito Freyre, 9 September 1663, BNRJ, 8,1,3, fs.3v–4. Cited in Schwartz, 'Rethinking Palmares', p. 112.

The sugar economy recovered: Damasceno, 'A ocupação das terras dos Palmares de Pernambuco (séculos XVII e XVIII)', p. 274.

veterans of Portuguese wars in Africa: see Felipe Damasceno, 'Guerra e escravidão: Palmares e a África centro-ocidental no século XVII', in *Anais do XV Encontro Regional de História da Anpuh-RJ*, 2012.

children, pregnant women and senior citizens: see discussion in Luiz Felipe Alencastro, 'História geral das guerras sul-atlânticas: o episódio de Palmares', in Gomes, *Mocambos de Palmares*, pp. 61–99.

121–2 *'the first loss felt by those countries ... they asked for peace with the whites'*: for the expeditions of 1672–7 and Ganga Zumba's embassy of 1678, see da Silva, *Relação*, 1678.

122 *further negotiations*: see DP 21/06/1678. Aires de Sousa de Castro, governador de Pernambuco to Provedor da Fazenda Real de Pernambuco. AUC, *Disposições dos governadores de Pernambuco, 1648–1696*. CCA, VI-III-I-1-31, fl. 334, doc. 5. For Cucaú being the place of the Palmarians' choosing, see *Papel que levaram os negros dos Palmares, em 22 de junho de 1678*. DP 22/06/1678. Aires de Sousa de Castro, governador de Pernambuco to Gana Zumba (Gana Zunbâ). AHU_ACL_CU_015, Cx. 011, D. 1116, anexo 01 (Pernambuco) 1. Transcribed in Lara et al., *Guerra contra Palmares*, pp. 176–8.

Ganga Zumba was duped: see Freitas, *Palmares*, p. 128; Cheney, *Quilombo dos Palmares*, p. 149.

Queen Nzinga of Ndongo: see Linda Heywood, *Njinga of Angola: Africa's Warrior Queen*, Harvard University Press, Cambridge, MA, 2017.

Palenque, Colombia: see Aquiles Escalante, 'Palenques in Colombia', in *Maroon Societies: Rebel Slave Communities in the Americas*, Baltimore: Johns Hopkins University Press, 1996, ed. Richard Price, pp. 77–80. See also the case of Yanga/San Lorenzo de los Negros, a free cimarron community recognised by the viceroy of New Spain (Mexico) in 1630. For British–Maroon treaties, see Herrmann, 'Consider the Source: An 1800 Maroon Treaty'.

the palenqueros: see Simon Romero, 'A Language, Not Quite Spanish, With African Echoes', *The New York Times*, 18 October 2007. The Saramaka also agreed to return fugitives in exchange for their freedom, but easily concealed runaways from Dutch colonial officials. See Richard Price, 'Palmares como poderia ter sido', presentation at 'Palmares, 300 años' conference, São Paulo, 1994, trans. João José Reis.

'live there forever': DP 24/08/1678. Carta do governador Aires de Sousa de Castro ao capitão Antônio Pinto Pereira, de 24 de agosto de 1678. AHU_ACL_CU_015, Cx. 019, D. 1863, anexo 16 (Pernambuco) 1. In Lara et al., *Guerra contra Palmares*, pp. 178–80.

Barely a thousand Palmarians: sources on the number of those who resettled at Cucaú vary, perhaps reflecting several waves of new populations arriving. See Cheney, *Quilombo dos Palmares*, p. 133.

destroyed the settlement: for a new assessment of Cucaú, see Silvia Hunold Lara, *Palmares & Cucaú: O Aprendizado da Dominação*, EDUSP, São Paulo, 2022.

His nation was fragmented: see Silvia Hunold Lara, 'O território de Palmares: representações cartográficas e dimensões territoriais', *Afro-Ásia*, 64, 2021, pp. 12–50 and Damasceno, 'A ocupação das terras dos Palmares de Pernambuco (séculos XVII e XVIII)'.

stormed a jail: Cheney, *Quilombo dos Palmares*, p. 147.

123 *'I, the King'*: Pedro II to Zumbi. 26/02/1685. Reproduced in Décio Freitas, *República de Palmares. Pesquisa e comentários em Documentos Históricos do século XVII*, Edufal, Maceió, 2004, p. 183, doc. 38. Freitas does not indicate the location of the original source. But subsequent documents confirm that a pardon was offered to Zumbi. See Ennes, *Guerras nos Palmares*, p. 150, doc. 7: 'Consulta do Governador de Pernambuco de 7 de Novembro de 1685'.

diplomat and priest: DP 02/07/1691. Antônio Vieira to Roque Monteiro Paim. In Gomes, *Mocambos de Palmares*, pp. 319–21.

An especially sanguinary paulista: for a detailed, if dated account of the career of Domingos Jorge Velho, see Virginia Freehafer, 'Domingos Jorge Velho Conqueror of Brazilian Backlands', *The Americas*, Volume 27, No. 2, 1970, pp. 161–84.

'so brave, reckless and steadfast': Domingos Jorge Velho to Pedro II. 15/07/1694. 'Carta autografada de Domingos Jorge Velho, escrita do Outeiro do Barriga, campanha dos Palmares em que narra os trabalhos e sacrifícios que passou e acompanha a exposição de Bento Sorriel Camiglio procurador dos Paulistas' [1694]. Gomes, *Mocambos de Palmares*, pp. 342–4.

Rio de Janeiro and Buenos Aires: Ennes, *Guerras nos Palmares*, p. 51.

124 *a fugitive North African*: see Ennes, *Guerras nos Palmares*, doc. 24, p. 194. 'Carta do Governador de Pernambuco Caetano de Melo e Castro, de 18 de Fevreio de 1694, sobre a gloriosa restauracao dos Palmares', 18 February 1694.

'almost impregnable': for the fortifications at Serra de Barriga, see Ennes, *Guerras nos Palmares*, doc. 54, p. 322. 'Requerimiento ... de Mestre de campo Domingos Jorge Velho ... na guerra dos Palmares'.

'admirable perfection and order': this account of the siege of Serra da Barriga in January–February 1694 draws on *Relação verdadeira da guerra que se fez aos negros levantados do Palmar, em 1694*. Reproduced in Maria Lêda Oliveira, 'A primeira Rellação do último assalto a Palmares', *Afro-Ásia*, 33, 2005, 300–24.

gnawing on roots: Ennes, *Guerras nos Palmares*, doc. 54, p. 324.

'our women and children made captives!': Ibid., p. 323.

125 *'an armed demon'*: 'Sermão feito na matriz do Recife de Pernambuco, estando o Santíssimo exposto na ação de graças que deu V. S. o governador e capitão general Caetano de Melo e Castro, pelo serviço feliz que alcançou dos negros dos Palmares, em 6 de fevereiro de ano de 1694', [*Sermões e poemas de matéria histórica e religiosa*], BNL-Res.Cód. 6751, fl.16v. Cited in Damasceno, 'A ocupação das terras dos Palmares de Pernambuco (séculos XVII e XVIII)', p. 14.

an informant ... 'Palmares ... is finished': 'Carta do governador de Pernambuco Caetano de Melo e Castro, dando conta de se ter conseguido a morte do Zumbi, a qual descreve' [1696], in Gomes, *Mocambos de Palmares*, p. 367.

125–6 *caffeine injections and sulphate of strychnine*: Marleide da Mota Gomes, 'The decline of Dom Pedro II's empire and health: neurophatogenic implications. Historical Notes', *Arq. Neuro-Psiquiatr.*, 65 (4b), December 2007.

126 *Pope sent her a golden rose*: Roderick J. Barman, *Princess Isabel of Brazil: gender and power in the nineteenth century*, Scholarly Resources, Wilmington, 2002, p. 190.

the true redeemer of men: cited in Edison Veiga, 'Cristo Redentor, 90 anos: como um monumento em homenagem à princesa Isabel quase foi erguido no Corcovado', *BBC News Brasil*, 11 October 2021; https://www.bbc.com/portuguese/brasil-58871798.

the president himself and his wife: 'Revogada por Lula, Ordem Princesa Isabel teve bolsonaristas como homenageados', *Folha*, 9 April 2023; https://www1.folha.uol.com.br/colunas/painel/2023/04/revogada-por-lula-ordem-princesa-isabel-teve-bolsonaristas-como-homenageados.shtml.

mounting pressure from below: for the historiographical debate over the causes of abolition, see *The Boundaries of Freedom: Slavery, Abolition, and the Making of Modern Brazil*, Cambridge University Press, 2023, eds. B. Fischer and K. Grinberg, pp. 17–18.

'Zumbi's successor … some whites': cited in Lara, 'O território de Palmares', p. 47.

as late as 1829: Damasceno, 'A ocupação das terras dos Palmares de Pernambuco (séculos XVII e XVIII)', p. 15.

Palmarians … transported to Rio de Janeiro: those transported in the wake of Carrilho's expeditions are testified as having escaped and formed new quilombos. See Stuart Schwartz, *Early Brazil. A Documentary Collection to 1700*, Yale University Press, 2009, p. 267. Some of those who were captured after the destruction of Barriga are likely to have done the same. Gomes, *Palmares: Escravidão e liberdade*, p. 154.

'new Palmares': Ibid., p. 160.

slashing the Achilles' tendons: Schwartz, 'Rethinking Palmares', p. 120.

127 *1.8 million enslaved Africans*: Fischer and Grinberg, *Boundaries of Freedom*, p. 8.

38,000 enslaved people: Schwarcz and Starling, *Brazil*, p. 201.

a cloak of toucan feathers … 2.5 million: Ibid., pp. 246–8.

Local oral histories: for Maria Felipa in fact and legend, see Evanildo da Silveira, 'Quem foi Maria Felipa, a escravizada liberta que combateu marinheiros portugueses e incendiou navios', *BBC News Brasil*, 6 August 2022; https://www.bbc.com/portuguese/brasil-62353785.

A further 700,000 Africans: Fischer and Grinberg, *Boundaries of Freedom*, p. 8.

London's banks profited: see Joseph Mulhern, 'Human collateral: British banking's long-neglected connection with slavery in Brazil', *LSE Blog*, 1 July 2020; https://blogs.lse.ac.uk/latamcaribbean/2020/07/01/human-collateral-british-bankings-long-neglected-connection-with-slavery-in-brazil/, and

Mulhern, *British Entanglement with Brazilian Slavery. Masters in Another Empire, c.1822–1888*, Anthem Press, London, 2024.

'it should be blacks': cited in Hendrik Kraay, '"As Terrifying as Unexpected": The Bahian Sabinada, 1837–1838', *Hispanic American Historical Review*, 72 (4), 1 November 1992, 501–27.

the conspiracies made it plain: for resistance from below prompting progress towards abolition on security grounds, see Dale T. Graden, 'An Act "Even of Public Security": Slave Resistance, Social Tensions, and the End of the International Slave Trade to Brazil, 1835–1856', *The Hispanic American Historical Review*, 76, No. 2, 1996, 249–82.

128 *'miserable African Ulysses'*: Hebe Mattos, '"The East River Reminds Me of the Paraná". Racism, Subjectivity, and Transnational Political Action in the Life of André Rebouças', in Fischer and Grinberg, *Boundaries of Freedom*, pp. 315–38.

Maria Firmina dos Reis: Helô D'Angelodiss, 'Quem foi Maria Firmina dos Reis, considerada a primeira romancista brasileira', *Revista Cult*, 10 November 2017; https://revistacult.uol.com.br/home/centenario-maria-firmina-dos-reis/.

pasted it into their copies of his books: Shannon Sims, 'In Brazil, a New Rendering of a Literary Giant Makes Waves', *The New York Times*, June 14, 2019; https://www.nytimes.com/2019/06/14/books/brazil-machado-de-assis.html.

proliferated from the 1870s: Fischer and Grinberg, *Boundaries of Freedom*, p. 13.

'with no kings and with no slaves': for Luís Gama and Luísa Mahin, see Lígia Fonseca Ferreira, 'Luiz Gama por Luiz Gama: carta a Lúcio de Mendonça Teresa', *Revista de Literatura Brasileira da USP*, n. 8/9, São Paulo, 2008, pp. 300–321 and the *Projecto Luiz Gama* by Bruno Rodrigues de Lima: https://projetoluizgama.hedra.com.br/TOP-en.

'Brazil's defining feature': Nabuco, *Minha formação*, cited in Fischer and Grinberg, *Boundaries of Freedom*, p. 1.

'little flu': https://www.cnnbrasil.com.br/politica/jair-bolsonaro-diz-que-nao-chamou-covid-19-de-gripezinha/; *turn people into alligators*: https://www.dn.pt/mundo/bolsonaro-sobre-a-vacina-de-pfizer-se-voce-se-transformar-num-jacare-e-problema-e-seu-13155253.html.

far more likely to die: P. R. Martins-Filho, B. C. L. Araújo, K. B. Sposato, A. A. S. Araújo, L. J. Quintans-Júnior and V. S. Santos, 'Racial Disparities in COVID-19-related Deaths in Brazil: Black Lives Matter?', *J Epidemiol.*, 5 March 2021, 31(3), 239–40. doi: 10.2188/jea.JE20200589. Epub 16 January 2021.

128–9 *'its legacy casts a long shadow'*: Schwarcz and Starling, *Brazil*, pp. xviii–xix.

129 Bedtime Stories for Grown-Ups: for Mangueira and Carnaval 2019, see Rafael Duarte, 'História pra ninar gente grande: a Mangueira em verso e prosa', *Saiba Mas*, 7 March 2019; https://saibamais.jor.br/2019/03/historia-pra-ninar-gente-grande-a-mangueira-em-verso-e-prosa/.

Black Troy . . . Iliad: the phrase is that of Joaquim Pedro de Oliveira Martins. Cited in Anderson, 'The Quilombo of Palmares', p. 550.

The hero of the story: Carvalho França and Alexandre Ferreira, *Três vezes Zumbi*, pp. 80–83.

Historians scoured foreign archives: the two massively influential accounts in this vein are Edison Carneiro, *O Quilombo dos Palmares*, Nacional, São Paulo, 1988 [1947], and Décio Freitas, *Palmares*, 1981.

'our black Spartacus': Astrojildo Pereira, *A Classe Operária*, 1 May 1929. Cited in Carvalho França and Alexandre Ferreira, *Três vezes Zumbi*, p. 96.

revolutionary figure of the Black Atlantic: for a new study of Toussaint Louverture drawing on a wide range of archival material, see Sudhir Hazareesingh, *Black Spartacus: The Epic Life of Toussaint Louverture*, Penguin, London, 2021.

130 *The Palmares Revolutionary Armed Vanguard*: see Luiza Villaméa, 'A verdadeira história do cofre do Dr. Rui', *Istoé*, no. 1555, 21 July 1999; https:// istoe.com.br/32795_A+VERDADEIRA+HISTORIA+DO+COFRE+DO +DR+RUI/.

'most glorious moment in the history of Black people': 'Entrevista publicada no *Jornal do Brasil*, do Rio de Janeiro, em 13 de maio de 1973', cited in Deivison Moacir Cezar de Campos, 'O Grupo Palmares (1971–1978): um movimento negro de subversão e resistência pela construção de um novo espaço social e simbólico', postgraduate thesis, Pontifícia Universidade Católica do Rio Grande do Sul, 2006, p. 185.

having their ashes scattered there: Funari and Carvalho, *Palmares, Ontem e Hoje*, p. 36.

Indigenous, European, Muslim and Jewish: Funari and Carvalho, *Palmares, Ontem e Hoje*. For the intriguing, if controversial hypothesis that Zumbi was gay, see Luiz Mott, *Crônicas de um gay assumido*, Editora Record, Rio de Janeiro, 2003, pp. 155–60.

purge it of 'Marxist' history books: Rafael Nascimento, 'Fundação Palmares foi encontrada "devastada fisicamente e moralmente", diz novo presidente', *G1*, Globo.com, 19 January 2023; https://g1.globo.com/rj/rio-de-janeiro/ noticia/2023/01/19/fundacao-palmares-foi-encontrada-devastada- fisicamente-e-moralmente-diz-novo-presidente.ghtml.

scrubbed from the website: 'Movimento negro é conjunto de escravos ideológicos da esquerda, diz Camargo', *UOL*, 16 June 2020; https://noticias. uol.com.br/politica/ultimas-noticias/2020/06/16/movimento-negro-e- conjunto-de-escravos-diz-camargo.htm.

130–31 *'a son of a bitch'*: 'Presidente da Fundação Palmares: movimento negro é "escória maldita". Ouça', *Metrópoles*, 2 June 2020; https://www.metro poles.com/brasil/presidente-da-fundacao-palmares-movimento-negro-e- escoria-maldita-ouca.

131 *'beneficial for the descendants'*: 'Novo presidente da Fundação Palmares minimiza racismo no Brasil em post; entidades criticam', *G1*, 28 November 2019.

the long afterlife of Palmares: see Flavio Gomes, Ana Carolina Lourenço Santos da Silva, 'A lei 10.639 e a patrimonialização da cultura: quilombos, Serra da Barriga e Palmares – primeiros percursos', *Revista Teias*, v. 14, n. 34, 2013.

'They destroy one Palmares': Gayl Jones, *Palmares*, Hachette, London, 2021.

'a huge past ahead': Millôr Fernandes, 'O Brasil tem um passado enorme pela frente', Acervo Millôr Fernandes/Instituto Moreira Salles, 2005.

132 *the story of the plantation*: for the archaeological and historical record on Camorim, see Sílvia Alves Peixoto and Tania Andrade Lima, 'Engenho do Camorim: arqueologia de um espaço açucareiro no Rio de Janeiro seiscentista', *Revista de Arqueologia Edição Especial*, Museu Nacional, Volume 2, 2020.

built atop his ancestors' cemetery: Daniel Gross and Jonathan Watts, 'Olympics media village built on "sacred" mass grave of African slaves', *The Guardian*, 21 July 2016; https://www.theguardian.com/world/2016/jul/21/olympics-media-village-sacred-grave-african-slaves-rio-games.

'unfit even to breed': Julia Affonso and Fausto Macedo, 'Justiça condena Bolsonaro por "quilombolas não servem nem para procriar"', *Estadão*, 3 October 2017; https://www.estadao.com.br/politica/blog-do-fausto-macedo/justica-condena-bolsonaro-por-quilombolas-nao-servem-nem-para-procriar/.

133 *'united by history'*: Pedro Henrique Gomes and Beatriz Borges, 'Bolsonaro recebe coração de Dom Pedro I na rampa do Palácio do Planalto', *Globo G1*, 23 August 2022; https://g1.globo.com/politica/noticia/2022/08/23/bolsonaro-recebe-coracao-de-dom-pedro-i-na-rampa-do-palacio-do-planalto.ghtml.

renames the Princess Isabel medal after Luís Gama: 'Brazil creates rights medal named after Black writer, replacing princess', *Reuters*, 3 April 2023; https://www.reuters.com/world/americas/brazil-creates-rights-medal-named-after-black-writer-replacing-princess-2023-04-03/.

'a wilful and premeditated coup attempt': Tom Phillips, 'Bolsonaro was engineer of "wilful coup attempt", Brazil congress inquiry alleges', *The Guardian*, 17 October 2023; https://www.theguardian.com/world/2023/oct/17/bolsonaro-brazil-coup-report.

134 *20,000 wildcat miners*: Mauricio Savarese and Carla Bridi, 'Haunted by post-election riot, Brazil's Lula reins in army', *AP*, 11 March 2023; https://apnews.com/article/brazil-lula-bolsonaro-military-bb26b6af649c21c046057ccde5f66823.

the 'kiss of death': 'Brazil's Congress weakens environmental, Indigenous ministries', *Al Jazeera*, 1 June 2023; https://www.aljazeera.com/news/2023/6/1/brazils-congress-weakens-environmental-indigenous-ministries.

at the very mouth of the Amazon: Eléonore Hughes, 'Brazil's Amazon megaprojects threaten Lula's green ambitions', *AP*, 7 May 2023; https://apnews.com/article/brazil-lula-amazon-indigenous-oil-belo-monte-d47e9bbf748d7b2477333b1b4a09a40b.

5: INCA, TAILOR, SOLDIER, SPY

138 *'boats that came from Europe'*: Mar Centenera, 'La cita fallida del presidente de Argentina: "Los mexicanos salieron de los indios, los brasileros de la selva, pero los argentinos de los barcos"', *El País*, 9 June 2021.

'a Brazilian problem': Rosario Gabino, '¿Hay negros en Argentina?', *BBC News*, 16 March 2007; http://news.bbc.co.uk/hi/spanish/specials/2007/esclavitud/newsid_6455000/6455537.stm.

more than doubled: 'El Censo 2022 registró en Argentina 58 pueblos indígenas y 53 lenguas ancestrales', *somos télam*, 11 March 2024; https://somostelam.com.ar/noticias/sociedad/el-censo-2022-registro-en-argentina-58-pueblos-indigenas-y-53-lenguas-ancestrales.

'a semi-European territory': Gastón Gordillo and Silvia Hirsch, 'Indigenous Struggles and Contested Identities in Argentina: Histories of Invisibilization and Reemergence', *Journal of Latin American Anthropology*, 8.3, 2003, pp. 4–30, p. 6.

rats, snakes, insects, shoe leather: for the foundation of Buenos Aires, see Ulrich Schmidel, *Historia y descubrimiento del Rio de la Plata y Paraguay; con una introducción y observaciones críticas por M. A. Pellizza*, Impr. y Librería de Mayo, Buenos Aires, 1881, Chapter XXXIV, pp. 89–114.

139 *'two distinct societies'*: D. F. Sarmiento, *Facundo*, Librería 'La Facultad', de Juan Roldan y Cia., Buenos Aires, 1921, p. 53.

further disproves the trope: for Diaguita territory as a 'black hole' where colonial rule disappeared, see Christophe Giudicelli, 'Indigenous autonomy and the Blurring of Spanish Sovereignty in the Calchaquí Valley, Sixteenth to Seventeenth Century', in *The Oxford Handbook of Borderlands of the Iberian World*, Oxford University Press, 2019, eds. Danna A. Levin Rojo and Cynthia Radding, p. 318.

140 *'with their mother's milk'*: Pedro Lozano, 1754, cited in Rodolfo Adelio Raffino, María Teresa Iglesias and Ana Igareta, 'Calchaquí: Crónicas y Arqueología (Siglos XV–XVII)', in *Investigaciones y Ensayos*, 58, Academia Nacional de la Historia, Buenos Aires, January–December 2009, p. 406.

Disciplined even in death: Juan and Judith Villamarin, 'Chiefdoms: The Prevalence and Persistence of "Señoríos Naturales" 1400 to European Conquest', in *The Cambridge History of the Native Peoples of the Americas*, Volume III: South America, Part 1, eds. Frank Salomon, Stuart B. Schwartz, pp. 642–3.

the angry ones: Raffino et al., 'Calchaquí: Crónicas y Arqueología', p. 404.

141 *the boy's arms are bound*: for an overview of mountain-top burials by the Inca, see Maria Constanza Ceruti, 'Frozen Mummies from Andean Mountaintop Shrines: Bioarchaeology and Ethnohistory of Inca Human Sacrifice', *Biomed Res Int.*, 2015, 439428, published online 6 August 2015; and Johan Reinhard, *The Ice Maiden: Inca Mummies, Mountain Gods, and Sacred Sites in the Andes*, National Geographic Society, Washington, DC, 2005, pp. 337–8.

'*very rebellious*': BNB Sucre, Correspondencia, Audiencia de la Plata, Sección Colonial [hereafter BNB Sucre, CAS], 358, 359, 14/04/1602, 'Carta del Cabildo Secular de Jujuy a la Audiencia de la Plata'.

a Dutch mapmaker: see *Paraguay, O Prov de Rio de la Plata, cum regionibus adiacentibus Tvcvman et Sta. Cruz de la Sierra, c.*1600.

'*going straight to hell*': BNB Sucre, CAS, 754, 6/12/1622, 'Carta del obispo de Tucumán a la Audiencia de la Plata'.

fomented resistance: Ana María Lorandi, *Spanish King of the Incas: The Epic Life of Pedro Bohorques*, University of Pittsburgh Press, 2005, trans. Ann de León, p. 201.

'*the total ruin*': BNB Sucre, CAS, 935, 24/05/1633, 'Carta de don Alonso de Rivera, Gobernador de Guerra de Salta, Jujuy, y Esteco, a la Audiencia de la Plata'.

gold, silver and jewels: for a planned mission to find hidden silver mines in the cordillera of Tucumán, see BNB Sucre, CAS, 917, 01/09/1631.

'*the richest province in the universe*': cited in Lorandi, *Spanish King of the Incas*, p. 154.

142 *fair skin and blond hair*: Ibid., 99, note 10, p. 225. Accarette du Biscay claims Bohórquez was a *morisco* and a native of Extremadura.

'*The Inca Don Cristóbal*': testimony of Bartolome Ramirez, AGI, Charcas, 122 (2), doc. 7, fs. 22v–23. Quoted in Ibid., p. 144.

some thirty-two children: Hemming, *Conquest of the Incas*, p. 510.

a realm of fabulously rich cities: Lorandi, *Spanish King of the Incas*, p. 112.

'*With all the fathers who served*': cited in Teresa Piossek Prebisch, *La Rebelión de Pedro Bohórquez, El Inca del Tucumán (1656–59)*, Juárez Editor, Buenos Aires, 1976, p. 15.

143 '*prostrated and humble*': Letter from Bohórquez to Mercado, 21 April 1657, Santa María de los Ángeles, Valley of Yocavil. For this and following narrative, see Lorandi, *Spanish King of the Incas*, pp. 151ff.

144 '*ancient, faithful hands . . . name has been lost*': J. B. Ambrosetti, *Exploraciones Arqueológicas en la Ciudad Prehistórica de La Paya. Campañas 1906–1907*, M. Biedma e Hijo, Buenos Aires, 1907, pp. 6–8, 27, 81.

Self-declared Diaguita: for a summary of these arguments, see Gabriel Levinas, 'El fantasma de los diaguitas, y una disputa absurda y cruel en los Valles Calchaquíes', *Clarín*, 4 April 2017.

145 *bows . . . wooden cannons*: BNB Sucre, CAS, 1181, 03/09/1658, 'Testimonio de carta de don Pablo Bernaldes de Obando a la Audiencia de la Plata. Relativa al alzamiento de los indios de Calchaqui y lo que se proveyó en su consecuencia'.

'*all will unfailingly be lost*': 'Representaciones que hacen a la Real Audiencia los Corregidores, Cabildo y Vecinos de Mendoza y San Juan, para que se les proteja contra un asalto que temen de los indios', 25 September 1658, Real Audiencia 487, pieza 1, Fs. 16, A.N.Ch. Cited in Horacio Zapater, 'Confederación bélica de pueblos andinos, amazónicos, cordilleranos, durante el dominio español', *Chungara: Revista de Antropología Chilena*,

No. 16/17, Actas X Congreso Nacional de Arqueología Chilena, October 1986, pp. 167–71.

'the only riches they give us': cited in Lorandi, *Spanish King of the Incas*, p. 167.

Bohórquez received a pair of Mercado's assassins: Prebisch, *La Rebelión de Pedro Bohórquez*, pp. 187–9.

146   *'enjoy it in peace'*: Bohórquez's speech as cited by Lozano is cited in Lorandi, *Spanish King of the Incas*, pp. 166–78.

a little white dog: for this account of the attack on the San Carlos *misión*, see Prebisch, *La Rebelión de Pedro Bohórquez*, pp. 191–206.

'the tyrant Don Pedro Bohórquez': BNB Sucre, CAS, 1181, 03/09/1658, 'Testimonio de carta de don Pablo Bernaldes de Obando a la Audiencia de La Plata'.

148   *the keys to his desk*: 'Relación Histórica de Calchaquí. Escrita por el misionero jesuita P. Hernando de Torreblanca y remitida al Padre Rector Lauro Núñez en 1696', Versión paleográfica, notas y mapas de Teresa Piossek Prebisch, Archivo General de la Nación, Buenos Aires, 1999, f.61.

'some coming forward': for the battle of San Bernardo, see Prebisch, *La Rebelión de Pedro Bohórquez*, pp. 216–18.

limping from a slash: Ibid., pp. 218–20; Torreblanca, *Relación Histórica*, f.60.

149   *'this is only the beginning'*: for the surrender, trial and execution of Bohórquez, see Lorandi, *Spanish King of the Incas*, pp. 182–97.

'one final quest for Paititi': Bohórquez would not be the last person to perish in pursuit of one variant of this legend or another. Well into the twentieth century, by which time its location had definitively shifted to the Amazon, explorers like Percy Fawcett (1867–?1925) went missing in search of the lost city of 'Z'.

'the obstinacy of this man': cited in Lorandi, *Spanish King of the Incas*, p. 198.

'a man without a place': cited in Ibid., p. 213.

150   *still pray to his First Lady*: 'Celebración escandalosa en Buenos Aires: "Santa Evita, jefa espiritual de la nación y del pueblo argentino, ruega por nosotros"', *InfoCatólica*, 8 May 2020; https://www.infocatolica.com/?t= noticia&cod=37622.

150–51   *'faked friendship ... fled to the depths'*: BNB Sucre, CAS, 1188, 24/06/1659, 'Carta de don Alonso de Mercado y Villacorta a la Audiencia de la Plata'.

to end their resistance: for the end of the Third Calchaquí War and the fate of the Quilmes, see Roxana Boixadós, 'El fin de las guerras calchaquíes. La desnaturalización de la nación yocavil a La Rioja (1667)', *Corpus*, Volume 1, No. 1, 2011; Lorandi, *Spanish King of the Incas*, p. 187.

152   *scarcely a thousand*: Raffino et al., 'Calchaquí: Crónicas y Arqueología', pp. 402–3. This extirpation was so thorough that some who had fought under Mercado were left embittered by the lack of captives. 'At the cost of shedding their own blood they served in that conquest without having any reward,' one veteran complained in 1684. AGI, Escribanía, 1044, 19v.

A Kakán dictionary: Prebisch, *La Rebelión de Pedro Bohórquez*, p. 205.

A royal decree: Raffino et al., 'Calchaquí: Crónicas y Arqueología', p. 408.

'I have wandered': 'He pasado a pie y a caballo el paraje en donde, según el historiador Herrera, estaban poblados los Diaguita; y aunque hable mucho de dicho Paraje con los sujetos prácticos en el, nadie me tomo en boca a los Diaguitas. ¿Que se ha hecho, señor, de tantos indios? Yo pregunto, leo, e inquiero, y ya no puedo hallar sino sus nombres.' Testimonio del obispo de Tucumán, Manuel Abad Illana, Córdoba, 23 August 1768. Quoted in Ibid., p. 377.

153   *returned to populate the valley*: for Diaguita survivors in the Andean north-west after the Third Calchaquí War, see Isabel Castro Olañeta, 'Las Encomiendas de Salta (Gobernación del Tucumán, Siglo XVII)', *Andes*, Volume 29, 2, 2018; and Sergio Facundo Rueda, 'Conflictos en las encomiendas y reducciones de pulares y guachipas de la jurisdicción de Salta: la participación indígena en el sistema judicial (fines del siglo xvii)', *Diálogo Andino*, No. 64, Arica, March 2021.

      a Royal Charter of 1716 ... tourist trap: see Karina Bidaseca and Santiago Ruggero, 'Disputas en torno a la Ciudad Sagrada-Ruinas de Quilmes. Memoria e identidad en la Comunidad India Quilmes', *Breves Contribuciones del I.E.G.*, 21, 2009/10, pp. 88–90.

154   *the rubble of an ongoing conflict*: see Gastón R. Gordillo, *Rubble: The Afterlife of Destruction*, Duke University Press, 2014.

      Ranquel ... Huarpes ... Selk'nam ... Diaguita: Gordillo and Hirsch, 'Indigenous Struggles', p. 20. For Indigenous peoples in Argentina's 2022 census, see 'El Censo 2022 registró en Argentina 58 pueblos indígenas y 53 lenguas ancestrales', *somos télam*, 11 March 2024; https://somostelam.com.ar/noticias/sociedad/el-censo-2022-registro-en-argentina-58-pueblos-indigenas-y-53-lenguas-ancestrales/.

      a different explanation: Cecila Castellanos, Paula Lanusse, Lorena Rodríguez, María Victoria Sabio Collado, Andrea Villagrá, 'Los Valles Calchaquíes y los Diaguitas: Procesos históricos, desigualdades y disputas identitarias', *Voces en el Fénix*, 8 (72), 2018, pp. 22–9.

      continuity of culture and place: see *Study of the Problem of Discrimination Against Indigenous Populations. Final report submitted by the Special Rapporteur, Mr. José Martínez Cobo*, United Nations, 1981.

155   *defiance that echoes down the ages*: *The False Inca*, a 1905 novel by the Argentine antiquarian Roberto Payró, popularised the legend that the last of the Diaguita had thrown themselves to their deaths rather than surrender.

      communes with his dead mastiff: Chad de Guzman, 'Argentina Just Elected an Eccentric Populist Who Seeks Counsel From His Cloned Dogs', *Time*, 20 November 2023; https://time.com/6337474/javier-milei-argentina-president-cloned-dogs-advice/.

6: THE AFRICAN ARMY OF THE ANDES

159 *'Garden of the Inca Monarchs'*: for this account of Castelli's campaigns in Upper Peru and their aftermath, see Fabio Wasserman, *Juan José Castelli. De súbdito de la corona a líder revolucionario*, Edhasa, Buenos Aires, 2011, pp. 187–203.

'the delicious enchantments of independence': [Bernardo de Monteagudo], 'Diálogo entre Atahualpa y Fernando VII, en los campos Elíseos', Archivo nacional de Bolivia (ANB), Rück-449. For Monteagudo's ethnicity, see Carlos Páez de la Torre H., 'El rostro de Monteagudo y una superchería', *La Gaceta*, 1 April 2012; https://www.lagaceta.com.ar/nota/484045/cultura/rostro-monteagudo-supercheria.html.

impeccable Inca lineage: Mara Espasande, '¿Un Inca como rey? Orígenes, gestación y base social del proyecto de la monarquía incaica de Manuel Belgrano', in *El legado de Manuel Belgrano*, Universidad de la Defensa Nacional, Buenos Aires, 2020, pp. 277–317, p. 302. See also Caleb Garret Wittum, *The Chasquis of Liberty: Revolutionary Messengers in the Bolivian Independence Era, 1808–1825*, PhD thesis, University of South Carolina, 2020, pp. 110–17.

'white-skinned Indians': María Luisa Soux, 'Insurgencia y Alianza: Estrategias de la participación indígena en el Proceso de Independencia en Charcas, 1809–1821', *Visiones y revisiones de las independencias americanas: los Indios y las independencias*, Volume 27, 2009, p. 62.

160 *'all the peoples of Peru'*: Ibid., p. 302.

imagined a sense of national identity: Benedict Anderson, *Imagined Communities. Reflections on the Origin and the Spread of Nationalism*, revised edition, Verso, London, 2006, pp. 50–64. Recent scholarship has questioned Anderson's claims about emerging criollo identity, instead only finding strong evidence for the emergence of nationalism far later in the nineteenth century – and not via newspapers or local government, but in novels, women's literary salons, university culture, archaeology and beyond. See *Beyond Imagined Communities. Reading and Writing the Nation in Nineteenth-Century Latin America*, Woodrow Wilson Center Press, Washington, DC, 2003, eds. Sara Castro-Klarén, John Charles Chasteen.

'el hombre necesario': Bartolomé Mitre, *Historia de San Martín y de la emancipación sudamericana*, Buenos Aires, 1950, Volume II, p. 258.

161 *'Bolívar here, Bolívar there'*: Elizabeth Bishop, *Prose: The Centenary Edition*, Random House, 2014, Chapter 3. Cited in Benjamin Moser, 'Elizabeth Bishop's Misunderstood "Brazil"', *The New Yorker*, 5 December 2012.

the lower end of the colonial hierarchy: for the experience of rank and file Rioplatense soldiers, see Alejandro Rabinovich, *Ser soldado en las Guerras de Independencia. La experiencia cotidiana de la tropa en el Rio de la Plata, 1810–1824*, Sudamericana, Buenos Aires, 2013.

'The rich and the landowners': cited in González et al., *Derechos de los pueblos originarios*.

162 *203,000 enslaved Africans*: Alex Borucki, '250 años de tráfico de esclavos hacia el Río de la Plata De la fundación de Buenos Aires a los "colonos" africanos de Montevideo, 1585–1835', *Claves. Revista de Historia*, Universidad de la República, Uruguay, Volume 7, No. 12, 2021. For slavery in Argentina, see Magdalena Candioti, *Una historia de la emancipación negra: Esclavitud y abolición en la Argentina*, Siglo Veintiuno Editores, Buenos Aires, 2021.

Antonio Porobio: Candioti, *Historia de la emancipación negra*, pp. 191–208.

a third of the population of Buenos Aires: Miriam Victoria Gomes, 'La presencia negroafricana en la Argentina: pasado y permanencia', *Boletín Digital de la Biblioteca del Congreso*, N. 9, 2006. For Afrodescendants in Paraguay, see Ignacio Tellesca, 'La historiografía paraguaya y los afrodescendiente', in *Los estudios afroamericanos y africanos en América Latina: herencia, presencia y visiones del otro*, CLACSO, Buenos Aires, 2008.

'excellent ear' . . . *the banks of the Plata*: José Antonio Wilde, *Buenos Aires desde setenta años atrás*, Imp. y Estereotipia de La Nación, Buenos Aires, 1908, Chapter XVIII.

the Pehuenche: Ibid., Chapter VIII.

'In all its provinces': intercepted letter from D. Bernardo Velasco, 12 July 1807, f.125 in BL Add, 32607 Buenos Ayres, 1806–7, f.129.

Bentura Patrón: Alex Borucki, *From Shipmates to Soldiers: Emerging Black Identities in the Río de la Plata*, University of New Mexico Press, Albuquerque, 2015, pp. 15, 84.

'entire population': Richard Cannon, *Historical record of the Eighty-Eighth Regiment of Foot, or Connaught Rangers: containing an account of the formation of the regiment in 1793, and of its subsequent services to 1837*, William Clowes and Sons, London, 1838, p. 10. For this account of the British assault on Buenos Aires, see also An Officer of the Expedition [Anonymous], *An Authentic Narrative of the Proceedings of the Expedition Under the Command of Brigadier-Gen. Craufurd, Until Its Arrival at Monte Video; with an Account of the Operations Against Buenos Aires Under the Command of Lieut.-Gen. Whitelocke*, Chapel Place, London, 1808.

Native militiamen: Wilde, *Buenos Aires*, Chapter VIII, Part III.

163 *Pablo Jiménez, an enslaved volunteer*: *Romance de la Gloriosa defensa de la Ciudad de Buenos-Ayres*, Buenos Aires, 1807.

Manuel Macedonio Barbarín: Florencia Guzmán, 'Identidades sociales y categorías raciales en la era de la esclavitud y la emancipación. El caso de Manuel Macedonio Barbarín (Buenos Aires, 1792–1836)', *Anuario de Historia de América Latina*, 57, 2020, pp. 190–225.

Captured British standards: a banner of the 71st Highlanders, captured during the reconquest of Buenos Aires in 1806 after the first British invasion, is kept in the museum of the Cabildo. Four other British standards are kept in the Church of Santo Domingo.

'the king and the patria': for popular participation in the defence of Buenos Aires, see Roberto L. Elissalde, *Historias ignoradas de las invasiones inglesas*, Aguilar, Buenos Aires, 2016.

'*the old master*': cited in *Escritos sobre educación*, Selección de textos, Manuel Belgrano, UNIPE, La Plata, 2011, ed. Rafael Gagliano, p. 39.

seventeen million people: John Lynch, *San Martín. Argentine Soldier, American Hero*, Yale University Press, 2009, p. 28.

fired the starting pistol: for the forgotten transatlantic impact of Condorcanqui's uprising, see Sinclair Thomson, 'Sovereignty disavowed: the Tupac Amaru revolution in the Atlantic world', *Atlantic Studies*, 13:3, 2016, 407–31.

164 *the world's first free Black republic*: Marlene Daut, *Baron de Vastey and the Origins of Black Atlantic Humanism*, Palgrave Macmillan, 2019, p. xxv.

'*flash of lightning*' . . . '*a new independent power*': *Authentic Narrative*, pp. 189, 196–9.

'*My beloved vassals*': cited in Rodolfo H. Terragno, *Maitland & San Martín*, Universidad Nacional de Quilmes, 2001, p. 146.

'*the turkey at a wedding*': cited in Julio Irazusta, *Tomás de Anchorena: prócer de la Revolución, la Independencia y la Federación*, La voz del Plata, Buenos Aires, 1950, p. 32.

José de San Martín: for San Martín's early life and conversion to the cause of independence, see Lynch, *San Martín*, pp. 1–27.

165 '*The Spaniards of Spain*': cited in Felipe Pigna, *Los mitos de la historia argentina*, Argentina: Grupo Editorial Norma, 2007, p. 236.

'*the staunchest supporters*': 'Documentos referentes a la insurrección de la ciudad de Buenos Aires en el año 1810', MS 7225, Biblioteca Nacional de Madrid, fol. 3. Cited in Carmen Bernand, 'Los olvidados de la revolución: el Rio de la Plata y sus negros', *Nuevo Mundo Mundos Nuevos* [online], workshops, January 2010.

telling his superiors: Terragno, *Maitland & San Martín*, p. 135.

'*anchored off Buenos Aires*': for San Martín in London and Buenos Aires, see Lynch, *San Martín*, pp. 28–54.

'*equal rights to all other citizens*': cited in Eric Denise Edwards, *Hiding in Plain Sight: Black Women, the Law, and the Making of a White Argentine Republic*, University of Alabama Press, Tuscaloosa, 2020, p. 39.

Juan Bautista Cabral: for a review of the evidence on Cabral, see Rolando Hanglin, '¿El sargento Cabral era negro?' *La Nación*, 5 June 2012. Available at: https://www.lanacion.com.ar/opinion/el-sargento-cabral-era-negro-nid 1479080/.

María Remedios del Valle: for del Valle and her treatment in subsequent historiography, see Florencia Guzmán, 'María Remedios del Valle. "La Capitana", "Madre de la Patria" y "Niña de Ayohuma". Historiografía, memoria y representaciones en torno a esta figura singular', *Nuevo Mundo Mundos Nuevos*, December 2016.

166 '*free and independent nation*': Luis Paz, *Historia general del Alto Perú, hoy Bolivia*, Volume 2, Imprenta Bolívar, Sucre, 1919, p. 397.

some later called it the United States: for example, Paz, *Historia general*, p. 313, refers to the Rioplatense nation that ceased to exist on 12 February 1820 as 'los Estados Unidos de Sud-América'.

sent far and wide: 'Periódico El Redactor (actas de las sesiones del Congreso de Tucumán de los días 9 a 31 de julio)'. Cited in Emilio Ravignani, *Asambleas Constituyentes Argentinas*, Peuser, Buenos Aires, 1937.

167 *'a constitution drawn from the best'*: Johan Adam Graaner, *Las provincias del Río de la Plata en 1816: informe dirigido al príncipe Bernadotte* [1816], El Ateneo, Buenos Aires, 1949, cited in Espasande, '¿Un Inca como rey?', p. 299.

sufficiently respectable . . . thrillingly radical: 'Actas de sesiones secretas del Congreso de Tucumán del día 6 de julio de 1816'. In Ravignani, *Asambleas Constituyentes*, p. 482. See also Irazusta, *Tomás de Anchorena*, p. 26.

'speedily concluding the revolution': Juan Manuel Quiroz, letter of 6 July 1816. Cited in Atilio Cornejo, 'Salta y el Congreso de Tucumán', *Trabajos y Comunicaciones*, 1966, Volume 15, pp. 146–7.

'many-sided advantages': San Martín to Godoy Cruz, 22 July 1816, in *Documentos del archivo de San Martín*, Imprenta de Coni, Buenos Aires, 1910, p. 546.

'ridiculous and extravagant idea': Irazusta, *Tomás de Anchorena*, p. 25.

entirely against public opinion: Bartolomé Mitre, *Historia de San Martín y de la emancipación sudamericana*, Peuser, Buenos Aires, 1952, p. 323.

Indigenous and popular demands: surprisingly, the fiercest opponent of the Inca plan was an Indigenous journalist from La Paz. As an Aymara, Vicente Pazos Kanki had little affection for the Quechua colonists from Cuzco. His newspaper, *La Crónica Argentina*, savaged the idea: 'to restore the grubby skeleton of the dynasty of the Incas to life after 300 years' would be 'an even greater miracle than the divine resuscitation of the mouldering corpse of Lazarus after three days'. Belgrano could hardly impose his Inca at bayonet-point, Pazos Kanki sniped: 'Better he stops writing and starts winning battles.' Paz, *Historia general del Alto Perú*, Volume 2, pp. 405–8.

'the Indians are grieving': Graaner, *Las provincias del Río de la Plata en 1816*, cited in Espasande, '¿Un Inca como rey?', p. 299.

'mingling my tears': William Bennet Stevenson, *A Historical and Descriptive Narrative . . .*, Volume 1, Hurst, London, 1928, p. 401. Cited in Alberto Flores Galindo, *In Search of an Inca: Identity and Utopia in the Andes*, Cambridge University Press, New York, 2010, ed. and trans. Carlos Aguirre, Charles F. Walker, Willie Hiatt, p. 126.

'expectations of the return of the Inca': Alexander von Humboldt, *Aspects of Nature . . .*, Lea and Blanchard, Philadelphia, 1849, p. 433. Cited in Ibid., p. 126.

travel guide: Sara Castro-Klarén, 'The Nation in Ruins: Archaeology and the Rise of the Nation', in *Beyond Imagined Communities*, eds. Chasteen and Castro-Klarén, pp. 163–95, p. 172.

planned a reprint: Felipe Pigna, *La voz del Gran Jefe. Vida y pensamiento de José de San Martín*, Planeta, Buenos Aires, 2015, pp. 262–3.

'his patria's ancient splendour': for criollo nativism, see Rebecca Earle, *The Return of the Native: Indians and Myth-Making in Spanish America, 1810–1930*, Duke University Press, Durham, NC and London, 2007, pp. 25–61.

168 *identified as Indigenous*: for example, see Osvaldo Otero, 'De amores, magro rancho y con harapos. Vida en los ejércitos en tiempos de la lucha por la independencia', in *Negros de la Patria. Los Afrodescendientes en las luchas por la independencia en el antiguo Virreinato del Río de la Plata*, Sb editorial, Buenos Aires, 2010, eds. Silvia C. Mallo and Ignacio Telesca, p. 321.

Mohawk-style headdresses: Rayna Green, 'The tribe called wannabee: Playing Indian in America and Europe', *Folklore*, 99.1, 1988, 30–55.

'*the Indian king and the Black King*': cited in Gabriel di Meglio [1816], *La trama de la independencia*, Planeta, Buenos Aires, 2016, pp. 229–37.

'*tears of joy . . . They arm themselves*': Graaner, *Las provincias del Río de la Plata en 1816*, pp. 65–6.

'*beautiful lady*': Graaner, *Las provincias del Río de la Plata en 1816*, p. 66.

169 *Legend would later tell*: for a biographical sketch of Juana Azurduy drawing on diverse sources, see Berta Wexler, 'Juana Azurduy de Padilla y sus amazonas en el ejército revolucionario', *La Aljaba*, Volume 6, 2001. Available at https://repo.unlpam.edu.ar/handle/unlpam/5251.

nine out of 102 republiqueta leaders: Gabriel Aníbal Camilli, 'Martín Miguel de Güemes y las operaciones de desgaste. Su contribución a la gesta sanmartiniana', 2002. Available online at: http://www.cefadigital.edu.ar/handle/1847939/2075.

'*enslave women and bar us from all ideals*': Estela Bringuer, *Juana Azurduy, teniente coronel de las Américas*, Editorial AZ, Buenos Aires, 1976, p. 78. Cited in Ana María Da Costa Toscano, 'La teniente coronela Juana Azurduy y las luchas de la independencia', Actas del II Encuentro Internacional Mujer e Independencias, Madrid, 2009; http://cvc.cervantes.es/literatura/mujer_independencias/dacosta.htm.

'*dynasty of the Incas*': [Martín Miguel de Güemes], *Proclama*. In *El Censor*, Biblioteca de Mayo, Volume VIII, Buenos Aires, 1960, pp. 6862–3.

Martín Miguel de Güemes: for the career of Güemes and his capture of the *Justine* in 1806, see Camilli, 'Martín Miguel de Güemes'.

more humble station: Sara E. Mata, 'Negros y esclavos en la Guerra por la independencia. Salta 1810–1821', in Mallo and Telesca (eds.), *Negros de la patria*.

María Remedios: 'Quién fue Remedios del Valle, la mujer que estará en los billetes de $500?', *La Nación*, 24 May 2022; https://www.lanacion.com.ar/sociedad/quien-fue-remedios-del-valle-la-mujer-que-aparecera-en-los-billetes-de-500-nid23052022/.

'*the humiliation of my patria*': 'Documento presentado a las Salas de Sesiones de Salta, 29 de abril, 1825', Archivo Nacional de Bolivia.

Diego Cala: Maira López, 'El rescate del papel de los indígenas en la guerra de la Independencia', *Página 12*, 11 October 2021; https://www.pagina12.com.ar/374012-el-rescate-del-papel-de-los-indigenas-en-la-guerra-de-la-ind.

170 '*To arms, Americans!*': for Campero, and his speech known as the *arenga de Santa Rosa*, see Rodolfo Martín Campero, *El Marqués de Yavi, Coronel del*

Ejército de Las Provincias Unidas del Río de la Plata, Editorial Catálogos, Buenos Aires, 2006.

'*confidence, self-assurance, and cold-bloodedness*': cited in Robert Harvey, *Liberators: Latin America's Struggle for Independence*, John Murray, 2000, pp. 329–30.

'*intrepidness and enthusiasm ... bold peasant patriots*': cited in Pacho O'Donnell, *Los héroes malditos*, Penguin Random House Grupo Editorial Argentina, 2017, Chapter 30.

great-grandchildren: see Chapter 5, and Sergio Facundo Rueda, 'Conflictos en las encomiendas y reducciones de Pulares y Guachipas de la jurisdicción de Salta: La participación indígena en el sistema judicial (fines del siglo XVII)', *Diálogo Andino*, No. 64, Arica, March 2021.

'*That's one cacique less*': *La Gaceta de Buenos Aires*, 19 July 1821. Cited by José Luis Busaniche, *Historia Argentina*, Solar-Hachette, Buenos Aires, 1976.

'*relegated to family life*': Carmen de Mora Valcárcel, 'Una mujer de armas tomar: la coronela Juana Azurduy', in *Milicia y sociedad ilustrada en España y América (1750–1800)*, XI Jornadas Nacionales de Historia Militar (501–508), Deimos, Sevilla, 2003, p. 507.

'*they who made it free*': cited in Rogelio Alaniz, *Hombres y mujeres en tiempos de revolución: de Vértiz a Rosas*, Universidad Nacional del Litoral, Santa Fe, Argentina, 2005, pp. 130–36.

171 *purloined their jewellery*: Juan Luis Ossa Santa Cruz, 'The Army of the Andes: Chilean and Rioplatense politics in an age of military organisation, 1814–1817', *Journal of Latin American Studies*, 46.1, 2014, 29–58, pp. 44–7.

'*fate of the revolution ... fortress of tyranny*'... '*el Rey José*': cited in Lynch, *San Martín*, pp. 66, 74.

The plan was in place: a variant of this strategy had been talked about in Whitehall for several years. Scottish Record Office (SRO), Maitland, GD. 193.6.4. fol. 28. Cited in Terragno, *Maitland and San Martín*, pp. 89–91.

English, Scottish and Irish riflemen: Carlos Campana, 'La historia secreta de los "Cazadores Ingleses" en la gesta sanmartiniana', *Ciudadano*, 1 June 2020; https://ciudadano.news/otro-punto-de-vista/la-historia-secreta-de-los-cazadores-ingleses-en-la-gesta-sanmartiniana.

Irishman turned viceroy of Peru: Tim Fanning, *Paisanos: Los Irlandeses olvidados que cambiaron la faz de Latinoamérica*, Sudamericana, Buenos Aires, 2017, trans. Jorge Fondebrier, pp. 195–7.

'*only the blacks are really good infantry*': cited in Lynch, *San Martín*, p. 87.

A third of the province's population: Candioti, *Historia de la emancipación negra*, p. 28.

a plot had been hatched: Beatriz Bragoni, 'Esclavos insurrectos en tiempos de revolución (Cuyo, 1812)'. In Mallo and Telesca (eds.), *Negros de la Patria*.

172 *2,500 Black soldiers*: Miriam Victoria Gomes, 'La presencia negroafricana en la Argentina. Pasado y permanencia', *Bibliopress*, 5 (9), Biblioteca del

Congreso de la Nación (BCN), Buenos Aires, October–December 2002, p. 5. Lynch, *San Martín*, p. 87, writes that 1,554 soldiers in the Army of the Andes were drawn from the enslaved; Blanchard, *Flags of Freedom*, p. 62 (see below) adds that the presence of Black freedmen and runaways from Mendoza and San Juan takes the total of Black soldiers to over half of the army of 4,000 regular troops (i.e. 5,000 minus 1,000 auxiliaries). Gerónimo Espejo, *El Paso de los Andes,* Imprenta y Librería de Mayo, Buenos Aires, 1882, p. 477, indicates that the combined strength of the (predominantly Black) 7th, 8th and 11th Battalions was 2,235 soldiers.

green piping and gold braid: for African and Afrodescendant soldiers in the Río de la Plata and the Army of the Andes, see Peter Blanchard, *Under the Flags of Freedom: Slave Soldiers and the Wars of Independence in Spanish South America*, University of Pittsburgh Press, 2008, pp. 37–41, 59–62, 118.

Juan Isidro Zapata: Abel Luis Agüero, 'Los médicos del Ejército de los Andes Desde los inicios de la Gobernación de Cuyo por el General San Martín hasta la batalla de Chacabuco', *Revista de la Asociación Médica Argentina*, 131 (2), 2018, pp. 31–6.

'*I sign with a white hand*': cited in Lynch, *San Martín*, p. 90.

Vicente San Bruno: Espejo, *Paso de los Andes*, pp. 612–14; Samuel Haigh, *Sketches of Buenos Ayres, Chile and Peru*, Effingham Wilson, London, 1831, p. 162.

173   *10,600 mules*: Harvey, *Liberators*, p. 340.

'*one single nation*': Ossa Santa Cruz, 'The Army of the Andes', p. 50, citing Pueyrredón to San Martín, 21 December 1816.

'*will become unified . . . to completion*': cited in Harvey, *Liberators*, p. 335.

a sheaf of . . . intercepted letters: Blanchard, *Flags of Freedom*, p. 63.

bullfights: see Florencia Grosso, *Remedios de Escalada de San Martín: Su Vida Y Su Tiempo*, Editorial Dunken, 1999, p. 140.

'*has need of these madmen*': Harvey, *Liberators*, p. 341.

a former seabed: Charles Darwin, *The Voyage of the Beagle*, Penguin, 1989, p. 245. Darwin journeyed through the Uspallata pass, taken by a detachment of the Army of the Andes, in 1835. Unlike the narrowly focused dispatches penned by patriot officers in 1817, he closely observed not only the geology, flora and fauna of these high-altitude Andean passes but also the beliefs and customs that were attached to them.

174   *evade the eyes of enemy spies*: H. Bertling, *Documentos históricos referentes al paso de los Andes* [hereafter DHRPA], Doc. 91, p. 103, Concepción, 1908.

raw onions and garlic: Darwin, *Voyage of the Beagle*, p. 247; Espejo, *Paso de los Andes*, p. 547.

scattered with the dead: Bertling, DHRPA, Soler to SM, 30 January 1817, Doc. 47, p. 54.

'*on foot and tired*': Las Heras, Santa Rosa, 8 February 1817. Cited in Hans Bertling, *El Paso de la Cordillera de los Andes efectuado por el General San Martín en los meses de enero i febrero de 1817 (campana de Chacabuco)*, 2nd edn, Talleres del Estado Mayor General, Santiago de Chile, 1917, p. 158.

Battered numb by hail: Ibid., p. 179.

'in peril from the intense cold': O'Higgins to San Martín, 1 February 1817. Cited in H. Bertling, DHRPA, 'Diario de campaña de la division O'Higgins', Legajo 1, Doc. 9, p. 10.

swigging laudanum: Harvey, *Liberators*, p. 344.

'these enormous mountains': cited in Lynch, *San Martín*, p. 85.

'an army travelling': Ibid., p. 179.

175   *sandals stuffed with rags*: Espejo, *Paso de los Andes*, p. 553.

all that is left is speculation: J. Roitman and K. Fatah-Black, '"Being speculative is better than to not do it at all": an interview with Natalie Zemon Davis', *Itinerario*, 3, 2015. Cited in Candioti, *Historia de la Emancipación Negra*, p. 190.

voyage with the Beagle *in 1834*: Darwin, *Voyage of the Beagle*, pp. 251–3.

'rather more lofty': Ibid., p. 241.

'The great mountains': Ibid., p. 248.

176   *native guides and mestizo militiamen*: Bertling, *El Paso de la Cordillera*, p. 161, suggests that the 'blandengue' militia who were stationed at San Carlos and traversed the Portillo and Piuquenes passes with Lemos were Pehuenche.

177   *'a triumph'*: Bertling, *El Paso de la Cordillera*, p. 179.

'Soldiers! Live with honour': cited in Lynch, *San Martín*, p. 94; cf. Espejo, *Paso de los Andes*, p. 593.

'Here's your sugar!': for this striking anecdote, see Espejo, *Paso de los Andes*, pp. 608–9.

'crying like a child': Haigh, *Sketches*, p. 162.

flimsily disguised . . . 'Give me that white hand': Ibid., pp. 612–14, 627–37.

'believed themselves in heaven': Florencia Guzmán, 'Bandas de música de libertos en el ejército de San Martín. Una exploración sobre la participación de los esclavizados y sus descendientes durante las Guerras de Independencia', *Anuario de la Escuela de Historia Virtual*, No. 7, 2015, pp. 18–36, p. 32.

'a continuous ill-humour': cited in Harvey, *Liberators*, p. 354.

178   *attack by night*: i.e. at the Battle of Cancha Rayada. Haigh, *Sketches*, p. 201.

pitched into panic: John Miller, *Memoirs of General Miller: In the Service of the Republic of Peru*, Volume 1, Longman et al, London, 1829, p. 178. For the rumour of San Martín's battlefield suicide at Cancha Rayada, see Haigh, *Sketches*, p. 194.

'the fate of all America': cited in Harvey, *Liberators*, p. 356.

'silent and gloomy ferocity': Haigh, *Sketches*, p. 214.

'the shock was tremendous': citations in this paragraph and below are from Haigh, *Sketches*, pp. 224–7.

soldier of the 8th: William Miller, letter to San Martín, Lima, 20 August 1830. In Mario Rodolfo Tamagno, without reference, cited by Carlos V. González Rivero, 'Falucho, entre la verdad y la leyenda', *La Ciudad*, 17 October 2016. Available at: https://www.lacapitalmdp.com/falucho-entre-la-verdad-y-la-leyenda/.

'obtained a complete victory': cited in Harvey, *Liberators*, p. 361.

179 *'the brunt of the action'*: Haigh, *Sketches*, p. 235.

Francisco Fierro: Luis Madrid Moraga, 'Soldados afrodescendientes y esclavos en el proceso de Independence de Chile', pp. 34–47. Available at: https://www.academia.edu/14854988/Luis_Madrid_Moraga_Soldados_afrodescendientes_esclavos_en_el_proceso_de_independencia_de_Chile_Esperando_la_libertad_en_transgresi%C3%B3n_y_lealtad_1817_1820.

'cannon fodder': Jorge Baradit, *Historia Secreta de Chile*, Volume 3, Sudamericana, Santiago, 2017, pp. 61–9.

'deserve the highest praise': Miller to San Martín, 9 April 1827, SMC, 70 (San Martín: Su correspondencia 1823–50). Quoted in Lynch, *San Martín*, p. 172.

'under the crown of Spain': Haigh, *Sketches*, p. 239.

'The day of America . . . has arrived': cited in Harvey, *Liberators*, p. 363.

Oliver Cromwell: Lynch, *San Martín*, p. 154.

scoured the sugar plantations: Seth Meisel, 'From Slave to Citizen-Soldier in Early-Independence Argentina', *Historical Reflections/Réflexions Historiques*, Volume 29, No. 1, 'Slavery and Citizenship in the Age of the Atlantic Revolutions', Spring 2003, pp. 65–82, p. 81.

180 *'Inglatierra . . . Ingas'*: 'that from Inglatierra those Ingas should be again in tyme to come restored and delivered from the servitude of the said Conquerors.' Cited in Christopher Heaney, 'A Peru of Their Own: English Grave-Opening and Indian Sovereignty in Early America', *William and Mary Quarterly*, 3rd series, Volume 73, No. 4, October 2016, p. 610. See also AGI, Cuzco, 29, N.58, 13 April 1781; Juan Manuel Moscoso y Peralta, Bishop of Cusco, to Areche: 'hablo de aquella que tiene el nombre de profesia [en] adoratiorios . . . sobre la restitución de este reyno a sus naturales asegurándola con la protección de la Inglaterra.'

'Inca mummy': Christopher Heaney, 'How to make an Inca mummy: Andean Embalming, Peruvian Science, and the Collection of Empire', *Isis: A Journal of the History of Science Society*, Volume 109, No. 1, March 2018, pp. 1–27. See also Heaney, *Empires of the Dead: Inca Mummies and the Peruvian Ancestors of American Anthropology*, Oxford University Press, 2023, p. 86.

'a memento of his sincere friendship': cited in Lynch, *San Martín*, p. 190.

left in limbo: for this account of the mutiny of El Callao in 1824 and Dámaso Moyano's military career, see Esteban D. Ocampo, 'De esclavo a Brigadier General en los Reales Exércitos', *Revista Histópia*, 1 (5), December 2019, pp. 50–58, and Ocampo, 'La bandera del Río de la Plata: Una historia llena de olvidos y confusiones', *Revista Histópia*, 15, 2021.

181 *'a divine impulse'*: quoted in Ocampo, 'De esclavo a Brigadier General', p. 55.

'the mere skeleton': Haigh, *Sketches*, p. 358.

181–2 *'a single nation . . . dissimilar characters'*: Simón Bolívar, 'Carta de Jamaica', Kingston, 8 September 1815. In Francisco Javier Yanes and Cristóbal Mendoza Montilla, *Colección de documentos relativos a la vida pública del Libertador de Colombia y del Perú Simón Bolívar para servir a la historia de la independencia de Suramérica*, Caracas, 1833, V, XXII, pp. 207–29. See also Bernardo de Monteagudo, *Ensayo sobre la necesidad de una federacion general entre los estados hispanoamericanos*, 1825, *Latinoamérica. Cuadernos de Cultura Latinoamericana*, 40, 1979, pp. 5–8. Monteagudo's assassination in Lima in 1825 dealt a heavy blow to dreams of Latin American unification.

182 *'We had better descend'*: Lynch, *San Martín*, p. 198, citing Gonzalo Pereyra de Olazábal, 'Manuel de Olazábal – su Amistad al General San Martín', *Investigaciones y ensayos*, 26, 1979, 453–68.

an elderly African pedlar: Espejo, *Paso de los Andes*, pp. 608–9.

as few as 143 returned: Gomes, 'La presencia negroafricana en la Argentina', p. 5.

to run a tavern: Marcos De Estrada, *Argentinos de origen africano*, Eudeba, Buenos Aires, 1979, pp. 79–80.

María Demetria: Wilde, *Buenos Aires*, Chapter XVIII.

Falucho … was living in Peru: 'Le aseguro que he tenido una verdadera satisfacción con la noticia que me da del célebre y nunca bien ponderado Falucho.' San Martín to William Miller, Paris, 10 July 1831, cited by González Rivero, 'Falucho, entre la verdad y la leyenda'. A tale of another soldier by the name of Falucho being shot by the Callao mutineers, related by Mitre, has been questioned by subsequent historians.

disabled and destitute: Blanchard, *Flags of Freedom*, p. 165.

183 *'singular in her patriotism'* and following: cited in Guzmán, 'María Remedios del Valle'.

'services to the King': cited in Ocampo, 'De esclavo a Brigadier General', p. 56.

weakened the institution of slavery: Blanchard, *Flags of Freedom*, p. 180.

'they conquered it': Candioti, *Historia de la Emancipación Negra*, p. 317.

they faded away: for Afro-Argentines in history and popular memory, see Roberto Pachecho, '"¡Pobres Negros!" The Social Representations and Commemorations of Blacks in the River Plate from the Mid-Nineteenth Century to the First Half of the Twentieth (and Beyond)', doctoral dissertation, Florida International University, 2015; available at: https://digitalcommons.fiu.edu/cgi/viewcontent.cgi?article=3242&context=etd.

the 'label of Africanness': cited in Paulina L. Alberto, *Black Legend: The Many Lives of Raúl Grigera and the Power of Racial Storytelling in Argentina*, University of Michigan, Ann Arbor, 2022, p. 48.

'foster European immigration': *Constitution of the Argentine Nation*, 1994, Section 25; http://www.biblioteca.jus.gov.ar/argentina-constitution.pdf.

'figures in a magic lantern': Wilde, *Buenos Aires*, Chapter XVIII.

'under the chains of slavery': *El Siglo*, 3 August 1880. Cited in Ibid., Chapter XVIII.

swerve the rigid hierarchies: for Black Argentine women as 'protagonists in their own erasure', see Edwards, *Hiding in Plain Sight*, p. 115.

184 *described as white*: Candioti, *Historia de la emancipación negra*, p. 192.

nearly one in ten: Uki Goñi, 'Time to challenge Argentina's white European self-image, black history experts say', *The Guardian*, 31 May 2021.

Available at: https://www.theguardian.com/world/2021/may/31/argentina-white-european-racism-history.

twelve per cent of the population: Celia Cussen, 'El paso de los negros por la historia de Chile', *Cuadernos de Historia*, No. 25, March 2006, 45–58, p. 53.

watercolour of the Battle of Chacabuco: *Batalla de Chacabuco*, José Tomás Vandorse, c.1863. Museo Histórico Nacional, Santiago, Chile, Exhibición Permanente, 3-239.

185   *'It matters little'*: cited in Ocampo, 'La bandera del Río de la Plata', p. 45.

an emperor 'with dirty shoes': cited in Walker, *Túpac Amaru Rebellion*, p. 257.

'drunk and covered in rags': cited in Julio Irazusta, *Tomás de Anchorena*, p. 26.

'A people that oppresses another': cited in Espasande, '¿Un Inca como rey?', p. 303. For more on Yupanqui, see Scarlett O'Phelan Godoy, 'El indio en los discursos, debates y proyectos políticos de la independencia del Perú', *Estudios de historia moderna y contemporánea de México*, November 2021.

'republicans and democrats': Juan Bautista Alberdi, *La monarquía como mejor forma de gobierno de Sud América*, A. Peña Lillo Editor, Buenos Aires, 1970, p. 83, cited in Espasande, Ibid., p. 308.

186   *settled on a republic*: Heaney, 'How to make an Inca mummy'.

censored all mention of Túpac Amaru II: Thomson, 'Sovereignty disavowed'.

dropped the reference to the Incas: Earle, *Return of the Native*, pp. 73–4.

luxurious sideburns: see Antonio Cisneros, 'Tupac Amaru relegated', trans. David Tipton, *TriQuarterly*, Evanston, IL, Volume 13, Fall 1968, 199.

'truly crazy idea ... theatrical nonsense ... burlesque': quoted in Walker, *Túpac Amaru Rebellion*, p. 71.

'like speaking to thin air': cited in Lynch, *San Martín*, p. 170.

'a great Republic': Cornejo, 'Salta y el Congreso de Tucumán', p. 148.

'They will miss us': quoted in Lynch, *San Martín*, p. 199.

187   *dispossession, civil wars and dictatorships*: on the other hand, as Hilda Sabato has argued, the mixed-race masses of the New World shaped their new nations through citizen-militias that defended order and the constitution, a rowdy court of public opinion and free press, and mass-suffrage elections that constrained strongman leaders. See *Republics of the New World: The Revolutionary Political Experiment in Nineteenth-Century Latin America*, Princeton University Press, 2018.

'accounts of civil broils': Haigh, *Sketches*, p. 316.

7: LORDS OF THE ENDS OF THE EARTH

191   *the Mapuche ... their country ... Wallmapu*: in this chapter I follow current usage in referring to the peoples south of the Biobío River and north of Valdivia, as well as their descendants, as Mapuche. This term has the drawback of obscuring differences between sub-groups like the Lafkenche and

Pehuenche, and was not used until the 1760s. However, present-day Mapuche historians tend to favour its retrospective application. See discussion by *Memoria Chilena*, Biblioteca Nacional de Chile (Servicio Nacional del Patrimonio): http://www.memoriachilena.gob.cl/602/w3-article-100855.html.

Mapuche tradition: for this version of the Mapuche origin myth, see José Bengoa, *Historia del Pueblo Mapuche (Siglo XIX y XX)*, Ediciones Sur, Santiago, 1997, pp. 9–12.

carved stone mace-head: Cabezal de maza de piedra: serpiente y lagarto, MCHAP, 0215.

192 *at least 15,000 years*: 'New clues emerge about the earliest known Americans', Vanderbilt University, *Research News*, 18 November 2015; https://news.vanderbilt.edu/2015/11/18/new-clues-emerge-about-the-earliest-known-americans/.

discover itself: Sergio Caniuqueo: Daniel Hopenhayn, 'El movimiento mapuche generó una élite enfrascada en su identidad', *La Tercera*, 18 September 2022; https://www.latercera.com/la-tercera-domingo/noticia/sergio-caniuqueo-el-movimiento-mapuche-genero-una-elite-enfrascada-en-su-identidad/A6WS3I56XVAQBEMTGKDWGH2QVA/.

Chicken bones with Polynesian DNA: for evidence of pre-Columbian contact between Polynesia and South America, see Alice A. Storey, José Miguel Ramírez, Daniel Quiroz, Elizabeth A. Matisoo-Smith, 'Radiocarbon and DNA evidence for a pre-Columbian introduction of Polynesian chickens to Chile', *PNAS*, 104 (25), 19 June 2007. See also Sebastián Montalva W., 'El vínculo polinesio de los mapuches', *El Mercurio*, 14 September 2008.

New genetic evidence: A. G. Ioannidis, J. Blanco-Portillo, K. Sandoval et al., 'Native American gene flow into Polynesia predating Easter Island settlement', *Nature*, 583, 2020, 572–7.

192–3 *Toki … kialu … kialoa*: Andrew Lawler, 'Beyond Kon-Tiki: Did Polynesians Sail to South America?', *Science*, Volume 328, Issue 5984, 11 June 2010.

193 *'with such impetus and yelling'*: cited in Armando De Ramón, *Historia de Chile. Desde la invasión incaica hasta nuestros días (1500–2000)*, Catalonia Ltda., Santiago, 2003, pp. 91, 26.

the chiliweke: see Paula Huenchumil, 'Chiliweke, el desconocido camélido extinto que fue clave en la sociedad mapuche', *Interferencia*, 24 December 2019; https://interferencia.cl/articulos/chiliweke-el-desconocido-camelido-extinto-que-fue-clave-en-la-sociedad-mapuche.

'more than half': Garcilaso, *Royal Commentaries*, Book VII, Chapter XXIX, p. 291.

winka … yanacona: Tom D. Dillehay, *Monuments, Empires, and Resistance: The Araucanian Polity and Ritual Narratives*, Cambridge University Press, 2007, p. 103.

probably drew on Inca warnings: Jorge L. Hidalgo et al., *Culturas de Chile, Vol. 2, Etnografía, Sociedades Indígenas Contemporáneas y su Ideología*, Editorial Andrés Bello, Santiago, 1996, p. 269.

194 *Lautaro, 'hawk'*: 'Líder de la primera gran rebelión mapuche. El toqui Lautaro (*ca.*1534–1557)', *Memoria Chilena*, Biblioteca Nacional de Chile (Servicio Nacional del Patrimonio). Available at: http://www.memoriachilena.gob.cl/602/w3-article-721.html.

five mares and two stallions: R. B. Cunninghame Graham, *The Horses of the Conquest. A Study of the Steeds of the Spanish Conquistadors*, The Long Riders' Guild Press, 2004 [1930], p. 143.

'such enormous troops': Felix de Azara, *Apuntamientos*, 1802, p. 214. Quoted in Cunninghame Graham, *Horses of the Conquest*, p. 115.

'most unhappy': Garcilaso, *Royal Commentaries*, Book VII, Chapter XXIX, p. 291.

swallowed up by the ground: Ibid., Chapter XXI.

'If you are such a friend to gold': Pedro Mariño de Lobera, *Crónica del Reino de Chile*, Atlas, Madrid, 1960, pp. 227–562 (Biblioteca de Autores Españoles, 569–75), Chapter XLIII. See also Francisco Núñez de Pineda y Bascuñán, *Cautiverio feliz, y razón de las guerras dilatadas de Chile*, Colección de historiadores de Chile y documentos relativos a la historia nacional, Tomo III, Imprenta del Ferrocarril, Santiago, 1863, p. 255.

typhus stalked: Bengoa, *Historia del Pueblo Mapuche*, p. 25.

The Mapuche population plunged: for population figures, see Roberto J. Campbell, 'Socioeconomic differentiation, leadership and residential patterning at an Araucanian chiefly center (Isla Mocha, AD 1000–1700)', PhD thesis, University of Pittsburgh, 2011, p. 18, citing Bengoa, 2003.

195 *'as you train a racehorse'*: cited in Pablo Marimán Quemenado, Sergio Caniuqueo Huircapán, Rodrigo Levil Chicahual, José Millalén Paillal, *Escucha Winka! Cuatro ensayos de historia nacional mapuche y un epílogo sobre el futuro*, Lom Ediciones, Santiago, 2006, pp. 68–9.

'They fled from us': 'Carta de Óñez de Loyola al Rey, Concepción, 17 de enero de 1598'. Mss. Medina, tomo 98, f. 47. Cited in Eduardo Cebrián, 'Curalaba: cuando la política no entiende la guerra', *Revista de Humanidades*, Volume 17–18, June–December 2008, 125–42, p. 130.

prepare for war: 'Óñez de Loyola para el virrey, Rancagua, 15-2-1593', Medina 394. Cited in Ibid., p. 133.

'sown the valleys': Alonso de Ovalle, *Histórica Relación Del Reyno de Chile y de las Misiones y Ministerios que exercita la Compañia de Jesus*, Francisco Caballo, Rome, 1646, p. 301.

a verse epic: 'La gente que produce es tan granada, Tan soberbia, gallarda y belicosa, Que no ha sido por rey jamás regida. Ni a extranjero dominio sometida'; 'estado araucano'. Alonso de Ercilla y Zúñiga, *La Araucana*, Imprenta Nacional, Madrid, 1866, pp. 2, 17.

drafted his stanzas: Cunninghame Graham, *Horses of the Conquest*, p. 6.

196 *took the missive to Pelantaro*: Cebrián, 'Curalaba', p. 135.

'sparrows in a net': cited, along with a description of the battle of Curalaba, in Diego Barros Araña, *Historia general de Chile*, Rafael Jover Editor, Santiago, 1883, Volume 3, Part 3, pp. 175–80.

Disaster of Curalaba: see, for example, Eduardo Arriagada A., '*Desastre de Curalaba*', Academia de Historia Militar: https://www.academiahistoria militar.cl/academia/desastre-de-curalaba/.

the heads of Spanish captains: AGI, Santa Fe, 99, fj. 204v.

chugging chicha: for the aftermath of Curalaba, see Francis Goicovich, 'Alianzas geoétnicas en la segunda rebelión general: génesis y dinámica de los vutanmapus en el alzamiento de 1598', Instituto de Historia, Pontificia Universidad Católica de Chile, *Historia*, No. 39, Volume I, 2006, 93–154.

struck through with penstrokes: AGI, mp-peru_chile, 172 (originally AGI, Patronato, 229). Cited in José Araneda Riquelme, 'Comunicando un desastre. Un mapa, diversos mensajeros y las noticias imperiales de una sublevación indígena (Arauco, 1598–1610)', *Revista Razón Crítica*, No. 10, 2021.

fled servitude: Bengoa, *Historia del Pueblo Mapuche*, p. 32.

196–7 '*Indian Flanders . . . seize their freedom*': Diego de Rosales, *Historia General del Reyno de Chile: Flandes Indiano* [1678], Imprenta del Mercurio, Valparaíso, 1877–8, Volume 1, pp. 18–19; Volume 2, p. 302.

200 '*Pigs and squaddies out of Wallmapu!*': 'Weichan Auka Mapu exhibe alto poder de fuego en video', T13, 4 November 2021; https://www.youtube. com/watch?v=EVicb7lkdo8&ab_channel=T13.

201 '*the rebel provinces*': AGI, Escribanía, 1026B, 'Antonio de Meneses Indio natural Araucano en el Reyno de Chile con dn. Alonso Perez de Salazar, sobre su libertad, 1648', fol. 21r–24v.

202 *a council of advisors*: British Library (BL) Egerton, 321, 'Consultas del Consejo de Estado Tocantes a indias', 1625, Volume II, 18 June–30 December, 102r-v.

'*not as barbarous*': Núñez de Pineda y Bascuñán, *Cautiverio feliz*, pp. 54, 70, 124, 211.

were the equal of their peers: see discussion in Daniel Palma Alvarado, 'La Rebelión Mapuche de 1598', tesis para optar al grado de Licenciado en Historia, Pontificia Universidad Católica, Santiago, 1995, and Kristine Jones, 'Warfare, Reorganization and Readaptation at the Margins of Spanish Rule: The Southern Margin, 1573–1882', in *The Cambridge History of the Native Peoples of the Americas*, Volume III: South America, Part 2, eds. Frank Salomon and Stuart B. Schwartz, p. 174.

a Basque highwayman: for Antonio de Erauso's (auto)biography and its authenticity, see Sonia Pérez Villanueva, 'Historia de la Monja Alférez: ¿escrita por ella misma?', AISO, *Actas*, VI, 2002, and Pérez Villanueva, *The Life of Catalina de Erauso, the Lieutenant Nun: An Early Modern Autobiography*, Rowman & Littlefield, 2014.

203 '*I ask for justice*': this paragraph draws on AGI, Escribanía, 1026B, 'Antonio de Meneses Indio natural Araucano', especially fol. 21r–24v. While catalogued in the AGI's PARES system, to the best of my knowledge this set of documents is not widely known.

two more independence revolutions: José Bengoa notes that Philip IV instructed colonial officials to sue for peace with the Mapuche explicitly because he could send no reinforcements in light of the Catalonian Revolt. Bengoa, 'Catalanes, Autonomías y Mapuche(s)', *The Clinic*, 4 October 2017; https://www.theclinic.cl/2017/10/04/columna-jose-bengoa-catalanes-autonomias-mapuche-s/.

their match cords lit: this account of the Treaty of Quillín draws on Ovalle, *Histórica Relación Del Reyno de Chile*, 1646, pp. 306–12.

204 *reinforce alliances*: Marimán et al., *Escucha Winka!*, pp. 68–9.

The principal Mapuche demands: see Ibid.; Diego de Rosales, *Historia General del Reyno de Chile, Flandes Indiano* [1678], Imprenta del Mercurio, Valparaíso, 1878, Volume 2, pp. 184–5; Felipe Gómez de Vidaurre, *Historia Geográfica, natural y civil del Reino de Chile*, Volume II. In *Colección de Historiadores y documentos relativos a la Historia Nacional*, Volume XV, Imprenta Ercilla, Santiago, 1889, pp. 239–40; and discussion in Bengoa, *Historia del Pueblo Mapuche*, p. 33.

fiercely debated: for differing views of Quillín, from an 'extraordinary acknowledgement of [Mapuche] sovereignty' and a landmark treaty kept out of the Chilean history books, to a commonplace encounter that helped bring the 'disorganised tribes' south of the Biobío to heel, see David J. Weber, *Bárbaros: Spaniards and Their Savages in the Age of Enlightenment*, Yale University Press, 2008, p. 208; Marimán et al., *Escucha Winka!*, p. 78; and Sergio Villalobos R., 'Nuevas fantasías y errores en la historia de la Araucanía', *Cuadernos de Historia*, No. 38, Santiago, June 2013.

would be remembered: for the discussion below, see Jorge Pinto Rodríguez, 'Presentación', in *Los parlamentos hispano-mapuches, 1593–1803: textos fundamentales*, Ediciones Universidad Católica de Temuco, 2015, ed. José Manuel Zavala Cepeda, pp. 13–15.

205 *'shameful peace'*: Tomás Guido, Buenos Aires, 20 May 1816. Cited in Espejo, *Paso de los Andes*, p. 691.

Dozens more parliaments: Marimán et al., *Escucha Winka!*, p. 79, puts the figure at twenty-seven between 1641 and 1803. Pedro Cayuqueo, *Historia Secreta Mapuche*, Catalonia, Santiago, 2018, loc. 203, puts the number of parliaments as over forty between 1593 and 1825.

'your Majesty's arms': letter from Manso to the king, Concepción, 28 February 1739, reproduced by Barros Araña, *Historia general de Chile*, Volume 6, pp. 102–3. Cited in Bengoa, *Historia del Pueblo Mapuche*, pp. 35–6.

'as with a foreign power': cited in Weber, *Bárbaros*, p. 208.

over most of Latin America: Ibid., p. 12.

'To conquer them by force': cited in Weber, 'Bourbons and Bárbaros. Center and Periphery in the Reshaping of Spanish Indian Policy', in *Negotiated Empires: Centers and Peripheries in the Americas, 1500–1820*, Routledge, 2002, eds. Christine Daniels, Michael V. Kennedy, pp. 79–105, pp. 79–80.

'Mapuche golden age': Cayuqueo, *Historia Secreta Mapuche*, loc. 217.

ran like clockwork: Jesse Zarley, 'Between the Lof and the Liberators: Mapuche Authority in Chile's Guerra a Muerte (1819–1825)', *Ethnohistory*, 66:1, January 2019, p. 128.

Ambrosio O'Higgins: Fanning, *Paisanos*, pp. 86–106.

206 *'eternal and lasting peace'*: Bernardo O'Higgins, 'Artículos de Paz hecha por el Director Supremo a los mapuches, signados con el Sello del Estado, y refrendados por mi Secretario de la Guerra, en la Plaza de Concepción, a 3 de agosto de 1817', Archivo Nacional, Ministerio de Guerra, Volume 27, fojas 12–13. Cited in Armando Cartes Montory, 'Bárbaros o ciudadanos? Los Mapuches en el albor republicano', in *Ciudadanía. Temas y debates*, Centro de Estudios Bicentenario, 2014, eds. Cartes Montory and Pedro Diaz Polanco, p. 227.

'bought with our blood': Bernardo O'Higgins, 'El Supremo Director del Estado a nuestros hermanos los habitants de la frontera del Sud', Santiago, 13 March 1819. *Gazeta Ministerial de Chile*, No. 83, Volume 1, pp. 111–14.

the Mapuche Wünelfe: Baradit, *Historia Secreta de Chile*, Volume 3, p. 119.

207 *'descendants of the latter ... wrongs they suffered avenged'*: cited in Earle, *Return of the Native*, pp. 29–44.

'will eventually achieve it': Bolívar, 'Carta de Jamaica'. Translated by Lewis Bertrand in *Selected Writings of Bolívar*, The Colonial Press Inc., New York, 1951.

'the first to charge': cited in Isabel Hernández, *Autonomía o ciudadanía incompleta: el pueblo mapuche en Chile y Argentina*, CEPAL, Santiago, 2003, p. 83. See also P. A. Cuadra Centeno and M. L. Mazzoni, 'La invasión inglesa y la participación popular en la Reconquista y Defensa de Buenos Aires 1806–1807', *Anuario del Instituto de Historia Argentina*, (11), 2011, p. 56.

lands and trading partners: see discussion in J. Crow and J. L. Ossa Santa Cruz, '¿"Indios seducidos"? Participación politico-militar de los mapuche durante la Restauración de Fernando VII. Chile, 1814–1825', *Revista Universitaria de Historia Militar*, 7(15), 2018, 39–58.

'these new allied brothers': for discussion of the Treaty of Tapihue, see Crow and Ossa Santa Cruz, Ibid., p. 7, and Marimán et al., Escucha Winka!, p. 83.

208 *When their merchants were wrecked*: see Manuel Llorca-Jaña, 'Of "Savages," Shipwrecks and Seamen: British Consular Contacts with the Native Peoples of Southern South America during the 1820s and 1830s', *International Journal of Maritime History*, 24(2), 2012, 127–54.

'amity and good-will': Richard Nugent, letter to George Canning, 9 October 1825. Quoted in Ibid., p. 145.

'a watery grave': G. A. Rothery, Walter J. Collins, *A diary of the wreck of his majesty's ship Challenger on the Western coast of South America in May 1835. With an account of the subsequent encampment of the officers and crew during a period of seven weeks on the south coast of Chili*, Longman, London, 1836, p. 8.

'exterminate the race of Indians': Ibid., pp. 90, 105–6.

'perfectly independent': cited in Llorca-Jaña, '"Savages," Shipwrecks and Seamen', p. 131.

equal confederation: see discussion in Joanna Crow, 'Troubled Negotiations: The Mapuche and the Chilean State (1818–1830)', *Bulletin of Latin American Research*, 36(3), 2017, pp. 285–98.

209 *'a living fire'*: cited in Zarley, 'Between the Lof and the Liberators', p. 127.

over 2,600 Mapuche chiefs: Crow, 'Troubled Negotiations', pp. 12–13.

'many of their civilisers on the border': Ignacio Domeyko, *Araucania I sus habitantes. Recuerdos de un viaje hecho en las provincial meridionales de chile, en los meses de enero I febrero de 1845*, Imprenta de Chile, Santiago, 1846, pp. 69–70.

'apt for mixing': cited in de Ramón, *Historia de Chile*, p. 86.

209–10 *'immense and virgin forest . . . work and needs'*: Vicente Pérez Rosales, *Recuerdos del Pasado*, Imprenta Gutenberg, Santiago, 1886, pp. 253–7.

210 *a Chilean damsel in captivity*: see Raymond Monvoisin's watercolours of Elisa Bravo, a fictional survivor of the *Joven Daniel*.

'stain on humanity': *La Tribuna*, 6 September 1849; 25 November 1849; 1 February 1850. Cited in Cayuqueo, *Historia Secreta Mapuche*, loc. 2757.

parcelling it out: Jones, 'Warfare, Reorganization and Readaptation', p. 167.

'strange to say . . . the difference': Edmond Reuel Smith, *The Araucanians: or, notes of a tour among the Indian tribes of southern Chili*, Harper & Brothers, New York, 1855, pp. 254–68.

'our territory and our independence': cited in Cayuqueo, *Historia Secreta Mapuche*, loc. 3231.

211 *have recently argued otherwise*: see discussion in Bruce Chatwin, *In Patagonia*, Vintage, London, 2005 [1977], p. 24; Cayuqueo, *Historia Secreta Mapuche*; and in Mat Youkee, 'Why the lost kingdom of Patagonia is a live issue for Chile's Mapuche people', *The Guardian*, 21 March 2018; https://www.theguardian.com/world/2018/mar/21/kingdom-mapuche-chile-patagonia-araucania.

'I may be reproached': Antoine de Tounens, *Orélie-Antoine 1er, roi d'Araucanie et de Patagonie: son avènement au trône et sa captivité au Chili, relation écrit par lui-même*, Librairie de Thevelin, Paris, 1863, pp. iii–iv.

212 *puppet ruler, Maximilian I*: for a recent study of Maximilian, see Edward Shawcross, *The Last Emperor of Mexico. A Disaster in the New World*, Faber & Faber, London, 2021.

'King Aurelio was afraid': Juan Calfucurá, cited in Cayuqueo, *Historia Secreta Mapuche*, loc. 2967.

'the price of a meal ticket': Chatwin, *In Patagonia*, p. 24.

'No one wants him': personal communication, 20 January 2022. For a recent reassessment of de Tounens drawing on new documentation, see Jean-François Gareyte, *Le rêve du sorcier. Antoine de Tounens, Roi d'Araucanie et de Patagonie. Une biographie*, La Lauze, 2018.

213 *'the submission that we seek'*: cited in Pablo Marimán Quemenado, 'La geostrategia en el conflicto chileno mapuche: la configuración del estado nación (1830–1869)', in *Revista anales, séptima serie*, No. 13, 2017, p. 47.

'How can justice be done?': Bengoa, *Historia del Pueblo Mapuche*, pp. 196–7.

a thousand years: 'Hallan el entierro en canoa más antiguo y austral de todo el continente', CONICET Patagonia Norte, 5 September 2022; https://patagonianorte.conicet.gov.ar/hallan-el-entierro-en-canoa-mas-antiguo-y-austral-de-todo-el-continente/.

214 *'a virile people'*: Kenneth M. Roth, *Annihilating Difference: The Anthropology of Genocide*, University of California Press, 2002, p. 45.

8.5 million hectares: Bengoa, *Historia del Pueblo Mapuche*, p. 316.

sent Calfucurá's skull: Gustavo Sarmiento, 'Después de 141 años, volverá a su tierra el cacique Calfucurá', *Tiempo*, 11 October 2020; https://www.tiempoar.com.ar/informacion-general/despues-de-141-anos-volvera-a-su-tierra-el-cacique-calfucura/; 'Restituirán dos ancestros de la comunidad Toki Calfucurá que están en el Museo La Plata', *Télam*, 6 December 2021; https://www.telam.com.ar/notas/202112/577072-restituiran-dos-ancestros-toki-calfucura-museo-la-plata.html.

Melín and his relatives: for this account of the 1881 uprising and its causes, see Bengoa, *Historia del Pueblo Mapuche*, pp. 270–71, 298–314.

'The dumb animals': Marimán et al., *Escucha Winka!*, p. 57, citing account of Alfredo Ebelet at Fort Aldecoa, 1875.

215 *'a great work of justice'*: F. A. Subercaseaux, *Memorias de la Campaña a Villarrica: 1882–1883*, Imprenta de la Librería Americana de Carlos 2° Lathrop, Santiago, 1883, pp. 26–34, 53–5.

500,000 hectares: Pablo Marimán Quemenado, 'El pueblo mapuche y la reforma agraria: una reforma entre cuatro contrarreformas', *Revista anales, séptima serie*, No. 12, 2017, p. 260.

216 *a further 200,000 hectares*: Marimán et al., *Escucha Winka!*, p. 11.

'We were right': cited in Bengoa, *Historia del Pueblo Mapuche*, p. 316.

'civilise the Indians … This wonderful monument': Matías González Marilicán, 'Civilizing Nature with the Spade and the Rifle: The Engineer Battalion in the Araucanía Region, Chile (1877–1891)', *Environment & Society Portal, Arcadia*, Spring 2020, No. 21, Rachel Carson Center for Environment and Society; https://doi.org/10.5282/rcc/9043.

'wheat crushed into a sack': cited in Marimán et al., *Escucha Winka!*, p. 125.

216–17 *'the Araucanian people'*: *Diario Austral*, Temuco, 2 January 1932. For the ongoing desire for an Indigenous Republic, see Cornelio Aburto, CEDM: 'Editorial Diario De La Federación Juvenil Araucana', in *Juventud Araucana. Diario de la Federación Juvenil Araucana*, Traitraico (Nueva Imperial), 27 December 1935, p. 4.

217 *Chile's exports plummeted*: Rosemary Thorp, *Latin America in the 1930s: the role of the periphery in world crisis*, Palgrave Macmillan, 2000, p. 332.

moved into caves: 'El impacto de la Gran Depresión en Chile (1929–1932)', *Memoria Chilena*, Biblioteca Nacional de Chile. Available at http://www.memoriachilena.gob.cl/602/w3-article-601.html.

The old cause: for discussion of the assembly and the subsequent history of Mapuche constitutionalism and separatism from 1990–2015, see Claudio Fuentes and Alfredo Joignant, *La solución constitucional. Plebiscitos, asambleas, congresos, sorteos y mecanismos híbridos*, Catalonia, Santiago, 2015.

the Araucano: Jorge Grove, *Descorriendo el velo: episodio de los doce días de la República Socialista*, Valparaíso, 1933, pp. 63, 4. Grove's later revolutionary career would take him to such exotic locations as Tahiti and Dover.

the conquistador snaps: 'Manifestantes derriban busto de Pedro de Valdivia y Diego Portales en Temuco', *24 horas*, 29 October 2019; https://www.24horas.cl/regiones/araucania/manifestantes-derriban-busto-de-pedro-de-valdivia-y-diego-portales-en-temuco-3691905.

218 *manhandled forward*: Werken Noticias, 7 August 2020; https://twitter.com/info_werken/status/1291809057897144321.

219 *'Chilean and Argentine uniforms'*: Paul Treutler, *Andanzas de un Aleman en Chile 1851–1863*, Editorial del Pacifico, Santiago, 1958, trans. Carlos Keller R., p. 394.

220 *$1.5 billion worth of land*: Benedict Mander, 'A new dawn in Mapuche fight for equality', *Financial Times*, 26 April 2021; https://www.ft.com/content/a42a3ae7-9603-4e9a-b8de-39b322702333.

222 *retreated by nearly two-thirds*: Andrés Rivera et al., 'Recent changes in total ice volume on Volcán Villarrica, Southern Chile', *Natural Hazards*, 75 (2015), 33–55.

'indigenist monarchy': Isidora Paúl, 'Convencional Zúñiga (UDI): "Se privilegió una Constitución para políticos y no para ciudadanos"', *Pauta*, 1 May 2022; https://www.pauta.cl/politica/convencional-arturo-zuniga-la-campana-silenciosa-derecha-rechazo.

Indigenous 'elite' . . . lost touch: Daniel Hopenhayn, 'Sergio Caniuqueo: "El movimiento mapuche generó una élite enfrascada en su identidad"', *La Tercera*, 18 September 2022; https://www.latercera.com/la-tercera-domingo/noticia/sergio-caniuqueo-el-movimiento-mapuche-genero-una-elite-enfrascada-en-su-identidad/A6WS3I56XVAQBEMTGKDWGH2QVA/.

2025 will mark 200 years: Pedro Cayuqueo, 'Volvamos a Tapihue', 2018; https://www.pedrocayuqueo.cl/post/volvamos-a-tapihue.

8: I DIE WITH MY COUNTRY

225 *a million dollars in bribes*: US Department of the Treasury, 'Treasury Sanctions Paraguay's Former President and Current Vice President for Corruption', 26 January 2023; https://home.treasury.gov/news/press-releases/jy1221.

227 *'hopeless lack of interest'*: Richard F. Burton, *Letters from the Battle-fields of Paraguay*, Tinsley Brothers, London, 1870, pp. vii, 1.

'an island surrounded by land': Augusto Roa Bastos, in *Memorias de la Guerra del Paraguay. Frente al frente Paraguayo. Recuperando lo Escrito*, Servilibro, Asunción, 2011.

227–8 *'brutal and sybaritic satrap'*: Carlos L. Isasi, foreword, in Dr Cecilio Baez, *La Tiranía en El Paraguay: Sus Causas, Caracteres y Resultados. Colección* de *Artículos Publicados en 'El Cívico'*, Asunción, 1903, p. 7. For comparisons between López and Hitler, see James Schofield Saeger, *Francisco Solano López and the Ruination of Paraguay: Honor and Egocentrism*, Rowman & Littlefield, Plymouth, 2007, p. 181.

228 *moral triumph*: the words are those of Juan Crisóstomo Centurión, *Memorias, o Reminiscencias históricas sobre la guerra del Paraguay*, Volume 4, J. A. Berra, Asunción, 1901, p. 169.

slaughtered Indigenous peoples: *Ventanas Abiertas. Informe de la Comisión de Verdad y Justicia sobre la dictadura en Paraguay 1954–89*, Versión esencial, Coordinadora de Derechos Humanos del Paraguay y Fábrica Memética, Asunción, 2023, pp. 116–21.

'Peace and Progress': *Correo del Paraguay*, Emisión No. 9, 27 December 1967, 631/67, 3867.

Stroessner remains honorary president: 'No hubo acto oficial para recordar la caída de Stroessner', *Última Hora*, 3 February 2024; https://www.ultima-hora.com/no-hubo-acto-oficial-para-recordar-la-caida-de-stroessner.

'Stroessner finished off the country': 'Entrevistas a Augusto Roa Bastos', in Antonio Pecci, *Roa Bastos. Vida, obra y pensamiento*, Servilibro, Asunción, 2007. Quoted in Damaris Pereira Santana Lima, 'O Intelectual Exilado em Augusto Roa Bastos', doctoral thesis, UNESP, 2013, pp. 62–3, 68.

English conquistadors: for English conquistadors in Paraguay, see Josefina Plá, *Los británicos en el Paraguay 1850–1870*, Arte Nuevo, Asunción, 1984, p. 22.

229 *'the measure of our armour and harquebuses'*: Schmidel, *Historia y descubrimiento del Rio de la Plata*, Chapter XXI, p. 77.

encouraged others to do the same: for Juliana, see Silvia Tieffemberg, 'La india Juliana: el enemigo dentro de la casa', in *Pensar América desde sus colonias: Textos e imágenes de América colonial*, Editorial Biblo, Buenos Aires, 2020.

nomadic peoples who ranged the Chaco: Bridget María Chesterton, *The Grandchildren of Solano López. Frontier and Nation in Paraguay, 1904–1936*, University of New Mexico Press, Albuquerque, 2013, p. 3.

hardships of the Chaco expeditions: Shawn Michael Austin, *Colonial Kinship. Guaraní, Spaniards, and Africans in Paraguay*, University of New Mexico Press, Albuquerque, 2020, pp. 29–30.

'would have been wiped out': Isabel de Guevara to Doña Juana de Austria, 2 July 1556. Archivo Histórico Nacional, ES.28079.AHN/5.1.8.// DIVERSOS-COLECCIONES, 24, N.18. Available at https://sites.google.com/site/bibliotecaunedviajes2/mujeres-viajeras/carta-de-isabel-de-guevara.

epidemics killed thousands: Olinda Massare de Kostianovsky, 'Salud e Higiene en Las Reducciones Jesuíticas', *Anuario de la Academia Paraguaya de la Historia*, Volume 37, 1997, pp. 37–56, p. 53.

keepie-uppies with rubber footballs: references to this game known as *manga ñembosarái* are made by Antonio Ruiz de Montoya, *Tesoro de la Lengua guaraní* (1639) and José Cardiel, *Las Misiones del Paraguay* (1771). See Veronica Smink, '¿Quién inventó el fútbol: los ingleses o los guaraníes?',

BBC Mundo, 29 August 2014; https://www.bbc.com/mundo/noticias/2014/08/140827_deportes_futbol_guarani_vs.

230 *republic of over 140,000 people*: Austin, *Colonial Kinship*, p. 6.

Black or mixed-race: cited in Ignacio Telesca, 'La historiografía paraguaya y los afrodescendientes', in *Los estudios afroamericanos y africanos en América Latina: herencia, presencia y visiones del otro*, CLACSO, Buenos Aires, 2008, pp. 175–6.

officially reserved for whites: *Expediente sobre pardos*, Archivo Nacional de Asunción (ANA), Sección Historia, Volume 166, No. 6, 1796, ff. 99–104.

'best saints to guard our borders': J. R. Rengger, *Ensayo histórico sobre la revolución del Paraguay*, Colección Historia, 25, Editorial El Lector, Asunción, 1996, pp. 117, 123.

pell-mell modernisation: Plá, *Los británicos en el Paraguay*, p. 11.

a buckled bedframe: Mario Pastore, 'State-Led Industrialisation: The Evidence on Paraguay, 1852–1870', *Journal of Latin American Studies*, Volume 26, No. 2, May 1994, pp. 295–324.

campesinos and the enslaved: see Magdalena López, 'El Estado en Paraguay durante el gobierno de Carlos Antonio López. Una propuesta teórica-histórica', *páginas*, 11, 25, January–April 2019. For slavery in post-colonial Paraguay and the *estancias de la patria*, see Mariana Katz, 'Slavery in an Authoritarian Republic: The Policing of Dissent and the Rise of State Slavery in Paraguay (1821–1840)', *Slavery & Abolition*, 44(4), 2023, 760–83, and Katz, 'El trabajo del Estado: lo público y lo privado según los trabajadores de las estancias de la Patria (1820–1850)', XII Taller/I Congreso, 'Paraguay desde las Ciencias Sociales', San Lorenzo, 12, 13, 14 April 2023.

231 *'worthy of its natural endowments'*: 'Reconocimiento de la Independencia del Paraguay por los Estados Unidos', ANA, Sección Historia, Volume 306, 38, 28 February 1853.

'with the pen': cited in Thomas L. Whigham, *The Paraguayan War, Volume 1, Causes and Conflict*, University of Nebraska Press, Lincoln, NE and London, 2002, p. 92.

'utterly depopulated' her adoptive country: George Masterman, *Seven Eventful Years*, p. 84.

stomp over it every day: Thomas L. Whigham, *Road to Armageddon: Paraguay versus the Triple Alliance, 1866–70*, University of Calgary Press, 2017, p. 158.

232 *'cause that Government to disappear'*: the Uruguayan version of the treaty was leaked to the British government, which ordered it to be printed and read before Parliament. See Lettsom to Earl Russell (1866), 'Treaty of Alliance against Paraguay', *Accounts and Papers of the House of Commons*, Session 1 February–10 August 1866, Volume 76, pp. 79–83.

'Asunción in three months': an example is kept by the Museo Histórico Nacional in Buenos Aires.

dives through the porthole opposite: George Thompson, *The War in Paraguay: With a Historical Sketch of the Country and Its People and Notes*

Upon the Military Engineering of the War, Longmans, Green and Co., London, 1869, p. 73.

pawn their jewellery for the war effort: Barbara J. Ganson, 'Following Their Children into Battle: Women at War in Paraguay, 1864-1870', *The Americas*, Volume 46, No. 3, 1990, pp. 335–71; https://doi.org/10.2307/1007017; accessed 22 September 2023.

shrapnel in cowhide and creepers: Burton, *Battle-fields of Paraguay*, p. 322.

his aura of invincibility: Thompson, *War in Paraguay*, p. 240.

'so lean that they would not burn': Ibid., p. 149.

233 *'thrown in the air in total confusion'*: these extracts by 'Dominguito' Sarmiento and Centurión are cited in Suzzi Casal de Lizarazu and Diego Gonzalo Cejas, 'Asalto a Curupayti. Visiones de una contienda', in *Memorias del 6to encuentro internacional de historia sobre la guerra de la triple alianza*, Asociación Cultural Mandu'arã, Asunción, 2014, pp. 341–3.

aftermath as a Boschian hellscape: Cándido López, *Después de la Batalla de Curupaytí*, 1893, Collection Museo Bellas Artes, Buenos Aires. See commentary by Roberto Amigo: https://www.bellasartes.gob.ar/coleccion/obra/7122/.

dies from sepsis two weeks later: for the life and legend of Díaz, see Herib Caballero Campos, 'En busca de un héroe: la construcción de la figura heroica del General José E. Díaz; Paraguay, 1867–1906', *Dossier Historias para la celebración: experiencias en la América Latina Contemporánea. Coordinado por Gabriela Dalla-Corte Caballero*, 32, 2014, pp. 22, 44.

can hardly afford to lose: Thompson, *War in Paraguay*, pp. 231–7.

every last Paraguayan was dead: Masterman, *Seven Eventful Years*, p. 140.

234 *forced to fight their comrades*: see, for example, Thompson, *War in Paraguay*, p. 77.

terrified of 'the American Attila': Burton, *Battle-fields of Paraguay*, p. 41.

enough Spanish to ask for quarter: Manuel Domínguez, *Causas del Heroísmo Paraguayo*, Talleres Nacionales de H. Kraus, Asunción, 1903, pp. 5–6.

'I have ever witnessed before': Martin Thomas McMahon, 'Paraguay and Her Enemies', *Harper's New Monthly Magazine*, 40, February 1870, 421–9. Cited in Michael Kenneth Huner, 'Saving Republics: General Martin Thomas McMahon, the Paraguayan War and the Fate of the Americas (1864–1870)', *Irish Migration Studies in Latin America*, 7:3, March 2010, pp. 323–38. Available online: www.irlandeses.org/imsla0907.htm; accessed 22 September 2023.

ugly racial overtones: for Paraguay's 'deeply engrained notions about the need to protect the community from invaders', see Whigham, *Road to Armageddon*, p. 429.

'lawless, godless and without Christ': see, for example, 25 November 1867 and 9 December 1867, in *Cabichuí. Periódico de la Guerra de la Triple Alianza*, 2nd edn, Servilibro/Biblioteca Nacional del Paraguay/Secretaria Nacional de Cultura, 2016, eds. Ticio Escobar and Osvaldo Salerno, pp. 59, 63. Paraguay had outlawed the trade in the enslaved and passed a free womb law in 1843, but it was only under allied occupation in 1869 that

slavery was abolished: by which time most of the male enslaved had been conscripted and killed. See Jerry W. Cooney, 'Abolition in the Republic of Paraguay: 1840–70', *Anuario de Historia de América Latina*, No. 11, 1974, pp. 149–66.

'semi-barbarous, almost "Indian"': Burton, *Battle-fields of Paraguay*, p. 168.

'Paraguayan of any age or sex alive': Thompson, *War in Paraguay*, p. 316.

'war of extermination': Masterman, *Seven Eventful Years*, p. 343.

235 *come upriver to rescue them*: Ibid., pp. 227–8.

terrified hordes to flight: *Cabichuí*, 24 July 1868, 94, San Fernando. In Escobar and Salerno, *Cabichuí. Periódico de la Guerra de la Triple Alianza.*

López executes hundreds: the existence of a concrete conspiracy against López has never been convincingly demonstrated. See Fabián Chamorro Torres, *El Mariscal. La vida de Francisco Solano López*, Editorial Goya, Lambaré, 2021, pp. 62–5.

a 'fleet of corsairs': 'Traducción de las cartas de James Manlove al Presidente sobre un Proyecto para la formación de una Flota corsaria y atacar la Costa Brasilera. Al ministro de Guerra respeto al mismo Proyecto y sobre su situación de prisionerio', ANA, Sección Historia, Volume 347, No. 39, 1866, Foj. 5. For Manlove's detention and execution, see Masterman, *Seven Eventful Years*, pp. 234–5.

monkey tails swinging from their helmets: Thompson, *The War in Paraguay*, p. 56.

Ramona Martínez . . . picks up a sabre: see Thomas Whigham, *La Guerra de La Triple Alianza*, Volume 3, *Danza de Muerte y Destrucción*, note 632.

'waiting for many years': Burton, *Battle-fields of Paraguay*, p. 340. Some opted out of the carnage. Reports circulated of a 'large quilombo' across the river in the Chaco where allied and Paraguayan fugitives were said to 'dwell together in mutual amity, and in enmity with all the world'. Ibid., p. 430.

236 *a tea party at her country house*: Carlos A. Von Horoch Benítez, 'Un combate insólito. Tren de asalto y recreo, Yuquyry, 10 de marzo de 1869', in Casal de Lizarazu and Gonzalo Cejas, *Memorias del 6to Encuentro*, pp. 185–98.

squaddies later reflected: Dionísio Cerqueira, *Reminiscências da Campanha do Paraguai: 1865–1870*, Biblioteca do Exército Editora, 1980, p. 317.

Nimia Candía, a twice-wounded veteran: R. Luisa Ríos de Caldi, *Diccionario de la mujer guaraní*, Editorial Siglo Veintiuno, Asunción, 1977, p. 73. Quoted in Ganson, 'Following Their Children into Battle', p. 367.

plays the piano: Alfredo de Escragnolle, Visconde de Taunay, *Recordações de guerra e de viagem*, Senado Federal, Conselho Editorial, Brasília, 2008, pp. 57–9.

incriminating secret archive: 'El presidente Franco exigió a Brasil la devolución de un cañón cristiano y de los archivos militares de la Guerra contra la Triple Alianza', *El Nordestino*, 1 March 2013; https://www.elnordestino.com/id-1681-cat-2-url-el-presidente-franco-exigi-a-brasil-la-devoluci-n-de-un-ca-n-cristiano-y-de-los-archivos-militares-de-la-guerra-contra-la-triple-alianza.html.

An Argentine surgeon: M. G., letter, *La Nación* (Buenos Aires), 29 January 1870, cited in Harris Gaylord Warren and Katherine F. Warren, *Paraguay and the Triple Alliance: The Postwar Decade, 1869–1878*, University of Texas Press, 1978, p. 39.

'fight like lions': for the battle of Campo Grande/Acosta Ñu, see de Taunay, *Recordações de guerra*, pp. 70–74.

237 *plant the seed*: for López's last words and national identity, see Ana Inés Couchonnal Cancio, 'Hija de mal padre. Identidad nacional y Dictadura en el Paraguay', *Nuevo Mundo Mundos Nuevos, Débats*, 24 February 2020.

'the pages of History': cited in María Eugenia Garay, *Río Escarlata: Guerra de la Triple Alianza*, Servilibro, Asunción, 2016.

239 *'I can compare Paraguay'*: — W., Asunción, 19 February 1870, in *The Weekly Standard*, 2 March 1870. Cited in Warren and Warren, *Paraguay and the Triple Alliance*, p. 39.

more than half the pre-war population: for this partial consensus figure on Paraguayan mortality during the Triple Alliance War, see Thomas L. Whigham and Barbara Potthast, 'The Paraguayan Rosetta Stone: New Insights into the Demographics of the Paraguayan War, 1864–1870', *Latin American Research Review*, 34 (1), 1999, Latin American Studies Association, 174–86.

'nor lock untouched': cited in Warren and Warren, *Paraguay and the Triple Alliance*, p. 17.

240 *still being repaid until 1964*: Fabián Chamorro, Humberto Trinidad, *Memorias de la Ocupación (1869–76)*, Editorial Goya, Asunción, 2014, pp. 97, 153.

'heroic but unfortunate': 'Asociación Nacional Republicana – Comisión Parroquial de la Catedral', circular, Asunción, 15 January 1904; Colección Jorge Gross Brown.

most lucrative export industries: Diego Abente, 'Foreign Capital, Economic Elites and the State in Paraguay during the Liberal Republic (1870–1936)', *Journal of Latin American Studies*, Volume 21, No. 1, 1989, pp. 61–88.

In 1902, he toppled: Carlos Von Horoch, *Páginas de Sangre. Las Cordilleras 1861*, El Lector, Asunción, 2016, p. 64.

'final injections of morphine': Rafael Barrett, *El Dolor Paraguayo* [1911], Fundación Biblioteca Ayacucho, Caracas, 1987, ed. Miguel A. Fernández, pp. 9, 55. For a new translation and introduction to Barrett, see *Paraguayan Sorrow: Writings of Rafael Barrett, a Radical Voice in a Dispossessed Land*, Monthly Review Press, New York, 2024, trans. and ed. William Costa.

on the hook for genocide: 'Piden que de declare genocidas a impulsores de la Guerra Grande', *ABC Color*, 1 March 2019; https://www.abc.com.py/nacionales/piden-que-se-declare-genocidas-a-impulsores-de-la-guerra-grande-1791449.html.

'Brazil fights with English capital': John George Witt, *The Times*, 20 May 1868.

241 *European powers were bystanders*: for alleged British responsibility for the Triple Alliance War, see discussion in Liliana M. Brezzo, 'La guerra de la Triple Alianza en los límites de la ortodoxia: mitos y tabúes', *Revista*

Universum, No. 19, Volume 1, 2004, 10–27; Leslie Bethell, 'The Paraguayan War (1864–70)', *Institute of Latin American Studies Research Papers*, 46, 1996, pp. 15–29; and Andrew Nickson, 'Gran Bretaña y la Guerra de la Triple Alianza: La tesis del "cuarto aliado"', *Última Hora*, 2 March 2024; https://www.ultimahora.com/gran-bretana-y-la-guerra-de-la-triple-alianza-la-tesis-del-cuarto-aliado.

'*nor very rich nor extremely poor*': Alexander K. Macdonald, *Picturesque Paraguay. Sport, Pioneering, Travel. A Land of Promise. Stock-Raising, Plantation Industries, Forest Products, Commercial Possibilities*, Charles H. Kelly, London, 1911, pp. 5–6.

'*does away forever with dictators*': William Mill Butler, *Paraguay: the Paradise of South America*, The Paraguay Development Company, Philadelphia, 1901, p. 57.

anarcho-syndicalist uprisings: Andrew Nickson, 'Toma de Encarnación, La', in *Historical Dictionary of Paraguay*, Scarecrow Press, Metuchen, NJ, 1993, pp. 581–2.

'*fifteen hundred revolutions*': *Crítica*, Buenos Aires, 3 January 1915, p. 1.

'*incapable of democratic life*': Báez, *La Tiranía en El Paraguay*, pp. 13–14.

242 '*history to bathe in light*': Chesterton, *Grandchildren of Solano López*, p. 11.

'*suffered by the son of Bethlehem*': Juan E. O'Leary, *Curupayty. Discurso Pronunciado en 22 de Septiembre de 1912 con motivo de la peregrinación patriótica*, Talleres Graficos M. Rodríguez Giles, Buenos Aires, 1912, pp. 8, 12.

'or with the Triple Alliance': Juan O'Leary, *Prosa Polémica*, Ediciones Napa, Asunción, 1982, pp. 152–5.

giant blocks of ice: Laura Daniela Ferrero and Mario Gustavo Parrón, 'La versión oral de la Guerra del Chaco en el testimonio de un excombatiente boliviano', in *Historia Regional, Sección Historia*, ISP No. 3, Año XIX, No. 24, 2006, pp. 151–71, p. 166 narrates Paraguayan planes dropping ice in bags at the Battle of Cañada Strongest.

against another invader: Chesterton, *Grandchildren of Solano López*, p. 119.

'*national hero without exemplar*': for Franco and López, see David Velázquez Seiferheld, *Relaciones entre autoritarismo y educación en el Paraguay 1869–2012. Un analisis histórico*, Volume II, Serpaj, Asunción, 2014, pp. 59–60.

243 '*There is an infinite, rending sorrow*': Arturo Bray, *Hombres y épocas del Paraguay*. Quoted in Warren and Warren, *Paraguay and the Triple Alliance*, p. 6.

Stroessner ... seized control: Peter Lambert and Andrew Nickson, *The Paraguay Reader: History, Culture, Politics*, Duke University Press, 2012, p. 6.

abducted and raped: *Ventanas Abiertas. Informe de la Comisión de Verdad y Justicia*, 2023.

244 *its 4 July garden party*: Document 5. Narcotics Control, from Asunción, June 14, 1972, Confidential. Under Secretary of State John Irwin II response, June 30, 1972, Confidential. Source: FOIA Lawsuit, National Security Archive v Department of State (17-cv-0770). Available at: https://nsarchive.

gwu.edu/dc.html?doc=4389153-Document-05-Narcotics-Control-from-Asuncion-June.

for city hall to demolish the property: Juan Carlos Lezcano, 'Lo que recupera el Estado', *ABC Color*, 4 August 2015; Phil Gunson, 'General Alfredo Stroessner', *The Guardian*, 17 August 2006.

almost blew up the dictator's motorcade: for Agustín Goiburú, see Alfredo Boccia Paz, *Goiburú: la odisea del insumiso*, Servilibro, Asunción, 2014.

245   *taken up arms against López*: Andrew Nickson, 'El Régimen de Stroessner (1954–89)', in *Historia del Paraguay*, Santillana, Asunción, 2010, p. 287.

an area the size of Panama: for these misappropriated lands, or *tierras malhabidas*, see Kregg Hetherington, *Guerrilla Auditors. The Politics of Transparency in Neoliberal Paraguay*, Duke University Press, 2011, pp. 70, 80.

greatest concentration of farmland: 'Paraguay – Notas de política 2018', World Bank Group, Washington, DC, p. 7. This is reflected in a Gini score for landholding of 0.93: almost perfect inequality.

246   *ballooned to US$79 billion*: Maximiliano Manzoni and Kevin Damasio, 'Energy, cash and climate shape talks over the giant Itaipú dam', *Dialogue Earth*, 8 May 2024; https://dialogue.earth/en/energy/energy-cash-and-climate-shape-talks-over-the-giant-itaipu-dam/.

US$77 billion: ' "Paraguay perdió USD 77 mil millones por Itaipú" ', *Última Hora*, 3 November 2022; https://www.ultimahora.com/paraguay-perdio-usd-77-mil-millones-itaipu-n3032135.

247   *'Use and abuse Paraguay'*: 'Cartes a empresarios brasileños: "usen y abusen de Paraguay" ', *Última Hora*, 18 February 2014; https://www.ultimahora.com/cartes-empresarios-brasilenos-usen-y-abusen-paraguay-n767800.html.

'the revival of a giant': 'Santiago Peña: su primer discurso completo como presidente de la República', *ABC Color*, 15 August 2023; https://www.abc.com.py/politica/2023/08/15/santiago-pena-su-primer-discurso-completo-como-presidente-de-la-republica/.

248   *the Quechua word for hunting-ground*: for this probable etymology of the Chaco, see Darién E. Prado, 'What is the Gran Chaco vegetation in South America? I: A review. Contribution to the study of flora and vegetation of the Chaco, V', *Candollea*, 48.1, 1993, 145–72, pp. 145–50.

249   *entire Ayoreo clans*: Lucas Bessire, *Behold the Black Caiman: A Chronicle of Ayoreo Life*, University of Chicago Press, London, 2014, p. 75.

stars falling to earth: for the Ayoreo and the Chaco War, see Volker von Bremen, 'Impactos de la Guerra del Chaco en la territorialidad ayorea', in *Mala Guerra. Los indígenas en la Guerra del Chaco, 1932–1935*, Servilibro, Asunción, 2008, ed. Nicolás Richard, pp. 333–55.

nation of pacifists: Peter P. Klassen, *Kaputi Mennonita. Arados y Fusiles en la Guerra del Chaco*, Editora Litocolor, 2018, trans. Kornelius Neufeld, p. 27.

displayed in a cage: Bessire, *Black Caiman*, p. 76.

helicopters and planes overhead: Rosie Blunt, 'Chagabi Etacore: The leader killed by contact with the outside world', *BBC News*, 11 August 2019; https://www.bbc.com/news/world-latin-america-49264245.

'*in accord to the Original Ideal of Creation*': for the size of the Unification Church's holdings in Paraguay – estimated at 590,000 hectares – see Arantxa Guereña and Luis Rojas Villagra, *Yvy Jára. Los dueños de la tierra en Paraguay*, Oxfam, Asunción, 2016. For Reverend Moon's plans, see The Leda Settlement, 'History and Motivation': https://www.ledaproject.com/history-and-motivation; and Michihito Sano and Kunihiko Shibanuma, 'The Words of the Sano Family. The Saints of Puerto Leda', September 2011; https://www.tparents.org/Library/Unification/Talks2/Sano/Sano-110900.htm.

250 *expire from a broken spirit*: this account of Mateo's early life draws on conversations in July 2017, December 2021 and March 2022, as well as that transcribed in Benno Glauser, *Huellas del futuro. El retorno de los Ayoreo a su territorio*, IWGIA, Paraguay, 2022, trans. Hugo Montes, pp. 127–35.

fragments of psalms: interview with Tagüide Picanerei, 14 December 2021.

killed five Ayoreo: for this incident, see Alan Riding, 'Asuncion Journal: In Paraguay's Jungle, No Letup In Battle For Souls', *The New York Times*, 1 April 1987.

251 '*As if we did not have a big country before*': cited in Lucas Bessire and Bernard Belisário, 'Visualizing a Post-Apocalypse: Notes on New Ayoreo Cinema', *Tipití: Journal of the Society for the Anthropology of Lowland South America*, Volume 17, Issue 1, Article 2, 2021, 16–35, pp. 25–6. *Ujirei* (2016) can be viewed here: https://vimeo.com/ondemand/ujirei. See also *Apenas El Sol/Nothing But the Sun*, dir. Arami Ullón, 2020: https://es.apenaselsol.com/.

fastest-vanishing forest on the planet: for calculating rates of deforestation in the Chaco, see *Grand Theft Chaco. The luxury cars made with leather from the stolen lands of an uncontacted tribe*, Earthsight, 2020, p. 10; https://www.earthsight.org.uk/grandtheftchaco-en.

'*journey of the conquistadors to a few hours*': Justo Pastor Benítez, 'Dos Jalones de Nuestra Soberanía', *Juventud*, Año II, No. 33, 15 August 1924, Biblioteca Nacional del Paraguay.

252 *across the Paraguay River to Brazil*: Carlos Almirón, 'Mano de obra paraguaya da 45% de avance al puente de la bioceánica', *ABC Color*, 29 April 2024; https://www.abc.com.py/nacionales/chaco/2024/04/29/mano-de-obra-paraguaya-da-45-de-avance-al-puente-de-la-bioceanica/.

to Chile's Pacific coastline: 'Corredor Bioceánico a dos tramos de culminar su primera etapa', Agencia IP, 13 January 2022; https://www.ip.gov.py/ip/corredor-bioceanico-a-dos-tramos-de-culminar-su-primera-etapa/.

'*win-win concept for everyone*': interview with Arnoldo Wiens, 13 December 2021, with Santi Carneri.

'*the realisation of a dream*': speeches by Mario Abdo Benítez and Reinaldo Azambuja Silva, 13 December 2021.

253 *newly-paved road into the trees*: see Miguel Lovera, Marcos Glauser and Marco Todisco, Informe CBA, *Carmelo Peralta bajo ataque*, Iniciativa Amotocodie, 2023, pp. 24–5. Available at: https://www.iniciativa-amotocodie.org/publicaciones/carmelo-peralta-bajo-ataque/. For BR-319,

see Leanderson Lima, 'A BR-319 highway in the middle of the road', *Amazônia Real*, 3 June 2023; https://amazoniareal.com.br/especiais/br319-highway/.

a thin latticework of trees: NASA Earth Observatory, *Deforestation in Paraguay*, 1 May 2018; https://earthobservatory.nasa.gov/images/92078/deforestation-in-paraguay.

254 *bloodletting spiralled out of control*: Bremen, 'Impactos de la Guerra del Chaco', p. 342.

at least ten small bands: for the 'uncontacted' Ayoreo-Totobiegosode and the signs they leave, see Miguel Lovera, Jieun Kang, Miguel Ángel Alarcón, Norma Flores Allende and Leonardo Tamburini, 'Los Ayoreo: los últimos aislados fuera de la Amazonía', *Debates Indígenas*, 1 July 2021; https://www.iwgia.org/es/noticias/4434-los-ayoreo-los-%C3%BAltimos-aislados-fuera-de-la-amazon%C3%ADa.html.

one of their uncontacted relatives: Santi Carneri, 'Entre el bosque y la muerte en Paraguay', *El País*, 12 January 2024; https://elpais.com/america/2024-01-12/entre-el-bosque-y-la-muerte-en-paraguay.html.

lamenting the destruction of their home: Ibid., pp. 8–9; and 'Los ayoreos apelan a la Comisión Interamericana de Derechos Humanos para salvar su bosque de la destrucción', *Survival*, 2021; https://www.survival.es/noticias/12666.

PNCAT: Patrimonio Natural y Cultural Ayoreo Totobiegosode.

a tall, near-naked figure: interview with Enrique Pebi, 13 December 2021.

destroyed for pasture since 2005: Lovera et al., *Carmelo Peralta bajo ataque*, p. 26.

255 *staging post for drug cartels*: Gabriel Stargardter and Daniela Desantis, 'Cocaine cartels encroach on Unification Church's Paraguayan paradise', *Reuters*, 10 August 2023; https://www.reuters.com/investigates/special-report/paraguay-drugs-unification-church/.

clandestine airstrips: Zully Rolón, 'El Chaco a la noche parece un árbol de Navidad', *La Nación*, 27 February 2021; https://www.lanacion.com.py/politica/2021/02/27/zully-rolon-el-chaco-a-la-noche-parece-un-arbol-de-navidad/.

in exchange for gifts: Paola Canova, *Frontier Intimacies: Ayoreo Women and the Sexual Economy of the Paraguayan Chaco*, University of Texas Press, 2020, pp. 6–11.

256 *lines luxury European cars*: see Earthsight, *Grand Theft Chaco*; and Aimee Gabay, 'Report links financial giants to deforestation of Paraguay's Gran Chaco', *Mongabay*, 13 April 2023; https://news.mongabay.com/2023/04/report-links-financial-giants-to-deforestation-of-paraguays-gran-chaco/.

257 *1,200 football fields' worth of forest*: https://www.earthsight.org.uk/news/investigation-analysis-paraguays-looted-lands.

soya and meat produced: Marina Aizen, 'Gran Chaco deforestation is an overlooked carbon bomb', *Mongabay*, 15 July 2021; https://dialogochino.net/en/climate-energy/44454-deforestation-in-the-gran-chaco-an-overlooked-carbon-bomb/.

fourteen times more biomass: F. Pötzschner, M. Baumann, N. I. Gasparri, G. Conti, D. Loto, M. Piquer-Rodríguez and T. Kuemmerle, 'Ecoregion-wide, multi-sensor biomass mapping highlights a major underestimation of dry forests carbon stocks', *Remote Sensing of Environment*, 269, 2022, 112849.

soybean and lithium frontiers are now expanding: J. Henderson, J. Godar, G. P. Frey et al., 'The Paraguayan Chaco at a crossroads: drivers of an emerging soybean frontier', *Reg Environ Change*, 21, 72, 2021; https://doi.org/10.1007/s10113-021-01804-z.

9: THE MAP OF CATASTROPHE

259 *200,000 guaraníes each*: Jack Nicas, 'One Secret to a Latin American Party's Dominance: Buying Votes', *The New York Times*, 15 May 2023; https://www.nytimes.com/2023/05/15/world/americas/paraguay-election-colorado-party.html.

261 *the Naval March*: Gastón Velasco Carrasco, *Marcha Naval*, available at https://cancioneroboliviano.com/marcha/marcha-naval/.

262 *down to the ocean*: https://gallica.bnf.fr/ark:/12148/btv1b530292266/f1.item.zoom.

'that vast empire': Félix Avelino Aramayo, *La Cuestión del Acre*, La Legación de Bolivia En Londres, Wertheimer, Lea and Company, London, 1903, pp. 7–9.

263 *suitable place for a harbour*: James Dunkerley, 'The Third Man: Francisco Burdett O'Connor and the Emancipation of the Americas', Institute of Latin American Studies, University of London, *Occasional Papers*, No. 20, 1999, p. 16.

bottled during Carnaval: Archivo Nacional de Bolivia (hereafter ANB), Jefatura del Mar, M416, 1858–1862, Cobija, 4 March 1862, f.5.

264 *the Bolivians barked orders*: Charles Weiner, *La Guerra en Sud America*, 1879. Cited in Sater, *Andean Tragedy*, loc. 163.

'the poncho and the cassock': Bolivia. El centenario de Voltaire, Imp. De El Litoral, E. Diaz, Numero Especial, Antofagasta, 30 May 1878, p. 4.

'administration has captured': El Litoral, Antofagasta, No. 87, Thursday, 17 January 1878, p. 3.

265 *'your exclusive responsibility'*: ANB, Ministerio de Relaciones Exteriores, 613, Carta al prefecto del Litoral (Enviada por la Comandancia del Escuadron a bordo del blindado Blanco Encalada, Chile), 21 March 1879, f.1.

one minister admitted: Memoria del Ministro de la guerra al congreso ordinario de 1883, La Paz, 1883, p. 24.

short on actual soldiers: Nathaniel Aguirre, *Informe del ministro de la Guerra a la convención nacional de 1881*, La Paz, 1881, p. 7.

'the stiff hands of the dead': Sara Neuhaus de Ledgard, *Recuerdos de la Batalla del Campo de la Alianza y de la Ocupación de Tacna en la Guerra del 79*, Lima, 1928, pp. 8–9, 14.

'Now I go calmly to die with our comrades': Zenón Dalence, *Informe histórico del servicio prestado por el Cuerpo de Ambulancias del Ejército boliviano*, La Paz, 1881, pp. 10–12.

266 *his battalions broke and scattered*: Narciso Campero, *Informe del General Narciso Campero ante la Convención Nacional de Bolivia como general en jefe del ejército aliado. Sesion Secreta del 13 de Junio, 1880*, La Paz, 1880, pp. 15–20.

'heart of the South American continent': André Bresson, *Bolivia: Sept Années d'explorations, de voyages et de sejours dans L'Amerique Australe*, Paris, 1886, pp. 167–78, 258.

'queerest man-of-war': 'Wonders of the Amazon', *The Chronicle-News*, Volume XIII, Number 138, 6 July 1899. Available at Colorado Historic Newspapers Association, http://tinyurl.com/5hyvr8dw.

267 *half a billion dollars*: for the Amazonian rubber boom and the Acre conflict, see Hecht, *Scramble for the Amazon*, pp. 165–81.

first X-ray machine: David Rey Cuellar, 'Cachuela Esperanza', Colección de Folletos Bolivianos de Hoy, 12, La Paz, 1982, pp. 5–10.

'I feel I am nearer to England': Valerie J. Fifer, 'The Empire Builders: A History of the Bolivian Rubber Boom and the Rise of the House of Suárez', *Journal of Latin American Studies*, Volume 2, No. 2, 1970, pp. 113–46, p. 142.

the only country . . . excluded: Sixto L. Ballesteros, *A Través del Amazonas*, La Paz, 1899, pp. 10–11.

'down to the base of the Andes': cited in Hecht, *Scramble for the Amazon*, p. 160.

British Empire in South Africa: Nicolás Suárez, *Anotaciónes y Documentos Sobre La Campaña del Alto Acre, 1902–1903*, La Académica, Barcelona, 1928, pp. 90–92.

268 *'to earn lots of pounds'*: Dr Elías Sagárnaga, *Recuerdos de La Campaña del Acre de 1903. Mis Notas de Viaje*, La Paz, 1909, p. 123.

the Amazonian rubber business: Clara López Beltrán, 'La Exploración y Ocupación del Acre (1850–1900)', in *Revista de Indias*, Dept de Historia de América, Fernandez de Ovideo Insituto de Historia, September–December 2001, No. 233, p. 587.

similar attempts in South America: Shawn William Miller, *An Environmental History of Latin America*, Cambridge University Press, 2007, p. 128.

'The only way left to us is space': Florian Zambrana, *El Acre. Notas y Correspondencias*, Geneva, 1904, pp. 23–4.

'a poor people without culture': Alcides Arguedas, *Historia General de Bolivia*, La Paz, 1922, pp. 14, 365; Arguedas, *Caudillos Letrados*, La Paz, 1922, pp. 74, 79–82.

'The memory, and the hope, are still there!': José Aguirre Achá, *De Los Andes al Amazonas. Recuerdos de la Campana del Acre*, La Paz, 1902, p. 272.

269 *'Five hundred years of resistance'*: https://www.pagina12.com.ar/diario/especiales/18-62330-2006-01-30.html.

271 *'facing the Pacific'*: Juana Gallegos, 'Arquitectura del cielo aimara', *La Republica*, 17 September 2023; https://larepublica.pe/domingo/2023/09/17/arquitectura-del-cielo-aimara-1214208.

272 *unveiling the change in 2014*: 'Bolivia congress clock altered to turn anti-clockwise', *BBC News*, 25 June 2014; https://www.bbc.co.uk/news/world-latin-america-28013157.

    Bolivia is a country-sized conundrum: James Dunkerley, 'Pachakuti en Bolivia (2008–2010). Un diario personal', *Revista de Estudios Bolivianos*, Volume 15–17, 2008–2010, p. 16, citing René Mercado Zavaleta, *La formación de la conciencia nacional*, Amigos del Libro, La Paz, 1990 [1967], p. 167.

273 *'We're here to govern ourselves'*: Evo Morales, Ceremonia Ancestral De Posesión De Mando, Tiwanaku, La Paz. Ministerio de Comunicación del Estado Plurinacional de Bolivia, 21 January 2015. Available at: https://www.somossur.net/documentos/I_21012015_EVOMORALES_Posesion_TIWANAKU.pdf.

274 *Katarismo rejects Western values*: see Olivia Arigho-Stiles, 'Landscapes of Struggle. *Katarista* Perspectives on the Environment in Bolivia, 1960–1990', in *Land Back: Relational Landscapes of Indigenous Resistance across the Americas*, Harvard University Press, 2024, eds. Heather Dorries and Michelle Daigle.

    'soulless, stinking corpse': 'Quispe: MAS "es cadáver sin alma y apesta" a corrupción', *Erbol archivo*, 13 November 2017; https://anteriorportal.erbol.com.bo/noticia/politica/13112017/quispe_mas_es_cadaver_sin_alma_y_apesta_corrupcion.

    'Kollasuyo has to liquidate Bolivia': '"El Kollasuyo tiene que liquidar a Bolivia, somos otra nación"', *Eju!/Página Siete*, 14 August 2018; https://eju.tv/2020/08/el-kollasuyo-tiene-que-liquidar-a-bolivia-somos-otra-nacion/.

275 *15,000 textbooks*: 'Armada distribuye 15.000 ejemplares de "Mi Primer Libro del Mar" para fortalecer conciencia marítima', *La Razón*, 21 March 2016; https://www.la-razon.com/nacional/2016/03/21/armada-distribuye-15-000-ejemplares-de-mi-primer-libro-del-mar-para-fortalecer-conciencia-maritima/.

278 *third year in a row*: Yvette Sierra Praeli, 'Planeta perdió 3.7 millones de hectáreas de bosques primarios en 2023: diez campos de fútbol por minuto', *Mongabay*, 9 April 2024; https://es.mongabay.com/2024/04/planeta-perdio-millones-bosques-primarios-en-2023/.

279 *blames demonstrations in Potosí on Chilean spies*: 'Desconfianza: Evo Morales cree que las protestas en Potosí son promovidas desde Chile', *Infobae*, 28 November 2017; https://www.infobae.com/2015/07/20/1742813-desconfianza-evo-morales-cree-que-las-protestas-potosi-son-promovidas-chile/.

282 *took their own lives*: Jorge Baradit, *Historia Secreta de Chile 3*, Penguin Random House, Chile, 2017, p. 178.

283 *trillion dollars of lithium*: Megan Janetsky, Victor R. Caviano and Rodrigo Abd, 'Native groups sit on a treasure trove of lithium. Now mines threaten

their water, culture and wealth', *AP*, 13 March 2024; https://apnews.com/article/lithium-water-mining-indigenous-cb2f5b1580c12f8ba1b19223648069b7.

284 *'nothing can exist'*: Charles Darwin, *Darwin's Ornithological Notes*, edited with an Introduction, Notes and Appendix by Nora Barlow, Cambridge University Press, 1960, p. 260.

288 *'absolutely and in perpetuity'*: International Court of Justice, 'Obligation to Negotiate Access to the Pacific Ocean (Bolivia v. Chile)', Judgement of 1 October 2018, p. 564. Available at: https://www.icj-cij.org/sites/default/files/case-related/153/153-20181001-JUD-01-00-EN.pdf.

289 *fomenting a coup*: for the contested events of 2019–20, see Thomas Becker and Linda Farthing, *Coup: A Story of Violence and Resistance in Bolivia*, Haymarket Books, 2021.
Aymara beliefs as 'satanic': Javier Biosca Azcoiti, 'Los tuits contra los indígenas de la presidenta autoproclamada de Bolivia: "¡Satánicos, a Dios nadie lo reemplaza!"', *elDiario.es*, 14 November 2019; https://www.eldiario.es/internacional/racistas-presidenta-autoproclamada-Bolivia-Aferrado_0_963454365.html.

290 *exhibits dedicated to Morales removed*: Denisse Rojas, 'Plantean traslado de piezas del "museo de Evo"; en Orinoca quieren "desvincularlo" de Morales', *Opinión*, 21 February 2024; https://www.opinion.com.bo/articulo/pais/plantean-traslado-piezas-museo-orinoca-pobladores-piden-desestigmatizarlo-como-museo/20240221123239937635.html.

291 *'history has paused'*: *Cartas de Abaroa*, La Paz, 1987, ed. Ronald MacLean Abaroa, p. xi.

EPILOGUE

294 *2024 is forecast to break records*: Milagro Vallecillos, 'Panamá prevé que este año la cifra de migrantes irregulares será superior a 2023', *Voz de América*, 17 February 2024; https://www.vozdeamerica.com/a/panama-preve-cifra-migrantes-irregulares-sera-superior-2023/7491137.html.
'key to the universe': The phrase is that of William Paterson, a Scottish trader who founded the Bank of England. Cited in Ignacio Gallup-Diaz, *The door of the seas and key to the universe. Indian politics and imperial rivalry in the Darién, 1640–1750*, Columbia University Press, 2005, p. 10.

295 *has reached full maturity*: cited in Pedro Portugal Mollinedo and Carlos Macusaya Cruz, *El indianismo katarista. Una mirada crítica*, Fundación Friedrich Ebert, La Paz, Bolivia, 2005, pp. 272–3. For the meaning of Abya-Yala, see Reuter Orán B. and Aiban Wagua, *Gayamar sabga, diccionario escolar, gunagaya-español*, Equipo EBI Guna, 2013.
'Byzantium might be for the Old World': Bolívar, 'Carta de Jamaica'.

296 *outside the Americas*: Peter Yeung, 'Disillusioned about China, more Chinese aim for US via risky Darien Gap', *Al Jazeera*, 22 February 2024; https://

www.aljazeera.com/economy/2024/2/22/disillusioned-about-china-more-chinese-aim-for-us-via-risky-darien-gap.

South America's homicide capital: Juliana Manjarrés and Christopher Newton, 'InSight Crime's 2023 Homicide Round-Up', 21 February 2024; https://insightcrime.org/news/insight-crime-2023-homicide-round-up/.

297 *right-wing paramilitaries*: 'Truth Commission of Colombia: Executive Summary', *ABColombia*, 15 July 2022; https://www.abcolombia.org.uk/truth-commission-of-colombia-executive-summary/.

Over 400 demobilised FARC fighters: Manuel Rueda, 'Colombians mourn the killings of hundreds of former rebel fighters and human rights leaders', *AP*, 20 February 2024; https://apnews.com/article/colombia-rebels-human-rights-cf2e9d2033c3dcd2a5e30aeed6ff7920.

298 *'chains that oppress us'*: Will Grant, *Populista*, p. 24.

299 *comparing himself to Tony Blair*: Ibid., p. 33.

left him an empty seat: Ibid., p. 25.

extracted some teeth and bone: Philip A. Mackowiak, 'Will we ever know for certain what killed Simón Bolívar?', *OUPblog*, 17 December 2015; https://blog.oup.com/2015/12/simon-bolivar-death/.

300 *'Our Chávez, who art in heaven'*: EFE, 'Oración "Chávez nuestro" se estrena en taller de formación de dirigentes', *Última Hora*, 1 September 2014; https://www.ultimahora.com/oracion-chavez-nuestro-se-estrena-taller-formacion-dirigentes-n825837.

around three cents: Stephen Gibbs, 'Venezuela's currency is so worthless there's no point hiding PINs', *The Times*, 26 February 2024; https://www.thetimes.co.uk/article/venezuelas-currency-is-so-worthless-theres-no-point-hiding-pins-zrd7xrjxf.

301 *political prisoners were tortured*: Grant, *Populista*, p. 68.

two-thirds of Venezuelans: Genevieve Glatsky, 'Venezuela's 2024 Presidential Vote: What to Know', *The New York Times*, 16 May 2024; https://www.nytimes.com/2024/05/16/world/americas/venezuela-president-election.html.

burned and decapitated: Eduardo Viloria, 'Severos daños causaron vándalos de Santa Apolonia al Bolívar pedestre de la plaza que guardia su memoria', *Diario Los Andes*, 19 February 2024; https://diariodelosandes.com/severos-danos-causaron-vandalos-de-santa-apolonia-al-bolivar-pedestre-de-la-plaza-que-guardia-su-memoria/; 'Quemaron estatua de Chávez en San Félix, Venezuela', *Noticias RCN*, 23 January 2019; https://www.noticiasrcn.com/internacional/quemaron-estatua-de-chavez-en-san-felix-venezuela-335871; Fabiola Sanchez and Hannah Dreier, 'Lawmaker: Hugo Chavez's childhood home burned by protesters', *AP*, 22 May 2017; https://apnews.com/article/85710834dfe045c6a4a5563d5fea6839.

eight million Venezuelans: 'Latin America and the Caribbean, Venezuelan Refugees and Migrants in the Region', *R4V*, 30 November 2023; https://www.r4v.info/en/document/r4v-latin-america-and-caribbean-venezuelan-refugees-and-migrants-region-nov-2023.

302 *'emotional and geographical void'*: Ramón, *Motherland*, p. 6.

Darién will be a cakewalk: Julie Turkewitz, 'In Record Numbers, Venezuelans Risk a Deadly Trek to Reach the U.S. Border', *The New York Times*, 7 October 2022; https://www.nytimes.com/2022/10/07/world/americas/venezuelan-migrants-us-border.html.

'We didn't think it would be so ugly': https://www.tiktok.com/tag/darien?lang=en.

'Write me': https://www.tiktok.com/@yeiiyeii/video/728209662265658906 2?lang=en.

escape with the powder: 'El Clan del Golfo cobra decenas de millones por paso de migrantes en el Darién', *AFP*, 9 November 2023; https://www.france24.com/es/minuto-a-minuto/20231109-el-clan-del-golfo-cobra-decenas-de-millones-por-paso-de-migrantes-en-dari%C3%A9n-informe.

305 *2.5 million people*: Jasmine Garsd, 'An unprecedented year in immigration, and in anti-immigration rhetoric', *NPR*, 22 December 2023; https://www.npr.org/2023/12/22/1221006083/immigration-border-election-presidential.

'largest deportation operation ... poisoning the blood of our country': Marianne LeVine and Meryl Kornfield, 'Trump's anti-immigrant onslaught sparks fresh alarm heading into 2024', *The Washington Post*, 12 October 2023; https://www.washingtonpost.com/elections/2023/10/12/trump-immigrants-comments-criticism/.

306 *twice the global average*: Brian Winter, 'A (Relatively) Bullish Case for Latin America', *Americas Quarterly*, 17 October 2023; https://www.americasquarterly.org/article/a-relatively-bullish-case-for-latin-america/.

'reproduced on the regional level': Galeano, *Open Veins*, p. 260.

Central America in the 1850s: Michel Gobat, 'The Invention of Latin America: A Transnational History of Anti-Imperialism, Democracy, and Race', *The American Historical Review*, Volume 118, Issue 5, December 2013, pp. 1345–75.

307 *uncertain future on the mainland*: Adri Salido, 'Gardi Sugdub: The Americas' disappearing island', BBC, 5 January 2024; https://www.bbc.com/travel/article/20240105-gardi-sugdub-the-americas-disappearing-island.

'obsession with the past': Andrés Oppenheimer, *Basta de Historias!: la obsesión latinoamericana con el pasado, y las doce claves del futuro*, Debaze, Montevideo, 2010, pp. 39–41.

'the past in our sight': Silvia Rivera Cusicanqui, *Un mundo ch'ixi es posible. Ensayos desde un presente en crisis*, Tinta Limón, Buenos Aires, 2018, pp. 103–4.

308 *'unmakeable by human beings'*: Galeano, *Open Veins*, p. 264.

Index

About the Author

Laurence Blair is an award-winning writer and journalist. He was born and raised in Dorset and studied Ancient and Modern History at the University of Oxford. Since 2014, he has reported from across Latin America for outlets including the BBC, *The Economist*, *Financial Times*, *Guardian*, *New York Times* and *National Geographic*. He currently lives in Asunción, Paraguay.